The Gospel According to Luke

BMSEC
BAYLOR–MOHR SIEBECK
Studies in Early Christianity

Wayne Coppins and Simon Gathercole
Series Editors

ALSO AVAILABLE

From Jesus to the New Testament
Early Christian Theology and the Origin of the New Testament Canon
Jens Schröter (2013)

Israel, Church, and the Gentiles in the Gospel of Matthew
Matthias Konradt (2014)

Christian Theology and Its Institutions in the Early Roman Empire
Prolegomena to a History of Early Christian Theology
Christoph Markschies (2015)

The Gospel According to Luke

Volume I (Luke 1–9:50)

Michael Wolter

Translated by
Wayne Coppins and Christoph Heilig

BAYLOR UNIVERSITY PRESS

Mohr Siebeck

Cover Design by Natalya Balnova

Originally published in German as *Das Lukasevangelium* (Tübingen: Mohr Siebeck, 2008) with the ISBN 978-3-16-149525-0.

This English edition is published in Germany by Mohr Siebeck with the ISBN 978-3-16-154932-8.

Distributors

For all other countries	*For Europe and the UK*
Baylor University Press	Mohr Siebeck
One Bear Place #97363	Wilhelmstr. 18, Postfach 20 40
Waco, Texas 76798	D-72010 Tübingen
USA	Germany

Library of Congress Cataloging-in-Publication Data

Names: Wolter, Michael, author.
Title: The Gospel according to Luke / Michael Wolter ; translated by Wayne Coppins and Christoph Heilig.
Other titles: Lukasevangelium. English
Description: Waco, Texas : Baylor University Press, 2016– | Series: Baylor-Mohr Siebeck studies in early christianity | "Originally published in German as Das Lukasevangelium (Tubingen: Mohr Siebeck, 2008), with the ISBN 978-3161495250." | Includes bibliographical references.
Identifiers: LCCN 2016006228 (print) | LCCN 2016016167 (ebook) | ISBN 9781481305921 (hardback: v. 1) | ISBN 9781481305969 (web pdf) | ISBN 9781481305952 (mobi)
Subjects: LCSH: Bible. Luke—Commentaries.
Classification: LCC BS2595.53 W6413 2016 (print) | LCC BS2595.53 (ebook) | DDC 226.4/077—dc23
LC record available at https://lccn.loc.gov/2016006228

Printed in the United States of America on acid-free paper with a minimum of 30 percent post-consumer waste recycled content.

To the memory of Abraham J. Malherbe (1930–2012)

Contents

Editors' Preface

The Baylor–Mohr Siebeck Studies in Early Christianity series aims to facilitate increased dialogue between German and Anglophone scholarship by making recent German research available in English translation. In this way, we hope to play a role in the advancement of our common field of study. The target audience for the series is primarily scholars and graduate students, though some volumes may also be accessible to advanced undergraduates. In selecting books for the series, we will especially seek out works by leading German scholars that represent outstanding contributions in their own right and also serve as windows into the wider world of German-language scholarship.

As Professor of New Testament at the University of Bonn, Michael Wolter is one of the most prominent scholars of early Christianity in the world today. He is especially well known for his work on the Corpus Paulinum, Luke–Acts, and the ethos and ethics of early Christianity. His major publications include *The Gospel According to Luke* (trans. W. Coppins and C. Heilig; BMSEC 4; 2 vols.; Baylor University Press, 2016/2017 [originally published as *Das Lukasevangelium*, HNT 5 (Tübingen: Mohr, 2008)]), *Paul: An Outline of His Theology* (trans. R. L. Brawley; Baylor University Press, 2015 [originally published as *Paulus. Ein Grundriss seiner Theologie* (Neukirchen-Vluyn: Neukirchener, 2011)]), and his commentary on Romans (*Der Brief an die Römer*, I, *Röm 1–8*, EKK 6.1 [Neukirchen-Vluyn: Neukirchener, 2014]; volume 2 is scheduled for publication in 2018). In addition to the information about his research provided at Michael Wolter's university webpage, a list of his English-language publications can be found at Wayne Coppins's blog, *German for Neutestamentler*.

As the fourth volume in the BMSEC series, we have consciously chosen a commentary, with the conviction that scholarship is advanced through the fruitful interaction between articles/book chapters, monographs, and commentaries. And we have chosen Michael Wolter's commentary on Luke because we regard it as an especially strong representative of this genre. By way of illustration, four strengths of his commentary may be highlighted here. First, Wolter often advances independent lines of argument that break new ground or challenge consensus views. For example, disputing the assumption that Luke places Jesus's birth during the reign of Herod, he argues that Luke has *not* assigned the census under Quirinius to the wrong period of time (see at 1.38 and 2.1-3). Moreover, with reference to the force of the imperfect ἔδει in 15.32 and his assignment of Luke 15 to the genre of controversy dialogue, he argues that the Parable of the Prodigal Son does *not* have an open ending. Secondly, Wolter effectively draws upon comparative material from the ancient world to illuminate numerous (key) texts in Luke. To name just one example, his interpretation of "this is my body" in 22.19b is informed by a striking comparison with the function of the words "this is the dream" in Daniel 2.36[Theodotion]. Thirdly, he frequently highlights the need to reassess the meaning of specific words and phrases. For example, while many scholars have claimed that ἀγωνία means "struggle" in 22.44, Wolter criticizes this interpretive tradition for focusing on the word in isolation and argues that when it occurs in syntagmatic connection with γενόμενος, it means "inner agitation" (see also at 1.4: παρακολουθεῖν; 2.19: συμβάλλουσα; 2.49: ἐν τοῖς τοῦ πατρός μου; 6.11: ἄνοια; 9.41: ἀνέξομαι ὑμῶν; 9.48: ἐπὶ τῷ ὀνόματι; 12.1d-3: ὑπόκρισις; 13.24: ἀγωνίζεσθε; 17.27 and 20.35: γαμεῖν/ γαμίσκεσθαι). Finally, Wolter is especially attentive to the structure of Luke and the relationship between different parts of the work. For example, he presents good reasons for ending the travel narrative at 18.34 and careful arguments against dividing it into three parts (see at 9.51–18.54; 13.22-35; 17.11; 18.35–19.46; 18.31-34).

With regard to the translators' divided allegiance to the source and target languages, Wayne Coppins and Christoph Heilig have generally attempted to adhere closely to the German wording, while allowing for some adjustments for the sake of clarity and readability in English. In some cases, of course, our communication with Michael Wolter has led to more extensive reformulations and ocassionally to minor additions or subtractions vis-à-vis the German version. Special note should be made of the fact that we have intentionally provided a rather wooden translation of Wolter's German translation of Luke rather than providing our own translation of the Greek text or adopting an existing English translation. More generally, we have usually provided our own translations of Wolter's translations of primary texts, quoting from existing translations only in cases in which he has quoted from an existing German translation.

Similarly, in most cases we have provided our own translations of German secondary literature rather than quoting from existing translations. Three specific points of translation may be mentioned here. First, in consultation with Michael Wolter, we decided to render *frohbotschaften* with "to gospel" rather than with "to proclaim the gospel" or the like. Second, Michael Wolter's distinction between *eschatologisch* and *eschatisch* has been retained. Parallel to the distinction between ontological and ontic or Egyptological and Egyptian, "eschatological" (*eschatologisch*) is used for matters that concern *speaking or thinking about the last things*, whereas "eschatic" (*eschatisch*) is used to signify *end-time events and conditions*. Third, despite the disadvantages of adopting a Germanism, Wayne Coppins decided to translate *Unheil* with "unsalvation" rather than with a (range of) term(s) such as disaster, calamity, misery, damnation, or condemnation.

Wayne Coppins would especially like to thank his cotranslator, Christoph Heilig, for his excellent work throughout the translation process. It would be difficult to overstate the many small and large ways in which Christoph contributed to the accuracy and readability of the translation, and the good *Zusammenarbeit* introduced a new level of enjoyment to this large project. As with previous translations, I am also grateful to Simon Gathercole for his careful reading of the entire manuscript, which included many good proposals for resolving specific problems of translation alongside his uncanny ability to catch minor slips in English, Greek, Hebrew, Latin, and Coptic. Likewise, Christoph and I are deeply thankful to Michael Wolter for providing us with such detailed feedback on the translation as a whole and for answering our many specific questions. We have gratefully incorporated many of his excellent suggestions, and appreciate the prompt and friendly manner with which he offered them. Finally, I am thankful to my wife, Ingie Hovland, and my daughters, Sophia and Simone, for creating space in our life for my translation work.

Both editors wish to express their thanks to Henning Ziebritzki at Mohr Siebeck and Carey Newman at Baylor University Press for their exceptional support and guidance in the continued development of this series. Likewise, we are thankful to the many people at Baylor University Press who have given us concrete assistance and guidance along the way, especially Diane Smith, Jenny Hunt, Jordan Rowan Fannin, David Aycock, and Cade Jarrell. We are also grateful to Elisabeth Wolfe for her helpful review of the English translation.

Wayne Coppins and Simon Gathercole
Athens, Georgia, and Cambridge, England,
October 2015

Author's Preface to the English Edition

The publication of the English edition of my commentary on the Gospel of Luke fills me above all with gratitude. I am especially grateful that during the last months I was afforded the opportunity to reread my own interpretation of Luke's gospel in a translation into a foreign language. Through this it has been brought again to my consciousness how excellent a theologian Luke is. Like no other gospel writer, Luke has managed to write his story of Jesus into the history of Israel and to integrate it into the history of the origin of Christianity. Not only is the theological and historiographical reflectiveness of his story of Jesus unrivalled, but the influence of Paul and his theology upon him is also most palpable.

However, the largest portion of gratitude goes to Wayne Coppins who together with Christoph Heilig performed the onerous task of translating the commentary. Having reread my own German text through their translation and become aware of the linguistic difficulties that had to be overcome (just to mention the German preference for compound words which cannot be reproduced in English), I can only express my highest admiration for the result they have produced with their translation. Thank you very much indeed!

Since I have learned so much from English and American scholarship on Luke, I am happy that the translation of my own commentary on the Gospel of Luke helps to make German scholarship more easily accessible to non-German speaking members of the community of Luke–Acts scholars.

I also wish to express sincere thanks to the editors of the "Baylor–Mohr Siebeck Studies in Early Christianity," Wayne Coppins and Simon Gathercole, for accepting this book into their series, and to the publishers of this book, Baylor University Press and Mohr Siebeck—represented by Carey Newman and Henning Ziebritzki—for their willingness to include this book in their publication programs.

I dedicate the translation of my commentary on the Gospel of Luke to the memory of Abraham J. Malherbe, whose death in October 2012 left a painful void. By doing this I want to express my deep gratitude for what I owe to him in scholarship and through friendship, and I explicitly want to also include in these thanks Abe's dear wife, Phyllis Malherbe.

Michael Wolter
Bonn, Germany
November 2015

Author's Preface to the German Edition

In recent years many good and comprehensive commentaries on the Gospel of Luke have appeared. Likewise, the numerous monographs and articles that are published each year also constantly increase our knowledge of the third gospel and contribute to a better understanding of its literary and theological distinctiveness. In this context, the composition of my own commentary was lightened by the fact that I had the privilege of writing it for the *Handbuch zum Neuen Testament*. I have attempted to implement the specific concept of this commentary series and limit the space given to tradition history in order to profile in this way the theological concerns of the Lukan Jesus story. In relation to the predecessor commentary of Erich Klostermann, which was first published in 1919 and appeared in a second edition in 1929, form-critical perspectives in particular have found stronger consideration. Because the commentary was not permitted to extend beyond one volume and because it also had to do without footnotes, it must be admitted that a text has arisen that is not especially pleasing to read at many points. This is above all the case whenever long sentences are interrupted by long parentheses. For this I beg the reader's indulgence.

A preface, however, exists above all for thanking the people who have had a part in the composition and publication of the book.

The first and greatest thanks are due to my coworkers, who have collaborated on the emergence of the commentary in the past four years with great engagement: Dr. Jochen Flebbe as research assistant as well as student assistants Martin Kessler, Gerd Maeggi, Sarah C. Prang, Verena Schlarb, and Nikolai Tischler. The collaboration with them has not only furthered the emergence of the commentary but was also a lot of fun. It is actually a shame that now it is all over.

I feel the same about the Bonn "Lukasübung" (Luke seminar), which has become legendary in the course of the years. For six consecutive semesters the participants in this course have read and critically discussed the Gospel of Luke and the growing commentary manuscript. I have thankfully adopted their corrections and suggestions into the manuscript (for the most part, at least), and I therefore wish to erect a memorial to the seminar and its members with the words of Luke 22.28: ὑμεῖς δέ ἐστε οἱ διαμεμενηκότες μετ᾽ ἐμοῦ ἐν τοῖς πειρασμοῖς μου. (Here the last genitive should, of course, be a *genitivus subiectivus*.)

My colleague Hans Dieter Bork (Cologne and Bonn) took it upon himself to read through the entire manuscript again before it went to press. It is due to him that the commentary was saved from many mistakes and linguistic follies and could be made more precise in terms of content at many points. Jens Schröter (Leipzig; now Berlin), who is to write the commentary on Acts in the same series, read the introduction, and I have gratefully taken up his comments and pointers.

I thank the *Deutsche Forschungsgemeinschaft* for generously supporting the work on the commentary.

The most important final thanks, however, should belong to those to whom the commentary directly owes its origin and its publication. This is above all Andreas Lindemann, who had so much faith in me that he first handed over the writing of this commentary to me many years ago and then stood alongside me with friendly advice at the completion of the manuscript after a long time of patient waiting. Dr. Henning Ziebritzki and Bettina Gade of Mohr Siebeck have cared for the volume with great reliability and friendliness. Therefore I wish to express sincere thanks to them as well.

Michael Wolter
Bonn, Germany
October 2, 2007

Introduction

1. Textual Tradition and Early Reception

1.1 At present $\mathfrak{P}^4$ (with Luke 1.58-59; 1.62–2.1, 6-7; 3.8–4.2, 29-32, 34-35; 5.3-8; 5.30–6.16), which probably was copied around 200 CE, is regarded as the oldest preserved textual witness to the Gospel of Luke.

$\mathfrak{P}^{75}$, the Bodmer Papyrus published by Martin/Kasser 1961, is likewise dated to the end of the second or the beginning of the third century. The following texts are preserved from it: Luke 3.18-22; 3.33–4.2; 4.34–5.10; 5.37–6.4; 6.10–7.32, 35-39, 41-43; 7.46–9.2; 9.4–17.15; 17.19–18.18; 22.4–24.53.

In the third century, the following additional copies were made: $\mathfrak{P}^{45}$ (with Luke 6.31-41; 6.45–7.7; 9.26-41; 9.45–10.1, 6-22; 10.26–11.1, 6-25, 28-46; 11.50–12.12, 18-37; 12.42–13.1, 6-24; 13.29–14.10, 17-33), $\mathfrak{P}^{69}$ (with Luke 22.41, 45-48, 58-61), and $\mathfrak{P}^{111}$ (with Luke 17.11-13, 22-23).

The oldest known *parchment manuscript* with a text of the Gospel of Luke is currently **0171** (Nestle/Aland[27], 699: "ca. 300") with the text of Luke 22.44-56, 61-64.

The Gospel of Luke is completely preserved for the first time in the great parchment manuscripts of the fourth and fifth century: ℵ **01** (Codex Sinaiticus), **A 02** (Codex Alexandrinus), **B 03** (Codex Vaticanus), and—though with extensive gaps—in the palimpsest manuscript **C 04** (Codex Ephraemi rescriptus). In the sequence of the New Testament writings, Luke always stands here in the third position after the Gospel of Matthew and the Gospel of Mark, and it also occupies this position in almost all of the canon lists. The only known exceptions are the canon list of Codex Claromontanus **D 06** and the so-called Cheltenham canon, which both probably come from the fourth century (cf. Zahn 1904, 81–84). In both of these lists the Gospel of Luke stands after the other three Gospels

(Codex Claromontanus: Matthew, John, Mark, Luke; Cheltenham Canon: Matthew, Mark, John, Luke) in the fourth position, followed by the Corpus Paulinum. There is not a single manuscript and no canon list in which the Gospel of Luke is directly followed by Acts. From this one can infer that from the beginning Luke–Acts existed in two physically independent units that were also published separately from each other and then fell into two different collections in the course of the New Testament canonization process; see also Schröter 2007, 314–15; 2013, 289–90; Sterling 1992, 338–39 with reference to Dionysius of Halicarnassus, *Antiquitates romanae* 7.70.2, whence it becomes clear that Dionysus published the first book of his Roman history separately (ἡ πρώτη γραφή, ἣν περὶ τοῦ γένους αὐτῶν συνταξάμενος ἐξέδωκα ["the first book that I wrote and published about their origin"]).

1.2 The oldest witness for the existence of the Gospel of Luke is Marcion, who in the middle of the second century published an anonymous "gospel" that was, on the one hand, very similar to the canonical Gospel of Luke—it evidently contained no pericopes that were not also in the Gospel of Luke—but was, on the other hand, much shorter. With the help of patristic quotations it can be reconstructed in fragmentary form (cf. Harnack 1996, 183ff, whose work admittedly requires revision; see Williams 1989, and now Roth 2015). At the time of the ancient church it was assumed that Marcion had obtained his "gospel" via a shortening of the existing Gospel of Luke, and this assessment is also widely held today (cf. recently U. Schmid 2002, 68–69 and the literature mentioned there; Vinzent 2002).

For a number of years, however, questions have been raised in relation to this consensus, which have been formulated most carefully by Gregory 2003, 173ff (see also Tyson 2006; Klinghardt 2006). In this framework, scholars have revived the old thesis that the "gospel" of Marcion did not arise as a shortening from the Gospel of Luke; rather, both writings were based on an older gospel, which was expanded, on the one hand, to the canonical Gospel of Luke and which Marcion, on the other hand, made into the basis of his own edition (cf. previously in the nineteenth century above all, Ritschl 1846, and in the twentieth century, Knox 1942, 77–113, 114–39).

Gregory 2003; 2005a assumes that it was a kind of 'Primitive Luke,' i.e., a first edition of the Gospel of Luke without Luke 1–2 and without Acts. This thesis has its weak point, of course, in the fact that it is based on an auxiliary hypothesis. Not only are there no indications for this hypothesis in the Gospel itself, but it is also unlikely on account of the overall plan of the Gospel of Luke (see section 6 below). In addition, it must, of course, presuppose not only that Luke 3–24 was written and published beforehand (on such a practice, cf. Dionysius of Halicarnassus, *Antiquitates romanae* 7.70.2 [see above]), but also that Luke subsequently supplemented and republished this version. And finally it can be added to this that with the omission of τῶν ἀγγέλων (cf. Tertullian, *Adversus Marcionem* 4.28.11 and Epiphanius, *Panarion* 42.11.6 [GCS *Epiphanius* II: 111.11–12]), the Marcion text in Luke 12.8, which has also left traces in Codex Sinaiticus (‫א‬), presupposes a reading that can probably be attributed to a harmonizing assimilation to Matthew 10.32.

On the other hand, Klinghardt's assumption that the Gospel of Luke is an expanded "redaction of the Marcionite gospel" (Klinghardt 2006, 499) founders above all on the fact that it ignores the textual evidence and does not take into account the fact that in many passages Marcion's gospel contains phrasings that must clearly be assigned to Lukan redaction. An especially conspicuous example of this is the typical Lukan syntagm βασιλείαν τοῦ θεοῦ κηρύσσειν/εὐαγγελίζεσθαι (Luke 4.43; 8.1; 9.2, 60; 16.16; Acts 20.25; 28.23, 31; attested nowhere else in the New Testament), which also stood, according to Tertullian, *Adversus Marcionem* 4.8.9; 33.7, in Luke 4.43; 16.16, in the "gospel" of Marcion. The same also applies to Luke 22.15 (ἐπιθυμίᾳ ἐπιθύμησα τοῦτο τὸ πάσχα φαγεῖν μεθ᾽ ὑμῶν πρὸ τοῦ με παθεῖν; in Marcion's "gospel" according to Tertullian, *Adversus Marcionem* 4.40.1 and Epiphanius, *Panarion* 42.11.17 [GCS *Epiphanius* II: 149.17–18]) and to Luke 24.25 (Marcionic according to Tertullian, *Adversus Marcionem* 4.43.4 and Epiphanius, *Panarion* 42.11.17 [GCS *Epiphanius* II: 154.10–11]). Also with regard to the bread petition of the Lord's Prayer (Luke 11.3), concerning which it says οἱ ἀπὸ Μαρκίωνος ἔχουσι τὴν λέξιν οὕτως· τὸν ἄρτον σου τὸν ἐπιούσιον δίδου ἡμῖν τὸ καθ᾽ ἡμέραν in Origen, Fragment on the Gospel of Luke 1801–1802 (GCS IL, *Origenes Werke* IX, 302), one would first have to explain how the Lukan phrasings δίδου and τὸ καθ᾽ ἡμέραν should have found their way into a pre-Lukan work. And even if one relies only on the critically secured minimal stock of the gospel of Marcion, as reconstructed by Williams 1989, 483ff, according to the principle of the double attestation in Tertullian and Epiphanius, it becomes clear that it contains not only Lukan special material and Q-material but also Markan material. Thus it also presupposes the fitting together of the Gospel of Mark, Q, and Lukan special material into a gospel writing. But in Klinghardt's hypothesis, how this gospel writing should be situated in the history of the synoptic tradition if it does not come from Luke remains completely unexplained.

1.3 Quotations from the Gospel of Luke that attest knowledge of it in other authors are not found until the writings of Justin Martyr shortly after the middle of the second century CE (cf. above all *BibPat* 319–78; Bellinzoni 1998; 2005; Gregory 2003, 211ff): *Apologia i* 15.8, 9 attests knowledge of Luke 5.32 and Luke 6.27-28; *Apologia i* 33.4–5 is based on the reading of Luke 1.26-35; Luke 20.35-36 is reworked in *Dialogus cum Tryphone* 81.4

and Luke 23.46 is taken up in *Dialogus cum Tryphone* 105.5. The series of examples could be extended further (cf. Gregory 2003, 225ff). A little later Justin's student Tatian incorporated the Gospel of Luke into a harmony of the four subsequently canonized gospels, namely in his *Diatessaron* (cf. Gregory 2003, 107ff), which was probably a revision of a gospel harmony by Justin based only on the three synoptic gospels. The only Greek fragment of the *Diatessaron* that we have thus far—which was discovered in 1933 and is named the Dura Europos Fragment after the place of its discovery—attests knowledge of Luke 23.49-51 (cf. Kraeling 1935).

2. Author, Date, and Provenance

2.1 Author

2.1.1 While the author of the "report of the events, which have been completed in our time" (Luke 1.1) speaks of himself (1.3), he does not mention his name. He has thus published his work anonymously (cf. Wolter 1988a, 13–14). The name Luke is found for the first time in $\mathfrak{P}^{75}$ (see section 1 above), namely in the phrasing εὐαγγέλιον κατὰ Λουκᾶν, which is placed as a *subscriptio* beneath the Gospel of Luke. In the great Bible manuscripts (see section 1 above) the name is then mentioned from the fourth century onward either as an *inscriptio* above or as a *subscriptio* beneath the text of the Gospel of Luke. Alongside the long form εὐαγγέλιον κατὰ Λουκᾶν ($\mathfrak{P}^{75}$ A D L W Θ Ξ Ψ 33 𝔐 lat sa^mss bo^pt) there is also the short form κατὰ Λουκᾶν (א B *pc* vg^st bo^ms), but that is very likely later in terms of textual history (cf. Hengel 1984, 10ff; Petersen 2006, 254). Other variants can be ignored. The phrasings εὐαγγέλιον κατά + *name* or κατά + *name* are the same in all the gospels. It can be inferred from this that they arose and were attached to the respective works at the earliest (not "at the latest" as Hengel 1984, 47 argues) at the point in time when at least two different gospels existed alongside one another. The superscripts had the task of distinguishing the gospels from one another and avoiding the confusion of one for the other. This procedure probably did not take place before the first half of the second century (see also Petersen 2006, 273), for in the superscripts the word εὐαγγέλιον is used as a designation for a literary work, and elsewhere this meaning is relatively certain only in the middle of the second century in Justin (*Apologia i* 66.3) and at best perhaps already attested in the 120s in the *Didache* (cf. Kelhoffer 2004; see also section 6.1 below).

Λουκᾶς is the short name for Λουκανός or Λουκάνιος (e.g., Plutarch, *Moralia* 675d, e; 676e) or Λούκιος, the Graecising of Latin *Lucanus*, *Lucanius*, and *Lucius* (cf. BDR §125$_6$). Deissmann 1923 has drawn attention to two dedication inscriptions from Pisidian Antioch, where one and the same person calls himself once Λουκᾶς and once Λούκιος. Among Jews the name was evidently not very common. Apart from Lucius of Cyrene (Acts 13.1), who is perhaps identical with the Jewish Christian Lucius mentioned in Romans 16.21, Ilan 2002, 334 lists only a single Jewish man with this name.

The earliest clear attestation for the ascription of the Gospel of Luke to a certain Luke is found ca. 180 CE in Irenaeus, *Adversus haereses* 3.1.1: *Et Lucas autem sector Pauli quod ab illo praedicabatur euangelium, in libro condidit* ("And Luke, however, the companion of Paul, has compiled the gospel preached by that one in a book"; see also *Adversus haereses* 3.10.1; 11.8; 14.1–3). A bit later the so-called Muratorian Canon (which should perhaps also not be dated until the fourth century; cf. Hahneman 1992; for criticism of this assumption, see Verheyden 2003; cf. also Markschies 2015, 203–8) writes: "The third book of the gospel is that of Luke. This Luke, a physician, whom Paul took to himself after the ascension of Christ as it were as somebody trained in the law (*quasi ut iuris studiosum*), wrote it up in his name on the basis of tradition [?] (*numeni suo ex opinione concriset*). However, he had not seen the Lord in the flesh and therefore begins to narrate, as he could 'follow,' from the birth of John onward" (lines 2–8); other texts from ancient church tradition can be found in Cadbury, *BoC* II: 210ff.

Along with the two texts cited, the whole church tradition assumes that the Gospel of Luke and the book of Acts were composed by the companion of Paul named Luke, who is mentioned in Colossians 4.14 (Λουκᾶς ὁ ἰατρὸς ἀγαπητός), 2 Timothy 4.11 (Λουκᾶς ἐστιν μόνος μετ' ἐμοῦ), and Philemon 24 (Luke stands at the end of a list of "coworkers" of Paul who send greetings) and that his voice can be heard also in the so-called "we" passages of Acts (Acts 16.10-17; 20.5-8, 13-15; 21.1-18; 27.1-8; 28.11-16).

Sometimes Lucius of Cyrene, one of the Antiochene prophets and teachers (Acts 13.1), and the Lucius who extends greetings in Romans 16.21 have been and still are identified with Luke (Origen, *Commentarii in Romanos* 10.39 [PG 14.1288C]; Ephrem the Syrian, *Commentarii in Acta Apostolorum* on Acts 12.25–13.3 in Conybeare, *BoC* III: 416; Ford 1920–1921, 219–20; Deissmann 1923, 374ff; Cadbury, *BoC* V: 489–95; Dunn 1988, 909; see also Stuhlmacher 1992/1999, I: 227–28). In both cases, however, the doubts are great and numerous. Beyond this, from the time of the ancient church, the anonymous "brother" whom Paul sends to Corinth with Titus and recommends to the community there with warm words has also been identified time and again with Luke (Jerome, *De viris illustribus* 7; see also those mentioned in Thrall 2004, 561–62).

Additional biographical specifications are found in the so-called Anti-Marcionite Prologue to the Gospel of Luke, which probably did not originate until the fourth century (cf. Regul 1969, 45): *Lucas Syrus natione Antiochensis, arte medicus, discipulus apostolorum, postea Paulum secutus usque ad confessionem eius, serviens Deo sine crimine. Nam neque uxorem umquam habens neque filios, LXXIIII annorum obiit in Bithynia, plenus spiritu sancto* ("The Syrian Luke, an Antiochene by birth, a physician by occupation, a student of the apostle, followed Paul later up to his martyrdom, serving God without reproach. He had neither wife nor children and died at the age of 74 in Bithynia, full of the Holy Spirit"; other versions have Luke die at the age of 84 in Boeotia).

Eusebius of Caesarea (*Historia ecclesiastica* 3.4.6) and Jerome (*De viris illustribus* 7; *Commentariorum in Matthaeum, praefatio* 35 [CChr.SL 77.2]: *Lucas medicus natione Syrus Antiochensis*) know of an Antiochene origin of Luke also in the fourth century, and this tradition probably arose at that time (see also Regul 1969, 200f). On the basis of Acts 13.1, Stuhlmacher 1992/1999, I: 228 also regards an Antiochene origin of Luke/Lucius as possible. Whether the "we" in Acts 11.28D presupposes this tradition (Kümmel 1973, 116) or whether the tradition was "spun out" of it (E. Plümacher, *TRE* 3: 520.53; see also already Lipsius 1884, 355) cannot be decided. Among more recent commentators of the Gospel of Luke, Fitzmyer I: 44ff still advocates Luke's origin from Syrian Antioch (see also Strobel 1958). Because Acts reveals detailed knowledge of the local conditions in Philippi and because the transition of the Pauline mission to Macedonia in Acts 16.6-10 is so extravagantly staged, Pilhofer 1995, 157–58 regards it as probable that Luke came from Philippi. According to Pilhofer, he "belonged there, however, not to the Latin speaking segment of the population (and was certainly not a *civis Romanus*), but to the group of the Greek speaking Macedonian inhabitants who had been at home in Philippi for centuries" (see also Pilhofer 1995, 248ff; for criticism of this thesis, cf. Broer 1998/2001, I: 134f). Lipsius 1884 compiles additional traditions about Luke (cf. also the overview in Kelly 1974).

2.1.2 Justified doubts are no longer possible concerning the traditional assumption that the Gospel of Luke and Acts come from the same author (cf. Parsons/Pervo 1993, 116; Verheyden 1999, 6 n. 13).

What is controversial is the question of whether the author of the Gospel of Luke and Acts is identical with the companion of Paul named Luke who is mentioned in Colossians 4.14; Philemon 24; 2 Timothy 4.11. The decisive question in this regard is how in the second century one came to the view that he was the anonymous author of Luke–Acts.

In the twentieth century, the equation of Paul's companion Luke with the author of the Gospel of Luke and Acts was called into doubt especially with the argument that Acts "is completely alien to Pauline theology" (Kümmel 1973, 118) and with the argument that for the following reasons alone he could not have been a companion of Paul, namely because he confuses the Pauline chronology, because he has resolutions composed at the apostolic council that contradict the Pauline account of it (cf. Acts 15.20-21, 28-29, on the one hand, and Galatians 2.6-10, on the other hand), and because he thinks Paul would circumcise Timothy (Acts 16.3) (E. Plümacher, *TRE* 3: 521.1ff). In the meantime, however, a change both in the interpretation of Paul and in the interpretation of Luke has led to the insight that the two authors are not as far from each other theologically as has long been assumed (cf. e.g., Porter 1999 and, more recently, the essays in Marguerat 2009). In this respect, it has become more difficult to contest the composition of Luke–Acts by the Luke mentioned in Colossians 4.14; Philemon 24; 2 Timothy 4.11 by appealing to the theological distance between Luke–Acts and Pauline theology.

The doubts about this identification are far from removed thereby, however. Two of these texts (Colossians 4.14; 2 Timothy 4.11) do not come from Paul himself but only arose after the death of the Apostle and were spun out of the greeting list in Philemon 24, which contains the only authentic mention of a Luke by Paul, in order to make the respective authorial fictions believable (cf. Brox 1969). Above all 2 Timothy 4.11 could have played an important role in this connection. When it states there that "only Luke is with me" and this letter also acts as if it were written by Paul when he was imprisoned in Rome with death before his eyes (1.17; 4.16ff), then it could only—so the conclusion had to run when 2 Timothy was still regarded as authentic—have been this Luke from whom the report of the Pauline imprisonment in Rome comes, which one can read in Acts 27.17-31. Correspondingly, Irenaeus writes also with reference to 2 Timothy 4.10-11: *Unde ostendit quod semper iunctus ei et inseparabilis fuerit ab eo* ("Through this he [sc. Paul] reveals that he [sc. Luke] was always connected with him and was inseparable from him"; *Adversus haereses* 3.14.1). And because one had recognized already in the second century that the Gospel of Luke and Acts were written by the same author, it is not to be ruled out that the name Luke was first inferred for the author of Acts from 2 Timothy 4.11 and then transferred to the Gospel. The sequence of the notes in Irenaeus, *Adversus haereses* 3.14.1 could perhaps be invoked in support of this order: "Luke, who always preached with Paul . . . *et creditus est referre nobis evangelium* (and who is regarded as having handed down to us the Gospel)." Thus, it would have been only the above-cited information from 2 Timothy 4.11 with whose help one was able to give a name to the anonymous author of Luke–Acts.

It is, however, also conceivable that the name Luke adhered to the Gospel already independently of Acts (in this vein, cf. now especially again Thornton 1991, 78; Jervell 1998, 80f; Schröter 2007, 312–13; 2013, 287–88). The consequences would be very far-reaching in this case, for this connection between the name Luke and the Gospel could only be traced back to historical recollection. How could one otherwise and without the detour via Acts explain that the composition of the Gospel of Luke was ascribed to Paul's companion Luke, of all people?

Taking all things into consideration, however, we cannot get around the diagnosis that, with respect to the person of the author of the Gospel of Luke and Acts, there are more questions than answers and earlier certainties have gone lost in the meantime, namely on both sides of the argument.

In this context, no role can be played by the thesis defended by Hobart 2004, according to which the intensive use of medical technical terms in the Gospel of Luke and Acts allows one to infer that the author was, in fact, the physician mentioned in Colossians 4.14. Most of the terms invoked by Hobart do not belong to specific medical technical terminology (cf. Cadbury 1926; 1933); moreover, the Lukan style displays "no more medical language and interest than the style of contemporary authors who were not physicians" (Kümmel 1973, 117). This has not been altered by the investigation of Weissenrieder 2003, who wants to ascribe more than average medical professional knowledge to Luke and in doing so does not pay attention to the fact that Luke also endeavors to use a correct professional terminological idiom in other spheres (cf. e. g., for the legal system Bormann 2001). Moreover, it is doubtful anyway whether the Lukan texts can really bear everything that Weissenrieder loads onto them.

2.1.3 What significance the so-called "we" passages in Acts 16.10-17; 20.5-15; 21.1-18; and 27.1–28.16 have in this context is yet another question. In any case, they do not allow inferences about the name and identity of the author of the Gospel of Luke and Acts. All attempts to reconstruct from them a source reworked by the author of Acts run aground on the fact that the linguistic character of the "we" passages is identical to that of the surrounding texts of Acts. Therefore, what Harnack 1906, 56 writes is really "incontrovertible—the 'we' passages and Acts have one and the same author" (see also E. Plümacher, *TRE* 3: 494.38ff), and this assessment also includes, of course, the author of the Gospel of Luke.

Therefore, the greatest probability remains with the explanation that is most suggested in any case when the author of a historical account writes in the first person on the authorial level of presentation, namely the explanation that he "himself participated in the events portrayed in the we-style" (E. Plümacher, *TRE* 3: 514.22f). This is not, of course, to say that "we" always means only "Paul and I." It refers instead always to the group formed by the author, Paul, and other companions.

Above all there is discussion over whether the *auctor ad Theophilum* really participated in the events narrated in the "we" style or whether he only acts as if he were present.

To be sure, Plümacher's own explanation, namely that with the "we" Luke wanted to demonstrate something like experience at sea (E. Plümacher, *TRE* 3: 514.27ff; 1977), falls apart on the fact that the "we" style does not "[appear] solely in the portrayal of sea journeys" (*TRE* 3: 514.28f; cf. against this Acts 16.12b-17; 20.7-8; 21.8-18; 28.14-16) and on the fact that not all the sea journeys are narrated in the "we" style. This fact contradicts all the more the thesis of Robbins 1978, who regards the "we" narrative as a stylistic device of ancient sea voyages. Wedder-burn 2002, 94ff (the "we" refers to an unknown companion of Paul whose student the author of Acts understands himself to be and in whose name he writes) wants to explain an *obscurum* by an *obscurius* and has therefore scarcely struck upon the correct interpretation. For criticism of other attempts at interpretation, cf. Wehnert 1989; Thornton 1991, 107ff.

Here too the most likely explanation is therefore the best one. The "we" comes from the author of the Gospel of Luke and Acts, who presents himself to the readers with his own "I" in Luke 1.3 and Acts 1.1 and has marked "his own share in the journeys of Paul" with the help of the "we" passages (Dibelius 1968, 93; then also Thornton 1991, passim). This means that the author of the Gospel of Luke and Acts did not always accompany Paul but was only present where he narrates in the first person plural. With this qualification one of the most serious objections against the identification of the "we" with the author of the Gospel of Luke and Acts then also loses its weight, namely that Acts evidently knows nothing of the Pauline letter writing and contains so little of the theological language of the Pauline letters. This matter finds a plausible explanation in the fact that all the letters of Paul were written between Acts 16.17 and 20.5, i.e., precisely in the time when the narrator responsible for the "we" was not with Paul— from 1 Thessalonians, which emerged during Paul's stay in Corinth (Acts 18.1-17), up to Romans, which was written at the time of Acts 20.3, i.e., immediately before the author of the "we" met up again with Paul. This explanation would also remain correct in the unlikely case that Philippians (or even Philemon) should have been written in Rome, for this could have happened in any case only after the situation narrated in Acts 28.16, where the "we" occurs for the last time. Plus, this identification is immune to the accusations that the author of Acts confuses the Pauline chronology, that he has Paul travel too often to Jerusalem, or that he evidently provides an inaccurate report concerning the apostolic council in Acts 15. For all these differences relate to periods of time in which the author of the "we" was not with Paul.

Accordingly, the author of the Gospel of Luke met Paul in Troas (Acts 16.10) and traveled with him to Philippi (16.11). There he was separated from Paul when Paul was put in prison with Silas (16.22). He then loses sight of Paul for a few years and meets him again in Philippi (20.5-6). From there he then accompanies Paul, via Troas (20.6-12), Miletus (20.15-38), Tyre (21.3-6), Caesarea (21.8-14), and other places, to Jerusalem. There, together with Paul, he visits James, the brother of the Lord (21.8). Due to the arrest of Paul in the temple (21.33), he is then separated from him again. He only meets him again in Caesarea Maritima (27.1), and he then accompanies him on the journey to Rome (27.1–28.14). After arriving there, he separates from Paul again only a short time later, namely after Paul has obtained his own dwelling in which he is watched by a soldier (28.16). This much, then, we know about the author of the Gospel of Luke. It must remain open whether he was identical with the "coworker" mentioned in Philemon 24 and whether he was named "Luke." Nevertheless, we will continue to call him Luke.

2.1.4 As a final point, we must also ask about the religious biography of Luke. Did he grow up in a Jewish or non-Jewish family? Was he a proselyte who grew up in a non-Jewish environment but then became a Jew and finally turned toward Christianity? Or did he belong prior to his turn to the Christian confession to the circle of the so-called God-fearers, who felt themselves drawn to Judaism as non-Jews, without becoming Jews themselves (see at Luke 7.5)?

About thirty years ago Kümmel 1973, 118 could still write, "The only thing that can be said with certainty on the basis of the Gospel of Luke about its author is the fact that he was a Gentile Christian." As evidence Kümmel referred to the fact that Luke "has no knowledge of the geography of Palestine and avoids Semitic terms apart from ἀμήν" (118). Scholars have also appealed to the disinterest in cultic questions (with reference to the excision of Mark 7.1-23) and the receding of the "typical Jewish conception of atonement" (Broer 1998/2001, I: 131). However, even if they are taken together, these elements cannot justify what they are intended to establish. Knowledge of the geography of Palestine is just as little an indicator of Jewish or non-Jewish identity or origin as the avoidance or use of Semitic words. The reasons for the absence of Mark 7.1-23 are completely different from a supposed disinterest in questions of purity (see at section 6.2 below). Luke did not borrow from Mark 7.24–8.26 either, and the fact that he is certainly interested in questions of purity can be seen in Acts 10.10-16; 11.1-10. Finally, the so-called conception of atonement is neither "typically Jewish" (cf. only Versnel 2005) nor alien to Luke, as Luke 22.19, 20; Acts 20.28 show. Moreover, its absence in the mission speeches of Acts finds its explanation in the fact that the interpretation of the death of Jesus as a salvific death was an element of early Christian internal language that would have been completely out of place in the mission discourses of Acts (see further at 22.19).

Beyond this, for a number of years scholars have rightly pointed to aspects that show that Luke was equipped with a cultural basic knowledge that was profiled in an unmistakably Jewish manner. His excellent knowledge of the Septuagint, which even extended so far that he could imitate Septuagintal style (see section 4.4.6 below; see further Plümacher, *TRE* 3: 506ff; Fitzmyer I: 114ff) and which placed him in position to narrate his story of Jesus as a continuation of the history of Israel (see at 1.5), his knowledge of the doctrinal differences between Pharisees and Sadducees (Acts 23.6-8), his precise portrayal of Jewish milieus in Luke 1–2 (Radl 1988a, 23), and above all the prominent interest in the Israel question, which probably first prompted Luke to write the history of the separation of Christianity and Judaism as a component part of the history of Israel (cf. Wolter 2004b, 262f), support the view that the author of the Gospel of Luke grew up in a Jewish family and, like Paul, experienced not only his primary but also his secondary socialization in a Jewish milieu (for the distinction between these two forms of socialization, cf. Berger/Luckmann 1966, 129ff).

2.2 Date

Terminus post quem is the composition of the Gospel of Mark in the years 69/70 CE, which Luke knew with great certainty (see section 3 below). If one wants to assume that he had it in a revised version, then one can, or rather needs to, add a few more years. Mittelstaedt 2006 has recently shown again that the announcements of the destruction of Jerusalem in Luke 19.43-44; 21.20-24 cannot function as dating criteria. However, his assumption that Paul was still alive when Luke ended Acts is based on a failure to recognize the genre of Luke–Acts. Luke is not writing a biography of Paul, and he can therefore end his work without reporting the death of Paul. A clear *terminus ante quem* is only given by the quotations from the Gospel of Luke in Justin Martyr in the middle of the second century (see section 1 above). Every more precise temporal placement is dependent on hypothetical auxiliary assumptions. If, for example, one ascribes the "we" passages to Luke (see section 2.1.3 above) and has him first meet with Paul already at the beginning of the 50s (the events narrated in Acts 16.10-17 are probably to be dated to this time), then it is advisable to estimate the completion of Luke–Acts at a good distance from the end of the first century. For this reason, nothing speaks against placing Luke's πρῶτος λόγος "concerning everything that Jesus did and taught" (Acts 1.1), which was finished first, at the beginning of the 80s of the first century.

2.3 Provenance

There was already uncertainty concerning the place of composition of the Gospel of Luke at the time of the ancient church. While Jerome had still spoken in *De viris illustribus* 7 of a composition of Luke–Acts in Rome, in his *Commentariorum in Matthaeum, Praefatio* 36f (CChr.SL 77.2) he has it originate *in Achaiae Boeotiaeque partibus*. More recently, consideration has been given to Antioch, Caesarea Maritima, Ephesus, Corinth, and Rome, among others (see Plümacher 1984, 169), without one of these locations being able to establish itself against the others. The author of the "we" passages comes with Paul to Rome, which could argue for a Roman origin, and the shepherd scene in Luke 2.8-14 could perhaps provide another indication (cf. ad loc. and Wolter 2000b), for with the announcement of the birth to the shepherds Luke takes up a politicized bucolic that is otherwise attested exclusively within *Roman* bucolic (see at Luke 2.8).

3. Sources

3.1 For the interpretation of the Gospel of Luke, the question of the sources and *Vorlagen* has lost much of its earlier significance in recent years. This is due above all to the insight into the methodological primacy of synchrony over diachrony in the interpretation of the gospels. Every evangelist has created his story of Jesus as a literary unity that is both structured and coherent, and he can therefore justifiably demand—even if his representation is based on *Vorlagen* that have also entered into it with their wording—that the present text be read as *his* text, i.e., as a linguistic expression furnished with meaning by him.

Despite this fact, it is, of course, not meaningless to inquire about the sources and *Vorlagen* of the Gospels, especially since Luke himself explicitly mentions that he composed his narrative on the basis of older presentations (Luke 1.1-2). For if we know these *Vorlagen* and know with which changes (supplements, deletions, rephrasings, rearrangements) the author has adopted them into his work, we obtain information that allows us to better understand the author, his mode of operation, and his intentions than if we interpreted his work solely on the basis of the existing final text. This insight, however, helps us only theoretically, for in practice the trust of earlier decades in our abilities to reconstruct *Vorlagen* via source criticism has rightly given way to a much more skeptical evaluation of the possibilities regarding this procedure. If older *Vorlagen* are not preserved, then there is scarcely a chance of reconstructing their form and wording from the presentations based on them.

These two caveats must be constantly kept in view in the quest for the sources and *Vorlagen* that underlie the Lukan story of Jesus.

3.2 The most plausible option is still to answer the question of the sources and *Vorlagen* of the Gospel of Luke within the framework of the two source hypothesis (on the proto-Luke hypothesis [cf. above all Streeter 1924, 199–222; Boismard 1997] and for other hypotheses, cf. Fitzmyer I: 73ff, 87ff, 89ff; Radl 1988a, 34–35; Schnelle 2007, 215ff; Tyson 1978). It reckons that two written sources are reworked in the Gospel of Luke and the Gospel of Matthew, namely the Gospel of Mark and the so-called Sayings Gospel Q, which is not handed down in any manuscript.

This framework, however, encompasses much more complex transmission circumstances than the two-source theory "in its ideal form" assumes (C. Heil 2001, 134; cf. the diagram, e.g., in Schmithals 1985, 182). Above all we cannot say that we know better than only rather approximately the text of the two copies of the Gospel of Mark and Q that were available to Luke in the composition of his story of Jesus.

3.2.1 In relative terms, the Gospel of Mark is best known to us. Here, however, the number and especially the quality of the so-called minor agreements (the clearest examples are listed at each respective passage; cf. further Ennulat 1994, 1–34, 417–30; Friedrichsen 1989; Kiilunen 2002; G. Strecker 1993; Neirynck 1974b, 11–49; 1982/1991/2001, II: 3–42) make it fairly likely that Luke and Matthew used this writing as a *Vorlage* not in the version known to us but in a 'deutero-Markan' version, which can perhaps even be designated as a "recension" (so already Sanday 1911, 21: ". . . by far the greater number of the coincidences of Mt Lk against Mk are due to the use by Mt Lk . . . *of a recension of the text of Mk different from that from which all the extant MSS. of the Gospel are descended*" [emphasis in original]). This does not mean, of course, that it was "an overall revision . . . , which revised the whole Gospel of Mark in terms of language and content" (A. Fuchs 2006, 210; on this cf. section 3.2.3). Moreover, we are far from being able to reconstruct this version even only approximately, for we cannot assume that all the minor agreements go back to this pre-Lukan–Matthean form of the Gospel of Mark. Some of them are probably due to a coincidentally identical redactional change of the Markan text by Luke and Matthew, others to the influence of oral tradition, and others are to be explained with reference to textual history. Conversely, one must, of course, assume that text elements of deutero-Markan provenance are present not only where there are discernable minor agreements. When the deutero-Markan text was redactionally changed by Luke or Matthew, then, though it remains preserved in the other one, it can no longer be recognized as deutero-Markan, because a Luke–Matthew agreement is no longer present. And if both have changed the deutero-Markan text, then nothing at all remains left over from it.

3.2.2 An adoption of text from the "Sayings Gospel" Q, which on account of its embedding of the Jesus tradition in narrative connections has been rightly referred to in this way for some time (cf. Hoffmann 2001, 288; S. Hultgren 2002), is especially probable where Luke and Matthew reproduce a common tradition that is not also preserved in Mark. Beyond this, of course, one must reckon with overlaps of Mark and Q, but the identification of these overlaps is difficult and controversial (on these cf. above all Fleddermann 1995; Laufen 1980; Schröter 1997a, 144ff). But only the minimal content of Q is thereby grasped, for it is highly likely that this writing had a very different form than the recent reconstruction attempts in *CEQ* and by Fleddermann 2005a suggest. This applies, first, with reference to the *extent*. If Luke and Matthew used Q in the way in which they used the Gospel of Mark, from which less than 50 percent is preserved in *both* of the large Gospels, then it must be assumed that a considerable portion of the Sayings Gospel is contained in the Lukan or Matthean "Special Material" (see section 3.3 below) and thus is no longer identifiable as Q-tradition. And just as 5 percent of the Gospel of Mark is preserved neither in Luke nor in Matthew, the same could, of course, apply also for Q-material. In addition, the proposed reconstruction of the *wording* is also doubtful, particularly in places in which different phrasings are encountered in the Luke–Matthew double tradition. The existing reconstructions consistently presuppose that the Q-wording is preserved in one of the two phrasings. But this is a completely ungrounded *petitio principii*, which produces very misleading results, as a comparison with the Luke–Matthew reception of the wording of the Gospel of Mark could immediately show. In almost half the cases the Markan phrasing is preserved neither by Matthew nor by Luke. Moreover, one must, of course, assume that as in the Mark material there are also Luke–Matthew agreements in the Q-material that were not due to the *Vorlage*, so that even when we find Luke–Matthew double tradition with identical wording, there is always a remaining uncertainty about whether we are really dealing with a Q-phrasing. For this reason the reconstruction of this *Vorlage* is burdened with great uncertainties and can be done only approximately.

3.2.3 The picture of the synoptic transmission history determined by the two source hypothesis has been critically accompanied for many years by Albert Fuchs and his students (see A. Fuchs 2004–2007). They start from the minor agreements and assume that the Gospel of Mark was initially revised into a "deutero-Mark" and that it was only available as such to Luke and Matthew as a source. The deutero-Markan redaction is said to be graspable above all in the minor agreements, but also to have encompassed material that is ascribed to the Sayings Source by the two-source theory.

For easily understandable reasons, this thesis has not been able to establish itself. Although Fuchs worked for more than thirty years on his model, he was never in a position to identify the additional material from the Luke–Matthew double tradition with which the original Gospel of Mark is to have been expanded to "deutero-Mark." As soon as this topic comes up he escapes into nebulous circumlocutions such as "it is only natural that on this occasion one inserted new materials into the Gospel of Mark as well (logia agreements)" (A. Fuchs 2006, 210) or these "logia" were inserted from "Q or other sources" "at all the places in the Gospel of Mark that appeared favorable to the reviser" (A. Fuchs 2004–2007, I: 1). Fuchs obviously does not know *which* texts should have been in view here. But so long as he cannot say which "new material, above all logia" it should be that "were inserted into the Gospel of Mark" in the deutero-Markan revision (A. Fuchs 2006, 240) and so long as he can provide no plausible picture of the literary form of the *whole*, his hypothesis cannot be regarded as a serious contribution to the solution of the Synoptic Problem.

With regard to the Sayings Source itself Fuchs assumes that "at least a portion of Q . . . was already available to deutero-Mark and (was) used *by him*, so that for Matthew and Luke only *the rest* of this source remained left over" (A. Fuchs 2004–2007, IV: 10; emphasis in original). But it could also be the case "that the logia inserted by deutero-Mark" do not come from Q, "so that under this presupposition the result would be not only . . . a division of Q, but a *shrinking* to the remainder left over" (IV: 10; emphasis in original). Apparently, Fuchs imagines the matter in such a way that there was only a single manuscript of Q and that "deutero-Mark" excised from it the logia that he wanted for his revision of the Gospel of Mark, so that only such a mutilated copy or a manuscript that depended on it remained left for Luke and Matthew, or that Q could only have contained such logia that deutero-Mark did *not* know from elsewhere. Who is supposed to believe this? And when Fuchs then claims on top of this "that *all* agreements without exception owe their origin to such a single process of revision" (A. Fuchs 2006, 240; emphasis in original), then this is just as misguided as the following statement of Cameron 1996, 352, which is formulated with regard to *CEQ*: "We do have a text of Q; what we do not have is a manuscript."

3.2.4 It is highly likely that Luke knew the Q and Mark material preserved in his presentation not only from the two sources available to him
in written form. One could reckon with an access to the Jesus tradition
mediated in such an exclusively literary manner only if one wanted to
assume that the oral tradition that found entrance into Mark and Q died
out once it was fixed in written form in these two writings. Although no
one, of course, claims this, many works on the history of the synoptic tradition implicitly presuppose this assumption. By contrast, one must start
from the assumption that over a long period, alongside and independently
of Mark and Q, there existed an oral tradition of the Jesus material that
also reached Luke and found entrance into his presentation of the story
of Jesus (on this topic, cf. now above all Dunn 2003). Plus, Mark and Q
were certainly not known in every Christian community. It need not be
stated separately that in light of these considerations the circumstances of
synoptic tradition become even more diffuse, so that it becomes even more
difficult and in most cases completely impossible to separate pre-Lukan
'tradition' from Lukan 'redaction' and to reconstruct the stock of the pre-
Lukan tradition according to its extent and wording.

3.3 The latter applies especially to the portions of the Gospel of Luke that
have parallels neither in the Gospel of Mark nor in the Gospel of Matthew,
i.e., for ca. 550 of the 1,149 verses, thus for almost half of the Gospel of
Luke. Today these texts are summarized under the umbrella term "Lukan
Sondergut" (S^{Lk}) or "Lukan Special Material" (Special L), and there is
analogously a "Matthean *Sondergut*" (S^{Mt}) or "Matthean Special Material"
(Special M). Both of these designations are so-called *remainder categories*. This term is used to designate categories under which phenomena
are subsumed that are associated with one another merely by a *negative*
characteristic, because within an existing categorical system they cannot
be assigned to the respective main categories and remain left over in the
truest sense of the word. In this sense the texts that are subsumed under
the heading "Lukan *Sondergut*" have as their only common feature the
characteristic that they have *a parallel neither in the Gospel of Mark nor
in the Gospel of Luke*.

But in a miraculous way the material designated with this umbrella
term was transformed quite quickly into an independent entity and in
parallel the term *Sondergut* mutated from a remainder category into a
main category. As such the Lukan *Sondergut* then made a rapid career. It
became a collection that was ascribed not only coherence in theme and
content but also a distinct theological profile (cf. the surveys of the history
of research in Schmithals 1985, 329ff; Rese 1985, 2275ff, 2284ff; Paffenroth 1997, 11ff). It was awarded the literary status of a written source (as

an independent source alongside Q and the Gospel of Mark for the first time, to my knowledge, in B. Weiss[7], 253), which then naturally needed also a name ("L"; for the first time in J. Weiss, 280). In this way it was awarded an individuality, the linguistic and theological distinctiveness of which could become the topic of investigations (Rehkopf 1959; Pittner 1991). According to H. Klein 1987 it even has a "message." "Bearers" and a "community" of the *Sondergut* arise (Schnelle 2007, 197). Riesner locates it in "conservative Jewish Christian circles . . . who gathered in Jerusalem and Judea around James, the brother of the Lord, and his successors" (Riesner 1999, 51; Manns 1996 is similar), while Habbe 1996, 116 attributes to it a female author in the form "of a well-off proselyte in a large city of Italy." It becomes the object of an academic commentary (Petzke), and finally a written source with regard to extent and wording is reconstructed from it (Paffenroth 1997).

All attempts to ascribe to the Lukan *Sondergut* the character of a source that has an independent literary or theological profile commit a grave error, however. They do not take account of the fact that the only feature that all the texts of the *Sondergut* have in common is merely a negative characteristic, namely their absence from the Gospel of Mark and the Gospel of Matthew, and they turn the remainder character of the *Sondergut* into a primary, positive characteristic that supposedly adheres to the texts as such and can be found in them. Against such a manner of proceeding one must raise not only positional and methodological objections but also scientific objections.

Paffenroth 1997, 65 represents an almost ideal-typical example of how this procedure of the transformation of a negative feature into a positive one functions and how this scientifically problematic construct is then used for further internal differentiation within the Lukan *Sondergut*: ". . . only 197 (sc. verses) have been judged as possibly from a pre-Lukan source other than Mark or Q." In his discussion of the origin of the material that comes into consideration (27ff) he repeatedly uses the argument "because not from Q, therefore not from another source." This is, however, a *petitio principii* that is grounded by nothing. The most likely possibility that there could be not only Mark–Q overlaps but also Mark–"L" and Q–"L" overlaps is not brought into consideration even once by him and the other authors who regard the Lukan *Sondergut* as a written source or as a coherent tradition.

This then results in a self-enclosed collection or even a written source whose borders are clearly defined by the extent of Mark and Q or, in other words, whose textual stock is established by the characteristic "not Mark and not Q." But this is a completely implausible construct. Actually, the exact opposite is probably the case, for it can scarcely be assumed that there were written sources or collections of Jesus tradition in the second half of the first century that displayed no overlaps. Thus, if the Lukan *Sondergut* should have been part of a written source, then it is more likely that this would have had the form of a gospel writing, which incidentally was already assumed by B. Weiss, for whom it was "highly probable" that the material of the Lukan *Sondergut* "belonged for the most part to *a* source that encompassed the whole life of Jesus" and is said to have included not only the passion story but also the Emmaus narrative (B. Weiss 1889, 543; emphasis in original). But such a claim would first need to be verified. And even if this were to succeed, one would still be far from being able to ascribe a certain theological profile to this text. This would be approximately like wanting to specify the theological peculiarity of the Gospel of Mark solely on the basis of the Markan material contained in Luke.

The term *Sondergut* should therefore remain what it is, a remainder category. It may by no means be made into a source designation by a sleight of hand, but rather needs to be used as an umbrella term for all the material that has a parallel neither in the Gospel of Mark nor in the Gospel of Matthew. Concerning the provenance of this material one can only say with some certainty that one "(may) not assume . . . a unified origin" (Schmithals 1985, 366): some of it is Q-material that was omitted by Matthew; some of it is scattered oral tradition brought together by Luke; and some of it goes back to Luke himself.

4. The Lukan Story of Jesus as an Episodic Narrative

4.1 Luke has narrated his story of Jesus as a sequence of individual stories (on the form of the episodic narrative, see also Breytenbach 1985). Although the sequence of the overall presentation seems arbitrary and interchangeable at many points, Luke has given it a well-ordered form. The sequence of events violates the narrative *verisimile* (τὸ εἰκός) neither in details nor as a whole. All the events that are constitutive for the plot of the macronarrative stand in the required position—the birth at the beginning and the suffering, death, and resurrection at the end (see also the introductory comments on 22.1–24.52[53]). The anointing with the Spirit and the proclamation as Son of God (3.21-22) stands at the right place as does the journey to Jerusalem. And the sequence of the episodes in 18.35–19.46 is unchangeable due to their topographical placement. In the sense of Aristotle, *Poetica* 10 (1452a14ff) Luke narrates a "simple action" (ἁπλῆ πρᾶξις), which "hangs together and forms a unity." He combines individual episodes into certain "narrative phases" or narrative "collecting basins" (terms from Lämmert 1975, 73), and he makes them recognizable as such by demarcating them from their respective literary contexts with the help of structuring markers.

For this structuring, however, Luke uses neither subheadings nor optical signals such as lacunae, paragraphs, or new page beginnings; rather, he *narrates* the structuring markers of his story. This fact, however, is also the reason why no two commentaries have the same outline for the Gospel of Luke. Every outline is brought to the Lukan story of Jesus from outside and is therefore already part of its interpretation. Accordingly, an outline is a text that the commentator writes. Therefore, it seems prudent that this commentary also give an account of the criteria that were used for the structuring of Luke's story of Jesus.

4.2 Narrated structuring signals are signals that make episodes into episodes, being characterized by a specific constellation of parameters involving *time*, *space*, and *people* that changes from episode to episode. Accordingly, one can recognize the end of the one and the beginning of a new episode by the fact that the narrator makes a change to these parameters and in this way establishes a new constellation. It is obvious that when all three parameters are changed (as, e.g., in 2.1-3; 3.1-2; 22.1-6), the structuring divisions are deeper than when only one changes (as, e.g., in 8.19). Moreover, the quality of a structuring division also depends, of course, on the quantity of the respective parameters. How large is the temporal or spatial distance? How many characters are exchanged?

4.3 This results in the following proposal for the outline of the Lukan story of Jesus according to its main parts (for further details and justification, cf. the discussions at the beginning of the respective sections). For reasons of space only the topmost structuring level will be described (for the subordinate structuring levels, cf. ad loc.).

1.1-4: The proem is a metanarrative text in which Luke provides the reader with information about the emergence, character, and intention of his narrative. It thus stands outside of the actual narrative.

1.5-79(80): Luke dates the events narrated in this section in the reign of Herod the Great (v. 5). The rhythm of the sequence of episodes is given by the chronology of Elisabeth's pregnancy (cf. vv. 24, 26, 56, 57). With the summary in v. 80, Luke goes beyond the temporal frame marked out in v. 5. Here he takes into view a time period of many years.

2.1-39(40-52): The narrative makes a temporal jump of unknown duration into the time of the census under the governorship of Quirinius. Luke dates the episodes narrated in vv. 1-39 in the time—which is taken into view in 1.80—of John the Baptist's growing up, for he refers to this period in 2.1 with "in these days." Moreover, the characters of the narrative are changed out. Verse 4 and v. 39 form a clearly recognizable *inclusio*. With a summary (v. 40, 52), which Luke illustrates—as in Acts 4.32–5.16—with the help of an embedded episode (vv. 41-51), the narrative is again led beyond the period of time mentioned at the beginning.

3.1-20: John the Baptist is the main narrative character in this section. Luke provides here a self-enclosed overview of the entire activity of the Baptist from his call (v. 2) to his placement in prison (v. 20). The synchronism in vv. 1-2 marks a deep caesura, with the introductory specification of time expressing that at least fifteen years have passed since the events narrated in 2.1-39.

3.21–4.13: Luke brings Jesus into the story and introduces him as a narrative figure. His narrated partners are only God (3.22) and the devil (4.1-13).

4.14-44: The narrative makes a temporal leap of unspecified duration and changes the location to Galilee (v. 14), namely to Nazareth (vv. 16-30) and Capernaum (vv. 31-42). In addition, the adult Jesus is now led among humans for the first time. Verses 42-44 mark not only the end of the stay in Capernaum but of the entire narrative collecting basin. Jesus's activity is expanded from Galilee to the entire Jewish land (v. 44).

5.1–6.49: In this section Luke narrates individual scenes that are exemplary for Jesus's proclamation of the reign of God "in the Jewish land" (4.44). Accordingly, not a single episode takes place in a specific place (in 5.17 Luke has even deleted Capernaum from Mark 2.1). A place name is not mentioned again until 7.1. It corresponds to this perspective that the section ends with Jesus's speech to "a great crowd of his disciples and a great crowd of the people from all Judea and Jerusalem and from all the coastal region of Tyre and Sidon" (6.17).

7.1-50: The narrative first returns to Capernaum and then changes to Nain, i.e., to two specific cities that are identified by name. Luke forms again a narrative collecting basin, which is comprised of events that are located in two places. The episodes in the two places are also joined together by the fact that Luke narratively parallels the Gentile Centurion (vv. 1-10) and the widow with the dead son (vv. 11-17) and places them in the light of 4.25-27.

8.1–9.50: With the summary of 8.1-3, not only the persons in the narrated environment of Jesus are switched but the angle of the narrative perspective abruptly widens from a small-scale localization in the house of a Pharisee into an extraordinary spatial breadth. The unspecified character of this spatial breadth (διώδευεν κατὰ πόλιν καὶ κώμην; 8.1) finds its counterpart in the fact that the individual episodes are connected with one another either only very loosely or not at all.

9.51–18.34: The fact that with 9.51 Luke narrates a structuring division that gives his story of Jesus a new orientation can be recognized above all in the fact that the perspective changes. While he had still directed the view of the readers into the spatial breadth with 8.1-3, he now directs it into the future. The reader receives the information that from now on the Lukan story of Jesus approaches its end. Jesus's journey to Jerusalem actually reaches its goal only in 19.45-46 and therefore one could also let this main section extend to this point. I prefer, however, to end it already in 18.34, for the character of the narrative fundamentally changes with the arrival in Jericho. While not a single place is identified by name between 9.51 and 18.34, with Jericho in 18.35 Luke not only mentions a place name again for the first time, one whose proximity to Jerusalem is known already from 10.30, but he also narrates the part of the journey of Jesus beginning in 18.35 very differently from the previous peregrination.

18.35–19.46: This section has its own character vis-à-vis 9.51–18.34, which is clearly recognizable and makes it into its own narrative phase. This is ensured not only by the frequent repetition of ἐγγύς and cognates (18.35; 19.11, 29, 37, 41) but above all by the non-interchangeable topographic succession of the individual scenes—from "shortly before Jericho" (18.5) via "Jericho" (19.1), "shortly before Jerusalem" (19.11), "shortly before Bethphage and Bethany at the Mount of Olives" (19.29), and "shortly before the descent of the Mount of Olives" (19.37), until the city finally comes into view (19.41) and Jesus enters into the temple (19.45).

19.47–21.38 can be recognized on the basis of the correspondence of beginning frame (19.47-48) and concluding frame (21.37-38) as a narrative unity that is clearly demarcated to the front and to the back. But the internal coherence is very strong as well, for scenically and thematically the same thing holds true for all the episodes of this narrative collecting basin. Luke narrates how Jesus teaches for many days in the Jerusalem temple before the Jewish people.

22.1–24.52(53): Luke narrates the story of the fulfillment of the two announcements of Jesus's passion and resurrection (9.22; 18.32-33). Luke has constructed the story of the "handing over" and death of Jesus as well as the narratives of the discovery of the empty tomb and the appearances on Sunday morning as two parts of a single fulfillment story. In v. 53 the Lukan story of Jesus ends with a summarizing prospectus, with which—as in 1.80; 2.40, 52—the temporal frame marked out at the beginning (24.1: "on the first day of the week") is transcended, and the narrative is opened up to a sequel. At the same time, Luke introduces the new main figures of his narrative here. The end of the story of Jesus has become the beginning of the story of the disciples.

4.4 The Lukan style of narration is additionally characterized in matters large and small by a whole series of characteristic features.

4.4.1 Luke often uses *(a)* "certain anticipations" (Lämmert 1975, 143) in order to announce what is coming, and *(b)* "inserted retrospections" (Lämmert 1975, 112), in order to take up again what lies behind. With the help of such arcs, which begin and end *within* the Lukan story of Jesus, its coherence is stabilized. Additionally there are also *(c)* retrospections into the time before the beginning of the narrative. They have the function of anchoring the Lukan story of Jesus in the history of Israel:

(a) Announcements that are realized within the narrative:
  1.13, 15-17: the birth, naming, and prophetic activity of John the Baptist (1.57-63; 3.1-20)
  1.20: Zechariah remains mute until the birth and naming of his son (1.64)
  1.31-33: the birth, naming, and installation of Jesus as messianic king, whose rule over Israel will have no end (2.7, 21; resurrection)
  1.76-78a: the prophetic activity of John the Baptist (3.1-20)
  1.78b-79: the visitation of Israel through a (sun)rise (sc. Jesus)
  2.34: the divided reaction of Israel to Jesus (*this announcement is not realized until the second volume of Luke–Acts*)
  3.16-17: the coming of the "Stronger One" (sc. Jesus)
  6.16: the handing over by Judas (22.47-48)
  9.22: the suffering, death, and resurrection of the Son of Man
  9.27: the "seeing" of the reign of God by the disciples (*this announcement is not realized until the second volume of Luke–Acts*; see at Luke 9.27)
  9.31: the "departure" of Jesus
  9.44: the handing over of the Son of Man
  18.32-33: the handing over, suffering, death, and resurrection of the Son of Man
  22.4-6: the handing over of Jesus by Judas (22.47-48)
  24.47-48: the proclamation of "repentance for the forgiveness of sins among all nations" by the apostles (*this announcement is not realized until the second volume of Luke–Acts*)
  24.49: the sending of the Holy Spirit upon the apostles (*this announcement is also not realized until the second volume of Luke–Acts*)

(b) Reminders of previously narrated material:
  2.21: of the mentioning of Jesus's name by Gabriel (1.31)
  22.35: of the equipment rule from 10.4
  23.8: of the fact that Herod Antipas had heard of Jesus and had wanted to see him (9.7-9)
  23.49: of the women who followed Jesus from Galilee (8.2-3)

24.6b-8: of the announcements of Jesus's handing over, death, and resurrection (9.22, 44)

24.22-24: of the discovery of the empty tomb (24.1-12)

24.44-46: of the announcements of Jesus's passion and resurrection (9.22, 44; 18.32-33)

(c) References to the past before the beginning of the narrative:
1.55: to the promises given to the patriarchs
1.70-71: to the prophets' promises of salvation
1.73: to the Abrahamic covenant
2.26: to the oracle given to Simeon
3.4-6: to the promises of Isaiah
4.18-19: to the promises of Isaiah
4.25-27: to Elijah and Elisha
6.3: to David's food theft according to 1 Samuel 21.2-7
6.23: to the persecution of the prophets by the fathers
6.26: to the approval of the false prophets by the fathers
7.27: to the witness of the Scripture about John
11.47-51: to the murder of the prophets by the fathers of the scribes
18.31: to the announcement of the fate of the Son of Man by the prophets
22.37: to the announcement of Jesus's fate by Isaiah
24.27: to the witness of Scripture about the Messiah
24.44: to the witness of Scripture about Jesus

4.4.2 Luke places similar material, themes, and narratives together, especially in the so-called travel narrative of 9.51–18.34. To the extent to which material from the Luke–Matthew double tradition is affected, this obvious clustering by Luke causes reconstructions of the structure of Q, as these have been presented by IQP with the *CEQ* and Fleddermann 2005a, which are based largely on the sequence of the Q-texts in the Gospel of Luke, to become doubtful. In detail the following thematic connections can be identified:

- The cycle of controversy dialogues in 5.12–6.11 is taken over from Mark 2.1–3.6, the cycle of miracle stories in 8.22-56 from Mark 4.35–5.43.
- In 11.1-13 Luke has placed together three tradition units on the topic of *prayer*.
- In 12.13-34 the concern is with dealing rightly with *wealth and possessions*, and in 12.13-21, 35-46, 54-59; 13.6-9 with the right evaluation of *time*. Both topics overlap in 12.13-21.
- In 14.1-24 all pericopes somehow have to do with *celebratory meals and banquets*.

- 15.1-32 deal with *what is lost* (sheep, drachma, son).
- In 16.1-31 the concern is once again with *money and possessions.*

4.4.3 Luke likes to form pairs, often with a male and a female component:

(a) Events that take place at two places form a narrative collecting basin:
2.4-21/22-39: Bethlehem and Jerusalem
4.14-30/31-43: Nazareth and Capernaum
7.1-10/11-50: Capernaum and Nain

(b) Narrative figures appear in pairs:
2.25-35/36-38: Simeon and Hanna
3.12-13/14: tax collectors and soldiers
7.1-10/11-16: the centurion and the widow
7.11-16/8.40-42, 49-56: the *only son* of a *mother* and the *only daughter* of a *father* are raised from the dead.

(c) Two examples illustrate one and the same idea:
4.25-27: the Syrian captain and the widow from Zarephath
6.44: figs from thorns and grapes from a bramble bush (par. Matthew 7.16)
11.31-32: the queen of the south and the Ninevites (par. Matthew 12.41-42 in reversed sequence)
12.24, 27: ravens and lilies (par. Matthew 6.26, 28b-29)
12.54-55: cloud and south wind
13.1-5: the Galileans killed by Pilate and the eighteen dead at the collapse of the tower of Siloam
13.18-21: mustard seed and leaven (par. Matthew 13.31-33)
14.28-32: tower building and going to war
15.4-10: lost sheep (man) and lost drachma (woman)
17.26-29: in the days of Noah and in the days of Lot
17.34-35: two men lie on one bed, two women grind together (see also Matthew 24.40-41)

4.4.4 Luke structures larger units by having two audiences alternate with each other; see the introductory comments to 9.51–18.34 and 14.25–18.34.

4.4.5 Luke is the only evangelist who introduces individual episodes with the phrasing ἐν μιᾷ τῶν πόλεων (5.12), ἐν μιᾷ τῶν ἡμερῶν (5.17; 8.22; 20.1), or ἐν μιᾷ τῶν συναγωγῶν (13.10). "This kind of compression, which must be called *eclectic*, narrates according to the principle '*pars pro toto*'" (Lämmert 1975, 84).

4.4.6 The most conspicuous features of the Lukan style of narration include—even more than in Acts—the imitation of the language of the Old Testament, namely in its Greek translation, the Septuagint. Luke even configures the first sentence of the narrative in close dependence on the episodic style of narration of the Septuagint (documentation in 1.5). Also, much of the whole section of Luke 1.5-79 calls to mind people and events of the Old Testament (for individual documentation, see the introductory comments on 1.57-79[80]). Thus, Luke obviously also makes an effort to narrate in the style of the Septuagint in the subsequent course of the narrative.

What follows is a small selection of examples (individual documentation at the passages mentioned; cf. further esp. Fitzmyer I: 114–25). The beginning of episodes with ἐγένετο δέ + infinitive or + *verbum finitum* or with καὶ ἐγένετο + *verbum finitum* (1.8-9; 2.1, 6; 3.21; 5.12, 17; 6.1, 6, 12; and elsewhere). καὶ ἰδού + *verbum finitum* (1.20, 31, 36; 5.12, 18; 7.12; and elsewhere). Inchoative ἀναστάς + *verbum finitum* (1.39; 4.29; 5.28; 6.8; 15.18, 20; and elsewhere). ποιεῖν ἔλεος (1.72; 10.37). πίπτειν ἐπὶ πρόσωπον (5.12; 17.16). εἰς μαρτύριον (5.14; 9.5; 21.13). δοχὴν ποιεῖν (τινι) (5.29; 14.13). ἐπαίρειν τοὺς ὀφθαλμούς (6.20; 16.23; 18.13). The introduction of episodic sequences through "so-and-so" παρεγένετο/παρεγένοντο πρός τινα (8.19). τὸ πρόσωπον στηρίζειν (9.51). ἐκζητεῖν τὸ αἷμα (11.50). ἐπὶ τὸ αὐτό (17.35). ὀρθρίζειν πρός (21.38). ἡ ὑπὸ τὸν/ἡ ὑπ' οὐρανόν (17.24). ἔρχονται ἡμέραι (23.29). οὗτοι οἱ λόγοι with a cataphoric orientation of the demonstrative pronoun (24.44).

This effort to adapt his story of Jesus stylistically to the narrative style of the Holy Scripture of Israel is guided by an interest in signaling to the reader that the narrated events are nothing other than a continuation of the history of Israel (see also section 6.1 below and the introductory comments on 1.5-79[80]).

4.4.7 A noteworthy characteristic of Lukan narration consists in the fact that in the narration of individual episodes he repeatedly combines genres of text sections with one another. Luke can narrate healings as chreiae (5.17-26; 6.6-11; 7.1-10; 14.1-6), simply add chreia-like elements (9.37-45; 13.10-17), or use an exorcism to set a chreia in motion (11.14-26). In 19.1-10 a conversion narrative is combined with a controversy dialogue.

4.4.8 Luke sometimes uses concentric ring compositions following the pattern a / b / . . . / n / . . . b / a. The following texts are most clearly configured according to this model.

The episodes of the first narrative collecting basin in 1.8-79 (see the introductory comments on 1.5-79[80]). The reading scene in 4.16d-20 (see ad loc.). In

10.25-37b ("The Scribe and the Merciful Samaritan") multiple ring compositions are even interwoven into one another (see the introductory comments on
10.25-37). 11.8 (see ad loc.). The scene with the hearing of Jesus before Pilate in
23.1-5 (see the introductory comments on 23.1-5). For the postulate of a chiastic
or concentric structure of the travel narrative, see the introductory comments on
9.51–18.34.

5. Intended Readers

"Intended Readers" are the readers whom the author imagines as readers
of his text or, rather, with whom he reckons as readers, and for whom
he writes his text. They exist in the consciousness of the author and are
constantly present there during the writing of his text. They must be distinguished from the so-called real readers (or empirical readers) who actually read a text—from its first readers (in the case of the Gospel of Luke
perhaps Theophilus) down to its present-day readers and interpreters. The
extent to which the Theophilus mentioned in Luke 1.3-4 as a fictive reader
also functions as a representative of the intended readers must remain
open (see the introductory comments to 1.1-4 and at 1.3). That this relation could be configured very flexibly is shown by Lucian's tractate *Quomodo historia conscribenda sit*, which is addressed, on the one hand, to a
friend (φιλότης [3] as metonymic *abstractum pro concreto*) by the name
of Φίλων (1, 22, 24, 29), but, on the other hand, wants—as "guidance . . .
for authors" (παραίνεσις . . . τοῖς συγγράφουσιν; 4), i.e., for "future history
writers"—not only to be read but also to be followed.

It is largely uncontroversial today that Luke writes for *Christian*
readers. Thus, he does not intend, as was long assumed (cf. those listed
in Plümacher 1983, 53), to practice political apologetics and "cleanse"
Christianity "from the suspicion of being subversive and seditious in disposition" (Plümacher 1983, 53).

The thesis that Bauckham 1998 put forward for discussion, according
to which the Gospels were written not for specific communities but for
all Christians (e.g., p. 46: "The Gospels have a historical context, but that
context is not the evangelist's community. It is the early Christian movement in the late first century"), is not really new with respect to Luke–
Acts. It was already emphasized time and again earlier that it "was not
directed to a specific community," but aimed at a "developing church with
its various branches scattered throughout the whole empire" (Riches 1987,
178; cf. already Plummer xxxiv: "for the instruction and encouragement
of all Gentile converts" and then also Maddox 1982, 15; O'Toole 1983, 2;
Allison 1988; R. E. Brown 1997, 271; and others).

Although Bauckham 1998 deserves credit for reinitiating an urgently needed discussion, and although he rightly criticizes (see below) the methodological deficiencies (of the inferences) of numerous redaction-critical and social-historical investigations, he has overdrawn his thesis to the extent that he constructs an antithetical dualism, whose poles could perhaps function as ideal-typical models but are much too undifferentiated for the description of historical processes (in this respect the questions put to Bauckham's thesis in the otherwise affirming article of Plessis 2000 and the sharp criticism of M. Mitchell 2005, forty-four are on target; for a summary of the debate, cf. Klink 2004). The greatest weakness of Bauckham's thesis consists in the fact that he throws out the baby with the bathwater and constructs an overly sharp alternative between the local community and all Christians in the *imperium Romanum*. For even if Luke should have written his story of Jesus "for any and every church to which their Gospels might circulate" (Bauckham 1998, 46), it cannot be effectively denied that he belonged to a certain Christian community, which was significant both for the experience and presentation of his Christian identity in particular and for his picture of Christianity in general. Beyond this it is problematic that Bauckham 1998 designates the intended readership of the Gospel of Luke as "not specific but indefinite" (1) or as an "open category of readers/hearers in any late first-century Christian church" (47), because in this way he levels out the distinction between intended and real readers: an intended readership is never "not specific, but indefinite." Rather, it can always be only a *specific* entity because it is a construction of the author. Even if—in this Bauckham is probably correct—one must reckon as the intended readership of the Gospel of Luke "any church . . . to which his work might find its way" (11), this readership can, for this reason, always be only *the very specific image* that Luke has of it.

However, Bauckham 1998, 26–27 is right to draw attention to the fact that due to their genre gospels do not have "addressees" or "recipients" and that it would therefore be a mistake to transfer the communication model of the Pauline letters to the gospels. Bauckham is also justified in his criticism of an uncontrolled "mirror reading," which uses the narrative as a mirror in order to reconstruct with its help specific conditions in the community of the author.

A small selection of examples may illustrate the legitimacy of this criticism. From Luke 12.13-15; 16.14-15 and other texts Schnelle 2007, 289 draws the following conclusion: "The rich in the community were self-righteous and greedy . . . they despised the poor (cf. Luke 18.9) and stood in danger of falling away from the faith through their striving for wealth (cf. Luke 8.14; 9.25)." Furthermore, it is time and again the Pharisees who are interpreted as an allegorical symbol for the rich of the Lukan community (cf. e.g., Petracca 2003, 198). From the brief narrative about Mary and Martha (10.38-42) it is inferred that in the Lukan community there were women "who literally worked hard for the community like Martha" and therefore "revolted against other women who were not so engaged" (Melzer-Keller 1997, 239), whereas others assume the story shows that in the Lukan community woman office holders were placed under pressure to relinquish their tasks to the men (Reid 1996, 157). On the basis of the parable trilogy on the theme of "the lost" in Luke 15, some conclude that in the Lukan community the relations between Jewish Christians and Gentile Christians were strained (e.g., Heininger 1991, 166; Pokorný 1998, 172ff), while others want to infer from the text that there were controversies over whether apostates could be received back again into the community (e.g., Bonnard 1980). Others think they can infer from the Lukan statements on the Torah that Jewish Christian community members were being accused of betraying the Jewish identity by other Jewish Christians or non-Christian Jews (cf. e.g., Esler 1987, 129).

None of this can be found in the texts. With the same method one could conclude from 1 Timothy 3.3 (whoever wants to become bishop may not be a drunkard) that there were alcoholic bishops in the community for which this instruction is specified. Plus, reconstructions of community circumstances such as those named above would, of course, have to be added up if they desired to be taken seriously. But this consequence is not taken into consideration in the reconstructions for obvious reasons. After all, it would immediately reduce this method *ad absurdum*, for this consequence allows to emerge such a complex web of problems and overlapping conflicts that could not even be assumed for Christian communities of the late twentieth and early twenty-first centuries. The picture of the Christian community that emerges on the basis of such reconstructions is downright monstrous and probably has nothing to do with reality. Furthermore, such "mirror reading" always leads to aporia. How should Luke 6.22 ("Blessed are you when people hate you . . . because of the Son of Man") and 6.26 ("Woe to you rich, for you have [already] received your consolation") be meant for the same group within the Lukan community, namely for *Christians* (v. 22) who are *rich* (v. 26)?

The preceding argument does not, of course, intend to deny that there are also texts in the Gospel of Luke that the community, to which Luke belonged, as a fellowship of *real* readers, could apply to their individual historical situation. But this applies equally to the real readers in every other Christian community. What must be decisively contested is the view that it is possible to infer from the text a specific individual situation of a specific individual community and that the identity of the *intended* readers is constituted by their membership in this community. Plus, it is time and again precisely the descriptions of *typical* situations, concerning which one can most likely say that Luke presents them to his readers for an actualizing reading. In this sense it is valid, for example, for every Christian community that there are Christians in it who "are increasingly choked by worries, riches, and the pleasures of life" (8.14) or "who are convinced concerning themselves that they are righteous and despise the rest" (18.19). This fits always and everywhere.

But we need not restrict ourselves to this negative result, for the intended reader of the Gospel of Luke can indeed be furnished with astonishingly precise contours. For this we simply need to orient ourselves to typical features, and this means to the image of Christianity that is recognizable in Luke–Acts itself. In this way the relative validity of Bauckham's thesis is then also recognizable. Luke writes his work with the knowledge that Christianity had been a supralocal entity spread throughout the entire Roman Empire for many decades already. According to the witness of Acts, there are Christian communities not only in the eastern provinces of the *imperium Romanum*—i.e., not only in Syria and in Cilicia, in Galatia and in Asia, in Macedonia and in Achaia—but also in Italy and in Rome itself. It would certainly be completely inappropriate if one wanted to keep this knowledge away from the Lukan story of Jesus and restrict the horizon of its author to the boundaries of a single Christian local community. Beyond this, however, this circumstance makes it also very probable that the Gospel of Luke was written not only *in the knowledge* that there were Christian communities everywhere in the Roman provinces, but also that in the view of its author its content was also relevant to every single (Bauckham 1998, 1: "any and every") one of these communities.

With this, however, an aspect has come into view that makes it possible to specify the Lukan picture of the readers of his story of Jesus with greater precision. The aspect of the diversity of early Christianity invoked against Bauckham by his critics (cf. Sim 2001, 9–10; M. Mitchell 2005, 39–40), which cannot, of course, be doubted, becomes meaningless if we view the communities not with the eye of a modern historian but instead ask about how they are perceived by a contemporary author such as Luke and about the picture that he has of Christianity. Then it is not difficult to give substance to this postulate of a unified identity—which is taken for granted by Luke—of *all* Christian communities in the Roman Empire, without having to revert to minimal contents such as the confession to Jesus Christ as Son of God and Messiah. For what, according to the Lukan conviction, *all* Christian communities, wherever they may be in the last quarter of the first century in the Roman Empire, have in common with one another amidst all diversity and what keeps them together is precisely that which Luke has written down in his "report" (Luke 1.1)—namely, a very specific foundation story: the story of the πεπληροφορημένα ἐν ἡμῖν πράγματα reaching from Luke 1.5 to Acts 26.29 (Luke 1.1; on this demarcation, see section 6 below). Thus, Luke intends as readers all those Christians and Christian communities who make up the "whole flock" (Acts 20.28) of Christianity, which owes its historical form to the events that he narrates in Luke–Acts. Besides this, however, the manifold anchoring of the story narrated by Luke in the history of Israel (see section 4.4.1 [c] above) shows that he reckons with readers who are well acquainted with the history of Israel and its Holy Scriptures.

Finally, one can possibly even reckon with the fact that Luke imagined this readership not only as a synchronic entity but also as a diachronic entity. His narrative would then be intended not only for the Christians of his own time but also for Christians of future generations. That history writing could be guided by such a perspective is already recognizable in Thucydides, who composed his history of the Peloponnesian War "more as an enduring possession than as a masterpiece for current hearers" (κτῆμά τε ἐς ἀεὶ μᾶλλον ἢ ἀγώνισμα ἐς τό παραχρῆμα ἀκούειν; 1.22.4). Lucian of Samosata also uses this phrasing (*Quomodo historia conscribenda sit* 5; 42), and in the summarizing advice at the end of his essay he gives the following instruction to future writers of history: "Write not only with a view to the present (καὶ μὴ πρὸς τὸ παρὸν μόνον ὁρῶν γράφε) in order that contemporaries praise and honor you; write instead in thoughts of permanence for the descendants (ἀλλὰ τοῦ σύμπαντος αἰῶνος ἐστοχασμένος πρὸς τοὺς ἔπειτα μᾶλλον σύγγραφε)" (61).

This does not mean, however, that with this expansion the picture of the intended readers becomes more diffuse, for with the Christian community of the Lukan present, Christian posterity enduringly shares the same characteristic feature that constitutes the identity of all intended readers, namely the foundation story of Christianity that Luke narrates in his "report." For this story is also their story.

Unlike in the other three canonical Gospels, however, this foundation story in Luke now encompasses not only the story of Jesus but also the time of the proclamation of the "witnesses" (see at 24.48). With this we stand before the question of the function of the story of Jesus within this foundation story of Christianity that Luke narrates in Luke–Acts.

6. The Theological Place of the Story of Jesus in Luke–Acts

6.1 The Gospel of Luke is the first part of a two-part historical work that narrates an epoch of the history of Israel and thus belongs to the historiographical genre of "epoch histories" (this view is grounded in detail in Wolter 2004b, 256ff; cf. also the diagram on p. 33).

It would therefore not be appropriate to the subject matter if one attempted with the help of the genre question to detach the Lukan story of Jesus from the literary and theological context of the Lukan work as a whole, as happens with many interpreters, who form-critically separate it from Acts on the basis of its similarity to the other three canonical Jesus stories and furnish it with the label "gospel" (cf. in this sense recently Shauf 2005, 62; Schröter 2013, 208–13; see also the overview in Verheyden 1999, 45ff). Against such attempts one must insist that Luke—like Mark, Matthew, and John—did not write his story of Jesus in the consciousness that he was writing a "gospel."

It already speaks against such an assumption that this term was used as as a literary category only from the second century onward and that it could therefore only be ascribed retrospectively to the canonical gospels as a genre designation (see section 2.1.1 above; cf. also Koester 1989; Dormeyer 1989; Kelhoffer 2004). Even in the superscription of the Gospel of Mark ἀρχὴ τοῦ εὐαγγελίου Ἰησοῦ Χριστοῦ . . . (Mark 1.1) the term εὐαγγέλιον is not used as a literary category, for the other uses of this term in the Gospel of Mark (cf. 1.14, 15; 8.35; 10.29; 13.10; 14.9) show clearly that by εὐαγγέλιον its author quite decisively understood an *oral* entity. Before Easter it is the εὐαγγέλιον τοῦ θεοῦ proclaimed by Jesus (1.14, 15), and after Easter it is the εὐαγγέλιον τοῦ Χριστοῦ, i.e., the salvific message of Jesus Christ, which is proclaimed in the whole world. Luke's usage corresponds to this. In his story of Jesus Luke does not carry over a single one of the seven Markan uses of εὐαγγέλιον. In Acts 15.7 and Acts 20.24, however, he places the term in the mouths of Peter and Paul as a summary designation of their respective proclamations of Christ.

The fact that already in his story of Jesus Luke also wants to narrate nothing other than a further part of the *story of Israel* can be recognized above all in three features:

- Luke narrates this story in a manner that recalls the Septuagint's narrative style in many respects (see section 4.4.6 above).
- Time and again he interprets events as fulfillments of the Holy Scriptures and Israel's hopes for salvation (e.g., Luke 1.55, 70-71, 73; 3.4-6; 4.18-19; 7.27; 18.31; 22.37; 24.26-27, 44-48; see then also Acts 2.16-21, 25-28; 15.15-17; 26.6-8; 28.26-27).
- He presents Jesus as the awaited "Savior" and messianic king of Israel and anchors him in the history of Israel (Luke 1.32-33; 2.11, 30; 3.6;

see then also Acts 13.17-23 with the series "our fathers," "Saul," "David," "Jesus").

One can, however, refer to Luke–Acts as a "sacred narrative" (Sterling 1992, 363) only insofar as solely the narrated events and not the narration of them is "holy," for Luke certainly did not intend to rank his work among the "Scriptures" in the sense of Luke 24.27, 32, 45; Acts 17.2, 11; 18.24, 32. Similarly, the classification of Luke's presentation as a "continuation of the Septuagint" (Sterling 1992, 363) can be maintained only with the qualification that this refers to the connection between promise and fulfillment and not to a specific literary claim.

Luke already announces in 1.1, when he speaks of "events that were completed in our time" (πεπληροφορημένα ἐν ἡμῖν), that he wants to write the story of an *epoch* in the strict sense of the word, i.e., as a presentation of a self-enclosed period of time with a distinct beginning and an end that is no less clearly defined. Accordingly, he begins with a portrayal of the salvation initiative that God takes up for the eschatic fulfillment of the prophetic promises and Israel's hopes for salvation by twice sending the angel Gabriel—first to an old priest in Jerusalem (1.5-20) and then to a Galilean virgin who is engaged to a descendant of David (1.26-38). Luke marks the end of this epoch with the imprisoned Paul's encounter with Agrippa II (Acts 26.1-29). He narrates this encounter as the crowning conclusion of the Pauline mission to the Jews and has it climax in v. 28 by having Agrippa so famously and mysteriously say: ἐν ὀλίγῳ με πείθεις Χριστιανὸν ποιῆσαι (perhaps: "you almost convince me to make myself a Christian"; cf. Barrett 1994/1998, II: 1170–71). But it remains at this "almost," and after the scene with Agrippa II there then follows only—separated by the distance-creating narrative of the adventurous sea journey to Italy—the narrative of the encounter with the Roman Jews (28.17-31). Luke has configured this scene as an epilogue, which explains with the help of Isaiah 6.9-10 why the overwhelming majority of Judaism has rejected the proclamation of Christ.

In schematic simplification the embedding of the Lukan narrative in the (hi)story of Israel can therefore be presented with the help of the overview on the following page. Luke sees the special profile of this epoch, which makes the narrated time period into an epoch in the first place, as consisting in the fact that the sending of God's eschatic salvation (σωτήριον; Luke 2.30; 3.6; Acts 28.28)—a sending that first took place through Jesus himself and then through his witnesses—was rejected by most of the Jews. Because, in contrast to this, the salvation of God was received by far more non-Jews, Luke can have Paul say with his last words in Acts 28.28: "And they will listen!" (αὐτοὶ καὶ ἀκούσονται; cf. also Plümacher 2004, 144).

The (Hi)story of Israel According To Luke

Fathers (Acts 13.17)
↓
Judges (Acts 13.20)
↓
Saul (Acts 13.21)
↓
David (Acts 13.22)
↓

↓
Jesus (Acts 13.23)
↓

↓

↓

↓

↓

↓

"Law and Prophets until John" (Luke 16.16)

The "events that have been completed in our time" (Luke 1.1)

First Book
John the Baptist
Jesus is the proclaimer
Jesus is on the earth
"in the land of the Jews and in Jerusalem" (Acts 10.39)
The apostles are "eyewitnesses" of the activity of Jesus
  (Luke 1.2; Acts 1.21)
Only Jesus has the Spirit

- -

Second Book
Jesus is the one proclaimed
Jesus in in heaven
"among all the nations" (Luke 24.47)
The apostles are "servants of the word" and "witnesses"
  of the resurrection (Luke 1.2; 24.48; Acts 1.8; 13.31
  and elsewhere)
The witnesses as well have the Spirit

Proclamation of the βασιλεία τοῦ θεοῦ

Parousia (Acts 1.11): "Reestablishment of all that God has spoken through the mouths of his holy prophets from the beginning on" (Acts 3.21); liberation of Jerusalem (Luke 2.38); reestablishment of the βασιλεία for Israel (Acts 1.8); "resurrection of the righteous and unrighteous" (Acts 24.15); judgment (Acts 17.31)

Thus, Paul formulates here "a contrast that can scarcely be surpassed in sharpness" (Plümacher 2004, 145). The fulfillment of the promises for Israel therefore led to a separation process, which had as a consequence the fact that "Israel" received a quite peculiar form in the Lukan time. On the one hand, Luke views the Christian church as standing in the unbroken continuity of the history of the people of God Israel, for it now includes also the Jewish and non-Jewish Χριστιανοί, who were called this for the first time in Antioch according to Acts 11.26. The Χριστιανοί are all those who believe that the promises of salvation given to the people of God are fulfilled in the sending and in the resurrection of Jesus from the dead (e.g., Acts 13.32-39; 23.6; 26.6-8). According to the Lukan understanding, the history of Israel finds its continuation in the history of the church. On the other hand, those Jews who deny the Christ proclamation also continue, of course, to belong to Israel, although they are—this may not be swept under the rug—threatened with eschatic exclusion from the people of God by Peter in Acts 3.23 with the words of Deuteronomy 18.19 and Leviticus 32.29.

From the perspective of the intended readers of Luke–Acts one can therefore say that Luke wants to write a prehistory of his present that seeks to explain the coming into being of a situation that exists in his time. According to his own self-understanding, Luke–Acts would then be something like a "foundation story" or "origin story" that intends to explain the origin and beginning of the current status quo and the historical development up until it was reached (cf. also Backhaus 2007, 31–32). Such a work of history can accordingly stop with the event with which this condition is reached—irrespective of how far back it lies. Correspondingly, many nineteenth- and twentieth-century Protestant portrayals of the history of the Reformation end with the Peace of Augsburg of 1555, in which the confessional geography of Germany, whose consequences reach into the present, was established. This would mean that Luke narrated the history of this epoch as going forth from the history of Israel in order to explain to his readers how it came to be that Christians and Jews became separated from each other in his present, although there is so much that binds them with each other.

On this basis, perspectives on Luke–Acts that want to see it merely as the story of Christianity's emergence (among others, Marguerat 1999, 63; Cancik 1997) are shown to be too narrow. These interpretations overlook the fact that Luke always narrates the history of the *expansion* of the witness of Christ also as a history of its *rejection*, which repeatedly leads to *separations*. Both movements—the movement of expansion and the movement of separation—are interdependent (details in Wolter 2004b, 263–64). The proclamation of Christ regularly causes separation, and the separation just as regularly enables the commencement of new proclamation. But above all it emerges from the concluding scene of Luke–Acts in Acts 28.23-28 that his perspective reaches beyond the Christian part of Israel, and at this prominent position of his presentation Luke directs the attention of the readers to the part of Israel that has not become Christian. With the help of Isaiah 6.9-10 he explains why the majority of the Jews have rejected the message of Christ. But precisely in this way, i.e., with recourse to the model of hardening formulated by the prophet Isaiah, the rejection is brought into the history of Israel. According to the Lukan view, the Jewish rejection of the Christ message can only be understood at all as part of the history of Israel.

6.2 Even though Luke has not taken over Mark 1.1 (the heading of the Gospel of Mark), the story of Jesus also functions in Luke as the prehistory of the post-Easter proclamation of Christ, so that the heading ἀρχὴ τοῦ εὐαγγελίου Ἰησοῦ could also stand over his story of Jesus. The difference consists solely in the fact that in Mark the story of the proclamation of the gospel, unlike in Luke, remained unnarrated. The same point applies to the story of Jesus in the Gospel of Matthew. With the mission command in Matthew 28.18-20 it is opened (like the Lukan story of Jesus in Luke 24.46-49) to the post-Easter proclamation, but (unlike Luke) Matthew has refrained from narrating the story of this proclamation.

This difference makes clear again and finds its explanation in the fact that the narrative aim sketched above, which caused Luke to expand his story of Jesus to Acts, differs characteristically from the intentions that guided Mark and Matthew.

That Luke did not come upon the idea of expanding his story of Jesus to a presentation of the history of the expansion of the Christian message of salvation and its rejection by most Jews only after completing the Gospel of Luke is shown above all by the configuration of the end of the "first book" in Luke 24.52-53, which introduces the disciples as the new protagonists of the narrative (see further there) and thus prepares for the sequel. Moreover, a whole series of indications make it probable that Luke had already planned such a continuation at the beginning of his story of Jesus. Of these, the proem of Luke 1.1-4 must be mentioned in the first place (see the introductory comments on 1.1-4). Beyond this, the omission of the controversy dialogue on "clean" and "unclean" from Mark 7.1-23 was probably caused by the fact that Luke wanted to save this topic for Acts 10.1–11.18, namely because he viewed it—historically no doubt correctly—as a circle of problems that did not become virulent until after Easter. The same applies analogously for the way in which Luke deals with Isaiah 6.9-10. In Luke 8.10, he has shortened the quotation of this text, in its adoption from Mark 4.12, to the point that it is almost unrecognizable because he wanted to utilize it only at the end of his overall presentation in order to be able to conclusively justify the rejection of the post-Easter proclamation by most Jews with its help (see also Barrett 1992, 1453ff; Marshall 1993, 174–75; Marguerat 1999, 73ff). Finally, Luke probably left out the false witnesses and the temple saying (Mark 14.58) in his version of the hearing before the Sanhedrin because he wanted to bring them into Acts 6.14 (cf. also Acts 13.45; 28.19, 22 with Luke 2.34 [see ad loc.]).

If one wants to bring this result into dialogue with the manuscript evidence discussed above (see section 1 of the introduction), one can say, on the one hand, that the Gospel of Luke and Acts were written and published successively from a publication-technical perspective, but that they are connected, on the other hand, by a unified theological and literary concept. The Gospel of Luke was written before but not independently of Acts.

6.3 Nevertheless, the story narrated in the Gospel of Luke of the divine sending of salvation to Israel does not become through Acts "something lying altogether in the past, real history [*Historie*]" (Käsemann 1970, I: 199). This judgment is contradicted already by the manner in which the story of Jesus appears in Acts:

(a) The *summary references to the entirety of the story of Jesus* can be identified as a first type of reference to the Gospel of Luke in Acts (Acts 2.22; 3.26; 10.36-38; 13.23). Common to them all is a profiled *interpretation* of the story of Jesus, which is clearly recognizable. They present *God* as the acting subject and portray *Jesus* as the instrument of the divine action of salvation toward *Israel*:

2.22 (Peter's Pentecost sermon): "Jesus of Nazareth, a man who was legitimated by God in relation to you through deeds of power, miracles, and signs, which God did through him in your midst (ἀνὴρ ἀποδεδειγμένος ἀπὸ τοῦ θεοῦ εἰς ὑμᾶς δυνάμεσι καὶ τέρασι καὶ σημείοις οἷς ἐποίησεν δι' αὐτοῦ ὁ θεός), as you yourselves know."

3.26 (Peter in Solomon's portico to the Jerusalem λαός): "For you first (ὑμῖν πρῶτον) God has raised up his servant Jesus Christ, and he has sent him as one who blesses you by turning every one of you from your wickedness (ἀπέστειλεν αὐτὸν εὐλογοῦντα ὑμᾶς ἐν τῷ ἀποστρέφειν ἕκαστον ἀπὸ τῶν πονηριῶν ὑμῶν)."

10.36-38 (Peter in the house of Cornelius): "He (sc. God) sent the word to the children of Israel by gospeling peace through Jesus Christ (τὸν λόγον ἀπέστειλεν τοῖς υἱοῖς Ἰσραὴλ εὐαγγελιζόμενος εἰρήνην διὰ Ἰησοῦ Χριστοῦ) . . . what happened in all Judea, starting from Galilee after the baptism that John offered: Jesus of Nazareth—how God anointed him with the Holy Spirit and power; he went around and did good and made well all who were oppressed by the devil (ὡς ἔχρισεν αὐτὸν ὁ θεὸς πνεύματι ἁγίῳ καὶ δυνάμει, ὃ διῆλθεν εὐεργετῶν καὶ ἰώμενος πάντας τοὺς καταδυναστευομένους ὑπὸ τοῦ διαβόλου), for God was with him."

13.23 (Paul in the synagogue in Pisidian Antioch): "From his (sc. David's) offspring God has brought Jesus as Savior for Israel according to the promise (ἤγαγεν τῷ Ἰσραὴλ σωτῆρα Ἰησοῦν)." Verse 26 takes this up with "the word of this salvation was sent to us (ἡμῖν ὁ λόγος τῆς σωτηρίας ταύτης ἐξαπεστάλη [*passivum divinum*])."

(b) These actualizations of the story of Jesus are continued in 2.23-24; 10.39-40; and 13.27-31 through recollections of *Jesus's fate of suffering and resurrection*, which Luke configures with the help of the so-called contrast schema (see also 3.13-15; 4.10; 5.30, where this schema stands alone; in 3.17b-18 it is related exclusively to the suffering of Jesus). Here too Jesus's fate of resurrection is constantly expressed as an action of *God* on him.

(c) By contrast, in Acts there are only very few references back to *details* of the story of Jesus:

This applies primarily to the *sayings tradition*. While in Acts 13.25; 19.4 the saying of John the Baptist from Luke 3.16 is quoted or, rather, referenced, there is not a single saying of Jesus from the Gospel of Luke that is recalled in Acts (the saying of Jesus quoted in Acts 11.6 is from Acts 1.5). The saying of the Lord that the Lukan Paul invokes in his farewell speech to the Ephesian presbyters in Miletus (20.35: "it is more blessed to give than to receive") stands neither in the Gospel of Luke nor does it come at all from Jesus, but is a proverb from Greco-Roman tradition (cf. Barrett 1994/1998, II: 983–84).

From the *narrative* tradition there are references—apart from the vague reference to Luke 3.22 in Acts 4.27 ("your holy servant Jesus whom you anointed")—only to events of the Lukan passion and Easter narrative. In Acts 1.16 (". . . Judas, who became a guide to those who arrested Jesus") there is a reference to Luke 22.47, in Acts 3.14 to Luke 23.13-25, and in Acts 4.27-28 (see at 22.66–23.56) in the very general sense to the events on the day of Jesus's death narrated in Luke 22.66–23.49, though an intentional reference back to 23.34 can perhaps be recognized in 3.17b (κατὰ ἄγνοιαν ἐπράξατε) and 13.27 (τοῦτον ἀγνοήσαντες). In 5.32; 10.41-42; 13.31 the readers can perceive a reference to the appearance reported in Luke 24.36-49, which made the disciples witnesses of the resurrection. The back references to this scene have the function of lending credibility to the resurrection witness of the missionaries in the narrated rhetorical situations.

It is obvious that these findings disprove the judgment of Käsemann quoted above. The concern is not with untheological "history" (*Historie*) in the sense of Käsemann, as is already shown by the fact that in the summary references to the entirety of the story of Jesus Luke consistently furnishes the activity of Jesus (section [a]) with a profiled theological interpretation, namely that God himself is the one who in the activity of Jesus acted toward Israel for salvation and that God is represented in an authentic way by Jesus. This interpretation is also attested in the Gospel of Luke at many points (e.g., Luke 1.17, 76; 5.17-26; 7.16; 8.39; 9.43a; 18.43; see further Squires 1993, 90ff), and, correspondingly, it establishes a fundamental theological continuity between the two books of Luke–Acts that encompasses the historical successiveness of the events narrated in them.

Moreover, this interpretation obtains its individual profile through the fact that Luke integrates Jesus's suffering and resurrection into it and presents them as part of God's salvific action toward Israel with which the promises of Scripture are fulfilled (cf. also Acts 17.2-3 and 26.22-23). The reason that Luke places the resurrection of Jesus preeminently at the center (cf. Acts 1.22; 4.2, 33; 10.40-41; 17.18, 31; 24.21) in the witnesses' proclamation of Christ probably resides in the fact that it is above all the resurrection that establishes the special character of the messianic reign of Jesus, namely that Jesus sits "on the throne of his father David" and "will rule over the house of Jacob into eternity and that his reign will have no end" (Luke 1.32-33). Without the resurrection the story of Jesus's activity and fate in Israel would remain threatened by the misunderstanding of the Emmaus disciples—namely, that Jesus was no more than a prophet who was "powerful in deed and word before God and the whole people" (Luke 24.19), but had otherwise suffered the same fate as many prophets already had before him, who were likewise put to death by the wielders of power in Israel (v. 20).

This meaning that Luke assigns to the story of Jesus is present wherever he characterizes the proclamation of Christ as proclamation of the kingdom of God (Acts 8.12; 19.8/10; 20.21/25; 28.23, 31), for he had already previously presented the proclamation of Jesus as such in the Gospel (Luke 4.43; 8.1; 9.11; 16.16; see also 9.2, 60). Beyond this, the same holds true for the texts in which Luke, in further theological compression, narrates only that "the Messiah Jesus" (5.42), "the Lord Jesus" (11.20), "the word of the Lord" (15.35), or even only "Jesus" (8.35) is proclaimed (see also Delling 1972/1973, 386). From this it also follows that this interpretation is to be supplied whenever Luke says that on the basis of this proclamation people believe "in Jesus," "in his name," "in the Lord," or simply "believe" (e.g., 3.16; 4.4; 5.14; 8.12; 10.43; 11.17; 13.12; 14.23; 16.15, 31; 18.8; 20.21; 24.24; 26.18). Luke indicates to the readers what is meant by this in the summary references to the entirety of the story of Jesus quoted above. Moreover, this interpretation also extends beyond the narrated world into the presents of all readers of Luke–Acts, since for Luke they too, of course, believe nothing other than what was proclaimed by the witnesses of Jesus. There should be no need to emphasize that this matter is of fundamental hermeneutical significance precisely because it places the story of Jesus narrated in the Gospel of Luke in the light of the faith of all readers of Luke–Acts.

Thus, the story of Jesus of the Gospel of Luke and its reception in Acts mutually interpret one another. First, the aforementioned texts of Acts function as exemplary theological interpretations of the story of Jesus. Their hermeneutical significance consists in the fact that they enduringly preserve the story of Jesus from sinking into mere *history*. The theological meaning that Luke attaches to the references to the story of Jesus in the mission speeches also demonstrates that he wants his narrative of Jesus to be understood not merely "as the historical basis, which comes to the kerygma as a second thing" (so Conzelmann 1977, 3). Rather, for Luke the narrative of Jesus is an integral component of the kerygma itself. Second, the Lukan story of Jesus unpacks for the believing readers of Luke–Acts what sort of words and deeds it was in which the sending of God's message of peace for Israel (10.36) and his salvific action toward Israel (13.23, 26) took form. Luke can restrict himself in Acts to reproducing only "the outline of the Jesus event" (Delling 1972/1973, 389) solely because he can presuppose that his readers known his πρῶτος λόγος (Acts 1.1) and therefore know what is meant in each case. Therefore, for Luke, without knowledge of the story of Jesus not only would Acts be incomprehensible at decisive points, but also the Christian faith would not know what it is directed toward. Here, the *historical* successiveness of the story of Jesus and the story of the proclamation of Christ, which is reproduced by the *literary* successiveness of the two books of Luke–Acts, is bridged *kerygmatically*: The story of Jesus is reactualized not only in the proclamation of its witnesses, whose story Luke narrates in the second book, but it "overtakes" in a way the time of the witnesses and is present in its Lukan interpretation wherever Jesus Christ is proclaimed and believed.

1.1-4: Proem

[1]**Because many have already undertaken to compile a report about the events that were** (already) **complete in our time,** [2]**as those who were from the beginning eyewitnesses and servants of the word handed on to us,** [3]**I also decided, having held to everything exactly from the beginning, to write it out for you in order, most excellent Theophilus,** [4]**in order that you may know the soundness of what has been told to you.**

The proem that Luke places before his story of Jesus is a single, artfully constructed period (cf. BDR §464 with n. 4), which was very popular in ancient rhetoric, especially within the proem, due to its cyclical structure (cf. Quintilian, *Institutio oratoria* 9.4.128: *periodos apta prooemiis maiorum causarum, ubi sollicitudine, commendatione, miseratione res eget* ["The period is fitting in the proems of larger trial speeches where the object requires solicitude, commendation and sympathy"]; see also Lausberg 1973, §924, §947). Its syntactic configuration and to some extent also its terminology are not only unique in the New Testament but also differ in character from Lukan style, as we otherwise know it from the Gospel of Luke and Acts. This can be seen, *inter alia*, in the frequency of New Testament *hapax legomena* (ἐπειδήπερ, ἀνατάσσομαι, διήγησις, αὐτόπτης). ἐπιχειρέω (see also Acts 9.29; 19.13), καθεξῆς (see also Luke 8.1; Acts 3.24; 11.4; 18.23), and κράτιστος (see also Acts 23.26; 24.3; 26.25) are attested exclusively in Luke–Acts.

Luke takes up here a convention that is widespread in historiography and in the literarily non-ambitious scientific and technical professional literature of the Hellenistic-Roman period (cf. Alexander 1993). It consists in the fact that the author prefaces his overall work and/or individual books with a personal explanation of the subject of his work and its methods and intentions (examples in Alexander 1993, 213ff; Eckey I: 56ff; Klein 76ff).

The proem has its place originally in rhetoric and was applied from there to literary works. The rhetorical proem had the task of making the hearers "well-disposed, teachable, and attentive" (*benevolum . . . facere et docilem et attentum*; Cicero, *De oratore* 2.80; see also Lausberg 1973, §266ff). But according to Lucian of Samosata, in his foreword the historian should forgo an appeal to the goodwill of the hearers and seek to awake only their attentiveness and desire for knowledge (*Quomodo historia conscribenda sit* 53).

In addition to the information concerning the content of the work, the following elements from the inventory of the *topoi* and forms of proems have found their way into the Lukan proem (the corresponding elements in Luke 1.1-4 have been placed in parentheses).

(a) The author points to earlier treatments of the subject matter and sets his own presentation over against them (πολλοί . . . ἔδοξε κἀμοί; vv. 1, 3): e.g., Isocrates, *Ad Nicoclem* 1–2; Diodorus Siculus 1.3.1–5; 4.1.2–4; Strabo 1.21.1; *Rhetorica ad Herennium* 1.1 (*Graeci scriptores . . . nos autem* ["the Greek writers . . . but we"]); Dionysius of Halicarnassus, *Antiquitates romanae* 1.6.1–5 (3: "for these reasons I decided [ἔδοξέ μοι] not to pass over a significant epoch of history, which was left unmentioned by the older [historians]"); Dioscorides Pedanius, *De materia medica*, praefatio 1–6; Josephus, *Bellum judaicum* 1.1–16; Tacitus, *Historiae* 1.1; Herodianus Historicus 1.1.1–6 (οἱ πλεῖστοι . . . ἐγὼ δέ ["the majority . . . but I"]); Arrian, *Anabasis* 1.3 ("Everyone who marvels over the fact that after such authors this composition came into my mind also [καὶ ἐμοὶ ἐπὶ νοῦν ἦλθεν ἥδε ἡ συγγραφή] should marvel only when he has read all their [presentations] and then picked up mine"); no criticism but rather positive connection to predecessors is found in Hero of Alexandria, *Pneumatica* 1, proem 2.4–10 (ed. W. Schmidt et al. 1976); further attestations in Herkommer 1968, 110–11.

(b) The predecessors are subsumed under a general πολλοί (v. 1): e.g., Strabo 1.21; Dioscorides Pedanius, *De materia medica*, praefatio 1; Josephus, *Antiquitates judaicae* 1.3; Thessalus of Tralles, *De virtutibus herbarum* 1, proem 1; Appian, *Praefatio 12*; Herodianus Historicus 1.1.1 (see above); see also Josephus, *Bellum judaicum* 1.17 (ἐπειδήπερ καὶ Ἰουδαίων πολλοὶ πρὸ ἐμοῦ τὰ τῶν προγόνων συνετάξαντο μετ᾽ ἀκριβείας ["because also many Jews before me have compiled with care the (history) of the ancestors"]), and also already the beginning of the funeral oration of Pericles in Thucydides 2.35.1 (οἱ μὲν πολλοὶ . . . ἐμοὶ δὲ . . . ἐδόκει ["the many . . . but I . . . decided"]). Further information in Cadbury, *BoC* I/2: 492–93; Fraenkel 1960; J. B. Bauer 1960; Alexander 1993, 109.

(c) The activity of the predecessors is designated as ἐπιχείρησις ("undertaking, venture, enterprise"; v. 1): e.g., Hippocrates, *De vetere medicina* 1.1; Diodorus Siculus 1.3.2 (ἐπεχείρησαν ἀναγράφειν ["they have undertaken to write out"]); 4.1.2; Ps.-Isocrates, *Ad Demonicum* 3; Thessalus of Tralles, *De virtutibus herbarum* 1; cf. also Josephus, *Vita* 40, 338; *Contra Apionem* 1.1. On the other hand, within the proem the author can also designate his own venture with ἐπιχειρεῖν in order to signal modesty (e.g., Isocrates, *Philippus* 2; Strabo 1.2.1; Polybius 2.37.4; 3.1.4; Thessalus of Tralles, *De virtutibus herbarum* 1, proem 2; Dionysius of Halicarnassus, *Antiquitates romanae* 1.7.1; see also Josephus, *Antiquitates judaicae* 1.5). Further information in Cadbury, *BoC* I/2: 493–94; Alexander 1993, 109–10.

(d) The author indicates what distinguishes his work from those of his predecessors (v. 3). Greater objectivity can be mentioned as a distinguishing feature (cf. Tacitus, *Annales* 1.1.3: *sine ira et studio*) as well as greater substantive nearness to the subject matter, which is established through ἀκρίβεια and αὐτοψία: Thucydides

1.22.1, 2; Dioscorides Pedanius, *De materia medica*, praefatio 5; Herodianus Historicus 1.1.3 (the ἀκρίβεια refers to the interaction with the sources, explicitly not to autopsy); Josephus, *Bellum judaicum* 1.9; Appian, *Praefatio* 13; Cassius Dio 1.2. Also, the specific ordering of the material is invoked (Dioscorides Pedanius, *De materia medica*, praefatio 5 [τῇ τάξει διαφόρῳ χρήσασθαι ("to make a deviating ordering")]; Josephus, *Bellum judaicum* 1.15; Herodianus Historicus 1.1.6) as well as shortening (2 Maccabees 2.23-24) or expansion, i.e., the intention to provide an overall presentation that reaches beyond previous individual presentations and closes gaps (cf. above all Polybius's program of a universal history in 1.4.3–11; see also 2.37.4; Diodorus Siculus 1.3.5–8; Hero of Alexandria, *Pneumatica* 1, proem). The information about the ordering of the material and the emphasis on the exactness (ἀκρίβεια) occur also independently of the demarcation from predecessors.

(e) The author mentions the benefit of his work (v. 4): cf. Thucydides 1.22.4; Dioscorides Pedanius, *De materia medica*, praefatio 5; Hero of Alexandria, *Pneumatica* 2.10–12; 2 Maccabees 2.25 ("for those who want to read we have aimed at edification [ψυχαγωγία], for those who want to memorize something at catchiness [εὐκοπία], but for all who [encounter our book] at benefit [ὠφέλεια]"); Herodianus Historicus 1.1.3; additional texts can be found in Herkommer 1968, 128ff.

(f) The author formulates a dedication (v. 3), as here with the address κράτιστε: Dionysius of Halicarnassus, *De antiquis oratoribus* 1; Hermogenes, *De inventione* 3.1; Josephus, *Contra Apionem* 1.1 (see also *Vita* 430); *Epistle to Diognetus* 1.1. The dedication of the work to an individual reader is uncommon within Greek historiography (uncertain exceptions are Callinicus of Petra, *FGH* 3c: 281, testimony 1; Manetho, *FGH* 3c: 609, testimony 11b, c; Berossus, *FGH* 3c: 680, testimony 2); it is found in none of the great historians (cf. Herkommer 1968, 25; Alexander 1993, 27ff), and it is also lacking in Sallust, Livy, and in the historiographical works of Tacitus. It could be directed to a friend as an expression of close personal attachment, but also as a sign of reverence and thankfulness toward benefactors or other people of higher standing, including the holder of the highest political power, from whose splendor something then fell upon the presented work itself. With a view to Luke 1.3 it is important to observe that the person named in the dedication is not addressed at a single point as a representative of the intended readers (when this is the case it is explicitly stated; cf. Josephus, *Contra Apionem* 2.296; on the concept "intended readers," see section 5 in the commentary introduction). Thus, the dedication address does not show for which reading public the author composed his work; on this cf. also the unconnected juxtaposition of the individual addressee and the intended readers in Lucian's essay on history writing (*Quomodo historia conscribenda sit* 1 and 4; see section 5 in the commentary introduction): Lucian wrote the treatise for a "friend" (φιλότης [3]) named Φίλων (1.22, 24, 29), but he conceives of it as a "guide . . . for authors"

(παραίνεσις . . . τοῖς συγγράφουσιν; 4), i.e., for "future writers of history." It cannot be ruled out that the individual address in this case is pure fiction.

Alexander 1993 has attempted to show that the Lukan proem corresponds less to the prefaces of historiographical literature than to the prefaces of scientific and technical-professional treatises. This thesis cannot totally be dismissed insofar as the aforementioned parallels make clear that the building blocks of the Lukan proem are, in fact, attested not only in the historiographical literature but also in other literary genres. On the other hand, however, one must also not overlook the fact that they can appear in historiographical proems, so that the alternative constructed by Alexander appears overly dualistic (cf. also Aune 2002, 140ff). Since with the phrasing ἀνατάξασθαι διήγησιν περὶ τῶν . . . πραγμάτων Luke also announces at the very beginning that he will present a *narration* of *events* and not a descriptive *treatise* on certain *issues*, it is difficult to dispute that with the help of his proem Luke wants to show his readers that they have a historiographical work before them. That the Lukan proem is much shorter than the proems to the historical writings of the great Greek historians (i.e., of Herodotus, Thucydides, Polybius, Diodorus Siculus, Dionysius of Halicarnassus, Josephus, Arrian, Appian, and Herodianus Historicus) need not contradict this, for one can explain in an entirely unforced manner that Luke–Acts is likewise much shorter than the presentations of the authors listed. Accordingly, the shortness of the Lukan proem finds its explanation in the fact that Luke follows a historiographical convention, namely that the length of the proem should correspond to the length of the history work (cf. Lucian of Samosata, *Quomodo historia conscribenda sit* 55).

The repeatedly advocated thesis that Luke only composed the proem after the completion of the Gospel or even Luke–Acts as a whole is not only unnecessary but downright misleading, for this is nothing other than a projection of the exegetical reception experience upon the author. Many interpreters read Luke 1.1-4 in the light of Luke–Acts as a whole and attempt to bring what is announced in the proem into concord with what they have discovered with the help of an exegetical analysis of the Lukan presentation (see the discussion of καθεξῆς in v. 3). They make the completed work into the hermeneutical key for the interpretation of the proem and are then, of course, compelled to postulate that Luke too proceeded in this manner. By contrast, the linguistic analysis of the proem will show that everything points to the view that Luke actually committed the proem to writing at the beginning, i.e., before he composed the πεπληροφορημένα ἐν ἡμῖν πράγματα. Its content is so conventional and general that it does not commit the author of the following presentation to anything. Rather, all possible options remain open to him, for he reveals only that he wants to reproduce literarily the diachronic sequence of the events in his history narrative, that he wants, in so doing, to orient himself closely to the traditions and previous presentations of the events, and that he wants to mediate reliable historical knowledge to his readers (see also Nolland I: 11–12: "The preface is very noncommittal about the subject matter of the work, beyond saying that Theophilus already knows what it is about"). A "theological program" (G. Klein 1969, 237–61) cannot be discovered in the Lukan proem, and the claim "that Luke binds the possibility of historical certainty that establishes for him the certainty of salvation to his work alone" (so G. Klein 1969, 260) certainly has no basis in the text.

It is yet another question whether the proem refers to both Luke and Acts (so Zahn 50; Cadbury, *BoC* I/2: 492; Klostermann 1, 2; Marshall 39) or only to the Gospel of Luke (so, e.g., Schürmann 4; Nolland I: 12; Klein 72). Luke will introduce Acts in Acts 1.1 with its own preface, in which he calls the Gospel of Luke the "first book" in which he gave an account "concerning everything that Jesus did and taught from the beginning" (περὶ πάντων . . . ὧν ἤρξατο ὁ Ἰησοῦς ποιεῖν τε καὶ διδάσκειν). By contrast, when Luke speaks in Luke 1.1 of a narrative περὶ τῶν πεπληροφορημένων ἐν ἡμῖν πραγμάτων, both the undetermined character of this specification of content and the fact that Luke mentions his own present as *terminus ante quem* for the end of the events that have to be presented (see ad loc.) make the first-mentioned assumption probable (see also section 6.2 in the commentary introduction). Luke has planned from the beginning to continue his presentation beyond the Easter appearances and up into the time of Paul. Whether the present form of Acts already stood before his eyes must remain open.

1 The causal conjunction ἐπειδήπερ "refers to an already known fact" (BDR §456.3).

It stands only relatively rarely at the beginning of the sentence as here; in addition to the two Galen texts mentioned by Alexander 1993, 108, cf. Heraclitus, *Allegoriae* 8.5; 56.6; Aristotle, *Magna moralia* 1.4.4 (1184b36); Diogenes of Babylon, Fragment 62 (*SVF* III: 224.6); Claudius Ptolemy, *Geographia* 8.2.3; Hero of Alexandria, *Liber Geeponicus* 45; Aelius Aristides, *Ars rhetorica* 120 (Lenz/Behr 1976, I: 182.13).

In Josephus, *Bellum judaicum* 1.17 ἐπειδήπερ is connected in a comparable way with the reference to "many" predecessors (πολλοὶ πρὸ πρὸ ἐμοῦ). It is not possible to infer the number of works that Luke alludes to, for the use of πολύς and derivatives is a rhetorical stereotype in prefaces and in general at the beginning of speeches and writings (cf. in detail section [b] above as well as Josephus, *Bellum judaicum* 4.238; Acts 24.10; Hebrews 1.1). The same also applies to the characterization of the predecessors' works as ἐπιχείρησις (see section [c] above), so that it is not possible to hear a critical subtext in the Lukan ἐπεχείρησαν (*pace* G. Klein 1964, 239; Bovon). This already seems doubtful on the basis of the parallelizing ἔδοξε κἀμοί in v. 3 with which Luke does not distance himself from the πολλοί but rather connects to them (see also van Unnik 1973–1983, I: 13). This interpretation is confirmed by the fact that in what follows Luke does not devalue his predecessors' works with a single word. He thus forgoes the use of a form-historical option that was certainly available to him.

The infinitive sentence ἀνατάξασθαι διήγησιν κτλ. indicates what the "many" predecessors did and what Luke also intends to do. Here Luke also brings his own project into view already, and therefore one cannot divide the proem in such a way that he speaks about the "attempts" of his predecessors in vv. 1-2 and does not speak about his own work until vv. 3-4. Like the "many," Luke also composes a διήγησις about the πεπληροφορημένα ἐν ἡμῖν πράγματα, and in this way he already provides information here about the literary character and content of his writing (*pace* Cadbury, *BoC* I/2: 494).

The *compositum* ἀνατάσσεσθαι, which is attested only very rarely, emphasizes the reproductive character of literary activity: Plutarch, *Moralia* 968c ("in the night . . . to repeat what is learned [ἀ. τὰ μαθήματα]"); Letter of Aristeas 144 ("in the Torah Moses has compiled everything in an impressive way for the sake of righteousness [πάντα ἀνατέτακται]"); Irenaeus, *Adversus haereses* 3.21.2 (God moved Ezra "to compile all the speeches of the earlier prophets" [τοὺς τῶν προγεγονόντων προφητῶν πάντας ἀνατάξασθαι λόγους]); see also Mansion 1930, 261. This semantic nuance finds its abutment in v. 2 (see there).

The term διήγησις does not designate a specific literary genre; even non-narrative texts can be brought under its roof:
It can designate the manner of presentation of historical writings (e.g., Lucian of Samosata, *Quomodo historia conscribenda sit* 55: τὸ λοιπὸν σῶμα τῆς ἱστορίας διήγησις μακρά ἐστιν ["the actual corpus of the history work is a detailed narrative"] or of myths and the works of poets (e.g., Plato, *Respublica* 392d: πάντα ὅσα ὑπὸ μυθολόγων ἢ ποιητῶν λέγεται διήγησις ["everything that is said by teachers of fables or by poets is a narrative"]; Plutarch, *Moralia* 133e: διηγήσεις ἄλυποι καὶ μυθολογίαι ["entertaining narratives and fables"]).
The same also applies to genres that are designated, as here, as διήγησις of πράγματα. These can include historical writings (e.g., Dionysius of Halicarnassus, *Antiquitates romanae* 1.7.4: περὶ τῆς ἱστορίας αὐτῆς, . . . περὶ τίνων ποιοῦμαι πραγμάτων τὴν διήγησιν ["concerning history itself, i.e., . . . concerning the

events about which I want to produce the narrative"]; see also Polybius 13.9: τῶν πραγάτων ἐξήγησις) as well as any other kind of narrative (cf. the general definition in Aelius Theon, *Progymnasmata* 78: διήγημά ἐστι λόγος ἐκθετικὸς πραγμάτων γεγονότων ἢ ὡς γεγονότων ["a narrative is an extensive presentation of events that have happened or as though they happened"]; Dio Chrysostom 7.10: "He narrated to me his matters [διηγεῖτό μοι . . . τὰ αὐτοῦ πράγματα] and the life that he lived with his wife and children"; see also Lausberg 1973, §289 on διήγησις of πράγματα in the forensic speech; Baum 1993, 107–8).

But beyond this, the term is also used for the designation of descriptive texts, such as, e.g., medical investigations, e.g., Hippocrates, *De ratione victus in morbis acutis* 392: ἡ τοῦ γλυκέος οἴνου διήγησις ("the investigation of the sweetness of the wine"); Galen, *De compositione medicamentorum per genera*, ed. Kühn 1964, XIII: 718.17: περὶ τοῦ φαρμάκου διήγησις ("investigation concerning medicine"); in his commentary on Hippocrates's *Epidemiae*, Galen calls his treatment διηγήσεις several dozen times (see further in Hobart 2004, 87–88), and for mere lists (e.g., Philo, *De specialibus legibus* 2.39: μυρία καὶ ἀναγκαῖα . . . νομοθετηθέντα, ὧν καὶ ἡ ἄνευ κόπου ψιλὴ διήγησις . . . ["innumerable important . . . legal regulations whose artless and plain listing . . ."]; 3.49: "the abhorrent lusts whose διήγησις would be already the greatest shame").

Accordingly, as such neither the term διήγησις nor the syntagm διήγησις περὶ τῶν . . . πραγμάτων are *termini technici* for history writing (so among others van Unnik 1973, 14; E. Plümacher, *EWNT* 1: 779–80). Nevertheless, the proximity of the Lukan phrasing to the above-cited texts of Dionysius of Halicarnassus, *Antiquitates romanae* 1.7.4 and Josephus, *Antiquitates judaicae* 20.157 cannot be denied, so that, at this point at least, there is a certain affinity of the Lukan phrasing to the language of Hellenistic history writing (*pace* Alexander 1993, 111, 112).

Luke designates these πράγματα as πεπληροφορημένα ἐν ἡμῖν. The meaning of this phrasing has been controversial for a long time (cf. the summary of the different positions in Fitzmyer I: 293–94). However, the perfect participle πεπληροφορημένα makes possible a relatively clear decision. It reveals that here Luke orients himself not to the schema of 'promise and fulfillment'; rather, he is concerned with designating, in a very intentional manner, the events that he and his predecessors narrate as *finished and completed* from both their perspectives (see also Lagrange 1912; Cadbury, *BoC* I/2: 496; Baum 1993, 112–13; Wolter 2004b, 258ff; Litwak 2006). This interpretation is supported above all by the fact that Luke speaks here of the πληροφορεῖσθαι of πράγματα and not of the "fulfillment" of λόγοι, ῥήματα, ἐπαγγελίαι, or γραφή, which he always does when he wants to designate an occurrence as a salvation historical fulfillment event (cf. Luke 1.20; 4.21; 24.44; Acts 1.16; 3.18; 13.27, 32-33; 26.6-7). The use of the resultative perfect used to express "the duration of what has been completed" (BDR §340 with reference to πεπληρώκατε in Acts 5.28; it could "be unpacked into ἐπληρώσατε καὶ νῦν πλήρης ἐστίν") also corresponds to this usage. Luke uses this phrasing to designate the events that his predecessors have narrated and he himself also intends to narrate as a sequence of events that not only he and his contemporaries but also his "many" predecessors *look back* upon as a completed whole. But with this a decision is also made about the meaning of ἐν ἡμῖν: it designates the Lukan present, and the ἡμεῖς are defined by the fact that they live outside of the epoch threshold marked by the end of the πράγματα narrated by Luke. The ἡμεῖς are the πολλοί, Luke himself, Theophilus, and the intended readers of the Gospel of Luke.

2 The subordinating conjunction καθώς is dependent on ἀνατάξασθαι διήγησιν (v. 1) and qualifies the accounts of the πολλοί. They are based on the traditions of those "who were from the beginning eyewitnesses and servants of the word." But Luke views this tradition also as the foundation of his own διήγησις, for he places the same circle of people as in v. 1 under the pronoun ἡμῖν, namely himself and his readers and the πολλοί (cf. also the similar phrasing in Irenaeus, *Adversus haereses* 3.1.1 with reference to the Gospel of Mark: "Mark handed down to us [*nobis tradidit*] what was proclaimed by Peter"). Luke thus regards the chronological distance between the πράγματα and the ἡμεῖς, which he had marked in v. 1, as bridged by the tradition of the "eyewitnesses from the beginning" and subsequent "servants of the word." That Luke used the definite article οἱ only once does not necessitate the assumption that he wishes to speak here of one and the same group (cf. BDR §276.1 with reference to Acts 19.21), although this remains, of course, possible to probable. What stands in the foreground, however, is the fact that the designations ἀπ᾽ ἀρχῆς αὐτόπται and ὑπηρέται . . . τοῦ λόγου mark different temporal periods. ἀπ᾽ ἀρχῆς αὐτόπται refers to the activity and fate of Jesus from the beginnings in Galilee to his resurrection from the dead and appearance before the disciples (cf. Acts 10.36-41; see also 1.21-22), while ὑπηρέται τοῦ λόγου takes the time of the post-Easter proclamation of Christ into view (cf. Acts 10.42-43). In 6.4 Luke describes the task of the circle of the twelve in Jerusalem as διακονία τοῦ λόγου (the absolute ὁ λόγος is also used elsewhere as a comprehensive designation for the Christian message: Acts 4.4, 29; 8.4; 10.36; 11.19; 14.25; 16.6; 17.11; 19.20; 18.5). The sandwich position of the participle γενόμενοι between ὑπηρέται and τοῦ λόγου shows that it should be connected only with this designation and not also with ἀπ᾽ ἀρχῆς αὐτόπται. The connecting of γενόμενοι with αὐτόπται made by Cadbury, *BoC* I/2: 498 and Alexander 1993, 119 (justification: "γίνεσθαι is almost invariably used in Greek writers with αὐτόπτης"; Cadbury, *BoC* I/2: 498) is mistaken, for according to the Lukan understanding, those designated here were certainly *not* 'from the beginning . . . servants of the word.' On the other hand, they remain, of course, "eyewitnesses from the beginning," even after they have become "servants of the word."

But even if Luke does not want to designate two different groups with these terms, the two circles of people are not identical. As indisputable as it is that the apostles unify both characteristics in themselves (Acts 1.21-22), it emerges from Acts 1.21-22 that not all the "eyewitnesses from the beginning" later also became "servants of the word." Moreover, there are also ὑπηρέται who were not "eyewitnesses from the beginning" such as Paul (cf. Acts 26.16) and all the others who "gospeled the word" (Acts 8.4).

Taking a broader perspective, it seems prudent in any case not to want to specify the extension (i.e., the reference of a term) of these two designations in an overly precise manner, for Luke is primarily concerned with their intension (i.e., the content of a term)—namely, that the temporal distance between the πράγματα and the authors of the reports of them (the πολλοί and Luke) is bridged by the tradition carried by this circle of people. That Luke has indeed interpreted the reference of ἀπ' ἀρχῆς quite generously is also recognizable in the fact that he does not have the first disciples and subsequent "eyewitnesses" attach themselves to Jesus until Luke 5.1-11. But when he wrote the preface, it need not yet have been clear to him that this would happen in this way later.

Syntactically this verse is related to the "reports" of the πολλοί, but with the help of the inclusive ἡμῖν Luke also places his own work in the light of the historical trustworthiness of the "eyewitnesses from the beginning and servants of the word."

3 Luke's presentation distinguishes itself from the theological programmatic anonymity of the other gospels (see Wolter 1988a) by the fact that he steps forth before the readers with his own "I" as the author on the surface of the text. The editor of the second edition of the Gospel of John does something comparable in John 21.25, though precisely not at the beginning but rather at the end of the book. In ancient historiography Josephus and Diodorus both abstain from mentioning their names in the proems to *Antiquitates judaicae* and *Bibliotheca Historica*. The phrasing (ἔδοξε) κἀμοί reveals that Luke wanted to emphasize the continuity with the efforts of the πολλοί, which were mentioned in v. 1, for he does not distance himself from them—for example with the help of the adversative phrasing (ἔδοξε) δέ μοι (e.g., Daniel[LXX] 4.37c; Lysias, *Orationes* 1.14; Galen, *De methodo medendi*, ed. Kühn 1964, X: 910.11; Vettius Valens, ed. Kroll 1973, 142.30; 241.16; Diogenes Laertius 7.9). ἔδοξέ μοι . . . γράψαι is a widespread Greek idiom (cf. Hippocrates, *Prorrhetica* 2.2;

[Ps.-]Speusippus, *Epistulae*, ed. M. I. Parente 1980, 158; 159.1; Galen, *De placitis Hippocratis et Platonis* 8.2.11 [de Lacy 1978–1984, 492.16]; *De curandi ratione per venae sectionem*, ed. Kühn 1964, XI: 312.11).

The series of the following six words belongs to the most intensively researched texts in Luke–Acts. This is the case because it was supposed that one could discover in them the historiographical principles and the theology-of-history program that Luke allowed himself to be led by in the composition of his portrayal. This supposition has resulted in the fact that almost every word has become the object of intensive discussion.

With the help of the *participium coniunctum* παρηκολουθηκότι ἄνωθεν πᾶσιν ἀκριβῶς that is coordinated with κἀμοί Luke provides information about his own approach.

The main problem is the meaning of παρακολουθεῖν. In the last decades a certain consensus has been established, according to which Luke uses this verb here to mean *"(eine Sache) verfolgen, (einer Sache) nachgehen"* (W. Bauer 1988, 1251) in the sense of *"erforschen," "(über)prüfen," "untersuchen,"* or "investigate," "trace" (cf. Schweizer; Wiefel; Fitzmyer; Ernst; Marshall; Klein; Baum 1993, 123–24, and many others). This interpretation is, however, untenable for philological reasons, for it lies beyond what is possible on the basis of the semantic spectrum of παρακολουθεῖν (for Luke 1.3, cf. especially the critical observations of Alexander 1993, 128n29 and Moessner 1999, 86ff in relation to the aforementioned consensus). When παρακολουθεῖν with the dative of the thing is used, it designates precisely *not* "subsequent investigations" (so Baum 1993, 124: *"nachträgliche Nachforschungen"*) and the critical attitude bound up with this, but rather the *affirmative* orientation that is designated with terms such as "follow closely," "attend to minutely," "trace accurately," "keep company with" (the last four translations are taken from LSJ 1313–14; see also Moessner 1999, 87: "follow with the mind"; Alexander 1993, "being thoroughly familiar with"). Accordingly, this meaning also left its traces in both the Lukan section of the Canon Muratori (line 7: *prout asequi* [sic!] *potuit* ["as he could follow"]; see section 2.1 in the commentary introduction) and in the translation of the Vulgate (*adsecuto*). As a dative object of παρακολουθεῖν both the πράγματα themselves (Josephus, *Contra Apionem* 1.53: "Whoever promises the presentation of facts must first have carefully [ἀκριβῶς] found them out—ἢ παρηκολουθηκότα τοῖς γεγονόσιν ἢ παρὰ τῶν εἰδότων πυνθανόμενον [either by accompanying the events or by inquiring about them from those who know them]"; for the interpretation of this text, cf. Moessner 1996, 108ff) and the reports about them can function with this sense (Josephus, *Contra Apionem* 1.218: some Hellenistic historians falsely represent the history of Judaism "because they do not μετὰ πάσης ἀκριβείας τοῖς ἡμετέροις γράμμασι παρακολουθεῖν [orient themselves with all possible care to our writings]"; that παρακολουθεῖν here cannot mean "critically investigate" is plain to see). For other examples, see the texts mentioned in LSJ 1313–14.

The two Josephus texts demonstrate that the semantic field of παρακολουθεῖν is associated with the adverb ἀκριβῶς, which also occurs in Luke, and its cognates. It always describes the care and precision with which one adheres to the facts or the representations of them; cf. in addition Demetrius of Phaleron, Fragment 201.7: μετὰ πάσης ἀκριβείας τοῖς ἡμετέροις γράμμασι παρακολουθεῖν ("to adhere to our writings with all exactness"); Demosthenes, *Orationes* 19.257: ὁ τὰ τούτου πονηρεύματ᾽ ἀκριβέστατ᾽ εἰδὼς ἐγὼ καὶ παρηκολουθηκὼς ἅπασι κατηγορῶ ("as one who knows the crimes of this [person] most exactly and is familiar with all I accuse"); 48.40: τοῖς εἰδόσιν ἀκριβῶς ἕκαστα ταῦτα τὰ πράγματα . . . καὶ παρηκολουθηκόσιν ἐξ ἀρχῆς ("to those who know all these events exactly . . . and have followed them from the beginning"); Hipparchus, *Commentarium in Arati et Eudoxi Phaenomena* 1.1.9 (ed. Manitius 1894, 6.19–20): ἵνα παρακολουθῶν ἑκάστοις ἀκριβῶς καὶ τὰς τῶν ἄλλων ἁπάντων ἀποφάσεις ἐν τούτοις δοκιμάζῃς ("in order that you, by following after all the details exactly, can also test the information of all the others about these things"; here the affirmative παρακολουθεῖν is what should make possible in the first place the critical δοκιμάζειν); Galen, *Hippocratis prognosticum commentaria*, ed. Kühn 1964, XVIIb: 190.3: ἀκριβῶς παρακολουθῆσαι τοῖς ὑφ᾽ Ἱπποκράτους εἰρημένοις ("following exactly what was said by Hippocrates"); cf. also Galen, *De locis affectis*, ed. Kühn 1964, VIII: 227.4–5, and Alexander 1993, 131 (see also Janse 1996, 97).

One is not permitted to ask what the neuter πᾶσιν refers to, for it means exactly what the word means, "everything"; namely, "everything" that Luke requires for the "compilation of a report about the events that have been completed in our time" (v. 1). How could he possibly be satisfied with less? πάντα therefore encompasses the reports of the πολλοί (v. 1a), the πράγματα (v. 1b), and the traditions of the eyewitnesses and servants of the word (v. 2; see also Moessner 1999, "events, traditions, and reports"). The same applies to the temporal adverb ἄνωθεν. It has no specific referent (e.g., the "infancy narratives" as is sometimes assumed; cf. G. Klein 1969, 251 and others), but rather makes a claim to completeness that is comparable with πᾶσιν ἄνωθεν ("from the beginning"), corresponds with the completedness of the events stated in v. 1 (πεπληροφορημένα . . . πράγματα), and expresses not only that Luke used all the sources available to him but also that his presentation encompasses the events in the entirety of their temporal extension—namely, "from their beginning" (ἄνωθεν) to their "completion" (πεπληροφορημένα). Thus, ἄνωθεν takes the beginning into view and πεπληροφορημένα the end.

The adverb καθεξῆς, which is attested only in Luke in the New Testament (see also Luke 8.1; Acts 3.24; 11.4; 18.23), is related directly to this temporal extension and announces that Luke intends to present the material available to him in a certain order, namely—this is at least suggested by the temporal perspective given by the interplay of ἄνωθεν and πεπληροφορημένα—in diachronic sequence, from the beginning to the end, as in Acts 11.4. This also corresponds to the use of the term in ancient historiography; cf. in this sense Thucydides 5.26.1: "Thucydides has recorded the same, in sequence (ἑξῆς), as each event came to pass"; see also Baum 1993, 135ff; Alexander 1993, 132: "a regular, connected account is in view." The thesis that with καθεξῆς Luke wanted to designate the "unbroken, namely continual connection of all parts to a logical whole" (so Völkel 1974, 298) overburdens the semantics of the term. It presupposes that Luke reckons with readers who not only know all of Luke–Acts but also the literature on it since Hans Conzelmann; for criticism, see also Schneider 1985, 129, whose own interpretation (καθεξῆς refers to "the working out of the promise and fulfilment line," 131), of course, also goes far beyond the meaning of the term that is accessible to the readers at this point. One can assume with great certainty that Luke announces here nothing else and nothing more than that he will orient his presentation to the *diachronic* sequence of the events. He announces that he wants to reproduce literarily the historical succession of the events. Even if one may not make the error of wanting to determine the intended meaning of καθεξῆς in this passage, so to speak, from 'the end,' i.e., from a subsequent literary and narratological analysis of Luke–Acts, one should not speak of a 'chronological' sequence, because Luke chronologically orders not the sequence of the principal macronarrative but rather only small-scale narrative collecting basins and because he quantifies temporal extensions (e.g., 1.24, 26, 56; 2.21, 46; 9.28; 22.66; Acts 18.11; 19.8, 10; 20.3; 24.27; 28.11, 17).

We know nothing else about the person to whom Luke dedicates his work and whom he also addresses in Acts 1.1, i.e., at the beginning of the second book (cf. now the comprehensive summary presentation of the literature in Heil/Klampfl 2005). Ever since Zahn 57n41, the Antiochene Theophilus mentioned in the Ps.-Clementine *Recognitiones* 10.71.2–3—which says that he belonged to the urban elite of his city (*erat cunctis potentibus in civitate sublimior* ["who was more elevated than all the powerful in the city"]) and that he placed at the Antiochene community's disposal a great gathering room in his private house—has been connected time and again with the Lukan Theophilus (cf. e.g., Klostermann; Schweizer; Bovon). On the other hand, there has been no lack of attempts to dispute his existence and understand Θεόφιλος as a symbolic name ('friend of God'; thus recently again Morgenthaler 1993, 395–96; Wargnies 2003, 78).

The name is attested for both Jewish and non-Jewish men. The most well known is the high priest Theophilus ben Ananus who was in office from 37–41 CE (cf. Josephus, *Antiquitates judaicae* 18.123; 19.297), who is, however, certainly not in view (*pace* Anderson 1997); see further Josephus, *Antiquitates judaicae* 17.78; 20.223; Ilan 2002, 287–88; Heil/Klampfl 2005, 23ff. Outside of Judaism the use of this name is attested for the first time in Plato, *Cratylus* 394e; 397b; see also Moulton/Milligan 1963, 288; Hemer 1990, 221n1; Head 2004, 34n12; Heil/Klampfl 2005, 16ff.

The question of whether Theophilus was Luke's patron or sponsor and perhaps wanted or ought to care for the dissemination of the Lukan work (cf. Goodspeed 1954) also cannot be answered (Alexander 1993, 190–91, 193ff). There is neither a positive indication for such an assumption nor can it be ruled out. His address as κράτιστε (Roman procurators are addressed in this way in Acts 23.26; 24.3; 26.25; see also Aristophanes, *Plutus* 230; Dionysius of Halicarnassus, *De Demosthene* 58.5; Galen, *De libris propriis*, ed. Kühn 1964, XIX: 8.2; and others) may allow the speculation that Theophilus was not without means and that he enjoyed a certain social prestige, but it does not allow more.

4 A number of possibilities are discussed (cf. Cadbury, *BoC* I/2: 508) for the syntactic resolution of the final sentence in which Luke says what intention he pursues with his presentation, but there are no great differences in content between them.

First, the joining of περί with κατηχήθης would be conceivable, taking one's orientation from Acts 21.21, 24 (in each case καθηχεῖσθαι περὶ σοῦ). In that case λόγων would be attributive to ἀσφάλειαν, and the lacking article τῶν would be replaced by the pulled forward relative clause περὶ ὧν κατηχήθης, which indicates which λόγοι are in view (". . . the ἀσφάλεια of the λόγοι, περὶ ὧν κατηχήθης"). But a rendering where περί is connected with ἀσφάλεια would also be possible, taking one's orientation from Acts 25.26 (περὶ οὗ ἀσφαλές τι): ". . . the ἀσφάλεια with reference (περί) to the λόγοι, which (οὓς) κατηχήθης" (the genitive of the relative pronoun would then be an attraction to the case of the antecedent λόγων [see also Acts 1.1: περὶ πάντων . . . ὧν ἤρξατο ὁ Ἰησοῦς ποιεῖν τε καὶ διδάσκειν]; cf. BDR §294). In any case, the inversion of the parts of the sentence dependent on the predicate shows that Luke is concerned to assign the elevated final position to the word ἀσφάλεια (see also Spicq 1994, I: 216; Fitzmyer).

For ἐπιγινώσκειν cf., in addition to Acts 21.34; 22.30 (in each case γνῶναι τὸ ἀσφαλές; see also 2.36), P. Giss. 27.8 (ἵνα τὸ ἀσφαλὲς ἐπιγνῷ ["in order that I know the certainty"]); P. Sarap. 80.3–4 (ἕως ἂν ἐπιγνῶ τὸ ἀσφαλὲς τοῦ πράγματος ["until I recognize the certainty of the matter"]).

There are also other places where ἀσφάλεια is regarded as a characteristic of λόγοι: Xenophon, *Memorabilia* 4.6.15 ("When he himself presented something in a speech [λόγῳ], he proceeded from what was most recognized, νομίζων ταύτην τὴν ἀσφάλειαν εἶναι λόγου [(for) he was of the opinion that this is the most certain basis of the reflection]"); Isocrates, *Antidosis* 143 ("I have said this to you ἵνα . . . τοῖς λόγοις ἀσφαλεστέροις χρῇ πρὸς αὐτούς [in order that you . . . use more substantive words in relation to them (sc. the judges)]"); Alexander, *De Figuris*, ed. Spengel 1953–1956, III: 15.22–23 (ὅταν . . . εἰπόντες ἀσφαλιζώμεθα τὸν λόγον ["when . . . we while speaking make certain the argument"]); Demetrius, *De elocutione*, ed. Radermacher 1967, 80.8 (οὕτω . . . εἰκασία γέγονεν καὶ ἀσφαλέστερος ὁ λόγος ["thus . . . there was a comparison and the argument became more certain"]).

Here λόγοι certainly does not mean the Christian message, for Luke always uses the singular for this (see at v. 2 above). This also makes it unlikely that the phrasing κατηχεῖσθαι περὶ (τῶν) λόγων should be understood in the sense of a 'catechetical' instruction, as in 4 Baruch 5.21; Galatians 6.6 (in each case κατηχεῖν τὸν λόγον; see also Testament of Joseph 4.4: κατήχησις, i.e., μαθεῖν λόγον κυρίου ["to learn the word of the Lord"]; Acts 18.25). Cadbury, *BoC* I/2, 509 has probably struck upon the right solution—the λόγοι have the same content as the πράγματα of v. 1 (cf. also the taking up of περὶ τῶν by περὶ ὧν), and it is implied that Theophilus has heard of them but knows nothing precise. Luke wants to address this shortcoming with his narrative and correspondingly he indicates with his phrasing that what Theophilus has previously learned is fundamentally accurate. The λόγοι are not corrected but furnished with ἀσφάλεια, i.e., confirmed. For this reason it is also not ἀλήθεια, which Luke wants to convey in distinction from inaccurate and incomplete presentations (cf. by contrast Josephus, *Antiquitates judaicae* 1.4; *Contra Apionem* 1.53; *Bellum judaicum* 1.6.16), but precisely ἀσφάλεια with respect to what Theophilus already knows; see also van Unnik 1973–1983, I: 13–14: "Luke does not make use of the word ἀλήθεια, but instead prefers ἀσφάλεια. This gives a different character to his preface. . . . Thus it is a feature of the ἀσφάλεια that it gives certainty to that which is generally accepted and recognized" (when, by contrast, J. B. Green 1995, 122 translates, "'That you may know the truth,'" then this is not only linguistically false but also misleading in terms of content).

The much-discussed question of whether one must imagine Theophilus as a person interested in Christianity who is not (yet) a Christian or as someone who has already been baptized cannot be answered. The latter is certainly not ruled out, for before the composition of Luke–Acts most Christians would have at best had scarcely more than a superficial

knowledge of the events reported in it. *Rebus sic stantibus* it is therefore
actually conceivable that Theophilus functions in this respect as a representative of the intended readers (see also Creech 1990 and section 5 in
the commentary introduction). In any case, there is no indication here that
Luke wants to correct false views or presentations.

1.5-79(80): "In the days of Herod, the King of Judea"

The transition to the narrative is characterized by an abrupt change of style.
It has the effect that one "slumps from a Greek that is quite passable and
well-structured and intends, in fact, to be graceful to the hardest Hebraizing expressions" (Schleiermacher 2001, 23). Luke begins with a series of
episodes that he dates during the reign of Herod the Great (37–4 BCE)
(v. 5). The narrative coherence of this section is established through three
factors: *(a)* through the placement of the reported events in the chronology of the pregnancy of Elisabeth, the mother of John the Baptist (cf.
vv. 24-25, 26, 56-57; the chronological unit that determines the rhythm
of the narrative is therefore *months*), *(b)* through the concluding summary
in v. 80, which encompasses a time period of a number of years (from the
birth to the public appearance of the Baptist), and *(c)* through the new start
in 2.1, which refers back via the phrasing ἐν ταῖς ἡμέραις ἐκείναις to the
undetermined intervening time mentioned in 1.80 (see at 2.1) and which
expands the narrative perspective from *Judea* as the sphere of *Herod*'s rule
to the *entire* οἰκουμένη as the sphere of Caesar *Augustus*'s rule. Luke thus
wants the sequence of the narratives contained in 1.5-79 to be understood
as a distinct literary unit that should initially be read for itself.

In addition, this chapter has the function of signaling to the readers
that in Luke–Acts the continuation of the history of Israel is narrated, for
it serves to integrate the πράγματα narrated by Luke into the history of
Israel. The style with which Luke begins his narrative in v. 5 finds its
immediate counterpart in the episodic style of the Septuagint (cf. C.-W.
Jung 2004, 45ff, 212–13; individual documentation ad loc.). In the story
narrated by him, things also proceed as in the history of Israel: like Abraham and Sarah, an old married couple still receives a child (cf. esp. Luke
1.7 with Genesis 18.11), and the fate of Elisabeth, who was regarded as
"unfruitful" (v. 36), calls to mind not only Sarah (Genesis 11.30; 16.1), but
also Rebekah (Genesis 25.21), Rachel (Genesis 29.31; 30.1), the wife of
Manoah (Judges 13.2), and Hannah (1 Samuel 1.2). Elisabeth comments
on her surprising pregnancy with almost the same words (κύριος . . .
ἐπεῖδεν ἀφελεῖν ὄνειδός μου ἐν ἀνθρώποις; Luke 1.25) with which Rachel
reacted to the birth of Joseph (ἀφεῖλεν ὁ θεός μου τὸ ὄνειδος ["God has
taken away my shame"]; Genesis 30.23). As in the history of Israel at that

time, now too angels repeatedly appear and speak with people (Luke 1.8-20, 26-38; 2.8-14). Mary's song of praise (1.46-55) calls to mind Hannah's song of praise (1 Samuel 2.1-10). The taking up again of these motifs is not intended to construct a typological correspondence between the individual persons, but through them Luke wants to establish an Old Testament atmosphere and engender the impression on the side of the readers that they are reading a book about the history of Israel.

The structure of this narrative complex is clearly recognizable. It is characterized by the sequence of three narrative phases that Luke demarcates from one another by having multiple uneventful months elapse between them. The first phase (vv. 8-24a) is followed, after a five month interval (v. 24b; see also vv. 26, 36), by the second phase (vv. 26-55), which is then separated through a distance of three months (v. 56) from the third phase (vv. 57-79). Luke then further divides these main phases into narrative subphases and measures the intervals between them in days (vv. 23-24a, 39, 59). The superordinated narrative rhythm corresponds with the narrative objects in such a way that the first and last main phase (vv. 5-24a and vv. 57-79) are each oriented toward John the Baptist, whereas the middle one is related to Jesus (vv. 26-55). In this respect the three phases are thus concentrically ordered according to the schema a-b-a. Once this structure principle is recognized it can be immediately made more precise. The Johannine portion begins with the narration of a birth announcement (vv. 8-23) and ends with a hymn that Luke places in the mouth of the recipient of that announcement (vv. 68-79). The same also applies to the Jesus portion (announcement: vv. 26-38; hymn of Mary: vv. 46-55). Luke thus makes a chiastic ordering of the sequence of the birth announcements related to John and Jesus and the hymns that answer them. Both lines come together in the scene that portrays the reactions of the still unborn John and his mother to the visit of the mother of Jesus (vv. 40-45). Viewed as a whole, Luke has configured the narrative unit as a concentric ring composition:

(a^1) Zechariah receives the announcement of the birth of John
(1.8-23)
    (b^1) Mary receives the announcement of the birth of Jesus
    (1.26-38)
        (ab) John and Elisabeth react to Mary's visit (1.40-45)
    (b^2) Mary answers with a hymn (1.46-55)
(a^2) Zechariah answers with a hymn (1.67-79)

Zechariah cannot answer the birth announcement communicated to him until the end of chapter 1, because he loses the ability to speak at the very beginning (vv. 20, 22) and only recovers it after the birth and naming of his son (v. 64). Thus, within the narrated time there arises an intervening period of at least nine months (cf. v. 20), which Luke probably created in order to place into it the Jesus portion of his narrative, i.e., the announcement of the birth of Jesus, Mary's visit to Elisabeth's place, and the Magnificat (vv. 26-56). With this principle of composition Luke also gives the overall narrative context a thematic slope. The two outer members signal that Luke orients the superordinated action narratively to John the Baptist, but he simultaneously orders it to Jesus as its actual center. This is recognizable first via the visit scene (vv. 40-45) in which the two lines running between birth announcements and hymns cross, for John and his mother obtain here the task of expressing the elevated position of Mary and her child. Second, with the help of this compositional ordering the readers are put in position to relate the Benedictus of Zechariah (vv. 67-79) with its messianic statements of salvation to Jesus and to understand it as an interpretation of the *entire* narrative sequence.

The preceding analysis of the narrative structure of chapter 1 entails an abandonment of the assumption, first presented by Dibelius 1911, 67ff, that the Lukan infancy narrative is to be read as a "diptych" (so, e.g., Laurentin 1967, 31; R. E. Brown 1993, 252; Radl 1996, 41), which Luke, on the one hand—thus Ernst 1989, 113 for all others—"constructs and structures according to the principle of the parallelism between John and Jesus," but on the other hand narrates in such a way that John is 'surpassed' by Jesus. Since that time, this interpretation of Luke 1–2 has been taken over almost unchanged (cf. e.g., Nolland I: 20: "No real improvement has been made on the structure proposed by Dibelius"; literature surveys that differ with regard to their extensiveness can be found in Laurentin 1967, 31–32; George 1970, 147ff; R. E. Brown 1993, 250ff, 623ff; Radl 1996, 43ff). However, this way of reading the Lukan 'prehistory' (one should not designate it as such anyway, for Luke 1–2 is, of course, an integral component of the πράγματα mentioned in 1.1 with whose narration Luke begins in 1.5) is untenable. The postulated parallelism does not match up in any case, for 2.8-20, 22-40, 41-51 have no equivalent in the John half. Besides that, while Luke does narrate the birth announcement (1.8-2 and 1.26-38), birth (1.57 and 2.4-7), and circumcision and naming (1.57-66 and 2.21) of both children, and the summaries in 1.80 and 2.40, 52 are also formulated identically in parts, these correspondences are not sufficient to make from them a composition principle that determines Luke 1–2 as a whole. The fact that Gabriel's visit to Mary is integrated into the chronology of Elisabeth's pregnancy (1.26) and Gabriel is introduced here as a narrative figure already known to the readers (see further in Wolter 1998b, 421) already reveals on its own that at this point Luke narrates not in two strands but in one strand and that the two birth announcements do not want to be read in parallel but successively. At no point do the Lukan birth narratives obtain that breadth (Lämmert 1975, 33) that the schematic sketches of its structure ever since Dibelius have repeatedly suggested, for the same space of time is never narratively passed through twice. Rather, the chronological longitude (Lämmert 1975, 33) of the narrative predominates. On the question of sources, cf. ad loc., respectively.

1.5-7: Exposition

⁵In the days of Herod, the king of Judea, there was a priest by the name of Zechariah from the daily service division of Abijah. He had a wife from the daughters of Aaron, who was called Elisabeth. ⁶Both were righteous before God, for they walked without blame in all the commandments and laws of the Lord. ⁷And they had no child because Elisabeth was barren and both were advanced in age.

These verses form the exposition of the narrative complex that reaches to v. 79. Luke integrates the narrated events into the historical chronology and introduces the people with whose fate the events are connected in this first narrative collecting basin of his work. In this way he provides for his readers the background information that they need to understand what follows. After the linguistically artfully stylized sentence period of the proem, Luke begins to narrate in a manner that unmistakably calls to mind the Old Testament.

5 The dating already corresponds to Old Testament narrative style, for the Old Testament also uses the phrasing ἐν (ταῖς) ἡμέραις + ruler's name to place events in the time of a king's reign (2 Samuel 21.1; 1 Kings 16.28^LXX; 2 Kings 15.28[29]; 1 Chronicles 4.41; 5.10, 17; 2 Chronicles 13.23; see also 1 Kings 10.21; 1 Chronicles 7.2; 2 Chronicles 9.20; 26.5 [see also C.-W. Jung 2004, 135ff]; this form of dating is not attested outside the Septuagint). When Luke takes up this linguistic convention at the very beginning of his presentation and dates the first sequence of events narrated by him during the reign of Herod the Great (37–4 BCE), he makes what follows into a continuation of the history of Israel. The fact that Herod is introduced here in a historically imprecise manner as βασιλεὺς τῆς Ἰουδαίας also corresponds to this, for in actuality he ruled over a much greater area from the beginning, to which non-Jewish territories were also assigned later. With "Judea" Luke designates both the territory of this name (roughly the former settlement of the tribe of Judah or the former southern kingdom or the Persian province "Jehud"; cf. 1.65; 2.4; 3.1; 5.17; 21.21; Acts 9.31) and in a comprehensive manner the area inhabited primarily by

Jews (thus including Galilee and Perea; cf. 4.44; 6.17; 7.17; 23.5; Acts 1.8; 10.37). Here, "Judea" stands as *pars pro toto* (R. E. Brown 1993, 257; see also Josephus, *Antiquitates judaicae* 14.280; 15.2) in order to signal the *material* reference of the events narrated in what follows.

The same also then applies to the introduction of the narrative figures. The introductory phrasing (ἐγένετο . . .) ἱερεύς τις ὀνόματι Z. corresponds to the episodic style that is common in Hellenistic history writing.

Cf. e.g., Josephus, *Bellum judaicum* 4.37: ἑκατοντάρχης δέ τις, Γάλλος ὀνόματι ("a centurion named Gallus"); 6.186, 387; *Antiquitates judaicae* 8.4.14; 12.265; 15.373; 20.34, 97; Polybius 3.98.2: ἦν δέ τις ἀνὴρ Ἴβηρ, Ἀβίλυξ ὄνομα ("there was an Iberian named Abilux"); Diodorus Siculus 17.45.6; 100.2; Dionysius of Halicarnassus, *Antiquitates romanae* 1.39.2; 3.46.3; Appian, *De bello Mithridatico* 353; see also Philo, *De vita Mosis* 1.250; Xenophon of Ephesus 3.9.4; Vita Aesopi 129; as distinct from the other gospels this usage is also frequently attested elsewhere in Luke: Luke 10.38; 16.20; Acts 5.1, 34; 8.9; 9.10, 36; 10.1; 16.1, 14; 18.24; 20.9; 21.10.

Ζαχαρίας is the Greek transcription of Hebrew זְכַרְיָה (e.g., 2 Kings 14.29; Zechariah 1.1). The name means "Yhwh has remembered"; see also Ilan 2002, 90ff.

With the exception of Job 1.1 and Bel and the Dragon 2 (here the introduction is ἄνθρωπός τις in each case), only narratively secondary characters are ever introduced in this way. Plus, these phrasings never introduce the main storyline but always only episodic subplots or individual scenes. Through the manner in which Zechariah is introduced narratively, what follows is qualified as an excerpt from an overarching event whose actual beginning already lies further back. With this special configuration of the beginning of his narrative, Luke wants to make clear that the narrated events are a continuation of the history of Israel (cf. also Wolter 2004b, 272ff).

Luke specifies the priestly status of Zechariah by also naming the division to which he belongs (cf. Josephus, *Antiquitates judaicae* 12.265: ἦν τις οἰκῶν ἐν Μωδαΐ . . . , ὄνομα Ματταθίας . . . , ἱερεὺς ἐξ ἐφημερίδος Ἰωάριβος ["in Modein . . . there lived one named Mattathias . . . a priest from the daily service division of Joarib"]). According to the list of priestly divisions in 1 Chronicles 24.7-18 (see also Nehemiah 12.1-7, 12-21; 4Q320–330), from which each was appointed to the priestly service for a week two times per year (cf. Josephus, *Antiquitates judaicae* 7.365; *Contra Apionem* 2.108; m. Tamid 5.1; see also Bill. II: 55–68; Winter 1954/1955a, 160ff; Schürer 1973–1987, II: 245ff, 292; Maier 1995–1996, III: 87ff), Zechariah belonged to the eighth division (Hebrew אֲבִיָּה according to 1 Chronicles 24.10).

The fact that Luke also introduces Zechariah's wife—she not only comes from the lineage of Aaron but also bears the same name as Aaron's wife (אֱלִישֶׁבַע = "my God is abundance" [?]; cf. Exodus 6.23; see also Ilan 2002, 239)—could, in view of what follows, already be a conscious allusion to Judges 13.2; 1 Samuel 1.1-2, where men with their barren wives are likewise introduced in this way before their childlessness is removed by God.

6 Zechariah and Elisabeth are characterized from the perspective of God. According to his judgment (on ἐναντίον in this sense, cf. W. Bauer 1988, 527–28; see also Genesis 7.1; Exodus 15.26; Job 32.1-2; 35.2), they are "righteous," because God finds their life conduct to be "blameless" (for the causal understanding of the participial construction, cf. BDR §418.1). In v. 6b the life conduct of the married couple is likewise described with recourse to the Septuagint, but without it being possible to identify specific texts. Here Luke takes up a few elements from the linguistic inventory of the semantic field that serves to designate the commission that God issued to Israel as part of her election (cf. e.g., Exodus 15.26; Deuteronomy 4.40; 6.2; 10.12-13; 27.10; 1 Kings 8.61; Ezekiel 11.20-21; 18.9; 20.19; 36.27; Psalm 119.1-6). Zechariah and Elisabeth are thus introduced as outstanding representatives of the people of God in whose life conduct this commission finds the realization for which God has promised his blessing (cf. Leviticus 26.3-4; Deuteronomy 7.11-14; 30.16).

7 In this light the information that the two had no child because Elisabeth was barren is at first glance surprising: cf. Exodus 23.26; Deuteronomy 7.11-14, on the one hand, and Leviticus 20.20-21; Hosea 9.11; Philo, *De specialibus legibus* 1.11; 1 Enoch 98.5 ("barrenness is not given to a woman, but because of the work of her hands she dies without children"), on the other hand. In the New Testament καθότι occurs only in Luke: see also Luke 19.9; Acts 2.24, 45; 4.35; 17.31. At the same time, however, this disclosure is meant to evoke the expectation that the narrative will now tell how God removes this bad state of affairs. For the readers are immediately reminded of analogous constellations in the history of Israel into which Luke has already ushered them with the first words of his exposition, namely of Sarah (Genesis 11.30; 16.1), Rebekah (Genesis 25.21), Rachel (Genesis 29.31; 30.1), the wife of Manoah (Judges 13.2), and Hannah (1 Samuel 1.2). In every case the barrenness of the woman is communicated as an expositional element only in order to recount how it is removed by God; cf. in this sense Genesis Rabbah 38.14 (on Genesis 11.30): "In every passage where it is said: אֵין לָה [she had not], יהוה לָה [she conceived]." This holds true all the more, of course, since Zechariah and Elisabeth already found themselves beyond the age in which one was able to reproduce (v. 7c), and the readers are thus directed to the fate of Abraham and Sarah (cf. Genesis 18.11: they were πρεσβύτεροι προβεβηκότες ἡμερῶν); the Lukan phrasing corresponds to Septuagintal style (cf. in addition Genesis 24.1; Joshua 13.1; 23.1; see also BDR §197.5; C.-W. Jung 2004, 179ff).

1.8-25: The Announcement of the Birth of John the Baptist

[8]It happened, however, when he provided the priestly service before God in the order of his division, [9]that he was drawn by lot according to the custom of the priestly service to present the incense offering, after he entered into the temple of the Lord. [10]And the whole multitude of the people prayed outside in the hour of the incense offering. [11]Then there appeared to him an angel of the Lord standing at the right side of the altar of incense. [12]And Zechariah was terrified when he saw (him) and fear fell upon him. [13]The angel, however, said to him, "Fear not, Zechariah, for your prayer has been heard and your wife Elisabeth will bear a son to you, and you are to give him the name John. [14]And he will be a joy and jubilation to you, and many will rejoice over his birth. [15]For he will be great before the Lord, and he will not drink wine and intoxicating drink. And from the womb onward he will be filled with the Holy Spirit. [16]And he will turn many of the children of Israel to the Lord, their God. [17]And he will go before him in the spirit and power of Elijah, to turn the hearts of the fathers to the children and the disobedient to think on what is right, in order to prepare for the Lord a ready people." [18]And Zechariah said to the angel, "By what will I know this? I am an old man and my wife is very advanced in age." [19]The angel answered and spoke to him, "I am Gabriel, who stands before God, and I was sent to speak to you and gospel this to you. [20]And look, you will be mute and not able to speak until the day on which this happens, because you did not believe my words, which will come into fulfillment in their time."

[21]And the people waited on Zechariah and wondered at his long stay in the temple. [22]When he came out, however, he could not speak to them and they recognized that he had seen an appearance in the temple. He gestured to them and remained unable to speak. [23]And it happened, when the days of his priestly service were complete, that he returned to his house. [24]After these days, however, his wife Elisabeth became pregnant and kept herself hidden for five months and said: [25]"So has the Lord done to me in the days in which he directed his attention to take away my shame among humans."

Luke narrates the first episode in vv. 8-23. He joins it with the exercise of the priestly service by Zechariah and localizes it in the Jerusalem temple. Since this is also the place to which he leads back the disciples at the conclusion of the Gospel (24.53), this localization functions as an element of a narrative *inclusio* that is of considerable theological significance.

Form-critically this is an appearance story around which a double frame is placed (v. 8 / v. 23 and vv. 9-10 / vv. 21-22). As genre-specific elements one can identify (documentation ad loc. respectively): *(a)* ὤφθη + dative as the first finite verb with the one who appears as the subject (v. 11); *(b)* the recipient of the appearance becomes frightened and/or afraid (v. 12); *(c)* the exhortation μὴ φοβοῦ or the like directed to the recipient of the appearance; *(d)* the self-identification of the one who appears with ἐγώ εἰμι (v. 19b); *(e)* the messenger statement (ἀπεστάλην or the like, v. 19c); *(f)* the one who appears speaks a shorter or longer text; in the present case we are dealing with a birth announcement (vv. 13b-17). It is not a 'call narrative' for the concern is not with the future task of Zechariah but with that of his son (see also at 1.28).

8-9 With the structure of the sentence Luke again imitates Septuagintal style. The construction ἐγένετο δέ + specification of time with the help of a substantivized infinitive (ἐν τῷ ἱερατεύειν αὐτόν) + *verbum finitum* (ἔλαχε) is also found in Genesis 24.52; 25.11; 35.17, 18; 38.28; Job 42.7. In the New Testament it is attested—like the sentence introduction with ἐγένετο δέ as such—only in Luke (2.6; 11.27; 18.35; see also 3.21; 5.1; 9.51; Acts 19.1; cf. Fitzmyer I: 118ff; Gault 1990). In two steps the readers are now led together with Zechariah to the event that Luke wants to narrate.

In **8** Luke initially picks out from the temporal frame, which has remained quite spacious in v. 5, the days in which Zechariah's priestly division provides the service in the temple and leads him from his place of residence to Jerusalem.

In **9-10** the event is then fixed temporally and spatially.

9 The individual liturgical functions were drawn by lot by the members of the priestly division that was on duty (cf. m. Yoma 2.1ff; m. Tamid 1.2; 3.1, 5.2; Schürer 1973–1987, II: 304). The Tamid offering (הַתָּמִיד = 'the continual [offering]'; cf. Numbers 28.10–29.38; Nehemiah 10.34; Daniel 8.11-13; 11.31; 12.11) was performed mornings and afternoons as an incense offering (the Septuagint correspondingly calls it ὁλοκαύτωμα; see also Exodus 3.7-8). m. Tamid 5.4ff describes the more exact course of the morning offering (see also Bill. II: 71ff; Winter 1954/1955a, 232ff); that Luke portrays here specifically the afternoon offering (so D. Hamm 2003) cannot be determined on the basis of the text. It took place on what the rabbinic literature calls the "inner altar" (הַמִּזְבֵּחַ הַפְּנִימִי), which was located in the actual temple building that was exclusively accessible to the priests (the הֵיכָל or the 'holy place'; see also Exodus 30.1-6; 37.25-28). Moreover, the golden menorah and the bread of the presence were also in it. This room was separated from the 'most holy place' (דְּבִיר) by a curtain. But Luke then has no more interest in the carrying out of the offering. He does not devote another word to it in what follows but instead notes the entrance into the temple, which is actually a given. Thus, what is important to him is not that Zechariah presents the incense offering but only that he enters into the temple. Contrary to the liturgical practice (multiple priests always participated in the incense offering and there was no point at which only a single person was in the הֵיכָל), he then has Zechariah also enter the temple building alone, for the appearance should be granted only to him. Thus, the actual goal of the narrative already influences the configuration of the frame.

10 In view of this narrative economy, the question arises of why Luke explicitly emphasizes that in the meantime the multitude of the people persists in prayer outside of the temple building, for it plays no role within the appearance story. Luke needs it, however, as a narrative figure in the concluding frame of the appearance story in order to be able to demonstrate (v. 22) the immediate realization of the muteness imposed upon Zechariah there (v. 20). Therefore, he has the multitude of the people appear already at the beginning at least in the background of the scene. When he presents them as praying, then this certainly does not happen in order to invite the readers to speculate about the content of the prayer (so, e.g., Green), but because he wants to characterize the people—as also often elsewhere—by communicating what they do. In this sense Luke portrays the people of God (it is also not without reason that in this passage he uses for the first time the theologically loaded λαός-term [see H. Frankenmölle, *EWNT* 2: 843ff], the "predicate of honor" [841]) as turned to their God here (see also Luke 2.37; Acts 1.14; 2.42; 9.11; 10.2; 12.12). In this way the people of God also simultaneously realize the purpose of the temple (cf. 19.46). The phrasing πᾶν τὸ πλῆθος, which occurs only in Luke in the New Testament (cf. in addition 8.37; 19.37; 23.1; Acts 6.5; 15.12; 25.24), occurs not only in the Septuagint (Exodus 12.6; 2 Kings 7.13; Ezekiel 31.6), but also elsewhere (e.g., Herodotus 8.34; Diodorus Siculus 2.41.2; 5.31.3; Herodianus Historicus 6.5.3; Letter of Aristeas 42; Ps.-Callisthenes 24.32; Josephus, *Antiquitates judaicae* 13.100; *Vita* 210, sometimes followed by a genitive as here).

11 ὤφθη is a *terminus technicus* for appearance stories (cf. e.g., Genesis 12.7; 17.1; 26.24; Mark 9.4). There is a special closeness to Exodus 3.2; Judges 6.12; 13.3; Testament of Issachar 2.1 (see also Tobit 12.22), where the appearance of an ἄγγελος κυρίου is reported with the same words. In Judges 13.3b-5; Testament of Issachar 2.1 there additionally follows a birth announcement as here. That Luke has the angel stand on the right side of the altar of incense is possibly meant to express his special dignity. Sitting or standing (angels always stand) at the right hand of God designates elevation and chosenness (cf. Psalm 110.1 and its reception in the New Testament [see at 20.42-43]; Testament of Benjamin 10.6; Testament of Job 33.3; Apocalypse of Abraham 22.6; Acts 7.55-56). Apart from this, the right side is regarded, of course, as the favorable side in general; cf. W. Grundmann, ThWNT 2: 37.21ff.

12 The information that the recipient of the appearance is frightened and falls into fear is specific to appearance stories (cf. Tobit 12.16; Daniel 8.17; 1 Enoch 60.3; Joseph and Aseneth 14.10; 2 Enoch 1.7; 20.1; Cicero, *De republica* 6.10; Mark 6.50par.; 16.5; Acts 10.4; see also Daniel 10.8; Revelation 1.17), as is the exhortation μὴ φοβοῦ from the side of the one who appears in v. 13b (cf. Genesis 26.24; 28.13^{LXX}; Daniel 10.12; Tobit 12.17; Joseph and Aseneth 14.11; 2 Enoch 1.8; Cicero, *De republica* 6.10; Mark 6.50par.; 16.16; Luke 1.30; 2.10; Acts 27.23-24; Revelation 1.17).

13-17 The short speech that the angel delivers belongs to the genre of birth announcement, which is widespread in ancient literature (cf. e.g., Homer, *Odyssea* 11.248–49; Homeric Hymns 5.196ff; Herodotus 5.92; Pindar, *Isthmionikai* 6.53ff; Euripides, *Iphigenia aulidensis* 1062ff; additional texts in Zeller 1992, 66ff). The following genre-specific elements can be identified: *(a)* The birth is announced to a parent (v. 13c). *(b)* The name of the child is mentioned or there is a commission to give it a name (v. 13d). *(c)* The future significance of the child is described (vv. 14-17). The concrete linguistic realization of the form by Luke is oriented, of course, toward the Old Testament instances of the genre (cf. the compilation in Radl 1996, 72f), but without a typological reference to a certain text being intended. The Lukan presentation contains, in particular, elements from the announcements of the births of Ishmael (Genesis 16.11-12), Isaac (Genesis 17.15-19), and Samson (Judges 13.3-5)—sometimes with word-for-word borrowings (cf. the overview in R. E. Brown 1978, 156; see ad loc. below). Thus, here too Luke is concerned to establish an Old Testament atmosphere, and in this way he simultaneously engenders the impression of unbroken salvation-historical continuity between the biblical events and the events that he describes.

13 When Luke has the angel justify the exhortation μὴ φοβοῦ in v. 13c with the message that God has heard the prayer of Zechariah (εἰσηκούσθη is a *passivum divinum*; see also Tobit 3.16; 2 Maccabees 1.8; Sirach 51.11; Daniel 10.12), this communication lacks a narrative abutment insofar as nothing has been previously recounted concerning such a prayer (cf. Dauer 1990, 15ff). The content of the prayer is, however, insignificant. Rather,

Luke wants here to characterize God's action alone and at the same time to remove the tension between deed and consequence built up in vv. 6-7. For when in the Old Testament and in early Jewish literature there is talk of God hearing the prayers of the pious and righteous, this always expresses his salvific turning to them (cf. above all the terminological parallels in 2 Kings 20.5; 2 Chronicles 6.19-21; 2 Maccabees 1.8; Tobit 3.16; Psalm^LXX 6.10; 27.6; 39.2; 65.19; Job 8.6; Proverbs 15.29; Sirach 51.11; Psalms of Solomon; 3 Baruch 1.5: ἡ γὰρ δέησίς σου ἠκούσθη ἐνώπιον αὐτοῦ ["for your prayer was heard before him"]; Life of Adam and Eve 29.12 as well as Numbers 20.16; Deuteronomy 26.7; Psalm^LXX 33.18; 151.3; Daniel 10.12; Liber antiquitatum biblicarum 32.7; 44.10; 1 Enoch 47.4; 2 Baruch 71.3; see also Jüng 2004, 193ff). Thus, what is being said is that God has begun to act in correspondence to Zechariah's righteousness. Verse 13d then indicates the consequence of this action (for the birth of children as a result of God's hearing, cf. Genesis 16.11; 25.21; 29.33; 30.6, 17, 22; Liber antiquitatum biblicarum 42.3 also adds a corresponding remark to the biblical *Vorlage* of Judges 13.3-5). The phrasing is oriented toward Genesis 17.19 (God says to Abraham: Σάρρα ἡ γυνή σου τέξεταί σοι υἱόν ["Sarah, your wife, will bear to you a son"]), i.e., to the only case of a birth announcement issued to the future father in the Old Testament (see also Genesis 18.10, 14). The following commission to name him finds its word-for-word counterpart in Genesis 16.11; 17.19; Isaiah 7.14 (see also Liber antiquitatum biblicarum 42.3, again as an addition to the *Vorlage*). Thus, Luke imitates the Septuagint again and signals in this way that God intervenes in the history of the people of God now, acting in the same way as he did then.

14 With a synthetic *parallelismus membrorum* Luke describes the reactions that the announced child will trigger among the persons in his environment. "Joy and jubilation" (also found as a lexical pair in Tobit 13.15; Psalm^LXX 95.11-12; 125.2; Habakkuk 3.18; Greek Apocalypse of Enoch 104.13; Testament of Abraham A 11.7, 10; Testament of Levi 18.5; 4 Baruch 6.17; Testament of Job 43.15; Matthew 5.12; John 8.56; 1 Peter 1.8; 4.13; Revelation 19.7) do not merely refer to the event of the birth but point to the salvific turning of God to his people (see Liber antiquitatum biblicarum 51.6–7, which appears also in an analogous context). The actual topic of the statement is John, who is characterized in this way as an integral part of God's salvific action (Luke has the angel provide the basis for this in vv. 15-17). The question of whether πολλοί in v. 14b should be understood inclusively (semitizing in the sense of 'all'; e.g., J. Jeremias, ThWNT 6: 541) or restrictively ('many,' but precisely not 'all'; e.g., Schürmann; Nolland) misses the intention of the text, for in this way the statement is made into a message about Israel by a sleight of hand. Instead, comparable sentences with πολλοί without an article or without an attribute always have the function of characterizing a person by describing their influence upon other people (cf. e.g., Judith 16.22 concerning Judith: πολλοὶ ἐπεθύμησαν αὐτήν ["many desired her"]; Psalm^LXX 39.4 concerning God: ὄψονται πολλοὶ καὶ φοβηθήσονται ["many will see (it) and fear"]; Sirach 39.9 concerning the wise man: αἰνέσουσιν τὴν σύνεσιν αὐτοῦ πολλοί ["many will praise his insight"]; see also 2 Chronicles 32.23; Matthew 12.15; Mark 11.8; John 2.23). Thus, Luke has the angel stress solely that John's birth becomes an occasion for great joy. With the help of five paratactically ordered sentences, vv. 15-17 unpack the basis for the joy.

15 The three statements of this verse characterize John with regard to his relation to God. First, v. 15a formulates God's judgment about him (for ἐνώπιον in this sense, cf. W. Bauer 1988, 546–47): John will enjoy great favor with him (cf. the analogous phrasings in Exodus 11.3; 2 Kings 5.1; Susanna^Theodotion 64; see also Testament of Joseph 15.5). The announcement that he will refrain from intoxicating drinks takes up the lexical pair οἶνος καὶ σίκερα, which is often attested in the Septuagint (cf. Leviticus 10.9; Numbers 6.3; Deuteronomy 14.26; 29.5; see also Testament of Reuben 1.10; C.-W. Jung 2004, 92ff). σίκερα is the Greek transcription of Hebrew שֵׁכָר, which probably designates an alcoholic drink that is not obtained from grapes. In the late Midrash Sifre to Numbers 6.3, שֵׁכָר is regarded as unmixed wine (Bill. II: 80), while יַיִן, which is always translated with οἶνος in the Septuagint, is taken as a designation for wine that is mixed (with water). Analogously formulated statements of abstention are found there in relation to the priests (Leviticus 10.9), the Nazirites (Numbers 6.3), Israel in the wilderness (Deuteronomy 29.5; see at Luke 7.33), the mother of Samson within a birth announcement (Judges 13.4, 7, 14), which is transferred to Samson himself in Liber antiquitatum biblicarum 42.3, and Samuel (1 Samuel 1.11^LXX: οἶνον καὶ μέθυσμα οὐ πίεται ["he will not drink wine and beer"]). Although John is not made into a Nazirite through this, the aforementioned texts flow into the picture of John insofar as they present the abstention from alcohol as a characteristic of people who are especially close to God. Finally, the third statement characterizes John by reaching back to two Old Testament motifs that converge with each other in the pretext but are not directly connected with each other, as they are here, in any other passage. On the one hand, there is the notion that God marks out certain individual persons by giving to them his Spirit ad hoc as a gift in order to make them mediators of his action toward his people. Luke could find this conception in the Old Testament, e.g., with reference to Joseph (41.38); Moses (Numbers 11.17; Isaiah 63.10ff); the so-called judges (Judges 3.10; 6.34; 11.29); Samson (Judges 14.6, 19;

15.14); Saul (1 Samuel 10.6, 10; 11.6); David (1 Samuel 16.13), and especially with reference to prophets (Numbers 11.25, 29; 1 Samuel 10.6, 10;
19.20; Nehemiah 9.30; Isaiah 42.1; 61.1; Ezekiel 11.5; 37.9; Hosea 9.7;
Joel 3.1; Micah 3.8; Zechariah 1.6; 7.12) (see also Jubilees 31.12; Liber
antiquitatum biblicarum 28.6; Josephus, *Antiquitates judaicae* 6.166, 222;
8.408). On the other hand, Luke takes up the motif of the calling of prophets "from the womb," which designates their prior election and installation
into their prophetic task in Isaiah 44.2, 24; 49.1; Jeremiah 1.5 (see also
Galatians 1.15 and Judges 13.5; 16.7). What is new in Luke and without
analogy is that he combines the two. The unprecedented conferment of
the Spirit while he was "still" (ἔτι) in the womb elevates John above all
previous prophets (see also 7.26) and confers upon him a status that surpasses all previous mediators (in v. 35 this is increased once more with
regard to Jesus). This status is also transferred to his prophetic task—he
becomes the mediator of an action of God toward his people that is unique
up to now.

In **16-17** Luke has the angel present what John's task toward Israel
consists in.

16 First, the 'classic' function of a prophet is transferred to him very
generally—to move Israel to turn to her God (cf. 2 Chronicles 24.19;
Nehemiah 9.26). To be sure, the fact that this is qualified here, unlike in
v. 14, should not be overlooked, but in view of the personal orientation of
the statement it should not be overvalued (see also Malachi 2.6), for it is
not the failure but the future success of the prophet that is emphasized (see
also Daniel 12.3).

In **17** Luke makes the prophetic task of John concrete by sketching it
into the traditional Elijah expectation. In Malachi 3.1, 23-24 the eschatic
return of Elijah is announced, who was translated to heaven before his
death and who will go before God, who comes in judgment, as a forerunner in order to ward off the wrath of God from Israel. Attestations for
this expectation are found in Sirach 48.10; 4Q588 IV; Lives of the Prophets 21.3 (Epiphanius 2); 4 Ezra 6.26; Sibylline Oracles 2.187–88; in the
New Testament it is reflected in Matthew 11.14; Mark 6.15par.; 8.28parr.;
9.11-12par. (see also Revelation 11.3ff) (cf. the overview in Öhler 1997,
1ff; see also Bill. IV: 779ff). With this link Luke also has the angel give
an extremely important signal, namely that the time of fulfillment of the
prophetic promises of salvation has dawned. At the same time, he thereby
communicates to his readers for the first time *expressis verbis* that he narrates not simply another epoch of the history of Israel in his history work
but that his presentation deals with the eschatic fulfillment of Israel's hope
for salvation. However, John is not equated with the expected *Elias redivivus*, even though Luke, taking up Malachi 3.1, initially presents him as

God's forerunner (v. 17a). When it says that John will carry out this task "in the spirit and power of Elijah," this means that he will act as the authentic representative of Elijah without being identical with him (cf. 2 Kings 2.9, 15 about Elisha). Πνεῦμα and δύναμις are often joined with each other (cf. just the genitive phrases in Wisdom of Solomon 5.23; 11.20; Liber antiquitatum biblicarum 27.10; 2 Timothy 1.7 [see also the texts mentioned at 4.14] or the coordinations in 1QH XV, 9-10; Luke 1.35; Acts 10.38; 1 Corinthians 2.4; 1 Thessalonians 1.5), so that one can indeed understand this lexical pair in this passage as a hendiadys (cf. BDR §442.9b). They are terms of legitimation and authorization insofar as one represents the one from whom one has received πνεῦμα and δύναμις (cf. e.g., in addition Isaiah 42.1/6^{LXX}; Micah 3.8; Liber antiquitatum biblicarum 36.2; Luke 24.49; Acts 1.8; Revelation 13.2; Epistle to the Apostles 30[41]; Martyrdom of Andrew 1 [Lipsius/Bonnet 1959, II/1: 46.11–13]: "And now there has fallen on every one of us the δύναμις that comes down from heaven and the gift τοῦ ἁγίου πνεύματος is poured out over us").

In v. 17b-c the goal of the prophetic task is described with the help of two cascading infinitive constructions. Verse 17b is configured as a zeugmatic *parallelismus membrorum*. The beginning refers thematically to Malachi 3.24(23), but in its linguistic form it orients itself less toward the Septuagint version of this verse (ἀποκαταστήσει καρδίαν πατρὸς πρὸς υἱόν ["he will bring back the heart of the father to the son"]) than toward Sirach 48.10 (ἐπιστρέψαι καρδίαν πατρὸς πρὸς υἱόν ["he will turn the heart of the father to the son"]) and to the Hebrew text to which the use of the plural forms πατέρων and τέκνα correspond. The frequently asked question of which text Luke uses (cf. C.-W. Jung 2004, 103ff) misses the intention of the phrasing, for he wants not to quote here but merely to apply Elijah typology to John.

The interpretation of the continuation in v. 17d-e and the way it should be related to the first part of the task description is controversial (cf. the overview of the different solution attempts in Marshall). Luke certainly does not want to relate the juxtaposition of "disobedient" and "righteous" to the juxtaposition of "father" and "children" (neither in parallel nor in a chiastic relationship). Rather, the generalizing terminology suggests that Luke goes beyond Malachi 3.24 here and no longer has only interpersonal relationships in view but the relation to God. 'Disobedience' characterizes the refusal of Israel to listen to God (cf. Leviticus 26.15; Numbers 20.10; Deuteronomy 9.23; Isaiah 30.9; 65.2; Ezekiel 3.27), whereas the opposite is true for the 'righteous.' Accordingly, in analogy to v. 16, it is the bringing about of conversion that is assigned to John as his prophetic task (as often in the New Testament ἐν stands here for εἰς; cf. BDR §218₃); see also Testament of Daniel 5.11: ἐπιστρέψει καρδίας ἀπειθεῖς πρὸς κύριον ("he will turn disobedient hearts to the Lord") as part of God's eschatic salvific action toward Israel. In this way Luke also establishes a connection with v. 17c, where the goal of the task to be embraced by John is encapsulated in summary form—he should ensure that God finds at his coming a people of salvation that corresponds to him. Luke probably adopted ἑτοιμάζειν and κατασκευάζειν from Mark 1.2-3 where both verbs are connected with each other with reference to John (Luke has then separated them from each other again in 3.4-6).

John is presented here without any qualification as the forerunner of God (see also v. 76), while later he functions *de facto* as the forerunner of Jesus. This tension is not due to the reworking of a written source or the dependence on oral tradition of a Baptist provenance. It points instead to an essential component of Lukan Christology, namely that Jesus is the one through whom the salvific turning of God to his people takes place. Its abutment within the Lukan Jesus narrative is found, e.g., in 7.16; 10.22; 11.20; 19.9.

18 Luke has Zechariah ask for a sign with the same words with which Abraham had already reacted to the promise of land (Genesis 15.8: κατὰ τί γνώσομαι ὅτι . . . ; ["by what will I recognize that . . . ?"]; see also Judges 6.36-37^LXX). And the objection with which he grounds his question also actualizes once more the story of Abraham and Sarah (cf. the analogous reactions in Genesis 17.17; 18.12). Thus, nothing surprising and uncommon adheres to this narrative element (for the Septuagintal style of the phrasing, see at v. 7). This then changes, however, in the answer of the angel.

19 In a way that is characteristic for appearance stories, the angel first makes known his identity (for the use of ἐγώ εἰμι in other instances of the genre, cf. e.g., Genesis 26.24; 31.13; Tobit 12.15; Joseph and Aseneth 14.8; 2 Enoch 69.5; 70.3; 72.5; Mark 6.50parr.; Luke 24.39; Acts 9.5; 22.8; Revelation 1.17; Corpus Hermeticum 1.2). Gabriel (Hebrew גַּבְרִיאֵל = "the strong one of God") is regarded in Jewish angelology as one of the four (see 1 Enoch 9.1; 40.9–10; 54.6; 71.8) or seven (1 Enoch 20) so-called archangels who stand as "throne angels" (cf. Revelation 1.4) or "face angels" (Isaiah 63.9; Ezekiel 1.6; Jubilees 1.27; 1Q28b IV, 25) in the immediate proximity of God (cf. Revelation 8.2) and thus participate in a special way in God's holiness (see 1 Enoch 20) and glory (see 2 Enoch 21.1, 3) (cf. K. E. Grözinger, *TRE* 9:587–88). Thus, he comes here, as it were, 'from the highest level.' A conscious reference to Daniel 9.21, where the same angel appears at the time of the evening offering in order to explain the mystery of the seventy weeks, is probably not intended. In Luke it remains open which of the two daily offerings is being offered. Unlike in Daniel 9, Gabriel appears here in the temple, and hence Luke has no interest in the time of the offering but only in the event as such, for otherwise he would not have been able to lead Zechariah narratively into the temple. What follows is the specification of the mission of the messenger (ἀπεστάλην is *passivum divinum*; cf. Daniel 10.11; Tobit 12.14; 3 Baruch 1.4; 4 Ezra 4.3; Testament of Abraham A 7.11; Apocalypse of Abraham 10.7, 14; see also 2 Enoch 1.8; 39.2; 72.5; 2 Baruch 56.1); within birth announcements εὐαγγελίζεσθαι is also attested in Josephus, *Antiquitates judaicae* 5.277, 282.

20 The narrative now takes a surprising turn. Zechariah is granted the requested sign, but it is a sign of punishment. The angel characterizes the request for a sign and its justification (v. 18) as an expression of unbelief (v. 20b) and punishes Zechariah with muteness (in Daniel 10.15 the falling silent has a completely different rationale; for the phrasing of the punishment, see at 13.11). ἀνθ' ὧν stands for ἀντὶ τούτων ὅτι; there are New Testament parallels in Luke 12.3; 19.44; Acts 12.23; 2 Thessalonians 2.10 (beyond this cf. Spicq 1994, I: 122ff). This reaction is surprising insofar as the request for a sign or the raising of objections from the side of the recipient of the appearance are never punished with sanctions of this sort elsewhere—and certainly not in the case of Abraham, who is the model for v. 18. Mary's objection in 1.34 also remains without consequences. Thus, with the abrupt reaction of the angel the narrative takes a quite extravagant turn. The narrative strategy that guides it becomes clear when one considers the consequences of Zechariah's falling silent and its temporal limitation (how long the temporal limitation lasts is not stated exactly here; but on the basis of the anaphoric ταῦτα the readers can already know now—at least until the birth of the child). First, this ensures that Zechariah cannot tell the words of the angel to anyone—especially not to his wife whose reactions to her becoming pregnant (v. 25) and to the jumping of the child in her body at the visit of Mary (vv. 41-45) are thus decoupled from the knowledge of her husband and from the knowledge of the readers. Therefore, only the readers can establish the connection between the narrated episodes. (That Zechariah could also have communicated in written form [cf. v. 63] is obviously not taken into consideration.) Second, in this way Luke creates within the narrated time an intervening period of more than nine months before Zechariah regains speech. With the temporal limitation of the punishment, this time period is characterized as limited from the start, and in this way Luke creates the expectation in the readers that how Zechariah can speak again will still be recounted. He will use this time to narrate within it the announcement of the birth of Jesus and Mary's visit at Elisabeth's (vv. 26-56).

The concluding emphasis that the announcements will be fulfilled εἰς (instead of ἐν; cf. BDR §206.1) τὸν καιρὸν αὐτῶν articulates for the first time the notion—which is central for Luke's understanding of history—that the events narrated by him will take place according to a plan that is determined by God (for the usage, cf. Testament of Naphtali 7.1: δεῖ ταῦτα πληρωθῆναι κατὰ καιρὸν αὐτῶν ["this must be fulfilled in its time"]; see also Testament of Joseph 19.15).

21 Luke now turns the view abruptly to the crowd of people waiting before the temple building, which he had narratively parked there in v. 10, and with the help of a thought report (cf. Vogt 1990, 157ff) he describes their perception of the situation (the plural ἐθαύμαζον after λαός is a *constructio ad sensum*; cf. BDR §134.1). According to m. Tamid 7.2, the priests, after the completion of the incense offering, give the Aaronic blessing from the steps of the forecourt of the temple (Numbers 6.24-26; see also Sirach 50.19-20). Apparently, Luke also assumes this practice here.

22 Thus, Zechariah would have had to speak now, but he cannot do so (v. 22a). Luke thus had the people wait before the temple building solely with the purpose of being able to create a scene that documented the immediate entering in of the imposed punitive sign. Luke can let the crowd infer from Zechariah's loss of speech that the marveling about the long stay of Zechariah in the temple building (v. 21b) gives way to the knowledge (v. 22b) that he encountered an appearance there because appearances can have such consequences (cf. Daniel 10.15-17; Acts 9.8-9). But of course, they do not have any clue about the actual reason for his falling silent and its temporal limitation. Both are known only by Zechariah and the readers. Finally, in v. 22c Luke reports additionally that Zechariah seeks to make himself understood with gestures; διανεύειν frequently designates the manner of communication of people who cannot or do not wish to speak (cf. Vita Aesopi 4; Didorus Siculus 17.37.5; Plutarch, *Moralia* 63b; Lucian of Samosata, *Vera historia* 2.44; *Bis accusatus* 15; *De saltatione* 64).

23 The note about Zechariah's return to his place of residence after the end of his priestly division's week-long period of service (see at v. 5) corresponds to v. 8 and marks the narrative conclusion of the first episode. The Septuagintal style of the sentence is attested with reference to καὶ ἐγένετο ὡς by Genesis 27.30; 39.13; Deuteronomy 5.23; Joshua 2.7; and elsewhere and with reference to ἐπλήσθησαν αἱ ἡμέραι by Genesis 25.24; Leviticus 12.4, 6; Esther 1.5; 2.12; Tobit 10.1; Isaiah 60.20 (see also 1.57; 2.6, 21, 22; Jüng 2004, 170ff).

24 An epilogue follows in which Luke switches from the episodic style of narration to the report style. This is characterized by a high degree of narrative compression, i.e., an intensified difference between time of narration and narrated time. A single sentence encompasses a time period of five months. The only event from this period that Luke regards as worthy of reporting is the fact that Elisabeth became pregnant after the return of her husband and thus that the first step toward the fulfillment of the announcement of the angel (v. 13c) is completed. But before he reports about the second step, i.e., the birth, he interrupts the passage of time of the narrative with the notice that Elisabeth kept herself hidden for five months. Through the specification of the time period the expectation is produced in the readers that something worth telling will take place in the sixth month. The reason for Elisabeth's behavior cannot be found within the narrated world but only by inquiring into its narrative function. With this notice Luke wants—and to this extent it follows the same intention as Zechariah's muteness—to make sure that no other narrative figure learns about Elisabeth's pregnancy in order that she can function as an authenticating sign in v. 36 (see also R. E. Brown 1993; Fitzmyer; C. F. Evans; and others). Otherwise it cannot be explained why Elisabeth changes her behavior after five months, i.e., exactly at the moment in which Luke requires the "unveiling" of her pregnancy for Mary's visit at her place.

2 Enoch 71.3 reports something similar about the mother of Melkizedek, who became pregnant although she was old, barren, and sexually abstinent; when she noticed this, she "was ashamed and she hid herself during all the days. And not one of the people knew about it" (translated by F. I. Andersen, *OTP* I: 205). Luke and the author of 2 Enoch 71 certainly would not have explained this behavior by stating that Elisabeth or the mother of Melkizedek hid themselves for five months or for the entire time of their pregnancy (cf. also the questions of Strelan 2003 regarding this). Both authors presumably imagined this action in such a way that the two women kept their pregnancy secret through appropriate clothing, which is not particularly difficult during the first five months. A text that speaks in favor of this interpretation and very decisively against the interpretation advanced by Strelan 2003, 94, namely that Elisabeth veiled only her face in order to make clear in this way "that the Lord looked down in mercy to remove her reproach by making her pregnant"—is Lucian of Samosata, *Dialogi mortuorum* 20.8 (this text was passed over by Strelan 2003): When the philosopher has to take off his coat in the beyond, a rash of vices come to light, whereupon Hermes says to him: οὐ λέληθεν γάρ με, εἰ καὶ μάλα περικρύπτεις αὐτά ("they are not hidden to me even if you would very much like to hide them").

25 Luke has Elisabeth interpret her pregnancy as a consequence of the gracious turning of God and in this way illustrates, first, her piety, and second, her ignorance of the words of the angel concerning the significance of the child for Israel (Zechariah had, after all, become mute and could tell her nothing about the appearance in the temple). Only Zechariah himself can provide the commentary pertaining to this, since only he knows what the child is all about. The phrasings that Luke places in Elisabeth's mouth follow the words with which Rachel reacts to the birth of Joseph (ἀφεῖλεν ὁ θεός μου τὸ ὄνειδος ["God has taken away my shame"]; Genesis 30.23) and are intended to give the narrative a biblical atmosphere. But cf. also 4 Ezra 9.45: "He (sc. God) saw my lowliness, took notice of my affliction and gave me a son."

1.26-38: The Announcement of the Birth of Jesus

[26]**But in the sixth month the angel Gabriel was sent by God into a Galilean town by the name of Nazareth,** [27]**to a virgin, who was engaged to a man named Joseph, who was descended from the house of David, and the name of the virgin (was) Mary.** [28]**And he approached her and said, "Greetings, favored one, the Lord (is) with you!"** [29]**But she fell into confusion on account of the address and reflected on what this could be for a greeting.** [30]**And the angel said to her, "Fear not, Mary, for you have found grace with God.** [31]**And look, you will become pregnant and will bear a son, and you will give him the name Jesus.** [32]**This one will be great and be called Son of the Most High. And God, the Lord, will give him the throne of his father David.** [33]**He will rule over the house of Jacob forever, and his rule will have no end."** [34]**But Mary said to the angel, "How should this happen, since I do not know a man?"** [35]**The angel answered and said to her, "The Holy Spirit will come upon you, and the power of the Most High will overshadow you. For this reason, also the child will be called holy, the Son of God.** [36]**And look: Elisabeth, your relative, she too has conceived a son—in her age—and she who is regarded as barren is in the sixth month;** [37]**for no word that comes from God will remain without effect."** [38] **But Mary said, "Look, (I am) the slave of the Lord; let it happen to me according to your word." And the angel left her.**

The correspondences with the first episode (1.8-23) are unmistakable. Almost throughout, however, we are dealing here with elements that are specific to the form of appearance reports in general (see the introduction to 1.8-25 above): *(a)* the fright of the appearance recipient (v. 29a/v. 12); *(b)* the appearing one's exhortation μὴ φοβοῦ (v. 30b/v. 13b); *(c)* the speech of the appearing one (vv. 31-33), which in both cases contains a birth announcement with the same elements: (α) announcement of the birth of a child (v. 31b/v. 13d); (β) a commission to give it a name (v. 31c/v. 13e); (γ) description of the child's significance (vv. 32-33/vv. 15-17). Besides this, in both narratives it is the angel Gabriel who is sent by God (v. 26/v. 19) and who delivers the birth announcements; moreover, both addressees react to the announcement with an objection (v. 34/v. 18).

The angel responds to this in different ways (cf. v. 19 with v. 35) and has a sign come to them both with the introduction καὶ ἰδού (v. 36/v. 20).

However, the form-critical findings do not allow any tradition-historical conclusions, although of course they rule out the possibility that the two texts emerged independently of one another (see Radl 1996). The parallels require, however, neither the assumption that the two narra-tives or a core of them were already connected with one another literarily prior to Luke nor a diachronic model of textual emergence, according to which Luke found one of the two versions already largely in place and then formed the other one according to its pattern. Instead, the correspon-dences find their sufficient explanation in the fact that we are dealing with form elements that are typical for the genre of appearance stories that were available to Luke as elements of his linguistic competence for the literary creation of appropriate genre specimens. A dependence of the second on the first narrative is to be taken into account only on the literary level insofar as Luke has written down the announcement of the birth of John before that of the birth of Jesus. Accordingly, he also gives the readers clear signals that should prompt them to a successive (and not compara-tive!) reading of the two narratives (vv. 26, 36). Therefore, one will also have to regard Luke as the first narrator of this episode. That he drew upon christological and biographical traditions from Christian tradition for the individual parts does not contradict this, for it should not be assumed that they were already connected with one another through a narrative complex prior to Luke.

But the differences between the two realizations of the form are just as conspicuous as the commonalities. The most important difference is that the messenger statement in the first episode was still part of the self-introduction of the angel addressed to Zechariah (v. 19), whereas it is now formulated as a disclosure of the narrator to the readers (v. 26). In this way it becomes an expositional element within the initial frame of the narra-tive, which even comes before the introduction of Mary and her betrothed. In this way only the readers learn who comes to Mary; she herself does not learn who her visitor is, not even at the end. And when, beyond this, Luke also forgoes further information about Gabriel, one can recognize in this that he presupposes among his readers the knowledge gained from the preceding episode and has the angel come upon the scene as an already known narrative figure. In this way the narrative thread that begins in 1.26-38 becomes identifiable to the readers as part of a superordinate main sto-ryline. This main storyline can, in turn, be recognized as such in the fact that both episodes have a common master of action, who sets the events in motion in a consistent way, and this is, of course, none other than God, who sends out Gabriel twice in succession. It is true that he sends him to

two different places and two different people, but both narrative threads
are intertwined with each other as two stations of *one* storyline. Another
convergence between the two episodes indicates which storyline this is—
the common reference of both texts to Israel and its eschatological expectation of salvation (vv. 16-17, 33). Both episodes portray two successive
sections of a single storyline in which Luke narrates how God takes the
initiative for the fulfillment of the eschatological hopes of his people.

26 Luke first fulfills the readers' expectation—which was evoked
in v. 24—that something would happen after five months of Elisabeth's
pregnancy had been completed by dating the renewed sending of Gabriel
in the sixth month. The preposition ἀπό (τοῦ θεοῦ) characterizes God as
the commissioner of the sending (cf. the linguistic analogies in [2] Ezra
7.14; 1 Maccabees 15.17; Plutarch, *Marcius Coriolanus* 30.4; Vita Aesopi
119: ἀπεστάλημεν ἀπὸ τοῦ θεοῦ λόγους τινὰς πρὸς σὲ ἀναγγεῖλαι ["we
have been sent by God in order to announce some words to you"]; see
also Galatians 1.1). Luke leads the readers to the goal of the sending in
a centripetal manner of narration in vv. 26b-27. The identification of the
individual to whom the sending applies occurs only at the end and thus
functions as the climax. Through the medium of the narrative imagination,
the way of the angel is traced in this manner: first there is only unspecific
talk of a town in Galilee, which is then identified by name in a second step.

The introduction of Nazareth by name with ᾗ ὄνομα N. (i.e., relative pronoun in
the dative + ὄνομα with the omission of ἐστίν [cf. BDR §123.3]) is presumably
a Septuagintism here (cf. Genesis 24.29; 38.1; Job 1.1; 42.17; Susanna[Theodotion]
45; Bel and the Dragon 2, 3; Hebrew in each case "so-and-so וּשְׁמוֹ"; see also
Testament of Levi 11.1). But it also occurs in non-Jewish Greek (e.g., Xenophon,
Anabasis 2.4.13; Arrian, *Anabasis* 1.29.1; Philostratus, *Vita Apollonii* 8.18; Diogenes Laertius 1.95). In the New Testament it is attested only in Luke (see also
1.27; 2.25; 8.41; 24.13; Acts 13.6).

Ναζαρέτ (Matthew 2.23; Mark 1.9; John 1.45, 46) or Ναζαρέθ (Matthew
21.11; Luke 1.26; 2.4, 39, 51; Acts 10.38) or Ναζαρά (Luke 4.16 par. Matthew
4.13), today En-Nāsira (Hebrew נצרת) is located in Lower Galilee, ca. 6 kilometers south of Sepphoris. Up until the third century CE it is mentioned neither
literarily nor epigraphically outside the New Testament. Therefore, it must have
been a small and entirely insignificant village, and it is sometimes even doubted
whether it existed at all as a place of residence at the beginning of the first century CE (e.g., V. Wagner 2001). Jesus's origin from Nazareth would then have
been derived from the designations Ναζωραῖος and Ναζαρηνός (see at 18.36-37),
which were no longer understood (see H. Kuhli, *EWNT* 2: 1117). But this is even
more unlikely, for no one can derive a place that no one knows from an epithet

that is not understood. For the archaeological situation, cf. Bagatti 1969/2002; V. Tzaferis/B. Bagatti, *NEAEHL* III: 1103–6; Tsafrir et al. 1994, 194.

27 Luke continues to approach the goal of the sending of the angel incrementally. The person to whom he has been sent is initially specified by mentioning her characteristics—she is a virgin who is engaged to a man. Luke has taken this biographical information, as the agreement with Matthew 1.18 shows, from the tradition. Nothing more can be said about its age and origin than that it probably comes from circles of Hellenistic Jewish Christianity. The reason that the institution of engagement was taken up in order to describe Mary's status is because it was necessary to reconcile the information taken over from the Jesus tradition, according to which Joseph was known to be Jesus's father (Luke 3.23; 4.22; John 1.45; 6.42) and Mary's husband (Matthew 1.16), with the notion of the birth of Jesus from a virgin. According to contemporary Jewish law, both partners were bound to each other in a legally binding way; the young woman continued to live in her parents' house and had no sexual intercourse with her betrothed but was regarded in a legal perspective as his "wife" (cf. Bill. II: 393ff).

Luke uses the opportunity to introduce, first, Mary's betrothed, specifically by name and with reference to his origin. With Mary, by contrast, such a specification, which was, by the way, also found with Elisabeth (cf. v. 5), is lacking. The emphasis on the Davidic lineage of Joseph (on the phrasing ἐξ οἴκου Δαυίδ, cf. 1/3 Ezra 5.5) is indispensable, because Luke, of course, imagines Jesus's Davidic sonship as mediated through Joseph, although Joseph plays no role in the conception. In connection with the motif of the virgin birth, it is ensured in this way that it was God alone whose initiative was responsible for the establishment of this connection (see also Strauss 1995, 128). Thus, God has very intentionally sought out a virgin who was engaged to a Davidide. Therefore, according to the Lukan understanding, it was her engagement with Joseph that made Mary suitable to be the mother of Jesus in the first place. At the very end of the exposition the addressee of Gabriel's mission is then also identified by name, and the readers have come together with him to Mary.

For the introduction of Joseph by name through ᾧ ὄνομα, see at v. 26. Ἰωσήφ is the Greek transcription of Hebrew יוֹסֵף (possibly a short form of יוֹסִפְיָה = "May Yhwh add" [cf. Ezra 8.10]; for the explanation of the name, cf. Genesis 30.23, 24); see also Ilan 2002, 150ff. Μαριάμ is the Greek transcription of Hebrew מִרְיָם (the meaning is unclear); cf. Exodus 15.20, 21 and elsewhere, as well as Ilan 2002, 242ff.

28 Gabriel's encounter with Mary is described not, as with Zechariah, with recourse to the vision term ὤφθη (see v. 11), but with the help of the commonplace expression εἰσελθὼν πρός (αὐτήν) (cf. in the New Testament Mark 6.25; 15.43; Acts 16.40; 17.2; Acts 3.20), which Luke uses in Acts 10.3 in connection with an angelophany (see also Genesis 20.3). It can, however, also refer to εἶπεν. Thus, the narrator describes an almost normal visiting scene. This will correspond to the fact that in v. 29 Mary, unlike Zechariah, is not frightened by the sight of the angel but by his greeting. In this way Luke undoubtedly pursues the intention of letting Mary's believing (see v. 45) affirmation of the birth announcement emerge with an even sharper profile.

The visit character of the scene also finds expression in the fact that, unlike with Zechariah, the angel greets Mary. The phrasing of the greeting has caused not only Mary in v. 29 but also the interpreters of Luke to ask about its particular nature and meaning. This applies already to the *salutatio* χαῖρε (cf. the discussion in R. E. Brown 1993, 321ff). Here we are dealing with the normal Greek greeting formula (cf. Strobel 1962, 92ff; H. Conzelmann, ThWNT 9: 251.15ff; 357.23ff; in the New Testament, see Matthew 26.49; 28.9; Mark 15.18parr.), but it is also attested in some Old Testament texts as a summons to joy over God's eschatic salvific action toward Israel (Joel 2.21; Zephaniah 3.14; Zechariah 9.9; see also 1QM XII, 13). In the last two or three texts mentioned, "(the daughter) Zion" is addressed, which has led to the assumption that Luke wanted to refer to these passages with the greeting (and above all to Zephaniah 3.14-17) and present Mary as 'daughter Zion' (e.g., Lyonnet 1939; 1964; Laurentin 1967, 64ff, 148ff). Such an allusion would, however, be much too unspecific, and beyond this the narrative position of χαῖρε at the beginning of the visit scene suggests nothing other than its understanding as a greeting. Moreover, the same greeting is also attested in other appearance stories, namely in the mouth of the one who appears and is followed by a predication of the recipient of the appearance (4 Baruch 7.2: χαῖρε . . . ὁ οἰκονόμος τῆς πίστεως ["Greetings . . . faithful manager"]; Greek Apocalypse of Ezra 2.2: χαῖρε, πιστὲ τοῦ θεοῦ ἄνθρωπε ["Greetings, faithful person of God"]; see also Testament of Abraham A 2.3: χαίροις τιμιώτατε πάτερ, δικαία ψυχή, φίλε γνήσιε τοῦ θεοῦ ["Greetings, most honorable father, righteous soul, true friend of God"]; 16.9; 3 Baruch 11.6-7).

The Lukan phrasing of this predication (κεχαριτωμένη; see Potterie 1987) takes up the *salutatio* paronomatically. Verse 30b explains the significance of this predication—Mary has found grace with God, i.e, God has chosen her (see below). The perfect of the extremely rare verb χαριτόω (cf. W. Bauer 1988, s.v.) brings the antecedent character of this election to expression, and the logical subject of the passive (*passivum divinum*) is God. The angel thus makes a statement about an action of God toward Mary that has already taken place.

In the concluding part of his greeting (ὁ κύριος μετὰ σοῦ) it is conspicuous that there is talk of God being with her as a statement and at the beginning of an appearance report, for normally it is pronounced as a promise for the future to the recipient of the appearance only at the conclusion (cf. Deuteronomy 31.23; 1 Chronicles 28.20; Jubilees 12.29–30; 1QapGen XXII, 30–31; Matthew 28.20; Epistle of the Apostles 30[41]; see K. Berger 1976, 434–35, 505–6, 535). This motif is found in the same position and as an affirmation within an appearance report only in Judges 6.12 (in Ruth 2.4 as a wish expressed as a greeting), which has often led to the assumption that Luke wanted to narrate a "calling" of Mary here (namely to motherhood; e.g., K. Stock 1980, 461ff; Ó Fearghail 1993; Rodríguez 1993; Radl 1996, 280–81). But this is probably inaccurate, for first, the remaining form elements that are adduced for this position ("fear not!"; objection; removal of objection) are not specific to call stories, and second, in the call texts that are repeatedly invoked as parallels, namely Exodus 3.11-12 and Jeremiah 1.4-8, there is talk of God being with the person only as a reaction to the objection (see also Judges 6.15-16). Moreover, unlike the aforementioned call stories, the Lukan narrative is oriented not to a future task of Mary but to that of her son (see also Muñoz Iglesias 1984). It is therefore much more advisable to connect the statement in this passage with texts such as Genesis 26.3; 28.14-15; 39.3; Deuteronomy 20.1; Joshua 3.7; Jeremiah 15.20-21; Haggai 2.4-6 (see also Acts 18.9-10 and the presentation of the Old Testament material in van Unnik 1973–1983, III: 362–91) and understand it as a pronouncement of election. The statement functions as a pragmatic counterpart to the preceding predication and bindingly promises Mary the enduring care and preservation of God (cf. also van Unnik 1973–1983, III: 377–78).

29 Mary becomes frightened according to the genre (see at v. 12), but unlike Zechariah it is not in relation to what she sees but what she hears. In this way Luke directs the attention of the readers back again to the words of the angel, and he strengthens this further by having Mary, on behalf of the readers, ask about the meaning of the greeting in the form of a thought report. In this way she makes the readers aware of an evident imbalance, namely that a greeting of an angel that is loaded with so much election theology is issued to a completely insignificant virgin in a completely insignificant Galilean town (cf. J. B. Green 1992, 461ff). By means of the reaction of Mary, Luke expresses that in the realization of his eschatological plan of salvation for Israel God takes surprising and unexpected ways. With this a theme is sounded here for the first time and with all restraint that will grow stronger later and run through the entirety of Luke–Acts until its end in Acts 28.23-28.

30 The introduction to the actual birth announcement (vv. 31-33; for the form, see at vv. 13-17) is formed largely in parallel to that of the first episode (v. 13a-c): μὴ φοβοῦ (see there), mention of name, justification. The only significant difference is that instead of speaking of the hearing of prayer (v. 13c), the justification speaks of the fact that Mary has found grace with God. This explains in the first instance the predication κεχαριτωμένη in v. 28. That "finding grace" means in general something like "pleasing" (εὐαρεστῆσαι) is noted by Philo, *Legum allegoriae* 3.78 (see also *Quod Deus immutabilis sit* 109). As the tradition-historical background for the use of this expression in the present context, one should assume the joining of "finding grace" and the communication of revelation or the disclosure of knowledge that is granted to God's elect (cf. Exodus 33.13; Sirach 3.18-19[LXX]; Joseph and Aseneth 15.13; 2 Baruch 28.6; 4 Ezra 4.44; 5.56; 6.11-12; 7.7; and elsewhere; cf. K. Berger 1973a, 5ff). Thus, the phrasing connects what precedes with what follows: Mary's electedness finds its expression in the fact that the content of the revelation speech that follows in vv. 31-33 is communicated to her.

In **31-33** there now follows the actual birth announcement with the three form specific elements that have already been mentioned (see at vv. 13-17, 30).

31 In comparison to vv. 13d-17, the birth announcement is expanded with the announcement of the conception, as this occurs also in the birth announcements of Genesis 16.11; Judges 13.3, 5; Isaiah 7.14 (see also Liber antiquitatum biblicarum 42.3). An intentional allusion to a single one of these texts (cf. the presentation in C.-W. Jung 2004, 121ff) may not be read into this phrasing, however, for the terminological correspondences are not close enough to do so. This also applies to Isaiah 7.14, even if λή(μ)ψεται is found in some manuscripts instead of ἕξει, for this also would not be sufficient for the recognition of an intertextual relationship (see also Fitzmyer 1981, 75–76; R. E. Brown 1993, 300). In Matthew 1.23 the readers must accordingly be referred explicitly to this link in order that they can perceive it.

In **32-33** Luke has the angel describe the future significance of the child in a series of five statements. As with the statements related to John the Baptist in vv. 13-17, they are paratactically joined to each other with καί. Here the first two (v. 32a, b) and the last three (vv. 32c-33b) are more closely connected with each other (cf. also the change of subject in v. 32c).

32 The first two statements form a *parallelismus membrorum* that describes the nature of the child, in which the content of the first member is further specified by the second one. οὗτος ἔσται μέγας varies v. 15a, but without marking the difference between John and Jesus, for when μέγας is used as an absolute predicate noun with respect to persons, it designates nothing more than their elevated position of power and/or dignity (cf. e.g., Esther 10.3^LXX; Testament of Levi 17.2; Matthew 5.19; Mark 10.43par.; Luke 9.48; Acts 8.9); it is only the continuation that clarifies what the μέγας-ness consists in. The closest parallels to v. 32a, b can be found in the horoscopes in Vettius Valens; attention should be given especially to the terminological and syntactical correspondence: 61.5 Kroll 1973 (μέγας ἔσται καὶ κυριεύσει ζωῆς καὶ θανάτου ["he will be great and will rule over life and death"]); 66.10 Kroll 1973 (ὁ γεννώμενος μέγας ἔσται καὶ ὄχλων ἡγήσεται καὶ νόμους θήσεται ["the one born will be great and will lead crowds and establish laws"]); 67.14 Kroll 1973 (ὁ γεννώμενος μέγας ἔσται καὶ πολλῶν ἀγαθῶν κυριεύσει ["the one born will be great and will rule over many good ones"]). Thus, the 'greatness' of Jesus will consist in the fact that he will be "Son of the Most High" (i.e., of God). As a title for God (ὁ) ὕψιστος occurs in the New Testament also in Luke 1.35, 76; 6.35; Acts 7.48 (see also at 8.28); in the Septuagint it is widespread as a translation for the Hebrew עֶלְיוֹן (see Numbers 24.16; Deuteronomy 32.8; 2 Samuel 22.14; Psalm^LXX 9.3; 17.14; 20.8; 45.5 among others; cf. with additional attestations Hengel 1973, 544ff; C. Colpe/A. Löw, *RAC* 16: 1035–56). κληθήσεται also designates the bestowing of a status elsewhere (e.g., Genesis 21.12; Exodus 12.16; 1/3 Ezra 3.7; Isaiah 56.7; Zechariah 8.3; Matthew 5.9; Luke 1.35; 2.23).

On this issue there is a much discussed parallel in 4Q246, a text that possibly arose at the same time as the book of Daniel (the manuscript comes from the early Herodian period). It is concerned with a king of whom it is initially said *inter alia*: "[and he will be] great over the earth" (רב להוה על ארעא [והוא]; 1.7). After this it says (2.1):

He will be called Son of God   ברה די אל יתאמר

and one will call him Son of the Most High   ובר עליון יקרונה כזיקא

Although the discussion of this text is not yet concluded (cf. U. B. Müller 1996, 2ff; J. Zimmermann 1998), one can nevertheless already say that this is not a description of a messianic savior but of a foreign tyrant who usurps the Son of God title (contrast among others J. Zimmermann 1998). This corresponds also to its use in the extra Jewish environment of early Christianity where, coming from Egypt (there the Pharaoh was regarded from days of old as the son of the sun god; cf. Kügler 1997, 15ff), the Son of God title had become a common element of the ruler ideology from the time of Alexander the Great, whereas the Judaism of the Hellenistic World—probably in order to separate itself from this kind of usage—remained guarded toward the connection of Messiah function and Son of God title; the only certain attestation for it is the eschatological interpretation of 2 Samuel 7.14 in 4Q174 III, 10–13. In addition, v. 32a, b stands much closer to the horoscopes in Vettius Valens (see above) than 4Q246 I, 7, which relativizes the significance of the Qumran parallels for the Luke text in a not insignificant way.

The transfer of the Son of God title to Jesus in 32b is usually understood as a predication of the messianic king who is regarded on the basis of his messianic enthronement as Son of God. As Romans 1.3, which is probably the oldest attestation for this christological conception, shows, it was originally formulated as an interpretation of the resurrection and exaltation of Jesus, and this probably took place in connection with the Nathan promise of 2 Samuel 7.12-14 (see also Acts 13.33; Hebrews 1.5). In the last two texts mentioned, Psalm 2.7 is also quoted where the connection between messianic king and Son of God title is also brought to expression. Moreover, this text stands in the background of the predication of Jesus by the voice from heaven in Mark 1.11 (see U. B. Müller 1996, 14ff). Although this christological tradition also shines through in Luke 1.32b-c, the two statements about Jesus's divine sonship (v. 32b) and his installation to the messianic function of the king over Israel (v. 32c) should not be prematurely intertwined with each other in this passage (see also Kremer 1991, 142; Marshall; Strauss 1995, 93). Here Luke more likely separates the two elements of this tradition from each other and has the angel first establish Jesus's divine sonship independently of his messianic enthronement (see also at 4.41 and in 22.67-70). This is recognizable, first, in the structuring of the christological complex of statements (see above and in what follows below) and, second, in the fact that in v. 35 only the coming into being of Jesus's divine sonship is justified. Jesus's divine sonship is made prior to his acquisition of the messianic regency and the latter is derived from the former.

The cohesion of the three statements in vv. 32c-33 is recognizable in the fact that the terms θρόνος, βασιλεύειν, and βασιλεία belong to one and the same semantic field. Beyond this, they display an irreversible temporal slope: v. 32c speaks of the installation of Jesus in his ruler function, and v. 33a-b thematize the exercise of the rule in its temporal extension. With the description of the function of John in vv. 16-17 these statements have in common, at first sight, the fact that both here and there the concern is with eschatic tasks that both have to carry out for Israel. The differences, however, are unmistakable. First, John will act as a prophet, while Jesus should acquire the function of the ruler. Second, the task assigned to John implies a temporal limitation, for as God's forerunner (v. 17a) he should prepare Israel for his arrival (v. 17c), while it is said concerning Jesus's reign that it will have no end.

32c "Throne of David" is already a metonymic designation for the institution of kingship in Israel in the Old Testament (1 Kings 2.23, 45; Isaiah 6.9; Jeremiah 13.13; 17.25; 22.2, 4, 30; 36.30; Psalms of Solomon 17.6). According to the Lukan understanding, the promise of Jesus's installment in the function of the kingly ruler over Israel will be realized with the resurrection and exaltation (cf. Luke 23.42; 24.26; Acts 13.33-34). In order to legitimate the acquisition of this position from a genealogical perspective as well, the descent of Jesus from David is emphasized in addition, which can even be expressed in biological categories in other passages (Acts 2.30: "fruit of his loins"; 13.23: "from his seed"; see also John 7.41; Romans 1.3; 2 Timothy 2.8). In 18.38-39 the designation of Jesus as "Son of David" corresponds to this notion. For the mediation of Jesus's Davidic sonship through Joseph, see at v. 27.

33 The two verse halves form a synonymous *parallelismus membrorum*. For οἶκος Ἰακώβ as a synonym for Israel, cf. Exodus 19.3; Isaiah 48.1; Psalms of Solomon 7.10; Liber antiquitatum biblicarum 44.8; 4 Ezra 12.46; and elsewhere. βασιλεύειν ἐπί τινα is a Septuagintism (from Hebrew מָלַךְ עַל; cf. Genesis 37.8; 1 Samuel 16.1; 1 Kings 8.9; 12.1; Psalms of Solomon 17.21; this expression is not attested in pagan Greek texts). The announcement of the eternal duration of Jesus's kingly rule over Israel formulates a high profile christological statement that goes far beyond the traditional messianic expectation. Two lines run together in it. The first line is the expectation of the eternal continuation of the Davidic dynasty grounded in the Nathan promise, i.e., the non-breaking of the chain of Davidic rulers over Israel (cf. 2 Samuel 7.13, 16; Psalm 89.3-5; 132.11-12; Isaiah 9.6; Ezekiel 37.25; Psalms of Solomon 17.4; 1 Maccabees 2.57). This expectation is now concentrated in the rule of a single Davidide, which simultaneously contains the implication that he will no longer have a successor. Luke expresses in this way that the biblical promise will find its definitive and final fulfillment in Jesus, which even surpasses the archegete of the Davidic dynasty himself. This christological concept has its abutment in Acts 2.25-36; 13.32-37.

The other line is no less significant. When it says in v. 33b that Jesus's βασιλεία will have no end, then in this way a traditional predication of God is transferred to him, for until now it had applied only to God's kingly reign that it would have eternal duration (e.g., Psalm 145.13; 146.10; Micah 4.7; Daniel 2.44; 3.33; 4.31; 6.27; Psalms of Solomon 7.1, 3, 46; Jubilees 1.28; 1 Enoch 84.2; Sibylline Oracles 3.49–50). Previously something similar was said only with regard to the Son of Man and the "people of the holy ones of the Most High" (Daniel 7.14, 27). The presupposition for this transformation of the traditional eschatological conceptions is to be seen, of course, in the fact that Jesus is the Son of God from the beginning of his existence (see v. 35).

34 Mary's question causes notorious problems of interpretation because it does not quite fit with the previous course of the narrative. When Mary asks about the realization of the announcement (τοῦτο refers to everything that Gabriel has said in vv. 31-33; see also Kilgallen 2001a, 413–14) and refers as an explanation to the fact that she has never had sexual intercourse with a man (on ἄνδρα γινώσκειν in this sense, cf. Genesis 19.8; Judges 11.39; 21.12), this is understandable only with difficulty in the mouth of a betrothed virgin, since things can always change. The attempted solutions are as numerous as they are fanciful (cf. the overview in R. E. Brown 1993, 303ff; Marshall; Landry 1995, 65ff; Radl 1996, 285–86). At present the majority of interpreters tends to view the question as a literary device that Luke has inserted for the readers so that he can give the angel an occasion to explain how Mary's child becomes the Son of God (cf. among others Schürmann; Schneider; Schweizer; R. E. Brown 1993, 307ff; Wiefel; the parallels to the phrasing in Demosthenes, *Orationes* 14.7; 22.26; Appian, *Bella civilia* 3.8.59; Epictetus, *Dissertationes* 2.14.9; 1 Clement 35.5 also have a purely rhetorical character). Mary does not formulate an objection but rather asks how the announcement of Gabriel can be accomplished without a man. This assumption has even more in its favor since Luke also likes to use the same literary technique elsewhere (e.g., Luke 2.48; 3.10, 12, 14; 10.29, 40; 12.41; 22.9; Acts 1.6; 2.37; 8.34; 19.3; 21.38; cf. Elbert 2004). In that case, the rationale for the question in v. 34b, which is otherwise difficult to understand, receives a good sense as indirect information for the readers that Mary will not conceive her son in the usual way (R. E. Brown 1993, 308).

In **35** Gabriel provides the requested explanation. Its subject matter is Jesus's divine sonship, and it therefore ends with the almost word-for-word taking up again of v. 32b in v. 35d. Here it is important to note that Luke does not have the angel explain how Mary's pregnancy comes about without a man, but why her child will be holy and Son of God. To this extent the answer of Gabriel does not quite deal with the question (which is usually not otherwise in the answers to the aforementioned literary questions), but contains a gap whose filling Luke leaves to the imagination of the readers (see at 2.5-6).

The explanation's structure of argumentation is transparent. With the help of a synonymous *parallelismus membrorum,* v. 35b, c describe what will happen, and the consequence is drawn out from this in v. 35d. For the description of the 'how,' Luke makes recourse again to the lexical pair πνεῦμα and δύναμις (cf. the attestations in v. 17a; 4.14), with the difference that these two entities now come into view as attributes of God, a usage that has a broad tradition-historical foundation (e.g., Wisdom of Solomon 11.20; Philo, *Legum allegoriae* 1.37; Josephus, *Antiquitates judaicae* 4.119; 8.408; see also W. Grundmann, ThWNT 2: 292ff; F. Baumgärtel, ThWNT 6: 363ff; E. Sjöberg, ThWNT 6: 379ff). When Luke brings Jesus's divine sonship into connection with the Spirit of God, he stands in continuity with the old christological tradition insofar as Jesus's installation to this status through his resurrection and exaltation was already interpreted at a very early point as a work of the Holy Spirit (cf. Romans 1.4: ἐν δυνάμει κατὰ πνεῦμα ἁγιωσύνης; Romans 8.11; 1 Corinthians 15.45; 1 Timothy 3.16; 1 Peter 3.18; see Horn 1992, 89ff). This connection is also recognizable in Mark 1.10-11, where Jesus's proclamation to divine sonship is connected with the descent of the Spirit upon him. Here, Jesus's installation to the status of Son of God is in a sense 'predated' to the beginning of his earthly activity. Luke now goes a step further by having Jesus's divine sonship be grounded in the influence of the Spirit upon his mother (this connection is not established in Matthew 1.18-23; see instead 2.15); in this way he sets his own accent.

Both members of the *parallelismus membrorum* undoubtedly characterize the same event; however, Luke intentionally does not say how the readers should imagine it. He also speaks of the ἐπέρχεσθαι of the Spirit in Acts 1.8 (as here in connection with δύναμις; see also Luke 24.49) and describes this event at Pentecost as being filled by the Holy Spirit (Acts 2.4); Isaiah 32.15 speaks in the same way about God's eschatic salvific action toward Israel. This, of course, rules out a sexual connotation in the sense of a spirit begetting, as the Egyptians imagine according to Plutarch, *Numa* 4.4 ("they regard it as not impossible that the πνεῦμα of a god approaches a woman and begets certain beginnings of emerging life [τινὰς ἐντεκεῖν ἀρχὰς γενέσεως]") as well as the assumption that ἐπισκιάζειν should be understood as a euphemism for sexual intercourse. The term is used not in the sense of a darkening (so Norden 1958, 92–93 with reference to Philo, *Quod Deus immutabilis sit* 3), but designates a dynamic notion of the manifestation of the presence and salvific activity of God (see also Kügler 1997, 281–82), as in Exodus 40.35 (Moses could not enter the tabernacle "because the cloud overshadowed it [ἐπεσκίαζεν ἐπ' αὐτήν] and the tabernacle was filled with the glory of the Lord"; see also Numbers 9.18, 22; 10.36; Wisdom of Solomon 19.7); Psalm^{LXX} 90.4; 139.8 ("Lord, Lord, power of my salvation [δύναμις τῆς σωτηρίας μου], you have overshadowed my head [ἐπεσκίασας; Hebrew סכך] on the day of war"); Mark 9.7parr. The announcement is rooted in the same notion of the Spirit as Acts 1.8 ("you will receive δύναμιν ἐπελθόντος τοῦ ἁγίου πνεύματος ἐφ' ὑμᾶς"). This way of speaking (about the Spirit) is connected with the notion of the effect of the shadow, which comes to light in Acts 5.15 (cf. Horst 1977), only insofar as it understands the δύναμις, the δόξα, or the Holy Spirit in a metaphorical manner as God's 'adumbration.' Correspondingly, v. 35c can formulate as a christological consequence that Jesus has a share in the holiness of God (cf. Luke 2.23; 4.34; Acts 3.14; 4.27, 30) and the status of divine sonship is conferred to him. The substantivized participle τὸ γεννώμενον is a common designation in Greek literature for the child who has been born (cf. e.g., Herodotus 1.108; Plato, *Leges* 775c, 930d; Plutarch, *Moralia* 140–41, 964e; Philo, *De plantatione* 15; see also Fridrichsen 1928).

Conclusion: For Luke, Mary has undoubtedly become pregnant neither through Joseph nor through another man. On the other hand, he neither says that Jesus was begotten through the Holy Spirit nor does he relate how Mary's pregnancy came about. Rather, he lets this aspect remain open and leaves it to his readers' imagination. Furthermore, it is not this aspect that stands in the foreground here but rather the fact that Mary's child is Son of God by God's Spirit and power from the first moment of his existence onward.

36 As in v. 20, the mention of a sign is introduced with καὶ ἰδού. With this Mary is the first person in the narrated world who learns of Elisabeth's pregnancy (the fact that those who belong to the heavenly world are, of course, informed about everything does not count). Συγγενίς designates a relative in the most general sense. Luke neither wishes to express that Mary also descended from Aaron nor invite the reader to speculate about the degree of kinship of the two women. Rather, it is for narrative reasons that Mary needs to know Elisabeth, since otherwise she would know neither about her barrenness nor her age and also could do nothing with the mention of the sign. Plus, Luke can motivate Mary's immediate journey to Elisabeth only under this presupposition.

In **37** Luke has the angel explain what Elisabeth's late-in-life pregnancy is a sign of, and he alludes again to the Abraham-Sarah material (cf. Genesis 18.14: μὴ ἀδυνατεῖ παρὰ τῷ θεῷ ῥῆμα; ["is anything impossible with God?"]; 2 Chronicles 14.10: κύριε, οὐκ ἀδυνατεῖ παρὰ σοὶ σῴζειν ["Lord, it is not impossible with you to save"]); see also C.-W. Jung 2004, 112ff. In terms of pragmatics the explanation is oriented to the fact that Mary should transfer the content of the sentence to the announcement pertaining to her and her child. The manuscript variant τῷ θεῷ (א² A C Θ Ψ f[1,]13 33 𝔐) is not only more poorly attested than the genitive τοῦ θεοῦ (א* B D L W Ξ 565 pc), but it is also an adjustment to Genesis 18.14. Thus, unlike in Genesis 18.14, παρὰ τοῦ θεοῦ is not an adverbial specification of ἀδυνατήσει, but, like in Genesis 41.32 (ἀληθὲς ἔσται τὸ ῥῆμα τὸ παρὰ τοῦ θεοῦ ["this matter, which is with God, will be realized"]), it is an adnominal attribute to πᾶν ῥῆμα; see also R. E. Brown 1993, 292; Green.

38 Mary has the last word in the appearance scene. This is surprising insofar as the one who appears speaks the concluding word in all other cases (Liber antiquitatum biblicarum 53.12 is not comparable because this is an embedded report of a narrative character). The nominal sentence in v. 38b finds its closest parallel in the declaration of submission in 2 Samuel 9.6 and is probably also meant in this way. With a phrasing that has numerous parallels in pagan Greek texts (e.g., Aeschylus, *Choephori* 386; Xenophon, *Cyropaedia* 6.3.11; Euripides, *Medea* 669; Lucian of Samosata, *Icaromenippus* 25; *Dialogi mortuorum* 7.2; Menander, *Aspis* 283), v. 38c articulates Mary's agreement, but without implying that the announcement is dependent upon it. The question of whether Mary agrees by necessity (e.g., Plummer) or enthusiastically (R. E. Brown 1993, 319) misses the intention of the text. Luke presents Mary as a person who does not doubt the realization of the announcement but rather gives it her unreserved trust (see v. 45)—irrespective of whether or not she rejoices over it. In this way Mary becomes not only a Christian model of faith (Räisänen 1989, 106), but also, above all, an ideal member of Israel. For she has done exactly what the majority of the people of God will later refuse, namely to believe the words of the messengers of God. This also makes clear why Elisabeth had to hide her pregnancy for five months, for if Mary had known of it, then her reaction in v. 38bc would have automatically been devalued.

Since the time of the ancient church it has been assumed that Mary became pregnant at the moment at which she pronounced her words (or at least shortly thereafter) (in the recent period, cf. Schürmann; Schneider; Nolland; opposed by Wolter 1998b). There is, however, not a word about this here. Unlike with Elisabeth (v. 24), Luke refrains entirely from fixing Mary's conception in the course of the time narrated by him. In view of the special circumstances under which it had to have taken place, this is also not very surprising (see at v. 35bc and 2.5). In v. 38d the angel leaves in the way in which he had come in v. 28a.

1.39-56: Elisabeth's Blessing and Mary's Praise of God

[39]But Mary set out in these days and went with haste into the hill country, into a town of Judah. [40]She came into the house of Zechariah and greeted Elisabeth. [41]When Elisabeth heard Mary's greeting, the child leaped in her womb. Elisabeth was filled with the Holy Spirit [42]and called out with a loud voice, "You (are) most blessed among women, and blessed (is) the fruit of your womb. [43]Whence does it happen to me that the mother of my Lord comes to me? [44]For behold, when the

voice of your greeting entered my ears, the child leaped with joy in my womb. [45]Blessed (is) the one who believed that what was spoken to her from the Lord will find fulfillment." [46]And Mary said:

"My soul praises the greatness of the Lord
[47] and my spirit exults over God, my Savior,
[48] for he has looked upon the lowliness of his slave.
For behold, from now on all generations will praise me,
[49] for the Mighty One has done great things for me
And holy (is) his name,
[50] and his mercy (is) for those who fear him for all times.
[51] He has exercised power with his arm,
and has scattered those who are arrogant in the thoughts of their hearts.
[52] He has dethroned mighty ones
and exalted lowly ones.
[53] Hungry ones he has filled with good things
and rich ones he has sent away empty.
[54] He has given help to his servant Israel,
remembering mercy,
[55] as he said to our fathers
(that it is) for Abraham and his seed forever."
[56] And Mary remained about three months with her and then returned home.

Luke has previously narrated two birth announcements. Both went out from God and were mediated through one and the same angel. In this way Luke has thus far expressed the connection of the two narrative threads as part of a superordinate main storyline exclusively *sub specie Dei* (cf. vv. 19, 26); now it is also realized *sub specie hominum*. The narrative function of this episode also emerges from its intermediate position. The pending continuations of the constructed arcs (Elisabeth's giving birth and Mary's conception) still remain unnarrated. Rather, the authorial sentences describing the action in this episode serve only the purpose of setting in scene the speeches of the narrative figures, which should mediate to the readers the interpretation of the superordinate storyline. This orientation of the scene is also recognizable in the fact that from its beginning to its end in v. 55 the narrative does not go beyond the situation of the greeting (v. 40).

39-40 Mary's journey to Elisabeth, like Gabriel's way to Mary (vv. 26-27), is traced narratively. Again it is only at the end that Luke mentions the name of the person to whom the journey leads. The temporal specification ἐν ταῖς ἡμέραις ταύταις appears only in Luke in the New Testament (see also 6.12; 23.7; 24.18; Acts 1.15; 6.1; 11.27) and only very sporadically in the Septuagint (Esther 9.22; Judith 14.8; Zechariah 8.9, 15). Also, it is too widespread in pagan Greek to be regarded as a Septuagintism (e.g., Xenophon, *Hellenica* 7.1.42; Thuycidides 4.91.1; Diodorus Siculus 5.4.7; Dionysius of Halicarnassus, *Antiquitates romanae* 7.71.3; Cassius Dio 73.16.2). ἀναστᾶσα (. . . ἐπορεύθη) is a Septuagintism (cf. BDR §419.2; see Genesis 13.17; 22.3, 24.10; 31.17; 2 Samuel 15.9; with few exceptions [Mark 1.35; 2.14parr.; 7.24; 10.1; 14.57] it occurs in the New Testament only in Luke: Luke 4.38; 15.18, 20; 24.12; Acts 5.6, 17; 8.27; 9.11, 38; 22.10; and elsewhere), and this also applies to the phrasing εἰς πόλιν Ἰούδα (49× in the LXX). The nominalized adjective ἡ ὀρεινή as a designation for the hill country between the Shfela in the west, the Jordan Valley in the east, and the Negev in the south is already common in the Septuagint (e.g., Numbers 13.29; Joshua 9.1; 10.40; Jeremiah 40[33].13; see also Josephus, *Antiquitates judaicae* 12.313; *Bellum judaicum* 1.41).

Luke is silent about the motive for the journey, and this should also be taken seriously (see Coleridge 1993, 77). Luke leaves it to the reader to imagine a plausible reason for Mary's journey to Elisabeth, and he can do this without further ado, since her motivation has no significance whatsoever for the continuation of the narrative. Apart from this, the imagination of the readers is placed here under considerable strain in general, for the journey of a virgin from Nazareth to a place located in the Jewish hill country alone is already a quite extravagant narrative move. Luke communicates this to his reader with the help of the prepositional phrase μετὰ σπουδῆς (v. 39b), which qualifies Mary's action as out of the ordinary; it can remain open whether he intends to designate the traveling speed or Mary's inner engagement (Hospodar 1956; Nolland). But it is probably precisely the narrative extravagance that is important to Luke here, for the doing of something extraordinary is presented time and again by him as the appropriate reaction to the proclamation of the message of salvation in the further course of his presentation (cf. e.g., Luke 5.5, 11, 28; 9.59-62).

41 Mary's greeting sets in motion a chain of reactions, but they are based not on the content of the greeting but solely on the fact that Mary's voice is heard (in v. 44 Elisabeth therefore also speaks only of the φωνή of the greeting; the difference from vv. 28-29 is evident; for καὶ ἐγένετο ὡς, see at v. 23 above). First, Luke has the still unborn child react and attributes its leaping to the fact that Elisabeth hears Mary's greeting. The readers can infer from this extraordinary coincidence that the announcement of v. 15c is fulfilled. The frequently encountered assumption that John, taking up his prophetic task already in the womb, points to Jesus as the Son of God and Messiah misses the intention of the text: Jesus is not present at all in this scene (see also Coleridge 1993, 81). On the basis of Elisabeth's

Spirit-effected interpretation in v. 44b, it is clear instead that Luke wants John's leaping to be understood as an expression of eschatic joy (for this connotation of σκιρτᾶν, cf. Wisdom of Solomon 19.9; Malachi 3.20; Luke 6.23; see also Nolland; Radl 1996, 334). Moreover, Luke has heaven intervene and fill Elisabeth with the Holy Spirit (ἐπλήσθη refers to an event that is occurring at the time of this episode, which therefore should not be interpreted from the perspective of 1.15c). In this way a narrative peripety is brought about. Mary leaves her role as protagonist of the scene's action, which was constructed in vv. 39-40, and becomes the person who is spoken about, while Elisabeth, who previously knew (almost) nothing (see at v. 25), now receives an advance in knowledge vis-à-vis Mary and even vis-à-vis the readers (see also Kozar 1990, 216). The phrasing ἐπλήσθη πνεύματος ἁγίου is typically Lukan and has here—as it also does in Luke 1.67; Acts 2.4; 4.8, 31 (see also 13.9)—the function of ascribing the content of the speech that follows to a heavenly origin.

42 The first part of Elisabeth's inspired speech is composed of two eulogies (v. 42b, c). The widespread explanation of this pairing, according to which the first eulogy, following the pattern of Genesis 14.19-20; Judith 13.18, finds its explanation or its basis in the second (e.g., Fitzmyer; R. E. Brown 1993, 342; Nolland; Bovon), truncates the tradition-historical findings and founders on 1 Samuel 25.32-33; Tobit 11.14, 17א; Psalms of Solomon 8.34; Joseph and Aseneth 15.12; Mark 11.9-10. Furthermore, it is also the case that eulogies tend to form series (cf. Deuteronomy 28.3-6; Tobit 8.15-17; Daniel 3.52-56). The two eulogies of Elisabeth should therefore be viewed as a synthetic *parallelismus membrorum*. The first states that Mary receives a prominent position among women because she is blessed (for the Hebraizing paraphrase of the superlative via the positive with ἐν, cf. BDR 245.2; see also Matthew 22.36; Deuteronomy 33.16^LXX; Judges 5.24א and above all Song of Solomon 1.8; 5.9; 6.1: in each case ἡ καλὴ ἐν γυναιξίν in the sense of "the most beautiful among women"), and the second states that God's blessing will also rest upon her child (cf. the promise of blessing in Deuteronomy 28.4: εὐλογημένα τὰ ἔκγονα τῆς κοιλίας σου καὶ τὰ γενήματα τῆς γῆς σου ["blessed are the offspring of your womb and the produce of your land"]). One may not, however, infer from this that Luke indirectly communicates to the readers in this passage that Mary is already pregnant (see also Spitta 1906, 282–83), for the expression καρπὸς τῆς κοιλίας is much too semantically unspecified to be able to establish the necessary unambiguity (cf. the overview in Wolter 1998b, 411–12). It can designate the child who has already been born (e.g., Micah 6.7; Lamentations 2.20; Testament of Abraham A 6.5; 4 Ezra 10.12); there is also talk of the 'fruit of the body' of the man (e.g., Psalm 132[131].11 [LXX: καρπὸς τῆς κοιλίας]; Testament of Abraham A

8.6; Liber antiquitatum biblicarum 32.2, 4; 39.11). There is unambiguous talk of a still unborn *fructus ventris* of a woman only in Liber antiquitatum biblicarum 9.5.

43 Elisabeth's question is rhetorical (one has to supply γέγονεν as the copula, and the ἵνα-clause replaces the infinitive as an epexegetical supplement to τοῦτο; cf. BDR §189.3, §394.3) and characterizes Mary's visit to her as a violation against societal norms, since the socially superior visits the socially inferior (see also 2 Samuel 24.21). But with this the question stands in obvious tension to the social status that Luke has assigned to the two women in his narrative, for Elisabeth undoubtedly occupies a higher rank in the social stratification of the narrated world due to her age and her husband. Besides this, the typically Lukan theme of the reversal of values, which Mary will soon take up in detail in her hymn (cf. York 1991, 44–45), is touched upon again after vv. 27-28 and already somewhat more clearly. By "my Lord" Elisabeth means, of course, Jesus (denotative meaning). It is more than doubtful that the significative meaning of this expression is charged in a titular-christological way (e.g., Nolland; Wiefel: "confession" [!]; R. E. Brown 1993, 344) from Psalm 110.1 (quoted in Luke 20.42-43; Acts 2.34); the same also applies to the assumption that the intention is to upvalue Jesus in relation to John (e.g., Marshall; Bovon; Böhlemann 1997, 21). Rather, what is in the background is probably the use of κύριός μου as a term of social relations, as it is attested above all in the Septuagint as a translation of the Hebrew אֲדֹנִי in the mouth of the person who is lower in rank (e.g., Genesis 24.12, 14, 27; 24.35-38; 39.8; 1 Samuel 25.25-31; see also Matthew 24.48par.; Luke 16.3, 5). In this way Luke has Elisabeth express with the authority of the Holy Spirit that God's eschatic salvific turning to his people is accompanied by a nullification and new ordering of the conventional assignments of status (cf. the Magnificat in what immediately follows and then 13.30; 22.25-27).

In **44** Elisabeth directs the view back to the event through which her speech was prompted (v. 44). She explains her reaction to Mary's greeting by referring to the leaping of the child in her womb and by characterizing it as an expression of eschatic joy (for ἀγαλλίασις in this sense, see at 1.14 as well as Isaiah 35.10; 51.3, 11; Greek Apocalypse of Enoch 5.9; Testament of Judah 25.5; Testament of Benjamin 10.6; Jude 24; see further R. Bultmann, ThWNT 1: 19–20.)

45 The concluding macarism (for the form, see at 6.20) directs the view even further back. Here Luke actualizes the readers' knowledge about the previous course of action, for he has Elisabeth not only evaluate Mary's reaction to Gabriel's announcement reported in v. 38 but also refers to the evaluation that Zechariah's reaction to the words of the same angel in v. 20 had received (οὐκ ἐπίστευσας). In this way he contrasts the recipients of the two birth announcements with each other. Unlike Zechariah, Mary had believed the words of the messenger sent by God. It is difficult to decide whether the subordinate clause introduced with ὅτι grounds the beatitude (like, e.g., Matthew 5.3-10; so, among others, Schweizer; Johnson; Fitzmyer) or is dependent on πιστεύειν (like Acts 27.25: πιστεύω . . . ὅτι + ἔσται + λαλεῖν perfect passive with dative; Tobit 14.4א: πιστεύω ὅτι πάντα, ἃ εἶπεν ὁ θεός, συντελεσθήσεται καὶ ἔσται ["I believe that everything that God has said will be completed and will take place"]; see also Mark 11.23; so, among others, Marshall; Bovon; Green). On the basis of the parallels and because the former understanding would say nothing new to the readers, more speaks for the assumption that with the ὅτι-sentence Luke wants to characterize the content of Mary's πιστεύειν. Almost without transition a hymnic song of praise then follows.

46-55 There is a large consensus that the Magnificat is entirely or mostly pre-Lukan in origin and that it originally existed as an independent hymn. Contrary positions that view it as a Lukan composition or regard this as at least possible are rare (e.g., Harnack 1931, 75, 84–85; Tannehill 1974; Schneider; Schmithals; Löning 1997/2006, I: 96–97; Green).

Opinions differ, however:

- in relation to the origin of the original version: Should one assume a general-Jewish (e.g., Gunkel 1921; Winter 1954/1955b; Bovon; Kaut 1990 [for Magnificat II]), a Jewish-Baptist (e.g., Klostermann; Kaut 1990 [for Magnificat I]), or a Jewish-Christian (e.g., L. Schottroff 1978; R. E. Brown 1993, 350ff; S. C. Farris 1985, 86ff; Mittmann-Richert 1996, 97ff) origin?
- in relation to the original language: Was there a Hebrew *Vorlage* (e.g., Gunkel 1921; S. C. Farris 1985, 31ff; Marshall; Mittmann-Richert 1996, 104ff)?
- in relation to the question of possible Lukan additions (above all, v. 48 is frequently regarded as a secondary addition; e.g., R. E. Brown 1993, 356–57; Fitzmyer; S. C. Farris 1985, 114).

All statements about a prehistory, whatever the specifications may be, have in common that they are highly speculative, and the respective decisions always are made outside of a methodological system of plausibility that can be made objective. Every statement about a pre-Lukan version of the text is additionally devalued by the fact that one must always also reckon with the possibility of omissions by the evangelist, which usually remains unconsidered in the numerous reconstruction attempts. Therefore, for the interpretation one must set aside a possible prehistory and start from the existing text within its literary context. The Magnificat should therefore be commented on exclusively as a Lukan composition (see also Tannehill 1974, 264–65, 275; L. Schottroff 1978, 303; Kennel 1995, 181).

With the integration of a poetic text into the narrative Luke orients himself to biblical models (cf. N. Lohfink 1994, 109ff); cf. above all Exodus 15.1-18, 19-21; Deuteronomy 32.1-43; Judges 5.1-31 (see also Liber antiquitatum biblicarum 32.1–17); 1 Samuel 2.1-10 (see also Liber antiquitatum biblicarum 51.3–6); 2 Samuel 22.2-51; 1 Chronicles 16.8-36; Jonah 2.3-10; Judith 16.1-17; cf. also Liber antiquitatum biblicarum 21.9–10; 59.4. A particularly close intertextual relationship exists to Hannah's song of praise in 1 Samuel 2.1-10 (cf. Meynet 1985). The Magnificat shares with the aforementioned texts the fact that it provides a hymnic answer to the intervention of God for his people that has previously been described in the narrated action (see also Green 101; Löning 1997/2006, I: 96).

It has also always attracted attention that the Magnificat is compiled throughout from linguistic pieces that occur in this way or similarly in numerous Old Testament texts (cf. the overview in Forestell 1961, 205ff; Mittmann-Richert 1996, 8ff; Kennel 1995, 155ff, as well as the individual documentation respectively ad loc.). Something comparable can also be observed, e.g., in Jonah's psalm (Jonah 2.3-10) and in the hymn of Judith (Judith 16.1-17). This collage technique is a literary stylistic device that is characteristic of cento poetry (cf. Schinkel 1999). Here the device has the function of anchoring Mary in the cultural tradition of Israel. Thus, Luke shows himself again to be a historian who demonstrates superb mastery of his craft, for he has his narrative figure, a Jewish virgin from Galilee, speak just as Lucian of Samosata requires: "as appropriate as possible to the person and the situation" (*Quomodo historia conscribenda sit* 58; cf. also Thucydides 1.22.1; see Johnson 43). No one expects her to think about poverty and riches in the exact same way as Luke. Correspondingly, it is also an integral part of the literary fiction that the Magnificat is free of any christological references, for Mary is neither an angel like Gabriel nor is she filled by the Holy Spirit like Elisabeth (v. 41) and then subsequently Zechariah (v. 67). Instead, Luke has her provide an interpretation of the narrated event in the light of Israel's history of election, and he has her do this with *the* words with which Israel has always praised the salvific intervention of God on behalf of his people.

In the literary context Mary's hymn functions as an answer to the announcement given to her by the angel according to which her son will be the one through whom God fulfills Israel's eschatological hopes of salvation. The Magnificat forms the climax of the Jesus portion of the episodes that take place under Herod the Great and therefore also stands at the end of this portion. This contextual relation also determines the structure of the text, which displays a remarkable cohesion. The most important coherence-creating feature is the talk of God, who is spoken of in every one of the fifteen other main sentences or subordinate clauses, with the exception of v. 48b. On the level of expression this coherence also overlaps the division between v. 50 and v. 51 (see below) insofar as God is referred to for the last time with a substantive (ὁ δυνατός) in v. 49a, and afterward only with anaphoric proforms (vv. 49b, 50, 51a, 54a), or he is hidden as the implicit subject in the predicate (vv. 51ab, 52, 53abc, 54ab, 55). After the doxological opening of the speech (vv. 46b, 47), there is also no predicate whose subject is not God (or his name and his mercy [vv. 49b, 50]), with the exception again of 48b. Another coherence-creating element is the repetition of terms (cf. Tannehill 1974, 264): μεγαλύνει/μεγάλα (vv. 46b, 49a), ταπείνωσιν/ταπεινούς (vv. 48a, 52b), γενεαί/γενεάς (vv. 48b, 50), ἐποίησεν/ἐποίησεν (vv. 49a, 51a), δυνατός/δυνάστας (vv. 49a, 52a), and ἔλεος/ἐλέους (vv. 50a, 54b). Finally, from a semantic perspective the fact that God's action reverses assignments of status, namely both with reference to the speaker of the hymn (vv. 48-49a) and in general (vv. 51-53), runs through the entire hymn.

With this the signals that indicate a subdivision of the text beneath this level are also in view—namely, the change between the references of God's action. After the performative introduction to the speech (vv. 46b-47), God's action toward the speaker of the hymn is first thematized (vv. 48-49a). This orientation is concluded by two qualifying nominal sentences (vv 49b-50). After a generalizing introduction (v. 51a), vv. 51-53 refer the action of God expressed in it to groups of people designated with appellative substantives, who are consistently named in the plural object accusative (ὑπερηφάνους, δυνάστας, ταπεινούς, πεινῶντας, πλουτοῦντας). In vv. 54-55 the object then changes again. Now God's action is related to Israel or the semantically equivalent "Abraham and his seed." This twofold change is held together by a semantic axis whose beginning and end points are marked by the terms δούλη αὐτοῦ (v. 48a) and παῖς αὐτοῦ (v. 54a), which are similar in meaning. This axis is constituted by the ones who experience a change to salvation through God's action—namely, the speaker of the hymn, the "lowly" (v. 52b), the "hungering" (v. 53a), and Israel (v. 54a).

46a Due to the manuscript tradition there continues to be debate about which of the two women Luke has sing the song (cf. the presentation of the discussion in Benko 1967):

While the overwhelming majority of the textual witnesses (including all the Greek ones) name Mary as the singer, it is ascribed to Elisabeth in three Old Latin Gospel manuscripts (a b l*), a few manuscripts of church fathers, and by Nicetas of Remesiana (fifth century CE). In support of this reading, primarily inner criteria are advanced. However the most important of these can also all be reversed: *(a)* Her being filled with the Holy Spirit (v. 41c) is said to raise the expectation that she will also speak in a Spirit-filled manner, but the parallelism between v. 41c and v. 67 (filling of Zechariah with the Spirit) equally suggests that one should also ascribe a hymn to Elisabeth alongside Zechariah, as does the fact that the two were married to each other. *(b)* In v. 56a Mary's name is mentioned, while reference is made to Elisabeth with an anaphoric personal pronoun. This actually indicates a change of subject, but precisely this makes the naming of Mary in v. 46a the *lectio difficilior*. *(c)* The Magnificat is oriented to the praise song of Hannah (1 Samuel 2), who was barren for a long time like Elisabeth; its ascription to her would give expression to this correspondence. Since there is also not a single textual witness for the assumption—which has been favored time and again since Harnack—that there was originally no name mentioned in v. 46a and since the Magnificat is also suitable to provide a substantial contribution *ad maiorem gloriam Mariae* (cf. the interaction of the Protevangelium of James with it, which knows it as a Mary-text but suppresses it with the exception of an allusion to v. 48b in 12.2; for this, see Kaut 1990, 272–73), the external evidence must remain decisive: Luke has placed the Magnificat in Mary's mouth.

46b-47 The Magnificat begins with a synonymous *parallelismus membrorum*. The change from present to aorist (see also Psalm^{LXX} 41.2-3) requires a gnomic understanding for the aorist (cf. BDR §333.2), as this is also frequently found in the Psalms (e.g., Psalm^{LXX} 15.9; 55.5, 12; 120.1; 121.1); Hannah's song of praise also begins in this manner (1 Samuel 2.1). The style corresponds to the opening of individual songs of thanksgiving (e.g., Psalm 9.2-3; 30.2; 31.8; 138.1-2; 1 Samuel 2.1; Sirach 51.1). In vv. 46b-47 the "I" of the one praying (i.e., Mary) is rephrased with ἡ ψυχή μου or τὸ πνεῦμά μου (this too is common in the Septuagint; from the Psalter, cf. Psalm^{LXX} 21.30; 33.3; 34.9; 41.2-3 or 76.7; 142.7; see also Job 6.4; Isaiah 26.9; 11Q05 XIX, 8; the same applies to the parallelizing of ψυχή μου and πνεῦμα μου: Job 7.15; Psalm^{LXX} 76.3-4; 142.6-7). μεγαλύνειν and above all ἀγαλλιᾶν are traditional terms for the praise of God (e.g., 2 Samuel 7.22, 26; Psalm^{LXX} 2.11; 9.3; 12.6; 31.11; 33.4; 68.31; 69.5; 103.1; see also Plutarch, *Lycurgus* 14.3; 26.3; Diodorus Siculus 1.20.6; and elsewhere; both verbs together: Psalm^{LXX} 34.27; 39.17). There is a special closeness to Psalm^{LXX} 34.9; Habakkuk 3.18; Isaiah 61.10 insofar as comparable syntagmatic relationships are present in these texts.

48 With the apposition τῷ σωτῆρί μου (see also Psalm^{LXX} 24.5; 26.1, 9; 61.3, 7; Micah 7.7; Habakkuk 3.18; Isaiah 12.2) the second part of the double statement contains a surplus in relation to the first. It describes God under the aspect of his salvific action toward the speaker and prepares the continuation, for in v. 48a the reason for the introductory praise of God is named, again in the style of Old Testament hymns (cf. e.g., also with extensive terminological points of contact Psalm 31.8). Luke makes a double reference here: *(a)* a *contextual* reference to Mary's self-designation as δούλη αὐτοῦ (v. 38a), which connects the Magnificat with its literary context, and *(b)* an *intertextual* reference to Hannah, namely with the help of the unmistakable allusion to 1 Samuel 1.11, "if you really will look upon the lowliness of your slave (ἐὰν ἐπιβλέπων ἐπιβλέψῃς ἐπὶ τὴν ταπείνωσιν τῆς δούλης σου) and give a son to your slave"; for the further use of ἐπιβλέπειν ἐπί, see at 9.38. Because Elisabeth—and not Mary—was barren like Hannah, this correspondence presumably led to the emergence of the textual variant in v. 46a (see above). It is, however, not the ending of Hannah's barrenness that forms the *tertium comparationis* but the changing of her social status by God through him giving her a son. This is recognizable in Genesis 29.32 where Leah, who was not barren but only unloved, reacts with almost the same words to the birth of Ruben (εἶδέν μου κύριος τὴν ταπείνωσιν ["the Lord has looked upon my lowliness"]). This also corresponds to the use of this expression elsewhere (e.g., Genesis 31.42; Deuteronomy 26.7; 1 Samuel 9.16; 2 Kings 14.26; 2 Ezra 19.9 [= Nehemiah 9.9]; Psalm^{LXX} 9.14; 24.18; 118.153; Lamentations 1.9; see also Joseph and Aseneth 11.12; 13.1; 1.3; 4 Ezra 9.45). The concern everywhere is that God nullifies an objectively existing negative condition (thus ταπείνωσις in v. 48b may by no means be translated with 'humility') and turn it into salvation.

48b makes plain that it is also a matter of status reversal with regard to Mary, for the inferential ἰδοὺ γάρ expresses her elevated position among humans with an allusion to the Leah saying in Genesis 30.13. The macarism from v. 45 is hyperbolically continued in the process. The dimension that comes into view here ("all generations") signals the unsurpassable eschatic character of God's action in the present (ἀπὸ τοῦ νῦν; cf. also the comparable use of this temporal specification in Luke 5.10; 22.69); in this respect it overlaps with the announcement of the eternal reign of her son over Israel in v. 32.

To ground this point v. **49a** refers again to God's action toward her (for the designation of God as [ὁ] δυνατός, cf. Psalm^{LXX} 23.8; Zephaniah 3.17; Joseph and Aseneth 8.9). The predication ἐποίησέν μοι μεγάλα places what God has done for Mary in a series with his liberation of Israel from Egypt (cf. Deuteronomy 10.21; 11.7; 2 Samuel 7.23; Psalm^{LXX} 70.19; 105.21; Letter of Aristeas 155 [taking up Deuteronomy 7.18]). 2 Samuel 7.21 (see also 1 Chronicles 17.19) probably stands in the background, where David, in his answer to Nathan's promise, says that God has brought about πᾶσαν τὴν μεγαλωσύνην ταύτην ("all this greatness") in order to make them known to him. Here David twice designates himself as δοῦλος (v. 20, 21; see Luke 1.48a), and the key word μεγαλύνειν (v. 46b) also occurs in the context (2 Samuel 7.22; the link to the Exodus event then follows in

v. 23). Since Luke has also already made reference to the Nathan promise in vv. 32-33, the term μεγάλα refers to the salvation initiative of God expressed there, namely to the election of Joseph's betrothed to be the mother of the messianic Son of God.

49b-50 Two chiastically structured nominal sentences (predicate, subject / subject, predicate) conclude the first part of the hymn. Comparable predications are also often found in the Old Testament psalms after a praise of God that describes his actions (e.g., Psalm 3.9; 111.9; 135.13). The terminology of the two statements corresponds to conventional language for the reaction to God's salvific intervention (for the holiness of the name, see, e.g., 1 Chronicles 16.35; Psalm 111.9; 145.21; Wisdom of Solomon 10.20; for the showing of mercy toward those who fear God, see Psalm 103.11, 17; Sirach 2.7, 9; Psalms of Solomon 2.33; 13.12). Here "his name" stands for God himself, for the name represents the person (see at 11.2d-e). The plural phrasing (εἰς) γενεὰς καὶ γενεάς finds its parallel in Psalm^{LXX} 99.5 (ἕως γενεᾶς καὶ γενεᾶς); Testament of Levi 18.8; see also Psalm^{LXX} 60.7 (ἕως ἡμέρας γενεᾶς). The question, which is sometimes posed, of whether Luke indicates a qualification in v. 50 with the phrasing τοῖς φοβουμένοις αὐτόν (only the God-fearing Israelites will have a share in the mercy; so, among others, Seccombe 1982, 82; Mittmann-Richert 1996, 201–2) or whether he already broadens the perspective beyond Israel and points to the group of non-Jewish God-fearers (so, among others, Bovon, 89; Klauck 1997), is based on a semantic misjudgment, for it asks about the extensional meaning of the term φοβούμενοι αὐτόν. But in the text the concern is with a predication of God that uses this term only in its intensional meaning.

In **51-53** the perspective is broadened and God's action is described in a generalizing manner. Hannah's praise song proceeds analogously, and vv. 51-53 also come into contact with Hannah's praise song in the fact that both here and there God's action is explicated as the reversal of fate and status (cf. 1 Samuel 2.4-5). A notorious problem is the understanding of the occurrences of the aorist (cf. Marshall 1991, 188–89; York 1991, 52). Due to the parallelism with the aorists in vv. 48a, 49a, 54a, and the analogy to the aorists in 1 Samuel 2.4-5, which likewise transcend the concrete situation, Luke undoubtedly wants to link the reversal statements with the salvific initiative narrated in vv. 26-38 (see also at v. 68). Two predications emerge in the process. First—this will become apparent in light of the parallels to vv. 52-53—Mary predicates God as the one who has shown his divine power and thus demonstrated his God-ness. Second, through the specific selection that is made from the inventory of possible predications of God, the event that kicked off the hymn is interpreted in a certain way, namely as being part of a universal reversal of the social status assignments that are in force among humans (see also York 1991, 53ff), i.e., as the establishment of a new order in which the criteria for the decisive distribution of salvation and unsalvation are newly determined by God's intervention. This verse finds its immediate abutment in the Lukan opposition of macarisms and woes (Luke 6.20-26), and the theme then runs right through the entire Lukan story of Jesus (cf. in addition 13.30; 14.11; 16.19-31; 18.9-14).

51 is a synthetic *parallelismus membrorum* and contrasts God's action toward Mary with the fate of the arrogant. This connection is established with the help of the common semantic opposition of ταπείνωσις (v. 48a) and ὑπερηφανία (cf. Additions to Esther 4.17k; Psalm^LXX 17.28; 88.11; 118.50; Proverbs 3.34 [quoted in James 4.6; 1 Peter 5.5]; Sirach 13.20^LXX; Isaiah 1.25; Joseph and Aseneth 21.21; Letter of Aristeas 263; and the like) and also finds expression in the taking up again of ἐποίησεν from v. 49a. Here Luke has Mary formulate the fact—which is also already emphasized time and again in the Old Testament—that God's action of salvation and deliverance is accompanied by his action of unsalvation and destruction toward his and Israel's enemies; accordingly, the terminology of this verse is also borrowed from the corresponding contexts; cf. e.g., Exodus 6.6; 15.6; Numbers 10.34; Psalm^LXX 58.12; 67.2; 88.11: "You have brought low . . . the arrogant (σὺ ἐταπίνωσας . . . ὑπερήφανον) and with the arm of your power (καὶ ἐν τῷ βραχίονι τῆς δυνάμεώς σου) you have scattered your enemies"; Judith 13.11: "to show . . . power against your enemies" (ποιεῖν . . . κράτος κατὰ τῶν ἐχθρῶν).

52-53 The two verses are composed of two chiastically structured antithetical parallelisms (unsalvation, salvation / salvation, unsalvation), in which the respective end syllables rhyme (twice ων, twice ους). With the statement that through his action God reverses the fate of the powerful and the powerless and of the poor and the rich, Luke takes up here an old motif that is widely attested in the environment of the New Testament (cf. e.g., 1 Samuel 2.7-8; 2 Samuel 22.28; Ezekiel 17.24; 21.31; Psalm 75.8; Sirach 10.14; 1QM XIV, 10–11; Homer, *Ilias* 20.242–43; *Odyssea* 16.211–12; Hesiod, *Opera et dies* 5–8; Pindar, *Pythionikai* 2.88–89; Euripides, *Troedes*, 612–13; Xenophon, *Anabasis* 3.2.10; Gnomologium Vaticanum 553 [on Zeus: τὰ μὲν ὑψηλὰ ταπεινοῖ τὰ δὲ ταπεινὰ ὑψοῖ ("high things he lowers, but low things he exalts")]; Herodianus Historicus 1.13.16; Horace, *Carmina* 1.34, 12–14; 35.1–4; 1 Clement 59.3; cf. with additional attestations Hommel 1983/1984, II: 3–9; Hamel 1979, 58ff). The intention of the antitheses regularly aims at characterizing divine power (see also Daniel 5.19). For this reason, an interpretation of the two antitheses that starts from the question of the denotation of the groups mentioned here, or reduces the understanding of the reversal of the relations to the alternative of sociopolitical vs. spiritualizing, misses the intention of the text. Rather, one must start from the assumption that this reversal was often formulated as a utopia or as an eschatological expectation; in addition to the afore-mentioned texts, cf. esp. P. Oxy. XXXI, 2554, Fragment I. 2 (third century CE): "It will go badly for the rich (τοῖς πλουσ[ίοις] κακῶς ἔσται; 5) . . . And the poor will be exalted, and the rich will be made low (καὶ οἱ π[τ]ωχοὶ ὑψωθήσοντα[ι, καὶ] οἱ πλούσιοι ταπεινωθήσονται; 10–11)." Against this background, the two verses are intended to express that God created this new reality with his intervention. It stands in discontinuity to previous reality insofar as in it the assignment of salvation and unsalvation is not in line with existing standards but rather implies breaks. Thus, according to the Lukan understanding, continuity and discontinuity go hand in hand in the realization of God's plan of salvation—a theological structuring prin-ciple that runs like a *cantus firmus* through Jesus's entire proclamation of · the kingdom of God in the Gospel of Luke (cf. Wolter 1995a, 549ff).

To a certain extent in a countermovement to this discontinuity, in **54-55** the salvation-historical continuity is emphasized again. At the end of her hymn, and therefore in a prominent position, Luke has Mary interpret God's salvation initiative as an expression of faithfulness to his election and his promises toward Israel, through her interpretation of the present action of God as the eschatic actualization of his original election with which God definitively bound himself to his people.

In **54** this takes place first in connection with Isaiah 41.8-9 ("But you, Israel, παῖς μου Jacob, whom I have chosen, σπέρμα of Abraham, whom I have loved, whom I have taken to myself [οὗ ἀντελαβόμην]— . . . I have called you and said to you: παῖς μου εἶ, I have chosen you, and I have not forsaken you . . ."; see also 42.1). The designation of Israel as God's παῖς also takes up Deutero-Isaianic language (cf. Isaiah 44.1-2, 21; 45.4; see also Psalms of Solomon 12.6; 17.21) insofar as this designation functions in all cases as the starting point of statements of salvation and deliver-ance. This saving action of God toward his people is then tied back to the tradition of the patriarchs in vv. 54b-55. The phrasing μνησθῆναι ἐλέους (the infinitive explains: see BDR §394) expresses, like the analogous syn-tagms above all in Psalm^LXX 97.3 (ἐμνήσθη τοῦ ἐλέους αὐτοῦ τῷ Ἰακώβ καὶ τῆς ἀληθείας αὐτοῦ τῷ οἴκῳ Ἰσραήλ ["he has remembered his mercy with Jacob and his faithfulness to the house of Israel"]; see also Ezekiel 2.24; 6.5; Leviticus 26.42, 45; 1 Maccabees 4.10; 2 Maccabees 1.2; Psalm^LXX 104.8-9, 42; 105.45; 110.5; Ezekiel 16.60; 4 Baruch 6.17-18), that it is the inviolable continuity of the covenant faithfulness of God and his holding fast to the election of Israel that have now caused him to take the ini-tiative to restore his people; on ἔλεος as a metonym for 'covenant,' cf. 1 Kings 3.6; Jeremiah 16.13^LXX; Habakkuk 3.2 and the lexical pair ἔλεος καὶ διαθήκη ("mercy and covenant"; Deuteronomy 7.9, 12; 1 Kings 8.23; 2 Chronicles 6.14; 2 Ezra 11.5; 19.32 [Nehemiah 1.5; 9.32]; Psalm^LXX 88.29, 34-35; Daniel 9.4).

In **55** God's present initiative of salvation is then also identified *expressis verbis* as the fulfillment of the promise given to the fathers (v. 55a; for καθὼς ἐλάλησεν in this sense, see, e.g., Exodus 12.25; Deuteronomy 1.11; Judges 6.36-37; 1 Kings 5.26; 8.20, 53; 2 Kings 17.23). The syntactical connection of v. 55b is unclear. Does τῷ Ἀβραάμ . . . refer back to v. 54b (v. 55a would then be a parenthesis), or should this part of the sentence be understood in apposition to πρὸς τοὺς πατέρας ἡμῶν and as dependent upon ἐλάλησεν? Final certainty cannot be obtained, but the stereotype character of the joining of ἔλεος and εἰς τὸν αἰῶνα (cf. just Psalm^LXX 135) and the correspondence to 2 Samuel 22.51 (= Psalm^LXX 17.51) and Micah 7.20 (see also 1 Kings 8.23) suggest that preference should be given to the first possibility mentioned.

56 Luke has Mary stay "about" (ὡς or ὡσεί with the specification of numbers is typically Lukan; cf. 3.23; 8.42; 9.14, 28; 22.59; 23.44; Acts 1.15; 2.41; 4.4; 5.7, 36; 10.3; 13.18, 20; 19.7, 34) three months at Elisabeth's house and then return home; ὑποστρέφειν is a favorite word of Luke (32 of 35 instances in the New Testament). Luke takes up the month numeration of v. 26 and in this way leads his readers back into the pregnancy chronology of Elisabeth and right up to her due date. Through the spatial distancing Mary is withdrawn from the action (Luke also proceeds similarly with John in v. 80 and with Paul in Acts 9.30; 18.22-23) in order to focus the readers' attention undividedly upon the birth of John and the following Benedictus of Zechariah, who takes Mary's place in the next episode (cf. Coleridge 1993, 96–97).

1:57-79(80): The Birth of John, His Name, and His Father's Praise of God

[57]**But for Elisabeth the time was fulfilled that she should give birth, and she bore a son.** [58]**And her neighbors and relatives heard that the Lord had shown his great mercy to her and they rejoiced with her.** [59]**And it happened that she came on the eighth day to circumcise the child, and they wanted to name him after the name of his father Zechariah.** [60]**Then his mother objected and said, "No, he should rather be called John!"** [61]**And they said to her, "There is no one from your tribe who bears this name."** [62]**But they signaled to his father, how he wanted to have it named.** [63]**And he asked for a writing tablet and wrote the words, "John is his name!" And all marveled.** [64]**Then immediately his mouth was opened, and his tongue and he spoke and praised God.**

[65]And fear fell on all who lived in their neighborhood, and these things were spoken about in the entire Jewish hill country, [66]and all who heard (of them) placed (them) in their heart and said, "What will this child become?" For indeed the hand of the Lord was with him!

[67]And Zechariah, his father, was filled with the Holy Spirit and began to speak prophetically:

[68]"Praised (be) the Lord, the God of Israel, for he visited and brought liberation for his people, [69]and he has raised up a horn of salvation in the house of David, his servant, [70]as he said through the mouth of his holy prophets from of old, [71]salvation from our enemies and from the hand of all who hate us, [72]in order to realize the mercy with our fathers and to remember his holy covenant—[73]the oath, which he swore to Abraham, our father—in order to grant us [74]to serve him without fear as ones delivered from the hands of the enemies, [75]in piety and righteousness before him all our days.

[76]But you too, child, will be called prophet of the Most High, for you will go before the Lord to prepare his ways, [77]to give knowledge of salvation to his people through the forgiveness of their sins [78]on the basis of the compassion-filled mercy of our God.

Through it a rising (of the sun) will visit us from on high, [79]to appear to those who sit in the darkness and in the shadow of death, to guide our feet into the path of peace."

[80]But the child grew and became strong in the Spirit. And he was in deserted regions until the day of his installation for Israel.

In the third main phase of narration Luke continues the thread of action begun in the first phase (vv. 8-25) and concludes part of the arc of suspense opened by the announcement of Gabriel, namely that Elisabeth, who has become pregnant in the meantime (vv. 24-25), will give birth to a son (v. 13d/v. 57), that her child will receive the name John (v. 13e/vv. 59-63), and that Zechariah regains speech as a result (v. 20a/v. 64). Luke divides this narrative phase into three scenes that he clearly demarcates from one another—namely, into *(a)* a report of Elisabeth's delivery (vv. 57-58), which is concluded (v. 58c) with an implicit acclamation from the side of the neighbors and relatives of Elisabeth in the form of a speech or thought report (cf. Vogt 1990, 145–46, 157ff); *(b)* a narrative of the naming of the child and the removal of Zechariah's inability to speak (vv. 59-66), which within the narrated time takes place eight days after the first scene and is concluded by an executed acclamation (v. 66bc); and *(c)* the hymn of Zechariah (vv. 67-79). This last part forms the climax of the whole, which is recognizable above all in the fact that the degree of compression is reduced from scene to scene and the narrative tempo increasingly slows. The difference between time of narration and narrated time becomes increasingly smaller. An indication of this is the portion of direct speech in the narrative. In vv. 57-58 Luke manages to do entirely without it, in vv. 59-66 he has his narrative figures come to speech at four points (vv. 60b, 61b, 63b, 66b-c), and, finally, vv. 67-79 are exclusively made up of direct speech with the exception of a short introduction (v. 67). It also corresponds to this that Luke uses here the rhetorical figure of *hysteron proteron* (cf. Lausberg 1973, §891: an "ordering of two ideas in a sentence that is opposed to the natural course of events") in order to be able to assign the decisive concluding position to the Bendictus. The εὐλογεῖν of Zechariah, which is conveyed already in v. 64, is only carried out from vv. 68 onward (εὐλογητός; Luke also proceeds analogously in Acts 28.25-28). In this way Luke separates the Benedictus from the last narrative scene and enables the reader to read the hymn of Zechariah as an interpretation of the whole narrative composition inaugurated in v. 5, i.e., including the second narrative phase (vv. 26-56).

57 Elisabeth's delivery is reported only with a few words; to this extent it receives only a prologue function in relation to what follows (Coleridge 1993, 102–3). Verse 57a has linguistic connections with Genesis 25.24 (concerning Rebekah: καὶ ἐπληρώθησαν αἱ ἡμέραι τοῦ τεκεῖν αὐτήν ["and the days for her to give birth were fulfilled"]; see further at 1.23). The replacement of αἱ ἡμέραι by ὁ χρόνος is probably due to Hellenistic usage where χρόνος is frequently linked in this way to forms of πληρόω (e.g., Plutarch, *Lucullus* 35.8: . . . πεπληρῶσθαι τὸν χρόνον [". . . that the time was fulfilled"]; Vettius Valens, ed. Kroll 1973, 260.10: πληρωθέντος τοῦ χρόνου ["when the time was fulfilled"]; Vita Aesopi 84: ὁ χρόνος ἤδη πεπλήρωται ["the time had already become fulfilled"]; Heliodorus, *Aethiopica* 1.22.2: τοῦ χρόνου πληρουμένου ["when the time had become fulfilled"]; see also Acts 7.23). Verse 57b takes up the phrasing from v. 13d.

58 Luke stops the continuation of the narrative (the durative imperfect συνέχαιρον in v. 58c lets it come to rest) and also brings the announcement of v. 14b to fulfillment. It is conspicuous that in v. 58b he does not communicate the fact, which becomes known to Elisabeth's neighbors and relatives, simply as such, but encodes it theocentrically (cf. Genesis 19.19; 1 Samuel 12.24; Psalm^LXX 56.11; 125.2-3) and thus lets his own presentation flow together with the subjective perception of the event by the narrative figures. Thus, the content of the communication functions simultaneously as an implicit acclamation, and this compressed manner of narration also enables Luke to preserve the prologue character of this scene without having to forgo a narrated interpretation of the birth of Elisabeth's son. Verse 58c is possibly an allusion to Genesis 21.6 (Sarah typology).

59-63 With the following scene Luke wants to show that God's plan of salvation establishes itself in a way that surprises the people of the narrated world because it does not meet their expectations. This will then intensify even more in the further course of Luke–Acts. Here too continuity and discontinuity go hand in hand (see also Löning 1997/2006, I: 103), and in order to illustrate this very thing Luke makes Elisabeth's neighbors and relatives in this scene into narrative antagonists and accepts some narrative extravagances.

59 The introduction with καὶ ἐγένετο + temporal specification with ἐν + *verbum finitum* is a Septuagintism; cf. Genesis 19.29; Exodus 12.51; Numbers 10.11; and elsewhere. Within the narrated time Luke makes a small jump to the day of the circumcision, which is to be performed eight days after the birth according to Genesis 17.12 and Leviticus 12.3 (see also m. Shabbat 9.5). The reference to the circumcision, however, serves merely the temporal specification and should not be interpreted as a demonstration of the information provided in v. 6 concerning the faithfulness to the law of the child's parents. Apparently, Luke presupposes that the day of the circumcision, as with Jesus (see at 2.21), is also the day of the naming (ἐκάλουν would then have to be understood as *imperfectum de conatu*; cf. BDR §326), although this connection is securely attested for the first time in post-Talmudic Judaism (PRE 48; cf. Blaschke 1998, 439–40). That a son receives the name of his father (on καλεῖν ἐπὶ τῷ ὀνόματί τινος, cf. Genesis 48.6; Deuteronomy 3.14; 1 Kings 16.24; 1/3 Ezra 5.38; [2] Ezra 2.61; 17.63 [= Nehemiah 7.63]; Testament of Naphtali 1.11; Jubilees [Greek Fragment] 11.15) is rather uncommon but possible (cf. Josephus, *Vita* 4; *Antiquitates judaicae* 14.10; 20.197; *Bellum judaicum* 4.160; 5.534; see also Krauss 1966, II: 13). More common was papponymy, i.e., naming a child after the grandfather (cf. Mussies 1988, 118ff; Ilan 2002, 32), so that with this suggestion Luke could dramatically intensify the transfer of the decision about the name to Zechariah (v. 62). The Lukan narrative interest is probably also responsible for the intensive participation of the neighbors and relatives in the naming (it actually fell within the parents' sphere of responsibility; cf. Krauss 1966, II: 13; the only exception is Ruth 4.17), for otherwise it would have been difficult to integrate Zechariah, who was still mute, into the decision making process and to realize narratively the announcement of v. 13e. Since the intention of the visitors contradicts this announcement, the narrative is placed in a state of tension (see also Löning 1997/2006, I: 103).

This tension is escalated further in **60** through the fact that Elisabeth objects to the suggestions of the neighbors and relatives and wants instead to name her child with the name given to him from God. This is somewhat surprising, for the readers do not actually expect that Elisabeth knows the name mentioned in v. 13c (Zechariah is, after all, still mute). There is thus another gap in the narrative here (see also Tannehill), which should be respected as such and not filled speculatively (cf. the survey in Coleridge 1993, 107).

61 The objection that the guests advance against the name mentioned by Elisabeth is based on a continuity mediated through bodily descent (on ἐκ τῆς συγγενείας in this sense, cf. Judges 17.7A; 18.11A; Ruth 2.1, 3; 2 Samuel 16.5; Tobit 1.22א; Job 32.2; Isaiah 38.12; Joseph and Aseneth 8.6) and documents in this way their lack of knowledge about the discontinuity established by God's initiative (see also Nolland). Luke, however, conversely uses the objection in order to make the readers aware of this discontinuity. In this way the giving of the name becomes a salvation-historical paradigm *en miniature*.

62 Through the transfer of the decision to Zechariah, he returns again to the narrative in which he had no longer played a role since v. 23 (or indirectly since v. 24). The substantivizing of the indirect interrogative sentence with τό is a Lukan and Pauline distinctive in the New Testament (otherwise in the New Testament only Luke 9.46; 19.48; 22.2, 4, 23, 24; Acts 4.21; 22.30; Romans 8.26; 1 Thessalonians 4.1; cf. BDR §267.2₃: "A difference in meaning between the presence and absence of the article is not evident").

63 ἔγραψεν λέγων is frequently regarded as a Hebraism (cf. BDR §420.3; Nolland); however, the phrasing is also attested in pagan Greek texts (e.g., Aristotle, *Protrepticus* 1; Theophrastus, *Physicorum opiniones*, Fragment 2 [Diels 1879, 477.7–8]; Plutarch, *Moralia* 568c; Diogenes Laertius 9.6). The text written by Zechariah on the writing tablet is not the actual naming ceremony, but functions as an identification of the child by name. The phrasing ἐστὶν ὄνομα expresses that the fixing of the name has already taken place—namely by the messenger of God in v. 13e. Luke has Zechariah acknowledge this very thing. With the concluding wonder motif (ἐθαύμασαν; cf. Theissen 1987, 78ff; Meiser 1998, 74ff), which plays a greater role in Luke than in Mark and Matthew (cf. 2.18, 33; 4.22 diff. Mark 6.2; 8.25 par. Matthew 8.27 diff. Mark 4.41; 9.43; 11.14 par. Matthew 9.33; 20.26; par. Mark 12.17; 24.12, 41; see also Acts 2.7; 3.12; 4.13 as well as Tobit 11.16; Plutarch, *Marcius Coriolanus* 24.3; Lucian of Samosata, *Abdicatus* 5), Luke ends the controversy and characterizes the perception of the event from the side of the visitors (see also v. 21). They observe that something extraordinary has happened, but without being able to fully understand it. Their original antagonistic certainty (vv. 59b, 61b) is thus shaken and placed in a state of uncertainty (see also Coleridge 1993, 111; F. Annen, *EWNT* 2: 334).

64 The announcement of Gabriel from v. 20 is immediately fulfilled in relation to Zechariah, and he regains speech (for the zeugmatic character of v. 64a, cf. BDR §479.2). That the healing comes to pass "immediately" (παραχρῆμα) belongs to the topics of healing stories (cf. Weinreich 1969, 197–98; Theissen 1987, 75). παραχρῆμα is typically Lukan and occurs in the New Testament, apart from Matthew 21.19-20, only in Luke–Acts (see also 4.39; 5.25; 8.44, 47, 55; 13.13; 18.43; Acts 3.7; 13.11; 16.26; for the historical-linguistic background, cf. Rydbeck 1967, 167ff, 184–85; Fabricius 1985). From a form-critical perspective we are dealing in v. 64b with the demonstration of the success of the miracle (cf. Theissen 1987, 75). The demonstration is formulated here and in Mark 1.31parr.; 5.42; 7.35; 8.25; Luke 5.6; 13.13; Acts 3.8; 14.10 in the durative imperfect. That the healed person praises God is a feature that is typical for the Lukan miracle stories (see also Luke 5.25 diff. Mark 2.12; Luke 13.13; 17.15; 18.43 diff. Mark 10.52: in each case δοξάζειν; Acts 3.8: αἰνεῖν). When Luke, on the other hand, uses εὐλογεῖν in this passage, this is because he wants to establish a connection with the Benedictus (cf. v. 68 and at v. 56 above).

In **65** Luke begins to report about the public reaction to these events. Form-critically we are dealing, in the first place, in v. 65a with the wonder motif that is frequently encountered at the end of miracle stories (with φόβος or the like: Matthew 9.8; Mark 4.41par; 5.15par.; Luke 5.26; 7.16; 8.37; cf. Theissen 1987, 78–79; H. Balz, ThWNT 9: 205); the phrasing with ἐγένετο . . . ἐπὶ (πάντας) is typically Lukan (cf. Luke 4.36: θάμβος; Acts 5.5, 11; 19.17: in each case φόβος; see also Genesis 35.5). Luke appears to connect with this the notion that such reactions seize people from outside (see also Exodus 15.16; Judges 11.29; 1 Maccabees 1.25). At the same time Luke expands the narrative perspective spatially and personally beyond those present at the events to "*all* neighbors" (cf. BDR §472$_6$). This is intensified further in v. 65b where he takes into view the entire region (see at v. 39) and with the help of the imperfect διελαλεῖτο lets the consequences also persist over a longer period of time. This notification finds its counterpart in the notes of dissemination that are also sometimes found after miracle stories (cf. Mark 1.28 par. Luke 4.37 [imperfect]; Mark 5.14 par. Luke 8.34; Luke 5.15 [imperfect]; 7.17; Matthew 9.26; Acts 9.42; 19.17 [imperfect]). For the phrasing πάντα . . . τὰ ῥήματα ταῦτα, see at 2.19.

In **66** Luke describes the reaction of those who receive knowledge of the events through the public dissemination (cf. the correspondence of διαλαλεῖν and ἀκούειν). τιθέναι . . . ἐν τῇ καρδίᾳ αὐτῶν is a Septuagintism (cf. above all 1 Samuel 21.13, but also 29.10; Sirach 50.28; Malachi 2.2; Jeremiah 12.11; Daniel[Theodotion] 1.8 as well as Luke 21.14; Acts 5.4) and designates here the inner involvement with which Luke has the reports of the events be taken up. Their reaction is put into words with the help of an acclamation that is carried out (v. 66b; cf. Theissen 1987, 80–81). It refers first in interrogative form (see also Mark 1.27par; 4.41parr.) to the future significance of the child and then gives the reason for the special expectations that are directed toward the future of the child in v. 66c. With the last sentence Luke continues the direct speech and does not provide, for example, a narrator's comment (so, among others, Klostermann; Marshall; Green). In the latter case one would have to assume that Luke wanted to give the readers a piece of information here that would be completely superfluous after what was previously reported about John the Baptist, for the readers have long known that God has acted in support of the child (for the understanding of the metaphor in this sense, cf. 1 Samuel 22.17; 2 Samuel 3.12; 14.19; 16.21; 2 Kings 15.19; 1 Chronicles 4.10 [from the hand of God]; Jeremiah 33[26].24; Testament of Abraham A 18.7). By contrast, the sentence receives a good sense as reflecting a theological interpretation within the narrated world, which refers to the extraordinary circumstances of the birth and naming of the future Baptist.

67-79 After Luke had already gone beyond the temporal and spatial situation of the scene with vv. 65-66, he returns to it once more and has Zechariah, who has regained the ability to speak in the meantime, carry out the praise of God touched upon in v. 64.

Like the Magnificat, the Benedictus is regarded by the majority of interpreters as entirely or mostly pre-Lukan. Contrary positions that view it as a Lukan composition or regard this as at least possible are rare (e.g., Harnack 1931, 80–85; Erdmann 1932, 33; Ernst; Schmithals; Löning 1997/2006, I: 106ff). In this context the same questions are controversially discussed as with the Magnificat (cf. the overview in S. C. Farris 1981, 128ff).

Is the Benedictus compiled from two hymns that were originally independent (e.g., Gunkel 1921; Vielhauer 1965; Gnilka 1962)? Has Luke provided more or less extensive additions to an existing hymn (e.g., Benoit 1956–1957; R. E. Brown 1993, 377; Dillon 2006, 458; Fitzmyer; S. C. Farris 1981, 26ff; Nolland; Bovon; Mittmann-Richert 1996)? It is astonishing that no one asks about possible deletions. Has Luke taken over the existing text without changes (e.g., Vanhoye 1965–1966; Auffret 1978; Rousseau 1986; Marshall)? Or is the tradition history even much more complex (e.g., Schürmann; Kaut 1990, 263ff; Radl 1996, 130–31)?

What is the provenance of the original hymn: General-Jewish (for 68–75[*] e.g., Gunkel 1921; Vielhauer 1965; Kaut 1990, 273ff; Radl 1996, 129–30), Jewish-Baptist (for 76–79[*], see, e.g., Vielhauer 1965; Gnilka 1962; Radl 1996, 128; for the entire *Vorlage*, e.g., Bovon; Dillon 2006) or Jewish-Christian (e.g.,

R. E. Brown 1993, 378; Marshall; Fitzmyer; S. C. Farris 1981, 95–96; Mittmann-Richert 1996, 63ff)?

Was there a Hebrew *Vorlage* (e.g., S. C. Farris 1981, 31ff; Mittmann-Richert 1996, 120ff)?

The methodological problems bound up with diachronic reconstruction endeavors have already been addressed in the interpretation of the Magnificat. For the reasons mentioned there, the Benedictus as well can be interpreted in a sensible and methodologically controllable manner only on the synchronic level of the text.

Like the Magnificat, the Benedictus is compiled in a collage-like way from pieces of language that come from the Old Testament (cf. the overview in R. E. Brown 1993, 386ff; Schmithals as well as the individual documentation ad loc. in what follows). Thus, here too the event of the narrated time is interpreted in the light of the past. Beyond this, some overlaps with the Magnificat can be identified: God's saving action as the occasion (σωτήρ; v. 47/σωτηρία; v. 71); the use of the aorist to speak about God's action (vv. 48-49, 51-54a/vv. 68b-69a); the reference to Israel (vv. 54a, 55b/v. 68); the reference to the Abrahamic covenant (μνησθῆναι or ἔλεος; v. 54b/vv. 72-73a); the presentation of the present action of God as fulfilling his promises (καθὼς ἐλάλησεν; v. 55a/v. 70).

The differences, however, are unmistakable. While the Magnificat is mostly characterized in terms of syntax by a paratactic ordering of the individual stichoi, hypotactic sentence structures predominate in the Benedictus. The entire text is not comprised of two parts as is usually assumed (cf. recently Dillon 2006, 458), but of three units that can be clearly distinguished from one another. In vv. 68-75 the concern is with what *God* does, in vv. 76-78a with the future task of the *child*, and in vv. 78b-79 with what the ἀνατολή will do. With this the subjects of the finite verbs are also already specified. Moreover, each of the three parts are based on the same syntactical structure—namely, the linking of *verbum finitum* + infinitive + an *infinitivus finalis* substantivized with τοῦ (cf. BDR §400.6):

vv. 68b-75	(God) ἐπεσκέψατο καὶ ἐποίησεν . . . καὶ ἤγειρεν	ποιῆσαι . . . καὶ μνησθῆναι	τοῦ δοῦναι
vv. 76-78a	(the child) προπορεύσῃ	ἑτοιμάσαι	τοῦ δοῦναι
vv. 78b-79	(the ἀνατολή) ἐπισκέψεται	ἐπιφᾶναι	τοῦ κατευθῦναι

Here we are dealing with a construction that in the New Testament is additionally attested in this form only in Acts 26.18 (the texts mentioned in

BDR §400₈ are not exact parallels; Matthew 2.13 is not either). It often occurs, however, in the Septuagint (e.g., Genesis 39.10; 43.18; Judges 19.3; 1 Samuel 19.11; 2 Samuel 14.11). God's action is spoken of in the aorist, while John and the ἀνατολή are spoken of in a future manner. In this way the entire text receives a temporal slope that consists of a sequence of three stages. Within this slope Zechariah, as the speaker of the Benedictus, is located between the first and second stage, i.e., between v. 75 and v. 76.

When we take a look again at the Benedictus at this point from the perspective of the Magnificat, yet another matter becomes important. While in the Benedictus God is the subject of the predicates only in the first part (vv. 68-75), this was consistently the case in the Magnificat and could be identified as a dominant coherence-forming factor for the entire text (see at 1.46-55). In contrast, in the Benedictus the coherence is established through the first person plural, which refers to the people of God Israel (cf. the parallelizing of τῷ λαῷ αὐτοῦ and ἡμῖν in vv. 68b, 69) and runs with this meaning like a red thread through the entire text (vv. 68b, 69, 71ab, 72a, 73ab, 75, 77a, 78ab, 79b). In the Magnificat there was talk of Israel and "us" only at the end (vv. 54-55). It corresponds to this further that the reference to the Abrahamic covenant, which was also spoken of in the last part of the Magnificat, is taken up again in the first part of the Benedictus (vv. 72-73a). In this way the two hymns are connected with each other (cf. N. Lohfink 1994, 119ff). In its first part the Benedictus builds upon the Magnificat (so in the temporal slope of the Benedictus, Mary also stands after v. 75) and develops it further in the second and third parts.

Thus, the Benedictus has a double task with regard to the literary context. First, the Benedictus is Zechariah's answer to the birth announcement given to him in vv. 13-17 (see there). This connection is established by the terminological link to the description of the future significance of the child (vv. 16-17) in vv. 76b, 77a. But because Zechariah also lost the ability to speak at the birth announcement that was given to him, Luke can present this answer only at the end of the entire event structure narrated in chapter 1. Second, this has the consequence that the Benedictus is also conceived as a Spirit-filled—i.e., authentic according to God— concluding comment on the events of chapter 1. For precisely this reason Luke has removed the Benedictus literarily from the John episode narrated in vv. 57-66 and placed it after that episode. In this way the readers are enabled to identify the announcement of the birth of Jesus as the event about which Zechariah speaks in vv. 68-69 (with the language of "house of David" in v. 69 they are also expressly referred back to vv. 27, 32). In this respect the readers know more than Zechariah, who appears here in two roles, namely as father of the Baptist and as representative of the eschatological salvific hopes of Israel. In this double function Luke has him integrate the announcement conerning his son into the salvific action of God connected with Jesus and provide a prophetic forward look at the future significance of the two figures of salvation—the eschatic prophet and the messianic king.

67 As with Elisabeth previously, Luke also has Zechariah be filled with the Holy Spirit (see at v. 41). In this way he signals to the readers that Zechariah's words are authorized by God, and that Zechariah interprets the previously narrated events according to God. For the connection between Spirit and prophecy, see at v. 15.

68 The introductory eulogy in v. 68a (the phrasing corresponds with 1 Samuel 25.32; 1 Kings 1.48; 8.15; 2 Chronicles 2.11; 6.4; Psalm^{LXX} 40.14; 71.18; 105.48; see also 1 Chronicles 16.36; 29.10; Tobit 13.18א; 1QM XIII, 2; XIV, 4; 4Q503 Fragments 1–6 II, VI, XVIII; and elsewhere) already has a signaling function, for from the inventory of possible God predicates, a phrasing is selected that predicates God decidedly as the "God of Israel." It is noteworthy that this designation for God, which accentuates the election of his people and is encountered at every turn in the Old Testament, has by contrast almost disappeared in the New Testament. It is still found only in Luke (cf. in addition Luke 1.16; Acts 13.17) and in the acclamation report of Matthew 15.31. This conspicuous phenomenon undoubtedly reflects the Christian-Jewish separation process that accompanied the missionary crossing over of the boundaries of Judaism (cf. also Romans 3.29-30). In this light, it becomes even more significant that Israel is established as the frame of reference here, right at the beginning.

68b provides the explanation, whose introduction with the preposition ὅτι (Hebrew כִּי) is relatively rare for eulogies (Exodus 18.10^{LXX}; Tobit 8.16-17; 13.2; Psalm^{LXX} 27.6; 30.22; Daniel 3.26-27; Joseph and Aseneth 3.3; 1QH V, 20; X, 14; XI, 32–33; 1QM XVIII, 6; cf. Deichgräber 1967, 40ff; Delling 1963, 2ff). The form of the sentence corresponds to Numbers 16.5; (2) Ezra 4.19; 6.1; Sirach 35.18; Testament of Levi 16.5 (in each case ἐπισκέπτεσθαι without accusative object + καί + *verbum finitum*). Luke takes up here a terminology that has a common semantic overlap with regard to the deliverance from a situation of unsalvation (referentially, e.g., the liberation of Israel from Egypt and from the exile: cf. Genesis 50.24-25; Exodus 3.16; 4.31; Zechariah 10.3; Zephaniah 2.7 as well as Exodus 6.6; 15.13; Isaiah 41.14; 43.1, 14; see further E. Zenger, *JSHRZ* I/6: 470n15c; Haubeck 1985, 98ff). This connotation is taken up again in vv. 71, 74. The aorists correspond to those of Exodus 4.31 and Isaiah 43.1; 44.23. The salvific initative taken by God can, because it is God's initiative, be characterized in such a way that it already includes its empirically perceptible result.

69 continues the explanation in a concretizing way. In the Old Testament God also often "raises up" persons in order to act with them toward Israel (e.g., 2.16, 18; 3.9, 15; 1 Kings 11.14, 23; Zechariah 11.16; see also Deuteronomy 18.15, 18; Jeremiah 23.4, 5 [messianic; likewise Ezekiel 34.23]; Greek Apocalypse of Enoch 89.42; Testament of Levi 18.2; Luke 7.16; Acts 3.22, 26; 13.22). κέρας is a metaphor for power and strength (e.g., 1 Samuel 2.1, 10; 1 Chronicles 25.5; Job 16.15; Jeremiah 31[48].25), but can also be used as a metaphorical designation for God himself (2 Samuel 22.3 = Psalm^LXX 17.3: "My God is . . . my shield and horn of my salvation [κέρας σωτηρίας μου]") or, as here, for the messianic ruler (Psalm^LXX 131.17; Ezekiel 29.21; Eighteen Benedictions [Babylonian Recension] 15). The closest parallel to the Lukan phrasing is Psalm 154.18-19 (Syriac Psalm 2): "Praise be to the Lord . . . who causes a horn to rise from Jacob and a judge of the people from Israel" (in 11Q5 XVII this psalm is also preserved in a Hebrew version, but the quoted lines are missing there). ἐν οἴκῳ Δαυίδ refers back to vv. 27, 32 and in this way makes it possible for the reader to identify the messianic ruler through whom God sets in motion the liberation of his people with the son of Mary, even if nothing is known yet about Jesus within the narrated world of Zechariah. It is therefore undoubtedly significant that within Luke–Acts the key word σωτηρία is encountered for the first time in this passage.

70 is a parenthesis that interprets the salvific initiative of God in the present as a fulfillment of the prophetic promises of salvation. It has an almost word-for-word connection with Acts 3.21. For the holiness of prophets, cf. Wisdom of Solomon 11.1; Greek Apocalypse of Ezra 1.1; 2 Baruch 85.1; 2 Peter 3.2.

71 Syntactically this verse is an apposition, but its reference is unclear. On the one hand, σωτηρία from v. 69 is taken up, though the accusative σωτηρίαν is not coordinated with its case. On the other hand, the sentence converges syntactically and semantically with ἐποίησεν λύτρωσιν (v. 68b), but the connection is broken by the paratactic in-between position of καὶ ἤγειρεν κέρας (v. 69). Even though this obscurity cannot be removed, the content of the sentence is easily understood as an explication of the consequences of God's salvific action for his people. Although the terminology comes close to Psalm^LXX 105.10 (concerning the deliverance at the Red Sea: καὶ ἔσωσεν αὐτοὺς ἐκ χειρὸς μισούντων καὶ ἐλυτρώσατο αὐτοὺς ἐκ χειρὸς ἐχθροῦ ["and he delivered them from the hand of those who hated them and he liberated them from the hand of the enemy"]), the verse does not make a specific allusion to this text but takes up a general linguistic usage. In the Septuagint, the lexical pair ἐχθροί and μισοῦντες designates those who stand against God (Numbers 10.34; Deuteronomy 32.41; Psalm^LXX 20.9; 67.2; 82.3), his people (Leviticus 26.17; Deuteronomy

30.7; 32.43; Psalm^LXX 43.11; 105.10, 42), and individuals (2 Samuel 22.18, 41 = Psalm^LXX 17.18, 41: David; Psalm^LXX 37.20; 54.13; 68.5; 88.24; see also Deuteronomy 33.11; Sirach 25.14; Daniel 4.19) as adversaries. Thus, God's saving intervention for his people is described here as liberation from foreign rule, without a certain contemporary-historical reference being intended (cf. also 1 Clement 60.3). This idea is then concretized further in a revealing way in vv. 74-75.

72-73a The finite verbs of vv. 68b, 69 are continued with an infinitive construction that specifies—analogously to v. 54—the intention that motivates God's action toward his people. ὅρκον (v. 73a) is, in parallel to διαθήκης, dependent on μνησθῆναι, but assimilated to the relative pronoun (*attractio inversa*; BDR §295). All three stichoi have the reference to the covenant with the fathers as a common center (for ἔλεος as a covenant term, see at v. 54; cf. further the parallels in Genesis 26.3; Exodus 2.24; Leviticus 26.42; Psalm^LXX 104.8-9; 105.45; Micah 7.20; 4 Baruch 6.18; for the holiness of the covenant, see 1 Maccabees 1.15, 63; Jeremiah 3.16^LXX; Daniel^Theodotion 11.28, 30). Without a reference being made to a specific one of the aforementioned Old Testament texts, Luke thus has Zechariah also interpret the salvific initiative taken by God with its christological center as a realization of the covenant promises and as an act of the covenant faithfulness of God. Through the statements in v. 69 (Jesus as Messiah), v. 70 (prophets), and vv. 72-73a (covenant), the slope of the Benedictus up to this point is carried by a theological substructure that Luke then expresses again in Acts 3.24-26 (see also 3.21) (cf. Vogel 1996, 346).

73b-75 The sentence is continued and concluded with another infinitive construction (see at 1:67-79 above). Comparable sentence structures as in vv. 73-74 (δίδωμι + *dativus commodi* + infinitive) are found, e.g., in Numbers 21.23; 1 Samuel 24.8; 2 Chronicles 20.10; Malachi 2.5. Thematically the concern is with the goal that God wants to reach with his saving intervention on behalf of his people for it (ἡμῖν).

According to **74** the goal is that Israel be placed in position to worship its God without disturbance and without interference from exterior enemies and thus to realize its purpose as God's people (cf. Deuteronomy 10.12; 11.13; Joshua 22.5; 24.14). Once again the Exodus tradition is probably actualized (cf. e.g., Exodus 4.23; 7.16, 26; 8.16). Here λατρεύειν certainly should not be understood in the narrow cultic sense (so Wiefel; S. C. Farris 1981, 138), but designates in a comprehensive way the entirety of Israel's orientation of her existence, which is exclusively directed to God (cf. Luke 2.37; Acts 24.14; 26.7; 27.23; see also Green).

75 This semantic orientation of the worship of God is now confirmed and given a characterizing specification. Here ἐνώπιον αὐτοῦ cannot be dependent on λατρεύειν (so, e.g., R. E. Brown 1993, 372; Mittmann-Richert

1996, 218), for the relevant valence of the verb is already occupied by
αὐτῷ (apart from this, λατρεύειν is connected with ἐνώπιον neither in the
Septuagint nor in Hellenistic-Jewish literature). Rather, the preposition
must be related to the modal specification ἐν ὁσιότητι καὶ δικαιοσύνῃ and
wants to express that in this phrase God's assessment of Israel's λατρεύειν
is pronounced (cf. the attestations and literature on vv. 6, 15). ὁσιότης and
δικαιοσύνη with their cognates are attested as a lexical pair in the whole
environment of the New Testament (e.g., Deuteronomy 9.5; Psalm^LXX
144.17; Wisdom of Solomon 9.3; Philo, *De sacrificiis Abelis et Caini* 57;
De specialibus legibus 1.304; *De virtutibus* 47; *De Abrahamo* 208; Greek
Apocalypse of Enoch 106.18; Plato, *Protagoras* 333b; Plutarch, *Moralia*
857a; Marcus Aurelius 12.1; Ephesians 4.24; cf. also the thematic discussions about the relations between the concepts in Plato, *Protagoras*
331a–3; *Euthyphro* 10e–12e). Beyond this, both terms also stand for the
traditional canon of those two virtues (cf. Dihle 1968; K. Berger 1972,
143ff) whose complementary dualism describes the entirety of human
behavior, first, with respect to the God relation and, second, with reference to the relation to one's fellow humans (cf. e.g., Dionysius of Halicarnassus, *Antiquitates romanae* 4.9.2; Plutarch, *Demetrius* 24.10; Marcus
Aurelius 7.66; Philo of Alexandria regards the entire law as summarized
in these two virtues; cf. *De specialibus legibus* 2.63 [cited at 10.27]). This
is all thoroughly Jewish of course, and yet Luke expresses this hope for
salvation in such a way that it is opened toward the Christian communities
and includes the Christian orientation of existence (cf. just Acts 24.14). In
this way he sets a clear signal of the unbroken salvation-historical continuity between the salvation hopes of Israel and the Christian communities
of his present. In them the people of God—mediated through the "horn of
salvation" raised up in the house of David (v. 69)—has found its purpose.

   76-78a Luke now has Zechariah look into the future and describe
the role that his son will play in the realization of God's plan of salvation. For this purpose Luke places genre-specific elements of a birthday
poem (*Genethliakon*) in Zechariah's mouth (cf. Erdmann 1932, 41–42; K.
Berger 1984b, 1197–98; Zeller 1992, 104ff).

   76 The particle δέ marks the new start, while καί places the child in
the series of prophets from v. 70 (cf. Lambrecht 2005a). At first the concern is with the status that is bestowed upon the child by God (cf. at v. 32
and 1/3 Ezra 4.42). προφήτης ὑψίστου is a context-dependent (cf. v. 32)
analogously coined phrase to προφήτης τοῦ θεοῦ/κυρίου (e.g., 1 Kings
18.22; 22.7; 2 Kings 3.11; 5.3^LXX; 2 Maccabees 15.14; Sirach 46.13; Josephus, *Antiquitates judaicae* 8.402; 10.92). Within the literary context, the
title 'prophet of the Most High' receives a threefold referential function.
(a) John is connected via the key word 'prophet' to the series of prophets

mentioned in v. 70, and with him this series is concluded at the same time (see also 16.16), for after him comes only the Lord (v. 76b); this corresponds to the expectation that was connected with the return of Elijah (see at v. 17). At the same time, the distinctiveness of the prophetic function of the Baptist is based on this (see also at 7.26-27). *(b)* The phrasing points to v. 32, where it says of Jesus that he will be called 'Son of the Most High.' The interlacing of difference and commonality is not meant to demote the Baptist in relation to Jesus but to express that both are assigned a different role in the one salvation plan of God. *(c)* The designation takes up the prophet typology from vv. 15c-16 and expresses it in a nutshell. This incorporation is continued in v. 76b, where the eschatological function of being a forerunner before the coming of God is taken over from v. 17a. The motif of the preparation of the way, which also shines through in v. 17c, comes from the synoptic Baptist tradition, while at the same time, Luke blends here the quotation from Malachi 3.1 (Mark 1.2; Luke 7.27 par. Matthew 11.10) with the quotation from Isaiah 40.3 (Mark 1.3parr.). With κύριος Luke certainly means God (see also at v. 17); that John then becomes *de facto* the forerunner of Jesus makes this statement into a characteristic feature of the Lukan Christology.

77 The infinitive substantivized with τοῦ indicates what the preparation of the way with which John is entrusted consists in. As in the description of the prophetic commission through Gabriel (vv. 16-17), the task of putting in order Israel's relation to God also falls to him according to the words of his father—"to give knowledge of salvation" here corresponds with "to turn to the Lord, their God" (v. 16) and refers to the baptism of repentance proclaimed by John (3.3; Acts 10.37; 13.24). Therefore, γνῶσις must be understood as a conversion term here (cf. R. Bultmann, ThWNT 1: 697.35ff; 701.14ff; 703.54ff; for the phrasing γνῶσίν τινος διδόναι ["to give knowledge of something"], cf. Wisdom of Solomon 7.17; 10.10; Barnabas 21.5). The phrasing ἐν ἀφέσει ἁμαρτιῶν αὐτῶν is then taken again from the synoptic Baptist tradition (cf. Mark 1.4 par. Luke 3.3; apart from Matthew 26.28; Colossians 1.4, it is otherwise attested only in Luke within the New Testament: Luke 24.47; Acts 2.38; 5.31; 10.43; 13.38; 26:18; outside the New Testament it is found in Philo, *De vita Mosis* 2.147; *De specialibus legibus* 1.190). It is dependent on σωτηρία and indicates the means by which salvation comes about.

The concluding expression in **78a** refers to v. 77 and specifies the enabling basis (διά + accusative; cf. BDR §222.2) for the salvific activity of the Baptist. Because God is merciful and full of compassion, he makes repentance possible for sinners and announces to them the remission of their sins. σπλάγχνα (literally: the innards; cf. H. Köster, ThWNT 7: 548ff; Spicq 1994, III: 273ff) is a metaphor for human emotionality and is often used in the sense of mercy and compassion. The phrasing σπλάγχνα ἐλέους is found in Testament of Zebulun 7.3; 8.2, 6 as a virtue of the pious (see also 1QS I, 22; II, 1; 4Q403 1 I, 23; 4Q405 3 II, 15; Colossians 3.12: σπλάγχνα οἰκτιρμοῦ). Viewed as a whole, the theological conception expressed in vv. 77-78a finds its closest parallel, also in terms of language, in Prayer of Manasseh 7: "You are the Lord, long-suffering, compassionate, full of mercy (εὔσπλαγχνος, πολυέλεος) . . . for you, God, have promised forgiveness from repentance (μετανοίας ἄφεσιν) to sinners, and in the fullness of your mercy you have appointed repentance (μετάνοια) for sinners unto salvation (εἰς σωτηρίαν)."

78b-79 The relative pronoun refers to σπλάγχνα, and the reading ἐπεσκέψατο, which is attested in numerous manuscripts (ℵ² A C D and others), should be explained as an adjustment to the aorist of the same verb in v. 68b. It is conspicuous that in the third part of the Benedictus the metaphorical character of the language skyrockets in density, which finds expression primarily in the fact that, unlike in the two preceding parts, a metonym (ἀνατολή) appears as the subject. With regard to the question of the semantic field of the source domain, on account of the specification of origin (ἐξ ὕψους) and the imagery of v. 79a ("appear," "darkness," "shadow"), one should more likely assume heavenly light phenomena (e.g., Isaiah 60.19; Greek Apocalypse of Enoch 18.15; Plutarch, *Moralia* 355b; Matthew 2.2, 9) than growth processes (e.g., Genesis 19.15; Ezekiel 16.7[LXX]; Psalms of Solomon 5.9).

The terminology is also already used metaphorically in early Judaism. In Zechariah 3.8; 6.12 ἀνατολή is a messianic title (cf. in this sense also Psalm[LXX] 131.17: ἐξανατελῶ κέρας τῷ Δαυίδ ["I will cause a horn for David to sprout up"]; Jeremiah 23.5; Numbers 24.17 and the receptions of this text in CD VII, 18–20; Testament of Levi 18.3; Testament of Judah 24.1. Philo, *De confusione linguarum* 62–63 interprets Zechariah 6.12 in relation to the Logos); syntagmatic metaphors are especially widespread: Malachi 3.20 (for the God-fearers the sun of righteousness will arise); Psalm 72.7 (righteousness and abundance of peace); Isaiah 60.1 (the δόξα of the Lord); Testament of Simeon 7.1 (τὸ σωτήριον τοῦ θεοῦ out of Levi and Judah; see also Testament of Dan 5.10; Testament of Naphtali 8.2; Testament of Gad 8.1; Testament of Zebulun 9.8: the κύριος himself as light of righteousness); Matthew 4.16 (modified quotation from Isaiah 9.1). The Babylonian king oracle conveyed in Dölger 1925, 152 reaches back even farther, though the "rising" here does not take place "from on high": "(From the house) he will shine forth. (From the) house he will become great. A king without equal. As the rising of the sun he will shine forth."

The semantic breadth of this metaphorical usage should warn one against exclusively asking about the reference of ἀνατολή in v. 78b in an allegorical manner. When this is done, it is usually assumed that Luke wanted to refer here to Jesus as the Davidic Messiah (so, in addition to most recent commentators, e.g., S. C. Farris 1981; Mittmann-Richert 1996, 121ff; Strauss 1995, 103ff; contrast, e.g., Zahn; Radl 1996, 125ff: God; Gathercole 2005: a preexistent, heavenly Messiah figure; see also Nolland). Although Luke refers here in a comprehensive way to the salvation event that accompanies the proclamation of Jesus (cf. the taking up again of ἐπισκέψεσθαι in Luke 7.16; 19.44; see also Tannehill 1986, I: 87), the intensional meaning of the imagery should not be overplayed. Thus, this imagery expresses that with Jesus God's salvation appears from heaven among his people. The use of ἐξ ὕψους in the Septuagint additionally suggests that one should not treat this expression as an appositional attribute of ἀνατολή but rather connect it with ἐπισκέψεσθαι. As in Psalm^{LXX} 17.17 (= 2 Samuel 22.17); 101.20; 143.7, it designates the origin of the salvation coming from God (see also Sirach 16.17; Lamentations 1.13).

To sum up, ἀνατολή refers to the sending of Jesus; significatively the term designates the salvation coming from God; and tradition-historically it is connected to Jewish light imagery (darkness is unsalvation [cf. v. 79a], light is salvation; see O. Böcher, *TRE* 21: 90ff). The fact that there is talk here not of 'light' in general but in a characterizing manner of its 'rising' could be connected with the semantic connotations of this term, for it marks the transition from darkness to light (the rising of the sun dispels the darkness) and in this way accentuates the sending of Jesus pointedly as the perceptible *beginning* of the eschatic time of salvation. The connection with ἐπισκέψεσθαι, which does not fit with this image but belongs in another context (see at v. 68 above), is a catachresis, which occurs frequently when metaphors are used.

In **79** the salvific consequences for Israel are described. Initially, the first infinitive in v. 79a, which picks up the description of God's saving intervention on behalf of his people in Psalm 107.10, 14, remains entirely within the image. Isaiah 9.1 also portrays Israel's experience of salvation with recourse to this imagery (cf. also the changes to this text in Matthew 4.16). To this corresponds also the verb ἐπιφαίνειν. It belongs to the semantic field of ἀνατολή (cf. τῆς κατὰ τὸν ἥλιον ἀνατολῆς ἐπιφαινομένης ["as the rising (of the sun) came into appearance"] in Polybius 3.113.1; 11.22.6), but its metaphorical reference describes here, as elsewhere too, "the experienceable intervention of God on behalf of his worshippers" (Lührmann 1971, 195–96). Verse 79d indicates the goal of the salvific action. The metaphor of 'way' indicates that the concern here is with Israel's behavior (cf. F. Hauck, ThWNT 5: 50ff). The genitive phrase ὁδὸς εἰρήνης stands only indirectly in connection with the reproach word of Isaiah 59.8—it would be more likely to assume a connection to Isaiah 41.3^LXX (διελεύσεται ἐν εἰρήνῃ ἡ ὁδὸς τῶν ποδῶν αὐτοῦ ["the way of his feet will come along in peace"]; see also v. 2a); we are probably dealing with a construction analogous to phrasings such as ὁδὸς ἀληθείας ("way of truth"; Genesis 24.48; Tobit 1.3; Psalm^LXX 118.30; Wisdom of Solomon 5.6: "We strayed from the way of truth and the light of righteousness did not illuminate us, and the sun did not rise for us [οὐκ ἀνέτειλεν ἡμῖν]"; 2 Peter 2.2), ὁδὸς ζωῆς ("way of life"; Psalm^LXX 15.11; Proverbs 5.6; 6.23; 15.24; Jeremiah 21.8; Acts 2.28) and the like, in which the genitive always characterizes the nature of the way, i.e., way of life (*genitivus qualitatis*). Thus, the goal of God's saving action is to make possible a behavior for Israel that is in accordance with behavior for which God has promised salvation and that corresponds to Israel's identity as the people of God. The use of εἰρήνη in Luke 19.42; Acts 10.36 shows clearly that Luke thinks, of course, of the proclamation of Jesus here. Viewed from this perspective, the 'way of peace' upon which Israel is to be led is nothing other than the acceptance of the proclamation of Jesus.

80 With the summary, which corresponds compositionally to the exposition of vv. 5-7, Luke ends the series of episodes that he had dated during the reign of Herod the Great (v. 5). He abandons the rhythmization of the narrative through months (cf. vv. 24, 26, 56) and encompasses a period of time that is to be measured by years (accordingly he uses imperfects). In v. 80c he even transcends the temporal framework marked out in v. 5, namely the time of Herod the Great's reign (Luke also proceeds in this way in 2.40, 52; 24.53), and in 3.1-2 he will take up the narrative thread again after the interruption of chapter 2.

The note about the growing up of the child is oriented to Judges 13.24-25 (Samson) and 1 Samuel 2.21, 26 (Samuel; see also 3.19). The plural ἐν ταῖς ἐρήμοις is here, as in 5.6 (diff. Mark 1.45: ἐπ᾽ ἐρήμοις τόποις); 8.29 (see also Sirach 9.7; Isaiah 5.17; Ezekiel 36.33; Malachi 1.4), an elliptical expression for ἐν ἐρήμοις τόποις ("in isolated places"; Josephus, *Contra Apionem* 1.306, 308, 314; cf. BDR §241.1). The concern is not with a "wilderness" in the actual sense of the word; rather, the word ἔρημος initially designates nothing more than an unsettled area. It does not follow from this that John spent his youth in Qumran (so, e.g., Fitzmyer). The concluding formula is probably also elliptical, for ἀνάδειξις, etc., is not otherwise connected with πρός. The reference of this term to a person suggests that it should be understood here in the frequently attested technical sense of the installation into an office (e.g., Plutarch, *Tiberius et Caius Gracchus* 33.7; Polybius 15.25, 11; 2 Maccabees 9.25; 10.11; Luke 10.1;

cf. Bikerman 1937; Spicq 1994, I: 103–4). The installation is narratively realized in 3.2; for the narrative technique, see at v. 56.

2.1-39(40-52): ". . . when Quirinius ruled over Syria"

Luke now starts anew and in doing so expands the political-geographical horizon in which he places the narrated events (see at 1.5). The literary configuration is comparable in some respects to chapter 1. After an exposition (vv. 1-3) there follows a series of episodes (vv. 4-39) that are then concluded with a summary (vv. 40-52) that leads the narrative beyond the temporal framework established in the exposition. With this, however, the commonalities already end. For apart from the fact that Luke enriches the concluding summary (vv. 40, 52) with an embedded episode (vv. 41-52), the spatial-temporal organization of the episode sequence differs from chapter 1. To be sure, Luke also sets time structuring signals (vv. 21, 22) in this chapter, but, first, he counts by days here (in chapter 1 the episodes were always separated by multiple months; cf. 1.24b, 26, 56), and, second, he provides merely an epilogue (v. 21) whose relation to what precedes is comparable with 1.24a. Beyond this, the structuring of the text in chapter 2 is determined by topographical specifications. This is already recognizable in the fact that the entire episode sequence is framed by an *inclusio* of two travel notes that correspond with each other—namely, Joseph's journey from Nazareth in Galilee to Bethlehem (v. 4) and the family's return to this same place from Jerusalem (v. 39b). In between, the scene changes in v. 22 from Bethlehem to Jerusalem, so that two spatial points of adhesion result from the episode sequence of chapter 2—in vv. 4-21 Bethlehem and in vv. 22-39 Jerusalem. Luke also organizes his narrative in this same way in 4.14-30, 31-44 (Nazareth and Capernaum) and in 7.1-10, 11-50 (Capernaum and Nain).

2.1-3: Exposition

¹But it happened in those days that an ordinance went out from Caesar Augustus that the whole world should be registered. ²This registration took place for the first time when Quirinius ruled over Syria. ³And everyone went to be registered, each in one's own town.

These verses correspond with 1.5-7, and they likewise have the function of placing the narrated event in its historical context. But unlike what we find there, the main characters are not introduced here, but in precisely the opposite manner, in a wide setting of the angle of narration, the general contemporary-historical context is sketched, which motivates the action of the individual persons upon which the narrative perspective then focuses from v. 4 onward.

The ἀπογραφή that Luke speaks of here is also mentioned in Josephus (cf. *Antiquitates judaicae* 17.355; 18.1–3; 20.102; *Bellum judaicum* 2.117–18; 7.253); in *Antiquitates judaicae* 18.26 Josephus dates it to the thirty-seventh year after the battle at Actium (31 BCE), i.e., in 6/7 CE. It was implemented after Archelaus was deposed by the Romans and his area of rule was allocated to the Roman province Syria. In the aforementioned passage (see also *Bellum judaicum* 2.433) Josephus reports that Quirinius, as newly named legate of the province of Syria, received the mandate to take a census to determine the value of the property of the population (ἀποτίμησις) and to sell the possessions of Archelaus (cf. *Antiquitates judaicae* 17.355; 18.1, 26); on Quirinius, cf. M. Wolter, *RGG⁴* 6: 1871). An analogy to the phrasing ἡγεμονεύοντος τῆς Συρίας Κυρηνίου is found in Josephus, *Bellum judaicum* 1.20 (after the death of Herod the people fell into rebellion Αὐγούστου . . . Ῥωμαίων ἡγεμονεύοντος ["when Augustus ruled over the Romans"]; see also *Antiquitates judaicae* 15.345; *Vita* 347; Luke 3.1). In *Antiquitates judaicae* 18.3–4 Josephus writes that the population of Judea was upset about the news of the intended registrations (ἐπὶ ταῖς ἀπογραφαῖς) but then complied, while a resistance movement led by Judas the Galilean violently fought against the action (see also Acts 5.37; Josephus, *Antiquitates judaicae* 20.102; *Bellum judaicum* 2.117–118, 433; 7.253–255; Judas demanded μὴ ποιεῖσθαι τὰς ἀπογραφάς ["that they carry out no registrations"], 7.253; see Hengel 1976, 79ff).

When Luke adds the observation that under Quirinius a census was organized for the first time (cf. Wolter 2000a) also in Judea, this makes good sense insofar as we know (cf. Brunt 1981, 164) that in the early imperial period the custom arose of making a census in newly established provinces as one of the first administrative measures (Ausbüttel 1998, 78: "initial census"). With its help the Roman provincial administration wanted to obtain a view of the conditions of the assets and possessions of the provinces so that they could fix on this basis the direct taxes (i.e., the head tax and land tax). This so-called provincial census recorded only the *peregrini*; therefore, it may not be confused with the census of the citizens of the empire that Augustus carried out in 28 BCE, 8 BCE, and 14 CE (cf. *Res Gestae* 8; Suetonius, *Divus Augustus* 27.5; see also W. Kubitschek, PRE 3/2: 1918–19; Braunert 1980, 214ff). These measures could be repeated in different extents (cf. Ausbüttel 1998, 79; on Egypt, see Palme 1993; 1994). A valuable source is the property declaration of Babatha, which was handed over on the occasion of a census carried out in 127 CE (see Rosen 1995). Although Babatha lived in Maoza in Zoara (a few kilometers south of the Dead Sea), she handed over her declaration in Rabbath Moab, which was forty kilometers away (P. Babatha 16 in Lewis/Yadin/Greenfield 1989). This means that, in contradiction to v. 1b, a provincial census was never carried out in all the provinces at the same time (see also Schürer 1973–1987, I: 407ff; Palme 1999). A new survey of the provincial censuses known in 1981 is provided by Brunt 1981, 171–72. See further at v. 3.

1 ἐν ταῖς ἡμέραις ἐκείναις does not refer back to 1.5 but resumes from 1.80 and thus dates the narrated events in the time of the growing up of the Baptist (cf. the analogous use of this temporal specification with reference to a preceding summary in 1 Samuel 4.1; 2 Chronicles 32.24; Matthew 3.1; Mark 1.9; see in detail Wolter 1998b, 414). Thus, the temporal distance between the events narrated in chapter 1 and the newly opened narrative collecting basin remains unspecified (the temporal schema of Dillmann 2000, 82, which has the birth of Jesus take place nine months after Gabriel's visit to Mary, founders on this fact). Therefore, there is also no reason to replace "Quirinius" with "Quintilius (Varus)" (*pace* Rist 2005). In v. 1b the issuing of an ordinance (for the phrasing, cf. Daniel^Theodotion 2.13) by Augustus is named as the point that stimulates the action. Luke transliterates here the Latin designation *augustus* "consecrated, elevated, majestic"—in Greek σεβαστός (cf. Acts 25.21, 25)—and uses it as a personal name (see also Josephus, *Bellum judaicum* 1.20; 2.168, 215). The specification of the name corresponds to the naming of Herod the Great in 1.5 and something analogous also applies to the political-geographical specifications: "Judea" as Herodian area of rule (1.5) corresponds with πᾶσα ἡ οἰκουμένη as the supposed scope of the ordinance (v. 1c). This information too is not correct historically (see above), and thus one will not err if one again ascribes a reader-guiding function to the specification. While 1.5 was concerned to characterize what followed consciously as a continuation of the history of Israel, it is now signaled to the readers that they are dealing with events with world-historical significance (see also Acts 26.26). However, the two perspectives may not be played off against each other, for through the embedding of the announcement of Jesus's birth in the chronology of Elisabeth's pregnancy (1.26-38[56]) Luke establishes an indissoluble interlocking between them. Out of the history of Israel an event grows that has a universal reach, or, to put it more precisely, through Jesus the history of Israel obtains world-historical significance. The continuation will show that in this way it is precisely also the ruler of the whole *orbis terrarum* ("circle of the earth") who becomes an instrument of God's plan of salvation (for οἰκουμένη as a component of the ruler ideology, cf. 1/3 Ezra 2.2; Josephus, *Bellum judaicum* 1633: the Roman Caesar as ὁ τῆς οἰκουμένης προστάτης ["patron of the whole world"]; OGIS II: 668.5: Nero as σωτὴρ καὶ εὐεργέτης τῆς οἰκουμένης ["savior and benefactor of the whole world"]; cf. with additional attestations O. Michel, ThWNT 5: 159; H. Balz, *EWNT* 2: 1231).

2 The structure of the sentence is somewhat obscure. But in all prob-ability αὕτη [ἡ] ἀπογραφή is the subject, πρώτη ἐγένετο is the predicate, and the *genitivus absolutus* ἡγεμονεύοντος τῆς Συρίας Κυρηνίου speci-fies the period of time in which this first census was carried out. Thus, Luke does not want to say that the concern is with the first of a number of ἀπογραφαί that Quirinius carried out (so Wiefel), but that this was the first census in Judea and that it took place when Quirinius was procu-rator (on the understanding of πρώτη, cf. Wolter 2000a). ἀπογραφή and ἀπογράφεσθαι (v. 1) are administrative technical terms and designate the registering in a list, the setting up of such a list, or the list itself (cf. Preisigke 1925–1931, I: 170ff; Preisigke/Kiessling/Rübsam 1969–1971, 30; E. Plümacher, *EWNT* 1: 301ff). Luke explains what is concretely in mind with the help of a narrator comment (cf. Sheeley 1992, 102ff) that informs the readers about the historical and chronological context of the events. This information has the function of clearly distancing the follow-ing sequence of episodes chronologically from the time of the reign of Herod the Great. Between his death and the provincial census carried out under Quirinius lay a time period of about ten years in which Herod's son Archelaus ruled as ethnarch over Judea, Samaria, and Idumea (cf. Jose-phus, *Antiquitates judaicae* 17.342; see also at 19.11–27). A contradiction to the relative chronology of the Lukan presentation does not arise through this (see on v. 1). The longstanding debate over this problem (cf. e.g., the surveys in R. E. Brown 1993, 547ff; Porter 2002) started, to this extent, from false presuppositions. Neverthless, there remains, of course, an irrec-oncilable contradiction to the dating of the birth of Jesus during the reign of Herod the Great by Matthew.

3 The information that everyone had to go "to their own town" to give their declaration of property value, which Luke interprets in v. 4 to mean that Joseph, together with his betrothed, had to travel from Nazareth to Bethlehem because he was descended from David, cannot be reconciled with the known census arrangements for three reasons:

(a) The registration took place not at the family's place of origin but at the place of the office of the responsible tax authority. And so a woman obligated to participate in the census who lived in Maoza in Zoara (a few kilometers south of the Dead Sea) handed over the ἀπογραφή of P. Babatha 16 (see above) in Rabbath Moab, which was about forty kilometers away.

(b) The institution, known from the province of Egypt, of the κατ' οἰκίαν ἀπογραφή ("registration by house"; see Hombert/Préaux 1952; Palme 1993, 2ff), to which reference is often made for the interpretation of v. 3b, because it can likewise make a journey necessary, is accompanied by completely different spec-ifications for implementation. Those obligated to participate in the census, who

currently reside outside of their main place of residence, at which they are registered and obligated to pay taxes, are exhorted to return there; P. Lond. III 904, 24: εἰς τὰ ἑαυτῶν ἐφέστια ("to their own hearths"); *BGU* 159.7 and elsewhere: εἰς τὰς ἰδίας (οἰκίας) ("to their own [houses]"); cf. Rostovtzeff 1910, 209–10; Palme 1993, 12ff. Thus, the circumstances here are precisely reversed vis-à-vis the event described by Luke.

(c) Joseph and Mary lived in Nazareth, i.e., in the tetrarchy of Herod Antipas (ruled 4 BCE to 39 CE). They were therefore not affected by the provincial census of 6/7 CE, which was carried out in Judea. In order to still be able to motivate the journey to Bethlehem, one must introduce the fanciful and improbable auxiliary hypothesis that Joseph possessed an inherited plot of land in Bethlehem or its environs (Zahn; Rosen 1995, 12; Smith 2000, 289–90). But even this would not yet explain Mary's participation in the journey.

If one nevertheless wants to allow the realia background an influence on the Lukan presentation, it can for this reason at best be said that the information that Augustus decreed an empire-wide census could have its background in the fact that the censuses in the imperial provinces were always carried out by the respective governors only on the basis of a special imperial empowerment from the emperor (cf. Braunert 1980, 219, 223–24; Kienast 1982, 332–33). Beyond this, Luke could also have known that an ἀπογραφή could possibly require a journey, because the people obligated to the census had to appear personally before the authorized authority. He uses this information in order to be able to motivate Joseph's and Mary's journey to Bethlehem. His goal is to reconcile two different traditions with each other—that Jesus was born in Bethlehem and that he came from Nazareth.

2.4-21: Bethlehem

⁴But Joseph also went up from Galilee from the town of Nazareth to Judea to the town of David, which is called Bethlehem, for he came from the house and lineage of David, ⁵in order to let himself be registered with Mary his betrothed; she was pregnant. ⁶But it happened, while she was there, that the days for her to give birth were fulfilled. ⁷And she bore a son, the first born, and wrapped him in swaddling clothes and lay him in a feed trough, for there was no place for them in the accommodation.

⁸And shepherds were in the same region in the field and kept night watches over their flocks. ⁹And an angel of the Lord came to them, and the glory of the Lord shone around them, and they fell into great fear. ¹⁰And the angel said to them, "Fear not; for look, I gospel to you

a great joy, which will be to the whole people: [11]for unto you a Savior was born today—namely, the Messiah, the Lord—in the town of David. [12]And this (is) the sign for you: You will find a child wrapped in swaddling clothes and lying in a feed trough." [13]And suddenly there was with the angel the multitude of the heavenly host, which praised God and said,

[14]"Glory to God in the highest and peace upon earth for people of the good favor!"

[15]And it happened when the angels went forth from them into heaven that the shepherds said to one another, "Let us go indeed to Bethlehem and see this thing which has happened (and) which the Lord has announced to us." [16]And they went on their way in haste and found Mary and Joseph and the child, which lay in the feed trough. [17]But when they saw (it), they reported the content of that which had been said to them about this child. [18]And all who heard it wondered at what was said to them by the shepherds. [19]But Mary kept all these things—whose meaning she understood—in her heart. [20]And the shepherds returned—praising and lauding God for everything which they had heard and seen, just as it had been said to them. [21]And when the eight days had become complete to circumcise him, then they called him Jesus, which name had been called by the angel before he was conceived in the womb.

The narrative complex is composed of three scenes. In vv. 4-7 Luke narrates how Mary gives birth to her first son in Bethlehem. In vv. 8-14 the birth and future significance of the child is proclaimed to a group of shepherds located in the vicinity of Bethlehem. In vv. 15-20 Luke brings together the protagonists of the first two scenes. Verse 21 concludes the birth story. The stress undoubtedly lies on the appearance story in vv. 8-14. The narrative degree of compression is smallest here and the portion of direct discourse is the highest (outside of this part the narrative figures speak only in v. 15b). At the same time the episode sequence in vv. 4-20 form a self-enclosed narrative unity. This is established by the fact that the individual parts of the text are connected with one another in several ways, namely through proforms (ἐκεῖ, v. 6; αὐτή, v. 8) and through analepses (σπαργανοῦν and φάτνη [v. 12/v. 7]; Bethlehem as city of David [v. 15/v. 11/v. 4]; τὸ βρέφος κείμενον ἐν τῇ φάτνῃ [v. 16/v. 12/v. 7]; the ῥῆμα spoken to the shepherds [vv. 15, 16, 19/vv. 10-12]; the indirect acclamation in v. 20 with its reference to vv. 10-12, 16).

In **4-5** Luke focuses the presentation, which was previously kept broad, on a single case. To be sure, the action-determining structure of the verbs was taken over from v. 3 (cf. ἐπορεύοντο . . . ἀπογράφεσθαι with ἀνέβη . . . ἀπογράψασθαι), but now the comprehensive pronouns are replaced by individualizing personal names and the *Aktionsart* changes from iterative imperfect to the punctiliar aorist. Luke introduces Joseph into the narrative with only his personal name and without further specification. He thus presupposes that the readers already know him, and in this way he refers them back to 1.26-38. The other topographical (Galilee, Nazareth; see 1.26) and personal information (origin ἐξ οἴκου καὶ πατριᾶς of David; this is a hendiadys, cf. Numbers 1.44; 3.24; 18.1; 25.14-15; Joshua 22.14; 1 Chronicles 23.11; 24.6; and elsewhere) also serves this purpose. It is surprising that Bethlehem is regarded as "David's city," for in the Old Testament and in Josephus only Zion or Jerusalem is designated in this way (e.g., 2 Samuel 5.7, 9; Josephus, *Antiquitates judaicae* 7.65). Bethlehem was, however, David's place of origin (see 1 Samuel 16.1-13; 20.6: "his city"), and according to Micah 5.1, the future messianic king should also be born there (see also John 7.42; Bill. I: 83). This identification is apparently such a given for Luke that he presupposes it also for the shepherds; cf. v. 15 ("Bethlehem") after v. 11 ("in the city of David").

Although in **5** Luke adds more in passing that Joseph was accompanied by Mary, the actual goal of the presentation thus far resides here, for actually only Mary—and not Joseph—must come to Bethlehem if Jesus is to be born there. But a journey there can be made plausible for her only as Joseph's companion, for only he—and not Mary—is of Davidic descent. Thus, the sketch of the contemporary-historical background in vv. 1-3(4) has no other function than to construct a plausible scenario for Mary's journey to Jerusalem. Luke has no interest in a correspondence with the actual basic knowledge of the readers, which was already seriously strained in v. 4. This is also recognizable in the fact that in what follows he does not devote another word to the census as the actual reason for the journey (see also 2.39 and at 1.9).

Mary's identification as Joseph's betrothed points back to 1.27 and informs the reader about the fact that in this respect nothing has changed since then. However, the statement that Mary is pregnant is all the more surprising. This information corresponds in a tension-filled way with Mary's designation as a virgin in 1.27. Only now do the readers learn that the announcement in 1.31 has been fulfilled (see also Spitta 1906, 284). Thus, both the how and the point in time of the conception remain unnarrated, and Luke again leaves it to the readers to fill out this narrative gap with the help of their imagination. And this should no longer be difficult for them on the basis of what follows.

6 During Mary's stay in Bethlehem, the time of her pregnancy ends (for the phrasing, see at 1.23), and accordingly Luke wants the readers to assume that the unnarrated time of conception fell in the time period of "those days" of the growing up of John the Baptist (1.80), to which he refers in v. 1. It falls in the intervening period, which separates the two narrative collecting basins of chapter 1 and chapter 2 (cf. Wolter 1998b, 416). In this way Luke has masterfully resolved a difficult problem of presentation narratively and theologically (see also at 1.35), for he places the virginal conception through the Holy Spirit in an open space and preserves its non-narratability and mysterious character in precisely this way.

7 The account of the birth of Jesus is unjustly described as sparse and terse (e.g., Nolland; Schürmann; Schweizer), for there is not a single child in the whole Bible that receives such extensive narrative attention right after his birth as Jesus does. The explicit statement that the child is the first born receives its good sense from the narrative distance extending over several years that lies between the birth announcement in 1.31 and its fulfillment (see above). It ensures that other births have not taken place in the meantime. In vv. 22-23 Luke uses this circumstance to be able to lead Jesus into the temple for the first time and document the Torah piety of his parents (see further there).

The fact that newborn children are wrapped in swaddling clothes was also a common practice in general in antiquity (Ezekiel 16.4 places it on a level with the cutting of the umbilical cord). Thus, Luke reports here something that is a completely normal, so that one must ask why he narrates this self-evident fact at all and how he wanted this to be understood. A plausible explanation is provided by the semantics of helplessness that is connected with the swaddling motif (Kügler 1995, 27; see also Schwemer 1994, 125–26). It is used, e.g., in Wisdom of Solomon 7.1, 4–5, to make clear that the king too is only a human being: "I am also mortal, a human being, who is like all. . . . ἐν σπαργάνοις and with care I was raised; for no king came differently into existence" (see also Plutarch, *Moralia* 638a: swaddling clothes are needed δι' ἀσθένειαν; Aeschylus, *Choephori* 755–56; *Agamemnon* 1606; Dio Chrysostom 6.16; Lucian of Samosata, *Dialogi deorum* 11.2; Apollodorus, *Bibliotheca* 3.10.2). Thus, the swaddling motif obtains a good sense with a view to Jesus's conception by the Spirit, for with the help of this communication of what was a given, Luke wants to express that although Jesus was conceived by the Spirit, he was nevertheless born as a completely normal human being, who shared the helplessness of all newborn children and was dependent on the care of others just like every other newborn child. In any case, neither here nor in v. 7c, d is Luke concerned to accentuate the lowliness of Jesus in contrast to the imperial claim of the Roman Caesar (so with many others, e.g., Schmithals 1973; Vögtle 1977, 86ff).

How Luke imagined the scene described in v. 7c, d cannot be determined with certainty. With φάτνη he means, with some certainty, a feed trough (the meaning 'stable' would also be possible, but this meaning is very unlikely here; cf. M. Hengel, ThWNT 9: 51–57). A φάτνη could be found inside or outside the house (the latter is presupposed in Luke 13.15). It could be movable, inset into the house wall, formed from clay, or cut into the rock (cf. Dalman 1964, VI: 286–87; M. Hengel, ThWNT 9: 54.9ff). Verse 7d does not intend to say that Jesus's parents were homeless (so e.g., R. E. Brown 1993, 3999; Radl 1996, 143n2); rather, Luke simply explains here why the newborn child had to be put down in such an unusual place (see also Dibelius 1953, 57–58). For a theological interpretation this narrative detail yields less than is usually assigned to it. There is neither a particular symbolism associated with feed troughs nor do they belong semantically to the shepherd milieu or to Bethlehem as the birth place of the Davidic Messiah (so, e.g., Dibelius 1953, 59; M. Hengel, ThWNT 9: 56; Radl 1996, 189; cf. against this just Luke 13.15). Lives of the Prophets 2.8 (the Egyptians "worship until today a virgin in the postpartum period and lay an infant [βρέφος] in a feed trough [φάτνη] and worship him [προσκυνοῦσι]") belongs with great probability to the posthistory of our text. Further, one may scarcely understand his placement in a feed trough as a pointer to the fact that Jesus is excluded from human society in the sense of Luke 9.58 and has therefore found his place only in the sphere of the animals (e.g., Marshall), for the explanation that Luke provides in v. 7d more likely identifies it as a solution to a problem that his *parents* had (οὐκ ἦν αὐτοῖς). Therefore, it is much more likely that Luke wanted the feed trough to be understood merely as an "uncommon place" (M. Hengel, ThWNT 9: 56) for putting to bed a newborn child, and therefore he can let it become a sign in v. 12. One also cannot rule out the possibility that Luke found v. 7c as an element of the tradition and in v. 7d provided it with a justification that was intended to provide a simple explanation for this detail (Radl 1996, 168).

The meaning of κατάλυμα is unclear only if one merely asks about the reference (cf. the overview in R. E. Brown 1993, 400). If, by contrast, one asks about the functional meaning of this term in the present context in light of its usual contextual usage, then a clear answer emerges. Time and again κατάλυμα designates a place where one stays temporarily, i.e., when one is on a journey and not at home (cf. e.g., Exodus 4.24; 1 Samuel 1.18^LXX; 2 Samuel 7.6 = 1 Chronicles 17.5; 1 Chronicles 28.13^LXX; Jeremiah 14.8; 40.12^LXX; Letter of Aristeas 181; Diodorus Siculus 36.13.2; Polybius 2.36.1; the denotation is different in every case, but the function is identical; see also LaVerdiere 1985, 552ff).

8-14 Form-critically we are dealing again with an appearance report. The features that are specific for this genre (see at 1.8-25) can also be identified here: *(a)* the recipients of the appearance become fearful (v. 9c);

(b) the exhortation μὴ φοβεῖσθε (v. 10a); *(c)* the speech of the appearing one (v. 10b-11), which is a birth announcement here (cf. Zeller 1992). The form is expanded by the mention of a sign (v. 12) and by a second appearance report (vv. 13-14).

8 The scene changes to the country. The shepherds are introduced as new narrative figures in a situation that is typical for them. They are situated in the open (cf. the speech of ποιμένες ἄγραυλοι in Homer, *Ilias* 18.162; Hesiod, *Theogonia* 26; Apollonius of Rhodes, *Argonautica* 4.317; see also Strabo 15.3.18) and keep the night watches over their herds. Whether Luke envisaged the shepherds in the immediate surroundings of Bethlehem does not necessarily emerge from the phrasing ἐν τῇ χώρᾳ τῇ αὐτῇ (cf. Burchard 1998, 332–33). Opinions differ with regard to the question of why Luke makes shepherds of all people the addressees of the birth announcement (cf. Dibelius 1953, 64ff; J. Jeremias, ThWNT 6: 489–90; Fitzmyer I: 395–96). Against the assumption, which is most prevalent today, that Luke actualizes the Old Testament David tradition here (cf. 1 Samuel 17.15; see also 16.11-13; Psalm 78.70-72) in order to point to Jesus's messiahship (e.g., Schürmann; Nolland) stands Marshall's objection, which is difficult to contradict: "it should be the child who is a shepherd, not the witnesses of its birth" (108). Therefore, it is more likely that Luke takes up here the *aurea aetas* expectation of Roman bucolic, as this is first attested in Virgil's Fourth Eclogue (see Wolter 2000b). This explanation is supported above all by the fact that Luke portrays the shepherds in the very situation of endangerment (see also Testament of Gad 1.3: "I . . . watched in the night the herds [ἐγὼ . . . ἐφύλαττον ἐν νυκτὶ τὸ ποίμνιον] and when a lion or a wolf . . . or any animal came, I pursued it . . ."), whose removal was expected from the golden age. The night watches over the flocks then become superfluous (cf. Calpurnius, *Eclogae* I: 37–42; see also Virgil, *Eclogae* IV: 22; Tibullus, *Elegiae* I: 10.9–10). Plus, the dawning of the golden age is also unveiled in the aforementioned Calpurnius text through a heavenly revelation. Here it is narrated that two shepherds discover an inscription on a tree trunk, which comes from Faunus, the god of the shepherds and farmers, and reveals Nero's ascension to power as the rebirth of the *aurea aetas* (42). It exhorts to rejoicing (*gaudete*; 36; see also 74: *exsultet quaecumque . . . gens* ["every people should rejoice"]) and speaks of the dawning of secure peace (*secura pax*; 42); cf. also Sibylline Oracles 3.372, where there is talk of the announcement of the time of salvation described in vv. 367–71: ὡς ἐν ἀγραύλοις ("as among field dwellers"; see H. Merkel, *JSHRZ* V/8: 1094).

9 In the New Testament only Luke uses ἐφίστημι for appearances of heavenly beings (Luke 2.4; Acts 12.7; 23.11). However, outside the New Testament it is frequently attested in similar contexts (e.g., Homer, *Ilias*

10.496; 23.105–6; Herodotus 7.14.1; Isocrates, *Orationes* 10.65; Diodorus Siculus 1.25.5; Josephus, *Antiquitates judaicae* 3.188; *IG* XIV: 1014.5; not, however, in the LXX). That the angelophany is accompanied by the earthly presence of the δόξα κυρίου elevates its significance far beyond the previously reported appearances. Luke will be able to report something comparable later only in the case of the transfiguration of Jesus (Luke 9.31-32) and the Christophanies (Acts 9.3; 22.6; 26.13). In the representation via his glory, no less than God himself is manifest upon earth. This, of course, evokes salvation-historical associations and raises this event to a level with the appearances of the כְּבוֹד יְהוָה in Israel's past, such as in the Exodus (Exodus 16.7, 10) and on Sinai (Exodus 24.16-17; Deuteronomy 5.24); but above all the readers will remember that the eschatological promises of salvation for Israel in Isaiah 35.2; 40.5; 60.1, 19 also involve the appearance of God's glory. It is therefore not surprising when the shepherds are seized by especially great fear in light of the unexpected encounter with God (cf. BDR §153.1; see also at 1.12).

10 The angel explains the genre-specific exhortation μὴ φοβεῖσθε (see at 1.13) by disclosing the intention of his proclamation. It is a joy-evoking event that he announces. This is represented by χαρὰ μεγάλη as a metonymy in the sense of the cause-effect relationship (cf. Lausberg 1973, §568.3).

The use of εὐαγγελίζεσθαι in this passage may be connected with the preference for using this verb and its cognates in the context of birth announcements (Zeller 1992, 127; e.g., Jeremiah 20.15; Theophrastus, *Characteres* 17.7: εὐαγγελίζεσθαι ὅτι υἱός σοι γέγονεν . . . ["to bring the joyful news: a son was born to you . . ."]; OGIS II: 458.41 [calendar inscription from Priene from 9 BCE]: ἦρξεν δὲ τῷ κόσμῳ τῶν δι' αὐτὸν εὐαγγελί[ων ἡ γενέθλιος] τοῦ θεοῦ ["the birthday of the god was for the world the beginning of the good tidings (proclaimed) on his account"]).

The relative sentence characterizes the content of the message that is to be passed on to the shepherds (cf. BDR §293.2b) by making χαρά an eschatic good of salvation (see also 1 Enoch 5.7, 9; 104.4; 2 Baruch 68.4; 73.1; John 16.20; Romans 14.17; 1 Peter 4.13). (πᾶς) ὁ λαός is used here in the same sense as in 1.68, 77. Thus, the shepherds become, on the one hand, recipients of a proclamation of salvation that applies to Israel (on the phrasing with ἔσται + dative, cf. e.g., Isaiah 11.16; Jeremiah 4.10; 23.17; 36.7[LXX]; Greek Apocalypse of Enoch 5.7), but, on the other hand, because of the *aurea aetas* semantic connected with them, they also represent the hopes of all humanity for universal peace. πᾶς ὁ λαός is a typically Lukan phrasing, for with the exception of Matthew 27.25; Hebrew 9.19

it is found within the New Testament only in Luke–Acts where it even occurs seventeen times.

11 The joyful event is the birth of the Savior for Israel. The *dativus commodi* ὑμῖν joins the shepherds with the whole people of God; in birth announcements the *dativus commodi* normally refers to the father or the parents (e.g., Judges 18.29; 2 Samuel 3.2; Jeremiah 20.15; Josephus, *Antiquitates judaicae* 3.87). That a child is born 'for' a people is known to us only in Plutarch, *Lycurgus* 3.4. Lycurgus presents his newly born nephew, whom he then additionally calls Χαρίλαος "joy of the people," to the public with the words "A king ὑμῖν γέγονεν (is born unto you), Spartans." But the linguistic form of this phrasing corresponds to those Old Testament texts in which there is talk of God "raising up" or "giving" a person as a σωτήρ 'for' Israel or the like: Judges 3.9, 15; 2 Ezra 19.27 (= Nehemiah 9.27); Isaiah 62.11^LXX; see also Testament of Gad 8.1; Acts 13.23. Here, the designation of Jesus with this predicate is not meant to be understood as a transfer of a typical designation of God to him, nor does Luke establish a targeted counterpoint to the imperial σωτήρ predications (cf. Karrer 2002), for they were not connected with a claim to exclusivity (cf. C.-W. Jung 2004, 7–176; K. H. Schelke, *EWNT* 3: 782: "Everyone who saves can be called savior [σ.]"). Although the σωτήρ designation increasingly assumes titular characteristics in the late writings of the New Testament (cf. John 4.42; Ephesians 5.23; 2 Timothy 1.10; Titus 1.4; 2.13; 3.6; 2 Peter 1.1, 11; 2.20; 3.2, 18; 1 John 4.14), in this passage it expresses through a noun no more than the function of Jesus; the readers learn nothing that they did not already know from 1.68ff (see also Strauss 1995, 113). The specification of the birth place (see v. 4; the Lukan shepherds know as a matter of course that Bethlehem is in view [see v. 15]) and a parenthetical explanation (with ὅς ἐστιν like, e.g., 12.1; 1 Corinthians 3.11; Galatians 3.16; Ephesians 1.14; 4.15; Acts 20.2) express that the newly born Savior is none other than the promised messianic king. σωτήρ is the topic, about whom a statement is made; χριστὸς κύριος is the comment, which defines the topic through the use of a predicate. The readers also already know this from 2.4 and 1.32. Luke now lets the significance of the birth of Jesus become known within the narrated world for the first time.

The juxtaposition of the two nominatives χριστὸς κύριος requires explanation (the variant χριστὸς κυρίου [β r¹] is too poorly attested to have a claim to originality; moreover, it is probably taken from v. 26 or 9.20—cf. the attestations mentioned at 2.26; in Lamentations 4.20 [Hebrew מְשִׁיחַ יְהוָה] χριστὸς κύριος is probably an error in the copying of ΧΡΙΣΤΟΣ K̄Ȳ which has been influenced by Luke 2.11). In Psalms of Solomon 17.32 (on the Messiah: "and he is a righteous king over them, taught by God, and in his days there is no unrighteousness in their midst, for all are holy, and their king is χριστὸς κύριος") יְהוָה מְשִׁיחַ should also be assumed as the Hebrew *Vorlage* and it should be emended to χριστὸς κυρίου against all preserved (Christian) Greek manuscripts (cf. Karrer 1991, 252n58 *pace* Hann 1985; see also Rowe 2006, 49ff).

Three explanations are linguistically possible for the Lukan phrasing: *(a)* Χριστός is a personal name and κύριος is an apposition ("Christ, the Lord"); *(b)* χριστός is an adjective to κύριος ("the anointed Lord"; χριστὸς βασιλεύς "anointed king" in 23.2 should be understood in this sense); *(c)* χριστός and κύριος are coordinated titular designations ("the anointed [i.e., the Messiah], the Lord"). In all probability the third possibility corresponds to what was intended by Luke. This is supported not only by the juxtaposition of the same titles in Acts 2.36 (God made Jesus κύριος . . . καὶ χριστός), but also similar title pairs with κύριος in the Septuagint (e.g., Psalm^LXX 28.10: κύριος βασιλεύς; or the address κύριε βασιλεῦ in 1 Samuel 24.9; 26.17; Daniel 2.4; and elsewhere).

Luke would scarcely have expected that his readers could understand the emphatically placed σήμερον ("today") as a signal for the beginning of the eschatic time of salvation (so most commentators; Marshall is rightly more sober). To be sure, Luke repeats this temporal adverb often later (Luke 4.21; 5.26; 19.5, 9 are comparable), but in every case it designates nothing more than the temporal and spatial particularity of a reality-changing historical event (cf. apart from that the form-critical analogies in Homer, *Ilias* 19.103; Epiphanius, *Panarion* 51.22.8: σήμερον ἡ Κόρη ἐγέννησεν τὸν Αἰῶνα ["Today Kore has given birth to Aion"]; see also Ruth 4.14; Psalm 2.7 or Genesis 41.41; Testament of Job 53.2).

12 Entirely in the style of the Septuagint (cf. the analogous phrasings in Exodus 3.12; 1 Samuel 2.34; 10.1-2^LXX; 2 Kings 19.29 = Isaiah 37.30; Isaiah 38.7; Jeremiah 51[44].29), a sign is named for the recipient of the message coming from God, which is meant to serve less as an authentication of the truth of the message than as a recognition sign for the shepherds (see v. 15), namely a swaddled child that lies in a feed trough. Here it is not, of course, the swaddling clothes, which are commonplace in the case of small children (see at v. 7), but solely the exceptional place where he is kept that makes the infant sufficient as a sign (and therefore only the feed trough is mentioned in v. 16). For the reasons mentioned at v. 7, it is improbable that Luke wanted to highlight in this way the contrast between the messianic majesty of the newborn and the lowliness of his current situation. Rather, the mention of the sign probably has the function of having the shepherds go to Bethlehem narratively, for whoever announces the "finding" of a sign also wants it to be looked for. It was no different with Mary (cf. 1.36, 39).

13 Something happens that never occured before in the history of Israel. Not only a single angel but the whole heavenly host, which surrounds the throne of God (cf. 1 Kings 22.19: στρατιὰ τοῦ οὐρανοῦ; Joseph and Aseneth 14.8 speaks of the στρατιὰ τοῦ ὑψίστου ["army of the Most High"], Greek Apocalypse of Ezra 6.16, 17 of the στρατιὰ ἀγγέλων ["army of angels"]), arrives on earth in order to perform its incumbent task of praising God (the plural αἰνούντων . . . καὶ λεγόντων is *constructio ad sensum*). There is frequently talk of a πλῆθος (τῆς) στρατιᾶς in Greek history writing (cf. already Herodotus 7.173; then Ctesias, *FGH* 3c: 688 Fragment 1e.5.5; Thycidides 1.106.2 in the sense of "the main part of the army"; Diodorus Siculus 2.5.5; 17.32.4; 25.19.1; Appian, *Hannibalica* 222; Dionysius of Halicarnassus, *Antiquitates romanae* 9.9.7; Arrian, *Anabasis* 2.6.3 and many others; significantly, in Jewish sources it is attested only in Josephus, *Antiquitates judaicae* 9.60). Luke describes what has never happened before and in this way expresses the significance of the birth of Jesus. The distance that separates heaven and earth from each other is removed for a moment; the earth becomes the place of the heavenly praise of God and humans become its earwitnesses.

14 The comprehensive orientation of the presentation, which encompasses heaven and earth, also corresponds to this.

The text-critical problem of this verse can be resolved with some certainty in favor of the originality of the genitive εὐδοκίας (ℵ* A B* D W and others). The result is then two lines in which the significance of the event for the heavenly world of God (as here, the expression ἐν [τοῖς] ὑψίστοις also stands for this heavenly world of God in Job 16.19; Psalm^LXX 148.1; Sirach 26.16; 43.9; Psalms of Solomon 18.10; Joseph and Aseneth 22.13; Mark 11.10 par. Matthew 21.9) and the earthly world of humans is explicated. δόξα and εἰρήνη, ἐν ὑψίστοις and ἐπὶ γῆς, and θεῷ and ἐν ἀνθρώποις εὐδοκίας correspond to one another.

In the first line the angels do what they or others are exhorted to do, e.g., in Psalm^LXX 28.1-2; 66.35; 95.7-8. They give glory to God by confessing that δόξα belongs to him alone, because he alone is God (cf. also *ex negativo* Acts 12.23; Romans 1.21). In Luke the doxology is thus connected with its occasion in such a way that the birth of the Savior for Israel is a work of God in which God once more (i.e, as in the creation, etc.) demonstrated his deity.

The second line, which explicates the significance of the birth for the world takes up the universal hope for peace that is connected with the birth of the eschatic bringer of salvation in the bucolic *aurea aetas* expectation (see v. 8). It is also proclaimed to the shepherds in Calpurnius that now *aurea secura cum pace renascitur aetas* ("the golden age with secure peace is born again," *Eclogae* I: 42; see also *Eclogae* I: 52–54; Virgil, *Eclogae* 4.17). In the expression ἐν ἀνθρώποις εὐδοκίας (ἐν stands for the simple dative; see BDR §220₁) the attributive genitive is meant not in a specifying but in a characterizing manner—over humans God's good pleasure is proclaimed (cf. also Psalms of Solomon 8.33). Therefore, 1QH IV, 32–33; XI, 9–10 ("sons of his/your good pleasure" [בני רצונו/רצונכה]) probably comes less into consideration as the closest parallel to what is meant here than the talk of πᾶν ζῷον εὐδοκίας ("every living thing of the good pleasure") in Psalm^LXX 144.16b, which is provided with nourishment from God (P.-R. Berger 1983, 144; see also Smyth 1987) or 4Q418 fragment 81 + 81a.10 ("in order to turn wrath from the people of the good pleasure [להשוב אף מאנשי רצון]"). In 19.38 the disciples of Jesus will give back this proclamation to the heavenly world.

In **15-20** Luke brings the protagonists of the two scenes together, who, in contrast to the readers, do not know about each other. The two narrative threads are meant to be joined with each other in this way, and the narrative goal of this episode also lies in this. Not much happens apart from that. The shepherds experience confirmation of the words of the angels (v. 16) and react by glorifying and praising God (v. 20). In between, those present in Bethlehem learn from the shepherds what was said about the child in the feed trough (v. 17) and react—with the exception of Mary (v. 19)—with astonishment (v. 18). The episode is thus constructed chiastically. What remains to be noted is that the information flows only in one direction. It is said of the shepherds that they disseminate what was revealed about the child by the messengers of God (v. 17). But, conversely, Mary does not do the same; rather, she keeps everything that she knows about Jesus to herself.

15 Unlike in 1.23b, 38b, Luke reports the return of the angels into heaven not on the narrative level of events but only as a subordinate temporal specification (on καὶ ἐγένετο ὡς, see at 1.23). The text-structuring caesura is therefore not as deep as elsewhere, and, therefore, the narrative also remains oriented toward the shepherds. Like Mary in 1.39, they now set out on their way after a sign has been mentioned for them. In the New Testament διέρχεσθαι is a typical Lukan word (31 of 43 uses) and is almost always found in clearly redactional sections; the same is true for the substantivized participle τὸ γεγονός, which is found, apart from Mark 5.14, only in Luke (Luke 8.34, 35, 56; 24.12; Acts 4.21; 5.7; 13.12; cf. especially the point of contact with 8.35). Unlike with Mary in 1.31, Luke does not leave the readers in the dark about the motive for the departure of the shepherds. They want to go to Bethlehem and see what was unveiled to them. The fact that they immediately identify the "city of David" spoken of in v. 11 with Bethlehem is actually, for the reasons mentioned at v. 4, a violation against what can be presumed for the basic knowledge of the narrative figures. Luke presents the shepherds in such a way that they do not doubt the truth of what is said for a moment. It becomes clear now, at the latest, that the sign of v. 12 was envisaged not as a sign of authentication but as a sign for recognition. That one can "see" a ῥῆμα or that it can "happen" is due again to Luke's endeavor to imitate the Septuagint (cf. Exodus 2.14; Deuteronomy 17.4; 1 Samuel 4.16; 12.16; 1 Kings 1.27; 12.24; but see also Joseph and Aseneth 17.1; Acts 10.37 as well as Burchard 1985).

16 Like Mary in 1.39 (μετὰ σπουδῆς), the shepherds are in a hurry (σπεύσαντες; with the exception of 2 Peter 3.12 [with transitive meaning], the verb is used in the New Testament only in Luke [5×; always intransitive]). It does not, of course, surprise the readers that the shepherds find everything just as it was announced to them. Through the bringing together of the two narrative threads the readers are faced with the question of what happens when the pieces of information about Jesus that were given to Mary and the shepherds by the angels of God come into contact with each other.

In **17-18** the shepherds are discussed first. The terminology partially takes up v. 15 (ὁράω, ῥῆμα, and γνωρίζω), so that ῥῆμα should be understood, as there and often in the Septuagint, to mean "content" or "thing" (see Burchard 1985). The shepherds are the first ones in the two Lukan prehistories to tell other narrative figures about what they have experienced through the angel appearances. Both Zechariah and Mary have kept their knowledge to themselves and Mary also continues to do so. Apparently, Luke wants to convey to the readers the notion that the shepherds narrated the message of the angel not only to Mary and Joseph but also disseminated it among many other people in Bethlehem. For their reaction (ἐθαύμασαν), see at 1.63.

19 If the readers expected that Mary would also narrate what was said to her about the child in 1.31-33, 35, Luke disappoints them. Nevertheless, this verse refers at least indirectly to the message of Gabriel, but this reference informs only the readers; within the narrated world its content continues to remain hidden. Beyond this, Mary, for precisely this reason, cannot simply be subsumed under those who can only "marvel" at what was said by the shepherds. For this reason, there is a report of her different reaction (v. 18). Contrary to most translations ἐν τῇ καρδίᾳ αὐτῆς should be connected with συνετήρει; cf. Daniel 4.28[LXX]; 7.28[Theodotion]; Testament of Levi 6.2; Luke 2.51; 4 Ezra 14.8; see also Deuteronomy 6.6; Proverbs 3.1 (an analogous joining with συμβάλλειν is never attested; see also Radl). The phrasing πάντα . . . τὰ ῥήματα ταῦτα, which is also found in 1.65 and can be identified without difficulty as a Septuagintism (cf. Genesis 20.8; Exodus 4.30; Deuteronomy 30.1; 1 Samuel 19.7; 25.9; Judith 10.1; Job

42.7; Isaiah 29.11; Jeremiah 16.10) probably refers very generally to the appearance of the shepherds and the content of their report (Fitzmyer).

But what does Luke have Mary do? The aforementioned linguistic parallels have their common denominator in the fact that the relevant people very intentionally keep in their memory and do not forget something that they have heard or seen. Apart from 1.66, this is also supported by the durative imperfect συνετήρει, which points temporally beyond the narrated episode. With reference to the usage in Euripides, *Medea* 675; Dionysius of Halicarnassus, *Antiquitates romanae* 1.24.1; Josephus, *Antiquitates judaicae* 2.72; 3.352; Arrian, *Anabasis* 1.20.1; Philostratus, *Vita Apollonii* 4.43.2, van Unnik 1973–1983, I: 72–91, was able to make probable the meaning "to grasp the sense," "understand" for the participle συμβάλλουσα, which should not be assigned a conative accentuation (contrast Räisänen 1989, 121; Fitzmyer; Nolland). In support of this view one could also invoke the semantic opposition of συμβάλλειν and θαυμάζειν (v. 18), which is attested, e.g., in Aelian, *De natura animalium* 11.19: ὁρῶντες τὰ πραττόμενα ἐθαύμαζον μέν, οὐκ εἶχον δὲ τὴν αἰτίαν συμβαλεῖν ("when they saw what happened, they marveled, but they were not in position to grasp the cause"). On the basis of the announcement of Gabriel, Mary knows more than those who know only the report of the shepherds and who can therefore only marvel.

20 forms the concluding frame for the episode opened in vv. 15-16 (see also 1.23, 56). The readers remain at the same place at which they already were in v. 7, for the story of Jesus has made no narrative progress since then. ὑποστρέφειν is a typical Lukan word (32 of 35 New Testament occurrences are in Luke–Acts). The information that the shepherds glorify and praise God and thus join in the choir of the angels (see v. 13-14; the parallelizing of δοξάζειν and αἰνεῖν, etc., corresponds to 1 Chronicles 16.27; Isaiah 12.2; Daniel 3.26.55) serves their characterization. They react in the way that is appropriate in light of the experience of God's salvific action. Numerous healing stories in Luke (cf. Luke 5.25; 17.15; 18.43; Acts 3.8, 9) also end in a very similar way (i.e., as here with a present participle of δοξάζειν or αἰνεῖν). ἐπί introduces the specification of the object and basis of the praise of God (cf. BDR §235.2; see also [2] Ezra 3.11; Psalm^LXX 150.2; Acts 4.21; 2 Corinthians 9.13); with the lexical pair "hear and see" (see also Isaiah 48.5; Acts 4.20) Luke explicitly wants *both* parts of the shepherd episode to be kept in mind, which is made unmistakably clear above all by the trailing specification of εἶδον. In 23.47 Luke writes, after the death of Jesus, about the centurion who witnesses the events at the crucifixion: ἐδόξαζεν τὸν θεόν. In this way Luke places, in a sense, a doxological frame around the life of Jesus.

With **21** Luke takes up again the narrative thread of v. 7, for the temporal specification refers to the day of the birth. Thus, the narrative makes a small temporal jump. Like John, Jesus is also circumcised eight days after his birth in accordance with Genesis 17.12 and Leviticus 12.3. Luke associates the naming with this ceremony (for the connection between naming and circumcision, see at 1.59). Here too the reference to circumcision functions merely as a secondary temporal specification (καὶ ὅτε). The main thing is the naming, which Luke again reports in the best Septuagintal style (ἐκλήθη τὸ ὄνομα αὐτοῦ + name; cf. Genesis 11.9; 25.30; 27.36; 31.48; Numbers 11.3; and elsewhere; see also at 1.23). Luke conveys to the readers quite succinctly that the name that is now given agrees with the one mentioned by Gabriel (see 1.31). How this coinciding is to be explained, i.e., how it came about and what it should make clear, is left again to the imagination of the readers. Luke has already indicated what possibilities exist in this respect in the narrative of the naming of John (see 1.59-64). With this the Bethlehem portion of the events that took place during the reign of Caesar Augustus ends.

2.22-39: Jerusalem

²²**And when the days of their purification were fulfilled according to the Law of Moses, they brought him up to Jerusalem in order to present him to the Lord—²³as it is written in the Law of the Lord: "every male that opens the womb should be declared 'holy to the Lord'"—²⁴and in order to bring an offering in accordance with what is said in the Law of the Lord: "A pair of turtle doves or two young pigeons."**

²⁵**And behold: There was a person in Jerusalem named Simeon; this person was righteous and pious, and he awaited the consolation of Israel, and Holy Spirit was on him, ²⁶and it was foretold to him by the Holy Spirit that he would not see death before he had seen the Anointed of the Lord. ²⁷And he came, (led) by the Spirit, into the temple. And when the parents brought in the child Jesus to do for him according to the custom of the law, ²⁸he took it in his arms and praised God and said:**

²⁹**"Release now your slave, Lord, as you have said, in peace. ³⁰For my eyes have seen your salvation, ³¹which you have prepared in the presence of all nations—³²light for revelation for the Gentiles and glory for your people Israel."**

³³**But his father and his mother were amazed at what was said about him. ³⁴And Simeon blessed them and said to Mary, his mother, "Behold, this one is destined for the falling and rising of many in Israel and to be a sign that is rejected—³⁵and a sword will penetrate**

through even your soul— in order that the thoughts of many hearts may be manifest."

[36]Anna also was there, a prophetess, daughter of Phanuel, from the tribe of Asher. She was advanced in years; after the time of her virginity she had lived together with a man for seven years, [37]and she was widowed for eighty-four years; she did not leave the temple and served (God) with fasts and prayers night and day. [38]And in the same hour she came, praised God, and spoke about him to all who awaited the liberation of Jerusalem.

[39]And after they had completed everything that the Law of the Lord prescribed, they returned to Galilee, to their town Nazareth.

This part of the narrative is framed by vv. 22-24 and v. 39. Verses 22-24 function as an introduction. They narrate that and why Mary and Joseph visit the temple in Jerusalem with Jesus (these verses thus have a similar function as the census in 2.1-4). The fulfillment of this purpose is not, however, narrated in detail, but merely stated summarily (v. 39a). Instead, the narrative of the encounter with Simeon (vv. 25-35) and the description of the reaction of Anna to Jesus's presence in the temple (vv. 36-38) stand at the center of this section. That Luke wanted the narrative presentation of these two people to be understood as a material unity is shown, on the one hand, by the frame that encloses the whole section with the help of the verb προσδέχεσθαι: at the beginning Simeon is introduced as awaiting (προσδεχόμενος) the "consolation (παράκλησις) of Israel" (v. 25), and at the end it says that Anna refers all προσδεχόμενοι the "liberation" (λύτρωσις) of Jerusalem to Jesus (v. 38). In doing so Luke makes both into representatives of the Jewish hope for the messianic liberation of Israel, and that is also why he locates the encounter with them in the Jerusalem temple. On the other hand, both parts of the section are held together by the complementary dualism of man and woman that is typical for Luke (cf. in addition 1.25-38; 4.25-27; 7.1-17; 8.42/9.38; 13.18-21; 15.4-10; see d'Angelo 1990, 444ff; Seim 1994, 11–24). Analogous contents are transported twice: first via a man, then via a woman. Verse 39 concludes the superordinate event sequence.

22a, 24 The journey to Jerusalem is dated with the help of the Torah for women who have recently had children (Leviticus 12; see also Jubilees 3.8–14). According to it, a woman who has become unclean through childbirth, in the case of the birth of a son, may not leave the house for thirty-three days after his circumcision (40 days total; 14 + 66 after the birth of a girl, i.e., 80 days total). After the end of this time (Luke formulates in dependence on Leviticus 12.4, 6: the "days of purification" are "fulfilled," i.e., they are completed; for the phrasing, see also at 1.23) she should bring an offering (Leviticus 12.6, 8). In v. 24 Luke evidently refers to this, and more specifically to the regulation for those who cannot afford a lamb to sacrifice (v. 8), though he is dependent in the phrasing on the Septuagint version of Leviticus 5.11 (ζεῦγος τρυγόνων instead of δύο τρυγόνας; see also C.-W. Jung 2004, 85ff). Although only the mother is regarded as unclean according to Leviticus 12, Luke speaks in the plural of "their" (αὐτῶν) purification (v. 22a); whom he had in mind and why or with what intention he uses the plural can be given only a hypothetical answer. It is possible that the Greek notion stands in the background, according to which mother and child become unclean through the birth (cf. Wächter 1910, 25ff; G. Binder, *RAC* 9: 85ff). But all attempts to explain it remain pure speculation, and the variants handed down in some manuscripts are nothing more than *lectiones faciliores*, which want to remove the thematic difficulty of the much better attested reading αὐτῶν. The bringing of the offering proceeds in such a way that the offering was handed over to one of the priests in attendance at the Nicanor Gate, i.e., at the transition from the "forecourt of women" to the "court of the Israelites" (women after childbirth were declared clean here, at least according to m. Sotah 1.5; see also at 5.14).

22b, 23 However, as the main reason for the journey, Luke specifies that Jesus was brought to Jerusalem in order to be introduced to God (v. 22b). For this he very freely quotes a Torah instruction obtained from Exodus 13.2, 12, which he enriches with phrasings of his own (v. 23). Here he does not refer with a single word to the redemption of the first born mentioned in Exodus 13.13c, 15b; 34.20c; Numbers 18.15-16 (pace Schmithals; Wiefel; and others). Instead, Luke interprets the intention of the parents of Jesus (v. 22b) as executing the instruction to consecrate the first born; cf. Exodus 13.2: "consecrate to me (LXX: ἁγίασόν μοι) all the first born! Everything from the sons of Israel, whatever first opens the womb among people and among animals belongs to me (LXX: ἐμοί ἐστιν)" (see also Numbers 3.13; Nehemiah 10.35-36; C.-W. Jung 2004, 68ff), without it being clear how he envisaged it. An independent christological significance probably should not be attributed to this quotation, for according to the Lukan understanding it is, of course, not just Jesus's status as first born that causes him to become ἅγιος τῷ κυρίῳ (on κληθήσεται as indicating a conferment of status, see at 1.32; the phrasing "ἅγιος καλεῖν someone or something" is found in Exodus 12.16; Isaiah 4.3; 35.8; Testament of Levi 18.2e17; Josephus, *Bellum judaicum* 5.195, 219; *Antiquitates judaicae* 3.125; and elsewhere), but the Holy Spirit, which already participated in his conception (1.35). Nor is it any more likely that this is construed after the model of Samuel (*pace* Schürmann; Marshall; Fitzmyer; Green), whom his mother consecrates to God and brings into

the temple (1 Samuel 1.11, 22, 24, 28; see also Liber antiquitatum biblicarum 51.1–2), for the differences are much too great (the motif of the
first born plays no role; Samuel is brought much later into the temple, and
he remains there). Beyond the narrative function that has already been
addressed, the Torah quotation therefore probably had for Luke merely the
not unwelcome secondary meaning that it shows the parents of Jesus to
be law-pious Jews on the one hand and confirms Jesus's special closeness
to God on the other hand. Similar phrasings are found, e.g., in Josephus,
Bellum judaicum 2.89; *Antiquitates judaicae* 7.382 concerning offerings
that are presented to God (Romans 12.1 in an ethicizing transference; see
also 6.13; 2 Timothy 2.15) and in Acts 23.33 concerning the presentation
of Paul before the Roman governor; see also Fragment of Ahiqar (= Vita
Aesopi) 103: Aesop made a Babylonian nobleman his son καὶ τῷ βασιλεῖ
παρέστησεν ὡς διάδοχον αὐτοῦ τῆς σοφίας ("and he presented him to
the king as his successor in wisdom"); it is often used intransitively for
the entourage or service personnel of important people (Numbers 11.28;
1 Samuel 25.27; 1 Kings 1.2; Isaiah 60.10) and then also for God's heavenly court (Daniel 7.10; Zechariah 4.14; 6.5; 4 Maccabees 17.18 for the
exalted martyrs: τῷ θείῳ νῦν παρεστήκασιν θρόνῳ; see also at 1.19).

In **25-26** Simeon is introduced as a new narrative figure. Via the information of his place of residence (Jerusalem), Luke narratively places him
in the path of the family who is going to this very place (v. 22) and prepares the readers for their encounter with him. The introduction of the
person in v. 25 is comprised of three elements and follows the narrative
style of the Septuagint: *(a)* ἄνθρωπος ἦν + specification of place with ἐν,
(b) naming, *(c)* characterization, sometimes through a number of characteristics; cf. in this sense above all 1 Kings 12.24h: *(a)* ἄνθρωπος ἦν ἐν
Σήλῳ ("there was a person in Selo"), *(b)* καὶ ὄνομα αὐτῷ Ἀχία ("and his
name was Achia"), *(c)* καὶ οὗτος ἦν υἱὸς ἑξήκοντα ἐτῶν ("and this one
was a son of sixty years"); Esther 2.5-6: *(a)* ἄνθρωπος ἦν Ἰουδαῖος ἐν
Σούσοις ("there was a Jew in Susa"), *(b)* καὶ ὄνομα αὐτῷ Μαρδοχαῖος
("and his name was Mardochaios"), *(c)* ὃς ἦν αἰχμάλωτος ἐξ Ἰερουσαλή
("who was a prisoner from Jerusalem"); Job 1.1: *(a)* ἄνθρωπός τις ἦν ἐν
χώρᾳ τῇ Αὐσίτιδι ("there was a man in the land Ausitis"), *(b)* ᾧ ὄνομα
Ιωβ ("whose name was Job"; on this phrasing, see at 1.26), *(c)* καὶ ἦν ὁ
ἄνθρωπος ἐκεῖνος ἀληθινός, ἄμεμπτος, δίκαιος, θεοσεβής ("and that man
was upright, blameless, righteous, God-fearing"; see also 1 Samuel 1.1-2;
25.2; 1 Kings 12.24b; Bel and the Dragon 2). The variability is greatest
with regard to the third element, i.e., in the characterization of the person.
This is hardly surprising, for the course setting that is decisive for the plot
of the narrative that follows occurs here.

Συμεών is the Greek version of Hebrew שִׁמְעוֹן (cf. Genesis 29.33; 34.25, 30; and elsewhere; for the meaning, cf. Köhler/Baumgartner 2004, s.v.; see also Luke 3.30; Acts 13.1; Revelation 7.7). Peter is designated with this name in Acts 15.14; 2 Peter 1.1 (see at 4.38 and BDR §53.2₅). For the bearers of this name mentioned in the New Testament, cf. G. Schneider, *EWNT* 3: 686–87; for Jewish usage, see Ilan 2002, 218ff.

Luke lets Simeon be distinguished at first by three characteristics. The lexical pair δίκαιος καὶ εὐλαβής mentioned *in the first position* is attested only here in early Jewish and Christian literature (it is found, however, in Plato, *Respublica* 311a, b), and, more generally, in the New Testament it is only Luke who characterizes people as εὐλαβής (cf. Acts 2.5; 8.2; 22.12: Ananias) and wants to express their conscientious Torah observance thereby (cf. R. Bultmann, ThWNT 2: 749–50). The *second* feature also characterizes Simeon as an authentic Jew. When Luke ascribes to him the expectation of the "consolation (παράκλησις) of Israel," he takes up in this way the promise of the eschatic restitution of Israel, which is connected with this terminology especially in (Deutero-)Isaiah (cf. Isaiah 40.1-2: "Comfort, comfort my people! . . . Speak in a friendly manner with Jerusalem and proclaim to her that her slavery has an end"; see also 49.13; 51.3, 12; 57.18; 61.2; 66.13; Jeremiah 31.13; Zechariah 1.17). Luke thus has Simeon await the fulfillment of the prophetic promises, and when one connects this feature with the preceding characteristic, the complementary dualism of "law and prophets" may be recognizable for the first time in Luke–Acts behind the characterization of Simeon (cf. then 16.16; 24.27, 44; Acts 24.14; 26.22-23; 28.23 and my comments on 9.30-31). The word placement is peculiar in the case of the *third* characteristic. Luke writes καὶ πνεῦμα ἦν ἅγιον ἐπ' αὐτόν. One should not assign too great a significance to the lack of the definite article, for it is also lacking in 4.1. Moreover, it is also said of Simeon that the Holy Spirit lastingly (imperfect!) rests on him. The possession of the Spirit is mainly necessary narratively, for without it the readers can scarcely understand how Simon is empowered to recognize the Messiah (v. 28) in the small child that parents who are completely unknown to him bring into the temple in v. 27.

26 The mode of the introduction changes from description, which is oriented toward typical characteristics, to narrative, which brings into view an individual event that is guiding for the continuation of the narrative. The Holy Spirit had announced to Simeon that he would encounter the Messiah before his death. With χρηματίζω Luke employs a term that is used especially in inspiration manticism (cf. C. Zintzen, KP 3: 968–76). It describes revelations that are issued primarily through oracles or dreams (e.g., Diodorus Siculus 15.10.2; Plutarch, *Moralia* 435c; Vettius

Valens, ed. Kroll 1973, 67.5; SIG 663.13; Josephus, *Antiquitates judaicae* 11.327–28; Matthew 2.12, 22); in Jewish texts often through God himself (e.g., Josephus, *Antiquitates judaicae* 3.212 [see Hebrews 8.5]; 5.42; 10.13; Hebrews 11.7) or through priests and prophets (e.g., Jeremiah^LXX 33.2; 36.23; Josephus, *Antiquitates judaicae* 6.255; Acts 10.22: through an ἄγγελος). The latter are also typical addressees of this term (Jeremiah^LXX 37.2; 43.2, 4; 2 Maccabees 2.4); see also W. Bauer 1988, 1765–66. The content of the revelation (for the grammar, cf. BDR §383.3: πρὶν ἄν, which is common in classical Greek, is found only here in the New Testament) plays with the word for "seeing": before Simeon dies (for the phrasing "to see death," cf. Psalm 89.49; John 8.51; Hebrews 11.5; see also Psalm 16.10 quoted in Acts 2.31), he will encounter ("see") the promised messianic king. An old age for Simeon is often inferred from this. But this does not necessarily follow from the text. The designation χριστὸς κυρίου is also found in 1 Samuel 24.7, 11; 26.9, 11, 16, 23; 2 Samuel 1.14, 16; 2.5; 19.22; Lamentations 4.20; Psalms of Solomon 17.32; 18, title, 7 and always refers to the king of Israel (cf. also the counterpart in 1 Samuel 2.10; 12.3, 5; 16.6; 2 Samuel 22.50-51 = Psalm 18.50-51; 23.1; Psalm 2.2; 20.7; 28.8; Sirach 46.19; Psalms of Solomon 18.5); in the New Testament there are comparable christological phrasings in Mark 1.24 par. Luke 4.34 (ὁ ἅγιος τοῦ θεοῦ); Luke 9.20; 23.35; Acts 3.18; 4.26 quoting Psalm 2.2; Revelation 11.15; 12.10. An analogous formation is, e.g., Matthew 25.34: οἱ εὐλογημένοι τοῦ πατρός μου; for the character of the genitive, see at 9.20. In terms of content this announcement refers to the second of the characteristics described in v. 25, namely the expectation of the consolation of Israel. Simeon has received the promise that this hope will find fulfillment still during his lifetime.

27-28 The Holy Spirit now brings about a meeting of Simeon with the family of Joseph in the temple; the readers know ever since vv. 22-24 that Mary, Joseph, and Jesus must visit this place. Also later Luke time and again has the Holy Spirit stage-manage the right choreography of his narrative figures (cf. 4.1, 14; see also Acts 8.39-40; 20.22). He brings the parents of Jesus together with Simeon even before they can carry out their purposes. The expression εἰθισμένον τοῦ νόμου refers to the quotations in vv. 23-24 (phrasings with κατὰ τὸ + ἔθος and cognates are found in the New Testament only in the Gospel of Luke: 1.9; 2.42; 4.16; 22.39). Due to the word placement περὶ αὐτοῦ should be connected with τὸ εἰθισμένον τοῦ νόμου; cf. also Philo, *De ebrietate* 18 ("the commandments that the law has made customary with regard to these things" [ὁ νόμος εἴωθε περὶ τούτων]) and the many other attestations with νόμος + περί (e.g., Leviticus 11.46; Philo, *De agricultura* 157; *De somniis* 1.92; *De specialibus legibus* 4.123). The fact that v. 24 refers to a Torah commandment that must

be fulfilled not for the sake of the child but for the sake of the mother—
thus the phrasing of v. 27c says less than vv. 22a, 24—makes visible the
Lukan disinterest in the ritual details (see also Salo 1991, 55). Luke does
not need to convey separately that Simeon immediately recognizes (v. 28)
Jesus as the promised messianic king (v. 26), the long awaited "consolation of Israel" (v. 25), for the readers can fill this in themselves thanks
to the detailed preparation. Simeon also needs neither a sign nor another
pointer; the possession of the Spirit (v. 25d) is completely sufficient to let
his behavior become plausible to the readers. That he places Jesus on his
arm can be regarded as an appropriate way to greet the messianic king,
when this one is still an infant. Luke has Simeon, like Zechariah in 1.64,
answer the fulfillment of the promise with a praise of God and makes him,
as one who represents Israel's hope for the fulfillment of the prophetic
promises of salvation, precisely in this way into an ideal picture of the
answer of Israel to the sending of Jesus. However, Simeon then signals in
vv. 34-35 that the answer will, to be sure, turn out completely differently.

29-32 Similarly to the Magnificat (1.46-55) and the Benedictus (1.68-
79), quite a few authors regard the Nunc Dimittis as a song that originally existed independently of its present literary context (in this sense,
e.g., R. E. Brown 1993, 446, 454–56; S. C. Farris 1981, 146). It speaks
against such an assumption, however, that the Nunc Dimittis is so closely
interwoven with its literary context (cf. above all the taking up again of
the key words "die" and "see" from v. 26 in vv. 29-30) that one is forced
to undertake further source-critical operations to uphold this assumption, which makes this hypothesis only more improbable. Therefore, the
voices that regard Simeon's song of praise as a Lukan composition are
also rightly predominant (cf. also the arguments in Grelot 1986 and Radl
1996, 224–25).

Like the Magnificat and the Benedictus, the Nunc Dimittis is also put
together in collage-like manner from textual pieces that come from the
Old Testament and especially from Deutero-Isaiah (cf. the overviews in
R. E. Brown 1993, 458; Schmithals and the individual documentation at
each passage).

Overlaps with the two hymns in Luke 1 exist especially in the respective references to "Israel" (1.54, 68/2.32) as well as in the talk of "his"
or "your" (sc. God's) "people" (1.68, 77/2.32). The κέρας σωτηρίας of
the Benedictus (1.68) is, of course, also referentially identical with the
σωτήριον of God (2.30), while God's predication as σωτήρ in the Magnificat (1.47) is christologically reinterpreted through this phrasing. In one
point, however, the Nunc Dimittis goes beyond the two other hymns. Here
a universal perspective of salvation is formulated that reaches beyond
Israel and includes "all nations" (v. 31) or the "Gentiles" (v. 32a), yet

without giving up the specific connection to Israel. This tension will run through Luke–Acts up to its last sentence in Acts 28.30-31.

K. Berger 1985, 27–28 has designated the small song of praise form-critically as a "thanksgiving prayer of one consecrated to death" and has invoked as parallels Cicero, *De republica* 6.9 (= *Somnium Scipionis* 1.1); Plutarch, *Marius* 46; Jubilees 22.7–9 and Martyrdom of Polycarp 14.2. Luke, however, gives no indication that Simeon stands at the threshold of death (see at v. 29). Beyond this, the texts are also much too heterogeneous to be grouped under a common genre. In Plutarch, *Marius* 46 the concern, as content and continuation show, is with the balance of one's life, and the same also applies to Jubilees 22.7–9 (moreover, here it is not the one praying but his son who is designated as "slave"); in Martyrdom of Polycarp 14.2 thanks is given for the fact that God receives the one praying into the circle of martyrs.

In Cicero, *De republica* 6.9.9 the prayer also has the function of characterizing the significance of the encounter with a specific person: *Grates . . . tibi ago, summe sol, vobisque, reliqui caelites, quod ante quam ex hac vita migro, conspicio in meo regno et his tectis P. Cornelium Scipionem, cuius ego nomine ipso recreor* ("I thank you, elevated sun god, and you, you remaining inhabitants of heaven, that I—before I depart from this life—see in my kingdom and under this roof Publius Cornelius Scipio, through whose name I already revive"; ahead there still comes an embrace). The same applies also to Pliny the Younger's account of the greeting that is given to Trajan when he enters into Rome (*Panegyricus* 22.3): *. . . alii se satis vixisse te viso te recepto . . . exclamabant* (". . . some shouted that they had lived enough, since they had seen you, had greeted you").

The closest correspondences are found, however, in Genesis 46.30 (Jacob says at his reencounter with Joseph: "Now I can die, after I have seen your face, that you still live"; see also Jubilees 45.3–4) and Tobit 11.9 (at the homecoming of Tobias his mother falls on his neck and says "I have seen you, child, from now on I can die"). Another tradition-historical point of contact is offered by texts that praise as happy those who "see," i.e., experience, the coming of the messiah or the dawning of eschatic salvation (cf. K. Berger 1985, 34–35): Psalms of Solomon 17.44 = 18.6; Sirach 48.11; see also Sibylline Oracles 3.371–72; 4.192.

29-30 refer back to the oracle of the Holy Spirit mentioned in v. 26.

In **29** the reference is explicitly established and the narrator now has Simeon himself identify as God's word what had been designated there as prophecy from the Holy Spirit. The motif of dying is also recoded— death is regarded as release from slavery (for the terminology of the image field, cf. Appian, *Bella civilia* 5.1, 7; Plato, *Menexenus* 245a; Josephus, *Antiquitates judaicae* 12.11, 46; *Gnomologium Epicteteum* 38; *Rhetores Graeci* [Walz 1968] VIII: 405; see also Matthew 18.27); on ἀπολύειν as a euphemism for dying, cf. Genesis 15.2 (where God is addressed as δεσπότης); Numbers 20.29; 2 Maccabees 7.9; Tobit 3.6, 13. The thematic emphasis of the statement undoubtedly lies on ἐν εἰρήνῃ, which is placed at the end. Just as it is promised to Abraham according to Genesis 15.15 that he will be able to die "in peace" because he does not remain without physical descendants, so Simeon also now characterizes his death in this way because the promise given to him is fulfilled (cf. also Tobit 14.2‭‮‬ℵ; Sirach 44.14; Jeremiah 41.5^LXX; Testament of Gad 8.3; Lives of the Prophets 4.23; 8.2; 11.4). It is not said that he has death directly before his eyes; it is merely expressed that his waiting for the "consolation of Israel" now has an end and in his life nothing more will come that could still surpass the current encounter. Luke has him formulate the explanation for this in vv. 30-32 (cf. the causal ὅτι at the beginning of v. 30).

In **30** Simeon repeats the key word "see" from v. 26b and replaces χριστὸς κυρίου with σωτήριόν σου. Luke has Simeon interpret his encounter with the promised messianic king as an encounter with the salvation of God itself (σωτήριον τοῦ θεοῦ according to Isaiah 40.5^LXX; see also Luke 3.6 diff. Mark 1.3; Acts 28.28 and Psalm^LXX 49.23; 66.3; 97.2, 3; 118.123; Isaiah 51.5 [with "light" as in v. 32; see also Testament of Simeon 7.1; Testament of Dan 5.10 with a view to Luke 1.78b]; Testament of Benjamin 10.5 [with "revelation" and "all nations" as in vv. 31-32]; 52.10) and thus as fulfillment of the (Deutero-)Isaianic promises of salvation. In this way Jesus's significance is increased even more, for he is identified here as the bringer of God's salvation. For the Lukan soteriology the reference precisely to the salvation prophecy of Deutero-Isaiah is of great thematic importance. For it has its special profile in an Israel-centric universalism. God's salvific action toward Israel obtains universal dimensions insofar as it is perceived by all the nations (cf. above all Isaiah 49.1-13), who are incorporated into this salvific action precisely through this means. Salvation for the whole world goes out from Israel. That Luke envisaged this in precisely this way is shown by the continuation.

The relative clause in **31** is dependent on τὸ σωτήριον. Noteworthy here is the talk of πάντες οἱ λαοί. Normally Luke always only uses the singular λαός, namely exclusively for the people of God Israel (see at 1.10) and for the Christian community (Acts 15.4; 18.10). Apart from Acts 4.25 (quotation of Psalm 2.1) the plural is found only additionally in 4.27 (λαοὶ Ἰσραήλ) as a designation for the tribes of Israel. The question of whether Luke likewise means the twelve tribes here (Kilpatrick 1965; Stegemann 1991a, 89; Rusam 2003, 80) or whether he wants to subsume all humanity under the term πάντες οἱ λαοί (Wilson 1973, 36ff; Miyoshi 1978, 114 as well as almost all recent commentaries; Wasserberg 1998, 140 is undecided) is undoubtedly to be answered in the sense of the second, universalistic interpretation. This view is supported by three observations. First, the usage in Acts 4.27 is determined by the fact that Luke has misunderstood the synonymous *parallelismus membrorum* of Psalm 2.1 quoted in 4.25, and for precisely this reason speaks of the λαοί of Israel in v. 27, while in Luke 2.31 there is talk of πάντες οἱ λαοί. Second, the phrasing κατὰ πρόσωπον πάντων τῶν λαῶν can be understood as an intentional modification of Isaiah 52.10, which speaks of the revelation of God's salvation ἐνώπιον πάντων τῶν ἐθνῶν ("before all nations") and thus takes the Gentiles into view as spectators in the restitution of Israel-Jerusalem. By contrast, the sting of Simeon's words lies in the fact that this overagainstness is now removed. The σωτήριον of God brought about with Jesus applies to Israel and the Gentiles equally.

Thirdly, this finds its confirmation in the fact that **32**, with the distinction between ἔθνη and the λαός . . . Ἰσραήλ, can be understood as a meaningful diaeresis of the umbrella designation πάντες οἱ λαοί (see also Nolland). This verse undoubtedly forms the climax of the Nunc Dimittis. In addition, it is distinguished by a plethora of references to the language of (Deutero-)Isaiah; cf. especially Isaiah 42.6 and 49.6 (φῶς ἐθνῶν); 46.13 (δόξα + Israel); 60.1, 19 (φῶς + δόξα). Syntactically this verse formulates a double apposition to τὸ σωτήριόν σου (v. 30): it is, first, φῶς εἰς ἀποκάλυψιν ἐθνῶν, and, second, δόξα of the people of God Israel (see also Klostermann; Schürmann; Nolland; Coleridge 1993, 170; most others understand only φῶς as in apposition and see in εἰς ἀποκάλυψιν and δόξαν further specifications related to it that are parallel to each other). This view is supported, first, by the lack of a preposition before δόξαν (this should be taken seriously), and, second, by the linguistic points of contact with Isaiah 42.6; 49.6 (see above); the last mentioned text is explicitly quoted in Acts 13.47 in order to justify the turning to the Gentiles in Pisidian Antioch (see also 26.18 with the exclusive reference to the Gentiles in v. 17). In this case, we would have a synthetic *parallelismus membrorum* that distinguishes the Gentiles and Israel in such a way (see also Nolland) that access to salvation is opened for the former through a transfer from darkness into light (i.e., through conversion), while Israel, which already occupies the status of people of God, receives through Jesus a share in God's own δόξα (see also Isaiah 35.2; 40.5; 60.1; Psalms of Solomon 11.7). In both cases we are dealing with a *genitivus obiectivus* (cf. BDR §163.1, 2). In v. 32a it stands in for the dative object of ἀποκαλύπτειν (cf. e.g., Sirach 4.18; Philippians 3.15); in v. 32b it stands in for the accusative object of δοξάζειν. Another reason that this verse is significant for the Lukan picture of history is that it makes clear that from the beginning the post-Easter Gentile mission was already an integral component of the realization of God's salvific action among humans. What Simeon recognizes here is disclosed to the Roman Jews in Acts 28.28.

33 Jesus's parents (a few manuscripts replace "his father" with "Joseph" in order to leave no doubt about Jesus's conception by the Spirit) react with just as little understanding as those who marveled at what had happened and been heard about in 1.63 (see there) and 2.18. Their reaction is certainly not an acclamation; it more likely corresponds to the motif of wonder that is typical of miracle stories (cf. Theissen 1987, 78ff and at 1.63 above). But this notification does not aim to disqualify Mary and Joseph either; rather, it has the function of additionally highlighting the unheard-of character of what was said by Simeon (see also Plummer; Schürmann; Coleridge 1993, 172). This becomes clear above all when one takes the previously narrated reaction of Mary as a benchmark (cf. 1.38; 2.19). The words of Simeon about the universality of the salvific activity of Jesus are not only more difficult for her to understand than the interpretation of the birth of Jesus through the angel in the field (see 2.17 with reference to vv. 9-14), but also more difficult than what was said to his mother by Gabriel about the conception of Jesus and his future significance.

34 After the reaction of the parents, Simeon speaks again. In this respect, the structure of the whole scene is similar to the narratives of Gabriel's visit to Zechariah and Mary, whose words are also interrupted by a reaction of the addressees (cf. 1.13-17/18/19-20 and 30-33/34/35-37). Luke has Simeon explicitly address only the mother of Jesus; the reason remains inexplicable. He first places a prophetic word in his mouth that describes the divinely appointed (κεῖται in v. 34b is *passivum divinum*; see also Philippians 1.16; 1 Thessalonians 3.3) effect that goes out from Jesus to Israel. Narratologically this is a "certain anticipation" (Lämmert 1975, 143; Vogt 1990, 123–24). It obtains its certainty (normally narrative figures can give only uncertain anticipations; see Lämmert 1975, 143) from the fact that Simeon has the Holy Spirit (v. 25). The first announcement, according to which Jesus will bring about a "falling and rising of many in Israel," certainly does not take up the saying of the "rock of stumbling" (Isaiah 8.14 [LXX: πέτρα πτώματι]), for this picture cannot explain the antithetical orientation of Simeon's statement. Texts such as Proverbs 24.16; Ecclesiastes 4.10; Isaiah 24.20; Jeremiah 8.4; Amos 8.14; Micah 7.8, where "falling and rising" are brought into temporal succession, more likely come into consideration. In that case Simeon's announcement would refer to the fact that Israel initially comes to a fall because of its predominant rejection of Jesus, but afterwards is set upright again (e.g., Schweizer 1981, 23; Marshall; Koet 1992, 1563 [with reference to Isaiah 51.17-23]; Radl [with reference to the "fallen booths of David," Acts

15.16]). But since the aforementioned Old Testament texts always have a different orientation, it is much more likely that "falling and rising" should be understood here as a description of two opposite consequences that the activity and proclamation of Jesus in Israel will draw after it. Precisely that reversal of status that Mary already spoke of in the Magnificat will come to pass in Israel and that will be explicitly brought to expression in the further course of the Gospel of Luke, e.g., in the juxtaposition of beatitudes and woes (6.20b-22 / 24-26), in the saying of the first and last (1.30), and in the parable of the Pharisee and tax collector (18.9-14) (see also L. T. Johnson 1977, 91; York 1991). In other words, Simeon announces that Jesus will unsettle Israel and bring about something like a paradigm change, insofar as he himself becomes the criterion for the allocation of salvation and unsalvation (that is what the metaphors of "rising" and "falling" stand for). The second announcement, which Luke likewise traces back to God's antecedent plan for history, is the designation of Jesus as a "sign that will be opposed." As the terminological taking up again of ἀντιλέγειν in Acts 13.45; 28.19, 22 shows, this is used to designate the Jewish rejection of the post-Easter proclamation of Christ. Thus, here the Lukan Simeon does not simply have the pre-Easter activity of Jesus in view but the complete narrative complex of the overall presentation (see also Radl 1999, 307–8). This ἀντιλέγειν will ultimately lead to a separation between Jews and Christians, and this process is already taken into view here. For the understanding of the designation of Jesus as "sign," one can refer above all to 11.30 (namely, to those phrasings in which the Lukan text deviates from the parallel in Matthew 12.40; see also already Klostermann): the function of Jonah as a "sign for the Ninevites" (τοῖς Νινευίταις σημεῖον) is regarded here as a model for the significance of Jesus for "this generation." Unlike "this generation," the Ninevites repented on the basis of the proclamation of Jonah (see v. 32), and therefore they will condemn it in the coming judgment. Here, what Luke imagines with the phrasing in v. 34c becomes graspable—that the status God has assigned to Jesus, namely to be his earthly representative, is not recognized in Israel and encounters rejection (cf. also Isaiah 8.18; Ezekiel 12.6; 24.24; Jubilees 4.24: the prophet as "sign" of God in Israel).

35 continues with a parenthesis that formulates a metaphorical prophecy about Mary. In prophetic threats there is sometimes talk of a sword going through (as here διέρχεσθαι or the like) a land, announcing destruction by means of this phrasing (cf. Ezekiel 14.17; Sibylline Oracles 3.316). There are also points of contact with Psalm 22.21 ("deliver my soul from the sword . . .") and the lament of Jeremiah 4.10 (although God has promised freedom to his people, ἥψατο ἡ μάχαιρα ἕως τῆς ψυχῆς αὐτῶν ["the sword has penetrated to their life"]). The meaning of this announcement with regard to Mary is controversial (cf. the overview in R. E. Brown 1993, 462–63; Bock I: 428ff). At present two interpretations are especially prevalent: *(a)* Simeon speaks here of the suffering that the mother experiences because of the rejection and death of her son (Mary as *mater dolorosa*; so e.g., Marshall; Nolland; Radl); *(b)* Simeon expresses that the division in Israel described in v. 34, which Jesus will bring about, also does not spare Mary and her own family (so, with reference above all to 12.51-53 and 8.19-21, R. E. Brown 1993, 464–66; Fitzmyer; Bock; Wasserberg 1998, 144). None of these proposed solutions completely does justice to the imagery of the text, and therefore one cannot say more than that Simeon announces painful experiences to Mary here. Perhaps Luke wants to refer back to the beginning of the Magnificat ("My soul praises the Lord"; 1.46) with the phrasing "your soul."

35b continues the thought of 34c with a purpose clause. That the heart is the place of thoughts corresponds to Old Testament anthropology (cf. Deuteronomy 15.9; Psalm 33.11; Daniel 2.30[Theodotion]; see also Mark 7.21par.; Luke 3.15; 5.22; 9.47; 24.38). Two things stand in the background of Simeon's announcement—that the thoughts of the heart are hidden to other humans and known only to God and that they are good for nothing (cf. e.g., Psalm 94.11: "The Lord knows the thoughts of humans that they are nothing"; Isaiah 59.7; 1 Maccabees 2.63; in the New Testament, see Mark 7.21par.). This would then mean that God makes Jesus into "a sign that is opposed," so that the hidden intentionality of the persons who reject him becomes manifest. When we place this "revelation" next to the "revelation" of the σωτήριον spoken of in v. 32a as illumination of the Gentiles, then we already have here precisely the same constellation before us as at the end of Luke–Acts (cf. Acts 28.26-28). On the one hand, it is stated that the Pauline proclamation of Christ has shown the hardening of the heart of those Jews who have rejected it, and, on the other hand, it is made known that precisely τοῦτο τὸ σωτήριον τοῦ θεοῦ was sent to the Gentiles who are willing to listen.

The narrative sequence that follows in **36-38** is peculiar. Luke first introduces the main figure Anna in detail (vv. 36-37) and then reports what she does (v. 39) with a few words and a high degree of compression with regard to the narrated time (cf. Lämmert 1975, 84). With forty-two words, the length of her introduction is more than double the description of her activity (seventeen words). Anna speaks, of course, on this occasion, but Luke does not let her get a chance to speak herself, but provides merely a summary report of her speech, which says *that* she speaks about Jesus; *what* she says about him remains unmentioned and left to the imagination of the readers. Luke also does not say that Anna meets with Jesus and his parents.

36-37 Unlike with Simeon, Anna's name is mentioned in the first position (Luke proceeded similarly with Gabriel in 1.26). In this it is recognizable that the two episodes should be understood as a unit. The introduction with καὶ ἦν (as predicate) + name is oriented again to the narrative style of the Septuagint (cf. Judges 13.2; 1 Samuel 9.1; 25.2; 2 Samuel 21.20; 1 Kings 12.24b^LXX; Esther 1.1r = Additions to Esther A 17). Anna is then introduced with an abundance of personal characteristics. Among them the beginning and end correspond to each other, for it is said here what she is and does at the time of the narrated event. She is a prophetess (like Miriam, Deborah, Huldah, Noadiah, and Isaiah's wife in the Old Testament; cf. Exodus 15.20; Judges 4.4; 2 Kings 22.14; 2 Chronicles 34.22; Nehemiah 6.14; Isaiah 8.3; see also Philo, *De vita contemplativa* 87; Josephus, *Antiquitates judaicae* 5.201; 10.59–60). Philo of Alexandria also calls Hannah, Samuel's mother, a prophetess (and "bearer of a prophet"; *De somniis* 1.254), and the Sibyl claims for herself the title θεοῦ μεγάλοιο προφῆτις ("prophetess of the great god"); Sibylline Oracles 3.818; see also Sibylline Oracles prologue 29. The hyperbolic statements in v. 37b present her as a woman of quite extraordinary and dedicated piety, for continually staying in the sanctuary (Psalm 23.6; 27.4) and serving God without interruption are regarded as Jewish piety ideals (the phrasing "night and day" reflects the Jewish understanding that the new day begins with the setting of the sun: see also Numbers 11.32; 1 Samuel 25.16; Esther 4.16; Mark 4.27; 5.5; Acts 20.31; 1 Timothy 5.5; and elsewhere). According to Josephus, *Antiquitates judaicae* 7.367, David ordered the priests and Levites δουλεύειν κατὰ νύκτα καὶ ἡμέραν τῷ θεῷ ("to serve God night and day in the temple"), and in Judith 11.17 Judith refers to herself as God's δούλη . . . θεοσεβής . . . θεραπεύουσα νυκτὸς καὶ ἡμέρας τὸν τοῦ οὐρανοῦ . . . ("slave . . . pious . . . serving the God of heaven in the night and in the day"); see above all, however, Acts 26.7 concerning Israel: ἐν ἐκτενείᾳ νύκτα καὶ ἡμέραν λατρεῦον. For the combination of fasting and praying as an expression of piety (often as a ritual of repentance), cf. Nehemiah 1.4; Psalm 35.13; Jeremiah 14.12; Baruch 1.5; Daniel 9.3; Tobit 12.8; Judith 4.7, 11; Testament of Joseph 3.3–4; 4.8; 10.1; Luke 5.33; Acts 13.3; 14.23.

Of the intervening biographical data, the first two pieces of information concern Anna's family. It is very improbable that Luke has fabricated the name of her father, Phanuel (from Hebrew פְּנוּאֵל ["God's face"]), and the belonging to the tribe of Asher (from Hebrew אָשֵׁר ["happiness, salvation"]) for reasons of theological symbolism. Rather, both details are indications of the presence of reliable historical recollection of a certain person who was in addition probably named Anna (from Hebrew חנן ["to be gracious, to show mercy"]); cf. Bauckham 1997, 186. The information about the age and duration of the widowhood of Anna (cf. J. K. Elliott 1988; for the phrasing προβεβηκυῖα ἐν ἡμέραις πολλαῖς, see at 1.7) is unclear and beyond this an invitation to number symbolic speculations (all the numbers are divisible by seven). Was she eighty-four years old (Plummer; Nolland; Bovon; Bock) or had she been widowed in the meantime for eighty-four years after seven years of marriage (Schürmann; Marshall; Radl)? In the latter case she would be—with the additional presupposition of a marriage at 14–105 years old, and thus exactly as old as Judith at her death (Judith 16.28). Should the reader thus recognize Anna as a woman of the type of Judith (cf. also Judith 11.17 quoted above)? In my opinion this is an overinterpretation that depends on too many hypothetical assumptions. It is relatively certain only that Luke speaks of an eighty-four-year widowhood (cf. the parallels for χήρα ἕως ἐτῶν + number in Josephus, *Antiquitates judaicae* 5.181; 6.18; 8.316; Dionysius of Halicarnassus, *Epistula ad Ammaeum I* 7; Diogenes Laertius 7.4; and elsewhere). If it were otherwise, the information about the duration of her marriage would also be without meaning. Coleridge 1993, 179 has pointed out that with regard to all the information that Luke communicates about Anna (in contrast to Simeon), we are dealing with "strictly public knowledge." Thus, there is some support for the view that here a "Jerusalem local tradition" has survived that referred to an old and pious widow named Anna, a daughter of Phanuel from the tribe of Asher, who was "a personality known to all visitors to the temple" on account of her age and temple piety (Schürmann I: 130). Luke must have somehow learned of her, and he could not miss the chance to give her a role in his story of Jesus.

However, when, after this detailed preparation, one reads further in **38**, this role proves to be downright meager. The temporal specification αὐτῇ τῇ ὥρᾳ (in the New Testament it is found only in Luke; cf. 10.21; 12.12; 13.31; 20.1; 24.33; Acts 16.18; 22.13; on its basis in the Septuagint, cf. Fitzmyer I: 117–18) coordinates Anna's activity with the Simeon episode. Luke introduces her with the same term with which he had narrated the appearance of the proclamation angel in 2.9 (ἐφίστημι), but here, unlike there, the object is lacking. Luke preserves a clear distance between Anna and the small group around Jesus. And he then recounts Anna's speech in the durative imperfect, i.e., he extends it beyond the punctiliar situation. The praise of God that he places in Anna's mouth (ἀνθομολογεῖσθαι is a *hapax legomenon* in the New Testament; but it is found in Psalm^LXX 78.13, at the end of a lament of the people, which prays for the restitution of Israel and Jerusalem; see also Daniel 4.34) stands in a series with the reactions of Mary, Zechariah, the shepherds, and Simeon, which the readers have already encountered previously (cf. 1.46, 68; 2.20, 28); for the characterization of the public as "all who awaited the liberation of

Jerusalem," see the introductory comments on 2.22-39. Concerning the content of Anna's speech, Luke only conveys that she somehow associates the hoped-for liberation of Jerusalem with Jesus. But he must not let it become more concrete. It is especially noteworthy that Luke does not let her explicitly announce that Jesus is the one who will liberate Jerusalem. There are, however, good reasons for this reserve. The Lukan Jesus will later have to correct many views that go in the same direction (cf. 19.11ff; 24.21ff; 24.21ff; Acts 1.6-8). He will, of course, liberate Jerusalem, but in an entirely different way than pious Jews could expect only a few days after his birth. This will emerge, however, only in the course of Acts. Plus, when Luke wrote his gospel, Jerusalem lay in ruins (see at 21.20-24). Thus, the unspecificity with which Luke surrounds the activity of Anna has its basis in the contemporary-historical experiences of the Jewish-Christian process of separation and the destruction of Jerusalem and corresponds on the level of the text with Simeon's announcement of the rejection of Israel (vv. 34-35).

39 ends two narrative complexes. Verse 39a concludes the narrative sequence begun in v. 22, which had brought Jesus's parents κατὰ τὸν νόμον Μωϋσέως into the Jerusalem temple (see also vv. 24, 27b-c). The readers know what they did there from v. 22b and v. 24. Verse 39b ends the narrative complex begun in v. 4 by having the young family return again to Nazareth, whence he had Mary and Joseph depart so that they could be registered in Bethlehem.

2.40-52: Jesus as a Wise Boy

[40]**And the child grew and became strong,** (and was) **full of wisdom, and God's grace was on him.**

[41]**And his parents were accustomed to travel each year to Jerusalem for the Passover festival.** [42]**And when he was twelve years old and they went up again according to custom,** [43]**and—after they had completed the days—returned again, the boy Jesus remained in Jerusalem, and his parents did not notice** (it). [44]**Because they thought he was** (somewhere) **in the traveling group, they traveled a day's journey and searched for him among the relatives and acquaintances.** [45]**And when they did not find him, they returned to Jerusalem and searched for him** (there). [46]**And it happened after three days that they found him in the temple sitting in the midst of the teachers, listening to them and questioning them.** [47]**But all who heard him were surprised at his insightful answers.** [48]**And when they saw him, they were astonished, and his mother said to him, "Child, why have you done such a thing to us? Behold, your father and I have searched for you in distress!"**

⁴⁹**And he said to them, "Why have you searched for me? Did you not
know that I must be in that which is my Father's?"** ⁵⁰**And they did not
understand the word that he had spoken to them.** ⁵¹**And he went down
with them and came to Nazareth. And he was obedient to them. His
mother kept all these things in her heart.**

⁵²**And Jesus increased in wisdom and age and in standing with
God and humans.**

As in 1.80, Luke concludes the narrative of Jesus's birth and its interpretations with a summary about the growing up of the child. This notice is
contained in v. 40 and v. 52. In this way Luke goes beyond the temporal
frame marked out at the beginning of this narrative collecting basin (the
governorship of Quirinius). He already proceeded in an analogous way
in 1.80, and in 24.53 he will use the same technique. An episode that is
meant to illustrate the content of the summary is embedded in it (vv. 41-
45), namely that the adolescent Jesus is already characterized by extraordinary wisdom and closeness to God. Luke also proceeds in a completely
analogous way in Acts 4.32–5.16. There he integrates the story of Ananias
and Saphira into a summary concerning the Jerusalem community in order
to document the presence of the Holy Spirit in the primitive community.

But the significance of the narrative goes beyond the function of illustrating Jesus's wisdom and closeness to God, for in v. 49 it contains the
first saying of Jesus in Luke–Acts. And after there had been talk about
Jesus only by others to this point, Jesus becomes his own interpreter for
the first time here (see also Coleridge 1993). There are comparable traditions in the Hellenistic environment of the New Testament about Augustus, Apollonius of Tyana, and Pythagoras; cf. Krückemeier 2004 (see also
de Jonge 1978, 339ff). The narrative of this episode in the Infancy Gospel
of Thomas (chapter 19; see Schmahl 1974) is dependent on the Lukan
narrative, but sets its own accents.

40 The summary about the physical growth of Jesus is identical in
wording with what Luke had written about John in 1.80 (see there). But
instead of speaking of growing strong "in the Spirit" (this is then promptly
added by some manuscripts) Luke then reports regarding Jesus that he was
"full of wisdom" and "God's grace" rested on him. It misses the intention
of the text to say that in this way he purposefully wanted to express Jesus's
superiority to John (so, e.g., Schürmann; Marshall). Moreover, Luke can
hardly have Jesus "grow strong in the Spirit" after the Holy Spirit already
participated in his conception. Apart from that, wisdom and grace are traditional attributes of men of God; both occur together, e.g., in Acts 7.10
regarding Joseph. The instrumental dative σοφίᾳ stands in for the genitive

(BDR §195.2); see also Acts 6.3; Philo, *De posteritate Caini* 137: ἀκράτου σοφίας πεπληρωμένη ("filled with pure wisdom").

41 serves the narrative preparation of the episode, which is meant to illustrate the characteristics that Luke has just ascribed to Jesus. He evidently does not want to send Jesus and his parents to Jerusalem for no reason and therefore mentions here an easily comprehensible reason—because each year (κατ᾽ ἔτος; this phrasing is widely attested in pagan Greek writings; for reasons of space I give only the attestations in Diodorus Siculus: 1.26.5; 34.2; 2.47.1; 3.2.3; 56.4; 62.7; 38/39.7.1; in Jewish sources it is attested only in Josephus: *Antiquitates judaicae* 4.69; 8.160, 396; 12.169; and elsewhere; thus, we meet again here the Hellenistic writer Luke) the parents of Jesus made a custom of traveling to Jerusalem for the Passover festival, which was one of the three Jewish pilgrimage festivals (alongside the festival of weeks and the festival of booths) for which every male Israelite had to appear in Jerusalem (cf. Exodus 23.14-17; 32.23; Deuteronomy 16.16; see also Jubilees 49.9–10, 16–21; Josephus, *Bellum judaicum* 6.421). No one knows how strictly this commandment was followed in New Testament times (Josephus, *Bellum judaicum* 6.422–27 mentions a counting that took place before the outbreak of the Jewish war and the number was 2.7 million participants; cf. Hengel 1976, 135). According to Josephus, *Vita* 269, it was possible to travel from Galilee to Jerusalem in three days. At any rate the Passover halakah is adequate to motivate a journey by Jesus's parents to Jerusalem; a reference to 1 Samuel 1.3, 7, 21; 2.19 (e.g., Nolland) is therefore unnecessary.

42-43 The twelve-year-old Jesus participates in one of these journeys. The specification of his age is very likely due to a great number of biographical traditions according to which the extraordinary characteristics of men who subsequently became significant already emerged at the age of twelve, such as with Cyrus (cf. Xenophon, *Cyropaedia* 1.3.1–18), Epicurus (cf. Diogenes Laertius 10.14), Samuel (cf. Josephus, *Antiquitates judaicae* 5.348), Augustus (cf. Suetonius, *Divus Augustus* 8.1), Solomon (cf. 1 Kings 2.12[LXX]); see also de Jonge 1978, 322–23).

It is recognizable in the high degree of compression that Luke has no interest in the course of the Passover festival (and Jesus's participation in it). Having scarcely arrived, he has Jesus's parents already depart again. What is most important to him in this sentence can be recognized in the fact that he first introduces the main clause with the communication of Jesus's remaining behind in Jerusalem. Luke will not provide an explanation for this until v. 49. Luke differentiates between the knowledge of the readers and the knowledge of his narrative figures with the information that Jesus's parents (some manuscripts show concern again for the virginity of Mary and correct it to "Joseph and the mother") do not initially

notice the remaining behind of their son. Unlike his parents, the readers
know what has happened; Luke first reestablishes an even level of understanding in v. 45.

In **44-45** Luke narrates the parents' search. Their assumption (v. 44)
that Jesus is somewhere in the travel fellowship causes them to search in
the wrong place and functions narratively as a retarding element. In Epictetus, *Dissertationes* 4.1.91 συνοδία is used in this sense with an interesting explanation—because a certain street is dangerous because of robbers,
one does not travel alone but waits until a συνοδία comes together. In any
case, the parents distance themselves spatially from their son by moving away from Jerusalem for a whole day and afterwards searching for
him—without success, of course—among relatives and acquaintances
(the imperfect ἀνεζήτουν describes the lasting character of the search; cf.
BDR §325, §327). Luke may have wanted to have this false assessment
of the parents be interpreted also as a theological alienation and as symbolic anticipation of the subsequent breaking of the traditional familial
relations (cf. 8.19-21; 11.27-28; 12.51-53). "Relatives and acquaintances"
on the one side and God as "my father" (v. 49) on the other side stand
over against each other. They mark out different symbolic universes, and
if one searches for Jesus not in God's symbolic universe but in the other
one, then one does not find him, of course (see also Räisänen 1989, 134ff).
With v. 45 Luke brings the knowledge of the parents together again with
that of the readers. What both do not yet know is the reason why Jesus
remained behind and the circumstances in which they will meet him.

46-49 are the climax and goal of the narrative, which obtains in this
way an apophthegmatic structure. To be sure, the narrative logic is not
stringent, for first, v. 47 does not fit with v. 46, and, second, the answer that
Jesus gives in 49 does not fit with the situation upon whose description in
vv. 46-47 so much value is placed.

46 This time, Luke makes a clear break with καὶ ἐγένετο (for the
phrasing, cf. Genesis 7.10; Exodus 12.41; Joshua 3.2; 9.16; 2 Chronicles
8.1; Ezekiel 3.16; see also Acts 28.17), so that we can probably assume
that the temporal specification refers to the duration of the search in Jerusalem. A relation to Jesus's resurrection (so Glombitza 1962, 2; Laurentin
1966, 95ff; J. K. Elliott 1971/1972) is not recognizable, the more so since
Luke (unlike Mark 8.31; 9.31; 10.34) never speaks of the resurrection of
Jesus "after three days."

The finding notification places Jesus in a situation that is artificial and
unrealistic to the highest degree, for normally a multiplicity of students
gather around *one* teacher and not the other way around. Moreover, students always sit only "at the feet" of the teacher (cf. Acts 22.3; see also
10.39) and not in their "midst." The intention that Luke follows with this

group picture is clear. The slope between those teaching and the one learning is leveled; Jesus is no longer a student, but rather a "conversation partner" (Wiefel; see also Green). The scene described in 1 Samuel 10.10-11 also corresponds to this. Saul is seen "ἐν μέσῳ of the prophets," which leads to the astonished question of whether Saul also belongs to them, i.e., whether he has become a prophet.

This perspective is confirmed by **47** insofar as an exchange of roles takes place. Jesus is no longer presented in the role of the hearer and questioner, but as one who answers. σύνεσις καὶ ἀποκρίσεις is a hendiadys and says that Jesus's σύνεσις is recognizable in his answers (cf. BDR §442$_{29}$). And in this way the claim of v. 40 finds its confirmation (on the reciprocal nearness of σοφία and σύνεσις, cf. Isaiah 10.13; 11.2; 29.14; Daniel 2.21; Daniel[Theodotion] 2.20; 5.14). It is not important to know what Jesus says (this is then different in the apocryphal Infancy Gospel of Thomas 19.2 [Schneemelcher 1990, 359] and in the Arabic Gospel of the Infancy 50–53 [Aland 2001, 18–19]). In the foreground stands only the impression that he makes upon the people and the fact that the Jerusalem temple is the place in which the twelve-year-old Jesus publicly demonstrates his wisdom (cf. de Jonge 1978, 330). πάντες οἱ ἀκούοντες (there with an aorist participle) appeared already in 1.66 and 2.18 (this occurs only in Luke within the New Testament: cf. also Acts 5.5, 11; 9.21; 10.44; 26.29), but they differ from those in the fact that they directly encounter Jesus. For the description of their reaction Luke reaches back to a term (ἐξίστημι) with which he later describes the reaction to Jesus's healings or the like (5.26; 8.56; Acts 2.7, 12; 3.10; 8.9, 11, 13; 10.10, 45-46; 12.16). It is worth mentioning that Luke also has the first public activity of Paul after his conversion call forth this same reaction word-for-word (ἐξίσταντο δὲ πάντες οἱ ἀκούοντες; Acts 9.21).

The beginning of **48** links syntactically—bypassing v. 47—to v. 46, for the subject can only be the parents of Jesus. But this should not become an occasion for regarding v. 47 as a subsequent addition (so van Iersel 1960, 169). In this verse the scene turns into a controversy dialogue, for Luke introduces the parents as antagonists, who reprimand the behavior of Jesus. Initially, it is noteworthy that they do not—as would actually be only natural after 15.6, 9, 23-24, 32—rejoice over the finding again of their lost son, but become astonished (ἐκπλήσσομαι; this need not necessarily be negative: cf. 4.32: at Jesus's teaching; 9.43: at the μεγαλειότης of God; Acts 13.12: at the Pauline "teaching of the Lord"). Mary's reproach begins with a rhetorical question (cf. the comparable phrasings in Genesis 12.18; 20.9; 26.10; 29.25; Exodus 14.11; Judges 15.1 as well as Pesch 1968; BDR §299.3), as is often the case in controversy dialogues (cf. e.g., Mark 2.18 par. Matthew 9.14; Mark 2.24 par. Luke 6.2; Luke 5.30

par. Matthew 9.11). The content of the reproach is interesting. It makes no reference to the situation in which the parents encounter the child (in this respect it deviates from the form of the other controversy dialogues), but exclusively thematizes Jesus's relation to his parents: "Why have you done such a thing to *us*? *Your father and I* have . . . searched for you!"

49 Jesus's counterquestion makes clear that his parents' error lies precisely here. It is, of course, equally rhetorical and implies a modest reproach of his parents. It was unnecessary to search for him, for they should have known where he had remained. But in detail Jesus's first statement creates some problems of interpretation. The phrasing of the question concerning the reason with τί ὅτι corresponds to Acts 5.4, 9 and occurs just under fifty times in the Septuagint (e.g., Genesis 3.1; 18.13; 26.9; 40.7; see BDR §299₃). However, the meaning of ἐν τοῖς τοῦ πατρός μου in v. 49c is especially controversial (cf. esp. Laurentin 1966, 38ff; de Jonge 1978, 331ff; Heininger 2005, 65–66). Two interpretations are primarily up for discussion: *(a)* in the sense of 'my father's house,' i.e., the temple (so the majority of recent commentators); attestations for this understanding are Tobit 6.2; Esther 7.9; Job 18.19; Josephus, *Contra Apionem* 1.118; cf. also Kügler 1997, 302: reference to "the kingly custom of dwelling with the deity" and therefore an "expression of the father-son relation between God and the king"; *(b)* in the sense of 'my father's affairs' (e.g., Johnson; Coleridge 1993, 202–3; attestations for this view are Mark 8.33; 1 Corinthians 7.32-34; 1 Timothy 4.15). Sylva 1987 combines them and sees here an announcement of the subsequent teaching of Jesus in the temple (19.45–21.38), and de Jonge 1978, 334–35 is also of the opinion that Luke consciously formulates ambiguously here (entirely different again is Weinert 1983, who wants to insert συνοδία from v. 44, which certainly founders, however, on the plural ἐν τοῖς). Now it is admittedly the case that in light of the correspondence with "seeking," one cannot effectively deny a local component to Jesus's ἐν τοῖς τοῦ πατρός μου . . . εἶναι. However, on the other hand, one also cannot dismiss the considerations of de Jonge 1978 that Luke—if he had wanted have Jesus refer to the temple in an unmistakable way—could have done so (332–33). This means that one must undoubtedly assume the temple as an extension of τὰ τοῦ πατρός μου; but the intensional meaning of this term allows for the fact that it can also point to other extensions. One can perhaps take the decisive pointer from Acts 3.20-21. With recourse to the δεῖ of the divine history plan that is fulfilled in Jesus (see also Luke 4.43; 9.22; 13.33; 17.25; 19.5; 21.9; 22.37; 24.7; 24.44), it says in Acts 3.20-21, as in Luke 2.49, that Jesus must be received by heaven. Also now, in the time of the Jerusalem community and then also of the readers, it thus applies that Jesus is ἐν τοῖς τοῦ πατρὸς αὐτοῦ, and it is precisely the fundamental necessity of this matter of fact that Jesus himself emphasizes in his first statement. Thus, the statement points beyond the world of the text into the world of the readers and the openness of the phrasing has its basis in the fact that Luke had to use a designation that fit both the temple and heaven. Correspondingly, Jesus is also translated thence at the end (24.51).

That Jesus calls God "Father" must be read as a reference to 1.32, 35 (there has not been talk of the divine sonship of Jesus in between), and it is primarily the special relationship binding him to God that functions as a motivation for his behavior. In the context of the individual episode, this reference makes clear that Jesus's behavior deviates from the expectations of his parents. Something analogous is repeated on a larger scale in the course of the Lukan story of Jesus and then, of course, in the context of the history of the spread of the message of Christ, which Luke relates in Acts. For the moment, however, the disclosure in **50**, according to which Jesus's parents react to what is said without understanding, lets the tragedy of the situation clearly come to light. In the conversation with the teachers, σύνεσις is credited to Jesus's answers by the earwitnesses, and his answer to the reproach of his parents also undoubtedly fulfills this criterion. In 18.34 Luke describes the reaction of the twelve to Jesus's second announcement of the passion and the resurrection (see also already 9.45) with this same verb. But ignorance is subsequently removed by the Risen One (cf. 24.45), and the same evidently applies also to Mary (cf. Acts 1.14). Verse 51a forms the concluding frame of the episode, which corresponds with v. 42.

51b, c then formulate an outlook into the narrated time after the return from Jerusalem. First, Luke makes a point of explicitly communicating to the readers that Jesus behaved in daily life in the manner that was generally expected from children, namely that they subject themselves to their parents or, more generally, elders (cf. 1 Timothy 3.4; 1 Peter 5.5; Marcus Aurelius 1.17.3; see also Ephesians 6.1; Colossians 3.20 and Spicq 1994, III: 424ff); the *coniugatio periphrastica* ἦν ὑποτασσόμενος expresses not only the temporal duration, but also "a certain emphasis" (BDR §353.2a; on its use in the Gospel of Luke, see Verboomen 1992). This note has a similar function as the notice about the swaddling clothes in 2.7 with regard to the conception by the Spirit—it wants to bring Jesus back into the sphere of human normality after the report of an extremely extraordinary event. On Mary's διατηρεῖν . . . ἐν τῇ καρδίᾳ and on πάντα τὰ ῥήματα, see at v. 19.

52 is a biographical note of development, as is found with the key word προκόπτειν in many biographical texts (in Apollonius, *Vita Aeschinis*, ed. Martin/Budé 1962, 5.20–21; Historia Alexandri Magni Recensio β, ed. Bergson 1965, 1.14; SIG³ 708.18; Clement of Alexandria, *Eclogae* *propheticae* 18.1 with τῇ ἡλικίᾳ, which always designates the person's age in this context; see also G. Stählin, ThWNT 6: 705.10ff, 18ff; 712.21ff, 44ff). But because this would be pointless, the meaning will be: 'the child becomes a man' (see also Radl). The note connects to the summary begun in v. 40 and continues it. With increasing age Jesus becomes ever wiser and more respected. The latter is developed with regard to the two fundamental human relations, namely the relationship to God and the relationship to other humans. Here the nearness to 1 Samuel 2.26 is unmistakable ("The boy Samuel increased in age and favor with YHWH and with humans" [LXX: καὶ τὸ παιδάριον Σαμουὴλ ἐπορεύετο καὶ ἐμεγαλύνετο καὶ ἀγαθὸν καὶ μετὰ κυρίου καὶ μετὰ ἀνθρώπων]; see also Proverbs 3.4 and Sirach 45.1 concerning Moses: "beloved by God and humans" [ἠγαπημένον ὑπὸ θεοῦ καὶ ἀνθρώπων]; Tobit 14.17; Romans 14.18 [in the background stands the ethical 'canon of two virtues'; see at 1.75]); for the translation of χάρις, cf. Acts 2.47. When one compares this verse with what Josephus, *Antiquitates judaicae* 2.228–31 can write about about Moses (cf. also the material compiled by de Jonge 1978, 339ff), the biography of Jesus's youth in the Lukan summary does not fall out of the framework of conventional biographies of unusually gifted youths.

3.1-20: John the Forerunner

[1]In the fifteenth year of the reign of Caesar Tiberius, when Pontius Pilate was governor of Judea and Herod tetrarch of Galilee, his brother Philip tetrarch of Iturea and Trachonitis and Lysanias tetrarch of Abilene, [2]at the time of the high priest Annas and Caiaphas, the word of God came upon John, the son of Zechariah, in the wilderness. [3]And he went in the whole surrounding land of the Jordan and proclaimed a baptism of repentance for the forgiveness of sins, [4]as it is written in the book of the words of the prophet Isaiah:
"A voice of one calling in the wilderness:
'Prepare the way of the Lord, make his paths straight!
[5] Every valley should be filled
and every mountain and every hill made low.
And the crooked should become straight,
and the rough paths should become level.
[6] And all flesh will see the salvation of God.'"
[7]He said to the many people who came out (to him) **in order to let themselves be baptized by him, "You brood of snakes, who has persuaded you into believing that you will escape the coming wrath? [8]Bring forth fruits that correspond to repentance, and do not say to yourselves, 'We have** (after all) **Abraham as Father,' for I say to you: God is in**

position to raise up children for Abraham from these stones! [9]The ax already lies at the root of the trees, and every tree that does not bring forth good fruit is cut down and thrown into the fire."

[10]Then the people asked him and said, "What then should we do?" [11]He answered them, "Whoever has two undergarments should give to the one who has none and whoever has food should do likewise." [12]But tax collectors had also come to be baptized, and they said to him, "Rabbi, what should we do?" [13]But he said to them, "Collect no more than what is set for you." [14]Soldiers also asked him and said, "And what should we do?" And he said to them, "Mistreat no one, do not plunder; be satisfied with your pay!"

[15]But the people were full of expectation, and all made thoughts in their hearts about John whether he was perhaps the Messiah. [16]Then John answered and said to all, "I immerse you in water; but there comes one who is mightier than I, whose sandal straps I am not worthy to loosen. He will immerse you in Holy Spirit and fire. [17]His winnowing shovel he has in his hand in order to clean his threshing floor and gather the wheat in his barn; but he will burn the straw with unquenchable fire."

[18]In this way he proclaimed with many other admonitions the message of salvation to the people. [19]But the tetrarch Herod, who had been criticized by him because of Herodias, the wife of his brother, and because of other evil deeds that Herod had committed, [20]added to all this that he put John in a prison.

The difference from the two narrative collecting basins in Luke 1–2 is unmistakable. The anchoring in history takes place at the beginning no longer through an unspecific ἐν ταῖς ἡμέραις (1.5; 2.1), but through a precise dating. The interplay of the summary biographical outlooks in 1.80 and 2.40, 52 with the beginning of 3.1 also makes clear that Luke does not want to establish a direct connection to what has been previously narrated, for Tiberius already reigns in the fifteenth year when the narrative continues. This makes clear to the readers that at least fifteen years have passed between the events narrated in chapter 2, which took place during the reign of Caesar Augustus (2.1), and what now comes. In this section Luke wants to provide a complete and self-enclosed overview of the activity of John the Baptist. This is recognizable in the fact that he brings forward the information about the placement of the Baptist in prison from Mark 6.17-18 and concludes his report about the Baptist's activity with it (vv. 19-20).

The structure of this text is clearly marked:

(a) In vv. 1-6 John comes upon the scene of the narrative. The detailed introduction that Luke provides for him gives a high level of attention to his activity.

(b) Vv. 7-18 are composed of three parts in which the παρακαλῶν εὐαγγελίζεσθαι (v. 18) of the Baptist is developed in relation to different thematic questions and concluded with a summary. John is thus presented as an ethical teacher. Correspondingly, all three units display an apophthegmatic structure. In each case, a short narrative exposition is followed by a dictum of the protagonist. Thus, from a form-critical perspective we are dealing with a series of chreiae or pronouncement stories (cf. especially *Semeia* 20 [1981] and 64 [1994]; Robbins 1994; Hezser 1996). In vv. 7-9 Luke portrays John as a prophetic preacher of repentance who exhorts the ὄχλοι, who want to let themselves be baptized by him, to a transformation of their life. In vv. 10-14 he answers the question concerning the actions that correspond to this exhortation (both textual units are joined with each other by the key word ποιεῖν: vv. 8, 9, 10, 12, 14), and in vv. 15-17 John clarifies his relationship to the expected Messiah. It is noteworthy that Luke consistently uses the imperfect not only for the concluding summary but also for the three report sections (cf. ἔλεγεν; vv. 7, 11; ἀπεκρίνατο; v. 16; ἐπηρώτων; vv. 10, 14). Thus, he wants not to recount individual events but to inform the readers about what was typical for the activity of the Baptist as a whole. The repeated practice not the individual deed stands at the center.

(c) In vv. 19-20 Luke has the Baptist depart again from the scene of the narrative.

Verses 10-14 are Lukan *Sondergut*. The provenance of this text can therefore be specified only in a hypothetical manner. It probably originates from Luke, like the synchronic introduction in vv. 1-2 and the summaries in v. 18 and vv. 19-20; Luke probably has formulated the last of these on the basis of Mark 6.17-18.

The relations in vv. 2b-17 are more complex (see also at vv. 21-22), for here there are many smaller and larger Luke–Matthew agreements against Mark. Unlike Mark 1.2, Luke and Matthew do not introduce the mixed quotation composed of Malachi 3.1 and Exodus 23.20 at this point, but in Luke 7.27 par. Matthew 11.10, i.e., within Jesus's speech about John the Baptist. In v. 4 par. Matthew 3.3 the quotation of Isaiah 40.3 stands not *before* (thus Mark 1.3) but *after* the content of the proclamation of John. The expression πᾶσα ἡ περίχωρος τοῦ Ἰορδάνου (v. 3a par. Matthew 3.5) is lacking in Mark 1.5. The chreia in vv. 7-9 par. Matthew 3.7-10 has no Markan equivalent. In v. 16b par. Matthew 3.11a John speaks of his own baptizing activity *before* he announces the "stronger one" (in Mark 1.7-8 the sequence is reversed). βαπτίζω (v. 16b par. Matthew 3.11a) occurs instead of ἐβάπτισα (Mark 1.8a). κύψας (Mark 1.7c) is lacking in v. 16d par. Matthew

3.11c. The "stronger one" baptizes according to v. 16e par. Matthew 3.11d ἐν πνεύματι ἁγίῳ καὶ πυρί instead of only ἐν πνεύματι ἁγίῳ (Mark 1.8b). The saying concerning the winnowing shovel and the barn floor (v. 17 par. Matthew 3.12) is without a Markan equivalent. Cf. further Neirynck 1974b, 55ff; 1991, 11–12. The explanations for these findings are very diverse. For some, the findings are due to a Deutero-Markan expansion of the original Mark text (A. Fuchs 1980b). For others, the Gospel of Mark has been influenced at this point by Q (Catchpole 1993b; Lambrecht 1992). Others suggest that Mark and Q could have independently taken up an older report about John and Jesus (Schröter 2003).

1-2a On the one hand, the very detailed synchronism differs clearly from the manner of dating with which Luke opened the first two chapters. But, on the other hand, it is also unmistakable that the geographical horizons that were named in 1.5 and 2.1—the sphere of Herod the Great's rule and the οἰκουμένη (see at 2.1)—are now brought together.

Luke begins with *Tiberius*, the successor of Augustus (ruled 14–37 CE). Close linguistic parallels are found almost exclusively in Josephus and the Septuagint; cf. Josephus, *Antiquitates judaicae* 18.238 (δευτέρῳ δὲ ἔτει τῆς Γαΐου Καίσαρος ἡγεμονίας ["in the second year of the reign of Caesar Claudius"]); *Bellum judaicum* 2.284 (δωδεκάτῳ . . . ἔτει τῆς Νέρωνος ἡγεμονίας ["in the twelfth year of the reign of Nero"]); the same also appears frequently with βασιλείας: 3(1) Ezra 6.1; Esther 3.7; Isaiah 52.4; Daniel 1.1[Theodotion]; 2.1; 8.1[Theodotion]; *Antiquitates judaicae* 8.254, 312; 9.186, 203, 205; and elsewhere. The dating in the fifteenth year of Tiberius, "the only absolute date within the entire New Testament" (Cancik 1982, 49) sounds more precise than it actually is, for no one knows whether Luke wants to have the reign of this emperor begin in the year of his coregency with Augustus (11/12 CE) (so Strobel 1995) or only with his appointment by the Senate (14 CE; so most others). Another uncertainty consists in the fact that we do not know exactly how Luke counted the years and to which calendars he oriented himself (for the different possibilities, cf. Dieckmann 1925; Fitzmyer; Bock I: 910ff).

Some of the other specifications refer to the territory ruled by Herod the Great, which was divided among his sons after his death in 4 CE.

As one of the successors of Publius Sulpicius Quirinius (2.2), *Pontius Pilate* was *praefectus Iudaei* (cf. the inscription printed in Barrett/Thornton 1991, 185; Lémonon 1981; Schwartz, *RGG*[4] 6: 1489–90) from 26 (perhaps also already since 19) to 36 CE. Judea, which originally fell to Herod Archelaus, had belonged to the province of Syria (for the phrasing ἡγεμονεύοντος Ποντίου Πιλάτου, see at 2.2) since 6/7 CE.

Herod's son (*Herod*) *Antipas* ruled as tetrarch from 4 BCE to 39 CE in Galilee and Perea (i.e., as a "small dependent ruler, whose rank and position of power are smaller than those of a king"; W. Bauer 1988, 1621; see also H. Volkmann, *KP* 5: 632–33; Josephus, *Antiquitates judaicae* 17.188, 318; Hoehner 1972). The inclusion of Perea in his territory is not mentioned here; this was, however, the presupposition for the fact that he had access to John the Baptist, who was active on the east shore of the Jordan.

According to Josephus, *Antiquitates judaicae* 17.189, at his father's death Antipas's half brother (*Herod*) *Philipp* received as a tetrarchy Gaulanitis, Trachonitis, Batania, and Pania (these are territories to the east and north of the Lake of Gennesaret; see also *Bellum judaicum* 1.668; 2.95). Iturea is north of Galilee, an area lying between Lebanon and Anti-Lebanon (cf. Strabo 16.2.10, 18; Schottroff 1982, 125–52), which is mentioned in Josephus, *Antiquitates judaicae* 17.319 as a territory of "a certain Zenodorus" (see also 15.360; *Bellum judaicum* 1.398). He governed it until his death in 34 CE.

We know much less about *Lysanias*, the tetrarch of Abilene (an area of this name is not mentioned anywhere else). In *Antiquitates judaicae* 20.138, Josephus reports that Caesar Claudius (ruled 41–54 CE) gave to Herod Agrippa II, *inter alia*, a tetrarchy named Abela that previously belonged to a Lysanias (cf. also 19.275: Ἄβιλα Λυσανίου; as well as *Bellum judaicum* 2.215, 247). This area is usually located north of Damascus and identified with the Abilene mentioned by Luke (cf. Schürer 1973–1987, I: 567–69; see also CIG 4521 = OGIS 606).

The mention of the two chief priests (Luke writes, however, ἐπὶ ἀρχιερέως, like 1 Maccabees 13.42; 14.27; Josephus, *Antiquitates judaicae* 12.157; 14.148; 16.163; Mark 2.26; see also Luke 4.27; Acts 11.28) presents us with riddles that are ultimately irresolvable (in many translations it is not observed that Luke uses the singular here). *Annas* exercised his office from 6–15 CE (cf. Josephus, *Antiquitates judaicae* 18.26, 33–35; see also A. Weiser, *EWNT* 1: 250). He was the father-in-law of *Caiaphas* (cf. John 18.13), who was in office from 18–36/37 CE (cf. Josephus, *Antiquitates judaicae* 18.35, 95; see also B. Chilton, *ABD* 1: 803ff). Luke also designates Annas as high priest in Acts 4.6 and places Caiaphas alongside others in the box "from high priestly lineage." According to John 18.12-14, Annas held a hearing of Jesus, and he is likewise designated high priest (contrast 11.49). In any case, the Lukan phrasing conveys the impression that only Annas was clearly the high priest, while the high priestly dignity of Caiaphas remains unclear. Normally the problem is resolved in a historicizing manner and it is assumed that even after his removal from office Annas still bore the high priestly title (as 'retired high priest,' so to speak; but only New Testament texts are ever named as sources; cf. Schürer 1978–1987, II: 232–33; Jeremias 1969, 178). This does not resolve the problem, however, for if one of the two was high priest at the end of the 20s/beginning of the 30s, it was Caiaphas. For this reason, it is to be assumed that Luke found the two names in his tradition of the passion narrative and assigned the high priestly title to the wrong person.

In any case, the dating, which is unusually precise in comparison with 1.5 and 2.1, has the purpose of precisely fixing historically the events that Luke will report henceforth and of identifying them as components of the history of Israel and world history.

2b takes up 1.80 and Luke now recounts the ἀνάδειξις of the Baptist for Israel announced there (cf. also the terminological link through ἔρημος). Since 1.14-17 the readers already think that John will be installed in the office of the prophet, and since 1.76 they know this for certain. Correspondingly, Luke now brings in the so-called word-event formula, which already designates the installation of the prophets in their commission in the Septuagint (cf. e.g., 2 Samuel 7.4; 24.11; 1 Kings 12.22; 13.20; 17.2, 8; 18.1; 2 Kings 20.4; Micah 11.1; Jonah 1.1; Zechariah 1.1; Isaiah 38.4; Jeremiah 1.4; Ezekiel 1.3; cf. Neumann 1973). However, unlike these examples, the word of God does not come "to" (πρός) but "upon" (ἐπί) John (so only 1 Chronicles 22.8 [with dative]; Jeremiah 1.1). It is understood as an event that comes down from God upon John and powerfully seizes him; Luke may orient himself consciously toward the beginning of the book of Jeremiah (cf. also the continuation in Jeremiah 1.2-3).

3 describes summarily how John carried out the commission issued to him, and in this way Luke indirectly communicates to his readers what this commission consisted in. First he names the area in which the Baptist was active; the phrasing πᾶσαν [τὴν] περίχωρον τοῦ Ἰορδάνου agrees in wording with Genesis 13.10, 11 (see also 2 Chronicles 4.17) and identifies the Baptist's sphere of activity with the area that Lot chose for his herds in his day. Genesis 13.10 credits this region with a richness of water, "before the Lord had destroyed Sodom and Gomorrah." It is possible that this additional observation has had an influence on the original phrasing of the geographical information (see also Matthew 3.5) in order to establish the connection to the destroying fire announced by John (see also Bovon; Böhlemann 1997, 49–50; Radl). The phrasing πᾶσα (ἡ) περίχωρος is a Septuagintism (see also Genesis 19.17; Deuteronomy 3.4 [plural], 13, 14; 2 Chronicles 16.4 [plural]; Judith 3.7), for it is not attested in other Greek literature. At any rate, with this geographical placement Luke wants to evoke the impression that John was active not only at a single location but that the place of his activity extended over a great stretch of land on both sides of the Jordan. That he was now no longer "in the wilderness" does not emerge from the text; rather, this assumption, which is sometimes advocated, rests on an inaccurate understanding of ἔρημος (see at 1.80).

In v. 3b Luke communicates, in a word-for-word adoption of Mark 1.4b, what John did in the aforementioned region. This is at the same time the carrying out of what Gabriel and Zechariah had named as his commission in 1.17 and 1.76-78a.

Here κηρύσσειν + accusative should probably be understood in the same sense as in Vita Aesopi 21–22: "When the offerer [at the market] offered the slaves (τοῦ δὲ κήρυκος τὰ σωμάτια κηρύττοντος) . . ." a woman heard this; she went to her husband and said, "Slaves are just being offered (εὐκαίρως σωμάτια κηρύσσονται); go there and buy for me a proper slave for the work."

What is new in relation to what is announced in 1.76b-78a and to this extent unexpected for the readers is only the term βάπτισμα, namely in two respects. First, Luke has previously not indicated with a single word that John would also carry out a ritual washing for the forgiveness of sins. Second, they could have previously encountered this term only in Romans 6.4 and Mark 1.4; 10.38-39; 11.30 par. Matthew 21.25, for outside of the New Testament (with reference to John's baptism, see also Matthew 3.7; Luke 7.29; 20.4; Acts 1.22; 10.37; 13.24; 18.25; 19.3, 4 and concerning Christian baptism, see Ephesians 4.5; 1 Peter 3.21) this word, which as *nomen rei actae* indicates the result of an action (cf. BDR §109.2), is not attested. Also the cognate *nomen actionis* (cf. BDR §109.1) βαπτισμός (in the New Testament: Mark 7.4; Colossians 2.12; Hebrews 6.2; 9.10) occurs outside of the early Christian literature for the first time in Josephus, *Antiquitates judaicae* 18.117, i.e., in the report about John the Baptist (!) (cf. then also Plutarch, *Moralia* 166a; Corpus Hermeticum, Fragment 25.8). In comparison with the ritual washings that were common in the environment, the "immersion" propagated by John (for the translation, cf. Wolter 2002a, 375n79) was distinctive not so much in the fact that it led to the forgiveness of sins (for the phrasing εἰς ἄφεσιν ἁμαρτιῶν, cf. Philo, *De specialibus legibus* 1.190: the he-goat is called περὶ ἁμαρτίας, but it is offered εἰς ἁμαρτημάτων ἄφεσιν ["for the forgiveness of sins"]; Luke 24.47: μετάνοια εἰς ἄφεσιν ἁμαρτιῶν; Acts 2.38: βαπτισθήτω ἕκαστος ὑμῶν . . . εἰς ἄφεσιν τῶν ἁμαρτιῶν ὑμῶν), for this was prepared by texts such as Isaiah 1.15-16; Psalms 51.3-4, 7-9; Life of Adam and Eve 4.3–6.2 (see also Klawans 2000; cf. in addition Ovid, *Metamorphoses* 11.132–43). Rather, the baptism of John obtained its specific profile through two features: first, through the active role that John played as *immerser* (ὁ βαπτίζων or ὁ βαπτιστής; these designations are correspondingly related exclusively to John in ancient literature: cf. Josephus, *Antiquitates judaicae* 18.116; Mark 1.4; 6.14; 6.24, 25par.; 8.28parr.; Matthew 3.11; 11.11-12; 17.13; Luke 7.20, 33), both in the carrying out and in the interpretation; second, by the fact that it took place only *one time*. This element of taking place only once is expressed through the genitive phrase βάπτισμα μετανοίας. The *genitivus qualitatis* μετανοίας (cf. BDR §165₂; see also Acts 13.24; 19.4) characterizes the "immersion" as an element of a non-repeatable and therefore eschatic repentance that leads to the forgiveness of sins and thus to deliverance in the advancing judgment of wrath.

4-6 Luke interprets the activity of John the Baptist—like the synoptic parallels—as fulfilling the prophetic promise of Isaiah and quotes for this Isaiah 40.3-5, though with small deviations. The introductory formula in v. 4a is formulated in a more stilted manner vis-à-vis the Markan *Vorlage* (for the phrasing "βίβλος λόγων of so-and-so," cf. Tobit 1.1; Assumption of Moses, Fragment e: ἐν βίβλῳ λόγων μυστικῶν Μωσέως αὐτὸς Μωσῆς προεῖπε περὶ τοῦ Δαυὶδ καὶ Σολομῶντος ["In the book of the secret words of Moses, Moses himself made predictions in relation to David and Solomon"]; Testament of Job 1.1; 1 Kings 11.41; Greek Apocalypse of Enoch 14.1). At the beginning of the quotation the mistake of Mark 1.2 is avoided, where a combination of Exodus 23.20 and Malachi 3.1 is quoted as an Isaiah text. The same applies to the parallel in Matthew 3.2; but in Luke and in Matthew the quotation that is missing here is then found in both with a reference to the Baptist in a Q-tradition (Luke 7.27 par. Matthew 11.10). There is no clear explanation for this circumstance. It is conceivable that Matthew and Luke have independently corrected an obvious error in Mark; but it also cannot be excluded that they both found the Isaiah quotation in Q (in this sense, e.g., Catchpole 1993b; Schröter 2003, 58), though without it being possible to say something about its extent.

In any case, Luke identifies John the Baptist with "the one crying out in the wilderness," who, according to Isaiah 40.3, announces the coming of God and in three synthetic parallelisms calls his hearers to prepare themselves for this (Isaiah 40.3-4 quoted in Luke 3.4b-5). Luke had already taken up the imagery of this call in the description of the task of the Baptist in the Benedictus (cf. 1.76b), and he had also already used the key word "prepare" (ἑτοιμάζειν) in 1.17c. These three texts (namely, 1.17c, 1.76b, and 3.4b-5) now work together in the more immediate literary context in such a way that the proclamation of the "baptism of repentance for the forgiveness of sins" (3.3) fuses semantically with the exhortation of "the one crying out in the wilderness" to prepare the way (see also Rusam 2003, 159). The imperatives in vv. 8, 10-14 then unpack what Luke understands by the preparing of the way to which Isaiah 40.3-5 exhorts (see also Bock).

At the end of v. 4, Luke replaces, following Mark 1.2, the phrasing τοῦ θεοῦ ἡμῶν from Isaiah 40.3 with αὐτοῦ. This results in a loss of unambiguousness, but that is probably precisely intended—is Jesus meant or God? One need not answer this question with an either-or, for there was

a comparable ambiguity already in 1.16-17, 76. God has his own coming announced, and it comes—Jesus; on this characteristic element of the
Lukan Christology, see at 1.76. For the universal visibility of the σωτήριον
τοῦ θεοῦ (v. 6), see at 2.30. The fact that Luke skips over Isaiah 40.5a
("and the δόξα κυρίου will appear") probably is not due to an oversight
(so Rusam 2003, 158 among others) but rather has been done deliberately.
The glory of God was present in the proclamation of the birth of Jesus
among the shepherds on earth (2.9), but precisely only on this occasion.
Otherwise, Luke painstakingly takes care that it remains a heavenly entity
and therefore accessible only in heaven (cf. 2.14; 19.38; Acts 7.55; see
also Luke 24.26). It will be encountered only once more, in a very special
situation, by a few chosen disciples at Jesus's transfiguration (9.31-32). It
will not be accessible on earth again until the parousia—then, however, as
δόξα of the Son of Man (cf. 9.26; 21.27). The difference from Johannine
Christology is clear (cf. e.g., John 1.14; 2.11; 5.44; 11.4, 40).

The quotation from Isaiah 40.3-5 in 3.4-6 obtains its special significance also through the fact that until the end of Luke–Acts it is the last
explicit quotation of Scripture with which the narrator directly addresses
his readers in order to furnish the narrated events with an interpretation
drawn intertextually from the Old Testament. After this, Scripture quotations appear only as elements of the narrative, i.e., the instances who quote
them are always only narrative figures who, of course, express the author's
mind (cf. the overview in Rusam 2003, 2–3).

7-9 The first chreia presents the Baptist as a prophetic preacher of
repentance, who in view of imminent judgment of destruction exhorts the
people to change their way of life. The *Leitwort* (leading word) is "to bear
fruit" (vv. 8a, 9b). In this respect, the Lukan presentation of the Baptist
comes into very close contact with the picture that Josephus, *Antiquitates
judaicae* 18.116–19 sketches of John. The baptizing activity of John is,
by contrast, just as little a narrative topic of its own here as it is in what
follows; it never comes out from the background of the narrated events.

In the narrative exposition at the beginning of **7**, this finds expression
in the fact that Luke uses the baptism only to explain why the people come
to John (here Luke has the neutral ὄχλοι, while Matthew 3.7 has Pharisees
and Sadducees come to John; there is a similar juxtaposition in Luke 11.29
diff. Matthew 12.38). But neither this intention nor the baptism itself go
on to play a role in the words of the Baptist; rather, the concern is exclusively with the way of life of those who wish to be baptized. The words
that John is accustomed to direct to them begin in v. 7b with an aggres-
sive insulting of the addressees. Its wording is without analogy (at least
apart from the fact that Matthew 12.34; 23.33 has Jesus title the Pharisees
[and scribes] in this way). The likelihood ranges from possible to probable

that the designation γεννήματα ἐχιδνῶν arose in the same way as ἔκγονα ἀσπίδων in Isaiah 11.8; 14.29, where it is a rendering of the Hebrew צֶפַע or צִפְעוֹנִי (see also 30.6; Nestle 1913, 267–68), i.e., as an attempt to translate an Aramaic designation for a certain animal into Greek. This verse is not, to be sure, a "reproach" (*pace* K. Berger 1984a, 195; Kirk 1998b, 6), for no actions are criticized. Rather, the propositional content of the rhetorical question in v. 7c consists solely in the observation that under the present conditions there is no possibility of escaping the coming destroying judgment of God; for the concept of judgment that is connected with the key word ὀργή, cf. Konradt 2003, 57ff; for the connection between wrath and fire (vv. 9, 17), see especially Isaiah 66.15-16 ("the Lord will come with fire . . . to avenge in the fury of his wrath and with reproaches in flames of fire; for the Lord will judge the whole earth through fire"; see also 5.25; 30.27; Jeremiah 4.4; 7.20; Ezekiel 21.36-37; 22.21: "fire of my wrath"; Zephaniah 1.15). Thus, "wrath" stands here metonymically for "fire" or in general for ruin or destruction.

8 John, however, points out, first (v. 8a), a way that preserves from ruin. But strangely he now summons not—as would actually be expected from v. 7b-c—to repentance but to the producing of deeds with which the already completed repentance will be made visible (see also Acts 26.20). While v. 7 assumed rhetorically that the addressees still had repentance before them, v. 8a presupposes it as already realized. This incoherence has arisen through the fact that Luke changed the singular καρπὸν ἄξιον, which stood in Q (see still Matthew 3.8) and was directed to the carrying out of the baptism (cf. also Sevenich-Bax 1993, 302), to a plural and in this way ethicized the summons (cf. the taking up again of the fruit metaphor in v. 9b and the imperative ποιήσατε in vv. 10-14). Luke has the Baptist speak now in the style of the post-conversion speech of admonition. The fruit metaphor is often found in paraenetic contexts in order to designate actions as consequences of an event or identity—in the New Testament, cf. also Matthew 7.16, 20; Romans 6.22; Galatians 5.22; Ephesians 5.9; Colossians 1.10; James 3.17. As the general use of "worthy" with the genitive shows (cf. just 2 Maccabees 4.25; 6.23, 24, 27; 4 Maccabees 5.11; 7.6) this adjective describes something like a relationship of appropriateness; accordingly, when used paraenetically it has the function of qualifying a certain "ought" as a consequence of a certain "is." Incidentally, Plutarch, *Moralia* 1117c also speaks of a "worthy fruit" in the sense of an intended consequence: οὐ μέντοι τὸ θεράπευμα τοῦτο . . . ἔσχε καρπὸν ἄξιον ("However, this homage did not bring corresponding fruit").

In terms of subject matter, v. 8b-c refers back to v. 7c. After what is said in v. 8a, the rejection of a potential objection that argues with the election of Israel reads like a radical destruction of any possibility of salvation that is not based on an action that gives credible expression to the repentance that has been put into effect. Luke takes over the theological disempowering of being children of Abraham from Q (cf. Matthew 3.9), though it stands in a certain tension with the idea of a salvation-historical continuity, which had always been important to him up to now—namely, that the activity of the Baptist is an integral component of God's eschatic fulfillment of the promise of Abraham (cf. 1.73; see also 1.55). In this way, however, there arises an interesting correspondence to his interaction with the election of Israel, e.g., in Acts 3.19-26. Both here and there we find an exhortation to repent, and both here and there criteria for having a share in the salvation that is brought with the fulfillment of the old promises are defined anew. With John they are "fruits that correspond to repentance," while in the Jerusalem speech of Peter it is the turning to Christ. It is common to both that God can establish belonging to Abraham ("Abraham's children") also on the basis of other criteria than the criterion of physical descent. Paul also says precisely the same in Romans 9.6-13 and Galatians 3.6-29. A wordplay may be hidden in v. 8c, for the Hebrew or Aramaic word for "stones" (אֲבָנִם or אַבְנִן) and "children" (בָּנִם or בָּנִין) are only slightly different (see also at 20.17-18).

9 takes up the imagery of v. 8a and intensifies the announcement of the coming judgment of destruction by bringing in a temporal factor via the temporal adverb ἤδη and with the help of the image of an ax that is already placed on the root of the trees (the tree feller need only raise his hand and strike). John states that the judgment of God has already begun and therefore no time remains for postponing the required action; for the image field, cf. von Gemünden 1993, 123ff; Reiser 1990, 163: "If one wishes to cut out the bad trees in an orchard, one must strike them under the earth at the roots. Therefore, the roots must first be carefully exposed. This is the situation presupposed in the parable. The roots are exposed, and the ax is placed for the first strike" (the assumption that the traditional image of Israel as the "planting of God" is taken up here [Reiser 1990, 161] is, however, unfounded). The tradition-historical background is graspable particularly in Daniel 4.14, 23[LXX]: ἐκκόψατε αὐτὸ καὶ καταφθείρατε αὐτό (sc. τὸ δένδρον) / ἐξᾶραι τὸ δένδρον καὶ ἐκκόψαι· ἡ κρίσις τοῦ θεοῦ . . . ἤξει ἐπὶ σέ ("strike . . . it . . . down! / tear out and cut down the tree: the judgment of God will come over you"). Beyond this, the agricultural practice of cutting down fruitless trees is also frequently used as an image for God's action of judgment elsewhere (cf. Matthew 7.17-19; Luke 13.6-9; for the metaphorical use of ποιεῖν καρπόν, see at 8.15). The explanation that God gives for the sparing of Nineveh in Ps.-Philo, *De Jona* 52–53 (216–18) is especially interesting: ". . . one cuts down a tree that is useless; but if it produces fruit, one lets it stand. Also the Ninevites were once without the fruits of piety . . . But now . . . How could I then uphold the judgment of death that was (once) announced without change in relation to those who have changed their life?" For the future meaning of the present forms ἐκκόπτεται and βάλλεται, cf. BDR §323. The announcement that the felled trees will also be burned intensifies the threat (from Sodom and Gomorrah onward the biblical tradition knows that God uses fire as a means for the punishing destruction; see Genesis 19.24-25; cf. further, e.g., Ezekiel 15.6-7). Not even its wood can still be used (cf. also the corresponding threat in Jeremiah 22.7: "Men of destruction will cut down your choicest cedars and throw them into the fire [ἐκκόψουσιν . . . καὶ ἐμβαλοῦσιν εἰς τὸ πῦρ]"). As another semantic feature one can add what is announced in 1 Enoch 48.9: "Like straw in fire . . . so they will burn . . . , and there will be no trace of them to find."

In **10-14** Luke has the Baptist concretize the material ethical content of the "fruits that correspond to repentance" (v. 8). The ὄχλοι of v. 7 return in v. 10, and the imperative ποιήσατε from v. 8 is taken up again through the threefold question τί ποιήσωμεν; (vv. 10, 12, 14). The textual unit is composed of three parts, which are clearly divided from one another through changing questioners. First, the aforementioned ὄχλοι come (vv. 10-11), then tax collectors (vv. 12-13), and finally soldiers (v. 14). All ask John the same question—a question that Luke also has his narrative figures pose time and again later; cf. 12.17; 16.3; 20.13; Acts 2.37; 22.10 (see also Luke 10.25; 18.18; Acts 16.30). The comparison with Acts 2.37 in particular shows that in his opinion this is the correct reaction to the message of the Baptist (see also Liebenberg 1993, 61).

If taken on its own, i.e., without a previous introduction of the person and message of the Baptist, vv. 10-14 would remain hanging in the air. It is therefore to be understood only within its literary context, and the assumption of an independent tradition as (pre-)Lukan *Sondergut* is rather improbable. If one does not wish to postulate that Matthew found it in Q but passed over it or that Matthew and Luke had two different Q-versions before them, then there remains as the most plausible solution only the assumption that Luke has created it himself.

10-11 The answer to the question of the ὄχλοι, which John gives in v. 11b-c, refers to clothing and food, i.e., to the absolutely indispensable necessities for human life. Accordingly, parallel groupings are found in many texts; in addition to Luke 12.23 par. Matthew 6.25 (τροφή and ἔνδυμα), cf. Genesis 28.20; Deuteronomy 10.18; Isaiah 4.1; Tobit 1.17; Jubilees 27.27; Diodorus Siculus 34/35.2.2; 1 Timothy 6.8 ("If we have food and clothing we will be content with these"); James 2.15. Here χιτών and βρώματα stand as examples for the basic needs of human existence. Thus, one should give to the needy what one has more of than one needs.

The instruction formulated in Sibylline Oracles 2.83 (ed. Geffcken 1967, 31.2) leads into the immediate proximity of the exhortation of the Baptist: ἔνδυσον γυμνόν, μετάδος πεινῶντ᾽ ἄρτων σῶν ("clothe the naked, give to the hungry from your bread"); cf. also the comparable phrasings in Tobit 1.17; 4.16 ("Give to the hungry from your bread and to the naked from your outer garments"); Isaiah 58.7; Ezekiel 18.7; Job 24.10; Testament of Issachar 7.5 (πτωχῷ μετέδωκα τὸν ἄρτον μου ["To the poor I gave away my bread"]). A χιτών is the undergarment worn on the skin or over a linen shirt. It reached to the knees or the ankles and had long or half-length sleeves (it was thus similar to the Roman *tunica*; cf. the image in *LAW* 1535; see also Krauss 1966, 161ff). Etymologically we are dealing with the Greek transcription of the Hebrew כֻּתֹּנֶת (cf. Genesis 37.23 and elsewhere; the piece of clothing that one put on over it was called ἱμάτιον; Luke 6.29 par. Matthew 5.40; Acts 9.39). The imperative ὁμοίως ποιείτω, etc., is found only in Luke within the New Testament (see also 6.31; 10.37). Thus, Luke has John demand nothing extraordinary or spectacular, but make a demand with regard to the care for the poor that had long been a given. We are really dealing "with a commonplace of ethical instruction" (Horn 1986, 94), which is anything but "extreme" (so Nolland). By contrast, the ethical demand with which Jesus later appears—namely, to sell all one's possessions and give the proceeds to the poor (12.33; 18.22)—is much more radical. And precisely this is the difference between "law and prophets until John" (16.16) and the proclamation of the reign of God with which Jesus connects the demand to separate oneself from all one's possessions (see at 16.16a-b).

12 Luke singles out the tax collectors from the ὄχλοι without wanting to give the impression that they appeared as a group before John. Rather, the informational content of this verse consists in the fact that tax collectors were also included among those who wanted to let themselves be baptized and bring forth the corresponding fruits (v. 8a) and the fact that they addressed John with the respectful title "Rabbi" (on this address, see at 7.40). Luke certainly does not mention this fact without also thinking of Jesus, for he is able to report various kinds of contact between him and the tax collectors later (cf. 5.29-32; 7.34; 15.1; 19.1-10). He thus makes visible here a piece of continuity between John and Jesus (cf. also 7.29).

The interest of the tax collectors in the message of the Baptist is also noteworthy because they had an extremely bad image in ancient society. In the New Testament this is expressed in the term pair "tax collectors and sinners" (Mark 2.15, 16; Luke 7.34 par. Matthew 11.19; Luke 15.1; cf. also the pair "tax collectors and prostitutes" in Matthew 21.31, 32) and in Luke 19.7, where the voice of the people can title Zachaeus ἁμαρτωλὸς ἀνήρ on the basis of his occupation alone; see also 18.11 (with the series "robbers, unrighteous, adulterers, tax collectors"); 18.13 with the self-designation of the tax collector as a "sinner"; Xeno Comicus, Fragment 1 (Kock 1880–1888): πάντες τελῶναι, πάντες ἅρπαγες ("all [are] tax collectors, all robbers"; similar series in Herrenbrück 1990, 81ff, 206). The bad reputation of the tax collector had its basis in the fact that the concern was with a tax-leaser (*Abgabenpächter*) working on his own behalf (or only with his employee; cf. Donahue 1971, 54), who had previously purchased the right to levy fees and taxes (cf. the description of the procedure in Josephus, *Antiquitates judaicae* 12.175ff) and had to see to it that he not only covered his costs but also made a profit. Thus, it was not the supposed "collaboration with the foreign occupying power" that was responsible for the tax collector's bad image, as one often hears, but rather their economic interest in pocketing the highest possible fees, etc. (i.e., beyond the set tariffs), for every "additional revenue . . . wandered into their own pocket" (Herrenbrück 1987, 190).

The ethical demand that the tax collectors get to hear from John in **13** also refers precisely to this; πράσσειν is a *terminus technicus* for the collection of money (cf. Luke 19.23; Theophrastus, *Characteres* 6.9; Demosthenes, *Orationes* 59.41; Appian, *Bella civilia* 1.232; Josephus, *Antiquitates judaicae* 9.233; and above all Cassius Dio, *Historia Romana* 53.15.6: μήτ' ἀργύριον ἔξω τοῦ τεταγμένου ἐσπράσσειν ["to collect no money apart from what is fixed"]). Thus, the Lukan John does not plead for the abolishment of taxes and fees but demands that those tasked with their collection not use them in a crooked manner for their individual enrichment. Here too we have a demand that undoubtedly does not move one millimeter beyond the prevailing ethical consensus.

The same applies to the instruction that John gives to the soldiers in **14**. The often discussed question of whether Luke thinks of Roman (and this would mean non-Jewish) soldiers or of soldiers from the army of Herod Antipas (these could then be Jews but need not be) is completely insignificant, for here the concern is solely with the question of how soldiers behave toward the civil population and this always arises in the same way—regardless of whom the soldiers fight for and by whom they are paid. They receive a paraenetic instruction that is composed of two parts, namely an apotreptic part (what they should refrain from doing) and a protreptic part (what they should do).

The two apotreptic admonitions find their common semantic feature in the fact that they each describe the use of force by the stronger against the weaker.

For διασείειν, cf. e.g., Polybius 10.26.4 (as behavior of soldiers: P. Oxy. II, 240.5–7). The use of συκοφαντεῖν in this passage finds its closest parallel in those texts of the Septuagint that use this verb and its cognates to translate the Hebrew עֲשֹׁק ("oppress, use force") and its cognates (Psalm^LXX 71.4; 118.122, 134; Proverbs 14.31; 22.16; 28.3, 16; Ecclesiastes 4.1 [3×]; 5.7; Job 35.9; cf. already Nestle 1903, 271–72). But here too the semantic spectrum is quite broad: for συκοφαντία it reaches, e.g., from "ill-gotten gains" (Ecclesiastes 7.7) to "violent oppression" (e.g., Psalm^LXX 118.134; Ecclesiastes 4.1). διασείειν and συκοφαντεῖν are also paralleled elsewhere; cf. P. Tebt 43.26, 36; Wilcken 1957, 161, col. II, 65–66; 162, col. V, 1 (see also Antiphon, *De choreuta* 43; Kinman 1993, 597, though without the apologetic intention that he wants to ascribe to Luke); Tabula Cebetis 40.3 (parallel, among others, to ληΐζεσθαι, ἀνδροφονεῖν, and ἀποστερεῖν ["rob, murder, and defraud"]).

The protreptic exhortation to be content with one's pay (cf. 1 Corinthians 9.7 and Spicq 1994, II: 600: "the wage paid in cash"; *pace* Caragounis 1974; on the plural, cf. BDR §141.6) is the positive counterpart to the two apotreptic instructions and corresponds to the exhortation to the soldiers to collect only "the fixed amount." Both groups should use the means of power at their disposal not for their own enrichment and to the detriment of the people who are at their mercy. On ἀρκεῖσθαι as an ethical ideal, cf. Ps.-Phocylides 5–6 ("Do not enrich yourself illegally but live from what comes to you legitimately; be content with your own things [ἀρκεῖσθαι παρ' ἐοίσι] and keep away from the possessions of others"); 1 Timothy 6.8; Hebrews 13.5 (parallel to ἀφιλάργυρος).

The most noteworthy feature in the ethical instructions that Luke has the Baptist give as καρποὶ ἄξιοι τῆς μετανοίας is undoubtedly their entirely ordinary character. Luke presents John as an ethical teacher who observes one of the most important ground rules of ancient paraenesis: "One should not strive after novel things, for in them [sc. in paraenetic speeches] one may say nothing foreign, nothing doubtful, and nothing uncommon" (Isocrates, *Ad Nicolem* 41). But in precisely this way John fulfills his salvation-historical function, as this is described in 1.16-17, 76b-78a: He turns "the disobedient to think on what is right, in order to prepare for the Lord a ready people" (1.17).

Luke has equipped **15-17** with his own narrative introduction (v. 15), which furnishes the words of the Baptist taken over from Q and Mark (vv. 16-17) with a specific occasion and through this, of course, also gives them a very specific thematic orientation. With the help of this introduction he has John correct the misunderstanding that he might possibly be the expected Messiah. This same technique is used by Luke at minimum in 19.11(-27) and Acts 1.6(-8), and perhaps also in Luke 10.17; 11.1; 17.5. Luke now leaves the scene constructed in v. 7, which portrays John in the circle of those wishing to be baptized, who had "come out" to him.

At the center stands now the impression that John makes—beyond the circle of those wishing to be baptized—upon the "whole" people (cf. διαλογιζομένων; the plural as further specification of λαός is *constructio ad sensum*; see at 1.21). Thus, the concern now is with the reputation that John enjoys in Israel as a whole. The use of the designation λαός (see at 1.10) expresses beyond this that we are now dealing with a topic that concerns Israel as the chosen people of God.

15 Luke begins with a thought report that is reminiscent of 1.21. In the first genitive absolute it is unusual that προσδοκᾶν does not have an object. The context from which the object must be added in such cases (W. Bauer 1988, 1427) is here undoubtedly the immediately following second genitive absolute (προσδοκᾶν and διαλογίζεσθαι also interpret each other in 2 Maccabees 12.43-44: ὑπὲρ ἀναστάσεως διαλογιζόμενος . . . , τοὺς προπεπτωκότας ἀναστῆναι προσεδόκα ["thinking about the resurrection . . . he expected that the fallen would rise"]; see also Polybius 8.18.1). The joining καί must therefore be understood as epexegetical (cf. BDR §442.6), and Luke ascribes to the people the expectation that it would get to see deeds from John that would show him to be the expected Messiah. While Luke sketches in the speculation aimed at John into the Jewish Messiah expectation (on this cf. Charlesworth/Lichtenberger/Oegema 1998; Oegema 1998), he formulates the question, of course, "in the knowledge of the Messiah Jesus" (Radl I: 187). In this way he identifies for his readers the person spoken of in the tradition preserved in v. 17 with Jesus Christ. John 1.19-20 also knows of a comparable expectation aimed at John, but it is probably more than doubtful that something like the revering of John as a messianic figure actually stood behind these texts let alone in the Lukan environment (cf. Backhaus 1991, 342ff).

16 Luke has John correct the misunderstanding (he formulates more clearly in Acts 13.25a, b). The object πᾶσιν (v. 16a) takes up πάντων from v. 15 and ensures in this way that a saying now follows that is intended for all Israel—even if one takes into account that both pronouns are hyperbolic. To whom the announcement of the "mightier one" coming after John refers for the historical Baptist is notoriously controversial. Is it God, the Son of Man, or another judging figure (cf. the presentation of the discussion in Dunn 2003, 369ff)? Luke at any rate transfers this designation to Jesus and then uses an image to illustrate how great the superiority of the coming ἰσχυρότερος is vis-à-vis John (see also John 1.27). The loosening of the straps with which the leather soles were fastened to the foot and sometimes also to the lower shank (cf. the images in Bruhn/Tilke 1955, 15–16, 20) belonged to the tasks of the slaves (for instance when their master wanted to recline to eat; rabbinic texts in Bill. I: 121). The Baptist thus describes the difference in social categories.

In vv. 16b and 16e the Lukan John contrasts his own "activity" with that of the coming "more powerful one." *Pace* Radl I: 187 one must maintain that the phrasing ὕδατι βαπτίζω (i.e., without ἐν) can, of course, also be understood locally, i.e., in the sense of "to immerse in water," and in view of the subject matter this is more likely at any rate (cf. Heraclitus Philosophus, *Allegoriae Homericae* 69.16 [Buffière 1962]; Hippocrates, *De affectionibus internis* 39; Plutarch, *Moralia* 950c). The problems of interpretation arise through the fact that here Luke has combined the Q and Mark traditions. Q had spoken (as presumably the historical Baptist had already done) only of an "immersion" in fire and in this way motivated the exhortation to accept water baptism by John: whoever refuses the water baptism is liable to the imminent destruction by fire. In Mark 1.8 the tradition is changed especially by the fact that Mark made those baptized by John the addressees of the word (namely, with the help of the aorist phrasing ἐβάπτισα ὑμᾶς). In this way the announcement of the baptizing activity of the "more powerful one" becomes a word of promise. Those baptized by John with water he will reward with the bestowing of the Holy Spirit. The combination of these two versions in v. 16e leads to the following question. Did Luke understand the juxtaposition of Holy Spirit and fire as a distinction between eschatic allocation of salvation and destruction (e.g., Schürmann; Radl), or does he have in mind here the Pentecost event described in Acts 2.1-4 (e.g., Marshall; Schneider; Wiefel; Bovon; Johnson; other possibilities can be found in Bock)? With a view to v. 17, where salvation and unsalvation are explicitly set over against each other and in view of the fact that the outpouring of the Spirit at Pentecost is not given to a single one of the ὑμεῖς whom Luke envisages here as present, the first interpretation mentioned is more likely. To be sure, the juxtaposition of these two manners of baptism is lacking in Acts 13.25, the epitome of this verse. In this it is evident that Luke's concern here is not primarily with a statement about the future fate of the addressees of the Baptist, but with the Baptist's relation to Jesus. Thus, v. 16e does not reflect the perspective of those being baptized. Rather, the statement wants to make clear why the ἰσχυρότερος coming after John is more powerful—because he carries out the eschatic judgment.

17 Luke has the Baptist sketch out a metaphorical timetable with another parabolic saying. With this he wants to make clear to his addressees where they find themselves in the sequence of the eschatic events that proceed with the same necessity as the production steps in the harvest (cf. especially Xenophon, *Oeconomicus* 18; Dalman 1964, III: 67ff; see also Schwarz 1981, 266). The fixed point is the burning of the straw (ἄχυρον) after the conclusion of all the other work stages (v. 17d; see also Genesis 24.25, 32; Judges 19.19; 21.18; Isaiah 11.7; Jeremiah 23.28). Many commentators speak of the burning of chaff, but this is blown away by the wind (cf. e.g., Job 21.18; Psalm 1.4; Daniel 2.35^{LXX}). This event is identified with the judgment of fire, which was already spoken of explicitly in v. 9 and implicitly in v. 7 and which the Baptist had announced as imminent. The parabolic saying describes the situation after the threshing, when the threshing lies on the threshing floor and the farmer throws it into the air with the shovel (πτύον) so that the wind carries away the chaff, and chopped straw and wheat fall next to each other on the floor (although the term ἅλων actually means the threshing floor, it can also designate metonymically what lies on it—namely, wheat, chaff, and chopped straw). John and his hearers find themselves at the very beginning of this work stage. The farmer or the coming "stronger one" already has the shovel in hand (v. 17a) and will soon begin separating the chaff and wheat (v. 17b). The harvest and the threshing already lie behind them, and after the winnowing there still comes (v. 17c) the gathering of the wheat into the storage place (ἀποθήκη; see also Matthew 6.26; 13.30; Luke 12.18, 24)—this process functions as a metaphor for the salvation fate of the baptized—and the burning of the straw (v. 17d). The designation of the fire as "unquenchable" (ἄσβεστος) bursts the picture, for as soon as the straw was burned, the fire went out of course. Thus, here the target domain protrudes into the source domain, namely the conception of the fire of judgment that never goes out (cf. Job 20.26; Isaiah 66.24; 1 Enoch 10.13; 18.11; 21.7; 90.24; Greek Apocalypse of Ezra 1.24; Matthew 25.41; Mark 9.48; see also Bill. IV/2: 1075ff; H. Lichtenberger, *EWNT* 3: 483–84); see also at 8.8b; 12.37, 46; 19.27.

According to some commentators, John has before his eyes a different point in time in the sequence of the work stages. In their view the winnowing has just taken place, and the farmer is now in the process of transporting the wheat with the shovel from the threshing floor into the storage place (so e.g., Schürmann; Nolland; Radl; see also Webb 1991a, 105ff). However, speaking against this view is, first, the fact that the term "clean/ purify" (καθαίρειν and cognates) can certainly designate the winnowing in this context: cf. Xenophon, *Oeconomicus* 18.6, 8; Alciphron, *Epistulae* 2.23.1 (ἄρτι μοι τὴν ἅλω διακαθήραντι καὶ τὸ πτύον ἀποτιθεμένῳ ὁ δεσπότης ἐπέστη ["I had just cleansed the threshing and put away the shovel then the master came to me"]); Columella, *De re rustica* 2.9.10 (*quicquid exteretur caphisterio expurgandum erit* ["everything that is threshed should be cleansed with a winnowing shovel"]); see also *De re rustica* 20.5 and Reiser 1990, 166–67. Second, in this case the shovel is placed on the salvation side as a work tool, namely in the gathering of the wheat (see above). In this case one would also have to introduce the auxiliary hypothesis that this saying functions as a salvation saying directed to those already baptized by John—which is, to be sure, by no means excluded (cf. Wolter 2002a, 377).

18 is a summary that generalizes the examples of the proclamation of the Baptist mentioned in vv. 7-17 (cf. again the imperfect). In this way Luke reveals to his readers that in what has preceded he has reproduced only an excerpt from the entire activity of the Baptist. For many the verb εὐαγγελίζεσθαι sounds out of place in light of the massive threats in vv. 7-9, 17, and therefore they would like to neutralize it ("to preach" instead of "to gospel" or "to proclaim good news"; so e.g., Liebenberg 1993, 64–65; Radl). But this interpretation does not do justice to the picture that Luke sketches of John the Baptist. Rather, Luke understands the message that John delivers as a carrying out of the task that John's father spoke of in the Benedictus: "to give his people knowledge of salvation" (1.77). There is no indication that Luke no longer wants to know anything of this now.

19-20 These two verses correspond to vv. 1-6. After Luke has brought the Baptist into his narrative there, he now withdraws him again. Narratively the notification of the placement of the Baptist in prison by Herod Antipas is connected to the preceding in such a way that a concessive structure arises (cf. BDR §447.2a). "It is true (μέν) that John gospeled . . . , but (δέ) Herod . . . placed him in prison." In this way Luke indicates that it was a familiar constellation that prepared a violent end to the activity of John, namely the confrontation of the prophet with the political ruler. As the reason for the imprisonment of the Baptist, Luke mentions, following Mark 6.17-18, his criticism of Antipas's marriage with Herodias, whom he had taken from his half brother Herod (a son of the daughter of Simon the high priest) after sending away his first wife, a daughter of the Nabatean king Aretas IV. Mark 6.17 erroneously regards her as the wife of Herod Philip (son of Cleopatra of Jerusalem; see at 3.1); but his wife was Salome, a daughter from the marriage of Herodias (cf. Josephus, *Antiquitates judaicae* 18.136). Josephus, *Antiquitates judaicae* 18.109–115 (this is the section that directly precedes the report about John the Baptist) provides orientation concerning the specific circumstances of the affair and its consequences, which were entirely disastrous for Herod Antipas. According to Leviticus 18.16; 20.21, marriage with the "wife of the brother"—as Luke formulates with Mark 6.18 in agreement with the two Old Testament texts—was regarded as a violation of the Torah's prohibition of incest. It is not at all inconceivable that the historical John did not let this behavior go without comment, even though Josephus mentions a completely different reason for his imprisonment by Herod Antipas (*Antiquitates judaicae* 18.118). According to Josephus, he feared that the extraordinary resonance of the Baptist among the population could become politically dangerous for him. Luke adds that Herod Antipas was not attacked by John only because of his marriage to Herodias but in general περὶ πάντων ὧν ἐποίησεν πονηρῶν (attraction of the relative pronoun; cf. BDR §294.3). Thus, Herod is made into a villain in a very intentional manner, and with this, of course, Luke also provides his readers with an understandable explanation for why John was thrown into prison despite his εὐαγγελίζεσθαι.

The linguistic harshness that exists through the asyndetic connection of vv. 20a and 20b without καί has led to the fact that καί was added subsequently (*pace* Nestle/Aland[27]); the manuscript tradition is therefore also divided (without καί: א* B D Ξ b e; with καί: א² A C L W Θ Ψ and others). Even with καί there admittedly remains a certain harshness; it can be reduced, however, if one understands it not in a coordinating manner but in a subordinating manner in the sense of BDR §442.4c (I have translated in a subordinating manner above).

In these two verses Luke takes up the news of the placement of the Baptist in prison by Herod Antipas (see at 3.1) from Mark 6.16-18 (for the phrasing κατακλείειν ἐν φυλακῇ, cf. Jeremiah 39.2[LXX]; Dionysius of Halicarnassus, *Antiquitates romanae* 7.37.3). Josephus, *Antiquitates judaicae* 18.119 writes that he was detained in the fortress Machaerus in Peraea. Luke leaves out the legend of the murder of John (Mark 6.19-27), though he certainly knew it. Instead, after v. 20 John's track gets lost in the narrative fog, for the reader does not learn what happens to him. In 7.18-19 he briefly crops up again on the margins, when he is informed about the deeds of Jesus by his disciples and after that sends two messengers to Jesus; but unlike Matthew 11.2, Luke does not mention with a word that John sits in prison. In 9.9 the readers then suddenly learn that John has been beheaded in the meantime. This neglectful handling of a narrative figure to whom Luke previously gave so much attention (cf. the interpretations of his activity in 1.13-17, 76b-78a; 3.1-6) shows that for Luke John is not interesting for his own sake but only in connection with Jesus. In the sense of the historiographical ideal of *brevitas* expressed in Lucian of Samosata, *Quomodo historia conscribenda sit* 56, the fact that Luke does not narrate the murder of the Baptist therefore also allows the inference that he reckoned it among the "insignificant and less important things" that a good historian passes over.

3.21–4.13: The Presentation of Jesus as Son of God

After the forerunner has made his exit, Luke can now bring into his narrative the one for whom he had John prepare the way and of whom John had last spoken in vv. 16-17. To be sure, the report of Jesus's public activity does not begin until 4.14. It is preceded by three textual units with the help of which Luke explains the character of Jesus's divine sonship. In this context it is especially significant that the initiative proceeds again from God. From the heavenly world the Spirit descends upon Jesus, and the Spirit is also the one who speaks first. The way that Jesus treads in this section is a mirror image of the way of the Baptist. While the Baptist came from the wilderness to the Jordan (3.2-3), Jesus takes the opposite way (4.1), before Luke leads him to Galilee in 4.14 and has him begin his public proclamation.

3.21-22: Spirit Anointing and Proclamation

[21]But it happened when the whole people were baptized and Jesus also was baptized and while he prayed that heaven was opened [22]and the Holy Spirit descended in bodily form upon him like a dove and a voice sounded from heaven: "You are my beloved son. In you I have taken delight."

While Luke had picked up John in 3.2 at the place where he had parked him after his birth, namely in the wilderness (1.80), the case is different with Jesus. Luke skips Mark 1.9 and thus does without the narrative bridging of the geographical distance between Nazareth, where Jesus grew up (2.51-52), and the Jordan, whence he then has Jesus set out again in 4.1. Without any narrative preparation Jesus is suddenly there. An important commonality between the two Lukan narratives of the beginning of the activity of John and Jesus undoubtedly resides in the fact that both here and there the word of God stands at the beginning and sets into motion the announced event (3.2, 22; cf. also 1.19, 26).

However, the different ways in which Luke has God come to speak in each case is just as revealing. In the case of John, it is merely recounted that God takes the initiative, while his words to Jesus are quoted word for word. It is also conspicuous that Luke narrates the episode of Jesus's proclamation to be Son of God only after he has concluded his presentation of the proclamation of the Baptist with a comprehensive outlook and reported about his imprisonment by Herod Antipas. Thus, also in this respect, Luke does not take over the Markan order of the narrative material. In Mark 1.14 the departure of the Baptist takes place only after the report about the baptism of Jesus and the events that follow it (1.9-11). The tension that arises through the Lukan manner of narration is obvious. In the sequence of the time of the narrative John is already in prison, whereas with regard to the time of what is narrated, it is presupposed that he is still active

(v. 21), though he is not present as a narrative figure—Luke omits the Markan reference that Jesus was baptized "by John" (Mark 1.9). In Acts 10.37-38 Luke makes this same separation of the event that took place in the context of Jesus's baptism from the activity of John the Baptist: Jesus's Spirit-anointing is presented as an event that took place temporally "after the baptism that John proclaimed." The Lukan understanding of the role of the Baptist can be invoked as the reason for this manner of presentation. It is a given that John, like Jesus, belongs to the time of the fulfillment of the ancient promises, but he differs from Jesus in the fact that he "goes ahead" of Jesus as one who prepares the way (Luke 1.17, 76) and "pre-proclaims" him (Acts 13.24). Correspondingly, Jesus comes "after" him (Acts 13.25; 19.4; see also 10.37; Luke 3.16). This functional ordering of the Baptist to Jesus now requires that the activity of the two does not overlap, for if they did John would not be a "forerunner." The prepositions πρό and μετά point toward each other, but they cannot meet. Luke has expressed this relation between Jesus and John with the tension-filled time-of-narration placement of the episode narrated in vv. 21-22.

Syntactically the entire episode consists of a single sentence whose structure is frequently encountered in Luke (e.g., 6.1, 6, 12; 16.22; Acts 4.5; 9.3; cf. Fitzmyer I: 118). The predicate is ἐγένετο δέ (v. 21a), which is continued through three *accusativus cum infinitivo* constructions: ἀνεῳχθῆναι τὸν οὐρανόν (v. 21d), καταβῆναι τὸ πνεῦμα τὸ ἅγιον (v. 22a), and φωνὴν . . . γενέσθαι (v. 22b).

Mark 1.9-11 is identifiable as a source; however, the narrative of the testing of Jesus (Luke 4.1-13 par. Matthew 4.1-11) makes it likely that there was also a parallel in Q (see the introductory comments on 4.1-13). Significant *minor agreements* are as follows: ἀνεῳχθῆναι or ἠνεῴχθησαν (v. 21 par. Matthew 3.16) instead of σχιζομένους (Mark 1.10); ἐπ᾽ αὐτόν (v. 22 par. Matthew 3.16) instead of εἰς αὐτόν (Mark 1.10); see further Neirynck 1974b, 58–59; 1991, 13; Ennulat 1994, 36–37. These agreements must be viewed in connection with the Luke–Matthew agreements in vv. 2b-17; on this point and for the different explanations, see the end of the introduction to 3.1-20.

21a-c What was never explicitly spoken of in 3.1-18—namely, that the people coming to John were also actually baptized—is now explicitly stated. This process, however, is not a component of the main storyline but merely serves to locate the main storyline situationally. With βαπτισθῆναι in v. 21b Luke takes up v. 7, while intentionally differentiating between the ὄχλοι mentioned there and the ἅπας ὁ λαός (see also 7.29; Acts 13.24). The former are not yet baptized, whereas the latter have already expressed their repentance through their acceptance of baptism and therefore can be designated with the predicate that is reserved for the people of God (see at 1.10). Here it again becomes clear what Luke meant in 1.17e when he had Gabriel speak of the fact that John had the task of "preparing for the Lord a ready people." This general background is now focused on Jesus (v. 21c; cf. also the transition from 2.3 to 2.4), who is singled out as part of the λαός with the help of a genitive absolute. The narrative remains with him, and the narrative tempo slows from the aorist βαπτισθέντος to the present προσευχομένου. Luke has Jesus, as it were, persist in prayer. In Luke the reference to Jesus's prayer stands in the position of Jesus's coming out of the water (Mark 1.10a) and makes visible for the first time a characteristic element of the Lukan story of Jesus. Time and again important events take place while Jesus prays or after he has just stopped praying. In general prayer is for Luke one of the most important marks of an existence oriented toward God (Luke 1.10; 2.37; 5.16 diff. Mark 1.45; Luke 6.12 diff. Mark 3.13; Luke 9.18 diff. Mark 8.27; Luke 9.28-29 diff. Mark 9.2; Luke 11.1; 18.1; 22.41, 44, 46; for the general significance of prayer in Luke, cf. Crump 1992a, 109ff).

During the prayer, the three aforementioned events take place, which are described in **21d-22**. With Matthew 3.16 and against Mark 1.10 (σχιζόμενοι οἱ οὐρανοί) Luke first speaks of (v. 21d) the fact that heaven "was opened" (ἀνεῳχθῆναι; this is a *passivum divinum*). He also does not give the event the form of a vision report as Mark does (1.10: εἶδεν), but he narrates it as an objective event. Here the event has nothing to do with the openings of heaven in apocalyptic literature, which grant the visionary insight or even entry into God's transcendence (e.g., Ezekiel 1.1; 1 Enoch 14.33; 34.2; Testament of Levi 2.6; Revelation 4.1); rather, a comparison can more likely be made to texts in which heaven opens in order that something or someone can come *down* to the earth: Genesis 7.11 and Deuteronomy (rain); Malachi 3.10 (blessing); 3 Maccabees 6.18 and John 1.51 (angels); Revelation 19.11 (the Messiah); Isaiah 63.19^{LXX} (God himself); cf. the collection of the tradition-historical material in van Unnik 1973–1983, III: 273–84 and Lentzen-Deis 1969. In that case, v. 22a would describe such an event—the opening of heaven should make possible the descent of the Holy Spirit upon Jesus. The special accent that Luke sets in relation to his Markan *Vorlage* resides in the fact that he explicitly ascribes a "bodily form" (σωματικὸν εἶδος) to the descending Spirit. In the first instance this affirms nothing other than the substance character of the Holy Spirit (cf. also Theophrastus, *De causis plantarum* 1.12.5: τι τῶν σωματικῶν . . . οἷον πνεῦμα ἢ πῦρ).

A notorious *crux interpretum* is the dove (cf. Dörrfuss 1991; Gero 1976; Huber 1995b; L. E. Keck 1970/1971; Schroer 1986; Schwarz 1997 as well as the overview of the previous attempts at interpretation, none of which has resolved the riddle of the symbolism, in L. E. Keck 1970/1971; Lentzen-Deis 1970, 170ff; Marshall; Fitzmyer; Bock; Radl). It is not even clear whether ὡς περιστεράν should be understood in an adverbial or adnominal manner. Is it meant to express the manner of the descent or the nature (but what sort?) of the Holy Spirit? And it is just as unclear whether a comparison is merely intended ("like a dove") or whether something like an incarnation of the Spirit in the dove ("as a dove") is in mind. And whether Luke has understood the matter of the dove in the exact same way as Mark is also questionable, for alongside the addition that has already been mentioned, he also changes the word placement. Yet the most likely assumption is that Luke did not ascribe any theological symbolic character to the dove because he could not. An indication for this is the word placement of the sentence. The phrasing σωματικῷ εἴδει stands exactly between the Holy Spirit and the dove and thus specifies the *tertium comparationis* that the two have in common in his view, namely the fact that they have substance. Luke thus imagined that the Holy Spirit looked approximately like a dove when it descended upon Jesus. That further connotations are connected with the dove apart from materiality (Marshall and Nolland: "gentleness"; Bock: "grace") is nothing more than vivid fantasy.

Luke has taken over the heavenly voice that proclaims Jesus as Son of God word for word from Mark. The phrasing connects elements from the proclamation of the servant of God in Isaiah 42.1[MT] ("Behold my servant whom I hold, my chosen one, in whom my soul has pleasure") with phrasings from Psalm[LXX] 2.7 (υἱός μου εἶ σύ). To be sure, the adjective ἀγαπητός is attested neither here nor there and would have to be added from Isaiah 44.2 (παῖς μου Ἰακὼβ καὶ ὁ ἠγαπημένος Ἰσραήλ). In Genesis 22.2, 12, 16 υἱὸς ἀγαπητός is a translation of בֵּן יָחִיד ("only son") and in Jeremiah 38(31).20 of בֵּן יַקִּיר ("precious son"). Apart from the Abraham-Isaac tradition, this expression is attested in Jewish writings only in 4 Baruch 7.23; but it is common in non-Jewish Hellenistic authors; cf. Antiphanes Comicus, ed. Kock 1880–1888, II: 260; Dionysius of Halicarnassus, *Antiquitates romanae* 8.48.1; Plutarch, *Moralia* 94a; Julius Pollux, *Onomasticon* 3.19; Artemidorus, *Onirocriticon* 5.37 (Pack 1963, 310.2).

The reading handed down in D it and some church fathers, which is aligned completely with the wording of Psalm[LXX] 2.7, is certainly secondary. Luke will later designate the event of the imparting of the Spirit to Jesus as "anointing" (Luke 4.18a, b; Acts 10.38), and this, of course, points, not without reason, to the connection between anointing and Spirit-reception in relation to David in 1 Samuel 16.13. Jesus would thus be authorized here to take over the task intended for him (cf. 1.32-33; 2.11). In that case, however, the narrative function of this scene is also clear. It does not consist in establishing the divine sonship of Jesus in the first place, for the Holy Spirit has brought it about (by whatever means) that he was already born as such (cf. 1.35). Nor should the readers be informed here about the identity of Jesus, for they have, of course, long been fully informed about this. Rather, this episode recounts that *Jesus himself* is informed of his identity and equipped for the carrying out of his task, and therefore Luke also takes over from Mark the direct speech by the heavenly voice in v. 22d.

3.23-38: Genealogy

[23]**And he, Jesus, was, when he began, about 30 years old, a son—as was thought—of Joseph,** (a son) **of Eli,** [24]**(a son) of Matthat,** (a son) **of Levi,** (a son) **of Melchi,** (a son) **of Jannai,** (a son) **of Joseph,** [25]**(a son) of Mattathias,** (a son) **of Amos,** (a son) **of Nahum,** (a son) **of Hesli,** (a son) **of Naggai,** [26]**(a son) of Maath,** (a son) **of Mattathias,** (a son) **of Semein,** (a son) **of Josech,** (a son) **of Joda,** [27]**(a son) of Joanan,** (a son) **of Rhesa,** (a son) **of Zorobabel,** (a son) **of Salathiel,** (a son) **of Neri,** [28]**(a son) of Melchi,** (a son) **of Addi,** (a son) **of Kosam,** (a son) **of Elmadam,** (a son) **of Er,** [29]**(a son) of Jesus,** (a son) **of Eliezer,** (a son) **of Jorim,** (a son) **of Matthat,** (a son) **of Levi,** [30]**(a son) of Simeon,** (a son) **of Juda,** (a son) **of Joseph,** (a son) **of Jonam,** (a son) **of Eliakim,** [31]**(a son) of Melea,** (a son) **of Menna,** (a son) **of Mattatha,** (a son) **of Natham,** (a son) **of David,** [32]**(a son) of Jessai,** (a son) **of Jobed,** (a son) **of Boos,** (a son) **of Sala,** (a son) **of Naasson,** [33]**(a son) of Aminadab,** (a son) **of Admin,** (a son) **of Arni,** (a son) **of Hesrom,** (a son) **of Phares,** (a son) **of Juda,** [34]**(a son) of Jakob,** (a son) **of Isaac,** (a son) **of Abraam,** (a son) **of Thara,** (a son) **of Nachor,** [35]**(a son) of Seruch,** (a son) **of Ragau,** (a son) **of Phalek,** (a son) **of Eber,** (a son) **of Sala,** [36]**(a son) of Kainam,** (a son) **of Arphaxad,** (a son) **of Sem,** (a son) **of Noe,** (a son) **of Lamech,** [37]**(a son) of Mathusala,** (a son) **of Enoch,** (a son) **of Jaret,** (a son) **of Maleleel,** (a son) **of Kainam,** [38]**(a son) of Enos,** (a son) **of Seth,** (a son) **of Adam,** (a son) **of God.**

Luke interrupts the narrative in order to provide the readers with biographical information about Jesus. In **23a** he begins by mentioning Jesus's approximate age; the relativizing ὡσεί with numbers is typically Lukan (cf. 9.14, 28; 22.59; 23.44; Acts 1.15; 2.41; 4.4; 10.3; 19.7; see also ὡς in Luke 1.56; 8.42; Acts 4.4; 5.7, 36; 13.18, 20; 19.34) and makes it difficult to see more in the number of Jesus's age than that he was "in the 'best age'" (C. G. Müller 2003, 499). Luke will later explicitly stress that the "beginning" of Jesus's public activity directly follows the activity of John the Baptist in time (Acts 1.22; 10.37). The parenthesis ὡς ἐνομίζετο (the same expression for an uncertain or false attribution of paternity is found in Appian, *Libyca* [= *Punica*] 111.525; Pausanias 2.10.3; Favorinus of Arles, *De exilio*, ed. Barigazzi 1966, 379.8; Harpocration, *Lexicon in decem oratores Atticos*, ed. Dindorf 1969, 68.18) between "son" and "Joseph" points to the extraordinary circumstances that accompanied the beginning of Mary's pregnancy (cf. 1.34). Although Jesus was, according to Luke's understanding, not the physical but—as we would say today—the social son of Joseph, Joseph is the mediator of Jesus's genealogical identity (see also Gordon 1977, 101), which is now unfolded.

23b-27 From Joseph to Rhesa: 19 names of people who are otherwise unknown. Zorobabel (cf. 1 Chronicles 3.19; Ezra 2.2; and elsewhere: Zerubbabel; Matthew 1.13). Salathiel (1 Chronicles 3.19^{LXX}; Ezra 3.2, 8; 5.2; Nehemiah 12.1; Haggai 1.1, 12, 14; 2.2, 23: Salathiel; Matthew 1.12; according to 1 Chronicles 3.19^{MT} Pedaiah was regarded as the father of Zerubbabel). Neri: not mentioned in the Old Testament (according to 1 Chronicles 3.17 [the text-critical tradition is, however unclear] and Matthew 1.12 the father of Salathiel was not Neri but Jechonias [Jojachin]).

28-30 From Melchi to Jonam: 14 names of people who are otherwise unknown. Eliakim (2 Kings 18.18 knows of a palace administrator with this name who fits in this time; the Eliakim mentioned in Matthew 1.13 is a grandson of Zerubbabel and belongs in the postexilic period).

31 From Melea to Mattatha: 3 names of people who are otherwise unknown. Natham (1 Chronicles 3.5: Nathan, David's third son by Bathsheba; see also 2 Samuel 5.14; 1 Chronicles 14.4; Zechariah 12.12; Matthew 1.6-7 has Solomon here). David (1 Chronicles 2.15; Ruth 4.17, 22; Matthew 1.6).

32 Jessai (1 Chronicles 2.12; Ruth 4.17, 22: Isai; Matthew 1.5-6). Jobed (1 Chronicles 2.12; Ruth 4.17, 21, 22: Obed; Matthew 1.5). Boos (1 Chronicles 2.11-12; Ruth 4.21: Boas; Matthew 1.5). Sala (1 Chronicles 2.11; Ruth 4.20, 21: Salmon; Matthew 1.4-5). Naasson (1 Chronicles 2.10–11; Ruth 4.20: Nachshon; Matthew 1.4).

33 Aminadab (1 Chronicles 2.10; Ruth 4.19, 20; Matthew 1.4). Admin, Arni: not mentioned in the Old Testament (according to 1 Chronicles 2.9-10; Ruth 4.19, Ram is regarded as the father of Aminadab and son of Hesron; see also Matthew 1.3-4).

The manuscript evidence deviates strongly with respect to these three names; the following readings are listed in Nestle/Aland^{27} (see further in Heater 1986, 26–27):

"Aminadab, Admin, Arni":	ℵ² L X [Γ] *f¹³ pc* bo (= Nestle/Aland²⁷)
"Admin, Arni":	B sy^s
"Aminadab, Aram, Admi, Arni":	(N) Θ (0102, 1) *pc*
"Aminadab, Aram, Joram":	K Δ Ψ 700, (892), 2542 *pm* b e (sy^h)

"Adam, Admin, Arni": 𝔓⁴ᵛⁱᵈ ℵ* 1241 *pc* sa *et v. l. al*

"Aminadab, Aram": A D 33, 565, (1424), *l* 2211 *pm* lat syᵖ

The reason for this state of affairs is the fact that in the Septuagint manuscripts of 1 Chronicles 2.9-10 and Ruth 4.19 as well as in Matthew 1.3-4, neither "Admin" nor "Arni" are mentioned between "Hesrom" and "Aminadab," but only Αρραν or Αραμ; this version corresponds to the last-mentioned variant. But with a view to textual critical considerations everything supports the sequence "Aminadab, Admin, Arni" as the oldest version (so also Nestle/Aland²⁷). It is clearly the *lectio difficilior* in relation to the variant just mentioned, and all the other readings can be derived from it.

Hesrom (1 Chronicles 2.5, 9; Ruth 4.18, 19: Hesron; Matthew 1.3). Phares (1 Chronicles 2.4, 5; Ruth 4.18: Peres; Matthew 1.3). Juda (1 Chronicles 2.1, 3; Matthew 1.2–3).

34 Jakob (1 Chronicles 2.1 ["Israel"]; Matthew 1.2). Isaac (1 Chronicles 1.28, 34; Matthew 1.2). Abraam (Genesis 11.26; 12.1ff; 1 Chronicles 1.27; Matthew 1.2). Thara (Genesis 11.24, 26; 1 Chronicles 1.26: Terach). Nachor (Genesis 11.22, 24; 1 Chronicles 1.26).

35 Seruch (Genesis 11.20, 22; 1 Chronicles 1.26: Serug). Ragau (Genesis 11.18, 20; 1 Chronicles 1.25: Reu). Phalek (Genesis 11.16, 18; 1 Chronicles 1.25: Peleg). Eber (Genesis 10.24, 25; 11.14, 16; 1 Chronicles 1.25). Sala (Genesis 10.24; 11.12, 14; 1 Chronicles 1.24: Shelach).

36 Kainam: not mentioned in the Hebrew Bible; here Arpachshad is always regarded as the father of Shelach (it is probably omitted for this reason from the Lukan text of 𝔓⁷⁵ D). By contrast the Septuagint versions of Genesis 11.12-13 and 1 Chronicles 1.18(A) (as Καινάν) as well as Jubilees 8.1–5 place him at exactly the same position as Luke, i.e., as son of Arphaxad and father of Sala. Bauckham 1990 was able to show that he is also counted in the second week of the Apocalypse of Weeks (1 Enoch 93.3–10; 91.11–17; here: 93.4), for without him one does not reach the required seven names (Bauckham 1990, 315ff; 1991, 98–99). Arphaxad (Genesis 10.22; 11.10, 12; 1 Chronicles 1.17, 24: Arpachshad). Sem (Genesis 5.32; 10.21; 11.10; 1 Chronicles 1.4, 17). Noe (Genesis 5.29, 32; 1 Chronicles 1.4: Noah). Lamech (Genesis 5.25, 28; 1 Chronicles 1.3).

37 Mathusala (Genesis 5.21, 25; 1 Chronicles 1.3: Metushelach). Enoch (Genesis 5.18, 21; 1 Chronicles 1.3). Jaret (Genesis 5.15, 18; 1 Chronicles 1.2: Jared). Maleleel (Genesis 5.12, 15; 1 Chronicles 1.2: Mahalalel). Kainam (Genesis 5.9, 10; 1 Chronicles 1.2: Kainan).

38 Enos (Genesis 5.6, 9; 1 Chronicles 1.1: Enosh). Seth (Genesis 5.3, 6; 1 Chronicles 1.1). Adam (Genesis 5.1, 3; 1 Chronicles 1.1). God.

From a form-critical perspective we are dealing with a *Geschlechtsregister* (genealogy or genealogical register—*Stammbaum* [family tree] and *Ahnentafel* [table of ancestors] mean something else)—and, more specifically, with a "rising" genealogy, for it begins with the youngest person and ends with the oldest. Matthew 1.2-16 is, by contrast, a "descending" genealogy, which begins with the oldest person (Abraham) and ends with the youngest (Jesus).

The closest form-critical correspondences to Luke 3.23-38 are found in the rising genealogies of the Old Testament and early Jewish literature: Ezra 7.1-5 and 5 Ezra 1.1-3SA (Ezra–Aaron); Judith 8.1 (Judith–Jacob/Israel); 1 Chronicles 6.19-23 (Heman–Jacob/Israel), 24-28 (Asaph–Levi), 29-32 (Etan–Levi); Josephus, *Antiquitates judaicae* 1.79 (Noah–Adam); 2.229 (Moses–Abraham); 1 Enoch 37.1 (Enoch–Adam); Apocalypse of Abraham title (Abraham–Jared); cf. also Herodotus 4.147 (Theras–Polyneikes); 7.11 (Xerxes–Achaimenes); 7.204 (Leonidas–Heracles); 8.131 (Leotychides–Heracles).

Descending genealogies in the Old Testament: Genesis 5.1-32 (Adam–Noah's sons); 11.10-26 (Sem–Terach's sons); Ruth 4.18-22 (Peres–David); 1 Chronicles 1.1-4 (Adam–Noah's sons); 1.24-27 (Sem–Abraham); 2.10-12 (Ram–Jesse); 3.10-14 (Salomon–Josia); cf. also Livy 1.8 (Latinus–Tiberinus); Plutarch, *Pyrrhus* 1 (Achilles or Tharrypas–Pyrrhus); *Lycurgus* 1.4 (Procles–Lycurgus).

An example of a joining of two subgenres is Diogenes Laertius 3.1 (Plato–Solon; Solon–Plato); for extra-Jewish parallels, cf. W. Speyer, *RAC* 9: 1172ff; Kurz 1984.

The genealogy of Jesus in the Lukan version is completely without analogy insofar as apart from it there is no other rising genealogy that extends the series of ancestors back to God as the creator of the first humans.

There has been no lack of attempts to discover (analogously to Matthew 1.17) something like a *structure-determining pattern* in the list. In many attempts a great role is played by the fact that the list from Jesus to Adam contains seventy-seven names, so that one could discover in it something like a genealogical week schema (eleven groups with seven names each). But this works only if it is presupposed that the group of three "Aminadab, Admin, Arni" in v. 33a-c is, from a textual critical perspective (see above), not only the oldest version of the text relatively, i.e., in relation to other textual variants, but is also the original version.

Other observations (cf. Nolland): The list begins behind Jesus with two groups of seven names each, at whose beginning and end the same name is listed, namely "Joseph" (vv. 23b-24e) and "Mattathias" (vv. 25a-26b).

Or: The lists mentions fifty-seven names from "Jesus" to "Abraham," and in position 29, i.e, exactly in the middle, there is again a "Jesus." The names before and after him can be divided into two parts of four groups of seven each: from "Jesus" (v. 23a) to "he" (v. 28e) and from "Eliezer" (v. 29b) to "Abraham" (v. 34c).

A *comparison with the genealogy in Matthew 1.2-16* (cf. Mayordomo-Marín 1998, 217ff) immediately reveals the differences: *(a)* The Matthean genealogy is oriented in a descending line, the Lukan genealogy in a rising line. *(b)* The Matthean genealogy begins with Abraham, the Lukan genealogy ends with Adam or, rather, with his creation by God; thus, Matthew directs the readers' view to Genesis 12, Luke to Genesis 1. *(c)* If one leaves aside Jesus's father Joseph, then between Abraham and Jesus Matthew and Luke agree, with very few exceptions, only where *Luke* mentions names that also appear in Old Testament genealogies. *(d)* Between the last biblical name ("Zorobabel"; Matthew 1.13; Luke 3.27c) and "Jesus" (Matthew 1.16; Luke 1.23b) Luke and Matthew not only have no names in common, but the numbers of generations also deviate spectacularly from one another. Only ten names are mentioned in Matthew 1.13b-16a, whereas no less than nineteen names are listed in Luke 3.23c-27d. *(e)* The most interesting difference resides, to be sure, in the fact that in Luke the post-Davidic sequence of generations runs not via Solomon and the kings of the Southern Kingdom who followed him from "Rehabeam" to "Jechonia"/ Joiachin (Matthew 1.6-11), but via David's son "Nathan" (Luke 3.31d), concerning whom we know only that he was likewise a son of Bathsheba (see above). He is then followed in a genealogical sequence in Luke 3.31c-27e (sic!) by a series of nineteen names whose bearers we do not know, until we encounter again two known names with Salathiel and Zorobabel, which Matthew also lists (1.12), who lists only thirteen names between "Solomon" and "Salathiel."

This, of course, gives rise to the question of why Luke chooses this subsidiary line for the genealogy of Jesus. The negative judgment on Joiachin (Jeremiah 22.24-30) is usually referred to as an explanation (e.g., Schürmann; Nolland; Fitzmyer). Above all the judgment word against Jechoniah/Joiachin in Jeremiah 22.30, which indicates that none of his descendants will sit on the throne of David (see also 36.30), probably led to the fact that he is not named as the father of Salathiel in v. 27e but rather an otherwise unknown "Neri." But this would have been sufficient to circumvent the difficulties associated with Jechoniah/Joiachin, and Luke would not have needed to have begun the genealogical redirection already with the direct descendant of David (see also Bauckham 1990, 327). There is, however, a plausible explanation if one considers christological reasons. The distinctive character of the Lukan version resides in the fact that the functional salvation-historical continuity between David and Jesus as the divinely appointed eternal ruler over Israel (Luke 1.32-33) completely passes by *all other* Davidides who already sat on the throne of David in the past. And it is certainly no accident that this reconstruction of the genealogical connection between David and Jesus finds its direct counterpart in the image that the Lukan Paul sketches of the history of Israel in his speech in Pisidian Antioch (Acts 13.16-41). In the series of mediators whom God had repeatedly given to Israel in the past (the judges, Samuel, Saul, and David), he does not have Paul continue after David with Solomon but jumps directly to Jesus (v. 23) and identifies him as the promised "Savior" from the seed of David. One may therefore view the series of names between David and Salathiel as a Lukan construction with whose help the genealogical line running via Solomon should be purposefully eliminated. The guiding interest is the establishment of a direct connection between Jesus and David. As ruler "over the house of Jacob" (1.33) Jesus can be regarded as the direct successor of David insofar as he is the first Davidide who sits again on the throne of David (cf. 1.32) within the lineage of the Davidic dynasty that ties him to David and genealogically mediates the continuity of the salvation-historical promise into the present. Between Jesus and David there is no other king in this line. Whence Luke obtained the material for the genealogical bridge between Salathiel (v. 27d) and Nathan (v. 31d) cannot be determined.

This brings us to the question of *sources*. One can assume that the sequence of generations between Adam (v. 38c) and David's son Nathan (v. 31d) (with the aforementioned exceptions in v. 33b, c) is completely documented by the different genealogical lists in the Septuagint: Genesis 5.1-32 and 1 Chronicles 1.1-4 (Adam–Sem); Genesis 11.10-26 and 1 Chronicles 1.17-27 (Sem–Abraham); Ruth 4.18-22 (Phares–David); 1 Chronicles 2.1-15 (Jacob/Israel–David); 3.1, 5 (David–Nathan). Beyond this, especially between "Thara" (v. 34d) and "Adam" (v. 38c), the close points of contact in the spelling of the names with the genealogies in Genesis 11.10-32 and 5.1-32 is conspicuous. Steyn (1989, 409–11; 1991, 103–4) concluded from this that Luke used the Septuagint as a source for this section (to this one can add the fact that the "Kainam" mentioned in v. 36a is lacking in the Hebrew version of Genesis 11.12-13, but is mentioned in the Septuagint). In the other parts the differences between the Lukan spelling of the names and their spelling in the respective Septuagint versions is not so large that one would need to rule out a use of Septuagint material. We are left with the questions of whether Luke found a preexisting genealogy (and possibly also reversed it, i.e, changed a descending order of generations into a rising one; so e.g., Bauckham 1991a, 102; Radl), whether he expanded and changed a source that was before him, or whether he created the existing list as a whole. The last possibility is the most probable, namely for form-critical reasons. The genre of genealogy is attested only as a subgenre of a superordinated framing genre and not as an independent text. It is therefore not conceivable that a genealogy of Jesus existed without being embedded in a Jesus narrative, and as things stand this could only have been the Gospel of Luke in the present case.

But what is *the theological meaning* of this text? The intention of the form of genealogies—especially rising ones—lies in construing identity, in which the creation of identity proceeds above all from the endpoint. In the present case this would be *God* in his role as the creator of Adam. But the genealogies of *all* people end virtually at exactly the same point, so that the tracing back of the origin of Jesus to God as the creator of Adam cannot have the function of emphasizing the distinctiveness of Jesus in relation to other people. What the Lukan Paul says in Acts therefore applies not only to Jesus but to all people—namely, that they "are God's offspring" (γένος οὖν ὑπάρχοντες τοῦ θεοῦ; Acts 17.29). The literature on Luke often interprets Jesus's genealogy as a sort of christological counterweight to the gift of the Spirit and the explanation of the voice from heaven that immediately preceded it. It is said that the concern is therefore to establish that Jesus was also 'true human being' (e.g., Marshall; Nolland; Bovon; Radl). This would certainly be correct if the genealogy only went to Adam; but it actually reaches to God (for the understanding of God as the father of Adam, cf. Philo, *De virtutibus* 204), and this fact suggests another interpretation. The line that the genealogy draws from Jesus to God does not wish to specify Jesus's genealogical origin. Instead, it wants to name the level on which Jesus's divine sonship has its significance. The concern is with God's relation to all humanity. Jesus does not become a new Adam through this, but Luke uses Adam's divine sonship as a model in order to mark out the framework of meaning for understanding Jesus's divine sonship.

4.1-13: Testing

[1]**But Jesus, filled by the Holy Spirit, turned from the Jordan and was led around by the Holy Spirit in the wilderness,** [2]**for forty days,** (and was) **tested by the devil. And he ate nothing in those days, and when they were over he was hungry.** [3]**But the devil said to him, "If you are the Son of God, tell this stone to become bread."** [4]**And Jesus answered him, "It is written: 'A person does not live from bread alone.'"** [5]**And he led him up and showed to him all the kingdoms of the earth in a moment.** [6]**And the devil said to him, "I will give you all this authority and their glory, for this has been granted to me. And I give it to**

whomever I wish. [7]If you fall down before me in worship, it will be completely yours." [8]**And Jesus answered and said to him, "It is written: 'You shall worship the Lord, your God, and you shall serve him alone.'"** [9]**But he brought him to Jerusalem and set him on the pinnacle of the temple and said to him, "If you are God's Son, cast yourself down from here,** [10]**for it is written: 'He will give instruction to his angels for your sake, that they protect you,'** [11]**and 'They will carry you upon hands in order that you not strike your foot upon a stone.'"** [12]**And Jesus answered and said to him, "It is said: 'You should not test the Lord, your God.'"** [13]**And after the devil had ended every testing, he departed from him until the (given) time.**

The coherence and structure of the narrative are clear. After an introduction with a change of location (v. 1a), there is a series of three episodes that each portray Jesus in dispute with the devil (vv. 2b-4 / vv. 5-8 / vv. 9-12). Verses 1b-2a and 13 are clearly recognizable as beginning and concluding frames. Here Luke communicates to his readers wherein the commonality of the three episodes consists and how they should be understood, namely as a "test" or "testing" (*vulgo* "temptation") of Jesus by the devil (cf. the *inclusio* through πειραζόμενος ὑπὸ τοῦ διαβόλου [v. 2a] and συντελέσας πάντα πειρασμὸν ὁ διάβολος [v. 13]). Form-critically all three episodes are chreiae. A *(a)* narrative exposition (v. 2b, c/v. 5/v. 9a, b) is followed by a *(b)* speech of the devil, which wants to move Jesus to a certain deed (v. 3/vv. 6-7/v. 9c-11) and which *(c)* Jesus does not—and this is the form-critical peculiarity of this chreia—answer with his own words but in each case with a quotation from Scripture (v. 4/v. 8/v. 12), which always comes from the book of Deuteronomy (8.3; 6.13 [see also 10.20]; 6.16). The first and third episodes are concerned with Jesus's divine sonship (cf. vv. 3, 9). This coherence indicates that the entire text appeared at once and that it was a literary product from the beginning. Moreover, the word-for-word Septuagint quotations in vv. 4, 8, 12 make it more than probable that the narrative existed from the beginning in Greek. Finally, because it is also extremely unlikely that such a text could have existed independently, i.e., without a literary context, one will probably have to assume that it was connected from the start with the narrative of Jesus's baptism, the bestowing of the Spirit, and the proclamation as Son of God. A historical point of adhesion in the life of Jesus is possibly recognizable in the overlap with Luke 10.18.

Since the narrative is also handed down in Matthew 4.1-11, we can assume that Luke has taken it from Q. It follows from this that there also must have been a parallel here to Mark 1.9-11, since in vv. 3, 9 the preceding proclamation of Jesus as

Son of God is presupposed. The most serious difference between the two versions concerns the order of the second and third episode, which differs in Luke and Matthew. It was presumably Luke who changed the original order of Q, because he viewed the third test as a provocation of God (see below) or because with the end position of Jerusalem he wanted to establish a correspondence to the end of the way of Jesus. In addition, there is also a short counterpart in Mark 1.12-13, but there Jesus is tested during the time of his forty-day stay in the wilderness and not after it as in Q and Matthew; Luke has combined the two.

In tradition-historical perspective one must distinguish between general and specific cross-connections. The *general* building blocks reworked in the narrative are found especially in narratives about the testing of the righteousness, faithfulness, or obedience of Jewish pious people (key words are especially πειρασμός and cognates). Correspondingly, foreign nations or sinners are never tested. Thus, being tested by God is always a consequence of election. The pious and righteous are tested to see whether they behave in correspondence to the status assigned to them by God also in situations of conflict (Wisdom of Solomon 3.5: whether they are "worthy" of God; cf. Korn 1937, 60ff; see also E. Aurelius, *TRE* 35: 44ff; M. Klein, *TRE* 35: 47ff; Spicq 1994, III: 82ff). Classic examples are the testings of Abraham (cf. Genesis 22.1; 1 Maccabees 2.52; Sirach 44.20; Hebrews 11.17; Jubilees 17.17–18; 19.3, 8; and elsewhere), Israel in the wilderness (cf. Exodus 15.25; 16.4; 20.20; Deuteronomy 8.2, 16; Wisdom of Solomon 11.9; and elsewhere), Joseph (Testament of Joseph 2.7), and of course Job (Job 1.6ff; though without πειρασμός or the like); see also 2 Chronicles 32.31: Hezekiah; Judith 8.25-26: the fathers; Wisdom of Solomon 3.5: the righteous in general; Sirach 2.1 ("My child, if you undertake to serve the Lord ἑτοίμασον τὴν ψυχήν σου εἰς πειρασμόν [prepare your soul for testing]"). The subject of the testing is usually God himself (Genesis 22.1; Exodus 15.25; Jubilees 17.17–18; 1 Enoch 67.3) or alternatively the devil or another opponent figure (Jubilees 10.8: Mastema; Apocalypse of Abraham 13.10: Azazel; see also 4Q504 1-2, V, 18; cf. Gerhardsson 1966, 38ff). According to 1 Kings 10.1-3, the queen of Sheba comes to Solomon "in order to test him with riddles" (πειράσαι αὐτὸν ἐν αἰνίγμασιν); see also John 6.6. Conversely, however, God can also be the object of the "testing" (see at v. 17 below and at 8.13; 11.4) or one can "test" oneself (cf. 2 Corinthians 13.5: ἑαυτοὺς πειράζετε εἰ ἐστὲ ἐν τῇ πίστει).

Prodicus's fable of Heracles at the crossroads, which likewise takes place in an "isolated place" and stands at the beginning biographically, is also not without a certain correspondence to the New Testament testing narrative (Xenophon, *Memorabilia* 2.1.21ff; Cicero, *De officiis* 1.118; 3.25); cf. also Hebrew Sirach 4.16-17 regarding the one who turns to wisdom: ". . . by disguising myself, I wander with him; at the beginning (לִפְנִם) I test him with testings. Afterwards his heart will be filled by me." Not only are there analogies with Buddha and Zarathustra (cf. Luz 1985–2002, I: 221), but it is in general a universal narrative motif that at the beginning of their careers heroes "have to fall into dispute with an adversary from the kingdom of the demons" (Dibelius 1971, 275).

The specific background is evoked by the three quotations from Deuteronomy, the key word "wilderness" (v. 1), and the mentioning of the forty days (v. 2). They congruently call to mind the three circumstances during the Exodus and the wilderness time of Israel in which the people of God was subjected in each case to a "testing" (cf. Brawley 1992).

1a Luke takes up the thread of the episodic narrative interrupted by the genealogy by making a change of scene (on ὑποστρέφειν, see at 1.56). He has never said that Jesus was previously at the Jordan, but with the help of the combination of 3.3 and 3.21 he makes it possible for the readers to infer such a stay. Further, it also becomes clear in this way that Luke wants to continue the narration directly after 3.21/22. The characterization of Jesus as πλήρης πνεύματος ἁγίου (v. 1a) also refers to this episode; this phrasing is also found in Luke in relation to the Jerusalem seven (Acts 6.3, 5), Stephen (7.55), and Barnabas (11.24); for the conceptual background, see at 1.15. In this way Luke indicates that the intentionality of Jesus is enduringly determined by the Holy Spirit, which—and behind it, of course, God—becomes the actual subject of the action of Jesus. For the leading of the narrative figures by the Holy Spirit, see at 2.27.

1b-2a The beginning frame of the whole narrative complex is syntactically unclear. The reason is that from ἐν τῇ ἐρήμῳ onward Luke continues with a Markan text and takes over the temporal specification and the *participium coniunctum* πειραζόμενος ὑπὸ τοῦ διαβόλου almost word for word from Mark 1.13. In this way the Markan conception of a testing of Jesus throughout the whole stay in the wilderness finds entrance into the Lukan narrative. Luke has apparently also imagined this in this way (with Nolland and Bock; most others advocate a different interpretation), for otherwise he would have had to introduce the devil into v. 3 narratively. Luke only returns to pathways of the Q-version in v. 2a, according to which the tests did not take place until the end of this period (see also Matthew 4.2). Thus, the Lukan presentation conveys the impression that Jesus was already tested by the devil before the three tests spoken of in what follows. With the phrasing πάντα πειρασμόν Luke then summarizes all the tests—both the ones that are not reported and the ones that are reported—in v. 13.

Luke has unmistakably designed the terminology of v. 2a as an allusion to the time of Israel's wilderness wandering. This accent is set much more clearly in Luke than in Matthew. The overlaps with Deuteronomy 8.2^{LXX} are the most far-reaching: "Remember the whole way, ἣν ἤγαγέν σε the Lord, your God, ἐν τῇ ἐρήμῳ in order that he . . . ἐκπειράσῃ σε and know what is in your heart, whether you observe his commandments or not" (see also 29.4: ἤγαγεν ὑμᾶς 40 years ἐν τῇ ἐρήμῳ). The Holy Spirit now stands in the place of God as the subject, and the forty years of Israel's stay in the wilderness are transformed into a temporal unit that fits individual biographies (cf. the analogous renumbering in Numbers 14.34; Ezekiel 4.6). Forty days are also a symbolically strongly loaded period of time elsewhere (cf. e.g., Exodus 34.38; Deuteronomy 9.9, 18: Moses stays for forty days and nights on Mount Sinai and Elijah's way to the mountain of God takes the same amount of time according to 1 Kings 19.18), but on account of the context one should assume that reference is made here to Israel's time in the wilderness (see also Gerhardsson 1966, 41ff).

In **2b-4** the first testing is narrated. The narrative exposition grows directly out of the time of the forty-day stay in the wilderness, which is portrayed as a time of abstention from food. In the other tests this fact no longer plays a role and therefore v. 2b-c belongs no longer to the frame but already to the first test. It is quite unlikely that Luke thought his readers would believe that Jesus ate nothing at all for forty days (cf. the intensifying double negation οὐκ ἔφαγεν οὐδέν; cf. BDR §431.2). Therefore, the specification is, of course, meant hyperbolically. Moreover, "not eating/eating nothing" can also designate merely a qualitative fasting (see also Matthew 11.18 with Luke 7.33; Romans 14.3; Klostermann; see also at 5.33). Beyond this, no independent significance is attached to this notice; it is merely intended to explain why Jesus is hungry and thus to provide the occasion for the dialogue that follows.

In **3** Luke, unlike Matthew 4.3a (προσελθών), no longer needs to have the devil specifically appear, for according to the scenario set forth in v. 2a, he has already been with Jesus the whole time. The devil does not want to persuade Jesus to perform a legitimating sign for his divine sonship (and thus to call it into question indirectly), for he formulates a real conditional sentence, which makes clear that he starts from it as a given (εἰ "with indicative of reality"; BDR §372). That Jesus is fundamentally in position to change a stone into bread is therefore not called into question by the devil. Sentences with the grammatical structure of an exhortation (εἰ + predicate noun + second person indicative present of εἶναι [thus εἶ or ἐστέ] + imperative) are found, apart from Luke 4.9 par. Matthew 4.6, also in Matthew 14.28; Luke 22.67; 23.37 par. Matthew 27.40 (with a minor agreement in the conditional sentence!); John 10.24; see also Luke 23.35; Matthew 19.21. It is common to all the texts that the one addressed is exhorted to an action that is congruent with his identity. In other words, the exhortation aims to make visible the person's own identity in a certain action. For the affinity between bread and stone, cf. also Epictetus, *Dissertationes* 2.24.16; Matthew 7.9; Proverbs 20.17. Interesting is the later Christian tradition on the "adversary" (ἀντικείμενος) who imitates the works of Jesus in Greek Apocalypse of Ezra 4.25–43 (v. 27: "This is the one who says: 'I am the Son of God who has made stones into bread and water into wine'" [with regard to the difference between Luke 4.3par. and John 2.1-10 this statement is quite astonishing]) and Ps.-Clementine Homilies 2.32.2 on Simon Magus ("he makes bread from stones"). That Luke has the devil, unlike Matthew 4.3 and probably also Q, speak only of *one* stone and *one* bread corresponds with the previously mentioned hunger of Jesus and is meant to express that the demand of the devil is not at all unreasonable.

In **4** Jesus answers with a quotation from Deuteronomy 8.3c, which follows the phrasing of the Septuagint word for word. This is the first Scripture quotation by a narrative figure in Luke–Acts (see at 3.4-6). Rhetorically this quotation functions as a justification for Jesus's implicit refusal to comply with the demand of the devil. Thematically the quotation in Deuteronomy 8.3 refers to the manna feeding narrated in Exodus 16. According to this text, God first let Israel be hungry and then gave her a foodstuff that no one knew because he wanted to give his people the teaching "that a person does not live by bread alone." The quotation in Luke is shorter than in Matthew 4.4 (some manuscripts therefore insert the Matthean longer version into Luke). The much discussed question of whether Matthew expanded the Q-wording or Luke shortened it (cf. Carruth/Robinson 1996, 137–47) cannot be decided, because we do not know whether both were using the same *Vorlage*.

5-8 The second test forms a spectacular contrast to the banality of the first one. The narrative exposition occurs in v. 5. A type of visionary translation is portrayed (for the use of ἀνάγειν in this sense, cf. 2 Kings 2.1^LXX; Testament of Abraham A 10.15; Justin, *Dialogus cum Tryphone* 32.3; Melito of Sardis, *Peri Pascha* 103.798). This is also suggested by ἐν στιγμῇ χρόνου, which is attested in Hellenistic literature (v. 5; cf. [Ps-]Plutarch, *Moralia* 13b; 104b = Demetrius of Phalerum, Fragment 79).

5 At any rate, Jesus is offered a view of the whole world (on οἰκουμένη, see at 2.1), which of course is not possible from any conceivable earthly point but only from outside or in visionary imagination. For this reason Luke has probably also deleted the high mountain (Matthew 4.8). There are various possibilities of filling the whole world, and the choice of paradigm is decisive for guiding the expectation of the readers and the continuation of the narrative. Luke (the same also already applies for Q) does not opt for humans, animals, or plants (options that would certainly have been available to him; cf. the filling of the world in 2 Baruch 76.3), but for "all kingdoms." This makes it clear that the concern is with political rule.

In **6-7** the devil presents his offer to Jesus. The word placement in the individual cola is carefully worked out, for in every sentence a pronoun is placed in the emphatic initial position (cf. BDR §472.2): σοί (v. 6b), ἐμοί (v. 6c), ᾧ (v. 6d), and σύ (v. 7a). Luke does not return to normal word placement until the concluding line (v. 7b), which is anacoluthically connected to the last pronoun (cf. BDR §466.2: *nominativus pendens*). A considerable part of what the devil claims for himself in v. 6bd is said of God in Daniel 4.31ᴸˣˣ: "The βασιλεία over Babylon . . . ἑτέρῳ δίδοται (is given to another); . . . I will set him over your βασιλεία and your ἐξουσία and your δόξα . . . in order that you know that the God of heaven has ἐξουσία over the βασιλεία of people and ᾧ ἐὰν βούληται δώσει αὐτήν (he will give it to whomever he wishes)." The phrasing δώσω τὴν ἐξουσίαν ταύτην in v. 6b causes one to think of a power-political event, for we often find such talk in relation to the installation of vassal kings or other authorized persons (cf. e.g., Diodorus Siculus 2.28.5; 1 Maccabees 10.32; Daniel 3.97ᴸˣˣ; 5.7, 29; 7.6ᵀʰᵉᵒᵈᵒᵗⁱᵒⁿ; 7.14; Josephus, *Bellum judaicum* 1.474; *Antiquitates judaicae* 2.90; 16.365; 17.239; Greek Apocalypse of Enoch 9.7; Matthew 28.18; Revelation 13.2, 4, 5, 7; see also at 9.1). The attributive specification αὕτη ἅπασα refers anaphorically to the kingdoms of the whole world and makes the ἐξουσία into a comprehensive *abstractum*. The concern is not with rule *over* all kingdoms but with power that is as great as the power of all the kingdoms of the whole world together. "Glory" (for δόξα as a characteristic of βασιλεία, cf. Esther 10.2ᴸˣˣ; Psalmᴸˣˣ 144.11, 12; Daniel 4.36; 11.21ᵀʰᵉᵒᵈᵒᵗⁱᵒⁿ; Testament of Judah 15.3; never in literature outside of Judaism and Christianity according to *TLG* #E). For Luke, of course, Jesus possesses his own δόξα, which is categorically superior to the glory offered by the devil since it has a heavenly provenance—he will "enter" into it (Luke 24.26) and "come" with it at the parousia (9.26; 21.27; see also 9.32).

6c is usually understood in such a way that here the devil clarifies the proprietary presuppositions of his offer, according to which the universal rule belongs to him (the thesis of Rudman 2004 in particular is based on this presupposition). This, however, overlooks the fact that παραδέδοται is used impersonally here and should be translated with "permit" or "allow" (cf. Mark 4.29; Xenophon, *Anabasis* 6.6.34), in which God is, of course, in view as the logical subject (the claim of Theissen 1992, 222 that the devil boasts of "power over all the kingdoms of the world" is thus precisely not accurate; the thesis that Jesus would be presented here as an antitype of Agrippa I—see N. H. Taylor 2001—also founders on this). The καί that follows in v. 6d is used to avoid another and thus redundant ὅτι (cf. BDR §442.4c).

In v. 7a Luke has the devil specify the conditions that Jesus must fulfill for πᾶσα (v. 7b)—i.e., as much ἐξουσία as all the kingdoms of the world together have (v. 6b)—to belong to him. He should worship the devil and in doing so fall before him; the latter aspect is accentuated through ἐνώπιον (cf. Psalm^LXX 21.28; 85.9; Isaiah 66.23; Revelation 3.9; 15.4; Joseph and Aseneth 28.9D; cf. also 1 Samuel 25.23; Psalm^LXX 21.30; Revelation 4.10; 7.11).

8 With the quotation from Deuteronomy 6.13 or 10.20 Jesus reveals that he is not willing to fulfill the condition. The quotation deviates from the original Septuagint version in two ways (so also already in Q; cf. Matthew 4.10). Instead of "worship" (προσκυνήσεις) both Septuagint texts have "fear" (φοβηθήσῃ). Moreover, the adjective "alone" (μόνῳ) is lacking in them. Whether the latter has entered in from the Shema, which appears in Deuteronomy 6.4, i.e., just before this quotation, must remain open. In both Old Testament texts the exhortation to worship Yhwh—which is, of course, meant just as exclusively here (as is emphasized by the adjective μόνῳ)—directly connects with the remembrance of the liberation of his people from Egypt and the admonition not to forget him (Deuteronomy 6.12). "Not to forget God" and "to fear/worship and serve him" are thus semantically isotopic.

9-12 The narrative exposition of the third test occurs in v. 9a-b. First, it is unclear here what is meant by the πτερύγιον τοῦ ἱεροῦ.

πτερύγιον is the diminutive of πτέρυξ = "wing" and designates things that are found on the edge or protrude outward (such as the tip of the nose). In literature outside the New Testament there is only rarely talk of a πτερύγιον in connection with the Jerusalem temple. Four texts are important with regard to our text:

(a) Hegesippus's report about the death of the brother of the Lord James (Fragment 2 in Eusebius of Caesarea, *Historia ecclesiastica* 2.23.4–18): James places himself on the πτερύγιον τοῦ ναοῦ in order to speak to the great crowd from there (11–13) and is thrown down by the scribes and Pharisees (16). He survives the fall and is then stoned (16) and finally struck with a wooden club (18).

(b) Testament of Solomon 22.7–8 (ca. third century CE): At the completion of the temple Solomon wants to put a large capstone on the πτερύγιον τοῦ ναοῦ, which he succeeds in doing with the help of a wind demon who then places the stone on the tip of the temple entrance (εἰς τὴν ἄκραν τῆς εἰσόδου τοῦ ναοῦ; 23.3).

(c) The report of the death of James in The Second Apocalypse of James (NHC V/4) 61.20–24, which reads like a combination of the two preceding texts (at least the connection to Testament of Solomon 22.8 is evident): "And they . . .

found him standing at the pinnacle of the temple (ⲡⲓⲧⲚⲎ Ⲛ̄ⲧⲉ ⲡⲉⲣⲡⲉ), at the strong cornerstone. And they decided to thrown him from the high place."

(d) The pilgrim of Bordeaux in his travel report from 333/334 CE evidently refers to the same architectural setup presupposed by the last two texts. First, the *angelus turris excelsissimae* ("very high corner tower") is mentioned as the place of the temptation, and he then continues: *ibi est et lapis angularis magnus* ("the great corner stone is also found there"; *Itinerarium Burdigalense* 589.11–590.3 [CChr.SL 175], 1965). Cf. in detail Jeremias 1936; Hyldahl 1961; Gerhardson 1966, 61; H. Balz, *EWNT* 3: 462–63; Schwarz 1992, 33–35; Luz 1985–2002, I: 226; Blumenthal 2005.

The plot of our story, however, manages without this information. The narrator probably imagined some point high up on the wall of the temple complex or on the roof of one of the temple buildings. What is decisive, however, is mainly the association that is called up from the basic knowledge of the readers in relation to this place: if one falls down from it, then one is dead or has at least broken many bones.

9c-e contain the actual test. It begins with an exhortation whose grammatical structure is identical to that of vv. 3b-c (εἰ + predicate noun + εἰ + imperative) and also repeats word for word the conditional protasis from v. 3b (εἰ υἱος εἶ τοῦ θεοῦ). Thus, the devil exhorts Jesus anew to an action that is suitable for proving his identity as Son of God, namely by jumping down from the πτερύγιον of the Jerusalem temple (v. 9e). This test functions according to the same logic as Wisdom of Solomon 2.16-18, where the godless say concerning the righteous: "He . . . boasts that God is his father. Let us see whether his words are true, and πειράσωμεν (let us investigate) the circumstances of the end of his life. For if the righteous one is God's son (εἰ γάρ ἐστιν ὁ δίκαιος υἱὸς θεοῦ) he will help him. . . ." Nevertheless, there is an important difference. The connection—established by the exhortation in v. 3—between Jesus's divine sonship and the transformation of a stone into a loaf of bread is comprehensible without further ado for an average cultural basic knowledge, especially when the concern is with the assuagement of hunger. By contrast, the plausibility of the connection—established in v. 9d-e—between divine sonship and jumping from the πτερύγιον of the temple is not necessarily obvious. Therefore, the narrator must have the devil explain what the one has to do with the other or, in other words, how such a jump is suitable to prove Jesus's divine sonship. This very thing takes place in the next two verses.

In **10-11** the devil quotes Psalm 91.11-12 in the version of the Septuagint (so Psalm[LXX] 90.11-12), in which Luke has divided the Old Testament pretext through an inserted καὶ ὅτι into two quotations. It was originally a promise that God would accompany the pious praying one on his way "in a protecting and saving manner" (E. Zenger in Hossfeld/Zenger 2000, 623); the last words of Psalm 91.11 ("in all your ways") are lacking. The devil thus suggests that Jesus identify himself with the σύ of the quotation, which is repeated four times. He should express his trust that God's promise of preservation applies to *him* by jumping down. No one will regard the explanatory potential of this quotation as especially convincing, but another usage may stand behind the use of the quotation, for precisely texts from Psalm 91 are attested from the first century CE onward on amulets, magical papyri, and inscriptions as magical texts with an apotropaic function (cf. Blau 1898, 95n4).

12 The narrator has Jesus formulate the rejection with reference to the Septuagint version of Deuteronomy 6.16 (if this is not conversely dependent on the two New Testament texts; the Hebrew version uses the plural at any rate). The pretext refers to the event of Exodus 17.1-7. It is said here that Israel "tests God" because it demands to receive water in the wilderness (v. 2), and connects this demand with doubt in God's faithfulness and succor (v. 7: "Is the Lord among us or not?"). If one adds other statements about the "testing" of God by Israel in connection with the Exodus event as the interpretive horizon, a rather clear semantic profile emerges. Although Israel has already often experienced the saving succor of its God and although God has already shown his God-ness in many powerful acts (in the Septuagint they can therefore also be called πειρασμοί metonymically; cf. Deuteronomy 4.34; 7.19; 29.2), his people compel him time and again anew to further demonstrations of his succor and his God-ness; cf. Numbers 14.22; Psalm 78.19-20 ("They tested God and said . . . He has struck the rock, so that water poured out and streams gushed out; but can he also give bread and provide flesh for his people?"); 95.8-9; Isaiah 7.12 ("to test the Lord" as interpretation of "to demand a sign from the Lord for oneself"; the same nexus is also found in Mark 8.11parr.). Accordingly, "to test the Lord" can also be connected in Psalm 78.41-43; 106.12-14 with forgetting his previous deeds of power. Tempting God therefore always grows out of doubting the God-ness of God.

13 functions as the concluding frame for the whole narrative complex (see the introduction above and at vv. 1b-2a). πάντα πειρασμόν are all the testings—the three that are narrated and those mentioned in v. 2a, which took place during the forty-day stay in the wilderness. The thesis—formulated especially by Conzelmann 1977, 20 and elsewhere—that Luke has the devil distance himself from Jesus (ἀπέστη ἀπ' αὐτοῦ) ἄχρι καιροῦ (the same phrasing is also found in Philo, *De Iosepho* 10; *Legatio ad Gaium* 260; Acts 13.11) in order to make a bridge to 22.3 and to construct in this way a "Satan free period" as "an epoch *sui generis* in the middle of the entire course of salvation history" (Conzelmann 1977, 70; see also

73) is rather unlikely. The devil does not return to Jesus in 22.3 but enters into Judas and ensures that Judas hands Jesus over to the chief priests and scribes. The linguistic cross-connections between these two texts are much too vague to be able to bear the weight of such a thesis. Beyond this, 10.19 also shows that for Luke the power of the devil was also present among people during the time of Jesus.

As one would expect, Jesus passes all the tests magnificently. But wherein does the significance of the narrative lie? This question has been controversially discussed for a long time (cf. the overview in Luz 1985–2002, I: 222–23, 228ff). An answer, however, is possible if we avoid the methodological error of wanting to first determine the meaning of the Q-version, which can be reconstructed only hypothetically, and instead direct our question to the present Lukan text. It is advisable to start from two indisputable facts.

(a) The allusion to Deuteronomy 8.2^{LXX} in the initial frame of the narrative complex (vv. 1b-2a) and the quotation from Deuteronomy 8.3; 6.13, 16 in vv. 4, 8, 12 create thematic coherence and should be viewed as the theological key to the whole. They connect the temptations of Jesus to Israel's wilderness period, which is interpreted as a time of the temptation of Israel by God. It corresponds to this that both here and there the temptations take place in the wilderness and that their positions in the respective relative chronology correspond to each other. Their placement in the biography of Jesus between Spirit-anointing and public activity corresponds to the placement in the history of Israel between election/deliverance and leading into the land. However, these intertextual connections provide only the interpretive categories for the shaping of the temptations of Jesus. This does not bring Jesus into a typological counterposition to the wilderness generation (so Dupont 1969).

(b) A semantic analysis of the term πειράζειν and its cognates shows that the so-called temptations primarily have a diagnostic function. Whoever "tempts" another (or "puts to the test" or "tests") wants to know whether this one really is what he is regarded to be (or wants to be regarded as) (see also Revelation 2.2). And whoever is "tempted" should prove this very fact. This function is explicitly emphasized, e.g., in Deuteronomy 8.2 ("in order to know what is in your heart, whether you keep his commandments or not") and in 2 Chronicles 32.31 ("so that he would know everything that was in your heart"; see also Exodus 16.4; Deuteronomy 13.2-4; Judges 2.22; 3.4; Judith 8.12–14: "to tempt" God in order to "search out" the Almighty; Jubilees 17.16–18).

(c) On these two foundations, the meaning of the temptation narrative in Luke 4.1-13 can be understood. As a whole it has the goal of giving Jesus an opportunity to prove his identity as Son of God. He has to pass

three individual testings, which are concerned with three different aspects of this identity. The common element is his relation to God, and the testings are meant to bring to light whether Jesus does everything correctly in this respect, i.e., behaves in the manner that corresponds to the nature of the Spirit-anointed Son of God (see also G. P. Thompson 1960). The "temptation" of the *first test* consists in having Jesus *himself* provide an empirical proof. His refusal means that only *God* can do this. In the *second test* Jesus is tested to see whether he is monotheistically ironclad (he is, of course). And in the *third test* Jesus is invited to confirm his divine sonship by making God prove it through his saving intervention. In this theological climax of the testings (and it therefore stands at the end in Luke) Jesus, however, rightly recognizes the temptation to tempt God and therefore rejects the suggestion.

(d) In the Old Testament the subject of the "temptation" of Israel is always God, and with him alone also resides the cognitive interest. But from time to time God can also use other people as instruments or agents of the temptation in order to test the faithful of Israel with their help. Such agents are mentioned in Deuteronomy 13.2-4 (false prophets), Judges 2.22; 3.4 (the people left in the land), and 2 Chronicles 32.31 (the envoys of the ruler of Babylon). According to Tobit 12.13א, the archangel Raphael even says of himself that he was sent to Tobit in order to test him (ἀπέσταλμαι ἐπὶ σὲ πειράσαι σε). It is not difficult to place the devil of the Synoptic temptation narratives in this very function. He does not act autonomously, but as the agent of God (see also at 6c). Therefore, one can neither speak of a "battle" between him and Jesus (Bock I: 382) nor of Jesus "conquering" him (Luz 1985–2002, I: 223).

4.14-44: The Beginning in Galilee

This part of the Lukan story of Jesus is meant when it is said in Luke 23.5; Acts 10.37 that the story of the activity of Jesus began in Galilee (ἀρξάμενος ἀπὸ τῆς Γαλιλαίας; see also Acts 13.31). This does not mean, of course, that Luke wants to give the impression that Jesus no longer sojourned in Galilee after this (cf. just Luke 17.11; 24.6). Moreover, he uses the name Judea in v. 44 and elsewhere (see at 1.5) in such a way that it also includes Galilee.

Luke forms again a narrative collecting basin that is enclosed by two framing notices (vv. 14-15 and vv. 42-44). The geographical terms in the beginning and concluding frames (Galilee and Judea) are related to one another. The events take place again in two places—namely, in Nazareth (vv. 16-30), which Luke had already designated as πόλις τῆς Γαλιλαίας in 1.26 (see also 2.4), and in Capernaum (vv. 31-41), which he introduces to the readers with the same words in v. 31 (diff. Mark 1.21). This narrative technique is already known to the readers from 2.4-21, 22-39 (Bethlehem/ Jerusalem); they will also encounter it in 7.1-10, 11-50 (Capernaum/Nain). But the topographical pair formation also has thematic implications that give the whole unit a paradigmatic character. First, Luke already portrays here *in nuce* the judgment of the Emmaus disciples about Jesus's entire activity—namely, that he was "powerful in deed and word" (δυνατὸς ἐν ἔργῳ καὶ λόγῳ; 24.19). The juxtaposition of the two cities is in this respect complementary. Luke presents Jesus in Nazareth as a speaker and in Capernaum as a miracle worker, and therefore he also emphasizes in v. 32 that Jesus teaches "with authority" (ἐν ἐξουσίᾳ). The parallelism of the two narrative parts also finds expression in the fact that they each begin with a synagogue visit on the Sabbath. But the two cities also stand over against each other antithetically. In Nazareth Jesus is rejected, whereas he meets with great approval among the inhabitants of Capernaum.

4.14-15: Exposition

[14]**And Jesus returned by the power of the Spirit to Galilee. And the news of him spread in the entire surrounding area.** [15]**And he taught in their synagogues** (and was) **praised by all.**

With the transfer of the setting to Galilee Luke orients himself to Mark 1.14. But in other respects the phrasing is his own. The assumption of another source (Schürmann 1968) cannot be justified (cf. Delobel 1989).

14 Luke lets Jesus's return to Galilee be caused by the Spirit and in this way makes this change of location into a component of God's plan of salvation (see at 2.27). The possession of the δύναμις τοῦ θείου πνεύματος is a mark of a true prophet according to Josephus, *Antiquitates judaicae* 8.408, and its absence is regarded as a mark of a false prophet according to Shepherd of Hermas, Mandates 11.2 (cf. also the analogous genitive phrases in Acts 1.8; Romans 15.13, 19). It is unusual that the remark about the public resonance of Jesus in v. 14b stands at the beginning of a narrative complex, for normally such notes stand in the concluding position (cf. esp. Philo, *De Iosepho* 268; *De vita Mosis* 1.265; Matthew 9.26; Luke 4.37; 7.17 and the other texts mentioned at 1.65). For the leading of narrative figures by the Holy Spirit, see at 2.27.

Verse 14b should therefore be connected with **15**. Luke wants to convey to the readers that Jesus found public attention from the beginning of his activity onward, and he concretizes this general information through the following summary about Jesus's teaching activity in the synagogues. In this way the pronoun αὐτῶν also obtains a good sense. As a *constuctio ad sensum* (cf. BDR §282.3) it refers to ὅλη ἡ περίχωρος, which stands here—as in Judith 3.7; Matthew 3.5; 14.35; Mark 1.28par.; Luke 7.17—as a metonym for the people living there. 15b indicates what kind of φήμη it was that spread about Jesus. Something similar is said in Esther 10.3ᴸˣˣ as a conclusion about Mordechai (δεδοξασμένος ὑπὸ τῶν Ἰουδαίων ["honored by all the Jews"]), and Sirach 25.5 writes, "How attractive is power of judgment in the aged and reflection and counsel in the esteemed (δεδοξασμένοις διανόημα καὶ βουλή)." With this Luke writes 2.46-47 forward into the time of the public activity of Jesus and in this way communicates indirectly to the readers that the content of Jesus's teaching concurs in the best way with the attitudes and expectations of the Jewish synagogue public. With a view to what follows, the general affirmation that Jesus experiences on all sides becomes a bright foil against which the reaction to his words in the synagogue of Nazareth has to be set off, and this is probably precisely what Luke intended at this point.

4.16-30: Nazareth

[16]And he came to Nazareth where he had grown up and went according to his custom on the Sabbath into the synagogue. And he rose to read, [17]and the scroll of the prophet Isaiah was given to him, and when he unrolled the Scripture scroll he found the place where it is written: [18]"The Spirit of the Lord is upon me, for he has anointed me.

To gospel to the poor,
he has sent me,
to proclaim freedom to the captives
and to the blind that they see again,
to release the mistreated in freedom,
[19]to proclaim the welcome year of the Lord."

[20]Then he closed the Scripture scroll, gave it back to the attendant and sat down. And the eyes of all in the synagogue were directed at him. [21]But he began to speak to them, "Today this Scripture word is fulfilled in your ears." [22]And all agreed with him and marveled at the pleasing words that came forth from his mouth, and said, "Is this not a son of Joseph?" [23]And he said to them, "Perhaps you will say this proverb to me, 'Physician, heal yourself! Everything which we have heard took place in Capernaum, perform here too in your hometown!'" [24]He said further, "Amen, I say to you: no prophet is welcome in his hometown. [25]Truly, I say to you: in the days of Elijah there were many widows in Israel, when heaven was closed for three years and six months and a great famine came over the whole land. [26]And Elijah was sent to none of them, except to Zarephath in Sidon to a widow woman. [27]And there

**were many lepers in Israel at the time of the prophet Elisha, and none
of them were cleansed—except Naaman, the Syrian." [28]And all in the
synagogue were filled with fury when they heard this. [29]And they rose
up, drove him out of the city, and led him to the edge of the mountain
upon which their city was built, in order to push him into the depths.
[30]But he walked through the midst of them and went on his way.**

The episode of Jesus's visit in his hometown Nazareth, which takes place
in Mark 6.1-6a par. Matthew 13.53-58 only after a longer activity of
Jesus at the Sea of Galilee is brought by Luke to the very beginning of
his account of the public activity of Jesus. If he had left this episode at
the same position within his own story of Jesus, it would stand between
chapters 8 and 9.

The narrative structure is clearly recognizable. After an *introduction*
(v. 16a-c) that leads Jesus to the place at which the episode takes place,
there follows the *exposition* (vv. 16d-17) with the communication of the
events that set into action the event that follows. As the *center* two events
follow, which are parallel insofar as in each of them a speech of Jesus
(vv. 18-21 and vv. 23-27) and the reaction of the hearers are narrated.
Verse 30 is the *finale* of the episode: Jesus goes from Nazareth and never
returns there again.

Although Luke has taken over the episode from Mark 6.1-6a, the agreements are
marginal. Only the information on time and place (on the Sabbath in the synagogue of Nazareth; v. 16 and Mark 6.1-2), the question of Jesus's family origin
(v. 22d; Mark 6.3), and the saying about the prophet who finds no acknowledgment in his hometown (v. 24c; Mark 6.4) allow one to recognize that the same
event is narrated here and there. It is usually assumed that Luke has strongly
reworked and expanded the Markan material (e.g., Klostermann; Rese 1969,
143ff; Fitzmyer; Radl). But there has also not been a lack of attempts to postulate
a different source than the narrative known to us in Mark 6.1-6a as *Vorlage* of the
Lukan narrative (an expanded Mark version or Q; cf. the overview in Schreck
1989). The fact that in Matthew 4.12-13 Jesus also only goes again to Nazareth
directly after his testing and this place is called Ναζαρά only in Luke 4.16 and
Matthew 4.13 (even though this name form is textually debated in both cases; cf.,
however, Goulder 2003, 366–88) can undoubtedly count as an indication for the
presence of Q-material. Therefore, the assumption that there was also an account
of Jesus's visit to Nazareth in Q cannot be excluded in principle (cf. above all
Tuckett 1982). It is dependent on the auxiliary hypothesis that Matthew deleted it,
however, and in any case, one cannot reconstruct it.

16a-c In the New Testament, Nazareth is called Ναζαρά after the Aramaic form only here and in Matthew 4.13 (cf. Rüger 1981). The participle τεθραμμένος is a biographical *terminus technicus* and refers to the entirety of the growing up of children from the age of infancy to the age of majority (cf. Acts 22.3; Plato, *Respublica* 572c; Isocrates, *Panathenaicus* 198; Plutarch, *Aemilius Paullus* 21.2; *Nicias* 5.3; *Alexander* 74.2; as here with specification of the place: Josephus, *Contra Apionem* 1.141; see also Spicq 1994, I: 115–16; III: 381–83). Within the Lukan story of Jesus this remark refers to 2.40, 51-52. The designation of Jesus's Sabbath synagogue visit as "custom" is a reference back to v. 15 (the youth of Jesus is not in view here; contrast Schürmann; Radl); later Luke will also report something analogous about Paul using almost the same words (Acts 17.2). The temporal specification (ἐν) τῇ ἡμέρα τῶν σαββάτων, which is extremely common in the Septuagint, is found only in Luke in the New Testament; see also Acts 13.14; 16.13.

Luke has configured the reading scene in 16-20 as a ring composition:

ἀνέστη (16d)	ἐκάθισεν (20a³)
ἐπεδόθη (17a)	ἀποδούς (20a²)
ἀναπτύξας (17b)	πτύξας (20a¹)
Quotation (18–19)	

We know that prior to 70 CE, in the Diaspora Jewish synagogue gatherings on the Sabbath, excerpts from the Torah were read and explained (and perhaps also discussed) from a whole series of texts; cf. Philo, *De somniis* 2.127: ". . . in your synagogues sit, hold the accustomed gathering (τὸν εἰωθότα θίασον) and without disturbance read (ἀναγιγνώσκειν) and . . . explain the holy books"; *Hypothetica* 7.12; Josephus, *Antiquitates judaicae* 16.43; *Contra Apionem* 2.175; Acts 15.21 (see also Philo, *De vita Mosis* 2.216; Josephus, *Bellum judaicum* 2.289). The analogous specification of function in the Theodotus inscription, which was attached to a Jerusalem synagogue, should probably be interpreted as an adoption of Diaspora Jewish custom: ". . . the synagogue for the reading of the law and for instruction in the commandments (εἰς ἀν[άγ]νωσ[ιν] νόμου καὶ εἰς [δ]ιδαχ[ὴ]ν ἐντολῶν)" (*CIJ* II: 1404); for Qumran there are two, admittedly textually unclear, references in 4Q251 1–2 5 and 4Q264a1 (Fragment 1) 4–5 (cf. Doering 1999, 246ff). The incorporation of texts from the Prophets into this practice is never attested prior to Luke 4.16-20 (see also Acts 13.27). This is also not altered by the fact that fragments of a scroll with the text of Ezekiel 37 were found in the Geniza of the synagogue of Masada (moreover the interpretation of this discovery is anything but clear; cf. Netzer 1991, 409–10); 4 Maccabees 18.10 ("he teaches you . . . the law and the prophets") refers to the instruction by the fathers. "The attempts of many biblical scholars to find traces of the reading cycle in the Gospels are an anachronism" (G. Stemberger, *TRE* 30: 559; for the corresponding efforts, cf. Monshouwer 1991 with older literature). The excursus "The ancient Jewish synagogue service" in Bill. IV/1: 153–88 is without value for the interpretation of Luke 4.16-30. For the preceding, cf. also Perrot 1988; D. D. Binder 1999, 399ff.

With the help of the markedly incremental preparation of the quotation in **16d-17** Luke successively slows down the narrative tempo (cf. Siker 1992, 77–78). In this way he sets a narrative signal that should increase the attention of the reader and underline the significance of the quotation that follows. The verb ἀναπτύσσω (א D[*] Θ Ψ *f*¹,¹³ 𝔐 et al.) in v. 17b suggests that Jesus has a scroll in his hands according to the Lukan understanding and not a codex (for this the variant ἀνοίξας attested by A B L Ξ 33 et al. would fit better; cf. Minnen 2001 with the correction of a false inference made by Bagnall 2000, 577ff).

Luke does not state that Jesus reads but he presents the quotation in **18-19** as the narrator's information for the readers concerning the place in the text to which Jesus unrolled the scroll. The reader reads the text as if it was read to him by Jesus, for in the moment in which s/he is finished with the reading Jesus also rolls up the scroll again (v. 20).

However, in contrast to what Luke claims, the quoted text is found at no point in the Old Testament, for it consists of a combination of Isaiah 61.1-2 and 58.6. Even though the phrasing of the Septuagint is taken over almost word for word, we are dealing with a Lukan construct. This is also recognizable in the fact that Luke *(a)* has left out from Isaiah 61.1 the phrasing "in order to heal those broken in heart" (ἰάσασθαι τοὺς συντετριμμένους τῇ καρδίᾳ; v. 1d), that he *(b)* has inserted Isaiah 58.6e (ἀπόστελλε τεθραυσμένους ἐν ἀφέσει ["send forth the oppressed in liberty"]; v. 18f) between Isaiah 61.1 and 2, and that he *(c)* has the quotation break off after the announcement of the "year of the Lord's favor" (Isaiah 61.2; in Isaiah the continuation of the sentence reads: ". . . and a day of retribution, to comfort all those grieving, to give the grieving of Zion glory instead of ashes"). There are also some smaller changes. In v. 18e he makes the finite verb form of Isaiah 58.6e (ἀπόστελλε) an infinitive (ἀποστεῖλαι) for reasons of syntactical adjustment, and in v. 19 he replaces καλέσαι (Isaiah 61.2) with κηρύξαι.

The decisive course setting undoubtedly takes place through the beginning of the quotation (v. 18a), for at this point every reader will immediately establish an analeptic connection with the descent of the Spirit on Jesus narrated in 3.22 (cf. there ἐπ᾽ αὐτόν with ἐπ᾽ ἐμέ here). In that case, with the help of this quotation this event is immediately interpreted as "anointing" (v. 18b / Isaiah 61.1b; see also Acts 10.38). Bestowal of the Spirit and "anointing" with it are identical, and possession of the Spirit is the consequence of the anointing (contra Radl). Beyond this, the anointing metaphor calls to mind again for the readers the titular Messiah statements of 2.11, 26 (see also Rusam 2003, 178–79). But these cross-connections between the quotation and what has already been narrated by Luke result in the two text worlds being read into each other—the "I" of the quoted text and the "I" of Jesus fuse with each other (see also v. 21b). Through this, then, the continuation with the four syntactically parallel infinitives (vv. 18c, e-f, 19), which are all dependent on "he sent me" (ἀπέσταλκέν με; v. 18d) can be read as a description of the commission of Jesus, to which he was authorized via the Spirit-anointing (see also 7.22): vv. 18a-b look back, vv. 18c-19 look forward. One will certainly not go wrong if one understands v. 18c (εὐαγγελίσασθαι πτωχοῖς) as the heading that summarizes the activities named in vv. 18e-19, or conversely, if one understands vv. 18e-19 as concretizing unfolding of v. 18c (see also Rusam 2003, 180–81). This would also mean that the πτωχοί are made concrete by way of example in the "prisoners," the "blind," and the "oppressed" (see also Green). Thus, Luke summarizes Jesus's entire activity in the phrasing εὐαγγελίσασθαι πτωχοῖς (v. 18c; cf. also 6.20; 7.22). In 4.43 Jesus will summarily describe his commission as εὐαγγελίσασθαι of the βασιλεία τοῦ θεοῦ. The denotative meaning of the two specifications is, of course, one and the same, and both phrasings mutually interpret each other.

The literature has devoted much effort to finding out which specific actions of Jesus or what kind of actions are referred to with the concretions in vv. 18e-19 (cf. e.g., Busse 1978, 33ff; Rusam 2003, 199ff). The search for such a reference, however, misses the intention of the quotation. Rather, Luke uses it *in its entirety* in order to express thereby that the content of Jesus's commission consists in nothing else than in carrying out the eschatic transformation of unsalvation into salvation, which God has promised to his people (cf. the corresponding use of Isaiah 61.2-3 in 11Q13). The quotation has the function of proleptically interpreting the actions of Jesus about which Luke will report in what follows as fulfillment of the prophetic promises of salvation (see also Strauss 1995, 226ff).

This, of course, raises the question of how the omission of Isaiah 61.1d, the breaking off before Isaiah 61.2b, and the insertion of Isaiah 58.6e are to be explained. Albertz 1983 has pointed the way to a possible answer, even though his phrasing (it is said that with the omissions Luke wants to liberate the prophetic promise "from its particularistic restriction, he wants to open it beyond the old people of God" [190]; see also J. A. Sanders 1993) overshoots the mark. Luke certainly does not want to introduce a universalistic perspective on salvation here, but the breaking off before the statement of retribution (Isaiah 61.2b) and his omission of Isaiah 61.1d do point to the fact that the salvation statements related to Israel are placed in a new context. The commission of Jesus is not liberation of Israel from Gentile foreign rule (this connotation was connected above all with Isaiah 61.1d; see also the corresponding connection of ἰᾶσθαι with συντρίβειν and cognates in Psalm^{LXX} 146.2-3; Isaiah 30.26; Jeremiah 3.22; 8.21-2; 14.17, 19; and elsewhere; see also Wolter 1995a, 555–56) but rather—and the addition of Isaiah 58.6e also points in this direction—the liberation of "humans in real social or corporeal distress" (Albertz 1983, 198) from their suffering. In vv. 25-27 Jesus makes clear in a provoking manner that God can turn this liberation in principle also past the distress in Israel to the Gentiles. To be sure, this is not yet carried out by him. Every one of the terms also has the potential for a metaphorical understanding.

In **20** Luke leads the readers back into the narrative by first closing in v. 20a the scene that was opened in vv. 16d-17 in an equally detailed manner. In v. 20b the narrative almost comes to a stop, for Luke describes a longer silence with the help of the phrasing πάντων οἱ ὀφθαλμοὶ . . . ἦσαν ἀτενίζοντες αὐτῷ (*coniugatio periphrastica*; cf. BDR §353; for its use in the Gospel of Luke, see Verboomen 1992; ἀτενίζειν is a typical Lukanism: Luke has 12 of the 14 attestations in the New Testament). The retarding interruption of the action should, first, certainly increase the level of tension, and yet second, it should also make the readers aware of the fact that unlike them, the inhabitants of Nazareth present in the synagogue do not yet know the connections and therefore the meaning of the quotation is still closed to them.

This situation, however, is not long in duration, for in **21** the information gap between the Nazarene synagogue visitors and the readers is balanced out. Jesus tells them that the word of Scripture that was read has spoken *about him*. The reader and the thing read are identical. The Isaiah text becomes Jesus's own text, i.e., it becomes a new text that in the hearers' present in Nazareth (i.e., "today") is no longer only a Scripture quotation, but also a self-statement of the Spirit-anointed Jesus. The significance of this is also expressed in the fact that within the narrated world this is the first time since the beginning of his public ministry that Jesus speaks with a statement of his own. Luke uses γραφή in the singular only here and in Acts 1.16; 8.32, 35, and in every case he means not Scripture, i.e., the Old Testament as a whole, but rather a specific statement (cf. also John 13.18; 19.24, 36, 37; James 2.23; 4.5; and elsewhere). The reference of ἐν τοῖς ὠσὶν ὑμῶν is only superficially unclear, for the usage in 2 Kings 23.2 = 2 Chronicles 34.30; Nehemiah 13.1; Jeremiah 43.14^{LXX}, where there is talk of "reading aloud (ἀναγιγνώσκειν) in the (your/their) ears" (see also Deuteronomy 5.1; Judges 9.2, 3; 17.2; 1 Samuel 3.17; 2 Samuel 3.19; 2 Kings 18.26: "speak in the [your/their] ears") makes it identifiable as a Septuagintism that must be connected with γραφὴ αὕτη via an elliptical form of ἀναγιγνώσκειν (the pointers of Ulrich 1999 are helpful only to a limited extent).

In **22** Luke narrates the reaction of the hearers in the synagogue of Nazareth (for the recourse to the motif of wonder, see at 1.63). It turns out to be much less rejecting than in Mark 6.3 par. Matthew 13.57. In the Lukan presentation, merely something like a dissonance between the perception of the activity of Jesus and the knowledge of his family background comes to expression. The latter, which already came up in 3.23 (ὢν υἱός, ὡς ἐνομίζετο, Ἰωσήφ), is clothed in the rhetorical self-question of v. 22d-e. In the phrasing it deviates again from Mark 6.3ab, but corresponds for the most part with Matthew 13.55a (Q-influence?). There is a quite close structural and partly also terminological correspondence in Acts 2.7 where Luke reports the reaction of the Jerusalem Jews to the Pentecost event: "ἐξίσταντο δὲ καὶ ἐθαύμαζον λέγοντες· 'Behold, are not all those who speak Galileans?'" (cf. also v. 12).

For the Lukan description of the impression that Jesus's words made upon his listeners, cf. Diogenes Laertius 1.23, where θαυμάζειν and μαρτυρεῖν + dative are used almost synonymously: "Xenophanes and Herodotus marveled at (θαυμάζει) him (Thales). Heraclitus and Democritus μαρτυρεῖ δ' αὐτῷ" (see also Plutarch, *Moralia* 457–58). It corresponds to this that the dative with μαρτυρεῖν is also used in a positive way without qualification in John 3.26; Acts 13.22; 22.15; 3 John 12, where there is also no supplement, and therefore should be interpreted both there and here as a *dativus commodi* (cf. BDR §188; see also Ó Fearghail 1984, 62–63, whose suggestion that the καί joining ἐμαρτύρουν and ἐθαύμαζον with each other should be interpreted adversatively [p. 71] tears apart, however, what belongs together). Instead, an epexegetical understanding of the καί would more likely correspond to the semantic interplay of the two verbs (cf. BDR §442.6a). Nolland 1979b, 219ff provides an overview of older proposed interpretations; his own interpretation (the θαυμάζειν of the hearers testifies to their guilt; p. 225) overlooks the joining of μαρτυρεῖν with the *dativus commodi* αὐτῷ, which refers to Jesus.

There is intensive discussion regarding how the λόγοι τῆς χάριτος are the basis and object of the marveling of the hearers. Does Luke use this to relay their assessment of the words of Jesus (so the majority) or does he communicate to the readers only his own judgment, which has nothing to do with the opinion of the hearers (Nolland 1984)? Is the genitive to be understood as *genitivus obiectivus* ("words about grace"; so, e.g., BDR §165$_2$; Plummer; Schürmann; Bovon) or as *genitivus qualitatis* ("words characterized by χάρις"; so, e.g., Marshall; Nolland 1984; Radl)? Does χάρις designate the grace of God in the theological sense (so the majority) or merely the outer form the speech as in Colossians 4.6; Proverbs 7.5; Ecclesiastes 10.12; Sirach 21.16 (e.g., W. Bauer 1988, 1750; Zahn)? It is in any case beyond question that we are dealing with a Septuagintism in the phrasing "words that came out of his mouth" (cf. Deuteronomy 8.3; Isaiah 55.11; Jeremiah 51.17^{LXX}; see also Numbers 30.3; 32.24; Judges 11.36; 1 Samuel 1.23; 2.3; 1 Kings 21.33; Judith 5.5; Isaiah 48.3 as well as Luke 11.54; 22.71; Acts 15.7; see BDR §217.3b: ἐκ τοῦ στόματος αὐτοῦ as Hebraizing paraphrase of a simple preposition). The answer to the last question decides everything: the attestations for the expression λόγος/ λόγοι (τῆς) χάριτος in the literature outside the New Testament show that this is an established idiom; cf. Isocrates, *Antidosis* 144; Plutarch, *Demosthenes* 7.5; *Cicero* 13.2; Athenaeus, *Deipnosophistae* 3.52 (v. 97c); *Epitome*, ed. Peppink 1937–1939, 2.1.17 (v. 97c); see also Plutarch, *Alcibiades* 10.3; *Moralia* 801c; 1097d (ῥήματα τῆς χάριτος) as well as the frequent mention of χάρις as a characteristic of a good speech (in addition to the aforementioned texts, cf. Demosthenes, *Orationes* 4.38; Plutarch, *Lycurgus* 19.1; Spicq 1994, III: 500; Radl I: 261n137). On the other hand, the parallels in Acts 14.3 and 20.32, which are often mentioned in this context, are not relevant, since these texts speak in a definite way of the "word of *his* (i.e., God's) χάρις." In Luke 4.22 χάρις thus means something like "charm," "pleasingness," "gracefulness." For Luke the concern is with a characteristic of the words of Jesus that is also already perceived by the hearers as such. And this is, of course, an error, for not the character but the content of the words of Jesus should have drawn their attention to itself.

The result of the impression that Jesus's words make upon those present in the narrative can also be described sociologically. It is a matter of cognitive dissonance between the *role* in which Jesus confronted the synagogue visitors and the *status* that is assigned to him in the place of his childhood and youth (see v. 16). Here, they all know him only as the "son of Joseph" (v. 22e). This is then also precisely the reason that their reaction is limited to a marveling over the shapely form of the words of Jesus (on θαυμάζειν, see at 1.63). Therefore, the πάντες in Nazareth do not fare better than those of 1.63 and 2.18 (and 9.43). They identify something extraordinary without comprehending it. The reason for this is obvious. They do not get past an uncomprehending marveling because they make the knowledge of the identity of Jesus that they have brought with them the taken-for-granted standard for evaluating his words instead of conversely deriving Jesus's identity from his words and correcting their knowledge accordingly. One should not lose sight of the fact that all three verbs with which Luke describes the hearers (ἐμαρτύρουν, ἐθαύμαζον, and ἔλεγον) are in the imperfect, whereas the surrounding action is narrated in the aorist. The reaction of the hearers is thus not narrated as a completed action but as a description of an open (precisely 'imperfect') situation (cf. Porter 1989, 188ff).

23-27 The words that Jesus addresses to his hearers form a clearly recognizable thematic nexus. The coherence arises through the structural parallelism of v. 23c-d and vv. 25-26, 27. The opposition between "near" and "far" is common to all four statements. In v. 23c this is carried out via the example of the physician who does **not** heal *himself* but only *others* (this half of the opposition has fallen away here but is implicitly present due to the proverbial character of the saying; see below). To this corresponds in v. 23d the opposition of Jesus's hometown *Nazareth*, where he does **not** do the sort of deeds that he does in *Capernaum*. Along this same line, in vv. 25-26 "many widows in *Israel*," to which Elijah is **not** sent, are set over against the one (non-Israelite) widow in *Zarephath*, and, finally, "many lepers in *Israel*," who were **not** healed, are juxtaposed with *the Syrian Naaman*. There are thus the following correspondences:

	on the one hand (near):	on the other hand (far):
23c:	the physician who does not heal himself	(the other sick people)
23d:	Nazareth as Jesus's hometown	Capernaum
25-26:	many widows	the widow in Zarephath
27:	many lepers in Israel	the Syrian Naaman

The sequence of these contrasts is also instructive, for it reveals a clear widening of the perspective from the first via the second down to the third and fourth—from the opposition of the person of the physician and the other sick people via the opposition of two places down to the opposition of Israel and the Gentiles. Beyond this, the first two contrasts involved *demands* (cf. the imperatives) *that are directed to Jesus* (ἐρεῖτέ μοι; v. 23b), while in the last two contrasts an action of God is described (*passivum divinum* in each case) that goes precisely in the other direction. God has done exactly the opposite of what is expected of Jesus according to v. 23c-d (cf. οὐδεμία and οὐδείς in v. 26a and v. 27b). Although there was great need in Israel, he sent his prophets to non-Israelites, i.e., he has precisely not done the thing that actually lay nearest at hand. Finally, the narrated situation (rhetorically: the *causa*; cf. Lausberg 1973, §411) is in view exclusively in v. 23d; in all the other oppositions we are dealing with rhetorical *probationes*, namely in the form of a παραβολή or *similitudo* (v. 23c; cf. Lausberg 1973, §422) and in the form of two *exempla* from history (vv. 25-27; cf. Lausberg 1973, §411). Here Luke introduces for the first time one of the so-called double examples (Morgenthaler 1948, I: 60ff) with which he repeatedly has Jesus illustrate his speech (see also 11.31-32; 12.24, 27; 12.54-55; 13.18-21; 14.28-32; 15.4-10; 17.26-29,

34-35 and 3.12-14; 13.1-5; see also section 4.4.3 in the introduction to this commentary). Verse 24 connects the *exempla* invoked in vv. 25-27 with the *causa* of v. 23d.

The narrative *function* of this verse has grown out of the Markan note ἐσκανδαλίζοντο ἐν αὐτῷ (Mark 6.3 par. Matthew 13.57): Luke has not adopted it in wording but probably in content, for in vv. 28-29 he highlights precisely this reaction of the hearers. And it is in relation to this result that the speech of Jesus narrated in vv. 23-27 was designed as a cause.

23 For the translation of πάντως with "perhaps," cf. Cadbury 1925, 223ff. παραβολή is the rhetorical *terminus technicus* for the *similitudo* (cf. Quintilian, *Institutio oratoria* 5.11.5-6), "which brings every similar phenomenon . . . into a credibility-seeking nexus of comparison with the *causa*," usually in the form of "the concise allusion" as here (Lausberg 1973, §422). This function is ascribed to a proverb that is widely attested since the time of Aeschylus (*Prometheus vinctus* 469–75) in ancient literature (cf. the presentation of the material in Nolland 1979a; Noorda 1982). This proverb normally confronts the person of the (sick) physician with the others (treated or healed by him) (e.g., Euripides, Fragment 1086: "A physician for others, but himself full of sores"; Cicero, *Epistulae ad familiares* 4.5.5: "bad physicians who in the sicknesses of others claim mastery of the medical science but cannot heal themselves"). The reference to the other side, i.e., to the healing of other sick people, is absent here, but it undoubtedly stands in the background (see above).

Verse 23d formulates the *causa* to which the proverb is related. The *tertium comparationis* is as follows. If Jesus does not also do in Nazareth what he has done in Capernaum, he is like a physician who can only heal other people but not himself, which, of course, calls into question his medical competence. An analogous comparison is found in Dio Chrysostom 49.13: "Whoever delays when his city calls him and exhorts him to take on responsibility and says he is not suitable, is like one who does not wish to heal his own body (τὸ . . . ἑαυτοῦ σῶμα θεραπεύειν μὴ θέλοι) but claims ἰατρὸς εἶναι and . . . readily treats other people."

Two matters, however, have traditionally made the understanding of this verse difficult. First, it is not the hearers in the synagogue of Nazareth who direct this request to Jesus. Rather, it is *Jesus himself* who announces to them that they will say these words to him. Second, it has always attracted attention that the people in Nazareth in Luke could know nothing about Jesus's deeds in Capernaum, since he (unlike Mark; see above) has not yet been there at all. To attribute the latter to a carelessness in the rearrangement of the Nazareth pericope (e.g., Klostermann; Johnson) would, of course, mean underestimating Luke. Decisive for an understanding of the Lukan intention is the future ἐρεῖτε in v. 23b. Luke has Jesus anticipate a future situation here, namely a situation that follows the likewise still-future deeds of power in Capernaum and therefore "(can) only be formulated in the future" (Busse 1978). There is thus a fictive looking ahead to a situation after 4.43 and of course, Luke cannot put such a looking ahead into the mouth of the people in Nazareth but only into the mouth of Jesus. In that case, the rather complicated rhetorical shaping can be traced back to a simple idea. In unpacking what he has said in v. 21 as an explanation of the Isaiah text that was read out (vv. 18-19), Jesus communicates to his hearers a key characteristic of his "mission" (see v. 18d): "My mission"—it can perhaps be paraphrased in this way—"will have the consequence that you will say: '. . .'" The propositional content of this disclosure thus consists in the fact that the Lukan Jesus announces to the inhabitants of Nazareth that among them he will do nothing for the "fulfillment" of the Isaianic promises of salvation. Thus, it is concerned only secondly with a statement about the inhabitants of Nazareth; in the foreground stands the peculiar character of Jesus's own mission. There can be no talk of a "change of mood," which is often discovered in this verse. And the announcement of Jesus is also not caused by the reaction described in v. 22. In vv. 24-27 a justification for this announcement is then given.

24 is set off from what precedes with the help of the speech introduction εἶπεν δέ. At the same time, this verse functions as a hinge. ἐν τῇ πατρίδι αὐτοῦ analeptically takes up the corresponding phrasing from v. 23d, while προφήτης is proleptically related to Elijah (vv. 25-26) and Elisha, "the prophet" (v. 27). This verse thus accomplishes what ancient rhetoric designates as *inductio* (cf. Lausberg 1973, §419ff). It connects the *exempla* that follow in vv. 25-27 with the *causa* of v. 23d. Luke takes up a proverb again, which he uses as a rhetorical *similitudo* (see at vv. 23-27). He has presumably adopted it from Mark 6.4 (par. Matthew 13.57; see also John 4.44), but there it is not only formulated differently ("A prophet is never ἄτιμος except in his hometown and among his relatives and in his house"), but also presents Jesus's reaction to the rejection that he has experienced from the side of the inhabitants of Nazareth. Parallels that correspond to the Lukan version with the adjective δεκτός are found in Gospel of Thomas 31 and in P. Oxy I, 1.9–12r, but there it is supplemented with another proverb: "A prophet is not welcome in his hometown, and a physician does not perform healings on his acquaintances." Dio Chrysostom 47.6 says something similar about philosophers ("All philosophers regarded life in the homeland as bad"); see also Philostratus, *Epistulae Apollonii* 44 ("Although other people regard me as equal to god, some even as god, μόνη μέχρι νῦν ἡ πατρὶς ἀγνοεῖ [alone the hometown ignores (me) down to the present]"). In Luke the proverb has a different function than in Mark, for it cannot explain the rejection of Jesus in his hometown, because this has not yet taken place. It is also not said that a prophet is rejected by the ones to whom he is sent (*pace* Nolland). Rather, the proverb functions as a bridge between the following examples from Israel's past and the narrated situation (Jesus in his hometown). It is intended to justify why Jesus's activity in Nazareth is, so to speak, suspended—namely, because his hometown, for the reason mentioned in this verse, is not included in his commission. All prophets are unwelcome in their hometowns, and therefore God does not send them there, and therefore Jesus also has no commission for Nazareth.

25-26 The incident that is narrated about Elijah in 1 Kings 17.7-24, who is sent into Phoenician Zarephath during a drought and there meets a widow whom he supplies with flour and oil that do not run out, functions as a first *exemplum* from history. There is, of course, not talk of a three-and-a-half-year drought in the Old Testament (1 Kings 18.1 recounts that it rained again in the third year), but there probably is talk of this in James 5.17; in all probability the temporal specification originates from Daniel 7.25; 12.7 (see also Revelation 11.2; 12.6, 14). Luke now develops this narrative so that its plot is determined by the opposition of the land of Israel and the city Zarephath, whose most important feature is the fact that it is not located in Israel. Although Elijah was a prophet of the God of Israel, he is appointed—contrary to expectations—not to alleviate the need in Israel but rather outside Israel. The disappointment of expectations via God's action is rhetorically intensified by the fact that a quantitative aspect is brought in. "*Many* widows . . . in *Israel*" are set over against the *one* widow woman in *Zarephath in Sidon*, and despite this God sent his prophet not to the former (not even to a single one of them: οὐδεμίαν αὐτῶν) but only to the latter. Although there were actually two reasons against sending Elijah to the widow in Zarephath, the commission that Elijah received from God passed by Israel.

27 The second example reaches back to the story, told in 2 Kings 5.1-14, of the Syrian (so Luke in dependence on the Septuagint) general Naaman, whom the prophet Elijah could free from his leprosy through seven immersions in the Jordan. The rhetorical realization of the plot of the retelling proceeds in parallel to that of vv. 25-26: *Many* lepers in *Israel* are set over against *one* leprous *Syrian*, and yet God had his prophet heal not the former (not even a single one of them: οὐδεὶς αὐτῶν) but only the latter. The two examples do not yet function as such as a proleptic pointer to the later Gentile mission (see also Busse 1978, 44; Wasserberg 1998, 162), though they are certainly open to this and this was probably also clear to the narrator (cf. at vv. 28-29). Rather, in the first instance they are intended to justify why Jesus does no miracles in Nazareth, namely because he does not serve the expectations of the people in his hometown but rather must solely fulfill the commission of God (see also Tannehill 1972, 62; Siker 1992, 84–85).

It is, however, also unquestionable that the Lukan Jesus performs a markedly idiosyncratic interpretation of the two Old Testament traditions. His interpretation says that in both cases God turned his salvation to Gentiles, passing by the distress of Israel. This also shows that Jesus does not anticipate the subsequent Gentile mission here, for it does *not* pass by Israel. At any rate, it is only this reasoning of Jesus that leads to an abrupt change of mood.

28-29 In these two verses Luke highlights the ἐσκανδαλίζοντο ἐν αὐτῷ from Mark 6.3, but he has provided it with different occasion through vv. 25-27. The indignation of hearers in the synagogue of Nazareth (for the phrasing, cf. Daniel 3.19; Xenophon of Ephesus 2.4.3) is triggered by what Jesus has said about God and the Gentiles. And this very thing is also the point that gives this episode paradigmatic significance, for this is also precisely the point at which Jewish opposition to the Christ proclamation of the witnesses is repeatedly ignited later in Acts (cf. 13.44-45; 17.4; 22.17-23). We have here the first example of the hardening of Israel that is stated in Acts 28.26-27. At any rate, exactly what Jesus announced in v. 24 takes place. Luke narrates the action of the synagogue visitors against Jesus in an extremely graphic way. For the use of ἀναστάντες, see at 1.39. In Acts 7.58; Plato, *Leges* 873b, the phrasing ἐκβάλλειν . . . ἔξω τῆς πόλεως introduces a stoning, prior to which the delinquent is frequently thrown down from an elevated point (see also Hegesippus, Fragment 2 in Eusebius of Caesarea, *Historia ecclesiastica* 2.23.4–18 [see at v. 9a-b above]). But Luke says nothing about this. The place to which Jesus is led and from which he is to be thrown down (for ὥστε as a designation of the intended consequence, cf. BDR §391.3) is not topographically verifiable, and ancient Nazareth was not located on a mountain but in a high valley. The details regarding this are pure fiction.

30 How Jesus managed to escape unharmed through the hostile crowd who wanted to kill him remains unnarrated. Luke intentionally does not narrate a sudden, miraculous disappearance through which, e.g., Apollonius of Tyana evades a similar situation (Philostratus, *Vita Apollonii* 8.5.3– 4). Rather, he again leaves it to the imagination of the readers to imagine the reason for Jesus's deliverance, and it would certainly not have been unwelcome to him if they had thought especially of a preserving intervention of God. On διέρχεσθαι as a typical Lukan word, see at 2.15.

The significance of this episode for the Lukan story of Jesus lies on multiple levels. *First*, it can be understood as an interpretive narrative elaboration of Mark 6.1-6a. This applies in particular to the note that the inhabitants of Nazareth "took offense" at Jesus (ἐσκανδαλίζοντο ἐν αὐτῷ;

v. 3c) and the note that he could perform no δυνάμεις there (v. 5a). Luke furnishes both with a new explanation. The offense is not traced back to the dissonance between Jesus's role as miracle worker and teacher of wisdom (v. 2) and the status assigned to him as roofer, etc. (v. 3a, b), but rather to Jesus's saying about the privileging of Gentiles by God (Luke 4.25-27). In addition, the absence of deeds of power in Nazareth is not presented as an impossibility but rather as the result of a very conscious intention (vv. 23-24). That this renunciation had its basis in the failure to recognize Jesus's true identity (so e.g., Wasserberg 1998, 163) does not emerge from the text. *Second*, this text contains the first public speech of Jesus with which he provides an overall interpretation of his activity for the first time within the narrated world, which remains, to be sure, without a reaction that corresponds to this interpretation from the side of the narrated public. For Luke and the omniscient readers, who already know how the whole story turns out and therefore read the Nazareth episode, so to speak, 'from the end,' Nazareth does, in fact, represent "Israel in miniature."

This applies both to the reaction to Jesus's word about the privileging of Gentiles, which is described in vv. 28-29, and to the perception of the identity of Jesus (v. 22). The inhabitants of Nazareth—like many other Jews after them—also do not get beyond an uncomprehending "marveling" when they encounter the self-interpretation of Jesus.

4.31-41: Capernaum

[31]**And he came down to Capernaum, a town in Galilee. And he taught them on the Sabbath.** [32]**And they were astonished at his teaching, for his word was powerful.** [33]**And in the synagogue there was a person with the spirit of an unclean demon. And he cried out with a loud voice:** [34]**"Hey! What do we have to do with you, Jesus of Nazareth? You have come to destroy us. I know who you are: the Holy One of God."** [35]**And Jesus shouted at him and said, "Shut up and come out of him!" And the demon flung him into the middle and came out of him without harming him.** [36]**And terror seized them all, and they said to one another, "What is this word? With authority and power he commands the unclean spirits, and they come out!"** [37]**And the news of him reached every place of the surrounding area.**

[38]**But he departed from the synagogue and went into the house of Simon. But the mother-in-law of Simon was gripped by a high fever, and they appealed to him concerning her.** [39]**And he stood over her and shouted at the fever, and it departed from her. On the spot she raised herself and provided for them.**

⁴⁰**Now at the setting of the sun all who had people suffering under various sicknesses brought these to him. And he laid the hands on every one of them and healed them. ⁴¹And demons also came out of many, who screamed and said, "You are God's Son!" And he shouted at them and did not let them speak, for they knew that he was the Messiah.**

Luke now aligns himself again with the Markan order and narrates the events that took place on a Sabbath in Capernaum. His *Vorlage* is Mark 1.21-34, and he follows it in the main. The coherence of this narrative collecting basin is clearly recognizable. At the beginning stands a summary report about Jesus's teaching activity and its impact on his hearers, which Luke traces back to the ἐξουσία of Jesus's words (vv. 31-32). In order to document the ἐξουσία of Jesus with examples, an exorcism (vv. 33-37) and a healing of a sick person (vv. 38-39) are then recounted. The narrative complex is concluded with a summary, which makes a generalization and in this way expresses that there was more than this one exorcism and this one healing of a sick person (vv. 40-41).

There are no significant minor agreements (cf. further Neirynck 1974b, 62–64; 1991, 15–17; Ennulat 1994, 41–47).

31-37 The narrative of the exorcism in the synagogue of Capernaum displays the usual structure: *introduction* (vv. 31-32), *exposition* (vv. 33-34), *center* (v. 35), and *finale* (vv. 36-37). Decisive for the assignment to the genre "exorcism story" is the semantics of the terms in vv. 33, 35 (πνεῦμα δαιμονίου ἀκαθάρτου, twice ἐξῆλθε[ν] ἀπ' αὐτοῦ, δαιμόνιον). However, there are clearly recognizable narrative thickenings in the introduction and—corresponding to this—in the finale: In v. 32 this applies to the description of the reaction to Jesus's teaching and in v. 36b-e to the verbal reproduction of the reaction to Jesus's exorcism. The terms λόγος and ἐν ἐξουσία occur both here and there. They function as a reading instruction and express how the narrative in between should be understood, namely as evidence for the "authority" of Jesus's teaching.

31 Luke knows that one must go down from Nazareth to Capernaum (for the spelling, cf. Lührmann 1987, 49; the manuscript tradition is also divided in v. 31a, and the evidence for the Hebraizing version is better). This is not as surprising as it is sometimes regarded (cf. e.g., Fitzmyer; Radl), since for him Nazareth is located on a mountain (see v. 29 as well as Conzelmann 1977, 32). Luke withholds from his readers the information that Capernaum is located on the Lake of Gennesaret (see already Conzelmann 1977, 32; Codex D therefore adds "τὴν παραθαλάσσιον [on the sea] in the region of Zebulon and Naphtali"). It is also noteworthy that

Luke calls this place a πόλις (town), while Josephus designates it from his own viewpoint as a "village" (κώμη; *Vita* 403; see also *Bellum judaicum* 3.519; Möller/Schmitt 1976, 128–29). In this way Luke undoubtedly wants to increase the significance of the activity of Jesus. This is guided by the same intention that has Paul say in Acts 26.26, "this has not taken place in a corner" (for the significance of the term πόλις in Luke, cf. the excursus in Hoffmann 1972, 278ff). In contrast, in 5.17 Luke will say concerning the Pharisees and scribes—i.e., the opponents of Jesus—that they come "from the villages." For the excavations in Capernaum, cf. S. Lofreda/V. Tzaferis, *NEAEHL* I: 291–96; Tzaferis 1989; M. Fischer 2001; see also the information in Tsafrir 1994, 97. Verse 31b describes a teaching activity of Jesus that extends over a longer period of time (*coniugatio periphrastica*; cf. BDR §353; for its use in Luke, see Verboomen 1992). Luke takes up vv. 14-15 (cf. the terminological cross-connections via "Galilee" and "teaching" and via "Sabbath"/"synagogue") and treats the stay in Capernaum as an episodic concretion of the previously formulated summary observation about the teaching activity of Jesus in Galilee.

32 Unlike in Mark 1.22, ἐξουσία is not a feature of Jesus's teaching, but rather designates the quality of his speech (εἶναι + ἐν + *dativus sociativus*, like Mark 1.23 [ἦν . . . ἐν πνεύματι ἀκαθάρτῳ]; Luke 8.43 [οὖσα ἐν ῥύσει αἵματος]; 23.12 [ἐν ἔχθρᾳ ὄντες]; see also BDR §198₂ with other examples). In v. 36 Luke has the people also ascribe the same characteristic to Jesus's exorcistic word. Thus, what is decisive for him is the fact that both come from one and the same mouth. Therefore, for Luke the point of the exorcism story lies in this judgment of the inhabitants of Capernaum, and for this reason he has most strongly altered the Markan *Vorlage* at this point and removed the distinction between the activity of Jesus as teacher and as miracle worker. In this way it also becomes possible for him to delete the Markan demarcation from the scribes (Mark 1.22c), for the concern in what follows is not with teaching controversies, as it is in Mark, which has the deeds of power in Capernaum merge into a series of controversy dialogues with the Jewish teaching authorities (2.1–3.6). In Luke the teaching conflicts do not arise until 5.17–6.1. It is of decisive importance, however, that Luke reminds the readers again of Jesus's activity in Nazareth, and the difference also immediately jumps out. While in Nazareth people had credited Jesus's words merely with χάρις ("gracefulness" or the like, v. 22; for the reasons, see there), the inhabitants of Capernaum perceive the teaching of Jesus immediately as 'λόγος τῆς ἐξουσίας' and then also have their judgment promptly confirmed by Jesus's exorcisms. In 7.7 the centurion will also ascribe the same quality to Jesus's word ("εἰπὲ λόγῳ and my servant will be healed"), whereupon Jesus attests his extraordinary faith (v. 9). It certainly is not too much of a stretch to refer in this context to Wisdom of Solomon 16.12-13, where the concern is with the ἐξουσία of God's word: "It is your word, Lord, that heals all, for you have ἐξουσία over life and death, and you lead down to the gates of Hades and you lead up."

33 With the narrative introduction of a possessed man, Luke sets the event into motion. In addition to some minor changes to the Markan *Vorlage* (deletion of the typically Markan εὐθύς, which Luke has also never taken over elsewhere; replacement of εἶναι . . . ἐν [see v. 32] with ἔχων; see also 8.27 diff. Mark 5.2), Luke says that the man "had the spirit of an unclean demon" (for this usage, cf. at 7.33). This designation is found nowhere else, and it is also not entirely clear why Luke chooses this phrasing. The usual explanation that in this way he wanted to explain the phenomenon of possession to Hellenistic readers is of little help, since for this he so often uses the phrasing ἀκάθαρτα πνεύματα that is replaced here (6.18; 8.29; 9.42; 11.24[Q]; Acts 5.16; 8.7; otherwise only 8.27 diff. Mark 5.2; Luke 8.33 diff. Mark 5.13; Luke 9.1 diff. Mark 6.7). A conception such as what is often attested in Josephus is presumably in the background. "The so-called δαιμόνια are πονηρῶν ἀνθρώπων πνεύματα that penetrate into the living and kill those who find no help" (*Bellum judaicum* 7.185); ". . . the evil spirit and the demons who take up residence in you" (ἐγκαθέζεσθαι; *Antiquitates judaicae* 6.211 about Saul); "There came to him again τὸ δαιμόνιον . . . πνεῦμα, which confused and disturbed him" (*Antiquitates judaicae* 6.214 about Saul). It belongs to the established motif inventory of exorcisms that the demon observes the approach of the exorcist and addresses him with the voice of the possessed, and this also occurs here.

34 Luke takes over the Markan phrasing word for word. He merely precedes it with an exclamation (ἔα), because he evidently imagines that the demon first wants to direct Jesus's attention to himself (cf. e.g., Epictetus, *Dissertationes* 2.24.22 with a comparable continuation: ἔα, ἄνθρωπε, ἐπὶ τί ἐλήλυθας; ["Hey, human being, for what have you come?"]; see also 3.20.5 as well as LSJ 465: "esp. before a question"); it would also be grammatically possible to understand it as an imperative of ἐᾶν ("Let!"; so e.g., Schürmann; Nolland), but this probably founders on the semantics of this verb (cf. Kirchschläger 1981, 37). The following question is a formulaic expression known from the Old Testament: cf. Judges 11.12 (Hebrew מַה־לִּי וָלָךְ); 2 Samuel 16.10; 19.23; 1 Kings 17.18; 2 Kings 3:13; 2 Chronicles 35.21 = 1/3 Ezra 1.24; and elsewhere; but see then also Mark 5.7; John 2.4; Epictetus, *Dissertationes* 2.19.16 and 19. Verse 34b can be understood as a question or as a statement. The latter is more likely because it results in a more meaningful connection with the information in v. 34c-d. Because the demon knows that Jesus is "the Holy One of God," he also knows what he is in for. In addition to the use of the defense formula in v. 34a, the expression of this double knowledge—namely, first, the knowledge of the identity of Jesus, and, second, the knowledge of the consequences of the encounter with him for its own fate—makes it appear extremely unlikely that the demon, for his part, attempts in v. 34c-d to gain power over Jesus in the way of a counterspell by pronouncing his name (the so-called Rumpelstiltskin motif; cf. also the convincing demolition of this assumption in Scholtissek 1992, 97ff). Here the demon mentions precisely not the *name* but rather the *title* of Jesus (ὁ ἅγιος τοῦ θεοῦ), and this can be understood only as a submitting recognition of the vastly superior power of Jesus, because he belongs on the side of God on account of his holiness (cf. 1.35). In this way the distancing attempt in v. 34a also obtains a good sense. Only if the "Holy One of God" keeps himself away from the "unclean demon" does the demon escape unscathed, and of course, it knows this.

35 Luke characterizes the command to be silent and come out (on the wording, cf. Acts 16.18; *PGM* IV: 1242–44, 3013), which Jesus addresses to the demon, as ἐπιτιμᾶν (v. 35a; see also Mark 9.25 par. Luke 9.42). He thus uses a word that describes God's exercise of his own power in Psalm^{LXX} 67.29-31; 103.7; 105.8-9 (see also 9.5-6; 75.7) or how God turns himself against his enemies (Psalm^{LXX} 118.21: against the proud, the cursed, apostates from the law; Zechariah 3.2: the devil; see also Jude 9) or how he, as creator, has bound the chaos power (Psalm^{LXX} 17.16; 103.6-7; Job 26.11; see also Mark 4.39parr.); see also Psalm^{LXX} 79.17 and for the Hebrew or Aramaic equivalent 1 נָעַר QM XIV, 10; 1QapGen XXVIII-XXIX. Because this word is lacking in exorcism stories and magical texts (e.g., magical papyri) outside the New Testament, it has here the function of characterizing Jesus not as a technically adept exorcist but as God's representative (see also Kee 1967/1968). Verse 35c portrays the circumstances that accompany the exiting of the demon and are regarded as proof that the demon has actually left the person; cf. Philostratus, *Vita Apollonii* 4.20.2 (the demon receives the command to come out ξὺν τεκμηρίῳ ["with a proof"], and offers to knock over a statue); Josephus, *Antiquitates judaicae* 8.48 (it must knock over a bucket of water). Luke apparently imagines the event in such a way that the possessed person is thrown to the ground before all who are present (εἰς τὸ μέσον, which is added here and in 5.19). Presumably for this reason he adds the comforting assurance that the possessed person is not harmed in the process (cf. Mark 9.26; Acts of Peter [Actus Vercellenses] 11: Peter gives the demon the command: ". . . come out of the youth without harming him [*nihil nocens eum*]. . . . When he had heard this, he came out and seized a great marble statue . . . and trampled it with kicks").

In accordance with the genre, **36-37** feature the wonder and accla-mation of the witnesses of the exorcism (cf. Theissen 1987, 78ff, 80–81; Wolter 1992, 171ff) and a note of dissemination (Theissen 1987, 81). Luke had already combined these elements with one another in 1.65-66 (see also 7.16-17). In the New Testament θάμβος (v. 36a) only occurs in Luke (see also 5.9; Acts 3.10); the verb (including *composita*) occurs only in Mark. It is a term that comes from the Jewish theophany tradition (cf. 1 Samuel 14.15; Ezekiel 7.18; Daniel 8.17[Theodotion]; Josephus, *Antiquitates judaicae* 6.92; see also W. Grimm, *EWNT* 2: 317–19). The realization of the acclamation in v. 36b-d reaches back via the terms λόγος and ἐξουσία to the introduction in v. 32 and conveys to the readers wherein the signifi-cance of this episode lies (see further at v. 32). Despite the word-for-word parallelism, the question τίς ὁ λόγος οὗτος; is most probably not an allu-sion to 2 Samuel 1.4[LXX] (see also at 24.17). The parallelizing of ἐξουσία and δύναμις is not uncommon in non-Jewish texts of the New Testament environment (cf. e.g., Thucydides 6.31.4; Plutarch, *Camillus* 1.2; *Sulla* 41.1; *Otho* 7.5; *Moralia* 283c; 337–38; Dio Chrysostom 1.46; Cassius Dio 55.18.5; and elsewhere; in Jewish texts it is attested only in Testament of Ruben 5.1).

38-39 When Luke has the narrative of the healing of the mother-in-law of Simon from Mark 1.29-31 follow, he accepts a narrative incoherence. Because he pushed back the narrative of the calling of the first disciples (5.1-11; in the Gospel of Mark it occurs in 1.16-20), Simon and Jesus are not yet known to each other within the narrated world, so that Jesus's visit in the house of Simon appears quite unmotivated. Beyond this Luke introduces him only with his personal name and thereby gives the impres-sion that he is a narrative figure known to the readers. Not mentioning the other disciples over against Mark 1.29 is meant to reduce this incoherence somewhat. Despite its brevity, the individual parts of this healing story are clearly identifiable. Verse 38a-b is the *introduction* and v. 38c-d the *expo-sition*. Verse 39a-b forms the *center*, and v. 39c the *finale*.

38 The introduction (v. 38a-b) portrays the change of scene with the Septuagintism ἀναστάς + *verbum finitum*, which occurs frequently in Luke (see at 1.39; the connection with ἀπό to designate the place from which one departs corresponds to general Greek usage: e.g., Genesis 46.5; 1/3 Ezra 9.1; Josephus, *Vita* 234; Dionysius of Halicarnassus, *Antiquitates romanae* 5.57.2; Pausanias 3.22.12).

Σίμων is an older Greek name (cf. already Aristophanes, *Equites* 242; *Nubes* 351, 399; cf. PRE 2/5 [1927], 162ff). In our passage and in many Jewish writings that were written in Greek (admittedly never in Philo but all the more often in Josephus) it functions as a Hellenistic substitution for the Jewish name Συμεών (see at 2.25 and BDR §53.3d) with the goal of assimilating to Greek language conventions. In the Septuagint Σίμων is used only in the independent writings (especially 1–4 Maccabees but also 1/3 Ezra 9.32; Sirach 50.1); in writings that were translated from the Hebrew canon, by contrast, we always find Συμεών; cf. also Fitzmyer 1971, 105–12; Ilan 2002, 218ff. In the Lukan story of Jesus the narrator calls Simon Peter "Simon" only up to 6.14; after this he always speaks of "Peter." He only continues to put the name "Simon" into the mouth of the narrative figures—namely, of Jesus himself (22.31) and of the disciples gathered in Jerusalem (24.34).

In the exposition (v. 38c-d) Luke describes the suffering with more technical terminology than Mark, for συνέχειν is what sicknesses do to people (concerning fever: e.g., Hippocrates, *De morbis popularibus* [= *Epidemiae*], 2.2.6; *De morbis* 1.18; Galen, *De typis*, ed. Kühn 1964, VII: 468.11; Philo, *De opificio mundi* 125; Josephus, *Antiquitates judaicae* 13.398; Diodorus Siculus 36.13.3; Pausanias 7.24.11; Acts 28.8; see further Hobart 2004, 3ff; Spicq 1994, III: 337ff; Luke is just as little identifiable as a physician by this as the other non-medical authors; see Cadbury 1926, 194–95, 203). Unlike Mark, Luke has people who remain anonymous ask Jesus for help (see also Mark 7.26; Luke 7.3 par. John 4.47) and indicates in this way that he was already regarded in the public as a miracle worker.

39 For the carrying out of the miraculous action (v. 39a) the narrator has Jesus stand upright alongside the woman envisaged as lying down (this is apparently what is meant by ἐπιστὰς ἐπάνω αὐτῆς) and then speak an exorcistic word of power (ἐπετίμησεν as in v. 35; see further there). The change of the Markan *Vorlage* at this place is probably caused less by a demonological understanding of the fever (so Derrett 1993; Kirchschläger 1981, 63 as well as many others with reference to Testament of Solomon 18.20, 23) than by the Lukan interest in a further demonstration of the ἐξουσία of Jesus's *word* (see at v. 32), connected with the establishment of a parallelism to the exorcism in the synagogue (see also Marshall; Klutz 2004, 80). In v. 39b Luke establishes the efficacy of the miraculous action, and in v. 39c he concludes the episode with a genre-typical demonstration of the healing's success (for this and the typically Lukan παραχρῆμα, see at 1.64); it is expanded vis-à-vis Mark 1.31c and in this way receives a greater weight within the episode. What Luke concretely imagines by διακονεῖν αὐτοῖς is actually unimportant for the narrative goal, for the note should demonstrate only the success of the healing. At any rate, the provision of 'table service' is not intended; cf. the destruction of this widespread assumption by J. N. Collins 1990, 73ff, whose own interpretation ("the root idea . . . is that of the go-between"; 194) replaces, of course, only one one-sidedness with another. Rather, διακονεῖν/διακονία designates any kind of activity that is carried out for the sake of another, at the behest of another, or for the benefit of another, and here the narrative thinks quite generally of the usual work that must be done when hosting guests (cf. also 10.39, 40; 17.8; John 12.2; Joseph and Aseneth 13.15). The plural αὐτοῖς in the concluding phrasing 39c should be noted as a narrative incoherence. Unlike in the parallel of Mark 1.31 it hangs in the air here, because in Luke, unlike in Mark, Jesus has not yet called any disciples.

The summary in **40-41** has a generalizing function. The *one* exorcism and the *one* healing of a sick person thus receive paradigmatic character. They are not special individual cases but are presented as typical for Jesus's activity as a whole; cf. also the corresponding formulas: ἅπαντες and ποικίλαι (v. 40) and ἀπὸ πολλῶν (v. 41).

40 The temporal specification is meant to refer to the fact that the Sabbath is over, even though this is less clearly marked here than in Mark 1.32 (present participle instead of aorist; the former can also, of course, designate relative anteriority; cf. BDR §339.2b). Luke now even has Jesus heal no longer with a word alone as previously but also with a laying on of hands (possibly an adoption from Mark 6.5). Healings by a laying on of hands are reported relatively rarely outside the New Testament; in Jewish sources it is attested only in 1QapGen XX, 22, 29: "I (sc. Abraham) laid my hands on his (sc. the Egyptian king's) [hea]d. Then the plague was removed from him and [the] evil [spirit] was driven [from him]" (cf. further Weinriech 1969, 94ff), but it occurs often in the Jesus tradition (cf. Mark 5.23 par. Matthew 9.18; Mark 6.5; 7.32; 8.23, 25; Luke 13.13). One may not, of course, infer from this that Luke also has an exorcistic activity in mind here (so e.g., Busse 1979, 79–80, who speaks of "mute" demons). This is contradicted not only by the healings via the laying on of hands in Acts 9.12, 17; 28.8, but also by the Lukan understanding of νόσοι (v. 40a), which are explicitly distinguished from "evil spirits" or "demons" in Luke 16.18; 7.21; 9.1; Acts 19.12. This is almost a complementary dualism by which sickness and possession are clearly distinguished from each other. The former is understood as a defect "on" the person, and the latter as a loss of one's identity to a foreign power (cf. Theissen 1987, 94ff). This is then admittedly different in 9.42.

41 For the description of the exiting demon Luke has made recourse to Mark 3.11-12 (he has therefore omitted these two verses in 6.17-19). The variant κράζοντα probably also has its origin there, which must be regarded as secondary for this reason, although it is somewhat better attested by ℵ B C K L N Θ Ξ Ψ *f¹* 33 and others than κραυγάζοντα (𝔓⁷⁵ A D E G H Q W Γ Δ *f¹³* and others). Luke apparently imagines the exiting of demons in such a way that these scream the Son of God confession as they come out. The logic of the narrative, to be sure, becomes somewhat unclear through the Lukan redactional activity, for it is difficult to discern a meaning in the note of v. 41c-d, which has been stitched together from Mark 1.34 and 3.12. Verse 41c (καὶ ἐπιτιμῶν οὐκ εἴα αὐτὰ λαλεῖν) should presumably refer to ἐπετίμησεν αὐτῷ . . . φιμώθητι in v. 35; Luke thus thinks here of the command to be silent *before* the exiting of the demons. But what then should the explanatory clause in v. 41d ground? While in Mark the command to be silent was still caused by the so-called messianic secret concept, according to which Jesus's identity as Son of God was not permitted to be made publicly known prior to the resurrection (cf. esp. Mark 3.12 in connection with 9.9), this connection has at least become unrecognizable in Luke 4.41d, which has been taken over from Mark 1.34. If one does not want to reach for untenable explanations (such as, e.g., Nolland with reference to a supposed Lukan theology of the cross; Marshall: Jesus does not want his messiahship to be made known by demons), and if one does not wish to assume that Luke has not paid enough attention to the coherence of his own narrative when he took over the Markan *Vorlage*, then only one other possibility remains: Luke distinguishes between Jesus's divine sonship and his messiahship and exclusively requires the Christ title to be kept secret. Thus, in this respect one can speak of a Lukan *messianic secret* in the actual sense of the word.

That we are on the right track with this interpretation is shown especially by the Sanhedrin hearing in Luke 22.66-71, where Luke divides the double question of Mark 14.61 into two separate questions (22.67-70) and has Jesus refuse to answer concerning the messiahship, whereas he has him explicitly confess his divine sonship. Acts 9.20-22 points in a similar direction. Here, the proclamation of the divine sonship is merely a preliminary step for the demonstration of the messiahship of Jesus and the latter requires a much greater argumentative effort by Paul than the former. And finally, if we examine how Luke deals with the remaining texts that are decisive for the Markan messianic secret in the actual sense (i.e., with Mark 1.25, 34; 3.11-12; 8.30; 9.9), it is immediately conspicuous that from the commands to silence in relation to the disciples he retains only the one that follows Peter's confession of Jesus as the Messiah (9.21). By contrast, Luke omits the prohibition of dissemination that follows the transfiguration (Mark 9.9), which refers to Jesus's divine sonship. Correspondingly, the commands to be silent refer in a very conscious manner to the fact that Jesus is the Messiah (χριστός). As in Mark, this fact is not unveiled until after the resurrection (cf. Luke 24.26-27, 44-46; Acts 2.31, 36; 3.18; 17.3; 26.23). The intention of keeping Jesus's mission free from narrative-internal political misunderstandings also certainly stands behind this handling of the messiahship of Jesus. Luke 23.2 also points in this direction. Here, Jesus's accusers bring forth the charge—namely, in the same breath with the obvious lie that he exhorts people to refuse the payment of taxes (see

20.20-26)—that he claimed to be the messianic king (χριστὸν βασιλέα εἶναι; *pace* Tannehill 1986, I: 220). However, the Lukan messianic secret is probably mainly motivated by the fact that the messiahship of Jesus characterized by the resurrection is closely connected with the incorporation of the Gentiles into the people of God (Luke 24.46; Acts 26.22-23; see also Schröter 2007, 257ff; 2013, 236ff). Thus, it is not only the eternal duration of the rule of Jesus, which he will exercise over the house of Jacob according to 1.33, but also the universal extension of this rule over Jews and Gentiles, which is only possible on the basis of the resurrection and therefore can also be proclaimed only after Easter. Since the Jewish messianic expectation is fundamentally altered by these two features, it is anything but a coincidence that the messiahship of Jesus, i.e., the demonstration "that Jesus [is] the Messiah," appears exclusively in the missionary sermons addressed to Jews (cf. Acts 9.22; 17.3; 18.5, 25 [quotation]; cf. also 3.20).

4.42-44: Departure to Further Proclamation of the Reign of God

[42]**At the break of day he departed and went to an isolated place. And the people sought him and they came to him and wanted to prevent him from leaving them.** [43]**But he said to them, "I must gospel the reign of God to other cities also, for I was sent for this."** [44]**And he preached in the synagogues of the Jewish land.**

At the beginning Luke places two light divisions on the levels of time and space in order to form a departure scene (of course, it has nothing to do with Homer, *Ilias* 6.405–502 [*pace* Bovon]). Mark 1.35-39 is recognizable as a source, although not much has remained from the Markan text. The most important change results from the fact that in Luke there are still no disciples at this point. Therefore, he must remove from them the role that they play in the Markan narrative. He gives it to the inhabitants of Capernaum by creating a scene from the disciples' statement in Mark 1.37 "all are looking for you." Beyond this, Jesus's description of his task in v. 43 becomes more loaded in terms of content vis-à-vis Mark 1.38.

42 The temporal specification γενομένης ἡμέρας occurs only in Luke in the New Testament (see also Acts 12.18; 16.35; 23.12); he always uses it when the preceding episode has taken place at night (see also Josephus, *Bellum judaicum* 6.141; *Antiquitates judaicae* 10.202; 13.359; *Vita* 406). Luke deletes the Markan indication that Jesus was praying in the isolation into which he had withdrawn; he presumably adds it later in 5.16 (diff. Mark 1.45). With his description of the ὄχλοι of Capernaum, Luke sets forth a clear counterpicture to the inhabitants of Nazareth. While the latter drive Jesus out of town and want to kill him, the former run after Jesus in order to prevent him from going away (κατεῖχον is *imperfectum de conatu*; cf. BDR §326). The description of their behavior is therefore not bound up with a negative evaluation, let alone a "conflict of interests between Jesus and the inhabitants of Capernaum" (Busse 1979, 77–78).

43 Jesus explains why he cannot remain in Capernaum and simultaneously makes an overall interpretation of his activity that both looks back to the entire time of the "beginning in Galilee" and looks ahead. The entity that already stood at the center of the proclamation of the historical Jesus and also runs like a red thread through Luke–Acts is now mentioned for the first time, namely the "kingdom of God" (βασιλεία τοῦ θεοῦ). The Lukan Jesus uses this phrase here to describe the content of his commission in a comprehensive manner.

Via the terms "to gospel" (εὐαγγελίζεσθαι) and "to send" (ἀπεστάλην; *passivum divinum*) Jesus's word points back to the Scripture reading in Nazareth (see v. 18c, d), and at the same time the entire proclamation of Jesus that is still to come is identified as proclamation of the kingdom of God. In his farewell speech (Acts 20.25) the Lukan Paul will very similarly designate his entire activity as a proclamation of the kingdom of God, and in the last verse of Luke–Acts (Acts 28.31) Luke presents him to the readers as "proclaiming the kingdom of God and teaching τὰ περὶ τοῦ κυρίου Ἰησοῦ Χριστοῦ." Thus, in Luke the kingdom of God has a very pronounced christological profile (cf. also 10.9, 11: the disciples should announce the coming of Jesus as the nearness of the kingdom of God). Another indication of the extraordinary significance of this verse for the Lukan story of Jesus is the fact that here the commission of Jesus is interpreted for the first time with the help of the impersonal δεῖ as the unchangeable fulfillment of the plan of history determined by God (cf. then also 9.22; 13.33; 17.25; 19.5; 22.37; 24.7, 26, 44; Acts 1.16; 3.21; 17.3; see Cosgrove 1984). In Acts this δεῖ is then also extended to the presentation of the history of the dissemination of the witness about Christ and the personal fate of the Apostle Paul (cf. Acts 1.16, 21; 4.12; 9.16; 19.21; 23.11; 25.10; 27.24, 26). In this way Luke has Jesus express that the separation from Capernaum does not go back to his free decision but rather stands under the command of his divinely issued sending commission, which he cannot evade.

44 provides an outlook that points temporally and geographically beyond the situation in Capernaum and leads back to the textual level of 4.14-15. The narrative phase of the "beginning in Galilee" (see the introduction to 4.14-44 above) is thus concluded. In the form of an iterative compression Luke summarizes a time period that is temporally undetermined but is at any rate longer in duration (with the *coniugatio periphrastica* as a distinguishing feature; cf. BDR §353; for its use in Luke, see Verboomen

1992) and characterizes it "through the specification of individual, regularly repeating events" (Lämmert 1975, 84), namely Jesus's proclamation activity in the synagogues of Judea (for the use of εἰς in the sense of ἐν, cf. BDR §205). When Luke replaces "Galilee" (so Mark 1.39) with "Judea" (a portion of the manuscript tradition harmonizes), he wants to express that the geographical radius of the activity of Jesus is expanding. Moreover, he uses the designation "Judea" with the same comprehensive meaning as in 1.5 (see further there). The content of the proclamation of Jesus is, of course, nothing other than what he has just said to the people in Capernaum—the kingdom of God. κηρύσσειν, εὐαγγελίζεσθαι (v. 43), and διδάσκειν (v. 31) are in this respect synonymous (Tannehill 1986, I: 78). However, Luke does not wish to convey the impression that the period of time taken into view by the summary ends with the events reported from 5.1 onward (cf. just 6.6; 8.1; 13.10). It merely has the function of naming a constant in the further activity of Jesus.

5.1–6.49: The Proclamation of the Reign of God in the Jewish Land

In 5.1 a series of episodes begins in which it is recounted that Jesus teaches, heals, and discusses at different places that nevertheless remain unnamed. Luke even deletes the place name in the narrative of the healing of a lame man (5.17-26), which Mark has located in Capernaum (2.1). He does not mention the name of a place again until 7.1 when he has Jesus return again to Capernaum. The scenario that Luke sets forth in 6.17-19 for the speech of Jesus (6.20-49) can also be understood as "a great representative scene" (Theobald 1984, 100) in which the presentation of the increasing spatial expansion of Jesus's public activity, which began in 4.44, culminates. The hearers of Jesus are not only the twelve apostles but also "a great crowd of his disciples and a great multitude of the people from all Judea and Jerusalem and from the coastal region of Tyre and Sidon" (6.17). In 7.1 the narrative then returns again to Capernaum. The individual episodes are only connected with one another by the the protagonist Jesus and not by a thread of action running through them or by spatial or temporal continuities. Only 5.17–6.11 is recognizable as belonging together. All the episodes in this part confront Jesus with Pharisees (and scribes) who criticize his behavior or the behavior of his disciples.

This part of the Jesus story is very strongly marked by the Gospel of Mark. In 5.1-11 Luke now adds the calling of the first disciples from Mark 1.16-20 and orients himself from 5.12 to 6.11 toward Mark 1.40–3.6 without a gap. He then omits the summary of Mark 3.7-12 (though he places parts of it elsewhere) in order to bring in Markan material once again in the appointment of the twelve apostles (6.12-16 par. Mark 3.13-19). The concluding speech of Jesus in 6.17-49 is mainly based on Q-material.

5.1-11: The Miraculous Catch of Fish and the First Disciples

¹**But it happened when the multitude pressed upon him in order to hear the word of God—and he was standing by the Lake of Gennesaret—** ²**that he saw two boats standing by the lake. But the fishermen had disembarked from them and were cleaning the nets.** ³**And he got into one of the boats that belonged to Simon, and he asked him to go out a small bit from the land. And he sat down and taught the multitude from the boat.** ⁴**But when he had stopped speaking, he said to Simon, "Go further out into deep water and throw your nets out for the catch!"** ⁵**And Simon answered and said, "Master, we have toiled the whole night through and caught nothing! But at your word I will cast the nets."** ⁶**And after they had done this they caught a great multitude of fish, and their nets nearly ripped.** ⁷**And they gave a sign to their colleagues in the other boat that they should come and help them; and after they had come they filled both boats so full that they nearly sank.** ⁸**When Simon Peter saw (that), he fell at the feet of Jesus and said, "Go away from me, for I am a sinful man, Lord!"** ⁹**For fright had seized him and all who were with him over the catch of fish that they had caught,** ¹⁰—**and likewise also James and John, the sons of Zebedee, whom Simon had as partners. And Jesus said to Simon, "Do not fear, from now on you will catch people!"** ¹¹**And after they had brought the boats to land, they left everything and followed him.**

Due to its numerous incoherencies, this narrative has given rise to a multitude of source-critical and tradition-historical hypotheses, though without a consensus having been reached with which all sides could be satisfied (in addition to the commentaries, cf. especially G. Klein 1969, 11–49 and Pesch 1969). It begins in vv. 1-3 with the exposition to a teaching scene that comes into rather close contact with Mark 4.1-2. The double narrative of the calling into discipleship of the two brother pairs Simon and Andrew and James and John (Mark 1.16-20) has also left clear traces; cf. the localization: "Lake of Gennesaret" (v. 1c) / "Sea of Galilee" (Mark 1.16); ἔπλυνον τὰ δίκτθα (v. 2) / καταρτίζοντες τὰ δίκτθα (Mark 1.19); the mention of the sons of Zebedee, James and John, in v. 10 and Mark 1.19; ἀφέντες πάντα ἠκολούθησαν αὐτῷ (v. 11) / ἀφέντες τὰ δίκτυα ἠκολούθησαν αὐτῷ (Mark 1.18; see also v. 20); plus, the Markan "fishers of people" (ἁλιεῖς ἀνθρώπων; Mark 1.17) can also still be recognized in the Lukan "catchers of people" (ἀνθρώπους . . . ζωγρῶν; v. 10d). (Simon's brother Andrew is, of course, passed over by Luke). Finally, elements of a narrative concerning an extraordinarily productive catch of fish can be recognized in vv. 4b-9, as this has also been handed down in John 21.1-14. Beyond the naming of the absolutely necessary requisites that such a narrative requires (water, fishers, fish, a boat, a net), there are in fact no overlaps between the two texts. As a correspondence one can note further only the fact that both here and there the same roles are assigned to Peter and Jesus and the fact that the superabundant catch of fish is preceded by a night of unsuccessful toil.

Aside from that, the following phenomena have been regarded as incoherencies that are said to make source-critical operations necessary: the change between singular and plural in the dialogue in vv. 4-6 and in the concluding discipleship scene (vv. 10-11); likewise the number of boats that are underway (vv. 2-3: two boats lie on the beach, explicitly only Simon's boat goes out; v. 7: the other boat is unexpectedly found on the lake).

The discussion concerning the tradition history of the episode has been determined for many decades by the alternative of whether they originated in a narrative of the first Easter appearance of the Risen One before Peter (G. Klein 1969, 11–49; see also Fitzmyer) or whether they were connected with the activity of the earthly Jesus from the beginning (Pesch 1969; see also Radl). One can regard as reasonably certain only that Luke *(a)* had knowledge of a tradition according to which Peter (and, more specifically, Peter alone) makes a superabundant catch of fish with Jesus's help, and that he *(b)* enriched this tradition in its literary realization with elements from Mark 1.16-20 (and possibly also from 4.1-2; from Mark 1.16-20 comes above all the insertion of the sons of Zebedee in v. 10). I regard it as not ruled out that *(c)* the pre-Lukan narrative of the superabundant catch of fish already concluded with a saying of Jesus with which Peter was called into discipleship or to mission. Nothing from any of this can be reconstructed.

1-3 The narrative begins with a scene that is strongly reminiscent of Mark 4.1-2. On the shore of the lake Jesus is pressed upon by a great multitude of people (ὄχλος both here and there), so that he climbs into a small boat (ἐμβαίνειν and πλοῖον both here and there), sits down (καθῆσθαι or καθίσας), and teaches (διδάσκειν) from there the people waiting on the shore. In Luke this scene would have to stand in 8.4. But it is lacking at this point so that one can assume that Luke used Mark 4.1-2 for the configuration of these three verses.

The linguistic form of the exposition in **1** (ἐγένετο δέ + ἐν + substantivized infinitive in the present + καί + *verbum finitum* [καὶ εἶδεν; v. 2a]) is again typically Lukan (see at 1.8-9; Kilpatrick 1979, 290 argues for the originality of the variant καὶ ἐγένετο 𝔓⁷⁵); for the sentence structure, see also at 5.17; 14.1. Luke has the multitude come to Jesus with the intention of hearing the word of God from him (καὶ ἀκούειν is not coordinated with ἐπικεῖσθαι but has telic force; BDR §442.3) and in this way connects the situation with the preceding departure scene on two levels—namely, first, through the semantic correspondence of ἀκούειν with εὐαγγελίζεσθαι and κηρύσσειν (v. 43-44), and, second, with the help of the term λόγος τοῦ θεοῦ, which is also typically Lukan. Since Jesus is underway in the commission of God and gospels the kingdom of God, what he says is, of course, "God's word." Luke is the only evangelist who presents Jesus as the proclaimer of the λόγος τοῦ θεοῦ (see also 8.11, 21; 11.28). Later he will designate the witnesses' preaching of Christ in this way (cf. Acts 4.31; 6.2; 8.14; 11.1; 13.5, 7, 46; 17.13; 18.11). For Luke the thematic continuity that connects the usage in the Gospel of Luke and Acts consists in nothing other than the fact that the "word of God" speaks of the salvation that God turns toward humans through Jesus (see also März 1974, 28ff; M. Wolter, *EKL*³ 4: 1328). The parenthetically inserted remark about the place where Jesus was standing was made necessary by 4.43-44. In 4.44 Luke had spoken of Jesus's proclamation "in the synagogues of Judea," and therefore he must lead his readers quickly to the Lake of Gennesaret, where the next episode takes place. And the concomitant geographical expansion (see there) was probably also the reason that he speaks here not of the "Sea of Galilee" like Mark but of the "Lake of Gennesaret." This also appears to have been the more commonly used designation (see also 1 Maccabees 11.67; Josephus, *Bellum judaicum* 2.573; 3.463, 506, 515–16; *Antiquitates judaicae* 18.28, 36; *Vita* 349; Strabo 16.2.16; Herodianus Grammaticus, *De prosodia catholica*, ed. Lentz/Ludwich 1965, III/1: 58.27).

2 Luke has the picture of a 'piscatorale' (fishing scene) emerge before the eyes of Jesus and the readers—two empty fishing boats on the shore and nearby the fishermen belonging to it who are cleaning their nets. Indeed, Luke uses the same words for the two boats as he uses for Jesus (ἑστῶτα παρὰ τὴν λίμνην; cf. the translation); of course, this is not yet an indication for the presence of a source (so, e.g., Dietrich 1972, 29–30; Marshall). It is not merely an "unattractive repetition" (Klostermann 69; Brun 1932, 39), but a completely unidiomatic phrasing. There is no Greek text in which boats are spoken of in this way. Luke intentionally mentions that there are two boats in number, for after he has sent Jesus with one of the vessels onto the water, he speaks in v. 7 in a certain way of "the other boat" and activates in this way the readers' knowledge about the number of the boats (for the correspondence of εἷς and ἕτερος, cf. BDR §247.3).

In **3** it is narrated, following Mark 4.1-2, how Jesus solves the problem described in v. 1a, b (cf. the taking up again of ὄχλος as well as the correspondence of "to hear the word of God" and "teach"). Sitting is the typical posture for the one teaching (cf. also Matthew 5.1; see C. Schneider, ThWNT 3: 446). Alongside these analeptic elements, the initially functionless information that the boat belongs to Simon serves to prepare for the continuation of the episode. Simon is now in the *same* boat as Jesus, and in this way the story becomes a Simon story (see also at v. 9).

4 Unlike in Mark 4.3ff, a rendition of Jesus's teaching does not now follow. Instead, Luke skips over Jesus's speech (v. 4a), and the narrative of the superabundant catch of fish begins, so to speak with a running start. Surprisingly, Peter does not receive the instruction to go back to the shore but to go further out into deep water (ἐπανάγειν; the same word as in v. 3c) and to throw out the nets there. Unlike the instruction to go out further, the latter exhortation is formulated in the plural (χαλάσατε). There is, however, no necessity to see indications for a tradition-historical growth of the narrative in this tension, for it lies much nearer at hand to explain the plural forms here and in vv. 5-7 with the help of the cultural basic knowledge of the narrator. Even an urbanite such as Luke will have known that a single person could not sail a fishing boat and that multiple people would be required to bring out a net, as this is presupposed in the narrative (cf. Bivin 1992: four men; cf. otherwise already B. Weiss 1901, 351). After all, Peter and Jesus were not traveling in a row boat, and Luke would have taken care that the atmosphere of his narrative was not too unrealistic. The fishing boat from the first century BCE/CE discovered in the Lake of Gennesaret between Ginosar and Magdala in 1986 was after all 8.8 meters long and 2.5 meters wide and would have had to be manned with a crew of five; it provided place for another ten people (cf. Wachsmann 1990).

5 Simon produces an objection in v. 5b, which also occurs in other miracle stories (cf. Mark 5.40; 2 Kings 5.11; see also Bultmann 1995, 236). He articulates skepticism based on daily experience in relation to the coming miracle event. Beyond this, the objection follows the logic of Mark 5.26 par. Luke 8.43 (cf. the parallels in Weinreich 1969, 195–97; see also Theissen 1987, 61). The reference to the futility of the previous effort to succeed with the help of conventional and daily methods functions as a foil for the miracle, which becomes even more spectacular in this way. The reference to the time and duration of the futile effort (here: "the whole night through") activates the readers' knowledge from experience, who probably would not have been unaware that one can catch fish much more easily at night than during the day (in John 21.3 this objection is formulated at the level of the discourse). The designation ἐπιστάτης for Jesus is found only in Luke in the New Testament, namely always only in the vocative as here and with the exception of 17.13 always only in the mouth of the disciples (8.24, 45; 9.33, 49). It is informative, however, that this address is also placed in the mouth of a group in 17.3 (see also Dietrich 1972, 40 with the not implausible inference that this address implies the presence of a ship's crew here). It is not a title but a designation of relation and function that is meant to express Jesus's elevated position within the group (Bovon: "boss"; cf. further A. Oepke, ThWNT 2: 619–20; W. Grimm, *EWNT* 2: 93–94). 5c is an expression of trust (cf. Sirach 41.16; Isaiah 30.12), for Simon allows himself to be moved by Jesus's word to a certain action. More should not be read into this word, for if Luke had wanted to establish a connection to the ἐξουσία of Jesus's word (cf. 4.32, 36), he would have had Simon say λόγος and not ῥῆμα.

6 Luke describes the event that takes place under water very idiomatically with συνέκλεισαν (cf. Aristotle, *Historia animalium* 533b25; Aelius Aristides, *Orationes* 13.142; 32.403 [Dindorf 1964]); πλῆθος . . . πολύ contrasts with οὐδέν (v. 5b). The reference to the threatening tearing of the nets (*imperfectum de conatu*; cf. BDR §326) serves the demonstration of the miracle and is meant to increase the miraculous character of the event even further (cf. Theissen 1987, 76).

The event that Luke portrays in **7** is also meant to demonstrate the staggering dimensions of the miraculous catch of fish. This narrative feature corresponds to the insufficient number of oil jars in 2 Kings 4.6 and the impossibility of hauling the net with the caught fish on board in John 21.6b. The speculations about how Simon and his crew conveyed to the other fishermen that they needed help (cf. e.g., Plummer; Nolland; Bock I: 457: "signaling with their heads or voices because their hands are busy"; Bovon I: 233 is certain that it was a "waving over," for "a 'calling over' would cause the fish catch to be diminished or even fail, since fish *hear* danger") are completely superfluous. Luke himself probably did not imagine this so exactly, and he can therefore also confidently leave it to the imagination of his readers (also those of the twenty-first century). When Luke designates those called for help as μέτοχοι (sc. of Simon and his ship's crew), he may have only wanted to express with this that they all have the same occupation as Simon and work with him (cf. Spicq 1994, II: 479). Whether Luke also wanted to convey the impression that they had mutualized their means of production and profits (Spicq 1994, II: 480: "they pooled their resources to pay for boats, nets, and the right to fish on the lake, and they divided the fishing revenues according to their respective interests in the partnership") does not emerge from the text. The narrative leaves open whether the other fishermen were also already on the lake with their boat when Simon's call for help reached them, or whether they were still on the beach (see also Marshall; Bock).

In **8-10** Luke describes a small epiphany scene. Genre-typical elements are: *(a)* the falling down of the recipient of the appearance (v. 8b), *(b)* the awareness of one's own sinfulness (v. 8c), *(c)* the petition for the departure of the one who appears (v. 8c), *(d)* fright and fear (v. 9), as well as *(e)* the appearing one's exhortation μὴ φοβοῦ (v. 10c). The appearance as such is, of course, lacking.

This element, which is decisive for the genre, is indirectly brought into the narrative at the very beginning of **8**, however—namely, through ἰδών (v. 8a), which Luke uses syntactically and semantically in the same way here as in 1.12 (in both cases without an object!). In connection with the description of Simon's reaction, Luke communicates to the readers in this way that Simon concludes from the event that in the person of Jesus he has the representative of God before him. His reaction is typical for the genre (see also K. Berger 1976, 592n466). He throws himself down (cf. e.g., Numbers 22.31; Ezekiel 1.28; Mark 3.11; Matthew 28.9; for the phrasing προσπίπτειν τοῖς γόνασίν τινος, cf. W. Bauer 1988, 1437) and asks the appearing one to distance himself from him (see also Mark 5.17), because he, as a sinner, must fear the encounter with the holiness of God (cf. classically Isaiah 6.5: "Woe to me, I perish! For I am of unclean lips and dwell among a people of unclean lips"). It is clear that this reaction (including the address κύριος in v. 8c) lies on a completely different level than that of Zechariah (1.12) or the shepherds (2.9). It makes clear that Simon Peter has recognized (the addition of the byname should direct the attention of the readers to him; cf. Dietrich 1972, 44–45) that with Jesus nothing less than God's power and holiness are before him.

With **9** Luke gives the reason for this reaction; for fear and fright as genre typical reactions to appearances, see at 1.12, 29; for the term θάμβος used here and its use in Jewish theophany tradition, see at 4.36-37. In 4.36 Luke uses it to describe the reaction of the inhabitants of Capernaum to the exorcism in the synagogue there (for the verb περιέχειν, see also Daniel 7.28^LXX as a reaction to the interpretation of the animal vision: σφόδρα ἐκστάσει περιειχόμην ["I was greatly seized by astonishment"]). In its place stands here the abundance of caught fish (the expression ἄγρα τῶν ἰχθύων also occurs in Diodorus Siculus 3.18.1; Pausanias 7.5.7; Dionysius Byzantius Geographus, *De Bospori navigatione* 17; Alciphron, *Epistulae* 1.15.1; Aristophanes Byzantius grammaticus, *Historiae animalium epitome subiunctus Aeliani Timothei aliorumque eclogis* 2.215). But Luke immediately abandons the focus on Peter and directs the readers' view to the whole group. None other than the "fishermen" of v. 2 are, of course, referred to, and yet the structure of the group has changed. They are now no longer described with the same appellative that makes them all equal, but rather they are now "Simon Peter and οἱ σὺν αὐτῷ." While Simon was still one of a nameless group of fishermen in v. 2 and came more by chance to his role in the narrative in v. 3 (actually Jesus only needed his boat), through the course of it he has become the center of the group (see also the description of analogous constellations with οἱ σὺν αὐτῷ or the like in Mark 2.26; Luke 9.32; Acts 5.17, 21; 19.32; 22.9; 26.13; and elsewhere).

10 Codex D has an interesting variant for vv. 10-11 in which there is no longer talk of Simon but only of the sons of Zebedee, James and John:

"His partners were James and John the sons of Zebedee. And he said to them: 'Up, and do not become fishers of fish, for I will make you fishers of people.' And when they heard that they left everything behind and followed after him." This reading is obviously secondary; unfortunately its intention cannot be discerned any longer (cf. Ruis-Camps 1999).

In the Lukan text James and John are attached at the end in a stylistically rather inelegant manner. It is unmistakable that they did not appear in the original narrative and Luke has given them a role only under pressure from Mark 1.19-20 (the historicizing explanation of Dietrich 1972, 63–76 requires too many auxiliary hypotheses). The narrative significance of their role, however, is greatly reduced vis-à-vis the Markan *Vorlage*, for James and John, the sons of Zebedee, are introduced in v. 10b only as part of a statement about Simon (εἶναι + *dativus commodi*; cf. BDR §190.1). The same holds true for κοινωνοί as for μέτοχοι (v. 7): in ancient business language it can designate, in the technical sense, the associates (e.g., P. Amh. 100.4; P.S.I. 306.3; see also Preisigke 1925–1931, II: 815–16; F. Hauck, ThWNT 3: 799; Horsley 1981, 84–85) or only those with whom one collaborates (e.g., Dionysius of Halicarnassus, *Antiquitates romanae* 20.4.4; Polybius 1.78.8; 2.45.4). In v. 10c-d the narrator returns to the original focus on Simon. Jesus's exhortation μὴ φοβοῦ, which is again directed only to him, belongs to the genre-specific elements of appearance stories (see at 1.12). The metaphor of "catching people" has possibly been formulated with a view to ἄγρα (v. 4c, 9b), for ζωγρεῖν is a composite of ζῷον ἀγρεῖν (cf. Spicq 1994, II: 161–63). The image of catching fish is also transferred to people in Amos 4.2; Habakkuk 1.14-15; 1QH X, 31; XI, 27; XIII, 10; CD IV, 15–16; Joseph and Aseneth 21.21 (Aseneth says concerning Joseph, "Through his beauty he caught me [ἤγρευσέ με], and through his wisdom he caught me like a fish on the hook"); Petronius, *Satyricon* 3.4: an *eloquentiae magister* "teacher of eloquence" is nothing other than a *piscator* (cf. also the use of the hunting metaphor in philosophical biographies in Diogenes Laertius 2.125; 4.16, 17; 8.36: Pythagoras as "hunter of people"; cf. further Wuellner 1967, 64ff). It is by no means always the case that the word has a "provoking, offensive undertone" (Hengel 1968b, 87). On the other hand, however, it is also not recognizable that here the preservation of life is stressed ("catch" and not "kill"; cf. Deltombe 1982; Spicq 1994, II: 163; Radl), for the imagery is based on the opposition 'animals—people' and not 'dead—alive').

In **11** it becomes clear that what is described in vv. 8-10 has still taken place for Luke upon the lake, for the boats only come to land now (κατάγειν forms together with ἐπανάγειν in vv. 3c, 4b an *inclusio*). Luke radicalizes the discipleship note in comparison with the Markan *Vorlage*. For "them" (for whom exactly Luke does not say; what he says is, 'at least Simon and the Zebedees') discipleship means leaving everything, i.e., not only "the nets" or "their father" (Mark 1.18, 20; but cf. then Mark 10.28). Luke will proceed in the same way with the discipleship of Levi (cf. 5.28 diff. Mark 2.14; cf. also 14.25-27, 33).

5.12-16: The Cleansing of a Leper

[12]**And it happened when he was in one of the cities—behold there was there a man full of leprosy. But when he saw Jesus he fell on his face and asked him, "Lord, if you are willing, you can make me clean."** [13]**And he stretched out his hand, touched him, and said, "I will, be clean!" And immediately the leprosy disappeared from him.** [14]**And he commanded him to say nothing to anybody, but, "Go, show yourself to the priest and make an offering for your cleansing as Moses prescribed as a witness to them."** [15]**And the news of him spread even more, and great crowds of people came together to hear and be healed from their sicknesses.** [16]**But he kept himself withdrawn in isolated places and prayed.**

The structure of the episode corresponds to the structure of other healing stories. The *introduction* (v. 12a) links the episode to the literary context, the *exposition* (v. 12b-d) describes the individual situation as a situation of need that must be removed by the protagonist, and in the *center* (v. 13) there is a description and statement of how and that the bodily defect was removed. The *finale* is composed of the instruction for the demonstration of the success of the healing (v. 14), which Luke cannot fit in elsewhere, and a note of dissemination (v. 15a). Verses 15b-16 are a small summary that changes from the mode of the episodic narrative into the mode of the intensely compressed description and presents Jesus to the readers in a situation that is typical for him. Mark 1.40-50 was most likely the *Vorlage*; a synoptic counterpart is found in Matthew 8.1-4.

A number of minor agreements are noteworthy: ἰδού (v. 12b par. Matthew 8.2a) is without a Markan equivalent; the same applies for the address κύριε (v. 12d par.

Matthew 8.2b); αὐτοῦ is an object of ἥψατο (v. 13a par. Matthew 8.3a) and not an attribute of τὴν χεῖρα (Mark 1.41); λέγων (v. 13a par. Matthew 8.3a) instead of καὶ λέγει αὐτῷ (Mark 1.41a); εὐθέως (v. 13c par. Matthew 8.3c) instead of εὐθύς (Mark 1.42a); cf. Schramm 1971, 91ff; Neirynck 1974b, 64ff; 1991, 17–18; Ennulat 1994, 50ff. The parallel in P. Egerton 2, Fragment 1ʳ (lines 32–41; text in Aland 2001, 60; Greek text and English translation in Ehrman/Pleše 2011, 245–53; date: not before 150 CE) is probably dependent on the Synoptic Gospels (cf. Neirynck 1982/1991/2001, II: 773–83; contrast Crossan 1992).

12 The Septuagintal style of the introduction (καὶ ἐγένετο ἐν τῷ + infinitive with subject; see also 9.18, 29, 33; 11.1; 14.1; 17.14; 19.15; 24.4, 15, 30) is attested by Genesis 4.8; 19.29; Joshua 15.18; Judges 1.14; and elsewhere. As here Luke also continues this introduction with a καὶ ἰδού sentence in 24.4. It connects via the key word πόλις to 4.43-44: Luke has the episode take place in some town of the Jewish land and in this way gives it the aura of an example chosen at random (namely, from among many examples) of Jesus's activity (for the correspondence with ἐν μιᾷ τῶν ἡμερῶν in v. 17, see there). The phrasing ἐν μιᾷ τῶν + specification of place is not a Hebraism (*pace* Schramm 1971, 96 and others); cf. the counterexamples in Thucydides 1.47.1 and 3.88.2 (in each case ἐν μιᾷ τῶν νήσων ["on one of the islands"]); Plutarch, *Themistocles* 8.5 (ἐν μιᾷ τῶν στηλῶν ["on one of the pillars"]); Philostratus *Vitae sophistarum* 2.547 (ἐν μιᾷ τῶν οἰκιῶν ["in one of the houses"]); Aesop, *Fabulae*, ed. Hausrath/ Hunger 1970, 42(1) (ἐν μιᾷ τῶν ἀμπέλων μου ["in one of my vineyards"]) and elsewhere (in the Septuagint: Deuteronomy 13.13; 15.7; 17.2; 1 Samuel 27.5; 1 Kings 8.37; Judith 6.7; however, the Hebrew equivalents sometimes vary here or are completely absent).

The Greek word λέπρα—although it has been translated with "leprosy"— should not be confused with the sickness called *morbus* Hansen. The concern is rather with one of the many skin anomalies described in Leviticus 13–14 (often the so-called psoriasis), which are summarized under the Hebrew umbrella term צָרַעַת (cf. Seybold/Müller 1978, 55–60, 116–21; Weissenrieder 2003, 133ff; Wohlers 1999a). Decisive for dealing with them was the fact that they made the person affected by them cultically unclean and led to his or her social exclusion. In Leviticus 13.45-46 the leprosy law prescribed the following: "The leprous person . . . should walk around in torn clothing, and his hair should be disheveled, and he should cover his beard and call out: 'Unclean, unclean!' . . . He should live alone, his dwelling should be outside of the camp" (see also Numbers 5.2). According to Josephus, *Antiquitates judaicae* 3.264, lepers "differ in nothing from a dead person"; cf. also 2 Kings 5.7; Job 18.13. The ellipsis of a finite form of εἶναι after ἰδού is a Hebraism (cf. BDR §128.7; the same is true for the introductory formula καὶ ἐγένετο . . . καί + *verbum finitum*, which is common to Luke; see BDR §442.4a and above at 1.8-9). The expression "to fall on the [or 'his'] face" is a Septuagintism (cf. Genesis 17.3, 17; Leviticus 9.24; Numbers 16.4; and elsewhere) and communicatively a gesture of submission (as here in connection with a request in 2 Samuel 14.4; Josephus, *Antiquitates judaicae* 10.11; Testament of Zebulun 2.1; Testament of Joseph 13.2; Joseph and Aseneth 28.2). This gesture directly corresponds to the address κύριε, which can also accompany it in the Septuagint, without the addressee always being God (cf. 1 Kings 1.23: David; 18.7: Elijah; Ezekiel 11.13: God). The request that the leper directs to Jesus, which is taken over word for word from Mark 1.40, is formulated as a statement. It says that his healing by Jesus is not a question of whether he is able but only of whether he is willing. The request is thus clothed in the linguistic form of a christological predication (see also Epictetus, *Enchiridion* 14.2: ἐὰν δὲ θέλῃς ὀρεγόμενος μὴ ἀποτυγχάνειν, τοῦτο δύνασαι ["if you as striver do not wish to founder, you are in position to do it"]).

13 The description of the action of Jesus in 13a agrees in wording with Matthew 8.3a against Mark 1.41a. The reaching out of the hand is not an allusion to God's acts of power narrated in the Old Testament (*pace* Marshall; Radl), for here (as, e.g., in Genesis 8.9; 19.10; 22.10) it has only the function of introducing another action—namely, the touching of the leper (cf. also Jeremiah 1.9; Joseph and Aseneth 16.16x; 17.3; 28.14: in each case as here "to reach out the hand . . . and touch"). The healing follows via touch and via the word; the assurance that the word alone would have sufficed (Bock) misses the intention of the text by a wide margin. Jesus acts similarly in 7.14; but often the touch alone suffices (cf. 6.19; 8.44-47; 22.51; see also Theissen 1987, 71–72, 73–74). Because God's holiness and power is present in Jesus, he is not made unclean by touching a leper, but he changes the uncleanness of the leper into cleanness. K. Berger rightly speaks in this context of "offensive [i.e., non-defensive] cleanness/holiness" (Berger 1988, 240 and elsewhere; cf. also Schröter 2014, 114).

14 The demonstration of the success of the healing should actually come now (see at 1.64; 4.39). For this, however, Luke would need to leave Jesus narratively and accompany the healed man to a priest, for according to the leprosy-Torah in Leviticus 13–14, a priest alone can establish whether the leprosy has really disappeared and the person affected by it is clean again. But because he wants to remain with Jesus scenically, Luke (like Mark already before him) has Jesus merely give him instruction for the demonstration of the success of the healing. This includes, first, the presentation to a priest (δεῖξον . . . τῷ ἱερεῖ corresponds to Leviticus 13.49) and then—if the priest establishes the cleanness—the bringing of offerings (cf. Leviticus 14.1-20 or the regulations for poor people in vv. 21-31). And insofar as the demonstration of the success of a healing always takes place through an action, it would only be the presentation of the offering in the temple of Jerusalem that could take over this form-critical function. In order to be able to preserve the scenic unity of his narrative, the narrator reduces all this to Jesus's instruction to proceed accordingly. The concluding εἰς μαρτύριον αὐτοῖς also refers to nothing other than this demonstration function of the priestly judgment and offering (and not to Jesus's faithfulness to the law; cf. Schürmann). εἰς μαρτύριον is a Septuagintism (as here with dative: Genesis 21.30; 1 Samuel 9.24; with ἐν: Deuteronomy 31.19, 26; Joshua 24.27; Micah 1.2; otherwise: Genesis 31.44; Proverbs 29.14; Job 16.8; Hosea 2.14; Amos 1.11; Micah 7.18; Zephaniah 3.8). The plural αὐτοῖς is *constructio ad sensum* (cf. BDR §134.1), which generalizes the singular ἱερεῖ taken over from Leviticus 3.49.

The introductory command to be silent, which Luke weakens by making it indirect speech and whose breaking he also does not narrate (cf., by contrast, Mark 1.45a), merely serves the rhetorical preparation of the instruction for the demonstration (*correctio* according to the pattern "not x, but y"; cf. Lausberg 1949, §785 [1]).

15 Luke changes from the episodic manner of narration to the mode of the durative compression (linguistic marker: imperfect). 15a is a note of dissemination (cf. Theissen 1987, 81), in which the comparative μᾶλλον marks the intensification in relation to the analogous statement in 4.37. This intensification also comes to expression in the fact that Luke no longer provides the note of dissemination with a specifying and thus limiting spatial qualifier. Verse 15b portrays the consequences. The dissemination of the news of Jesus going out from him (διέρχεσθαι) evokes a complementary countermovement toward him (συνέρχεσθαι). Many people flock to him (cf. also 14.25). Luke ascribes to them a double intention. First, they want to "hear." This was already the case in v. 1, and the readers can effortlessly supply from there what the people want to hear—"God's word." Second, they want "to be healed from their sicknesses," and so what Luke had already reported about Capernum in 4.40 is repeated in much greater measure.

16 Again as a kind of countermovement Luke portrays the reaction of Jesus. He does not have the ὄχλοι πολλοί meet with Jesus (ἔρημος designates the semantic opposition to them) and accordingly there is also not a note corresponding to 4.40b. Luke reverses the sequence of Jesus's withdrawal and the people's movement toward him vis-à-vis Mark 1.45c, d, and in this way manages to bring the narrative to rest.

5.17–6.11: Controversy Dialogues over Various Themes

A new group that has thus far not been spoken of now turns up, namely the Pharisees (for them cf. Schürer 1973–1987, II: 381–403; Stemberger 1991; Deines 1997, esp. 534ff; for the Lukan presentation of Pharisees, see Ziesler 1978/1979; Carroll 1988). Luke introduces them into the narrative in 5.17 (together with so-called teachers of the law, whom he calls "scribes" in v. 21), and they then appear in each of the four scenes that follow up to 6.11. Luke has taken over these scenes *en bloc* from Mark 2.1–3.6. The emergence of the Pharisees as narrative figures is accompanied by a change in the linguistic form of the individual texts. Luke no longer recounts manifestations of Jesus's authority (with the exception, to be sure, of 5.17-26 and 6.6-11—i.e., revealingly enough—the two outer episodes) but rather "conflict stories" or "controversy dialogues" (for the form, cf. Wolter 2002b).

5.17-26: Authority to Forgive Sins

[17]**And it happened one day when he was teaching and Pharisees and scribes were sitting there, who came from every village of Galilee and Judea and from Jerusalem, and the power of the Lord was there, so that he** (could) **heal.** [18] **And behold, men were bringing on a bed a man who was lame. And they attempted to bring him in and place him before Jesus.** [19]**And because they found no way by which they could bring him in on account of the crowd, they climbed onto the roof and lowered him on the bed through the tiles into the middle before Jesus.** [20]**And he saw their faith and said, "Man, your sins are forgiven."** [21]**And the scribes and Pharisees began to consider, "Who is this, who speaks blasphemies? Who can forgive sins except God alone?"** [22]**But Jesus knew their thoughts; he answered and said to them, "What do you consider in your hearts?** [23]**What is easier—to say, 'Your sins are forgiven you,' or to say, 'Stand up and walk around'?** [24]**But in order that you may know that the Son of Man has authority on earth to forgive sins." He said to the lame man, "Stand up, take your bed, and go into your house!"** [25]**And going around he rose up before them, took what he had lain on, and went forth into his house and praised God.** [26]**And fright seized all, and they praised God and said full of fear, "Today we have seen something incredible."**

In this episode elements that are specific to healing stories (vv. 18-19, 24b-26) are mixed with form characteristics that we know from controversy dialogues (vv. 21-24a). Luke prepares both lines in the *introduction* (v. 17): v. 17c-d belong to the controversy dialogue, v. 17e to the narration of the healing. The latter continues with the *exposition* (vv. 18-20a) and is continued after the dialogue between Jesus and his critics with *the center* (v. 24b-c), in which Jesus's saving action is described, and concluded with the *finale* (vv. 25-26), which consists of the demonstration of the healing and the description of its effect on those present. Within the line of the controversy dialogue, vv. 18-20 function as a description of the *starting situation*, and the two lines only separate with the Jesus word in v. 20b. Here the behavior is then described in relation to which the *criticism of the antagonists* follows in v. 21. Luke then portrays the *reaction of the protagonist Jesus* in vv. 22-24.

In light of these form-critical findings, the question of which of the two genres dominates arises. It can be answered rather clearly in favor of the controversy dialogue. This can be seen in the fact that Luke already introduces the Pharisees and scribes, i.e., the antagonists of the later controversy dialogue, in the introduction to the whole text (v. 17). Since the constellation Jesus vs. Pharisees, etc., determines the entire narrative collecting basin up to 6.11, the narrative of vv. 17-26 is identifiable as the first example of these episodes. With this functional coordination of the healing elements to the controversy dialogue, the main points are brought out much more clearly in the Lukan version than in Mark 2.1-12, where the opponents of Jesus are introduced only after the exposition of the healing story. Through the association with the controversy dialogue, the healing receives a legitimating function in relation to the controversy between Jesus and the Pharisees. However, this does not yet make the healing of the lame man into a "norm miracle" (Theissen 1987, 114ff, 319), for there is no reference whatsoever to a specific behavior that would be confirmed or criticized. Instead, we are dealing with a classic "therapy," which receives the function of the legitimation of personal authority through the context in which it is placed. One can therefore speak at most of a *legitimation miracle*.

Luke took over the narrative from Mark 2.1-12 and greatly altered it, especially in the introduction and in the exposition to the healing story; a synoptic counterpart is found in Matthew 9.1b-8.

A few minor agreements must be registered: ἰδού (v. 18a par. Matthew 9.2a) is again without a Markan equivalent (see also already v. 12b par. Matthew 8.2a); ἐπὶ κλίνης (v. 18a par. Matthew 9.2a) is likewise without a Markan equivalent (on κλινίδιον [vv. 19b, 24c] and κλίνη [Matthew 9.6c] instead of κράβαττος [Mark 2.4b, 11b] cf. ad loc.); εἰς τὸν οἶκον αὐτοῦ (v. 25c par. Matthew 9.7) is without a Markan equivalent; τῷ παραλυτικῷ and καὶ ἆρον τὸν κράβαττόν σου (Mark 2.9) are lacking in v. 23 par. Matthew 9.5; cf. Schramm 1971, 99ff; Neirynck 1974a; 1974b, 67ff; 1991, 19–20; Ennulat 1994, 58ff.

17 The introductory formula καὶ ἐγένετο + indication of time with ἐν + *verbum finitum* joined with καί is a Hebraism and is also found elsewhere in Luke (cf. BDR §442.4a and Luke 8.1; 17.11; 24.15). The whole verse functions as an introductory sentence to v. 18 that is enriched by many parentheses (see also 5.1-2; 14.1-2 [the apodosis is introduced with καὶ ἰδού both here and there]). Unlike Mark, Luke does not have the episode take place in Capernaum but somewhere in the Jewish land (cf. 4.44). Having articulated the episodic unspecified character of the event with regard to space in v. 12 (see further there), he now does this in a complementary manner with regard to time. Both specifications want to be read together and this means that this episode also takes place "in one of the cities (sc. of the Jewish land)"; for the phrasing ἐν μιᾷ τῶν ἡμερῶν cf., in addition to 8.22; 20.1, Vita Aesopi 75 as well as the parallels mentioned in Burchard 1998, 335 (see further at v. 12). This impression of the "as-always" is also strengthened through the statement that Jesus teaches (see also 4.31, 44; everywhere *coniugatio periphrastica*; for its use in the Gospel of Luke, see Verboomen 1992). But this changes immediately, for Luke brings Jesus together with a group who has not yet cropped up, namely "Pharisees and scribes" (νομοδιδάσκαλοι; see also Acts 5.34); he calls the latter γραμματεῖς in v. 21.

With the reference to the origin of the Pharisees and scribes in v. 17c, Luke gives the readers two important pieces of information (the indisputable hyperbolism of this statement allows a corresponding interpretation). First, he indirectly communicates to them that the news of Jesus has advanced by now even as far as Jerusalem. The series of the geographical designations corresponds exactly to the sequence of the Lukan story of Jesus: Galilee (4.14-43)–Judea (4.44–9.50)–Jerusalem (9.51ff/19.28ff). Second, Luke characterizes the Pharisees and scribes as a village movement and in this way devalues them in relation to Jesus, whom he has had appear thus far only in towns (cf. 4.29, 31, 43 [in more detail there]; 5.12). The lexis and syntax of v. 17d are somewhat unclear. We are dealing with a telic substantivized infinitive with a subject, so that αὐτόν functions as subject (as, among others, εἰς τὸ παρακαλέσαι ἡμᾶς in 2 Corinthians 8.6; the misunderstanding of αὐτόν as object has led to the variant αὐτούς [A C D (K) Θ Ψ 33 𝔐]). In terms of content, Luke certainly does not wish to express with this sentence that God's dynamis was only temporarily present in Jesus and that his being fulfilled by it was a more or less contingent occurrence. Accordingly, semantically it is not a characterization of Jesus but rather a characterization of the δύναμις of God that was constantly present in him (on δύναμις as an attribute of God, cf. Joshua 4.24; 1 Chronicles 29.11; Psalm^{LXX} 67.35; 150.1; see also at 6.19 and 10.13). With the help of the telic or consecutive εἰς τό it is specified more precisely as power to heal (cf. BDR §402.2; see also §145.1). However, the narrative function of this remark stands in the foreground. Luke wants to use it to direct the attention of the readers away from the Pharisees for the moment and toward the healing that now follows.

18 Only now does it become clear that Jesus is in a house. The communication of this fact in Mark 2.1, which is not unimportant for the plot of the healing story, has not been carried over by Luke. Also the number of men who carry him remains open in Luke (and in Matthew 9.2).

The most striking minor agreement is, however, the fact that the lame man in Mark 2.4 lies on a κράβαττος, whereas he lies on a κλίνη in Matthew and Luke (on this topic, see now Wolter 2011). The difference is not so easy to recognize, for one lies on both when one sleeps (Luke 17.34; Epictetus, *Dissertationes* 1.24.14) and when one is sick (Mark 6.55; 7.30; Acts 5.15; 9.33; Acts 2.22; see also John 5.8ff). And just as one can place a light under a κλίνη, so one can hide under a *grabatus* (Petronius, *Satyricon* 97.3–4; 98.5)—both can thus have legs. The κράβαττος is wrongly regarded as the "bed of the small man" (W. Bauer 1988, 909; see also Klostermann 1971, 23), for after all, in Testament of Job 25.8; 32.4 there is mention of "golden and silver κράβαττοι"; a κράβαττος is therefore by no means necessarily a "mat or straw sack" (Radl I: 316). Multiple inscriptions from Epidaurus that report about the healing of lame people always have them come upon a κλίνη into the sanctuary (cf. Herzog 1931, W 35.64.70; different again is Lucian of Samosata, *Philopseudes* 11 [see at v. 25]). κλίνη is probably simply the more common expression, for κράβαττος or κράββατος does not appear at all in the Septuagint, Philo of Alexandria, or Josephus and almost never in pagan Greek literature (it appears somewhat more often only in the papyri; cf. Preisigke 1925–1931, I: 834).

The fact that Luke replaces the term παραλυτικός with παραλελυμένος has nothing to do with him wanting to avoid the impression that we are dealing with a person who was lame from birth (so Busse 1979, 120). The latter is simply the more common expression in medical professional literature.

19 The fact that the miracle worker can be reached only with difficulty and only after the arduous overcoming of obstacles (ποίας is a genitive of location; one must supply ὁδοῦ; cf. BDR §186.1) is a narrative motif that is also found elsewhere in the exposition of healing stories (cf. Mark 5.24par.; 10.48parr.; cf. Theissen 1987, 63). Apart from that, the crowd that presses around Jesus functions not only as hindrance but also as an indication of the great resonance that Jesus finds with his teaching activity (cf. v. 17a after 4.42; 5.1, 15). Luke narrates the same story as Mark 2.4, and yet with completely different details. In Luke the roof of the house has tiles, whereas the bearers of the sick man in Mark "dig it up" (ἐξορύσσειν).

One can probably infer from this that Luke did not think of an oriental flat roof composed of loam and wattle as Mark did (cf. Dalman 1964, VII: 75, 118–21), but rather a Hellenistic-Roman tile roof (see also McCown 1939, 213ff; Cicero, *Orationes philippicae* 2.45: *per tegulas demittere* ["to lower through the tiles"]).

20 Luke has Jesus interpret this action in v. 20a as a visible expression of faith, which is not in itself viewable. After Mary (see 1.45), they are the first people within Luke–Acts who are credited with faith. An understanding of faith that is also found elsewhere in the Synoptic tradition becomes recognizable here. Faith precedes the intervention of Jesus and is understood as Jesus-directed trust in his healing or saving power (7.9; 8.48, 50; 17.19; 18.42); correspondingly, a lack of trust in him is regarded as a lack of faith (8.25). Another attestation for this understanding of faith is the behavior of the woman sinner according to Luke 7.36ff (cf. v. 50), although there the connection to a miracle is lacking. In v. 20b the narrative takes a surprising turn. There follows no healing action in word or act (this comes then in v. 24), but Jesus says that the sick person is forgiven his sins. Unlike the parallels in Mark and Matthew, Luke does not use the present but the resultative perfect (see also v. 23; 7.47, 48), which gives the statement more strongly the character of a declaration than a performative speech act. Jesus declares that God has forgiven the sick person his sin (*passivum divinum*)—though on the basis of the word of Jesus (see also John 20.23; 1 John 2.12; in the same way God was, of course, also the subject of the forgiveness of sins in the case of John the Baptist—though on the basis of the immersion ritual carried out by John). The lame man and the woman sinner of 7.36-50 are the only people to whom Jesus makes such a disclosure in the Gospel of Luke. Beyond this, in both cases it is faith that leads to the forgiveness of sins (cf. 7.49-50; see also Acts 10.43; 26.18). The connection between sickness and forgiveness of sins, often postulated with reference to John 9.2 and Bill. I: 495, plays no role here, for if it were the case that the narrative made use of this connection, the sick man would have to become well immediately and not only after another word of Jesus (the same applies to 7.36-50, for the woman sinner is not sick); for the tradition-historical background, cf. C. Breytenbach, *ThBNT* 2: 1737–42 with additional literature).

21 makes clear that the narrative has changed into a controversy dialogue, for now the Pharisees and scribes, who were prepared for narratively in v. 17b-c, come onto the scene. They become antagonists by raising the accusation of blasphemy against Jesus (v. 21b). However, Luke narrates their criticism of Jesus not as the inauguration of an open dispute but rather as a report of their thoughts (see at 1.21; 3.15). While they only raise questions, these are rhetorical questions for which the answer is not in doubt. With the pronouncement of the forgiveness of sins Jesus has, in their eyes, claimed a prerogative of God for himself. For this is the reason that they formulate no real question, for it has already long been clear to them who Jesus is—one who is not entitled to forgive sins, for that belongs only in the authority of God (see also Isaiah 44.22; 4Q242 1, 3–4 [on this see Klauck 1981, 239–40]; but see 2 Samuel 12.13; Zechariah 3.4); on the linguistic form of v. 21c (τίς + εἰ μή;) cf. Judith 6.2; Psalms of Solomon 5.11. Jesus's word is not, however, a blasphemy in the sense of Leviticus 24.15-16 (cf. also the intensification of this regulation in Philo, *De vita Mosis* 2.206 and its limitation in m. Sanhedrin 7.5: "A blasphemer is only guilty if he pronounces the name"). The question in v. 21c with the emphatically placed adjective μόνος signalizes a probable tradition-historical point of contact, for an association of the accusation of blasphemy with the violation of the exclusivity of the deity of God is also attested elsewhere (cf. e.g., John 10.36; Revelation 13.1; 17.3).

22 makes immediately clear how little the Pharisees and scribes actually know about Jesus, for the knowing of the thoughts hidden in the heart belongs already in the Old Testament to the specific distinguishing features of God (cf. 1 Samuel 16.7; 1 Kings 8.39; Psalm 94.11; 139.2; Psalms of Solomon 14.8; Testament of Levi 2.3[e]). The question of his critics is basically already answered through this, for in this way Jesus demonstrates that he represents God. Luke here presents to us an essential element of his Christology, which he often adds to his sources (cf. also 6.8 diff. Mark 3.2; 9.47 diff. Mark 9.33; 11.17 par. Matthew 12.25; 24.38). Plus, the announcement of Simeon from 2.35 is now fulfilled: Jesus makes manifest the hidden intentionality of those who reject him.

23 In relation to the Markan *Vorlage* the statement of Jesus is raised more onto a fundamental level by Luke (and Matthew) through the omissions. But due to the context it is clear that. for him as well, the concern is with the lame man who is found before Jesus. The line of the controversy dialogue and the line of the healing story begin to approach each other again. The question with which Jesus answers his critics is equally rhetorical. It is mostly assumed that the exterior visibility is presupposed as a point of comparison. According to this view, it would be easier to pronounce forgiveness, because the effectiveness of such a word cannot be publicly verified. Thus, the concern would not be with the question of whether it is easier to forgive or to heal (so Radl), but with the εἰπεῖν (see also Plummer) in the sense of "just *saying* is easy." However, the question arises of whether this interpretation is not too modern in its thinking and thus based on anachronistic presuppositions. In fact, the question formulates no real alternative, but it merely functions to pave the way for the narrative-internal discursive value of the successful healing described in

vv. 24-25 (cf. W. Weiss 1989, 139). This is also supported by the continuation in the next verse.

24 If the critics of Jesus do not know how to answer the question posed in v. 23, they should at least know that God has authorized the Son of Man to forgive sins on earth. The telic clause placed at the front (see also Matthew 17.27; Acts 24.4) ends as an anacoluthon. It is not continued as a Jesus word through a main sentence, but interrupted through authorial speech with which a change of addressee is made. The word that effects the healing then follows. This was also already the case in Mark 2.10, and not only Luke but also Matthew took over this text without correction. One should therefore proceed from the assumption that all three narrators understood this construction not as a solecism, i.e., as a violation against the syntactical idiom, but as a meaningful Greek text. That this is, in fact, the case can be seen via a whole series of parallels in which, as here, a telic clause introduced with ἵνα δὲ εἰδῆτε is followed not by the main sentence but with a change of addressee; cf. e.g., Demosthenes, *Orationes* 45.19 (ἵνα δ' εἰδῆθ' ὅτι ταῦτ' ἀληθῆ λέγω, λαβὲ τὴν τοῦ Κ. μαρτυρίαν ["In order that you see, that I say these things truthfully—take the testimony of K."]); 46.10 (ἵνα δὲ εἰδῆτε ἀκριβῶς, αὐτὸν τὸν νόμον μοι ἀνάγνωθι ["But in order that you see exactly—read to me the law itself"]); Aeschines, *In Ctesiphonem* 93 (ἵνα δ' εὖ εἰδῆτε ὅτι ἀληθῆ λέγω, λαβέ μοι τὴν Καλλίου γραφήν . . . ["But in order that you see clearly that I speak truthfully— bring to me the writing of Callias . . ."]). If the speeches were embedded in a narrative, then between the telic clause and the injunction there would have to be supplied in each case: 'and he said to so-and-so' or the like (see also with additional references Wolter 2004a). Thus, the healing of the lame man attests the authority of the Son of Man to forgive sins on earth. The phrasing ἐπὶ τῆς γῆς is decisive. It names the sphere in which Jesus is active as the authentic representative of God and therefore can also do what is actually exclusively reserved for God (cf. also the special accentuation in Matthew 16.19; 18.18, 19; 23.9). At the same time, however, it also means that the authority of Jesus is always only an authority bestowed by God. Luke too has certainly understood the Son of Man designation, which he has taken over in this passage from Mark 2.10, as a title (for the origin of the Son of Man conception and its christological reception in the Synoptic tradition, cf. the excursus in Lührmann 1987, 147–48). The authority to forgive sins is a component of the special dignity of the Son of Man—to be sure, only here and nowhere else in early Judaism or in the Christian tradition (cf. Klauck 1981, 236ff). Then again, the Son of Man is defined by the ἐξουσία bestowed by God and thereby demarcated as God's representative in an entirely analogous manner elsewhere (cf. Daniel 7.13-14; John 5.27). For the Lukan conception of the Son of Man, this scene is specific insofar as it corresponds with the self-statement of 19.10: "The Son of Man has come to seek and to save the lost." This saying applies to the tax collector Zachaeus, who is called a "sinner" by "all" (v. 7).

In **25** the demonstration of the success of the healing is narrated (on the typically Lukan παραχρῆμα, see at 1.64). Lucian of Samosata narrates the same thing about a vine-grower named Midas who was bitten by a snake and was brought by his colleagues on a pallet (ἐπὶ σκίμποδος) to the miracle worker. He is healed, and at the end it says: ἀπάμενος τὸν σκίμποδα ἐφ' οὗ ἐκεκόμιστο ("He took the pallet on which he had been brought"; *Philopseudes* 11). It is theologically or christologically significant that Luke places the acclamation in the mouth of *the healed man* and that he has him glorify *God* (in Mark 2.12 the public does this). This is a typical Lukan narrative motif (see also 1.64; 9.43; 13.13; 17.15; 18.43 diff. Mark 10.52; Acts 3.8). Luke has them all be filled with the knowledge that in Jesus none other than God himself has acted on them for salvation (see also 7.16; 8.39; 19.37).

The description of the wonder and acclamation typical to miracle stories (see Theissen 1987, 78–81) in **26** is portrayed by the mixture of fright and joy, as is characteristic for the encounter with the holy. There is a considerable terminological overlap with Wisdom of Solomon 5.2, where the reaction of the godless to the deliverance of the righteous is described (seeing, φόβος, ἐξίστημι, and παράδοξος; only the praise of God is lacking; cf. also Diodorus Siculus 17.41.7: "incredible signs [σημεῖα παράδοξα] that cause the people consternation and fear [διατροπὴν καὶ φόβον τοῖς ὄχλοις]"). Events that lie beyond human experience (cf. classically Plutarch, *Moralia* 305a; see also Phlegon of Tralles, *De mirabilibus* 26: a man brings a child into the world) are regarded as παράδοξα; in the New Testament this term only appears here. The *Testimonium Flavianum* (Josephus, *Antiquitates judaicae* 18.63) refers to Jesus as a παραδόξων ἔργων ποιητής ("doer of incredible deeds"; cf. also Weinreich 1969, 198–99).

5:27-39: Eating and Drinking

²⁷And after this he went out and saw a tax collector named Levi at the tax booth. And he said to him, "Follow me!" ²⁸And he dropped everything, stood up and followed him.

²⁹And Levi organized a great banquet for him in his house, and there was a great crowd of tax collectors and others who reclined at table with him. ³⁰And the Pharisees and their scribes grumbled and said to his disciples, "Why do you eat and drink with tax collectors and sinners?" ³¹And Jesus answered and said to them, "It is not the

healthy who need a doctor, but those who are sick. [32]I have not come to call the righteous but sinners to repentance."

[33]But they said to him, "The disciples of John fast strictly and say prayers, as also the Pharisees, but yours eat and drink." [34]But Jesus said to them, "Could you make the wedding guests fast while the bridegroom is with them? [35]But days will come when the bridegroom is taken away from them, then they will fast, in those days."

[36]But he also told them an example, "No one cuts a patch from a new piece of clothing and sows (it) on an old piece of clothing. Otherwise, he will tear the new and the patch from the new will not fit with the old. [37]And no one puts new wine in old wineskins. Otherwise, the new wine will tear the wineskins, and it will pour out, and the wineskins will be ruined. [38]One must instead put new wine in new wineskins. [39]And no one drinks the old and wants the new, for he says, 'The old is pleasant.'"

Luke combines two controversy dialogues into one scene (vv. 27-32, 33-35) and at the end has Jesus comment on the controversy with an "example" (παραβολή; vv. 36-39). Vis-à-vis Mark, he establishes the coherence of the first two units in two ways. First, he replaces the narrative introduction of Mark 2.18a-b, which marks there a spatial-temporal distance and a change of narrative figures (in Luke it would have to stand between v. 32 and v. 33), with a phrasing (v. 33a) that creates the impression that Jesus was still dealing with the same conversation partner as in vv. 30-32 and that all the participants were still in the house of Levi. Second, he changes the topic of conversation in each case so that in both rounds of conversation, unlike in Mark (and Matthew 9.9-13, 14-17), the concern is with the same topic—namely, the eating and drinking of the disciples. The first controversy dialogue deals with the fact that the disciples eat with—as the Pharisees and scribes say—"tax collectors and sinners" (v. 30b: ἐσθίετε καὶ πίνετε diff. Mark 2.16d: ἐσθίει; the concern there is thus with Jesus's behavior). The second round of conversation deals with the fact that the disciples do not fast but rather "eat and drink" (v. 33c diff. Mark 2.18d: οὐ νηστεύουσιν). Luke deals in a completely different manner with the double parabolic saying in vv. 36-39. While Mark had directly linked it to the controversy dialogue about the non-fasting of the disciples, Luke sets it off as a narrative speech in v. 36a via the insertion of an introduction and in this way relates the double parabolic saying about the incompatibility of old and new to *both* controversy dialogues.

Noteworthy minor agreements (apart from the reconfiguration of the introductory note in Mark 2.13): Mark 2.15c is lacking in v. 29 par. Matthew 9.10; Mark 2.16b is lacking in v. 30 par. Matthew 9.11; διὰ τί (v. 30b par. Matthew 9.11b) instead of ὅτι (Mark 2.16); Mark 2.18 is lacking in v. 33 par. Matthew 9.14; Mark 2.19c is lacking in v. 34 par. Matthew 9.15; ἐπιβάλλει (v. 36b par. Matthew 9.16a) instead of ἐπιράπτει (Mark 2.21a); cf. further Schramm 1971, 104ff; Neirynck 1974b, 70ff; 1991, 21–22; Ennulat 1994, 68ff.

Verses 33-35 has a parallel in Gospel of Thomas 104 and vv. 36-39 in Gospel of Thomas 47. However, in both cases one must assume a dependence on Lukan redaction. In Logion 104 it is the combination of fasting and prayer (cf. v. 33 diff. Mark 2.18) that can be identified as specifically Lukan, and in Logion 47 it is the combination of the double parabolic saying about the incompatibility of old and new with the saying about old and new wine.

27-32 The characterization of the question of the Pharisees and scribes as ἐγόγγυζον ("grumbling"; v. 30a) goes hand in hand with the controversy dialogue character. We have the genre typical *narrative exposition* in vv. 27-30a. The *starting situation* thematized in the controversy dialogue is, however, not described until v. 29. The narrative of the calling of Levi to discipleship (vv. 27-28) merely has the function of explaining how it could come to a great meal celebration in his house. Thus, it is a kickoff scene. In v. 30 Luke narrates the criticism of the antagonists, and in vv. 31-32 Jesus's concluding speech follows, which defends and explains the criticized behavior.

27 The small narrative of the calling of Levi into discipleship has the same pattern as many other call stories—namely, he is encountered while practicing his occupation and is torn out from the midst of it (see also Mark 1.16-20parr.; 1 Samuel 16.11-13: David; 1 Kings 19.19-21: Elisha; Amos 7.15: Amos; Aristotle, Fragment, ed. Rose 1967, 64: Nerinthus; Pliny the Elder, *Naturalis historia* 18.20: Cincinnatus; cf. with additional examples Schult 1971). Within the Lukan story of Jesus he is the first person whom Jesus calls into discipleship (cf. then also 9.59 par. Matthew 8.21; 18.22 following Mark 10.21 and Mark 1.16, 20; John 1.43). Jesus's call to follow differed from contemporary eschatological 'prophetic or messianic movements' led by charismatic prophets (see Acts 5.37; 21.38; cf. Hengel 1968b, 23ff) in that he always appealed only *to certain individuals* and exhorted them to share the itinerant-charismatic manner of life and the concomitant social uprootedness with him (in addition to the texts mentioned above, cf. Mark 8.34parr.; Luke 9.57-58 par. Matthew 8.19-20; Luke 9.61-62; 14.27 par. Matthew 10.38; see also Hengel 1968b, 66; H.-W. Kuhn 1980). Thus, "follow me" effectively means "come along with me!" (cf. also Acts 12.8; Lucian of Samosata, *De morte Peregrini* 24: ἕπεσθαι τῷ διδασκάλῳ καὶ συνοδεύειν ["to follow the teacher and go along (with him)"]; *Dialogi meretricii* 9.4[304]; Diogenes Laertius 7.3

describes with the term how Zenon became a student of Crates; see also 9.21). The summons to follow never became a general ethical admonition.

28 The reaction of Levi to the call of Jesus corresponds to that of the fishermen of 5.11 (see also 14.25-27, 33). The specifically Lukan accent is recognizable again in the radicalization: "he dropped everything" (καταλιπὼν πάντα; diff Mark 2.14) and went along with Jesus (on the inchoative ἀναστάς as a Septuagintism, see at 1.39-40). The use of the durative imperfect ἠκολούθει (diff. Mark 2.14 par. Matthew 9.9) reveals that for Luke not only the individual event is significant but also the characterization of the person. Elisha, whom Elijah made into a prophet when he was plowing, also acted in a similar manner as Levi. He "left the oxen behind (κατέλιπεν) and ran after Elijah" (1 Kings 19.20); clearer still is Josephus, *Antiquitates judaicae* 8.354: καταλιπὼν τοὺς βόας ἠκολούθησεν Ἠλίᾳ ("He left the oxen behind and followed Elijah"; cf. also Lives of the Prophets 9.4 on Obadiah: "He left [καταλιπών] the service of the king, followed Elijah [ἠκολούθει τῷ Ἠλίᾳ] and began to speak prophetically"). A Hellenistic parallel is found in Philostratus, *Vita Apollonii* 1.19.1; here the disciple says to the master, "Let us go, you follow God, but I you." As in 5.10-11, here too Luke has presented Jesus's call to discipleship and Levi's prompt reaction as an authentic component of the narrated world of the story of Jesus. This event was just as singular as the activity of Jesus on earth as a whole. One should therefore not project it unjustifiably onto the world under discussion and make Levi into a paraenetic model for the readers, with which Luke wants to exhort the reader "to resolute discipleship of Jesus" (Radl I: 328; see also Wiefel). Luke certainly did not understand following Jesus in such a formal and, basically, empty way. Following Jesus, as Levi and the other disciples did, was tied to the presence of Jesus. Accordingly, it disappears after Easter in Luke, both as a demand and as an ethos of the disciples of Jesus.

29 Levi gives a banquet for Jesus, which Luke probably understood as an illustration of his discipleship. The expression δοχὴν ποιεῖν (τινί) appears only in the Septuagint (Genesis 21.8; 26.30; 1/3 Ezra 1.3; 5.4, 8; Daniel 5.1[Theodotion]) and then in Luke 14.13. The meal scene that Luke sets forth in v. 29b is somewhat unclear with regard to the participants, for one does not learn exactly who reclined with "them" at table ("with them" means not 'with Jesus and Levi,' but, due to v. 30b, 'with Jesus and the disciples'). Luke speaks merely of anonymous ἄλλοι. He has consciously established this fuzziness with a very specific intention. In this way he sets an accent that characteristically differs from Mark 2.15, where it was not "tax collectors and others" who eat and drink with Jesus and the disciples, but "tax collectors and sinners." Thus, in Mark 2.15 it is the narrator himself who brings this religious stigmatization onto the discourse level and thereby makes it his own. By contrast, Luke speaks neutrally of ἄλλοι and thus leaves it to the Pharisees and scribes, i.e., the narrative-*internal* antagonists of Jesus, to disqualify the table society of Jesus and the disciples as "sinners." Thus, Luke distinguishes between the situation and its evaluation by the Pharisees and scribes. He communicates to the readers merely that certain people *were viewed* by the Pharisees and scribes as sinners; whether they also *were* that remains open. Thus, "sinner" functions here not as a term of the narrator's language of description but as a category of the narrative-internal polemic (see also Neale 1991, 134).

30 Luke still does not yet let the Pharisees criticize Jesus directly (that was also already the case in Mark 2.16). They criticize (and this is different from Mark 2.16) not Jesus's behavior but that *the disciples* practice meal fellowship with the—as they say—"tax collectors and sinners." The fact that Luke has "Pharisees and their scribes" turn up can be explained as a reconfiguration of the *Vorlage* of Mark 2.16 ("the scribes of the Pharisees") that is guided by the interest in having the Pharisees also turn up clearly in this episode. In Luke the "grumbling" ([δια]γογγύζειν) is a reaction to the behavior of Jesus, which is characteristic of the Pharisees and yet also for the *vox populi* (see also 15.2; 19.7). It always refers to Jesus's dealings with tax collectors (and sinners). In the Old Testament it describes above all Israel's discontentedness in the wilderness (Exodus 15.24; 16.2, 7-9, 12; 17.3; Numbers 11.1; 14.2, 27, 29, 36; 16.11; 17.6, 20, 25; Deuteronomy 1.27; see also Psalm 106.25; 1 Corinthians 10.10), but Luke probably does not wish to establish a typological relationship of correspondence to that. The possibility that Luke alludes to Isaiah 29.24 with this element ("And those who go astray in spirit will understand and the γογγύζοντες will learn to obey") is probably also too far-fetched, though at least worthy of consideration. If one had asked him, he would certainly have had no objection to the establishment of such a cross-connection. While the lexical pair "eat and drink" is used as a merism (cf. e.g., Genesis 26.30; 2 Samuel 19.36; Ecclesiastes 5.18; Isaiah 22.13; Matthew 6.25; 11.18-19; 24.49; Luke 10.7), the situation is different in the case of "tax collectors and sinners." This collocation, which is found only in the Synoptic Gospels (cf. also Luke 7.34 par. Matthew 11.19; Luke 15.1; 19.2/7), combines not two different groups of people with each other but two categories from two different sign systems—namely, the socio-economic ("tax collector" as designation of occupation) and the religious ("sinner" as designation for the status in the relation to God). Only "tax collector" points to a clearly specifiable *denotatum* as an object of reality (namely, people who practice this occupation), whereas no specific extension can be assigned to the category "sinner" as such. Its meaning can be specified only via its *designatum* and in this sense functions as an umbrella term for people who, according to the judgment of the one using the term, do not fulfill God's demand, either as a self-designation (e.g., 5.8; 18.13) or as a designation assigned by others (e.g., Genesis 13.13; Luke 7.39; cf. Dunn 2003, 528ff). One can combine "sinners" with "tax collectors" because the significative semantic profile of both terms display overlaps (on the tax collectors, see at 3.12). Thus, the Pharisees accuse the disciples of sojourning in the society of those rejected by God and in this way of also not aligning themselves with God's judgment.

31-32 Jesus's answer consists of two parts that correspond to each other structurally (in each case "not . . . , but"). The first half (v. 31b) formulates a general fact of experience, which Jesus then uses to interpret his own work by way of an allegorizing transference.

31 The commonplace that a physician is there for the sick and not for the healthy comes from the Hellenistic environment of early Christianity (see Klauck 1978, 153–54; Ebner 1998, 150ff); cf. e.g., Plutarch, *Moralia* 230–31: "The physicians are not accustomed to stay among the well but where there are sick" (as an answer to the question of why Pausanias did not remain in Sparta but went to Tegea into exile); Dio Chrysostom 3.100: "Medicines are necessary for the sick, but superfluous for the healthy" (see also Artemidorus, *Onirocriticon* 4.22 [Pack 1963, 258.2]); Diogenes Laertius 6.6: "When he (sc. Antisthenes) was once reviled because he was together with bad people (ἐπὶ τῷ πονηροῖς συγγενέσθαι), he said, 'The doctors too are among the sick, but they receive no fever'" (see also Gnomologium Vaticanum 37). Additional passages: Diogenes Laertius 2.70; Philo, *De providentia* 2.70; Dio Chrysostom 8.5; Joannes Stobaeus, *Anthologium* III: 13.43 (Wachsmuth/Hense 1958, III: 462.12–15). Luke has adjusted the Markan phrasing to the usage outside the New Testament insofar as he calls the healthy not οἱ ἰσχύοντες (so Mark 2.17) but οἱ ὑγιαίοντες. The phrasing κακῶς ἔχειν in the sense of 'to be sick' (see also Ezekiel 34.4; Plutarch, *Pericles* 38.2; *Moralia* 588a; Matthew 4.24; Mark 1.32, 34 par. Matthew 8.16; Mark 6.55 par. Matthew 14.35) is only an excerpt from a broader linguistic use that describes with it very generally a bad condition; cf. e.g., Josephus, *Antiquitates judaicae* 11.161 (Jerusalem and its inhabitants); 16.270 (political relations); Demosthenes, *Orationes* 14.38 (Greece); see also Euripides, *Medea* 533.

By means of **32** it comes to a metaphorical fusion of the two sign systems or symbolic universes (for the understanding of ἔρχομαι + aorist infinitive as a self-statement of Jesus, see at 12.49). There emerges a semantic relation of determination in which the religious symbolic universe, with which the Pharisaic criticism operates, functions as the topic, while the symbolic universe of the Hellenistic parabolic saying of the physician is used as the comment. The semantic change that takes place with reference to the sinners is of decisive importance. They suddenly become sick people whose healing is desired in every case and by every person (i.e., also by the Pharisees). Thus, the concern is with the assignment of identity. The Pharisees should be brought to see the sinners as sick people who need healing and are capable of being healed (entirely analogously 15.1ff is concerned with seeing them as people who are lost; see there). The specific accent that Luke gives to the answer of Jesus consists in the addition of εἰς μετάνοιαν, which implies two aspects. First, on the linguistic surface Jesus solicits the assent of the Pharisees, for there is little that can be objected against Jesus's intention to move sinners to repentance. Thus, it is clear that Luke does *not* have Jesus confront the position of the Pharisees. And second, Jesus's answer displays an often-missed christological substructure that is contained in it. Here repentance is precisely *not* thematized as a prior "condition . . . for fellowship with Christ" (so Zimmermann/Kliesch 1982, 100). Rather, the repentance of sinners takes place when they turn to Jesus as the authentic representative of God's salvation and/or enter into his discipleship like Levi (see also at 7.36-50; 15.1-10). This gives rise to a considerable gain in theological precision, for the thematic provocation that goes forth from Jesus's answer is now found where it belongs, namely in Christology. The central point of the controversy dialogue also lies here. It has nothing to do with supposed controversies about the table fellowship of Jewish and Gentile Christians, for these had probably already not been a problem for quite some time in Luke's day.

33 Luke marks the transition to the question on fasting with maximal brevity. The anaphoric transition οἱ δέ refers to the same questioners as in v. 30 (cf. also BDR §251). In comparison to Mark 2.18 the question is reformulated especially in the description of the ethos of the disciples of John. With the help of the combination of fasting and prayer, Luke had already characterized the piety of Anna (cf. 2.37 with additional attestations for this combination; for the expression δεήσεις ποιεῖν, cf. 3 Maccabees 2.1; Philo, *De posteritate Caini* 169; Josephus, *Antiquitates judaicae* 18.276; *Bellum judaicum* 7.107). Luke thus characterizes the adherents of the Baptist as strict (πυκνά) fulfillers of Jewish piety norms. At the center stands, of course, the fasting, as the description of the ethos of Jesus's disciples as "eating and drinking" makes clear (the comparison of Jesus with the Baptist in Luke 7.33-34 par. Matthew 11.18-19 also makes use of the same terminology). According to Luke 18.12, the Pharisees fasted twice a week (probably on Monday and Thursday; cf. Didache 8.1; Bill. II: 242–44; IV/1: 77–114; see further at 18.11-12).

Νηστεύειν means either a sustained renunciation of certain foods (cf. e.g., Jeremiah 35.6-7; Philo, *De vita contemplativa* 73; Mark 1.6; see also Daniel 1.5, 8, 12; Tobit 1.10-12; 2 Maccabees 5.27; Josephus, Vita 14) or a temporally limited forgoing of food on certain days or for a given occasion (e.g., for the support of prayer or as fasts of repentance or grief; cf. Leviticus 16.29, 31; 23.27, 29, 32; 1 Kings 21.27; Joel 1.14; 2.15ff; Isaiah 58.1-9; Daniel 9.3; 10.3; Judith 8.5-6; Psalms of Solomon 3.8; Testament of Ruben 1.10; Testament of Joseph 10.1; Testament of Benjamin 1.4; 2 Baruch 9.2). With the exception of the fast on the Day of Atonement (cf. Leviticus 16.29ff; 23.27ff), fasting was not a requirement of the written Torah. It was practiced as a ritual of self-abasement and as an expression of humility in which the pious bows down, mindful of his sinfulness, before God; sin-removing power was therefore also ascribed to it (cf. Ezra 8.21; Isaiah 58.3-5; Sirach 31.31; Psalms of Solomon 3.7; 1 Enoch 108.7; 1 Clement 53.2; 55.6; Barnabas 3.1; Shepherd of Hermas, Visions 3.10.6); see also at 18.12 and Arbesmann 1929.

34-35 As in Mark 2.19-20, Jesus's answer is two-leveled. First, a rhetorical metaphorical question is used to justify why the disciples of Jesus do not fast. This would be just as absurd as if one had the guests fast at a wedding celebration. The expression "sons of the wedding chamber" as a designation for the wedding guests is a Semitism (literal translation of בְּנֵי הַחוּפָּה; cf. J. Jeremias, ThWNT 4: 1096; for the reference, see R. Zimmermann 2001, 286; see also at 10.6). Luke brings the questioners into the source domain through the change of the predicate from the third person (δύνανται; so Mark 2.19b par. Matthew 9.15b; subject is the "sons of the wedding chamber," thus the disciples on the subject matter level) to the second person (δύνασθε). Their answer can, of course, only be "No!" and with this they have already agreed with Jesus. The point of the parabolic saying, however, consists in the allegorizing identification of the presupposed situation with the present qualified by Jesus (see also Klauck 1978, 168–69; Kingsbury 1991, 88)—namely, that it becomes a time of celebration through his appearance and is like a wedding celebration at which Jesus plays the role of the groom and the disciples are his guests. For the allegorizing presentation of Jesus as groom, cf. also Matthew 25.1, 5-6, 10; John 3.29 (see also 2 Corinthians 11.2); there, however, reference is made to other parts of the wedding celebration than in our text. From a tradition-historical perspective the metaphorical description of the time of salvation as a time of celebration stands in the background (cf. Isaiah 25.6; Zephaniah 1.7; 1 Enoch 62.14; 2 Enoch 42.5; Testament of Isaak 8.11; Revelation 19.9: "wedding banquet"; 5 Ezra 2.38; see Volz 1934, 367–68, 388–89), which was also taken up elsewhere in the Jesus tradition (cf. Matthew 22.3: as wedding celebration; Luke 14.16; Matthew 8.11par.).

Of course the subject matter itself also already impacts the picture. When the wedding celebration is described as the presence of the groom with the wedding guests (ἐν ᾧ . . . μετ᾽ αὐτῶν ἐστιν), its temporal limitation is already implied in this emphasis on simultaneity (cf. BDR §455.3a₅)—the groom will leave his guests at some point and this will end the time of celebration.

This idea is made explicit in **35**, and at the latest the readers now know that Jesus speaks here about his own future fate and refers to the time of his forced separation from the disciples; the latter, in turn, now become transparent for the post-Easter Christian community. It is above all the expression καὶ ὅταν ἀπαρθῇ ἀπ᾽ αὐτῶν that no longer fits with the image field. Luke will probably have related it to the ascension, for this phrasing functions grammatically as a further specification of ἡμέραι (cf. BDR §442.6) and stands in a conscious antithesis to the talk of Jesus's with-ness in v. 34c. Unlike in Mark 2.20, a restricted fast on a certain day (ἐν ἐκείνῃ τῇ ἡμέρᾳ) is not now justified. Rather, Luke takes into view the time after the death and resurrection in its entirety (ἐν ἐκείναις ταῖς ἡμέραις) and qualifies it as an epoch of fasting, which differs precisely in this respect from the time of the presence of Jesus on earth. Thus, unlike in Mark, this verse does not serve to justify a certain Christian practice of fasting, but rather has the function of retrospectively designating the time of the earthly presence of Jesus as a time *sui generis*—namely, as a unique, temporally limited time of celebration in which there was no fasting.

36-39 With the help of a transition that is characteristic for him (cf. 6.39; 12.16; 13.6; 14.7; 15.3; 18.1, 9; 21.29), Luke has a metaphorical commentary follow, which consists of three parabolic sayings, and he wants his readers to connect it with the two previously discussed questions (for the rhetorical significance of παραβολή, see at 4.23). The conversation situation remains unchanged. All three parabolic sayings thematize the opposition of "new" (καινός or νέος) and "old" (παλαιός). Luke has Jesus begin with two examples that have parallel sentence structures (οὐδείς . . . εἰ δὲ μή γε) and have their commonality in the fact that with the help of daily experiences they want to express that old and new cannot be physically combined with each other without both suffering harm. The key word is βάλλειν and its cognates.

36 Unlike in Mark 2.21, it is not the damage to the old piece of clothing but the damage to the new that stands at the center. Correspondingly, the senselessness of the behavior does not consist in sewing (ἐπιράπτειν) an unshrunk piece of cloth onto an old garment, which would damage this even more, but in tearing (σχίζειν) a new garment for the sake of the old. First, the new clothing is destroyed, and second, the old also gains nothing from this. Thus, the interest here clearly lies with preserving the new without damage.

The same applies to **37**. No winemaker would put new wine in old wineskins (i.e., in depilated skins of goats or sheep; cf. Habbe 1996, 96 with the indication that this always took place only for the purposes of transportation and never for storage), because they were no longer sufficiently elastic and strong to withstand the pressure that results from the process of fermentation (cf. Job 32.19; see also Joshua 9.4). But here it is not the concern for the destruction of the old wineskins but the interest in the preservation of the wine that stands at the center.

This very thing is illustrated by the pragmatic conclusion in **38** where there is talk of the new wine only (βλητέον is the only verbal adjective in the New Testament that ends in -τέος; cf. BDR §65$_5$).

The intended sense of the two examples is clearly recognizable. The concern is with the characterization of the time that has dawned through Jesus's appearance. It requires from people a behavior that is fully and wholly adjusted to this new time and makes no compromises. Every attempt at accommodation would be as absurd 'as if . . .' Some identify the old with Judaism and the new with Christianity (e.g., Nolland; Bock), but this misses the point by a wide margin. Rather, the new stands for the kingdom of God, which requires people to completely change the orientation of their existence (as this is displayed, for example, by the clever manager in 16.1-8 and refused by the rich man in 18.18-23).

39 is a notorious *crux interpretum*, because here the old is obviously priviledged vis-à-vis the new and thus a certain tension appears to arise in relation to what has been said in vv. 36-38. (For this reason and because this verse is lacking in the parallels it was deleted by D it Mcion Iren Eus). Some interpreters even make the statement of this verse the key for the understanding of the preceding double parabolic saying (e.g., Steinhauser 1981, 50ff; Good 1983). This is certainly not possible, however, for Jesus expresses himself here not with regard to the quality of old and new wine, but with regard to the practice of drinking wine. Luke expresses oenological knowledge that was also already common in antiquity, and connects it via a terminological (παλαιός vs. νέος) and thematic (wine) link to the preceding; cf. Pindar, *Olympionikai* 9.48; Athenaeus, *Deipnosophistae* 1.47 (v. 26a): "Old wine serves not only enjoyment but also health"; Sirach 9.10; Plutarch, *Marius* 44.1; Lucian of Samosata, *De mercede conductis* 26; m. Avot 4.20; b. Berakhot 51a; see also Diogenes Laertius 2.84 and the discussion of new and old wine in Plutarch, *Moralia* 655e–656b; for χρηστός as an attribute of wine, cf. Plutarch, *Moralia* 240d; Athenaeus, *Deipnosophistae* 13.49 (585e); Inscription of Abercius 15. An understanding that is not forced results if one has the aorist participle πιών in connection with the present λέγει designate a punctiliar *action* rather than a timeless *attitude* (cf. Flebbe 2005). The meaning of the statement would then be that no person requests new wine after he has just drunk old, which would involve mixing old and new wine. For this would be just as absurd as if one lit a light and then hid it (8.16) or if one looked backward while plowing (9.62; all the texts display the same structure: οὐδείς + aorist participle + present). The example does not, of course, function the other way around, for everyone would have liked to drink (better) old wine after drinking (worse) new wine; but this was evidently clear to Luke, for otherwise he would not have formulated this sentence in this way. With this qualification this example also goes in the same direction as the two others—old and new are not compatible with each other.

6.1-5: Sabbath I

[1]**It happened on a Sabbath that he went through wheat fields. And his disciples plucked off heads of grain, rubbed them with their hands, and ate them.** [2]**But some of the Pharisees said, "Why do you do what is not permitted on the Sabbath?"** [3]**And Jesus answered and said to them, "Have you not read what David did when he and his companions were hungry,** [4]**how he entered into the house of God and took the bread of presence, ate (it) and gave it also to his companions, although no one is permitted to eat (it), except for the priests alone?"** [5]**And he said to them, "Lord of the Sabbath is the Son of Man."**

The individual elements of the controversy dialogue form are clearly identifiable: vv. 1-2 is the *narrative exposition* with the description of the starting situation (v. 1) and the criticism that "some of the Pharisees" make of this situation (v. 2). In vv. 3-5 Luke brings in a two-part answer of Jesus that argues with a historical *exemplum* (vv. 3-4) and formulates a saying about the authority of the Son of Man. Unlike in Mark 2.24, the Pharisees do not directly address Jesus in v. 2b but criticize the behavior of the disciples (as in 5.30, 33). In doing so they also turn to the disciples themselves (as in 5.30).

Luke's *Vorlage* was Mark 2.23-28, though the number and nature of the minor agreements make it probable that Matthew and Luke had a revised version of the Gospel of Mark before them: ὁδὸν ποιεῖν (Mark 2.23) is lacking in v. 1 par. Matthew 12.1; καὶ ἤσθιον or καὶ ἐσθίειν (v. 1c par. Matthew 12.1) is without a Markan equivalent; the same is true for εἶπαν and εἶπεν (v. 2a, 3a par. Matthew 12.2, 3); the prohibition formula ὃ οὐκ ἔξεστιν occurs not *after* (Mark 2.24) but *before* the temporal specification (2b par. Matthew 12.2); χρείαν ἔσχεν (Mark 2.25c) is lacking in v. 3 par. Matthew 12.3; ἐπὶ Ἀβιαθὰρ ἀρχιερέως (Mark 2.26a) is lacking in v. 4 par. Matthew 12.4 (this was incorrect in Mark); τοῖς μετ' αὐτοῦ (v. 4c par. Matthew 12.4) instead of τοῖς σὺν αὐτῷ (Mark 2.26); μόνους or μόνοις (v. 4d par. Matthew 12.4) has no equivalent in Mark 2.26; Mark 2.27b is lacking in v. 5 par. Matthew 12.7; in v. 5b par. Matthew 12.8 ὁ υἱος τοῦ ἀνθρώπου is placed at the end (diff. Mark 2.28); cf. further Schramm 1971, 111–12; Neirynck 1974b, 74–75; 1991, 23–24; Ennulat 1994, 77ff.

1 The linguistic form of the exposition (ἐγένετο δέ + ἐν + temporal specification + substantivized infinitive with subject + καί + *verbum finitum* [καὶ ἔτιλλον]) is typically Lukan (see also 6.6, 12 and at 1.8-9).

For the temporal specification there is a peculiar text-critical problem. In A C L W Θ Ψ (*f¹³*) 𝔐 lat syʰ Epiph the episode takes place not on just any Sabbath but on the "second-first" Sabbath (ἐν σαββάτῳ δευτεροπρώτῳ). This word is not attested anywhere else, and the variant is almost certainly secondary. A persuasive explanation does not yet exist (cf. the survey of previous attempted solutions in Bock I: 534–35; Radl I: 338). This applies also to the currently favored explanation of Metzger 1971, 139. According to this explanation, a scribe, with a view to 6.6 (ἐν ἑτέρῳ σαββάτῳ), added πρώτῳ in v. 1, which another copyist, with a view to 4.31 (the Sabbath in Capernaum) corrected to δευτέρῳ ("deleting πρώτῳ by using dots over the letters"). A third copyist is said to have overlooked the dots and combined both words with each other. It would, of course, be simpler to assume that with a view to 6.11 πρώτῳ was added in one manuscript, and δευτέρῳ in another on the basis of 4.31. Another copyist found the two in different manuscripts and combined them with each other. A variation of this view is found in H. Klein 1996a: Luke himself already wrote ἐν σαββάτῳ πρώτῳ, which a first copyist corrected to ἐν σαββάτῳ δευτέρῳ. A second copyist then harmonized the two specifications with each other.

The action of the disciples is described in much greater detail than in Mark 2.23b. Despite the unclear syntactic relations in the sentence, it is nevertheless clear what happens. The disciples tear heads from the stalks (Diodorus Siculus 5.21.5 is the only literary parallel for τίλλειν . . . στάχυ[α]ς, although a completely different event is described there; cf. further Spicq 1994, III: 379–80). They rub them between their hands in order to separate husks and grains from each other and then eat the latter (see also Delebecque 1976, 76ff).

2 Against the background of the halakic differentiation of the Sabbath Torah of Exodus 20.8-11; 31.12-17 and elsewhere in Judaism (cf. Goldenberg 1979; Doering 1999) it was possible to accuse the disciples of violating two Sabbath halakoth. First, by the otherwise allowed (cf.

Deuteronomy 23.26) tearing off of the heads they could be accused of violating the prohibition of harvesting on the Sabbath (cf. already Exodus 34.21; see also m. Shabbat 7.2; Bill. I: 617–18). Second, by the rubbing of the heads they could be accused of violating the prohibition of preparing on the Sabbath (cf. e.g., Jubilees 2.29; CD 10.22–23; see also m. Shabbat 7.2). Unlike Mark 2.24, Luke speaks of "some (τινές) of the Pharisees" and differentiates in this way within this group (see also 13.31; 19.39; Matthew 12.38; John 9.16; Acts 15.5; see also Mark 12.13; Acts 23.9). Whether he wants to indicate in this way that other halakic evaluations of the action of the disciples are possible (so Safrai 1990) must remain open. After all, the disciples would not necessarily offend against the Sabbath Torah according to another rabbinic tradition, but one which is preserved only in the much later text b. Shabbat 128a: "One may pinch off with the hand and eat but not with a tool; one may crush something and eat but not with a tool. Words of R. Yehuda, 'The wise say: one may crush with the fingertips and eat, but not a great amount with the hand, as one does on a weekday.'"

3-4 The first part of Jesus's answer wants to legitimate the behavior of the disciples with the help of an example from the history of Israel by referring to the event reported in 1 Samuel 21.2-7 (Jesus thus argues not with recourse to the Scripture but with recourse to the event behind the Scripture). That passage recounts how at the Yahweh sanctuary at Nob David requisitioned for his troop the twelve breads of the presence whose consumption was reserved for the priests alone according to the Torah (cf. Exodus 25.30; Leviticus 24.5-9). The conditions in the Jerusalem temple, which did not yet exist at the time of David, were joined with the David narrative in an anachronistic way by a redactor of the story told in 1 Samuel 21 and by Mark 2.25-26. Here there was originally talk only of "holy bread" (1 Samuel 21.5, 7a). These breads have something to do with the Sabbath only insofar as they were always renewed on this day (cf. Leviticus 24.8; 1 Chronicles 9.32); that David took the loaves of the presence on a Sabbath is a late rabbinic construction that was invented to exonerate David (cf. Bill. I: 618–19). Jesus's answer overlaps with the description of the starting situation (v. 1) only in the key word ἐσθίειν and with the accusation of the Pharisees (v. 2) in the phrasing οὐκ ἔξεστιν (for the use of ἔξεστιν in this context, see at 20.22). Unlike in Matthew 12.1, it is not said that the disciples, like David, were hungry. Thus, in Luke Jesus argues not from the analogy of the situation but with the help of the authority of David, who overrides an instruction of the Torah. Cohn-Sherbok 1979 has shown that such an argument would not be valid within the halakic discussions of early and rabbinic Judaism. But this controversy—at least Luke's version of it—is not concerned with this point anyway, for it argues implicitly christologically. The concern is not with the question of what situations of distress override a Torah commandment (cf. e.g., in 1 Maccabees 2.29-41), but with the right that David may presume for himself in relation to the Torah.

The continuation in 5 extends this line further and elevates it by means of an *argumentum a comparatione* ('if already David . . . how much more the Son of Man'; cf. Lausberg 1949, §395–97) to the level of explicit Christology. This background was probably also responsible for the fact that Luke deleted Mark 2.27. This is at any rate more likely than an explanation in the framework of the Deutero-Mark hypothesis and more likely than the assumption that this saying was omitted "because it was no longer understood among the addressees of the Gospel or could be misunderstood as a general rejection of the Sabbath command because of the existing distance to Judaism" (so Mayer-Haas 2003, 309). Syntactically κύριος τοῦ σαββάτου is the subject (thus topic), while "the Son of Man" functions as a predicate noun (thus comment; cf. the very similar statement in Epictetus, *Enchiridion* 14.3: κύριος ἑκάστου ἐστὶν ὁ . . . ἔχων τὴν ἐξουσίαν εἰς τὸ περιποιῆσαι ἢ ἀφελέσθαι ["whoever has the power to allow or prohibit . . . is lord over everyone"]). Luke does not say that the Sabbath is "abolished" (Schürmann I: 305). It is merely expressed that the question of the Sabbath observance is placed in the Son of Man's authority of disposition and decision.

Codex D places Luke 6.5 after v. 10 and inserts a chreia at this point: "On the same day he saw someone who was working on the Sabbath, and he said to him, 'Man, if you know what you are doing, you are blessed. But if you do not know, you are accursed and a transgressor of the law.'" The much-discussed question of whether this is an authentic saying of Jesus (Jeremias 1965, 61ff; see also Bammel 1986) must be answered with great probability negatively. Though there is no tradition-historical connection, this saying has a strong theological connection with Romans 14.23 and therefore belongs in the context of the post-Easter Christian-Jewish process of separation; cf. also Delobel 1985; Nicklas 2002; see also Derrett 1995; Doering 1999, 438ff.

6.6-11: Sabbath II

⁶But it happened on another Sabbath that he went into the synagogue and taught. And there was a person there whose right hand was withered. ⁷But the scribes and Pharisees watched him furtively, whether he would heal on the Sabbath so that they might find (a reason) to accuse him. ⁸But he knew their thoughts and said to the man who had the withered hand, "Rise and stand in the middle!" And he rose

and stood. ⁹But Jesus said to them, "I ask you: Is it permitted on the Sabbath to do good or evil, to save life or to destroy (it)?" ¹⁰And he looked around at them all and said to him, "Stretch out your hand!" And he did it, and his hand was restored. ¹¹But they were filled with want of understanding and were discussing among themselves what they could perhaps do to Jesus.

As in 5.17-26, the first episode of this series, the form elements character-istic of controversy dialogues are also connected with a healing story here, in the last episode. After the *introduction*, with whose help the episode is embedded in the overarching literary context (v. 6a), there follows first an *exposition*, which causes one to expect that the narrative will now continue as a healing story (v. 6b). But it does not initially do so, for there follows in another *exposition* the introduction of scribes and Pharisees, whom the readers already know to be antagonists of Jesus from the previous epi-sodes (v. 7). After this the two lines alternate: verses 8a, 9, 10a belong to the controversy dialogue line, vv. 8b-d, 10b-d belong to the line of the healing story. The narrative is concluded with a *finale* that is configured as a parody of the usual note of wonder (v. 11). This verse concludes not only this episode but the entire narrative collecting basin from 5.17. Luke does not have the Pharisees turn up again until 14.1, where he says concerning them that they "watch furtively" (παρατηρεῖν) Jesus. They thus do the same there as here in v. 7; moreover, both here and there we are dealing with a healing on the Sabbath. This terminological and material correspon-dence is probably anything but a coincidence. This narrative is also not (see also the introductory comments on 5.17-26) a "norm miracle" (The-issen 1987, 114ff, 319), though the concern here is with the observance of the Sabbath and thus (in contrast to 5.17-26) with a question of the supra-individual ethos. But at the center of interest stands not the legitimation of the halakic norm but the legitimation of the person of Jesus, so that with regard to this miracle one also should speak instead of a *legitimation mir-acle* or a "*demonstration miracle*" (Busse 1979). The latter designation is based especially on vv. 8b-d. Within its literary context this episode can be understood in this respect as an illustration of the christological state-ment of v. 5.

Luke's *Vorlage* was Mark 3.1-6. The number of noteworthy minor agreements is average: ξηρά(ν) (v. 6c par. Matthew 12.10a) instead of ἐξηραμμένην (Mark 3.1b); εἶπεν δὲ ὁ Ἰησοῦς or ὁ δὲ εἶπεν (v. 9a par. Matthew 12.11a) instead of καὶ λέγει (Mark 3.4a); Mark 3.4c (οἱ δὲ ἐσιώπων) is lacking in v. 9 par. Matthew 12.12; likewise μετ' ὀργῆς, συλλυπούμενος ἐπὶ τῇ πωρώσει τῆς καρδίας αὐτῶν from Mark 3.5a is lacking in v. 10 par. Matthew 12.13; the enclitic possessive pronoun σου with τὴν χεῖρα (v. 10b par. Matthew 12.13b) is lacking in Mark 3.5b; cf. further Neirynck 1974b, 76ff; 1991, 24–25; Ennulat 1994, 84ff.

The story was also in the apocryphal gospel of the "Nazarenes and Ebionites," about which Jerome says that he "recently" translated it from Hebrew into Greek (*Commentariorum in Mattheum* II: 30 on Matthew 12.13 [CChr.SL 77.90.367f]). But only a fragment from the exposition of the healing story is preserved. Here the handicapped person himself turns to Jesus by introducing himself as a bricklayer (*caementarius*) and asks for healing so that he would not have to beg (text: Aland 2001, 158; Schneemelcher 1990, I: 134).

6 The linguistic form of the introduction corresponds to that of v. 1 (see further there), and the situation that Luke sets forth is the same as in 4.31 (see also 4.44; 5.1, 3, 17). Jesus teaches (diff. Mark 3.1), and he does so on a Sabbath in the synagogue, i.e., the readers meet him in the carrying out of his mission. The encounter with a person who displays a bodily defect sets the narrative course in the direction of a healing story. In the terminology of today's folk medicine one would probably regard the hand as paralyzed; that it is designated in the narrative as "withered" (ξηρά; cf. also Testament of Simeon 2.12 and the corresponding verb ξηραίνειν for Hebrew יָבֵשׁ in the punitive miracle in 1 Kings 13.4) must be attributed in the context of ancient humoral pathology (cf. Schöner 1964; I. Müller 1993) to the fact that people thought of a lack of the body fluid that provided for the mobility of the hand. In the inscription of Epidaurus there is possibly a report of the healing of a "withered" leg (W 60 [Herzog 1931, 32]). Luke lets the right hand (diff. Mark 3.1) be "withered" and intensifies the hardship in this way (but see also 22.50 par. John 18.10 diff. Mark 14.47).

7 The description of the scribes and Pharisees now identifies them from the outset as opponents of the person of Jesus and no longer only as critics of his or his disciples' action. According to Psalm^LXX 36.12, παρατηρεῖν ("watch furtively") characterizes the behavior of the sinner against the righteous (see also Daniel^Theodotion 6.12; Susanna^Theodotion 12.15-16 and then Luke 14.1; 20.20; Acts 9.24). Thus, they have arrived in their opposition upon the level on which the whole series of controversy dialogues is situated, namely on the level of Christology. The expression ἵνα εὕρωσιν κατηγορεῖν is not an Aramaism (so Fitzmyer), but good Greek, for εὑρίσκειν without an accusative object but with an infinitive is widely attested in Greek (cf. the presentation of the material in J. A. L. Lee 1991). The thought report that Luke provides here of the intention of the scribes and Pharisees presupposes that the healing of a "withered" hand on the Sabbath could be viewed as an offense against the Sabbath Torah (see at v. 2). To be sure, the question of whether one may heal on the Sabbath was never discussed as such in Jewish texts, i.e., in this generality—let alone in pre-rabbinic times (see further at 14.3-4a).

8 Vis-à-vis his *Vorlage* Luke first supplements the same motif as in 5.22. Jesus knows the hidden intentions of his opponents—this is what the scribes and Pharisees in Luke have become by now (see at 5.22 for the theological connotations of this knowledge and its significance with regard to the announcement of Simeon in 2.35). The exhortation to the sick person to stand in the middle (see also already 4.35; 5.19) still belongs to the expositional motifs of the healing story and has the function of establishing publicness. Luke thus has the healing take place very intentionally before the eyes of all those present, and it is this narrative move that gives the miracle a demonstration character. *What* it should demonstrate is obvious—that *Jesus* is "Lord of the Sabbath" and not the Pharisees (v. 5). Although this part of the episode is a component of the healing story, it fulfills an important dramaturgical function with regard to the line of the controversy dialogue.

9 The rhetorical question that Jesus addresses to the scribes and Pharisees formulates a double antithesis and is certainly not meant comparatively (*pace* BDR §245.3b$_4$; Schürmann). In a *formal* respect the conjunction ἤ is "sharply disjunctive" (BDR §446$_1$) and "separates what is mutually exclusive" (BDR §446$_1$). From the perspective of *content*, the decisive achievement of the two antitheses consists in the fact that they transfer the halakic question of what is permitted on the Sabbath into another symbolic universe and thus make a paradigm change. First, the concern is no longer with the *kind* of action but with its *consequence*, and second, this consequence is described with recourse to categories that are taken from the symbolic universe of ethics and there is a universally valid consensus concerning their evaluation—even between Jesus and his opponents. Through this placement of the Sabbath observance in a general ethical sign system, not only is the halakic problematic subordinated to the ethical orientation, but the special character of the Sabbath is *de facto* annulled, for the propositional content of the question of Jesus is, of course, equally valid for every day. Not only on the Sabbath but on every day one should do good and not evil, save life and not destroy it. Therefore, the question that is placed in Jesus's mouth here belongs in the context of the Christian-Jewish process of separation. It makes use of a figure of argumentation that gives reason for the suppression of the exclusive Jewish ethos by an inclusive ethic in which the differences between Jews and non-Jews are nullified (cf. in detail Wolter 1997a). Luke has reformulated the second antithesis (ψυχὴν σῶσαι ἢ ἀπολέσαι) vis-à-vis Mark 3.4 and inserted the common opposition of σῴζειν and ἀπολλύναι (cf. in the New Testament Mark 8.35parr.; Luke 19.10; 1 Corinthians 1.18; 2 Corinthians

2.15; 2 Thessalonians 2.10; James 4.12; Judges 5). Here ψυχή means not the soul as the unique self of the person but stands instead, like Hebrew נֶפֶשׁ, for the human life in its entirety (cf. Dautzenberg 1966, 13ff, 158–59; E. Schweizer, ThWNT 9: 635.24ff).

10 The event of the healing is not narrated without irony. It consists in the fact that Jesus does not actually make a healing-effecting action. Instead, it says merely that the hand "was restored" (ἀπεκατεστάθη; cf. also Exodus 4.7), with the *genus verbi* being identifiable without further ado as a *passivum divinum*. In this way the narrative gives the impression that it was none other than God himself who healed on the Sabbath. In this way Jesus's opponents, as portrayed in v. 7, are blamed.

11 functions both as a conclusion to the healing story and as a conclusion to the series of controversy dialogues opened in 5.17. As the finale of the preceding miracle story the readers expect a reaction of the eyewitnesses (as a note of wonder, acclamation, or dissemination; cf. Theissen 1987, 78–81). And indeed, the first two form elements mentioned are present in this verse. However, Luke has configured them as a parody, and this has its reason in the fact that this verse functions simultaneously as the conclusion of the overarching narrative complex. This is already recognizable in the note of wonder in v. 11a, which Luke probably conceived of as a counterpart to the description of the reaction of the healing of the lame person in the first episode of this series (5.26), for both here and there the wonder is designated as a "being-filled" (ἐμπλήσθησαν). However, while the people there react with "fear"—as is also common elsewhere (cf. 1.65; 7.16; 8.37; Mark 9.8; Mark 4.41; 5.5 par. Luke 8.35) and as is appropriate for the encounter with the representative of God on earth—Luke has the "ignorance" (ἄνοια) gain entrance into the Pharisees here. But this also distinguishes them, on the other hand, from the visitors of the synagogue in Nazareth, who "were filled with fury (θυμός)" as a reaction to the words of Jesus according to 4.28-29 and wanted to put him to death.

Astonishingly, this interpretation must be justified, for in many lexicons and commentaries ἄνοια is not translated with "ignorance" (so only Wiefel; Radl; T. Söding, *ThBNT²* 1: 273) but with "rage"/"fury"/"madness" (cf. F. Behm, ThWNT 4: 960: "In the pathological sense they became entirely mad [with anger over Jesus]"; W. Bauer 1988, 140; *EWNT* 1: 252; Klostermann; Grundmann: "full of blind anger"; Fitzmyer; Nolland; Bovon; Schürmann: "filled with blind madness"; Schweizer; Kremer; Schneider; Johnson: "anger"; Bock: "mindless rage"; Eckey). In the background stands evidently the distinction in Plato, *Timaeus* 86b: "There are two sorts of ἄνοια, madness (μανία) and lack of knowledge (ἀμαθία)." The decision in favor of μανία is, however, not only arbitrary but also false, for in the Hellenistic world of early Christianity ἄνοια is always used only in the sense of ἀμαθία; cf. the attestations mentioned in Radl I: 348, namely Philo, *Legum alle-goriae* 3.164; *De ebrietate* 93; *De confusione linguarum* 54; *De somniis* 2.115, 169, 191, 200, as well as the uses in parallel with ἀφροσύνη or μωρία in *Legum allegoriae* 3.211; *De sobrietate* 11, the antithesis to wisdom in Proverbs 14.8 ("It is the wisdom of the intelligent to grasp his way, but the ἄνοια of the fool is deception") or to "shrewdness" (ἀγχίνοια) in Philo, *De mutatione nominum* 193, and the distinction between μανία and ἄνοια in Josephus, *Antiquitates judaicae* 16.260. ἄνοια is also to be understood not affectively but cognitively in 2 Timothy 3.9, as the context clearly shows.

Verse 11b also points in this same direction, where Luke concretizes the Pharisees and scribes' lack of understanding with regard to the identity of Jesus by reporting—though with much more restraint than Mark 3.6—conversations (διαλαλεῖν) directed against Jesus. Even though Luke reveals via the use of the potential optative ἂν ποιήσαιεν (cf. BDR §385.1: "for the designation of what is merely thought") that these remarks are still a long way from concrete plans, through this he nevertheless makes an unmistakable reference to the death of Jesus in Jerusalem. Of the groups mentioned in v. 7 the Pharisees are, of course, no longer involved in the implementation of these "conversations" into concrete action (they are lacking altogether in the passion narrative), but only the scribes, namely in connection with the chief priests (cf. 22.2, 66; 23.10).

If we view again the controversy dialogues together and in so doing take Jesus's answers as coherence-creating instructions for interpretation, it becomes clear that they are concerned with ethos questions and halakic norm conflicts, first, only at a superficial level, and second, only in the perception of the opponents of Jesus. For Luke it is precisely this that also comprises their "ignorance" (cf. also Klumbies 1989, 170). In substance, the concern, from the first to the last episode, is instead with nothing other than the question of the identity of Jesus and of the ἐξουσία and authority of the Son of Man. If we tentatively place this profile into the terminology of Pauline theology, it becomes clear that here Luke developed in narrative form nothing other than what Paul attempted to express with the termino-logical opposition of ἔργα νόμου and πίστις Χριστοῦ.

6:12-49: The Sermon on the Plain

Luke localizes the Sermon on the Plain, which concludes this part of his story of Jesus, in the same temporal and spatial vagueness as in the previous episodes. He has it take place at some time (cf. the introduction v. 12) and at some place "in Judea" (4.44), i.e., in the Jewish land. After Luke had previously already mentioned numerous times *that* Jesus taught (cf.

4.31, 44; 5.1, 3, 17; 6.6), the readers now learn for the first time something about the content of this teaching. Plus, the Sermon on the Plain contains the first public words of Jesus that do not thematize his own identity and task—everything that Jesus had said previously was related to this—but go beyond this.

The scenic preparation is correspondingly elaborate. As always, temporal, spatial, and person-related structuring signals work together and configure the rhythm of the narrative course. Before the narrator has his main character speak in vv. 20-49, he prepares the scene on the aforementioned three levels: *(a) temporally* through the sequence of night (v. 12) and day (vv. 13-49), *(b) spatially* through the sequence of mountain (vv. 12-16) and plain (vv. 17-49), and *(c) with reference to the characters* through a successive expansion of the persons in the narrative. Initially Jesus is alone (v. 12), then the circle of the twelve apostles is added (v. 13), thereafter "a great multitude of his disciples" (v. 17b), and finally, in a mighty crescendo, "a great multitude of the people from all Judea and Jerusalem and the coastal region of Tyre and Sidon" (v. 17c). Up to the end of the narrative in v. 49 it remains *day* and all the persons remain on the plain together. All three levels are carefully coordinated with one another. In the *night* on the *mountain* Jesus is *alone*. In the *day* on the *mountain* the *twelve apostles* are added. The *disciples* join on the *plain*, and, finally, the *crowd* too then follows here.

6.12-19: Scenic Preparation

¹²**In these days he went out onto the mountain to pray, and he spent the whole night in prayer to God.**

¹³**And when it was day he called his disciples and picked out twelve from them, whom he gave the designation "apostles":** ¹⁴**Simon, whom he gave the designation "rock," and Andrew, his brother, and James and John and Philip and Bartholomew** ¹⁵**and Matthew and Thomas and James** (the son) **of Alphaeus, and Simon, whom one called Zealot,** ¹⁶**and Judas** (the son) **of James, and Judas Iscariot who became a traitor.**

¹⁷**And he descended with them and stopped on a level place, in addition a great crowd of his disciples and a great multitude of the people from all Judea and Jerusalem and the coastal region and Sidon,** ¹⁸**who came to hear him and to be healed from their sicknesses. And those afflicted by unclean spirits were made well.** ¹⁹**And everyone sought to touch him, for a power went forth from him and healed all.**

It is unmistakable that this section displays a particular closeness to Mark 3.7-19. With this, of course, the actual questions begin in the first place, for Luke has not only reversed the sequence of the Markan text—unlike in Mark, the installation of the circle of the twelve (vv. 13-16 par. Mark 3.13-19) precedes the pressing of the crowd and the healing summary (vv. 17-19 par. Mark 3.7-8)—but there are also unmistakable agreements between this section and Matthew. The most noteworthy is certainly the fact that the Sermon on the Mount in Matthew evidently stands in the same context as the Sermon on the Plain in Luke, namely after the note, corresponding to Mark 3.7-8, about the inflow of many people from very different cities and regions (Matthew 4.25 par. Luke 6.17). Both also report summarily of healings. Luke 6.18-19 displays only a very punctiliar overlap with the corresponding note in Mark 3.10-11 ("touch" and "unclean spirits"), while Matthew 4.24b-c strongly agrees with Mark 1.34. The latter is again quite interesting, for it should be called to mind—and with this the illusion of a simple solution finally falls away—that Luke has placed the note about the subjection of the unclean spirits from Mark 3.11-12 in Luke 4.41, i.e., in the Lukan counterpart to Mark 1.34. Correspondingly, he omits it here, while Matthew shortens it and brings it into 12.16 with a changed addressee. All this indicates that the tradition circumstances at this point are much too complex to be explained through the assumption of a common Matthew–Luke dependence on the Gospel of Mark that we have (or even on a Deutero-Mark). The assumption that another tradition stands in the background here is more than only possible, and that would then probably be Q. That Jesus's request to have a boat ready (Mark 3.9) is lacking in Matthew and Luke cannot, of course, be invoked as an indication for this, for the omissions can be explained as redactional changes that were made independently of each other. In Matthew and Luke, the scene does not take place on the water, and therefore a boat is of no use to them. In the healing summary Matthew and Luke agree against Mark that Jesus healed not only "many" (Mark 1.34; 3.10) but "all" sick people or "sicknesses" (v. 19c par. 4.24).

One can discuss whether vv. 13-18 are designed as a single sentence or whether they must be divided into two sentences, namely into vv. 13-16 and vv. 17-18a (cf. Beutler 1991). In the first case, the two participles ἐκλεξάμενος (v. 13b) and καταβάς (v. 17a) would be related to the main verb ἔστη (v. 17a). In the latter case, the sentence beginning in v. 13b would be an anacoluthon, for the participle ἐκλεξάμενος is not followed by a main clause with a *verbum finitum*. This solution is clearly to be preferred on the basis of the thematic complexity of the sentence structure that would emerge otherwise, in which the selection of the twelve represents only a subordinated action.

In Matthew there is no narrative about the choosing of the twelve. In 10.1-4 he mentions merely their names, and there are also some minor agreements here: ὅν ... ὠνόμασεν Πέτρον or ὁ λεγόμενος Πέτρος (v. 14 par. Matthew 10.2) instead of ἐπέθηκεν ὄνομα τῷ Σίμωνι Πέτρον (Mark 3.16); the placement of Andrew in the second position (v. 14 par. Matthew 10.2); his identification as ἀδελφὸς αὐτοῦ (sc. Simon's; v. 14 par. Matthew 10.2) is lacking in Mark 3.18; cf. Schramm 1971, 113–14; Neirynck 1974b, 79–82; 1991, 27–28; Ennulat 1994, 93–107.

12 The linguistic form of the introduction corresponds to that of v. 1 (see there for more details). The temporal specification with the anaphoric ταύταις connects what follows closely with what precedes (cf. further at 1.39). By having Jesus spend the whole night in prayer to God, Luke announces that an event that is important to Jesus is nevertheless approaching. In Luke, important events repeatedly happen during or after a prayer of Jesus (cf. 3.21-22 with further references; 9.18-19, 28-29; 11.1; 22.41, 44, 46), where the significance of the following event is announced by the extraordinary duration of the prayer. It is usually assumed that the prayer of Jesus is related to the selection of the twelve that follows from v. 13 on (e.g., Plummer; Dietrich 1972, 86; Crump 1992a, 145; Radl), and that is probably also the case, for according to Acts 1.23-24, there is, analogously, prayer before the election of Matthias into the circle of apostles. An attributive objective genitive with προσευχή is not attested elsewhere (but cf. as analogical form εὐχαριστία θεοῦ or the like: SIG³ 798; Wisdom of Solomon 16.28), but here τοῦ θεοῦ clearly stands in for the objective dative, which is occasionally found with προσεύχεσθαι (τῷ θεῷ or the like: e.g., Diodorus Siculus 13.16.7; Testament of Joseph 3.3; Testament of Benjamin 1.4; Josephus, *Antiquitates judaicae* 10.252; *SGUÄ* 3740 [first century CE]; Matthew 6.6; 1 Corinthians 11.13). Luke has taken over the mountain as a place of prayer from Mark 3.13. It may be regarded as certain that he wanted special theological connotations to be associated with it (cf. Radl I: 355: "As already in the Old Testament . . . the place of encounter with God"). After all, Jesus also goes to pray on a mountain in 9.28-29 (transfiguration) and 22.39-42 (relocation of the Gethsemane scene to the Mount of Olives!).

13 Luke describes the course of the emergence of the circle of the twelve in dependence on Mark 3.13-14, but he interprets this event not as installation into a task (for the Markan ἐποίησεν, cf. 1 Samuel 12.6; 1 Kings 12.31, 33; 2 Chronicles 2.17), for Luke has omitted the two telic clauses that describe the function of the twelve in Mark 3.14. Therefore, one should not speak of a "calling" (so, among others, G. Klein 1961, 203; Dietrich 1972, 83; and elsewhere; Radl). Luke describes the event merely as a selection of a narrower circle from a greater group, for which he makes recourse to the theologically not entirely insignificant verb ἐκλέγεσθαι (cf. also John 6.70). Luke can use this verb to designate both the election of the fathers (Acts 13.17) and the naming of deliverers of letters (Acts 15.22, 25); thus, one probably needs to be reserved in relation to an exclusively election-theological interpretation. The apostles are distinguished from the disciples by the fact that only they are furnished with a specific distinguishing mark—namely, with the designation (one could almost speak already of a "title") "apostle." We are dealing here with a substantivized verbal adjective (derived from ἀποστέλλειν) that identifies a person (or more people) functionally as a sent one (or sent ones; e.g., Herodotus 1.21; 1 Kings 14.6^{LXX}; Josephus, *Antiquitates judaicae* 17.300; cf. further J.-A. Bühner, *EWNT* 1: 342ff; Lohmeyer 1995, 133ff; Spicq 1994, I: 186ff). This term became a title only in the post-Easter period. The "apostles" of primitive Christianity knew themselves to be sent by the Risen One to proclaim the gospel (cf. e.g., Romans 1.1-5; Galatians 1.1). Within the narrated world of the Gospel of Luke, they receive a commission that corresponds to their designation in the first place in 9.2. In addition to the naming, the identification of the apostles with the members of the circle of the twelve is also a subsequent theological construction. It has the purpose of integrating the circle of the twelve, which had already lost its significance a few years after Easter, into the continuity of the early Christian apostles and to strengthen its value in this way (cf. also Haacker 1988, 10).

14-16 In addition to this listing, there are three more lists with the names of the twelve in the New Testament—namely, in Mark 3.16-19, Matthew 10.2-4, and Acts 1.13. None of these lists completely agrees with another, not even the two Lukan ones. But all three lists in the Gospels have in common that they name Peter in the first position and Judas Iscariot in the last, thus clearly making a valuation from a post-Easter perspective (in Acts 1.13 Judas is lacking for well-known reasons).

In v. 14a Luke makes a noteworthy accentuation. Just as the twelve are distinguished from the other disciples by the fact that Jesus gave the designation "apostle" *only to them* (οὓς καὶ ἀποστόλους ὠνόμασεν), so Simon is lifted out from the circle of the twelve by the fact that Jesus gives the designation Πέτρος *only to him*, as Luke communicates with a phrasing that is almost identical in wording (ὃν καὶ ὠνόμασεν Π.). This expresses that the same "selective principle" is active both here and there (Dietrich 1972, 93). In contrast to the function of a byname, which merely assigns a certain characteristic to a person (often also only to distinguish them from other bearers of the same name), the designation takes place here in both cases with regard to a *titular* unique position. Simon is not merely *called* "rock"; rather, this is what he *is*. Historically this designation arose either

from the translation of the Aramaic word כֵּיפָא ("stone, rock") or from
its Greek transcription Κηφᾶς (cf. John 1.42), and it probably originally
functioned merely as an individualizing byname. This name was brought
into connection with the special position of Simon within the primitive
community only after Easter, and an aftereffect of this correlation is found
here (cf. also Matthew 16.18; see Böttrich 2001, 42ff).

"Thomas" is also not the personal name of someone but the Graecising of Aramaic תְּאוֹמָא ("twin," Greek δίδυμος; cf. John 11.16; 14.5D pc; 20.24; 21.2; Gospel of Thomas 1; Dalman 1989, 145n6a; see also Ilan 2002, 416). His real name is
Judas (cf. Acts of Thomas 1; 11; Book of Thomas [NHC II 7] title; and elsewhere;
Gospel of Thomas [NHC II 2] 1 [title]; John 14.22syr[s.][c] [instead of "Judas, not
the Iscariot" it has "Thomas"]). As in the case of Simon Cephas (see above), this
designation most probably had a historical basis, especially insofar as there are
two more bearers of the name Judas in the circle of the twelve. As a personal
name, Thomas was not yet common in New Testament times anyway.

It must, of course, remain open whose twin this Judas was. The designation
of a person with such an epithet without specifying further the distinguishing
characteristic through an attribute (thus "twin of so-and-so") makes it probable
that the other twin was not only known in the circle of those who gave Judas this
byname but also played a prominent role. Otherwise Judas would not have been
one-sidedly identified by the relation to his twin brother (see also Harris 1927, 45:
"the less is defined with reference to the greater"). Acts of Thomas 31, 39 (Lip-
sius/Bonnet 1959, II/2: 148.9; 156.12) and Book of Thomas 138.9 designate him
as Jesus's twin brother, and it is, in fact, not ruled out that this is also correct (cf.
also and partly with skepticism in relation to this assumption Klijn 1970; Gunther
1980; Bauckham 1990, 32–36).

Apart from the differences in the sequence of the names and in the configuration (after Philip, who always stands in the fifth position, Matthew 10.2-
4; Acts 1.13 order by pairs), the lists differ in the fact that the two Lukan
versions lack Thaddeus and in his stead have "Judas, (the son) of James"
(v. 16). A plausible explanation for this deviation does not yet exist. Since
the time of the ancient church, the problem has repeatedly been solved by
regarding "Judas" and "Thaddeus" as two names for the same person (cf.
now also Plummer; Schürmann; Nolland; and others). But this is probably
a somewhat too easy harmonization. There is no real difference in the case
of the deviation with Simon, who is called ὁ Καναναῖος in Mark 3.18 par.
Matthew 10.4, while Luke calls him ζηλωτής in Luke 6.15 and Acts 1.13,
for the former is the transcription and the latter the translation of Aramaic

קַנְאָנָא (on this cf. also Mézange 2000). Judas Iscariot is designated as "traitor" (προδότης) only in Luke 6.15; elsewhere it always only says that Judas "handed over" (παραδιδόναι) Jesus.

The meaning of the byname Ἰσκαριώθ, which Judas has in all four lists, is still controversial. Only two possibilities seriously come into consideration (cf. further with older literature M. Limbeck, *EWNT* 2: 491–92; Klauck 1987, 40ff; Schwarz 1991; Klassen 1996, 32ff): *(a)* Judas is identified by his place of origin as "man from Kerioth" (Aramaic אִישׁ קְרִיֹּת; cf. Joshua 15.25; Jeremiah 48.24, 41; Amos 2.2) (see also John 6.71; 13.2, 26). *(b)* The designation is based on Hebrew שֶׁקֶר ("lie") and means "*the* liar, *the* false one" (M. Limbeck, *EWNT* 2: 492). In John 6.71 Judas's father, Simon, is given the same byname, and this makes it very likely that it designates the place of origin in the sense of the first possibility mentioned.

17-18a The listing of the groups who come together at the foot of the mountain gives rise to the image of concentric circles that gather around Jesus: the *apostles*, a great crowd of his *disciples*, and many persons from the *people*, which Luke refers to here, certainly not without reason, with the theologically loaded term λαός (see at 1.10), thus supplementing the phrasing that is otherwise taken over from Mark 3.7. With the geographical differentiation of the "great multitude of the people" (cf. also 23.27) the story also broadens narratively and obtains through this a rhetorical intensity (cf. Lausberg 1949, §665ff). If Mark 3.7-8 was the *Vorlage*, Luke has shortened the geographical information by removing "Galilee," "Idumea," and "from beyond the Jordan"—possibly because he saw these regions as covered by "Judea" (cf. at 1.5). With the naming "of the coastal regions of Tyre and Sidon" he is most certainly not thinking of Gentiles (so Fitzmyer; Radl; rightly opposed by Bovon; Nolland), for he identifies also the people who come from there as part of the λαός. The relative pronouns at the beginning of v. 18a refer to πλῆθος πολὺ τοῦ λαοῦ (the plural is *constructio ad sensum*; cf. BDR §134.1). The description of the intention that causes people to stream to Jesus calls to mind 4.40 and 5.1, 15; now, however, everything takes place in a much greater dimension. The same also applies for the summary that follows.

18b-19 In v. 18b ἀπὸ πνευμάτων ἀκαθάρτων should be related to οἱ ἐνοχλούμενοι and not to ἐθεραπεύοντο (cf. also Acts 5.16) because the verbal phrase would otherwise not be congruent with the subject (here ἀπό stands for ὑπό, as also in Matthew 11.19; 16.21 par. Luke 9.22; Acts 15.4; and elsewhere; cf. BDR §210.2). A clearly recognizable line of constant expansion of Jesus's activity in Israel runs from the first exorcism and healing in Capernaum (4.33-36, 38-39) via the same deeds of power toward many other persons in the same town (4.40-41) up to what Luke now reports of Jesus, and it reaches an initial high point here. The background of the note that all the people want to touch him because a healing power proceeds from him is the dynamistic worldview of antiquity, according to which objects and persons could be loaded with "power" (δύναμις) that can have the potential to harm but also to heal and that is transferred through touch (cf. 8.44 and 5.17; 18.15; Mark 6.56 par. Matthew 14.36; Acts 19.12; Theissen 1987, 71 with other examples; for the general background, cf. W. Grundmann, ThWNT 2: 288ff; Nilsson 1950, 534ff; see also at 10.13).

Luke abruptly ends this turbulent scene by having Jesus turn to his disciples.

6.20-49: The Speech of Jesus

In this speech the Lukan Jesus speaks for the first time not about himself and his commission but turns to the people around him, namely to his disciples (v. 20a) and the many others about whom Luke had already often reported that they had come to "hear" (v. 27a with 5.1, 15; 6.18). Correspondingly, the speech can be divided into two main parts. Verses 20b-26 apply, first, only to the disciples. In 27a the circle of the addressed people is then expanded for vv. 27b-49 *expressis verbis* to all those present.

This division also corresponds to the form-critical evidence. Verses 20b-26 are composed respectively of a series of beatitudes (vv. 20b-23) and woes (vv. 24-26) that are antithetically set over against each other. From a rhetorical perspective these verses would have to be assigned to the *genus demonstrativum* (for this rhetorical genre, cf. Lausberg 1973, §224ff). In vv. 27b-49, by contrast, we are dealing with a paraenetic speech that wants to move the hearers to a certain behavior and should therefore be assigned to the rhetorical *genus deliberativum* (cf. Lausberg 1973, §224ff). With the help of the structuring signal in v. 39a we can divide this speech into two parts. Verses 27-38 exhort to an action that is not oriented to the friendship-ethical principle of reciprocity, and as the heading in v. 39 shows, Luke has designed vv. 39-49 as a series of parabolic sayings that are without thematic coherence. In this series vv. 46-49 function as a generalizing conclusion to the whole λόγος παραινετικός ("admonition speech"). This conclusion takes up the key word ἀκούειν from the introduction in v. 27a and in this way places a frame around this part of the speech.

The speech of Jesus displays extensive overlaps with the Sermon on the Mount in Matthew 5–7. The findings are represented in detail as follows:

20b-c:	Matt 5.3	29b:	Matt 5.40	37a:	Matt 7.1	44b:	Matt 7.16b
21a-b:	Matt 5.6	30:	Matt 5.42	38c:	Matt 7.2	46a:	Matt 7.21a
22a-c:	Matt 5.11	31:	Matt 7.12	41:	Matt 7.3	47a:	Matt 7.24a
23:	Matt 5.12	32:	Matt 5.46	42a-c:	Matt 7.4	48a-b:	Matt 24b-c
27a-b:	Matt 5.44a-b	35c-d:	Matt 5.45	42d-e:	Matt 7.5	48c-d:	Matt 7.25
28b:	Matt 5.44b	36:	Matt 5.48	43:	Matt 7.17, 18	49:	Matt 7.26-27
29a:	Matt 5.39b						

Beyond this, there are also the following parallels with other texts of the Synoptic Gospels:

—only with Matt:	39b-c:	Matt 15.14	43:	Matt 12.33a, b	45a-b:	Matt 12.35
	40a:	Matt 10.24a	44a:	Matt 12.33c	45c:	Matt 12.34b
	40b:	Matt 10.25a				
—also with Mark:	38c:	Mark 4.24c par. Matt 7.2b				

Accordingly, the following verses are without a parallel in Matthew or Mark:

21c-d	27c	33a, b	35a-b	38a-b	46b
24-26	28a	34	37b-c	(39)	47b

There are parallels in the Gospel of Thomas to the following verses:

20b-c:	Gos. Thom. 54	34a, 35b:	Gos. Thom. 95	42d-e:	Gos. Thom. 26.2
21a-b:	Gos. Thom. 69.2	39b-c:	Gos. Thom. 34	44b:	Gos. Thom. 45.1
22a-b:	Gos. Thom. 68.1	41a-b:	Gos. Thom. 26.1	45a-c:	Gos. Thom. 45.2–4

The extensive agreements with the Sermon on the Mount, especially in the order of the instructions (only the Golden Rule [Luke 6.31] is located in a different place [7.21], and Luke 6.35b-c is found a few verses further ahead [Matthew 5.45]), can be best explained through the assumption of a *written* source that both gospels had in at least similar form. An explanation of the relationship of the Sermon on the Plain to the Sermon on the Mount in the framework of the Q-hypothesis still finds the most advocates. According to this view, the two speeches are based on a speech of Jesus handed down in Q, whose *extent* is identified in the main with the Lukan version of the speech of Jesus.

However, there is a need for explanation with regard to the numerous and sometimes clear differences in the *wording* of the Matthew–Luke double traditions. The spectrum of the attempted solutions reaches from relatively simple proposals (such as, e.g., those of the *CEQ* of the IQP, according to which, in the case of deviations, one of the two versions always reproduces the Q-wording and the other is correspondingly redactional in each case) via the assumption that the two evangelists had different Q-recensions, thus Q^{Lk} and Q^{Mt} (e.g., G. Strecker 1984,

9ff), down to more artificial explanations such as that of Bergemann 1993, 236 (the two speeches rest on one *Grundrede* [basic speech] that existed in different versions and "was never part of the sayings source") and that of H. D. Betz 1992; 1995 (the two speeches were originally independent summaries of the proclamation of Jesus that then found entrance into Q^{Lk} or Q^{Mt}). In light of the methodological problems associated with the reconstruction of non-preserved texts, it is advisable with regard to the question of the relation of the two speeches to work with a model that is as open as possible. With reference to *wording* the deviations in the double traditions could thus have multiple causes, without it being possible in many cases to say which. The following are possible: redactional change or addition to the Q-*Vorlage* by Matthew and/or Luke, different Q-recensions, influence of oral tradition alongside Q. The wording of Q is accessible with relative (!) certainty only where Luke and Matthew do not deviate from each other ("relative" because in the Q-material we must, of course, also reckon with Matthew–Luke agreements against the *Vorlage*, as with minor agreements in the triple tradition). With regard to the *extent* we do not know much more. It is at any rate unlikely that Q-material is present only where there is a parallel in the Lukan Sermon on the Plain to the Matthean Sermon on the Mount. It could be the case (but need not be) that material from the Q-speech has also been preserved in the so-called Matthean or Lukan *Sondergut* (for this issue, see the section on sources in the introduction to this commentary). Therefore, the only thing that can perhaps be said in this respect with some probability is that the extent of the speech of Jesus in Q comes closer to the extent of the Lukan Sermon on the Plain than the extent of the Matthean Sermon on the Mount.

6.20-26: Beatitudes and Woes

²⁰**And he lifted his eyes to his disciples and said:**
   "Blessed (are) **the poor,**
   for to you belongs the kingdom of God!
²¹**Blessed** (are) **those who hunger now,**
   for you will be satiated!
   Blessed (are) **those who now weep,**
   for you will laugh!
²²**Blessed are you when people hate you and when they exclude you and revile you and put about your name as something evil on account of the Son of Man.** ²³**Rejoice on that day and dance, for behold, your reward** (is) **great in heaven. For their fathers treated the prophets in the same way.**
²⁴**But woe to you, the rich ones,**
   for you have (already) **received your comfort.**
²⁵**Woe to you who are now well-fed,**
   for you will hunger.

Woe to you who laugh now,
for you will mourn and weep.
[26]**Woe, when all people speak well of you; for their fathers treated**
the false prophets in the same way."

Luke has carefully coordinated the two series of macarisms and woes (4×
μακάριοι and οὐαί, respectively) formally and semantically in relation to
each other. The introduction of the narrator in v. 20a and the structuring
signal that he has Jesus give in v. 27a make certain that this part of the
Sermon on the Plain is concerned with the disciples. They are directly
addressed in the macarisms, and the rich, who function as fictive addressees of the woes, are conceived as their counterimage. A comparable opposition of beatitudes and woes is not attested elsewhere within or outside
the New Testament.

The first three macarisms and woes are first recognizable as self-
enclosed units, for a front-placed clause is grounded in each case by a
trailing clause in the future—introduced by ὅτι—that announces the future
reversal of the present fate. As here, in vv. 20b-21 "the poor" function as
the principal term that is then further specified as "those who hunger" and
"those who weep." In vv. 24-25 Luke specifies "the rich" as "those who are
well-fed" and "those who are laughing." The future reversal of their present situation is announced to both groups. (The narrative of the rich man
and Lazarus in Luke 16.19-31 looks like an individualizing illustration of
this opposition of beatitudes and woes.) There follows then a fourth macarism (vv. 22, 23c) and a woe (v. 26) that provide a description—introduced
with ὅταν—of the opposite fates that will be bestowed upon "the people"
(οἱ ἄνθρωποι), the "disciples," and the "the rich" at the present time. The
explanation that is pronounced only with regard to the disciples in v. 23ab
consists in the fact that this experience too will be reversed in the future.

The first three Lukan beatitudes differ from those in Matthew 5.3-10
especially *(a)* through the use of the second person (Matthew consistently
uses the third person), *(b)* through their number (Matthew has eight, Luke
has only three), *(c)* through the description of objective hardships in the
front-placed clause (with the exception of 5.4 Matthew always formulates
ethical rules), *(d)* through a νῦν in the front-placed clauses—formulated
in the present—of the second and third beatitude, which is lacking in Matthew, and *(e)* through the woes, which do not exist in Matthew.

The question of which version may have stood in Q cannot be decided
with respect to the first difference mentioned (cf. the compilation of the
opinions in Hieke 2001, 141ff). With great to very great probability it is
to be answered in favor of the Lukan version with respect to the second
and third *(b–c)* and in favor of the Matthean version for the last two *(d–e)*.

20 By means of the introduction, Luke makes sure that his readers relate what follows to the disciples (ἐπαίρειν τοὺς ὀφθαλμοὺς εἰς is a Septuagintism; cf. Genesis 13.10; 2 Samuel 18.24; 1 Chronicles 21.16; Ezekiel 18.6; but see also Chariton of Aphrodisias 1.4.7; it also occurs at the beginning of a speech in Luke 18.13; John 17.1). When Jesus designates the disciples as πτωχοί and promises them the salvation of the rule of God, he puts into practice within the Lukan narrative what he had formulated in 4.18 with recourse to Isaiah 61.1 as his sending commission—namely, εὐαγγελίσασθαι πτωχοῖς. If one asks about how the disciples are identifiable as a group of πτωχοί, one will be able to point to the fact that upon entering into the discipleship of Jesus they "left everything" (cf. 5.11, 28; see then also 18.28-29 and 14.26).

The term πτωχός designates above all the so-called begging poor. In this sense it says in Aristophanes, *Plutus* 551–52 that the πτωχός "has nothing," while the πένης must save and work. Cf. also Marcus Aurelius 4.29.2: "A πτωχός is one who needs another and does not himself possess everything that is necessary to live"; see also Kloft 1988: "The one who cannot satisfy by himself the three human basic needs, namely shelter, i.e., a home, food, and clothing, but rather is dependent upon the help of others is regarded as ptochós in the strict sense" (see further: Hands 1968, 62ff; Prell 1997, 48–49).

It was the semantic characteristic of dependence upon help from others that made it possible to load the term πτωχός with a theological connotation, for in this meaning it came into contact with the meaning of the Hebrew terms דַּל and עָנִי (עָנָו) (cf. D. Michel, *TRE* 4: 72–76; J. Maier, *TRE* 4: 80–83). In this way the term became suitable for designating those for whom in their objectively existing situation of hardship only the help of God remains (e.g., Psalm 9.10; 12.6; 22.25; applied to Israel, e.g., Isaiah 41.17; 49.13; 61.1; Zephaniah 3.12).

The beatitude of the poor probably also had the connection mentioned last in the mouth of the historical Jesus. The term could therefore also be given a positive meaning, for the persons designated by it articulated with its help their religious self-understanding. They called themselves "poor" and expressed in this way that they expected everything from God; "poor" meant as much as "pious" (Psalm 9.19; 25.9; 34.3; Psalms of Solomon 10.6; often in the Qumran texts: 1QH XIII, 22; 1QM XI, 9, 13). When the beatitude of the poor says to them that God will change their present fate of unsalvation into salvation, it is therefore not as paradoxical as is repeatedly claimed (e.g., by Mineshige 2003, 18). In the sense of the tradition sketched above, "the poor" are always those who may be certain of the salvific turning of God to them, for the conviction that God receives precisely the "poor" is a fixed component of the early Jewish image of God (e.g., Psalm 113.7-8; Psalms of Solomon 5.2, 11; 15.1). It is probable that both aspects play a role for the picture of the disciples that Luke sets forth here. The disciples are poor in economic terms, and they are poor with reference to their relation to God. They have left *everything*, and they have expressed in this way that they expect *everything* only from God.

This complex obtains its theologically distinctive profile, however, by the fact that it has a christological center. The disciples have become all this only because they have turned to *Jesus* and followed *him*. In this vein the exhortation to the rich ἄρχων in 18.12 also shows that the Lukan poverty theology is based on Christology.

The dialectic of "already now" and "not yet" dwells in the promise in v. 20c. The certainty of having a share in salvation exists already in the present. The transformation into real events is still outstanding; the future statements in v. 21b-d refer to the transformation (for this dialectic, see also Tobit 8.21א: with the words ὑμέτερόν ἐστιν an inheritance is already bindingly promised now, but it will be fulfilled only in the future). In this sense, James 2.5, where the "poor" are designated as "heirs of the kingdom" (κληρονόμοι τῆς βασιλείας), stands right in the middle between Luke 6.20 and Tobit 8.21א. This certainty, of course, does not give the present the signature of the absence of the future; rather, it is nothing other than the mode of the presence of the eschatic salvation in the midst of the unsalvation of the world.

21 describes the concretization of the promise of v. 20. "Hungering" (v. 21a) and "weeping" (v. 21c) in the front-placed clauses of the two following beatitudes are invoked as typical consequences and accompanying phenomena of unsalvation and hardship (cf., on the one hand, L. Goppelt, ThWNT 6: 14ff; W. Bauder/W.Grimm, *ThBNT*[2] 1: 426–27 and, on the other hand, K.-H. Rengstorff, ThWNT 3: 722–23; J. Frey, *ThBNT*[2] 1: 532–33). The salvation of the reign of God will be accompanied by the transformation of the present situation of unsalvation of the disciples into its opposite (the tradition of the eschatic banquet is not invoked here). This element is foreign to the eschatological beatitudes of the Jewish tradition, for there we always have a continuity between present and future. Luke (and before him probably also already Jesus) make recourse here to another tradition and combine it with the form of the beatitude, namely the expectation of the eschatic reversal of the present fate of unsalvation into salvation (cf. e.g., Testament of Judah 25.4 with clear proximity to the Lukan beatitudes: "And those who die in mourning will rise in joy, and those who are poor for the sake of the Lord will become rich").

22-23 The fourth beatitude differs from the first three in multiple respects. The predicate in the front-placed clause is not a nominal sentence, and instead of the explanatory (ὅτι) promise of salvation in the trailing clause (vv. 20c, 21b, d), two temporal clauses occur here (ὅταν) that portray the situation of unsalvation of those praised as blessed. Semantically the trailing clauses do not go beyond what is said in the front-placed clauses of the first three beatitudes. They describe the present fate of unsalvation of those to whom the beatitude applies. The beatitude itself does not go as far as a promise of salvation (this happens frequently, however: e.g., Psalm 40.5; Wisdom of Solomon 3.13; Sirach 28.19). It is added only in v. 23b, without being syntactically connected with the beatitude; however, with the help of the anaphoric κατὰ τὰ αὐτά in 23c it is tied back to it text-semantically.

22 I have not found elsewhere a macarism that is continued with a temporal clause (ὅταν or the like) in the trailing clause. The disciples' fate of suffering is described here as an everyday experience of rejection, social exclusion, and discrimination. These are the typical reactions that a marginalized minority experiences from the majority society.

The first temporal clause (v. 22b) is probably a heading of sorts that is then concretized in what follows via diaeresis. The rejection that the group of Jesus adherents experiences in its environment is also interpreted as "hating" (μισεῖν) in Mark 13.13parr.; Matthew 10.22; John 15.18-19; 17.14; 1 John 3.13. It corresponds to this that hate is encountered in the Psalms as a topos in the description of the enemy of the one praying (cf. Psalm 25.19; 34.22; 35.19; 38.20; 41.8; and elsewhere; cf. Ruppert 1973, 111ff). From among the verbs that concretize this rejection in v. 22c (they also occur in the description of the enemies of the suffering righteous; cf. Ruppert 1973, 111ff), ὀνειδίζειν has a conspicuous parallel in 1 Peter 4.14a: "When you are insulted in the name of Christ—(you are) blessed!" The two other terms are probably also taken from this same context. With ἀφορίζειν Luke certainly does not mean the temporally limited synagogue ban nor, specifically, the exclusion from the synagogue (cf. Schürmann; Wiefel), nor the twelfth Benediction of the Eighteen Benedictions, the *Bir-kat ha-Minim* (on this see Horbury 1998, 67ff; Kellermann 2007, 132ff), but very generally the experience of social exclusion and isolation of Christians from the beginnings into the Lukan present (see also Hoffmann 1995, 183). The last two actions mentioned are certainly included in this. Luke probably formulates in such an open manner so that his contemporaries can also find their own experiences here. An interesting parallel is Isaiah 66.5 where the Hebrew and Greek texts admittedly deviate strongly from each other. In the Hebrew text it reads, "Your brothers speak, who hate you and cast you out (שֹׂנְאֵיכֶם מְנַדֵּיכֶם) for my name's sake"; LXX: "Speak, our brothers, to those who hate and abominate us (μισοῦσιν ἡμᾶς καὶ βδελυσσομένοις) so that the name of the Lord may be glorified" (for the connection with our passage, cf. Horbury 1998, 53). That Luke has specific events in his time in mind (so Stegemann 1991b, esp. 133–34) is an unjustified reduction (cf. also the criticism in Hoffmann 1995, 170, 185ff).

It cannot be completely clarified what the third action involves. There is only a very distant parallel in Deuteronomy 22.14, 19 ("to bring against her an evil name [19: against an Israelite virgin]"; LXX: καταφέρειν αὐτῆς [19: ἐπὶ παρθένον Ἰσραελῖτιν] ὄνομα πονηρόν). Here, however, the concern is not that *persons* are made bad but rather a *name* that is a group designation. Therefore, τὸ ὄνομα ὑμῶν stands with great certainty for the *nomen Christianum* (cf. Acts 11.26 and above all 1 Peter 4.14: "reviled ἐν ὀνόματι Χριστοῦ"; see also 1 Peter 4.16 and Hoffmann 1995, 179); an example for what is meant here could be Suetonius, *Nero* 16.2, where it is explained to the readers what *Christiani* are: a *genus hominum superstitionis novae ac maleficae* ("a kind of people of a new and harmful superstition").

The concluding reference to the Son of Man as the one for whose sake the disciples experience this fate comes into contact with statements such as Mark 8.35parr. (to lose one's life ἕνεκεν ἐμοῦ); 13.9parr. (to be brought before rulers and kings ἕνεκεν ἐμοῦ; Luke 21.12: ἕνεκεν τοῦ ὀνόματός μου); cf. also John 15.21; Acts 5.41; 9.16; 15.26; 21.13; and elsewhere. This explanation of experiences of suffering has a prehistory in the literature of early Judaism where such statements are found in the context of the suffering righteous; cf. Psalm 44.23; 69.8; 4 Maccabees 9.8; 16.19, 25 (other texts and literature in M. Wolter, *TRE* 20: 679).

23 ἐν ἐκείνῃ τῇ ἡμέρᾳ is anaphoric and refers to the temporal ὅταν in v. 22b, c (see also Mark 2.20 [with reference to ὅταν]; Acts 2.41; 8.1; contrast Luke 10.12; 17.31 and BDR §291.1: the day of retribution). In tradition-historical perspective Luke takes up here the motif of joy in suffering (cf. Jeremiah 31.13; Tobit 13.16BA; Testament of Judah 25.4; Josephus, *Bellum judaicum* 1.653; 1 Enoch 103.3; 4 Ezra 7.96; in the New Testament: 1 Peter 1.6; see also W. Nauck 1955; Ruppert 1973, 176ff). As in the aforementioned texts, here too the eschatic salvation, which is given to the pious and righteous who also stand firm in suffering, is the basis and object of joy (for σκιρτᾶν as an expression of the jubilation of the saved, cf. Wisdom of Solomon 19.9; Malachi 3.20; see also Philo, *De plantatione* 38: paradise as a symbol of the soul ὑπὸ πλήθους καὶ μεγέθους χαρᾶς ἀνασκιρτώσης ["which leaps up on account of the abundance and greatness of joy"]; Josephus, *Bellum judaicum* 5.120).

Elsewhere the metaphorical use of μισθός often designates the salvation or unsalvation that God allows to result from the corresponding deeds of the humans (e.g., 2 Maccabees 8.33; Wisdom of Solomon 5.15; Sirach 2.8; 1 Corinthians 3.18; 2 Peter 2.13). The semantic connotation of the metaphor consists in accentuating the equivalence of deed and consequence and thereby in underlining the justness of the retributive action of

God (cf. also the overview in Spicq 1994, II: 502–15). The talk of eschatic reward is not related here, in contrast to what we find elsewhere, to a specific behavior but formulates an unconditional promise of salvation. Thus, the pragmatic of this statement is not aimed at inculcating a specific action but seeks to mediate comfort and assurance. A sideways glance at the corresponding woe in v. 26 shows that the summons to joy in suffering and its rationale (v. 23a-b) has no correspondence there.

Verse 23c refers back to the deed of the persons described in v. 22 (the unspecific ποιεῖν should encompass all four verbs of v. 22b-c). Despite this, it remains unclear what this sentence is meant to establish; the conjunction γάρ somehow comes to nothing. Luke takes up here the tradition of the violent fate of the prophets (cf. 1 Kings 19.10, 14; 2 Chronicles 36.15-16; Nehemiah 9.26; Jeremiah 2.30; in the New Testament also Luke 11.47-51 par. Matthew 23.29-36; Luke 13.34 par. Matthew 23.37; Mark 12.5 par. Matthew 21.35; Acts 7.52; Romans 11.3; 1 Thessalonians 2.15; see Steck 1967, 60ff; Weihs 2003, 15ff). However, unlike Mark 5.12c, he emphasizes not the continuity of the *victim*, but the continuity of the *perpetrator*. Luke sets this accent with the help of the phrasing οἱ πατέρες αὐτῶν, which refers back to οἱ ἄνθρωποι (v. 22b). In a rather analogous way he has Stephen in Acts 7.51-52 place what the Jews of *Jerusalem* (sic!; Acts 2.23; 3.15; 4.10; 5.30 with 10.39; 13.27 as well as at 13.33) had enforced against Jesus in continuity with the murdering of the prophets by "your fathers" (see also Luke 11.47-48). It is often inferred that this back reference results in an identification of οἱ ἄνθωποι in v. 22b as Jews and that thus the action described in v. 22b-c would also be directed "from the Jewish side" against the Christians (cf. Schürmann; Nolland; Radl; Stegemann 1991b, 118; Hoffmann 1995, 185 speaks of a "Jewish atmosphere"). But there is no basis for such a reduction, for the semantic specification of the relation runs over the doing and not over a genealogical connection that would exist independently of it (Luke has Jesus speak precisely not of "our" or "your" fathers). The ones who once treated the prophets in the way in which "people" now treat the disciples become their "fathers" precisely through that action. Correspondingly, the iterative imperfect ἐποίουν has the function of characterizing the fathers and making them into a model for "people."

24-26 A tradition-historical connection point for the four woes are the woes of the prophetic announcements of judgment (e.g., Isaiah 1.4; Jeremiah 13.27; 27[50].27; Hosea 7.13; Amos 6.1; Habakkuk 2.6; 2.12; 2.19; but see then also Ecclesiastes 10.16; Sirach 41.8; Judith 16.17; Sibylline Oracles 3.303, 319, 323, 480, 492, 504, 508, 512; Revelation 9.12; 11.14; 18.10, 16, 19; cf. Westermann 1971, 137ff; Gerstenberger 1962). We are dealing with an anticipated lament. Like the macarisms, they tend to form series (cf. Isaiah 5.8-23; Habbakuk 2.6-19; Sirach 2.12-14; 1 Enoch 94.6–8; 95.4–7; 96.4–8; 98.9–99.2; 99.1–15; Matthew 23.13ff, 23ff; Luke 11.42-44, 46-47, 52). Apart from the last attestations mentioned, additional woes occur in Luke–Acts only in Luke 17.1; 21.23; 22.22; they are found only in the mouth of Jesus and are correspondingly lacking in Acts.

24 The woe against the rich is justified with reference to their current fate. The rich man in 16.25b, who laments the conditions in Hades, also receives a similar answer (ἀπέλαβες τὰ ἀγαθά σου ἐν τῇ ζωῇ σου). ἀπέχειν is a metaphor that is taken from the same image field as μισθός in v. 23b (cf. P. Mich. 337.8; *BGU* 1647.13; Matthew 6.2, 5, 16; see also Spicq 1994, I: 162–68). It designates the receipt of money or goods and appears above all on receipts (P. Hibeh 97.5; P. Phil. 11.13; see also Philippians 4.18; other attestations in Spicq 1994, I: 163). It corresponds to this that ἀπέχειν excludes all other claims. This is now related here to the παράκλησις, with which the term πενθεῖν (v. 25) is contrasted (Genesis 37.35; Sirach 48.24; Isaiah 61.2; Jeremiah 16.7; Matthew 5.4). Further, we should note that this word can be used in manifold ways. It can designate not only the experience of the turning of God in situations of unsalvation (e.g., Testament of Joseph 1.6), but also the changing of unsalvation into salvation (cf. O. Schmitz/G. Stählin, ThWNT 5: 771–98, esp. 790.9ff). The best explanation of this text, however, is found in 16.25 (παρακαλεῖται vs. ὀδυνᾶσαι; see also already Psalm^LXX 93.19). Apparently, behind both texts stands the notion that "comfort" and "pain" are balanced before and after death and that, correspondingly, after death a balancing out takes place.

The two woes in **25** are partly formulated as terminologically exact reversals of the two beatitudes of v. 21. This scheme is modified at two points. In v. 25 it is—so literally—"the fully fed" (ἐμπεπλησμένοι) to whom "hungering" is announced (πεινάσετε). Luke thus establishes the same terminological opposition as in 1.53a (see also Proverbs 6.30; Isaiah 9.19; 58.10; Jeremiah 38.25^LXX; 4 Baruch 9.18). In v. 25b Luke supplements the opposition of "laughing" and "weeping" taken over from v. 21a with "mourning" (πενθεῖν) in the trailing clause. This, of course, probably points not to a knowledge of the second Matthean beatitude (5.4) and is probably due instead to the fact that "mourn and weep" is a stereotypical word combination (like "hunger and thirst" in Matthew 5.6; cf. Wrege 1968, 16): see Deuteronomy 34.8; 2 Samuel 19.2; 2 Ezra (Nehemiah) 1.4; 18.9; Sirach 7.34; Baruch 4.11, 23; Testament of Judah 25.5; Josephus, *Antiquitates judaicae* 7.40; Mark 16.10; James 4.9; Revelation 18.11, 15, 19. The poor shoemaker Micyllus also speaks of a reversal in the beyond in Lucian of Samosata, *Cataplus* 15Q (ἡμεῖς μὲν οἱ πένητες γελῶμεν, ἀνιῶνται δὲ καὶ οἰμώζουσιν οἱ πλούσιοι ["we the poor laugh, but the rich moan and wail"]).

26 is conceived as a counterpart to vv. 22-23, though v. 23a-b remain without a correspondence. This verse rules out the view that Jesus wanted the woes to be related to rich members of the community and designed them as "admonition or warning to well-off Christians" (Schottroff/Steggemann 1978, 128; see also Stenger 1986, 57). This assumption would require that that addressee would have to feel addressed by v. 22c and v. 26a *simultaneously*, but that is difficult to imagine. καλῶς εἴπωσιν is antithetically related to ὀνειδίσωσιν and ἐκβάλωσιν τὸ ὄνομα ὑμῶν ὡς πονηρόν; for the language, cf. Diogenes Laertius 2.35 about Socrates: when someone told him "So-and-so speaks badly about you (κακῶς ὁ δεινά σε λέγει)," he answered, "He never learned to speak well (καλῶς . . . λέγειν οὐκ ἔμαθε)."

The woes have two addressees—first, the disciples as narrated hearers of Jesus's speech, and, second, "the rich ones" as *fictive addressees*. We also have this same difference in many other woes (so e.g., in 1 Enoch 94.6–8; 95.4–7; 96.4–8; 98.9–99.2; 99.1–15; see also Judith 16.17; Sibylline Oracles 3.303, 319, 323, 480, 492, 504, 508, 512; 4.143). They are always directed against addressees who do not come into consideration as readers of this text and in addition are even hostile toward the addressees who are actually addressed. Correspondingly, the woes in these texts and in Luke 6.24-26 are part of an internal communication, and their confrontational stance against shared opponents gives them the function of stabilizing the cohesion within the group by demarcating it to the outside. The Lukan woes thus belong in the narrated world and want to be understood as part of the Lukan story of Jesus. The stereotype character and the semantic unspecificity of these characterizations ("the rich," "the well fed," "those who laugh") also speak against an application to rich Christians in the Lukan present. It excludes the possibility that anyone in the Lukan community could feel addressed, even by a single one of them. Rather, one sticks labels like these only on others. Luke has extrapolated the characteristics out of the beatitudes as antitheses in order to do two things. First, in connection to 1.52-53 he wants to interpret Jesus's proclamation of the reign of God as a reversal of the assignments of status that are in force. Just as the disciples are poor (vv. 20-21) and experience rejection (v. 22) *for Jesus's sake*, so the completely different fate of the rich in the present also receives its signature from their stance toward Jesus. Their riches (v. 25) and their reputation among humans (v. 26) are based on the fact that they keep away from Jesus, unlike the disciples who are poor for precisely this reason. The decisive difference between the poor and the rich is therefore marked solely by Jesus. Second, Luke marks out here the general framework for the subsequent controversies with the Pharisees, whose "greed" and rejection of Jesus are directly connected with each other (cf. 16.14-15). It is no accident that they are the ones whom Luke constructs in a completely intentional manner as a counterimage to the disciples through the organization of his narrative from 14.25 onward and to whom he has the parable of the rich man and poor Lazarus narrated, which stages the opposition of beatitudes and woes.

6.27-38: The Nullification of the Principle of Ethical Reciprocity

[27]"But I say to you who are listening:
Love your enemies!
Do good to those who hate you!
[28]Bless those who curse you!
Pray for those who revile you!
[29]To the one who strikes you on the cheek, hold out the other one as well,
And to the one who takes your outer garment do not refuse the undergarment as well!
[30]To everyone who asks you, give,
And from the one who takes what belongs to you, do not demand it back!
[31]And as you wish that people treat you . . . treat them in the same way!
[32]If you love those who love you, what do you receive as a return? For even sinners love those who love them.
[33]And if you do good to those who do good to you, what do you receive as a return? Even sinners do the same.
[34]And if you lend to those from whom you expect to receive, what do you receive as a return? Even sinners lend to sinners in order to receive back the same.
[35]Instead, love your enemies and do good and lend without hoping for restitution. For your reward will be great, and you will become sons of the Most High, for he is friendly to the unthankful ones and evil ones.
[36]Be merciful just as also your Father is merciful!
[37]And judge not, then you also will not be judged.
And condemn not, then you also will not be condemned.
Acquit, then you also will be acquitted.
[38]Give, then it will be given to you. One will give into your lap a measure that is good, pressed down, shaken, and overflowing. For with the measure with which you measure it will be measured again to you."

Luke has configured the structure of the section with extremely great care (see also Lührmann 1972a, 421–22). There are two ethical main parts: vv. 27b-30 and vv. 32-34.

The first part (vv. 27b-30) consists of a series of eight imperatives, which show a clear commonality. They are consistently concerned with how one should react to the curtailment and diminution of one's own life by other people. This series is divided into two groups with four imperatives each (thus, as in the beatitudes and woes, Luke also forms two series of four here), which differ from one another in multiple respects. In the first group (vv. 27b-28) the imperatives are *placed at the beginning*, and the concern is with the behavior of *groups* (recognizable in the use of the *plural*). The second series (vv. 29-30) consists of two double sayings that are directed to individuals (recognizable in the use of the *singular*) and in which the imperative is *placed at the end*. They begin in each case with a *protreptic* exhortation that speaks of the ethical Other [*Gegenüber*] in the dative, and are then continued via an *apotreptic* admonition that characterizes the ethical Other in each case as a person who wants to have something from one (in both cases with the phrasing ἀπὸ τοῦ αἴροντος).

The second part (vv. 32-34), which is separated from the first by the Golden Rule (v. 31), consists of three parallel explanatory statements that characterize the breaking of the reciprocity of interpersonal action as an ethical identity marker of—as it says in v. 35c—the "children of the Most High."

27a Luke has Jesus now explicitly turn beyond the circle of the disciples to the πλῆθος πολὺ τοῦ λαοῦ (v. 17). Its designation as οἱ ἀκούοντες looks back to v. 18 (ἦλθον ἀκοῦσαι) and makes the addressees of what follows clear to the readers. Luke takes up this same phrasing again in v. 47, and in 7.1 he marks the conclusion of the speech of Jesus with the words εἰς τὰς ἀκοὰς τοῦ λαοῦ.

27b-28 The exhortation to love of enemies (v. 27b) must be interpreted together with the three other imperatives (vv. 27c-28b), for Luke speaks here not of four different groups but of a single group. "Your enemies" are the same people as those "who hate you," "who curse you," and "who revile you." Here the relational appellative "your enemy" is elucidated by the three verbs (Luke thus applies the same procedure as in the beatitudes and woes in vv. 20-22, 24-26): the enmity comes to expression in the actions, or put the other way around, in these actions the addressees recognize their enemies. Correspondingly, the last three imperatives in vv. 27c-28b, "do good!" "bless!" and "pray for!" are ethical illustrations of "love!" Thus, the corresponding exhortations are meant to be read as concretizations of the command to love one's enemies, which functions here as a heading. Justin Martyr then also drew together v. 27b-c crosswise resulting in "love those who hate you" (*Apologia i* 15.9; see also Epistle to Diognetus 6.6).

27b The exhortation to love one's enemies is also found with the same wording in Matthew 5.44b and can be traced back to Jesus himself with great certainty (cf. Lührmann 1972a, 412; Becker 1996, 313; contrast, however, Sauer 1985, 26–27). It was regarded from an early point on as *the* specific distinguishing feature (*differentia specifica*) of the Christian ethic (in this sense, e.g., Tertullian, *Ad Scapulam* 1.3: *diligere inimicos . . . sit perfecta et propria bonitas nostra, non communis* ["To love enemies . . . should be our perfect and special quality, not a general one]")—and this is probably also justified, for nowhere else do we find a phrasing that exhorts one to *love* one's *enemies*.

Nevertheless, in the environment of early Christianity we find many exhortations that go in a similar direction. From Plato onward people had called into question the widespread principle that "it is just to treat the friend well but the enemy badly" (δίκαιον εἶναι τὸν μὲν φίλον εὖ ποιεῖν, τὸν δ' ἐχθρὸν κακῶς, *Respublica* 335a and elsewhere; additional attestations in H. D. Betz 1995, 305; cf. also Plato, *Crito* 49a–e; *Meno* 71e; Plutarch, *Moralia* 218a as well as Gill 1991, 246–62). In addition, there is the admonition to answer evil not with evil but with good (Seneca, *De beneficiis* 4.26.1 with a revealing justification: "If you . . . want to imitate the gods, show benevolent deeds also to the unthankful [*si deos . . . imitaris, da et ingratis beneficia*], for the sun also rises over the criminals and the seas are also open to sea robbers"; *De beneficiis* 7.31,1; *Testament of Joseph* 18.2; *Testament of Benjamin* 4.3; see also Proverbs 24.29; Philo, *De virtutibus* 116–118; Romans 12.21). Biblically, reference must be made above all to the text of Proverbs 25.21-22 quoted in Romans 12.20 (give bread and water to the hungry and thirsty enemy; see also Bill. I: 353ff; Nissen 1974, 304ff; Radl I: 400ff; Waldmann 1902; on the Jewish background as a whole, cf. Zerbe 1993, 33ff). If one orients oneself toward the terminology of the Synoptic texts, however, then the finding is clear; cf. in this respect, e.g., Polybius, *Historiae* 1.14.4 ("A good man should . . . with the friends hate the enemies and with [them] love the friends [συμμισεῖν τοῖς φίλοις τοὺς ἐχθροὺς καὶ συναγαπᾶν τοὺς φίλους]"); 9.29.12 ("You may not love [ἀγαπᾶν] the Macedonians, but you must regard and hate [μισεῖν] them as enemies"); *Anthologia Graeca* 10.36 (one should guard oneself before a false friend as before an enemy [ὡς ἐχθρὸν προφυλάσσεσθαι] and not love him as a friend [ἀγαπᾶν ὡς φίλον]); Josephus, *Antiquitates judaicae* 7.254 (Joab accuses David as he grieves for Absalom of loving the worst enemy [στέργειν . . . τοὺς ἐχθροτάτους]; 1QS I, 9–10 ("To love all the sons of light . . . and to hate all the sons of darkness").

27c-28b In order to work against the abstractness of the general exhortation to love one's enemies, Luke has provided it with concretizing specifications. Luke knows from his Bible (cf. Leviticus 26.17; Numbers 10.35[34]; Deuteronomy 30.7; 32.41, 43; 2 Samuel 22.18, 41; Psalm 18.18, 41; 38.20; 44.11; and elsewhere) that "enemies" do "hate" and ἐχθροί can accordingly be elucidated by οἱ μισοῦντες (v. 27c). And what "doing good" to people means in terms of content requires no elucidation, for this is known by everyone. It refers to the way in which one treats friends. Here the principle quoted above, according to which one should treat enemies badly, is thus reversed; cf. Lysias, *Orationes* 9.20: τοὺς μὲν ἐχθροὺς κακῶς ποεῖν, τοὺς δὲ φίλους εὖ ("to treat enemies badly but friends well"). The experience of marginalization that Christians suffered from their environment is also described with ἐπηρεάζειν (v. 28b) in 1 Peter 3.16. Philo, *In Flaccum* 52 uses this term to describe the anti-Jewish pogrom in Alexandria, and Josephus, *Antiquitates judaicae* 16.27 uses it to summarize the experience of the Ionian Jews who are not permitted to live according to their own laws and are forced to appear in court on the Sabbath.

29 The exhortation to let oneself be struck not only on the one check but also on the other in addition is without analogy. To be sure, in the environment of early Christianity the renunciation of retribution and revenge was sometimes propagated or there was a demand that one should suffer injustice rather than commit it (e.g., Plato, *Gorgias* 469c; *Crito* 49c; Proverbs 20.22; 24.29; Sirach 28.1-5; Seneca, *De ira* 2.32.1; 34.1; see also Romans 12.9 as well as Dihle 1962, 41ff, 61ff; L. Schottroff 1975, 208ff), but all this remains far behind what is required here. Only two texts move in a similar direction. In Isaiah 50.6 the words of the servant of God ("My back I gave to the beatings, the cheeks, however, to blows [εἰς ῥαπίσματα], my face I have not turned from the shame of spitting") and in Lamentations 3.28-30 the words of the prophet ("He should sit alone and be silent, if he [sc. the Lord] places it [sc. the yoke] on him. δώσει τῷ παίοντι αὐτὸν σιαγόνα [He shall hold the cheek to the one who strikes him] . . ."). It is common to both texts that the view of the one struck is directed solely to *God*. They both do not avoid suffering for *God's* sake—and not for the sake of the perpetrator of violence or for the improvement of the world. Jesus could have meant the word in this sense; for Luke at least it was a further concretion of love of enemies.

The same also applies to v. 29b, where the situation of a robbery is presupposed, as this is described by Luke in 10.30. Apparently, the clothing was also always taken from the victim, and his outer garment was, of course, taken off first and then the undergarment. The admonition now exhorts that one should not fight to keep the undergarment in such a situation but to readily hand it over to the robber (for ἱμάτιον and χιτών, see at 3.11; for the phrasing κωλύειν τι ἀπό τινος, cf. Genesis 23.6^LXX). This could, of course, also be a completely sensible survival strategy, but the rationale of the exhortation certainly does not reside in this.

30 makes a generalization. The paronomasia αἰτοῦντι / μὴ ἀπαίτει at the beginning and end binds the two halves together. In this vein παντί, which is placed emphatically at the beginning (diff. Matthew 5.42a), is interpreted by v. 30b. One should not refuse the request even of one from whom one knows that he or she will not give back what is asked for. Nor should one demand back his or her property from him or her afterward; despite the parallelism with ἀπὸ τοῦ αἴροντος in v. 29b, an exclusively violent αἴρειν ἀπό is not in view here. On the whole, however, the concern is also not specifically with the exhortation to care for the poor or with charitable activity, for in v. 34 this instruction is reinterpreted with recourse to the verb δανίζειν "lend" (cf. also Sirach 20.15: σήμερον δανιεῖ καὶ αὔριον ἀπαιτήσει ["Today he lends and tomorrow he demands it back"]). This verb probably already stood at this point in Q (cf. Matthew 5.42b), and Luke has omitted it in v. 30b for the sake of the aforementioned paronomastic accentuation. What is at issue in this verse is clear: even in relation to possessions in general one should align one's actions not with the principle of reciprocal retribution but with the principle of one-sided renunciation. This instruction has in common with the exhortation to love one's enemies and its concretion the fact that both here and there one should act not "connectively" but "disjunctively" (see at v. 35).

The Golden Rule, which follows in **31**, is known in all cultures of the world.

It formulates a formal-ethical, common-sense principle (cf. Dihle 1962, 85ff, who ascribes its emergence to the Greek Sophistic of the end of the fifth century BCE; but according to Diogenes Laertius 1.36 ,Thales already formulated a similar proverbial saying). For the dissemination, see the surveys in Philippidis 1929; Wattles 1996; a concise review of scholarship is found in H. D. Betz 1995, 508ff. In Greek literature it is first found in Herodotus 3.142; 7.136, namely in the negative version; the oldest attestation for the positive version is Isocrates, *Ad Nicolem* 49. Within Judaism it is first encountered in Tobit 4.15 and Hebrew Testament of Naphtali 1.6 in the negative version (see also Ps.-Menander 250–51 [*OTP* II: 599]). For Philo of Alexandria there are ἄγραφα ἔθη καὶ νόμιμα ("unwritten customs and laws"; *Hypothetica* 8.7.6). Letter of Aristeas 207 offers a combination of both versions. According to b. Shabbat 31a, it is "the whole Torah, and the rest (i.e., what stands in the Torah) is elucidation" (see Nissen 1974, 390ff).

In the literature, the placement of the Golden Rule at this point is regarded as "strange," since it is said to be oriented "toward the principle of retribution" (Dihle 1962, 113, 113–14) or to be aimed "at the idea of mutual correspondence" (Horn 1986, 105) and therefore allegedly does not fit with the exhortation, formulated in vv. 29-30 and vv. 32-34, to nullify the principle of ethical reciprocity. This misunderstands the intention of the Golden Rule, however, for according to it the standard of one's own actions should not be what "people" *de facto* do to the hearers of the words of Jesus, but the way in which the latter *wish* to be treated by the former (cf. also G. Strecker 1984, 158; Wattles 1996, 63ff; Radl), and that is something totally different. Therefore, this phrasing of the Golden Rule has nothing to do with the principle of retribution. For this reason, it also fits excellently with the demands formulated in vv. 29-30, which it not only characterizes as behavior *wished by all people* and makes this behavior the material norm of the ethical reciprocity, but it also anticipates this utopia in one's own actions. The distinctiveness of the Golden Rule, as it is formulated here and in Matthew 7.12, consists above all in the fact that here there is not merely talk, as is otherwise always the case, of individuals and anonymous "others" or the like, but rather it is "humanity" that functions here as an ethical Other (*Gegenüber*) to *a group*. Thus, in Luke, the same opposition is established as in the fourth beatitude (v. 22), namely the opposition of marginalized minority and majority society. The Golden Rule is thus contextualized and placed in the situation of the Christian community that is discriminated against by its non-Christian environment. The imperative ποιεῖτε . . . ὁμοίως is typically Lukan (see also 3.11; 10.37).

32-34 The three parallel constructed lines of justification make recourse to three of the ethical demands from vv. 27-30: v. 32 to v. 27b (love enemies), v. 33 to v. 27c (do good to the haters), and v. 34 to v. 30 (do not demand back what is given away; see there for further observations on the connection between the two verses; ἀπολαμβάνειν τὰ ἴσα [v. 34c] with reference to the sum of money that is lent probably means an amount at the same level; cf. Plato, *Leges* 774c: ἴσα ἀντὶ ἴσων λαβεῖν ["to receive equal for equal"]). Luke brings these three exhortations into confrontation with the popular ethical principle of the reciprocity of action (cf. especially Bolkestein 1967, 156ff; Hands 1968, 26ff, 49ff; van Unnik 1966).

In this sense Hesiod, *Opera et dies* 349 already writes, εὖ μὲν μετρεῖσθαι . . . εὖ δ' ἀποδοῦναι ("Measure well . . . give back well"); cf. further Xenophon, *Memorabilia* 2.6.28 (φιλῶν . . . ἀντιφιλεῖσθαι . . . καὶ ποθῶν ἀντιποθεῖσθαι ["As one who loves . . . to be loved in return . . . and as one who desires to be desired in return"]); *Memorabilia* 4.4.24 ("To act well in return [ἀντευεργετεῖν] to those who act well is law everywhere . . . but those who do not act well in return [οἱ δὲ μὴ ἀντευεργετοῦντες] are hated by them because of unthankfulness [διὰ μὲν τὴν ἀχαριστίαν μισοῦνται]"); Epictetus, *Dissertationes* 2.14.18 (τὸν εὖ ποιοῦντα ἀντευποιῆσαι καὶ τὸν κακῶς ποιοῦντα κακῶς ποιῆσαι ["To treat well in return those who act well and to treat badly those who act badly"]); cf. also Mott 1975; Kirk 2003.

The core of the principle of the reciprocity of action is the word χάρις taken up in the rhetorical questions of vv. 32b, 33b, 34b, which in this context denotes something like a return or restitution; cf. Sirach 12.1: "If you do good . . . there will be thanks for your good deeds (ἔσται χάρις τοῖς ἀγαθοῖς σου)"; Aristotle, *Ethica nicomachea* 1164b.26: εὐεργέτῃ ἀνταποδότε χάριν ("Repay the well-doer with thanks"); Ps.-Aristotle, *Rhetorica ad Alexandrum* 1421b38–39; φίλους εὖ ποιεῖν καὶ τοῖς εὐεργέταις χάριν ἀποδιδόναι ("To treat friends well and repay well-doers with thanks"); Moretti 1967/1976, I: 55.23–24: ἀνταποδιδόναι χάριτας τοῖς εὐεργέταις ("Repay well-doers with thanks"); see also Thucydides 3.67.6; Sirach 3.31; 30.6: τοῖς φίλοις ἀνταποδιδόναι χάριν ("Repay friends with thanks"); 35.2; Josephus, *Antiquitates judaicae* 14.212 (see also van Unnik 1966, 295ff; Spicq 1994, III: 503ff; Harrison 2003, 50ff, 80ff, 128ff, 140ff, 179ff and below at 14.12-14). The answer that the rhetorical questions require is undoubtedly "None!" for it is God who comes into view as the giver of the χάρις dealt with here. This change of perspective is also expressed in the fact that Luke introduces the questions with the help of the qualitative interrogative pronoun ποῖος, and it is also recognizable in the phrasing of the grounds in vv. 32c, 33c, 34c. An orientation toward the principle of reciprocity would distinguish the hearers in nothing from all other persons, whom Luke designates here as "sinners" (ἁμαρτωλοί) and thereby defines them with reference to their relation to God. With a view to the Christians in the world under discussion, whom Luke has in mind as the intended readers, nothing less is described here than that which comprises the ethical identity of Christian communities. Christians receive their ethically unique position through the fact that in their interpersonal actions they do not orient themselves toward the principle of reciprocity, but one-sidedly do what all humans wish from one another (v. 31).

After the nullification of the principle of ethical reciprocity in vv. 32-34 with respect to its function as a *boundary marker* (demarcation in relation to what is outside) has been treated, **35** thematizes its function as an *identity marker* (i.e., as a *darstellendes Handeln* [embodying behavior] that brings to expression the *gemeinsamen christlichen Zustand* [collective Christian condition]; Schleiermacher 1999, 50, 51). Luke now has Jesus explain *why* an action, as he demanded it in vv. 27-30 and repeated by way of summary in v 35a, differs from the ἁμαρτωλοί and makes those acting in this way identifiable as non-sinners (this contrast finds expression in the adversative πλήν, which Luke places before the summary)—namely, because being a child of God is promised to such an action as a "reward" (v. 35c; for this understanding of being a child that is established through action, cf. already at v. 23c); only Luke uses ὕψιστος as an antonomasia for God (see at 1.32). Thus, the υἱοὶ ὑψίστου and the ἁμαρτωλοί (vv. 32c, 33c, 34c) are juxtaposed with each other as group designations. Here we are dealing with a constellation that every Christian community in Luke's time could transfer to its own situation without problem.

One question is still open: why do the people who follow the words of Jesus and no longer orient themselves in their actions toward the principle of reciprocity but rather love their enemies, etc., become children of the Most High? Verse 35d gives the answer—because in his actions God also does not orient himself toward this principle; rather, he is "friendly" even to the unthankful ones and evil ones (on χρηστός as a predicate of God, see, e.g., Psalm^{LXX} 85.5; 99.5; 105.1; 118.68; Wisdom of Solomon 15.1; Jeremiah 40.11^{LXX}; K. Weiss, ThWNT 9: 474–75; Spicq 1994, II: 512).

With great admiration the commentator looks at the systematic coherence of the ethical concept that Luke has presented here.

36 still belongs to the preceding—namely, for three reasons. *(a)* The designation of God as "Father" (v. 36b) is complementary to "children of the Most High" (v. 35c). *(b)* "Friendly" (χρηστός; v. 35d) often stands alongside "merciful" (οἰκτίρμων; 36b)—namely, both as a predicate of God and in general: Psalm^{LXX} 68.17-18; 145.7-8, 9; 111.5; 144.8-9; Josephus, *Antiquitates judaicae* 7.184; Theocritus, *Eidyllia* 15.75; Memnon Historicus 3 (Orelli 1816, 8); Plutarch, *Camillus* 17.5; Aelian, *Varia historia* 1.30; Colossians 3.13; cf. also the rendering of our text in Justin, *Apologia i* 15.13 ("Become χρηστοὶ καὶ οἰκτίρμονες as also your Father is χρηστὸς . . . οἰκτίρων"). *(c)* This verse argues exactly like v. 35. The addressees should orient themselves to God, and the correspondence between God's being merciful and the action of those addressed is described with the help of the phrasing καθὼς καί, which is also found in other paraenetic texts of the New Testament in an analogous manner and has a grounding function in every case (cf. BDR §453.2): Romans 15.7 (προσλαμβάνεσθε ἀλλήλους, καθὼς καὶ ὁ Χριστὸς προσελάβετο ὑμᾶς); Colossians 3.13 (χαριζόμενοι . . . καθὼς καὶ ὁ κύριος ἐχαρίσατο ὑμῖν); see also Ephesians 4.32; 5.2, 25; Matthew 5.48. Argumentatively, these instructions function in the same way as the guiding paradigm of the Torah formulated in Leviticus 11.45: "You should be holy, for I am holy" (see also 19.2; 20.24-26); for the content, cf. Letter of Aristeas 208 (ἔλεον τραπήσῃ ["you will practice mercy"], for God is also ἐλεήμων ["merciful"]); Targum Ps.-Jonathan to Leviticus 22.28 ("as our father is merciful in heaven, so you should be merciful on earth"); see also Sifre Deuteronomy 11.22 (§49).

37-38 Without transition, Luke attaches a series of proverbial sayings whose commonality consists in the fact that in orientation to the schema of the *talio* they formulate the correspondence between (present) conduct and (eschatic) consequence (for the tradition-historical background, cf. Dihle 1962, 12ff; see also Testament of Zebulun 5.3 ["Have mercy in your hearts. For as someone acts with his neighbor, so the Lord will also do to him"]; Jubilees 4.31–32). The four exhortations in vv. 37a-38a are identifiable as belonging together *formally*. For they are each composed of a pair of apotreptic (v. 37a, b) and protreptic (vv. 37c, 38a) imperatives. Luke presumably understood them as concretions of the demand for mercy advanced in v. 36.

First Clement 13.2 also quotes as a saying of Jesus a series that is very similar thematically and formally: "Be merciful in order that you find mercy. Forgive in order that it be forgiven you. As you do, so it will be done to you. As you give, so it will be given to you. As you judge, so you will be judged. As you show friendliness, so one will show friendliness to you. With the measure with which you measure it will be measured to you." The overlaps with the Lukan series are unmistakable. A literary dependence of the one on the other is usually ruled out; it is often assumed that the series in 1 Clement 13.2 reproduces an independent tradition (e.g., H. D. Betz 1995, 615; Lindemann 1992, 52 [literature]). *Ignoramus, ignorabimus.*

The first three imperatives in **37** formulate not three different demands but one and the same demand: "The μὴ κρίνειν is first equated by Luke with μὴ καταδικάζειν and then understood positively as ἀπολύειν" (Kollmann 1997, 175). This is supported particularly by the antithetical opposition of καταδικάζειν ("condemn") and ἀπολύειν ("acquit") in Aristotle, *De respiratione* 1268a3; Achilles Tatius, *Leucippe et Clitophon* 8.8.10; Athenaeus, *Deipnosophistae* 4.18 (141a); Diogenes Laertius 2.41; Athenagoras, *Legatio pro Christianis* 2.3. An attractive parallel is the metaphorical use of the terminology with reference to public opinion in Dio Chrysostom 66.18: "Without knowing the case, without taking witnesses, and without being drawn by lot, he judges, and it does not bother him to vote while drinking or bathing. . . . For the one whom he acquits today he condemns tomorrow (ὃν γὰρ ἂν ἀπολύσῃ τήμερον, αὔριον καταδικάζει)." Therefore, a fixation to the "exercising of ecclesiastical disciplinary authority" (Kollmann 1997, 176) overly narrows the spectrum of what is meant by Luke.

In **38** the theme of ready giving from v. 30a is taken up again; for the connection with v. 36 and the theological characterization of the giving, cf. Psalm^LXX 36.21: "The righteous . . . is merciful and gives." The argumentative substance of the statement of v. 38a is clearly recognizable. God will bestow upon the giver the retribution that he is denied on earth (cf. v. 30b). This does not backhandedly reintroduce the principle of reciprocity, for God is brought into play, and therefore no bilateral exchange of giving takes place, for God gives without having received himself. Verse 38b provides a specification of δοθήσεται ὑμῖν: Luke describes metaphorically the generosity of the divine giving (the third person plural stands either for God or for the impersonal "one"; cf. BDR §130.2). The picture portrays the filling of a measure with grain or the like. It is shaken and rocked; it is pressed down from above in order that even more comes in; and finally, a heap is added on top, so that it even falls down to the side. For the metaphor of "giving-into-the-fold" as a designation for the divine retribution, cf. Isaiah 65.6-7; Jeremiah 39.18. Via the key word μέτρον the saying—taken over from Q (cf. Matthew 7.2b)—about the equivalence of the eschatic retribution is attached. It is nothing other than a metaphorical phrasing of the *talio* principle (there are a plethora of correspondences that are almost identical in wording in rabbinic literature; cf. Rüger 1969).

6.39-49: "He also told them a parable speech"

³⁹He also told them a parable speech.

"Can a blind man lead a blind man? Will they not both fall into a pit? ⁴⁰A disciple is not above the teacher. But when he is finished, everyone will be like his teacher.

⁴¹Why do you pay attention to the splinter in the eye of your brother, while you do not notice the beam in your own eye? ⁴²How can you say to your brother, 'Brother, let me remove the splinter that is in your eye,' without paying attention to the beam in your eye? You dissembler, remove first the beam from your eye, and then you will see clearly to remove the splinter from your brother's eye.

⁴³There is no good tree that produces bad fruit, and conversely, no bad tree that produces good fruit. ⁴⁴For each tree is known by its own fruit. One does not gather figs from thistles, and one does not harvest grapes from a thornbush. ⁴⁵The good person brings forth good from the treasure of the good heart, and the evil (person) brings forth evil from the (treasure) of the evil (heart), for from the overflow of the heart the mouth speaks.

⁴⁶Why do you call me 'Lord, Lord' and do not do what I say?

⁴⁷Everyone who comes to me and hears my words and does them—I will explain to you whom he is like: ⁴⁸He is like a person who builds a house after he has excavated and dug deep and laid a foundation on the rock. When high water came, the river crashed against that house. But it could not be shaken because it had been built well.

⁴⁹ But whoever has heard (my words) and not done (them), he is like a person who has built a house on the earth—without a foundation. The river crashed against it, and it immediately fell, and the fall of that house was tremendous."

With the help of a transition (**39a**) that is characteristic for him (cf. 5.36; 12.16; 13.6; 14.7; 15.3; 18.1, 9; 21.29), Luke has a metaphorical commentary follow that is composed of a series of multiple parabolic sayings (for the rhetorical meaning of παραβολή see at 4.23). The portion of texts that have no parallel in the Sermon on the Mount is much higher here than elsewhere in the Sermon on the Plain (cf. the overview in the introductory comments on 6.20-49). One cannot know what parts of this were in the speech in the Sayings Gospel Q.

39b-c That a blind person is not suitable as a guide on a journey is a picture that is not unknown in the environment of the New Testament; cf. Xenophon, *Memorabilia* 1.3.4; Dio Chrysostom 62.7 (an unrighteous king would be the same as a blind guide); Philo, *De virtutibus* 7; Sententiae Pythagoreorum 40; Diogenes Laertius 5.82. Horace, *Epistulae* 1.17.1–7 applies it to the teaching of another: "Although you . . . require . . . no instruction, hear nevertheless . . . what your *docendus . . . amiculus* can say about this, as if a blind person wants to show the way (*ut si caecus iter monstrare velit*)." The closest parallel is found in Sextus Empiricus, *Adversus mathematicos* 11.235: "An ἄτεχνος cannot teach (διδάσκειν) an ἄτεχνος, as the blind cannot guide the blind (ὡς οὐδὲ ὁ τυφλὸς τὸν τυφλὸν ὁδηγεῖν)" (see also *Pyrrhoniae hypotyposes* 3.259). The parabolic saying also comes into contact with Romans 2.19-22, although Luke certainly has intra-community relations in view here. The basic idea is that for the ὁδηγεῖν of blind people one necessarily requires a person who can see. And if "to guide the blind" should be a metaphor for "to teach beginners" (see also Acts 8.31; John 16.13), the parabolic saying could be wanting to say that a Christian community cannot manage without teachers (according to 2 Timothy 2.2, it would be the πιστοὶ ἄνθρωποι who are distinguished from others in the fact that they are in position to teach others). But the emphasis could also point in the other direction: 'If in the Christian community there should be one who fancies that he would like to teach others, this would be like if a blind person would guide a blind person, since all are equal.' Everything thus depends on who of the two blind people mentioned in v. 39b is the metaphorical addressee of the parabolic saying.

40 is often interpreted in connection with v. 39 (cf. Wanke 1981, 21–31), which is indeed suggested on account of the imagery of v. 39. The meaning of this saying is clear. The student will never surpass his teacher; he can at best become like him. The goal of being a student thus consists in becoming like the teacher (for the understanding of καταρτίζειν in this sense, cf. Spicq 1994, II: 273; H. D. Betz 1995, 624–25). But what does this mean? With all caution this much can perhaps be said: after Luke has mentioned so often in the meantime that Jesus "teaches" (4.15, 31; 5.3, 17; 6.6), he will probably scarcely have assumed that a reader would *not* think of Jesus when reading διδάσκαλος, and something analogous probably also applies in the case of μαθητής (cf. 5.30, 33; 6.1, 13, 17, 20). But in what way can *these* disciples (i.e., the disciples) become like *this* teacher (i.e., Jesus)? Probably through nothing else than that they teach the same thing as what their teacher has taught them. This would correspond to what Schürmann I: 369 writes, "The teaching of Jesus, as it was presented in 6.27-38, is and remains the standard." Thus, the phrasing εἶναι ὑπὲρ τὸν διδάσκαλον refers not to social status or the like, but must be understood materially and contains the accusation that a certain "teaching" no longer stands in continuity with the received teaching tradition, about which one can, of course, always be divided.

41-42 are clearly demarcated from the immediate context by the address in the second person singular and by the high recurrence of their terminology (κάρφος, ὀφθαλμός, ἀδελφός, δοκός, ἐκβάλλειν). Moreover, it is an admonition and not a statement. The metaphor is extremely hyperbolic. But for this very reason it was successful. After almost 2,000 years people who never read the Bible still know this saying. This admonition, however, has nothing to do with the warning against judging (v. 37a), for it lacks any reference to one's own fate in the final judgment. The meaning is clear: before one aims at removing flaws from others, one should first separate oneself from one's own flaws. There is a rabbinic parallel in b. Arakhin 16b: "R. Tryphon said: It would amaze me if in this age there were one who receives correction. If one says to someone: 'Take the splinter away, which (is) between your eye,' this one responds: 'Take away the beam, which (is) between your eye.'" The nearness to Plutarch, *Moralia* 515d is unmistakable: "Why (τί; for comparative rhetorical "why" questions, whose intention consists in criticizing the behavior of the respective addressee, see at 2.48) . . . do you look so sharply at a foreign error (ἀλλότριον κακόν), but overlook your own (τὸ δ' ἴδιον παραβλέπεις)?" The repeated designation of the other as ἀδελφός shows that Luke has the scene take place in the Christian community.

43-45 are a combination of sayings compiled by Luke. In vv. 43-44 realities from the world of plants are described, which are transferred to the level of human behavior in v. 45. The attachment to the preceding verse could have come about through the paronomasia κάρφος/καρπός (H. D. Betz 1995).

43-44 The narrator first refers to the clear relation of correspondence between the condition of a (fruit) tree and its fruit (vv. 43-44a). In the New Testament, σαπρός is attested only in connection with this parabolic saying, in the parable of Matthew 13.48 (concerning fish; opposite term: καλός; see also the same opposition in Vita Aesopi 23.33 with reference to slaves), and in Ephesians 4.29 (concerning a λόγος; opposite term: ἀγαθός; cf. further Lindhagen 1950). Verse 43 describes this situation as a *context of emergence* (ποιεῖν: what the tree does). On the other hand, v. 44 formulates the same situation as a *context of perception* (γινώσκειν:

what the person perceives). Verse 44b then makes a further intensification by transferring the context of perception to plants that do not produce any fruit at all (for the parallelizing of ἄκανθα with βάτος, cf. e.g., Theocritus, *Eidyllia* 1.132; Lucian of Samosata, *Quomodo historia conscribenda sit* 33; Appian, *Libyca* [= *Punica*] 559; Aelian, *De natura animalium* 7.14).

45 transfers the relation of correspondence described in v. 43 to people in an ethicizing manner. The opposition of καλός and σαπρός is replaced in v. 45a, b with the opposition of ἀγαθός and πονηρός (for the conception of the ἄνθρωπος ἀγαθός and its development in the ancient world, cf. H. D. Betz 1995, 630ff). Here, "heart" stands metonymically for the nature or identity of a person. Therefore, this is also where the accent lies, which distinguishes the Lukan phrasing from Matthew 12.35; as a semantic overlap, "treasure" and "heart" have the characteristic of hiddenness in common (cf., on the one hand, Matthew 13.44; Colossians 2.3, and, on the other hand, Deuteronomy 15.9; Psalm 44.22; Romans 2.29). Verse 45c concretizes this idea not in relation to human action but rather in relation to *speaking*. It is the words that come from the mouth that reflect the condition of the heart (according to v. 45a, b: either "good" or "evil"). This is somewhat astonishing, for it was also already known in Luke's time that there is a great difference between the words that leave the mouth and the heart; cf. Pittacus in Diogenes Laertius 1.78: "The tongue speaks nothing reliable through the mouth, for in the heart it has a διχόθυμος . . . νόημα (a divided . . . thought)." But precisely the talk of the "overflow" of the heart (the ending -μα makes περίσσευμα into a *nomen rei actae*, which characterizes the result of an action; cf. BDR §109.2) probably wants to set another accent, which also differs from Martin Luther's translation (*Wes das Herz voll ist, des geht der Mund über* ["whose heart is full, his mouth overflows"]), namely that the mouth sooner or later discloses what is in the heart, because no heart is absolutely receptive; sooner or later the mouth brings it (good or evil) forth (προφερει); cf. also Sirach 21.26, but there a distinction is made in this respect between the fool and the wise: ἐν στόματι μωρῶν ἡ καρδία αὐτῶν, καρδία δὲ σοφῶν στόμα αὐτῶν ("in the mouth of the fools [is found] their heart, but the heart of the wise [is] their mouth"). This conception has only the term in common with the Stoic distinction between the *logos prophorikos* and the *logos endiathetos* (cf. H. D. Betz 1995, 633; cf. also Sirach 27.6). What is lacking in this verse vis-à-vis v. 43 is the correspondence to v. 44a, namely the mention of the context of perception, which would have had to read in a similar way to Matthew 7.16a: 'For every person is known by their words.' This conclusion, of course, applies only in a very qualified way (see also Duplacy 1981). Luke may have not written it for this reason and in this way left the pragmatic of this combination of sayings quite vague. It cannot, however, be an exhortation to self-testing directed to the disciples (von Gemünden 1993, 149), for this contradicts the orientation of the parabolic sayings.

46-49 The parable of the two houses also concludes Jesus's speech in Matthew 7.24-27. In the form of a metaphorical syncrisis, two models of behavior are set over against each other. Verses 47-48 portray the fate of those who align their behavior with the instructions of Jesus ("hear and do"), v. 49 the fate of those who "hear and do not do." This opposition corresponds—also with respect to the concluding position—to the opposition of blessing and curse in the observance or non-observance of the commandments in Leviticus 26.3-13, 14-17; Deuteronomy 28.1-14, 15-44 (see also 30.15-20); Assumption of Moses 12.10–11; 1 Enoch 91.18–19; as at the end of the Sermon on the Plain/Sermon on the Mount, there too the positive example is always mentioned first (see also Luke 8.18; 13.9). The function of the parable consists in inculcating the binding nature of the preceding ethical instruction. Above all, the points of contact with James 1.22-25 are conspicuous. In both cases the concern is with "hearing and doing" in opposition to "hearing and not doing," and both here and there the consequences of these two opposing patterns of behavior are described in the form of a metaphorical syncrisis. The two texts engage with a problem that is characteristic for early Christianity. It already surfaces clearly in the first verse.

In **46** the opposing position, which the pragmatic of the following parable is intended to correct, is criticized. This criticism goes in the same direction as the one made by James 2.14-26 in relation to a "faith without deeds" (v. 26). Such a perception could arise because in the early Christian communities it was faith that was assigned the function of an identity-creating ethos, and apart from the worship service there were no specific institutionalized actions through which Christian identity was made visible in an exclusive way (cf. Wolter 1997a). What James calls "faith without deeds" is the same thing that is designated here with "calling me 'Lord, Lord' and not doing what I say." Although Paul would have certainly (and rightly) rejected such a labelling, texts such as Romans 10.9 ("If you confess with your mouth, κύριος Ἰησοῦς . . . you will be saved") or 10.13 ("everyone who calls upon the name of the Lord will be saved") make this problem clear. For τί in the sense of "why?" see at 7.24-26.

47 "To come to me and hear my words" refers to what Luke had often reported about the crowd (cf. 5.1, 15; 6.18; see also 6.27). The hearing is now concluded, and the view is directed to the doing that follows it. That what matters is not merely hearing but *doing* what has been heard is an old biblical *topos* (cf. Deuteronomy 5.27; 6.3; 30.12-13; Ezekiel 33.31-32; Sirach 3.1; Josephus, *Antiquitates judaicae* 20.44; Romans 2.13; James 1.22; see also Luke 8.21). The consequences of doing or not doing the words of Jesus are now explained with the help of two contrasting examples (ὑποδείξω; cf. Spicq 1994, III: 403ff); the anacoluthon after πᾶς is a Semitism (cf. BDR §466.3). A parallel that is taken from this same image field is found in Avot of Rabbi Nathan 24 (Bill. I: 469).

48-49 Luke narrates the two stories somewhat differently than Matthew. While in Matthew 7.24, 26 it depends on whether the house is built on rock or on sand, in the Lukan version it is decisive whether it was built καλῶς (v. 48d), i.e., whether one has dug down through the ground and laid a foundation on bedrock (v. 48b), or whether it was placed "without foundation" directly on the earth (v. 49b). Thus, in Matthew the two houses were built in different places, whereas in Luke they stand in the same place and their respective technical process of construction differentiates them from each other (these two aspects are not distinguished clearly enough from each other in Franz 1995). And while in Matthew a cloudburst falls on both houses, which—as in a wadi—results in wrenching torrents, in Luke the current of an overflowing river breaks upon them (προσέρηξεν; for the picture, cf. Marcus Aurelius 4.49.1: "Be like a crag [ἄκρα] upon which the waves break [προσρήσσεται]").

The negative example not only stands at the end but also contains a narrative incongruity at the very end. It ends not with an explanatory statement parallel to v. 48e (διὰ τὸ καλῶς οἰκοδομῆσθαι αὐτήν), but rather intensifies the information about the collapse of the house (ἐγένετο τὸ ῥῆγμα . . . μέγα; v. 49e). Thus, the emphasis lies on the description of the *negative* consequence of human action, and the text is focused more on making threats than making promises. This emphasis corresponds, however, to the introduction in v. 46 with the fictive address of the parable to those who "do not do" Jesus's words (the key word ποιεῖν is correspondingly repeated in vv. 47a and 49a).

7.1-50: In Capernaum and in Nain

In 7.1 Luke makes a deep structuring division, for he not only directs the view in the direction in which the narrative continues (v. 1b: 'episode opening signal'), but also ends the preceding narrative section *expressis verbis* (v. 1a: 'episode concluding signal'). The structuring signals characteristic for episodic narratives (specifications of place, time, and persons) show that here Luke has opened an episodic complex, which is only concluded by the summary in 8.1-3. Luke first leads Jesus back again to Capernaum (vv. 1-10) and then to Nain. To the end of the chapter the narrative appears to remain in this town, though it is mentioned only in v. 11. However, with ἐν τῇ πόλει (v. 37) Luke refers to εἰς πόλιν καλουμένην Ναΐν (v. 11) and does not mention a change of location again until 8.1. Moreover, the four appearances of the term προφήτης in the three Nain episodes obviously establish coherence (vv. 16, 26 [2×], 39).

Beyond this, there are indications that Luke wanted the narrative of the healing of the slave of a Gentile centurion (vv. 1-10) and resurrection of the son of a widow (vv. 11-17) to be read together. This is supported by the following observations. *(a)* The pair formation of man and woman is typical for Luke (cf. 4.4.3 in the commentary introduction and the introductory comments on 2.22-39). *(b)* Luke brings in the motif of wonder and note of dissemination only at the conclusion of the second "deed of power." *(c)* The juxtaposition of Gentile centurion and widow refers to the two examples from the history of Israel that Jesus had mentioned within his inaugural address in Nazareth in 4.25-27 (the agreement of v. 15c with 1 Kings 17.23 shows that Luke has very consciously established this connection). Therefore, quite a lot speaks for the view that Luke has joined together the two narratives, which come from two different tradition contexts, with a view to 4.25-27.

The readers already know that Luke constructs a narrative collecting basin from episodes that occur in two places from the topographical pair formations in 2.4-39 (Bethlehem/Jerusalem) and 4.16-42 (Nazareth/Capernaum). Thus, we again have before us a typical element of Lukan narration.

7.1-10: The Faith and the Slave of the Centurion

[1]**After he had completed all his words** (given) **to the people for hearing, he went to Capernaum.** [2]**Now the slave of a centurion was sick and was dying, who was precious to him.** [3]**But when he heard of Jesus, he sent elders of the Jews to him and asked him to come and save his slave.** [4]**When they came to Jesus, they asked him and said urgently, "He is worthy that you grant this to him,** [5]**for he loves our people, and he had the synagogue built for us."** [6]**And Jesus went with them. But when he was already no longer far away from the house, the centurion sent friends and said to him, "Lord, do not trouble yourself! For I am not worthy that you come under my roof.** [7]**Therefore, neither did I regard myself as worthy to come to you. But speak with a word; then my lad must be healed.** [8]**For I am also someone who is set under authority, and I myself have soldiers under me. And when I say to this one, 'Go!', then he goes. And to another, 'Come!', then he comes. And to my slave, 'Do this!', then he does it."** [9]**But when Jesus heard this, he marveled at him and turned and said to the crowd that followed him, "I say to you: Not even in Israel have I found such faith."** [10]**And when the messengers returned to the house, they found the slave healthy.**

This narrative is a mixture of healing story and chreia (pronouncement story). This already becomes clear in the exposition (v. 2), where the narrator cannot quite decide whom he should introduce as the dramatic main character—the centurion (he is spoken of in the first place) or the sick slave (he is the subject of the sentence; but the relative pronoun in v. 2b then acts as if the centurion is the subject). Viewed as a whole, however, the elements that make the text into a pronouncement story clearly dominate. On this level, most of the narrative attention is devoted to the centurion. He is first introduced in detail (vv. 4-5), he then gets a chance to speak himself (vv. 6c-8), and finally, Jesus's saying, to which the whole narrative leads (v. 9), also refers to him. By contrast, the elements that are typical for healing stories remain underdetermined, and above all, the most important feature is missing, namely the center with a saying or action that effects the healing. The connection between the healing, which is established in v. 10, and the saying, which Jesus has spoken in v. 9b, is anything but clear.

The agreements with Matthew 8.5-13 make it probable that there was a *Vorlage* in Q (cf. S. R. Johnson 2002). But the differences should also not be overlooked. Unlike in the Matthean parallel, in the Lukan version there is no encounter of Jesus with the centurion, who is portrayed as a God-fearer in v. 5. Luke lets both the request for healing (vv. 3-6a) and the suggestion to heal the slave from a distance with its rationale (vv. 6-8) be addressed to Jesus through intermediaries—first through the "elders of the Jews" (v. 3a) and then through "friends" (v. 6b). Both groups were probably inserted into the narrative by Luke himself (cf. especially Gagnon 1994), and the same also applies to the characterization of the centurion by the Jewish elders in vv. 4-5. This assumption is at any rate more probable than the tracing back of these elements to Q (so, e.g., Dauer 1984, 114–15), or to a pre-Lukan special tradition such as Q^{Lk} (so, e.g., Sato 1988, 55) or Lk[s] (so, e.g., Schramm 1971, 40–43); Wenger 1985 advocates a combination of the last two positions (cf. further the presentation of the discussion in S. R. Johnson 2002).

It is hard to say what relationship John 4.46b-53 has to that synoptic tradition. Unlike here, we are dealing there with a healing story in pure form. It lacks precisely those elements from which the two synoptic versions draw their chreia-like character. With the judgment "secondary" (Luz 1985–2002, II: 13), the tradition-historical relationship of the Johannine version to its parallels in Matthew and Luke is, of course, only very inadequately characterized, for it unmistakably goes back to the same origin as its synoptic counterparts. That the plot of an original healing story was subsequently enriched with chreia-elements (so, e.g., Loos 1965, 532; Bovon; Landis 1994) is just as conceivable as the reverse—namely, that

John has made the form-critically 'mixed' tradition into a pure healing story again (in this sense, e.g., Wilckens 1998, 89).

1 An episode conclusion signal that is followed by a corresponding opening signal is also introduced with ἐπειδή in Genesis 50.4; Exodus 34.33, and πληροῦν with reference to λόγοι or ῥήματα and in the sense of "end," "conclude" is also found in 1 Kings 1.14 (cf. also Luke 1.1; Acts 12.25; 14.26; 19.21). For the function of εἰς τὰς ἀκοὰς τοῦ λαοῦ in the context, see at 6.27a (for the phrasing, cf. Acts 17.20; Philo, *De somniis* 1.36; Josephus, *Bellum judaicum* 5.378 [τὰ ἔργα τοῦ θεοῦ λέγων εἰς ἀναξίους ἀκοάς ("presenting the deeds of God before unworthy ears")]; Vita Aesopi 5.9).

2 introduces the main characters on both narrative levels (see above). On the level of the pronouncement story, Luke names the characteristics of the centurion that are decisive for the continuation of the narrative—namely, that he had a deathly ill slave and that this slave was ἔντιμος to him. The latter piece of information functions as an explanation for the initiative that Luke has the centurion make in v. 3. The text does not, of course, indicate that Luke wanted through this to let "a good light fall on his character" (Schnider/Stenger 1985, 61), for the semantic profile of ἔντιμος also allows the effort on behalf of the slave to be traced back to considerations of usefulness (cf. e.g., Philippians 2.29; Isaiah 13.12^{LXX}; Isocrates, *Panegyricus* 49, 159; Plutarch, *Moralia* 208d; see also Green with reference to Xenophon, *Memorabilia* 2.10.1 and Columella, *De re rustica* 12.3.6; Hengstl 2004, 122 with reference to the fact "that in everyday life slaves were a rare possession for ordinary people"); for the narrative function of this information see at 9.38. The claim that the text suggests a pederastic relationship of the centurion to his slave (so Gowler 2003, 116ff and others) is far-fetched. It stands in blatant contradiction to the witness that the Jewish elders give him.

To be sure, the military rank ἑκατοντάρχης/ἑκατόνταρχος corresponds to the Latin *centurio* (cf. A. Neumann, KP 1: 1112; Dobson 1974; Wegner 1985, 60ff). But there were also "leaders of a hundred" in other armies (cf. e.g., 1 Maccabees 3.55); moreover, armies of Jewish rulers were not, of course, composed of only Jewish soldiers (cf. Josephus, *Antiquitates judaicae* 17.198). Nevertheless, Luke could, of course, have imagined him (like Cornelius in Acts 10.1) as a Roman soldier.

On the level of the healing story the narrative of a deathly ill slave functions as a signal that causes the readers to expect a healing story. For the phrasing κακῶς ἔχειν see at 5.31, and for ἤμελλεν τελευτᾶν (a short form of μέλλειν τὸν βίον τελευτᾶν; cf. Isocrates, *Aegineticus* 31; Aeschines, *In*

Timarchum 145; Timaeus of Tauromenium, *FGH* 3b: 566, Fragment 93b, Dionysius of Halicarnassus, *Antiquitates romanae* 13.10.1) cf. Plato, *Gorgias* 523b; Diodorus Siculus 6.5.3; 13.102.3; 2 Maccabees 6.30; Philo, *De fuga et inventione* 107; Josephus, *Antiquitates judaicae* 17.178.

3 The action is continued on the narrative level of the healing story. That a miracle worker is asked for help through intermediaries is also attested elsewhere (e.g., Mark 5.22-23parr.; 7.25-26; John 11.3; Acts 9.38; Philostratus, *Vita Apollonii* 4.10.1; b. Berakot 34b). However, the distinctiveness of the Lukan narrative consists in the fact that the centurion uses yet another group to convey his request—namely, members of the gerousia of Capernaum (for the usage, cf. 1 Maccabees 14.28; Judith 6.16, 21; 7.23; 8.10; 10.6). Their designation as "elders *of the Jews*" signals the non-Jewish outsider perspective, but that is not the perspective of the author but of the centurion. With the help of this identification of the embassy, which is not necessary for the healing story, Luke announces that the narrative will also be concerned with the topic of 'Israel and the Gentiles' (especially since the concern is not with just any Jews but with representative Jews).

4 The delegation of the Jewish elders passes on not only the request of the centurion, but also even makes it their own, for *they* are the ones who now come before Jesus as petitioners (on παραγενόμενοι + *verbum finitum* see at 14.21). Luke also has the intensity of their effort come to expression in the fact that he describes it with recourse to the durative imperfect παρεκάλουν (see also 8.41; Mark 6.56 par. Matthew 14.36) and strengthens it through the adverb σπουδαίως. In the form of a direct quotation Luke reproduces the argument with whose help they want to move Jesus to comply with their or the centurion's request. Many regard the relative clause as a grammatical Latinism (subjunctive in the relative clause; cf. BDR §5.4; 379₁; see also Moule 1959, 192; Marshall; Fitzmyer; Radl). Two things are worthy of note. First, it is the centurion and not the slave for whose sake Jesus is petitioned for help. Thus, the concern is less with preserving the slave from dying and more with preserving the centurion from the loss of his slave. Second, the emphasis on the worthiness of the centurion reflects unspoken doubts concerning this. This is something completely new within a healing story, for such considerations have never played a role previously in Jesus's healing activity. The two things are, of course, connected with each other, and to this extent it is already recognizable here that this narrative is mainly concerned to let Jesus do something good to a Gentile—though not passing by Israel like Elisha did in his day (cf. 4.27), but rather at the prompting and with the accompaniment (cf. v. 6) of the representatives of the local Jews.

5 provides the explanation for the ἄξιός ἐστιν of v. 4b. Now the centurion is also identified *expressis verbis* as a non-Jew, for with the phrasing "he loves our people" he is placed outside of it. Elsewhere the phrasing τὸ ἔθνος ἡμῶν (the pronoun includes Jesus here with the speakers) also repeatedly accentuates the contrast to non-Jews from a Jewish perspective (e.g., 1 Maccabees 3.59; 16.3; Josephus, *Antiquitates judaicae* 12.7; 14.114, 186, 189; 20.184, 231, 254; *Contra Apionem* 1.5, 161, 172; 2.43). The description of the centurion by the delegation also shows that Luke wants him to be understood as a so-called God-fearer.

The term "God-fearers" is used with reference to people who were inclined to Judaism for different reasons (usually aniconic monotheism and Jewish ethics are mentioned) and kept a connection to the Jewish communities in the Greco-Roman diaspora (*inter alia*, by visiting the synagogue services and observing the Jewish festival calendar, the Sabbath, and the most important food commandments). They were distinguished from proselytes by the fact that they did not formally convert to Judaism (which would have included circumcision for men). Jews therefore continued to view them as "Gentiles." There were, of course, different forms and levels of drawing near to Judaism and its institutions, and the Greek words θεοσεβεῖς, φοβούμενοι, and σεβόμενοι (τὸν θεόν; cf. Acts 10.2, 22; 13.16, 26, 43, 50; 16.14; 17.4, 17; 18.7) are informal rather than formal designations. Early Christianity gained the majority of its new converts from this group. Cf. Siegert 1973; F. Siegert, *NBL* 1: 931–32; Wander 1998; S. Mitchell 1998.

Another God-fearer mentioned in Luke–Acts is Cornelius—likewise a centurion (cf. Acts 10.1-2) and, according to the presentation of Acts, the first "Gentile" upon whom the Holy Spirit falls and who is then baptized. The two share the fact that they give financial expression to their connection to the Jewish communities. It says of Cornelius that he "gave the people many alms" (Acts 10.2), and the Jewish elders report concerning the centurion of Capernaum that he had a synagogue built for them (ᾠκοδόμησεν is to be understood as a causative active; cf. Kühner/Gerth 1890–1898, II/1: 99–100; Moulton/Turner 1963, 52–53; see also 9.9; 20.9, 16; 22.11; 24.20). Numerous honorific inscriptions use this same term to designate the sponsorship of the building of synagogues by specific people (e.g., Lifshitz 1967, numbers 1.1; 63.3; 79.3-4; see also 31.2 and OGIS 96, 101, 129; Reynolds/Tannenbaum 1987, 5–24). Financial support of Jewish communities was apparently a common expression of the special relationship of God-fearers to them (see also Josephus, *Antiquitates judaicae* 14.110), and the collection of the Gentile Christian communities in support of the Jerusalem Jewish Christians agreed upon at the apostolic council (Galatians 2.10; cf. K. Berger 1977a) probably also belongs in this context.

6-7a Since it is essential for the central point of the narrative—which Luke is, of course, aware of and does not wish to spoil—that Jesus does *not* reach the house of the centurion, he must take narrative measures to prevent this. Moreover, it is important to him that Jesus and the Gentile do not meet each other. He therefore invents another delegation, which is composed this time from friends and has the task of keeping Jesus away from the centurion's house. He has not been especially successful with this narratively; this is recognizable, *inter alia*, in the fact that Luke narrates the direct discourse of the centurion as though he were speaking with Jesus himself. Luke has him ground the petition to keep away from his house (vv. 6-7) in his personal unworthiness (v. 6e; its correlate is the respectful address of Jesus as κύριος in v. 6d; cf. Spicq 1994, II: 343ff), and in v. 7a he appeals to this unworthiness to explain why he himself did not come to Jesus, but always only sent intermediaries. The explanation—adduced with reference to Acts 10.28; 11.3; m. Ohalot 18.7 ("the dwellings of the non-Jews are unclean")—that Jesus would defile himself in a Gentile house has no basis in the text (see also Marshall). But neither is there a tension between the Jewish elders' evaluation of the centurion formulated in vv. 4-5 and his self-evaluation (see also Haapa 1983, 76). The former refers to the petition for the rescue of his slave, the latter to an encounter with Jesus. A "paradoxical situation" (Busse 1979, 158; see also Radl I: 445: "opposition") is by no means recognizable. The description of his own unworthiness is oriented instead toward the person of Jesus, and in this way the words of the centurion are charged with implicit Christology (see also Catchpole 1992, 530).

7b-8 The phrasing εἰπὲ λόγῳ (7b) is a *figura etymologica* (cf. BDR §153: strengthening of the verb through a "substantive that is related in its root or meaning"), which is also very common outside the New Testament (e.g., Thucydides 1.22.1; Demosthenes, *Orationes* 6.11; Herodianus Historicus 8.6.8; Aristotle, *De Xenophane* 980a21; Achilles Tatius, *Leucippe et Clitophon* 8.14.2). In Luke the slave is called παῖς μου only in the mouth of the centurion (v. 7c). This designation is also frequently used for slaves elsewhere (cf. W. Bauer 1988, 1223–24). In contrast, Luke always calls the slave δοῦλος (vv. 2a, 3d, 10; this is different in Matthew 8.13c) in the authorial speech. With the help of this difference between the designation of the slave by the narrator (it stresses the personal relation) Luke illustrates the ὃς ἦν αὐτῷ ἔντιμος of v. 2b.

In the foreground, however, stands the christological basic tone that is clearly present in the words of the centurion, for he ascribes an ἐξουσία to Jesus's word that corresponds in terms of its effect to the commanding authority that military commanders possess. What he says definitely takes place (cf. also the description of the ἐξουσία of the king in 1/3 Ezra 4.7-9). A familiar theme is introduced for the readers in this way, for ever since the first Capernaum episode they have known that Jesus's "word" is character-ized by ἐξουσία (see at 4.32; cf. also 4.36; 5.24). The centurion's judgment about Jesus is recognizable in the description of his own commanding authority. Because he himself stands under an ἐξουσία (v. 8a), those under him obey his word (v. 8b-f). Thus, his commanding authority is grounded solely in the fact that he himself is subjected to a superordinated ἐξουσία. A christological statement lies beneath this self-presentation. Jesus's word (v. 7b) will necessarily lead to the recovery of his slave (v. 7c) because it owes its power to Jesus's subordination under the ἐξουσία of God (see also Marshall).

9 With reference to the centurion's speech reproduced in vv. 6-8, the concluding saying of Jesus specifies what faith is—namely, the certainty that Jesus brings salvation. After the men who lower a lame man through the roof (cf. 5.18-20), the centurion is the second person who is credited with faith. The two narratives also share the fact that in both cases the narrative figures whose faith is mentioned have the same function, being intermediaries between Jesus and the sick. In contrast to Matthew 8.10, Jesus's evaluation of the faith of the centurion is not critical of Israel. Nevertheless, with a view to 5.18-20 the question arises of how Luke dis-tinguishes the faith of the centurion from the faith of those men in such a way that he can have Jesus say that not even in Israel had he found "such a faith." Is it the insight into the ἐξουσία of the *word* of Jesus? Or—far more simply—is it the trust that Jesus is also in position to heal from afar? But perhaps Luke no longer thought of what he had written in 5.20. Thus, we cannot get beyond speculations.

10 The story then takes a surprising turn once more upon the narrative level of the healing story. The sick person has become well even without a word of power of Jesus, and this does, in fact, distinguish this healing from that of the lame man, for which such a word of Jesus was needed (5.24). Thus, there is here a very massive narrative gap, whose filling Luke leaves once again to the readers. It would presumably be alright with him if they would come to the conclusion that it was the faith of the centurion that saved him.

7.11-17: The Son of the Widow

[11]**And it happened after this that he went into a town called Nain, and his disciples and a great crowd of people accompanied him.** [12]**But when he drew near to the town gate, behold, the only son of his mother**

was brought out dead there. She was a widow, and a considerable crowd of people from the town was with her. ¹³When the Lord saw her, he had compassion on her and said to her, "Weep no longer!" ¹⁴He approached and touched the coffin. The bearers, however, stopped, and he said, "Young man, I say to you, wake up!" ¹⁵And the dead man sat up and began to speak. And he gave him (back) to his mother. ¹⁶But fear seized all, and they praised God by saying, "A great prophet has arisen among us," and "God has visited his people." ¹⁷And this news about him spread into all Judea and in the whole surrounding area.

We are dealing here with a constellation of figures that is similar to those of vv. 1-10. Jesus–widow–son here corresponds to the constellation Jesus–centurion–slave in vv. 1-10. The *structure* of the narrative displays a few distinctive features. The *introduction* (v. 11) is followed by an extensive *exposition* (vv. 12-13). On the one hand, Luke makes here a form-critical turn in the direction of a raising-of-the-dead narrative (v. 12b), but on the other hand, he places the widow in the center of the narrative. She is mentioned no less than six times in vv. 12-13. In this way Luke makes her a parallel to the centurion of the preceding episode and simultaneously points to 4.45-27 as the hermeneutical key of this double narrative. The *center* of the narrative, in which the successful action of the miracle worker is described, follows in vv. 14-15a. Verses 15b-17 form the *finale*. It is narratively configured quite opulently with a demonstration (v. 16a), a variant of the dismissal motif (v. 15c), the motif of wonder (v. 16a), two performed acclamations (vv. 16b-d), and a note of dissemination (v. 17).

From a form-critical perspective, the narrative corresponds to the type of raising-of-the-dead narrative (cf. the cataloguing of the genre-specific elements in Fischbach 1992, 22ff) in which the miracle worker encounters the funeral procession on the way to the interment and brings the dead person back to life again at this occasion (see at v. 12). By contrast, people send for Jesus in the other New Testament raising-of-the-dead narratives (cf. Mark 5.21-24a, 35-43parr.; John 11.1-44; see also Acts 9.36-42); the same also applies to 2 Kings 4.8-37 and the rabbinic parallel handed down in Leviticus Rabbah 10 (cf. Bill. I: 560). However, it is also unmistakable that Luke wanted this episode to be understood as a typological correspondence to the bringing back to life of the son of the widow of Zarephath, for v. 15c is a word-for-word quotation of 1 Kings 17.23b, which underlines once more the connection to Luke 4.25-27.

11 The introduction with καὶ ἐγένετο + specification of time + *verbum finitum* is a Septuagintism (see at 1.59). One has to supply χρόνῳ (see also Vettius Valens, ed. Kroll 1973, 269.36–37) to the phrasing ἐν τῷ ἑξῆς (see also Strabo 2.1.39; Aelius Aristides, *Ars rhetorica* I 4.1.14), which in the New Testament occurs in this way or similarly only in Luke (cf. 8.1; 9.37; Acts 21.1; 25.17; 27.18). Luke designates Nain too, where Jesus now arrives, as a πόλις (see at 4.31).

To be sure, he probably did not know which place was in view, and we also do not know much more. The Bible does not otherwise know of a place with this name (the identically named Idumean village mentioned by Josephus, *Bellum judaicum* 4.511, 517 [cf. Möller/Schmitt 1976, 8–9] has nothing to do with it). Eusebius (*Onomasticon*, GCS XI/1, *Eusebius Werke* III/1, 140.3ff) and Jerome (*Epistulae* 46.13 [CSEL 54.344]; 108.13 [CSEL 55.323]; PL 23.961) identify it with a locale of Lower Galilee (today's Nēn), located ca. ten kilometers southeast of Nazareth on the north side of the Ğebel ed-Dahī, about forty kilometers from Capernaum (cf. also Kopp 1964, 294ff; Tsafrir 1994, 192).

The notion that Jesus moves from place to place with a great crowd in tow or that a crowd comes together wherever he stays (the combination μαθηταὶ καὶ ὄχλος occurs elsewhere only in Mark 10.46) is a scenic idea that Luke retains until Jesus's entrance into Jerusalem (cf. 5.19; 7.9; 8.4; 9.11; 14.25; 18.36).

12 Linguistically the construction with καὶ ἰδού + *verbum finitum* is again a Septuagintism (cf. BDR §442₁₅). The dead are interred outside the town (with ἐκκομίζεσθαι πύλης Josephus, *Bellum judaicum* 5.567 describes the carrying out of dead from the town; see also Plutarch, *Moralia* 271a; Cassius Dio 72.21.3), and on the way to the cemetery the miracle worker also encounters the funeral procession in other raising-of-the-dead narratives (cf. 4 Baruch 7.13–17; Philostratus, *Vita Apollonii* 4.45.1; Pliny the Elder, *Naturalis historia* 26.15; Apuleius, *Florida*, Fragment 19 [with B. T. Lee 2005, 179]; *Metamorphoses* 2.21–30; Lucian of Samosata, *Philopseudes* 11; see also Weinreich 1969, 171ff). The suffering of the mother of the dead man, however, is placed in the foreground. The two pieces of information—that it was precisely her only son (literally "the only-born son of his mother"; for the ellipsis of the copula, cf. BDR §190.4) who was being carried to the tomb and that she was a widow (v. 12b-c)—correspond with each other and convey to the readers that the woman is now without a provider (for the narrative function of this information see at 9.38).

13 It is the widowed mother and not her dead son for whose sake Jesus becomes active (ἰδών αὐτήν and ἐσπλαγχνίσθη ἐπ᾽ αὐτῇ); the same sequence is also found in Mark 6.34 par. Matthew 14.14; 9.36; Luke 10.33; 15.20; Testament of Zebulun 7.1 (for the theological connotation of ἐσπλαγχνίσθη see at v. 16). What is especially noteworthy about this verse is the fact that the *narrator* designates Jesus as κύριος for the first

time here. Among the Synoptic Gospels, this occurs only in the Gospel of
Luke and, more specifically, only in the Lukan *Sondergut* (7.13; 10.39, 41;
13.15; 16.8; 18.6; 19.8) and as a redactional addition to Q-material (7.19;
10.1; 11.39; 12.42; 17.5, 6) and to Mark-material (22.61; 24.3). Thus,
this is a Lukan peculiarity (cf. de la Potterie 1970; George 1978, 237ff;
Rowe 2006, 119–20). With respect to the history of Christology, this title
is rooted in the earliest Easter confession (cf. Romans 10.9; 1 Corinthians 12.3; 16.22; Philippians 2.9-11), but in Luke's time it had long since
become part of the name of Jesus (but see now Novenson 2012, 174).
Thus, Luke employs here the usage of his time and gives up the terminological distinction between the earthly Jesus and the kyrios of the confession, which was still preserved in the other gospels. Perhaps it is no
accident that Luke introduces this usage into his story of Jesus precisely
on the occasion of a raising of a dead person (cf. Radl). μὴ κλαῖε exhorts
her to stop weeping (present imperative; see also in 8.52 with reference to
Ovid, *Fasti* 7.746–47; see further 23.28; Revelation 5.5; Nehemiah 8.9;
Babrius, *Fabulae Aesopae* 78; Plutarch, *Moralia* 459a; Philogelos 25;
Anthologia Graeca 5.43).

14 Luke presumably imagined that the dead man lay in an open
wooden box (σορός is elsewhere always closed in Jewish texts; cf. Genesis 50.26 [translation of Hebrew אֲרוֹן]; Philo, *De migratione Abrahami*
16.23; Testament of Reuben 7.2; Testament of Levi 19.5). Plutarch, *Numa*
22.1, 4–5 distinguishes between the "bier" (λέχος) on which the dead
person is carried from the "coffin" (σορός) in which he is interred (see
also Phlegon, *De mirabilibus* 17; 18). But the term can also designate
an open wood box (so already Herodotus 2.78). Luke now narrates very
incrementally by dividing the course of the event into multiple individual
actions. In this way he wants less "to increase the suspense of the reader"
(Busse 1979, 164), for what will happen is, of course, long known to the
reader. Rather, the slowing of the tempo should pave the way for the direct
speech in which the time of narration and the narrated time become almost
equally long. The passive imperative ἐγέρθητι occurs only here in the New
Testament. However, the verb ἐγείρω often designates the raising of dead
people (cf. Luke 7.22; 9.7; 20.37; 24.6, 34; Acts 3.15; 4.10; 26.8; and
elsewhere). It functions as a metaphor that presents death as sleep and the
raising of dead people as awakening from sleep.

15 Luke establishes the immediate effect of the word of Jesus (v. 15a;
the successful raising of Tabitha is likewise established with ἀνακαθίζειν),
and he also immediately adds a demonstration of the success of the healing (v. 15b; see also Philostratus, *Vita Apollonii* 4.45.1). The agreement in
wording of v. 15c (καὶ ἔδωκεν αὐτὸν τῇ μητρὶ αὐτοῦ) with 1 Kings 17.23b
(see also 9.42) is important on several levels. First, Luke makes a bridge

to vv. 12-13, where he had placed the mother in the foreground, and calls to mind in this way the fact that Jesus raised the dead man for his mother's sake. Second, through this the entire narrative is again placed explicitly in the horizon of 1 Kings 17.17-23. However, Luke certainly does not activate this recollection in order to show that Jesus is superior to Elijah, for by now this should no longer be necessary. Instead the reminder is necessary because Luke wanted the raising of the son of the widow in Nain and the story narrated in 7.1-10 to be read within the horizon of 4.25-27. Such a reading is made more difficult, however, by the fact that in 4.25-26 Jesus had introduced the widow Elijah had been sent to as a *Gentile* woman, while he himself brought back from the dead the son of a *Jewish* widow. In order to compensate for this incoherence Luke explicitly establishes the connection to Elijah again.

16 The description of the wonder in 16a resembles 1.65 and 5.26 (see there with additional attestations); above all "fear" is the typical reaction to the epiphany of the divine (cf. H. Balz, ThWNT 9: 191, 202, 205ff). As in 5.26 the fear changes into praise of God, which Luke gives the form of a performed double acclamation (16c-d). He places an interpretation of the event in the mouths of the eyewitnesses that interprets Jesus's action as part of God's salvific action toward *Israel* (see at 8.39), even though their christological insight remains far behind the knowledge of the readers. The witnesses of the deed of power regard Jesus as a "great prophet" (cf. also Sirach 48.22; Luke 1.15; Aeschylus, *Septem contra Thebas* 611; Ps.-Lucian, *Amores* 23). Luke makes clear in this way that on the basis of his deed they place Jesus on the same level as Elijah. *For the readers*, of course, the two acclamations establish a completely different connection, for they are reminded immediately of the Benedictus of Zachariah (1.68-79). Both here and there it is said that God "has visited" (ἐπεσκέψατο; 1.68; see also v. 78) his people. Both texts speak of "his people" (λαὸς αὐτοῦ; 1.68) and of the "raising up" (ἐγείρειν) of the bringer of salvation (1.69). Within the narrative, the stress on Jesus's σπλαγχνίζεσθαι (7.13) points back to the talk of the σπλάγχνα ἐλέους of God (1.78). With the acclamation the witnesses of the raising of the dead man attest the fulfilment of the prophecy (cf. 1.67b) of Zechariah. However, the readers know that the people have recognized only half the truth when they see Jesus merely as "great prophet" (Croatto 2005 repeats this error again in the present). This is what John the Baptist was (cf. 1.15-17, 76), whereas Jesus is God's son and Messiah (see also at 9.19-20; 24.19c-21a).

When we ask in conclusion what significance the two acclamations receive from the perspective of 4.25-27 and with a view to the specification of the relation between Gentile centurion and (now Jewish!) widow, the answer is obvious: the faith of the centurion is directed toward Jesus as the one through whom God acts for the salvation of Israel. Therefore, both narratives also receive the character of a narrative staging of Simeon's oracle (above all of 2.32).

The note of dissemination in **17** belongs to the typical inventory of forms of miracle stories (for additional texts, see at 1.65b); for ἐξέρχεσθαι in the sense of "to spread," cf. 1 Thessalonians 1.8. With this summary the narrative widens geographically. Through this Luke already paves the way for the continuation in v. 18, which will begin in a completely different place.

With the raising of a dead person, a high point of the activity of Jesus is reached that can scarcely be surpassed. This narrative gains its implicit christological content above all through the fact that God alone and no one else can make the dead alive again (cf. in this sense the conclusion of the second benediction of the Eighteen Benedictions: "Praise be to you, Yahweh, the one-who-makes-the-dead-alive" [Babylonian recension: מחיה מתים; Palestinian recension: מקים מתים ("the-raiser-of-the-dead")]; see Kellermann 2007, 58ff). It is therefore not surprising that Luke has this narrative follow a text that thematizes Jesus's identity.

7.18-35: Jesus and John the Baptist

This textual complex consists of three different individual traditions that have a common denominator in their reference to John the Baptist. Verses 18-23 report Jesus's answer to the Baptist's question of whether he is the announced ἐρχόμενος. In vv. 24-28 Jesus identifies the Baptist as Elijah having come again (via him the three texts are joined with 7.11-17). Verses 29-35 thematize the reaction of the Pharisees and scribes to John's and Jesus's proclamation. All three pieces are also found in this sequence in Matthew 11.1-19; thus, Luke again aligns himself here with Q. Verses (20-)21 and vv. 29-30 have no counterpart in Matthew.

There has been no lack of attempts to ascribe a coherent theological message that goes beyond the thematic connection to John the Baptist to the entire textual complex already in Q (cf. Kee 1996; see also Cameron 1990, 50ff), but in doing so the individual profile of the three texts have sometimes been leveled out too forcefully.

7.18-23: Who Is Jesus?

[18]**And his disciples reported to John about all this. And John called two of his disciples** [19]**and sent them to the Lord to say, "Are you the coming one or should we wait for another?"** [20]**And when the men had come to him they said, "John the Baptist has sent us to you and says,**

'Are you the coming one or should we expect another?'" [21]In that hour he healed many from sicknesses and afflictions and evil spirits, and he gave many blind people sight. [22]And he answered and said to them, "Go and report to John what you have seen and heard: The blind see, the lame walk, lepers become clean, the deaf hear, the dead are raised, the poor are being proclaimed good news. [23]And blessed is the one does not take offense over me."

Form-critically, this text is a chreia (pronouncement story). At the beginning stands a narrative exposition (vv. 18-21), which functions as a concrete occasion for a dictum of Jesus (vv. 22-23), whose content points, however, beyond the individual situation. In the present case the exposition reflects the original difference between the "stronger one" announced by John (Mark 1.7; see at 3.16) and the historical Jesus, who was identified with this figure only in retrospect, i.e., by the post-Easter Christian tradition. This tension comes to expression in the phrasing of the question of the Baptist in v. 19b (and v. 20c). On the one hand, the activity of Jesus does not fit with the action profile of the "fire baptizer" announced by John. On the other hand, among his contemporaries his activity could certainly have given rise to the question of whether Jesus's claim to be the authentic representative of God was justified after all. Within the present text this tension finds expression in the fact that neither the question of the Baptist fits with his proclamation (that Jesus was not the announced "fire baptizer" must have been clear to everyone) nor does the answer of Jesus fit with the question, which therefore is not really answered. For this reason, the narrative exposition cannot have been developed from the dictum. Plus, the saying of Jesus in v. 22 cannot stand for itself, but is only meaningful as an answer to a question about his identity. These incoherencies speak for an old, i.e., pre-Easter, age of the tradition, without one needing to assume that John himself was the originator of the question.

There are form-critical reasons for the fact that a reaction of the Baptist to the answer of Jesus remains unnarrated, for chreiae (pronouncement stories) regularly lack such a reaction. In them the questioner always functions only as a cue-giver for the protagonist, and the present pericope is a story of Jesus rather than a story of John.

The exposition is more extensive in Luke than in Matthew 11.2-6 where the sequence of question and answer is narrated much more compactly. In the literature it is usually assumed that the shorter Matthean version is closer to the Q-*Vorlage* than the cumbersome Lukan version. It is, however, equally possible that Matthew shortened it (cf. Davies/Allison 2001–2004, II: 235) or that Luke expanded it at one place (v. 21?) and Matthew shortened it at another (v. 20?) (see also Schürmann; Marshall; Bock).

18-19 Luke interrupts the scenic and temporal cohesion of his narrative, for he shifts to the location of John the Baptist, whose placement in prison by Herod (Antipas) he had last reported (3.20). He now narrates the prehistory of the question, which he has the messengers of the Baptist direct to Jesus in v. 20. Whether the comprehensive phrasing περὶ πάντων τούτων (18a) is meant to refer to the episodes narrated in 7.1-17 (cf. 24.9; Acts 24.8; 1 Thessalonians 4.6) or to the entirety of the previous activity of Jesus cannot be determined with certainty. In any case, the attention of the readers is withdrawn from Jesus for a short period. The difference between time of narration and narrated time is substantial. The adaptation to the context has also not been particularly successful because the duration of the narrated event implies a long uneventful stay of Jesus in Nain. (Matthew has resolved the problem of the adaptation of the tradition to the context better by placing a summary before it in 11.1). The fact that John sends *two* disciples to Jesus (v. 18b; diff. Matthew 11.2) finds its counterpart in the sending in pairs of other messengers (cf. Mark 6.7; 11.1parr.; Luke 10.1; Acts 8.14; 9.38; 13.2; 19.22; Revelation 11.3). This is always intended to secure the authenticity of the communication (cf. Jeremias 1966, 132–39). In the background stands the fact that only a statement confirmed by two witnesses is valid in court (cf. Deuteronomy 19.15; Matthew 18.16; 26.60; John 8.17; 2 Corinthians 13.1; 1 Timothy 5.19; Hebrews 10.28). For the typical designation of Jesus as κύριος in the narrator speech in v. 19a, see v. 13.

With ὁ ἐρχόμενος and προσδοκῶμεν (ἕτερον—although it is better attested in the manuscripts than ἄλλον—must be explained as influenced by Matthew 11.3) Luke takes up two key words that he had already used in 3.15-17, where the concern was with the messiahship of the Baptist and the announcement of the coming "stronger one." Therefore, the definite article neither has titular meaning nor does it point to the Jewish expectation of a messianic figure (cf. the different proposals in Nolland and Bock). Rather, here ὁ ἐρχόμενος means none other than "the stronger one about whom John said that he comes after him."

20 The disciples sent by John act in the manner that was required of ancient messengers (for παραγενόμενοι + *verbum finitum*, see at 14.21). They legitimate themselves by naming their commissioner (v. 20b; cf. the correspondence in wording in 1 Samuel 25.40: Δαυὶδ ἀπέστειλεν ἡμᾶς πρὸς σέ ["David has sent us to you"]) and repeat the message given to them word for word (v. 20c; as here it appears as a question in 2 Kings 8.9). For the designation of John as βαπτιστής, see at 3.3b.

With **21** Luke wants to inform the readers about the context of the events. This information differs from the previous healing summaries (4.40-41; 6.18-19; see also 5.15) in two respects. First, it does not grow out of a note about the coming of the people to Jesus, and, second, it is dated to the event narrated in v. 20 with the help of the anaphoric temporal specification ἐν ἐκείνῃ (cf. also Mark 13.11 par. Matthew 10.19; Matthew 8.13; 18.11; 26.55; John 4.53; Acts 16.33; Revelation 11.13). Thus, the summary describes the circumstances under which the messengers encounter Jesus. It undoubtedly functions to give a real foundation to the appeal to the seeing and hearing of the messengers in v. 22 and to make them into eye- and earwitnesses. This is not enough, however, to make this verse into the center of the whole pericope (so Craghan 1967). For the typically Lukan talk of "evil [instead of 'unclean'] spirits," see at 8.2-3. Luke has separated the reference to the healing of the blind in v. 21b from the other healings and provided it with its own summary. In this way he wants to give it special emphasis and direct the attention of the readers to it, for without this reference v. 22 would remain floating in the air—Jesus speaks here of the healing of the blind, without it previously appearing in the Lukan story of Jesus.

22 Jesus's answer is formulated in such a way that the answering of the question is given back to the original questioner John. If they hand on to John what they have perceived as eye- and earwitnesses with Jesus's interpretation (v. 22c), he can answer his own question. The lexical pair "see and hear" in v. 22b may not be torn apart (Völkel 1973b, 171: "separation of deed and word of Jesus"; it is said that the seeing refers to v. 21 and the hearing to vv. 22-23), for as a merism, it describes the entirety of human capacity for perception (cf. the analogous pair formation in Matthew 13.13-17parr.; Acts 4.20; 7.34; 22.14-15; Philippians 1.27; 1 Peter 3.12). Thus, the relative pronoun ἅ is cataphoric and refers to what follows. The aorist form of ὁρᾶν and ἀκούειν (the present occurs in Matthew 11.4) must be understood as a 'report aorist' (in analogy to the "epistolary" aorist; cf. BDR §334). From the fictive situation of the messenger's reporting to John there is a looking back to the narrated present.

In 22c Jesus communicates to the messengers what they should say to their commissioner. He provides at the same time an interpretation of his activity. The text is carefully configured linguistically. Luke forms a catalogue-like double series of three two-word sentences that are each perfectly parallel syntactically. These sentences describe in a generalizing manner the nullification of different human diminutions of life. As elsewhere, here the intention of the catalogue form seeks to convey the impression of completeness. The series finds its counterpart in 4.18-19 where the commission of Jesus is described proleptically. Luke now provides the analeptic counterpart here. The change of εὐαγγελίσασθαι πτωχοῖς to πτωχοὶ εὐαγγελίζονται has taken place for the sake of the formal coherence of the series and therefore may not be taken as an argument for an original Aramaic form of the text (cf. also the analogous use in Joel 3.5[LXX] and Hebrews 4.2 as well as BDR §311.1 on the passive use of transitive *deponentia*). The items conveyed in the list receive their meaning through the fact that through the context they give information about Jesus's identity without being formulated linguistically as statements about Jesus's actions. Rather, healing events are described in which it is only implicitly presupposed that they are carried out by Jesus. Thus, in the first place it is above all *what* happens that is decisive. In this respect the list receives its semantic specificity through the fact that they bundle together prophetic promises of salvation that are based especially on Isaiah 26.19; 29.18; 35.5-6; 42.7, 18; 61.1 and describe in these texts the eschatic salvific action of *God* toward his people or function as metaphors for the reversing of Israel's unsalvation into salvation brought about *by God*.

A comparable catalogue-like concentration is found in 4Q521 2 II, 4–13, where the salvific action of God is likewise described: ". . . freeing prisoners, giving sight to the blind, straightening out the twis[ted]. . . . He will heal the badly wounded and will make the dead live, he will proclaim good news to the poor . . . and he will lead the . . . and enrich the hungry" (translated by Martínez/Tigchelaar 1998, 1045; cf. Maier 1995–1996, II: 684; see also with additional literature Kvalbein 1997; Niebuhr 1997).

The christological punch line resides in the fact that while it does not put Jesus in the place of God, it does let him *act* in God's place. What the prophets announced as *God's* action is realized through *Jesus*. In this respect we do not simply have here a listing of individual actions of Jesus; rather, a christological overall interpretation of his activity is made. Plus, on account of their anchoring in the prophetic promises (see above), the list lets Jesus's healings point beyond themselves and gives them an additional salvation-historical value. They do not merely remove individual human suffering, but they signal the dawning of the eschatic time of salvation for Israel.

23 Against this background the concluding macarism, which points beyond the particular situation of the question of the Baptist, receives a plausible sense. Its propositional content consists in the fact that the rejection of the christological claim formulated in v. 22c results in condemnation (cf. the analogous usage in Sirach 9.5; 23.8; 32.15). Accordingly, its pragmatic is aimed at the acceptance of this claim (see also Matthew 26.31, 33; Mark 6.3 par. Matthew 13.57; and G. Stählin, ThWNT 7: 338–58, esp. 348.35–36: "σκανδαλίζεσθαι ἐν αὐτῷ [can] form the counterpart to πιστεῦσαι εἰς αὐτόν").

7.24-28: Who Is John?

[24]**When the messengers of John had gone, he began to speak to the crowd about John, "Why did you go out into the wilderness—to look at a reed moved by the wind?** [25]**Or why did you go out—to see a person clothed in soft clothing? Behold, those who live in magnificent clothing and in luxury are in palaces!** [26]**Or why did you go out—to see a prophet? Yes, I say to you, (you see) more than a prophet!** [27]**This is the one about whom it is written, 'Behold, I send my messenger before your face; he will prepare your way before you.'** [28]**I say to you: among those born of women there is none greater than John, but the smallest in the kingdom of God is greater than him."**

The structure of this section is clear. Jesus's judgment on the identity of the Baptist (vv. 26c-27) is prepared for with the help of three parallel structured rhetorical questions (vv. 24b-c, 25a-b, 26a-b). Yet another saying is then added, which sets John in relation to the kingdom of God. The wording of the text mostly corresponds to the parallels in Matthew 11.7-11. Verses 24-27 and v. 28 were probably originally handed down independently of each other and connected for the first time by Q. There is a parallel to vv. 24-25 in Gospel of Thomas 78 and to v. 28 in Gospel of Thomas 46.

24-26 Syntactically the three questions in vv. 24b, 25a, 26a can also be understood in such a way that the pronoun τί asks not about the reason for the ἐξέρχεσθαι (so my translation in line with Luke 2.48 [see there]; 6.46; 19.33; 24.28a; Acts 1.11; 14.15; 26.8; see also W. Bauer 1988, 1633 with additional attestations; BDR §299.3; Gospel of Thomas 78.1), but about the object of the seeing: "To see what did you go out?" (so, e.g., Fitzmyer; Nolland; Radl). But the interrogative pronoun and the reference word (θεάσασθαι or ἰδεῖν respectively) are too far away from each other for this allocation. With regard to the addressed ὄχλοι, the questions do not fit particularly well in a town of Lower Galilee, whose population probably did not "go out to John in droves" (Radl I: 470); the parallel in Matthew 11.7-9 localizes the scene in an unspecified somewhere. All three questions are rhetorical, for the answer is clear from the beginning, and in the third question Jesus then provides it himself (v. 26a-c). In all three questions the concern is with the motives and expectations that led the people to John.

The answer that is required by the first two questions is "no." Their propositional content resides in the fact that Jesus reminds his hearers that they went out into the wilderness neither to see how a reed blows back and forth in the wind (v. 24b-c; κάλαμος can designate the individual reed and the reed bed as a whole; for the latter meaning, cf. Job 40.21; Psalm[LXX]

67.31; Isaiah 19.6; 35.7; Joseph and Aseneth 24.19–20; 27.8; 28.7–8) nor to meet a person "in white clothing" there (v. 25a-b).

The wording of **24c** corresponds to what Aesop writes in his famous fable about the character of the reed that justifies its superiority over the oak tree: "When a strong wind came, the reed swayed" (*Fabulae*, ed. Hausrath/Hunger 1970, 71.1). The blowing back and forth of reed by the wind is regarded as such a natural process that it can be used time and again as a comparison (cf. 3 Maccabees 2.22; Lucian of Samosata, *Hermotimus* 68). For this reason, everything favors the view that reed blown by the wind functions as an example rather than having a metaphorical meaning. It stands as an example for a natural and absolutely unexciting event that could attract no person into a desolate place (see also Davies/ Allison 2001–2004, II: 247: "an everyday sight"). This also fits the meaning of θεάσασθαι (cf. W. Bauer 1988, s.v.). By contrast, the suggestion that one should see in this an allusion to Herod Antipas (Theissen 1992, 26–42) is not plausible. It is based not only on a highly controversial interpretation of the emblem of a Herodian coin as a reed, but it also depends on too many hypothetical auxiliary hypotheses. ἔρημος may by no means be translated "desert," since reeds only grow where there is also water.

25 argues with a somewhat different logic. No person expected to find John in "soft," i.e., in expensive clothes, because such people are not found in the wilderness but in palaces. Thus, the exclamation in v. 25c is related to the addressees' behavior at that time and does not intend to communicate a new insight to them. Thus, the concern now is with the image that people had of John. The question is based on an opposition between ἔρημος and βασίλειον ("palace"), and it reflects the Baptist's conspicuous clothing and food ethos (cf. Mark 1.6 par. Matthew 3.4). As a characteristic of "garments" (ἱμάτια), "soft" (μαλακός) is attested only in pagan Greek texts; cf. Kock 1880–1888, Fragment 534: ἱμάτιον ἐφόρει μαλακόν ("he wore a soft garment"); Ps.-Diogenes, *Epistulae* 28.1; Galen, *In Hippocrates de victu acutorum*, ed. Kühn 1964, XV: 521 (μαλακὸν ἢ πολύπτυχον ἱμάτιον ["a garment that is soft or has many folds"]); Diogenes Laertius 5.67 (μαλακότης ἱματίων ["softness of garments"]); see also Artemidorus, *Onirocriticon* 1.78 (Pack 1963, 87.24); Chariton of Aphrodisias 1.4.9. But this does not yet make John into a Cynic (so Cameron 1990, 42ff), for while Cynics are indeed not found in "palaces," they are also not found in the "wilderness."

The third rhetorical question in **26** first records the expectation with which people did, in fact, go to the "wilderness"—namely, because they counted on meeting a prophet there. This image of the Baptist in public opinion is, on the one hand, confirmed by Jesus (ναί), and yet, on the other hand, immediately corrected by having him maintain that John is, in reality, more than a prophet.

27 clarifies that "more than a prophet" does not mean "something better than a prophet" but "not an ordinary but a special prophet." Luke now adds Mark 1.2, i.e., the mixed quotation from Malachi 3.1 and Exodus 23.20, which he had omitted at the relevant place at the beginning of chapter 3 (for the quotation introduction, cf. the parallels in CD I: 13; 4Q174 1, I, 3, 16). This quotation must have been connected very early with the Baptist tradition, for in 27c it reproduces the Hebrew text of Malachi 3.1 and not the text of the Septuagint. Both texts are connected with each other in Exodus Rabbah 32.9 (cf. Bill. I: 597). Thus, John is again sketched into the expectation of the eschatic return of *Elias redivivus* (cf. already 1.17, 76; see further there and at 3.4-6). This understanding of "more than a prophet" finds its abutment in 1.15c (see there): no other prophet was already filled with the Holy Spirit in the womb.

28 The concluding commentary-saying places John in relation to the kingdom of God. We are dealing with an antithetical *parallelismus membrorum*, in which the two cola end with the same word (ἐστίν). Beyond this, the rhetorical figure of the *redditio* ("repetition as . . . bracket"; Lausberg 1973, §625) is formed by the placement of μείζων at the beginning and the end. The social hierarchies of the human world and the kingdom of God are set over against each other. The latter is understood here as a future entity that is spatial and transcendent (see also Matthew 5.19, 20; 7.21; 8.11par.; 18.1, 3-4; 21.31; 23.13; Mark 9.47; 10.23-25parr.; thus, the concern is not with the church) in which the allocation of prestige is oriented to a different system of value than in the human world, though there too the allocation is made, of course, by God. The phrasing "born of a woman" or "born of women" is also found elsewhere as a metonymic description for "human being" (cf. Job 14.1; 15.14; 25.4; 1QS XI, 21; 1QH V, 31; XXI, 2, 9-10; XXIII, 13-14; Galatians 4.4; Bill. I: 597–98). It is always used when the concern is to accentuate human estrangement from God or the distance of humans from God. This connotation is also present here, for the hyperbolic placement of John at the highest position that God has to give within the world of humans serves to define the kingdom of God as a reality whose social hierarchy is categorically different from that of the earthly world. In the kingdom of God even the smallest (for the understanding of μικρότερος as a superlative, cf. BDR §60) is superior to the greatest in the world of humans. In this way John is excluded *de facto* from the kingdom of God or it is presupposed that he does not belong to it. This firm delineation of a boundary makes it probable that this saying was constructed only after Easter and belongs in the context of the differentiation of the first "Christians" from the Baptist movement.

7.29-35: Jesus's Judgment about His and the Baptist's Contemporaries

[29]**"And all the people—when it heard** (him)**—and even the tax collectors acknowledged God to be just and let themselves be baptized with the baptism of God.** [30]**By contrast, the Pharisees and the scribes rejected God's plan for them by not letting themselves be baptized by him.**

[31]**With whom should I compare then the people of this generation? With whom are they comparable?** [32]**They are like children who sit at the market place and call to one another and say, 'We played the flute for you, and you did not dance. We sung a dirge for you, and you did not weep.'** [33]**For John the Baptist has come; he eats no bread and drinks no wine, and you say, 'He has a demon!'** [34]**The Son of Man has come; he eats and drinks, and you say, 'Behold a glutton and a drunk, a friend of tax collectors and sinners!'** [35]**And wisdom has been vindicated by all her children."**

The third part is composed of a parabolic saying with introduction and application (vv. 31-34; parallel in Matthew 11.16-19) and a narrative introduction (vv. 29-30), to which the concluding saying in v. 35 refers. Its status in the literature is controversial. Does the authorial narrator, i.e., Luke, speak (e.g., Marshall; Nolland; Bock) or does he have Jesus speak (e.g., Plummer; Schneider; Radl)? The better arguments support the second assumption, for it is quite unlikely that πᾶς ὁ λαός (v. 29) refers to the ὄχλοι of v. 24, i.e., to the hearers of the preceding words of Jesus about the Baptist (see also Ernst 1991b, 198). These two verses are filled with typical Lukan phrasings—πᾶς ὁ λαός (v. 29; see at 2.10), τὸ βάπτισμα Ἰωάννου (apart from Mark 11.30parr., it only occurs elsewhere in Acts 1.22; 13.24; 18.25; 19.3) and the talk of the βουλὴ τοῦ θεοῦ (cf. also Acts 2.23; 4.28; 5.38; 13.36; 20.27; see Christ 1970, 78). Therefore, a great deal favors the view that Luke did not find these verses but formulated them himself (cf. the presentation of the arguments for and against this view in Ernst 1991b). Moreover, the concern is exclusively with background information for the readers by means of which Luke wants to give a very specific orientation to the parabolic saying that follows from v. 31 on. It is easy to recognize what it consists in. The sweeping way in which v. 31—as the handed-down introduction to the parabolic saying—charges all contemporaries of Jesus and the Baptist with having reacted to their respective proclamation with rejection very clearly contradicts the Lukan presentation in chapter 3 with respect to John. According to 3.12, it is precisely the tax collectors mentioned in v. 29 who responded to the call of the Baptist. Thus, by placing vv. 29-30 before vv. 31-35, Luke wants to indicate to the readers against whom the accusation made in the latter verses is really directed—namely, against the Pharisees and scribes. And these are, not without reason, the same people whom Luke has introduced as opponents and critics of Jesus in his narrative.

29-30 By contrasting their respective reactions to the proclamation of John the Baptist in the form of a syncrisis (cf. K. Berger 1984b, 1175ff), the groups of the tax collectors, on the one hand, and the Pharisees and scribes, on the other hand, are differentiated out from the πᾶς ὁ λαός. At the center stands the behavior of the Pharisees and the scribes. The positive reaction of the tax collectors functions merely as a bright foil (in the sense of: "Even those who have such a bad reputation [see at 3.12] let themselves be baptized by John"; for this use of καί, cf. BDR §442.8) against which the rejection of the Pharisees and the scribes appears even darker. Accordingly, John the Baptist already brought about a division in Israel (see at 2.34), which resulted in a status reversal (see at 3.1-20). In 7.36-50 this Lukan *topos* is then realized in the narrative on two levels.

The reaction of the tax collectors, described in **29** with ἐδικαίωσαν τὸν θεόν, should not be translated merely with "affirm that God is right" or the like. The use of this expression in Psalms of Solomon 3.5 ("The righteous stumbled, he acknowledged the Lord to be just [ἐδικαίωσεν τὸν κύριον]"); 8.7 ("I have acknowledged God to be just [ἐδικαίωσα τὸν θεόν] . . . God has revealed their sins before the sun") and its linguistic convergence, e.g., with the confession of sins in Psalm[LXX] 50.6 ("against you alone have I sinned, and I have done evil before you—in order that you may be proved just in your words [ὅπως ἂν δικαιωθῇς ἐν τοῖς λόγοις σου]"); Psalms of Solomon 8.23-26 ("God has been proved just in his judgments . . . , we have justified your name [ἐδικαιώθη ὁ θεὸς ἐν τοῖς κρίμασιν αὐτοῦ . . . , ἐδικαιώσαμεν τὸ ὄνομά σου]"); 9.2 (dispersal of Israel among the nations "according to the word of God, in order that you may be proved just, O God [ἵνα δικαιωθῇς ὁ θεός]") support the view that this phrasing is used here as an allusion to the acknowledgment that God is just in the confession of sin, and thus that Luke wants to express specifically with this that the tax collectors have met the Baptist's demand for repentance.

30 Luke describes the reaction of the Pharisees and scribes (νομικοί) as a mirror image. With the exception of Matthew 22.35 (par. Luke 10.25), the νομικοί are found in the Gospels only in Luke (see further 11.45, 46, 52; 14.3 and Titus 3.13 as individual occupational designation, i.e., "Zenas the lawyer"; see also Plutarch, *Sulla* 36.3; *Moralia* 271e). As here, Luke also places them together with the Pharisees in 11.42-44/45-52; 14.3 (like the νομοδιδάσκαλοι in 5.17).

In Jewish texts this term is attested elsewhere only in 4 Maccabees 5.4. From this text, however, it follows that νομικός is simply another word for γραμματεύς ("scribe"), for here the subsequent martyr Eleazar is introduced as "according to origin, a priest, according to education, a scribe (τὸ γένος ἱερεύς, τὴν ἐπιστήμην νομικός)," while he is designated in 2 Maccabees 6.18 as "one of the leading scribes" (τις τῶν πρωτευόντων γραμματέων). To this corresponds the fact that after the woes against the Pharisees and νομικοί in 11.42-52, Luke continues in v. 53 with οἱ γραμματεῖς καὶ οἱ Φαρισαῖοι. In pagan Greek texts νομικός is attested, starting in the first century BCE, as an occupational designation; cf. Arius Didymus, *Epitome of Stoic Ethics* 11d (Pomeroy 1999, 68.7–8): "a νομικός is an interpreter of the law (ἐξηγητικὸς τοῦ νόμου)"; Strabo 12.2.9: "an interpreter of the law (ἐξηγητὴς τῶν νόμων) like the νομικοί among the Romans"; cf. also Plutarch, *Cicero* 26.9: "Publius Costa wanted to be a νομικός, but he was ungifted and uneducated." Luke probably took this term from this technical usage (see also Bormann 2001, 153ff).

On the basis of its position, εἰς ἑαυτούς should be connected not with βουλὴ θεοῦ but with ἠθέτησαν. If it were otherwise, the personal pronoun rather than the reflexive pronoun would have had to be used. Moreover, there was no special plan for the Pharisees and scribes. The summons to the baptism of repentance applied equally to all. Thus, Luke wants to say that the Pharisees and scribes rejected the summons of John and in this way opposed the will of God (for the phrasing, cf. Psalm^{LXX} 32.10c: κύριος . . . ἀθετεῖ βουλὰς ἀρχόντων ["The Lord . . . confounds the resolutions of the rulers"]). This is the first mention of the "plan" (βουλή) of God in the Lukan work (cf. then Acts 2.23; 4.28; 13.36; 20.27: metonymically for the content of the Pauline proclamation). It consists in nothing other than the fulfillment of the promises issued to Israel. What is said here in relation to the Pharisees and scribes with reference to the proclamation of the Baptist is repeated in Acts 28.26-27 in relation to the greatest portion of Israel with reference to the Pauline proclamation of Christ.

31 In addition to the parallel in Matthew 11.16, the (double-)question as a parable introduction also occurs in Mark 4.30 par. Luke 13.18; 13.20; see also (though with a different rhetorical intention) Isaiah 40.18 (τίνι ὡμοιώσατε κύριον καὶ τίνι ὁμοιώτατι ὡμοιώσατε αὐτόν; ["With whom do you compare the Lord, and with what comparison do you compare him?"]) as well as the formulaic introduction to many rabbinic parables: ל דומה הדבר למה‎ ("To what may it be compared? To one . . ."; Exodus Mekilta 5 on Exodus 20.2 and the examples mentioned in Bill. II: 8). The designation γενεὰ αὕτη (literally: "this generation") for the contemporaries of Jesus is attested in the whole Jesus tradition (cf. Luke 11.31-32 par. Matthew 12.41-42; Mark 8.12 [2×], 38; 13.30 par. Luke 21.32; Matthew 12.45; 23.26; 24.34; Luke 11.29-30, 50-51; 17.25; see also Genesis 7.1; Psalm 12.8; Jubilees 23.16, 22; Hebrews 3.10; in the two Old Testament texts "this generation" as sinful and hostile to God stands over against the individual devout person who is preserved by God; see also at 9.41 and Meinertz 1957).

32 How the picture of the children playing at the market place (v. 32) should be understood and what it should illustrate with regard to the subject matter—i.e., the reaction of "this generation" to the activity of John and Jesus (vv. 33-34)—is controversial. Today the interpretation that has found the broadest acceptance equates "the people of this generation" with the children who are respectively addressed in vv. 32c-d and who want to play neither "wedding" nor "funeral," i.e., neither a joyful game nor a sorrowful game, although both were offered to them (for other proposals, cf. the overviews in Zeller 1977a; Bock; Luz 1985–2002, I: 184ff). Thus, the scene, which is described in v. 32c-d, recounts that there is a group of children who cannot motivate another group to play with them, namely neither through playing the flute nor through songs of lament, and who now complains about them. The *tertium comparationis* of the imagery and subject matter would then lie in the fact that one cannot satisfy the people of this generation. They find fault with both John (v. 33) and Jesus (v. 34). "If John is too ascetic for the present generation, Jesus is not ascetic enough" (P. Müller 1992, 252). Expressed again in terms of the picture, it is *not only a certain kind of game* that they do not like, but they do not want to join their game *at all*. It is this fundamental stance of refusal that is illustrated with the help of the opposing game suggestions (dancing and mourning). There is, in fact, much that supports this interpretation, but one must guard oneself at any rate against a point-by-point allegorizing that identifies the children playing dance music with Jesus and the children asking for mourning with John. Although the opposition of αὐλεῖν / ὀρχεῖσθαι, on the one hand, and θρηνεῖν / κλαίειν, on the other hand, finds its analogy in v. 32 in the opposition of the characteristics that are attributed to John ("eats no bread, drinks no wine"; v. 33a) and Jesus ("eats and drinks"; v. 34a), the parabolic saying and application do not intend a point-by-point substitution that goes beyond this. Against this speaks not only the different sequence but also the introductory formula in v. 32a, which indicates an analogous relation of correspondence of the *situations* as, e.g., in Matthew 13.45 ("The kingdom of heaven is like a merchant who . . ."). Thus, one would need to translate as follows: "With the people of this generation the situation is like when children . . ." (cf. Zeller 1977a, 255).

The relative sentence at the end of the verse is text-critically disputed. The grammatically correct phrasing ἃ (sc. τὰ παιδία) λέγει is supported by its manuscript attestation by ℵ* B and by the fact that it was uncommon, while λέγοντες (D L *f¹³* and others) is grammatically incorrect and thus the *lectio difficilior* in this respect, but is, on the other hand, used so often that the assumption of a secondary adjustment to other passages is likely. One can derive the origin of the other readings from this variant (καὶ λέγουσιν, A Θ Ψ 33 𝔐 and others; λέγοντα, א² W Ξ and others), but not the relative clause. The latter observation contradicts, among other things, the argumentation in favor of the originality of ἃ λέγει in Victor 2009, ad loc.

33-34 The descriptions of the Baptist and Jesus in vv. 33b, 34b are reduced to a single distinguishing feature in order to illustrate in this way the peculiar character of the "people of this generation." *They* are in the focus here, not John or Jesus. Consideration is thus given to the same difference that was thematized in 5.33 in relation to the disciples of the two. There it was described as a difference between the "fasting" (νηστεύειν; 5.33b) of the disciples of John and the "eating and drinking" (5.33d; the phrasing corresponds to 7.34b) of the disciples of Jesus: John practices food asceticism and Jesus does not. This difference is expressed even more pointedly in Matthew 11.18-19 insofar as it says concerning John there that he "neither eats nor drinks" (μήτε ἐσθίων μήτε πίνων; v. 18b) while Luke says that he "neither eats bread nor drinks wine" (μήτε ἐσθίων ἄρτον μήτε πίνων οἶνον; v. 33b). This is nothing more than a linguistic difference, however, for in the Lukan version the concern is not with an abstinence from specific foodstuffs. Rather, "(eating) bread and (drinking) wine" form a fixed lexical pair that can be used in a metonymic way for eating and drinking as such; cf. e.g., Jubilees 45.5: "And Joseph and his brothers *ate bread* before their father, and they *drank wine*. And Jacob rejoiced very greatly because he saw Joseph *eating* and *drinking* with his brothers before him" (translated by O. S. Wintermute, *OTP* II: 136; see also Genesis 14.18 (translated in 1QapGen ar XXII, 15 as מאכל ומשתה ["food and drink"]); Judges 19.19; Proverbs 4.17 ("They eat the bread of wickedness and drink the wine of violence"); 9.5; Nehemiah 5.15; Ecclesiastes 9.7; Isaiah 36.17 ("a land in which there is wheat and wine, a land in which there are bread and vineyards"); Testament of Levi 8.4–5 (cf. also the texts mentioned at 5.30). Thus, the concern is not at all with the respective "material." (Thus, Böcher's hypothesis [Böcher 1971/1972] that ἄρτος is a false translation of the Hebrew לֶחֶם, which could mean "bread" *and* "flesh," starts from false presuppositions; moreover, the Matthean version probably stood in Q.) But the Lukan description of the food asceticism of the Baptist may also be due to a rereading of Deuteronomy 29.5^LXX (on Israel's stay in the wilderness [sic!]: ἄρτον οὐκ ἐφάγετε, οἶνον καὶ σίκερα οὐκ ἐπίετε ["Bread you have not eaten, wine and intoxicating drink you have not drunk"]) in the light of Luke 1.15 (see there).

The second person plural λέγετε in vv. 33c, 34c (diff. Matthew 11.18-19) shows that Luke apparently now envisages the Pharisees and the scribes (v. 30) as addressees of Jesus's speech. They are characterized as inconsistent insofar as they react to two opposing modes of behavior equally with rejection. They explain the food asceticism practiced by John as a consequence of demonic possession (v. 33c; the phrasing δαιμόνιον ἔχει has correspondences in 7.33; John 7.20; 8.48-49, 52; 10.20 [together with μαίνεται]; see also Mark 3.22, 30; 5.15; 7.25; 9.17; Luke 4.33; 13.11; Acts 8.7; 16.16; 19.13; cf. H. Hanse, ThWNT 2: 820–22), and they react to the non-ascetic behavior of Jesus by accusing him of excessiveness in eating and drinking (v. 34c). Jesus's accusation also implies that the Pharisees and scribes stigmatize his and the Baptist's relation to food, which is different, to be sure, but still does not transgress the framework of what is societally acceptable.

Behind the phrasing (ἄνθρωπος) φάγος καὶ οἰνοπότης presumably stands a lexical pair such as זוֹלֵל וְסֹבֵא in Deuteronomy 21.20 and Proverbs 23.20-21 (without an exact counterpart in the LXX; the Greek noun φάγος appears elsewhere only in Zenobius Paroemiographus 73 [Leutsch/Schneidewin 1958, I: 26]: ἄλλοισι μὲν γλῶττα, ἄλλοισι δὲ γόμφιοι· παρόσον οἱ μὲν γὰρ λάλοι, οἱ δὲ φάγοι ["For some it is the tongue, for others the teeth: in this respect the some are gossips, others gluttons"]). The tag "friend of tax collectors and sinners" fits the theme of "eating and drinking" insofar as Jesus's nearness to "tax collectors and sinners" (on this lexical pair, see at 5.30 and Völkel 1978) is also described as table fellowship in Mark 2.13, 16 parr.; Luke 15.1-2. Precisely the linking of these two verdicts and their appearance in Q, the Gospel of Mark, and Lukan special material therefore makes visible something typical in the activity of the historical Jesus and in the perception of Jesus by his contemporaries (criterion of multiple attestation).

35 With the metaphorical talk of "all the children (of Wisdom)," the concluding words sketch the positive counterpicture to the rejection of the Baptist and Jesus by "the people of this generation" (cf. Christ 1970, esp. 77ff). What Luke had called the "plan of God" in v. 30 is now called "Wisdom." In the background stands the motif of the inviting Wisdom who encounters rejection and acceptance (cf. e.g., Proverbs 1.20-33; 8.1-21; Sirach 4.11-19). In this connection the ones who are regarded as "children of Wisdom" are consistently the people who follow the call of Wisdom and allow themselves to be led by her (cf. Proverbs 2.1; 8.32; Sirach 4.11). In contrast to the "children (of Wisdom)" the "people of this generation" are assigned the role of those who have rejected Wisdom, who was present in the messengers John and Jesus; for the notion of the presence of Wisdom in her messengers, cf. Proverbs 9.3; Wisdom of Solomon

7.27. After those who receive the call of Wisdom become her "children" in this way, Wisdom becomes recognizable in their way of life and in this way "legitimated" as such (cf. Kilgallen 2003b). Thus, ἐδικαιώθη means more than that Wisdom merely "experiences affirmation" from the side of her children or "is said to be just." Therefore, the preposition ἀπό can be understood best as a marker of the indirect originator (in the sense of "because of, due to"; see also Matthew 18.7: "Woe to the world ἀπὸ τῶν σκανδάλων" as well as W. Bauer 1988, 176); *pace* Gathercole 2003b, who wants to understand ἐδικαιώθη ἀπό from Romans 6.7; Sirach 26.29 ("Wisdom has been separated from her children"; 487). One must, however, pay attention to the fact that here we find precisely not ἀπὸ ἁμαρτίας; moreover, Acts 13.38-39 is not comparable grammatically. Despite the rejection by the people of this generation, Wisdom is (and above all, of course, her messengers are) vindicated by the existence and way of being of "all her children"—namely, as *God's* wisdom. In this affirmation it is therefore also implied that God's wisdom is accessible in the proclamation of the Baptist and Jesus.

7.36-50: The Pharisee and the Woman Sinner

[36]Now one of the Pharisees asked him to eat with him. And he went into the house of the Pharisee and reclined at table. [37]And behold, there was a woman in the town, a sinner. And she learned that he reclined at table in the house of the Pharisee, and brought an alabaster flask with aromatic oil [38]and placed herself, weeping unceasingly, under his feet and began to wet his feet with the tears, and with the hair of her head she wiped (them), and she kissed his feet and anointed (them) with the aromatic oil. [39]When the Pharisee who had invited him saw this he said to himself, "If this one were really a prophet, he would know who and what sort of woman she is who touches him; for she is a sinner." [40]And Jesus answered and said to him. "Simon, I must say something to you." But he said, "Rabbi, speak!"

[41]"A moneylender had two debtors. One owed him five hundred denarii, the other fifty. [42]Because they were not in position to pay it back, he cancelled (both debts). Who of them will love him more?" [43]Simon answered and said, "I assume, the one to whom he cancelled more." He said, "You have judged rightly."

[44]And he turned to the woman and said to Simon, "Do you see this woman? I came into your house, (and) you have poured no water on my feet, but she has wet my feet with tears and has wiped (them) with her hair. [45]You did not give me a kiss, but since I entered, she has not ceased to kiss my feet. [46]You did not anoint my head with oil, but she

anointed my feet with aromatic oil. [47]**For this reason I say to you: her many sins are forgiven, for she has loved much. But the one who is forgiven little loves little."** [48]**And he said to her, "Your sins are forgiven."** [49]**And the other guests began to say among themselves, "Who is this who even forgives sins?"** [50]**But he said to the woman, "Your faith has saved you. Go forth in peace!"**

This episode functions as a narrative illustration of Jesus's designation as "friend of tax collectors and sinners" (v. 34). It explains what this friendship is based upon—knowledge of Jesus as "Savior" (cf. 2.11), in this case from sins. That Luke brings a "woman sinner" together with Jesus in the house of a Pharisee of all places is evidence of his subtle irony—as is the fact that Jesus was invited to eat by a Pharisee of all people, after he had previously been spoken of as a "glutton and drunk" (see also Neale 1991, 141–42).

The narrative's constellation of figures is the same as in the controversy dialogues of Luke 5.29-32 and 15.1-32. In all three texts Jesus interacts on the one hand with so-called sinners and on the other hand with Pharisees, and he always does so in the same way. First, in a narrative exposition the nearness between Jesus and "sinners" is highlighted, then the criticism that the Pharisees advance is narrated, and finally, Jesus meets this criticism with shorter or more extensive remarks. Moreover, all three texts connect the controversy dialogue with a meal situation (5.29-30; 7.36; 15.2) and have Jesus answer 'in parables' (5.31; 7.41-43; 15.3-32). The current episode differs from the two other texts, which end with a saying addressed to the Pharisaic critics, through the fact that Jesus turns once more to the "woman sinner" at the end (vv. 48-50).

The threefold structure is clearly recognizable. After the introduction (v. 36), *(1)* vv. 37-38 narrate the event that is discussed in what follows. *(2)* Verses 39-47 report a dialogue between Jesus and the Pharisee over the correct understanding of the event, which is again composed of three parts: *(a)* the interpretation of the Pharisee (v. 39); *(b)* the narration of a parable by Jesus (vv. 40-43); *(c)* the application of the parable to the present case (vv. 44-47). *(3)* Verses 48-50 narrate Jesus's reaction to the behavior of the woman. Parable and controversy dialogue are interlocked through the key word "love" (v. 42/v. 47) and via the semantic connection of "fifty" and "five hundred" (v. 41) or "more" to the opposition of "much" and "little" (v. 47), so that the two cannot be separated from each other in terms of tradition history.

The episode has two different counterparts in Mark 14.3-9 (Luke has no parallel to this) and John 12.1-8. It is common to all three narratives that Jesus reclines at table in a house and a *woman* applies *aromatic oil* (μύρον) to him, which is followed by a dialogue with other meal guests. Luke has the following elements in common with one of the two versions:

- *with Mark 14.3-9*: *(a)* the host is named *Simon* (vv. 40, 43, 44/Mark 14.3);
  (b) the woman brings an *alabaster flask with aromatic oil* (ἀλάβαστρον μύρου; v. 37/Mark 14.3),
- *with John 12.1-8*: *(a)* the woman *anoints the feet* of Jesus (v. 38/John 12.3);
  (b) she *wipes the feet with her hair* (v. 38/John 12.3; with the difference, of course, that she does this in Luke before the anointing and in John after it).

The following features of the narrative exposition (vv. 36-39) are only attested in the Lukan version: *(a)* The narrative does not take place in Bethany and also is not situated in the vicinity of Jesus's passion; *(b)* the host is a Pharisee (v. 36); *(c)* the woman is designated as a "sinner" (vv. 37, 39); *(d)* she weeps and wets Jesus's feet with her tears (v. 38); *(e)* she kisses Jesus's feet (v. 38); *(f)* the commentary on the behavior of the woman criticizes not her but Jesus (v. 39).

How should the commonalities and differences between the three narratives be explained? It is entirely unlikely that Luke 7.36-50 is nothing but a transformation of Mark 14.3-9 (e.g., Wellhausen; Klostermann; von Bendemann 2000), for there are too many differences for this to be the case, and the dependence on auxiliary hypotheses, which are then required to explain the Johannine version, is too great. Two possibilities then remain. *(a)* The origin of the three different versions was the tradition of a single anointing that took place in the house of a certain Simon and was not localized in the context of the passion of Jesus. In the oral tradition three different versions of the narrative arose from this, which then found their literary expression in the Markan, Lukan, and Johannine versions. Luke was familiar with the narrative both from Mark 14.3-9 and independently of it (so e.g., Holst 1976; Oberlinner 2003; Fitzmyer). *(b)* From the beginning there were two independent traditions of anointing events—namely, a narration of the anointing of the feet that was not fixed biographically and a narrative of the anointing of the head of Jesus in Bethany shortly before his death. In the course of the oral tradition, motifs from the one narrative drifted into the other and vice versa. This resulted in the three existing versions (so e.g., Marshall; Nolland). Both are conceivable (with a slightly higher likelihood for the first model).

The episode is the first of three meal scenes in which Jesus is invited into the houses of Pharisees (see also 11.37-52; 14.1-24). They are found only in Luke. One can add to this that the comparison between the Pharisee and the "woman sinner" (vv. 44-47), attested only in Luke, is connected to the syncrisis between Pharisees and tax collectors in the preceding speech of Jesus (7.30), which is also attested only in Luke. All this makes it likely that the setting and the configuration of the controversy dialogue starting in v. 39 come from Luke. With their help Luke recounts the tradition of the turning of a woman regarded as a "sinner" to Jesus as part of the story of Jesus's conflicts with the Pharisees (see also Neale 1991, 142). He picks up from 5.29-32 and will then take up this thematic thread again in 15.1-32.

36 The new episode is closely connected to what precedes. The change to the house of a Pharisee lies on a more specific level than the one marked in 7.11 with the reaching of the "town" Nain (cf. also the analogy in 4.38); the narrative will not return to this level again until 8.1. The occasion and intention of Jesus's invitation by the Pharisee can remain open, for they play no role in what follows. Rather, the decisive guidance of the reader takes place through the fact that from the inventory of characteristics that were available to him for characterizing the person who issues the invitation, Luke chooses of all things his belonging to the group of the Pharisees.

37-38 The linguistic configuration of the introduction of the woman in 37a (καὶ ἰδού + nominal sentence; cf. BDR §127) resembles the expositional introduction of new narrative figures in Matthew 12.10; Luke 5.12, 18; 13.11; 19.2; 23.50; Acts 8.27. As here, there follows also in Acts 8.27 the specification with the help of an imperfect relative clause (ὃς δέ; on ὅστις as a substitute for the definite relative pronoun, cf. BDR §293). A certain linguistic analogy is found in Josephus, *Antiquitates judaicae* 8.236 (ἦν δέ τις ἐν τῇ πόλει πρεσβύτης πονηρὸς ψευδοπροφήτης ["There was in the town a wicked old man, a false prophet"]). The designation of the woman as a "sinner" characterizes her with regard to her relation to God, for this tag makes her into a person who acts against the will of God. The narrator is only interested in this. What makes her a "sinner" in the eyes of God is left to the readers' imagination. One usually imagines her to be a prostitute (πόρνη) or courtesan (ἑταίρα; cf. Melzer-Keller 1997, 119ff), and Luke may also wish to evoke this impression. However, this is irrelevant for the content (see also Oberlinner 2003, 264–65). Rather, it is only important here that through her designation as ἁμαρτωλός the woman is placed at the side of those of whom it was said in 5.32 that Jesus came to call them to repentance. With ἐν τῇ πόλει Luke emphasizes that the woman was known in the whole town as a "sinner." This information is required to explain to the readers the corresponding recognition of the woman by the Pharisee in v. 39d.

In vv. 37b-38a, with the help of three aorist participles (ἐπιγνοῦσα . . . κομίσασα . . . στᾶσα), Luke first describes a sequence of actions that the woman undertakes in preparation for the main storyline narrated in 38b-e. A fourth participle (κλαίουσα), which is now present, merges into the main storyline. The fact that the woman learns about Jesus being in the house of the Pharisee is the point that stimulates the action. Thus, the initiative starts solely from her and she is solely concerned with Jesus. Luke does not provide her with the characteristics of the so-called uninvited guest (ἄκλητοι), which were not uncommon at ancient symposia (cf. e.g., Plato, *Symposium* 174b; Xenophon, *Symposium* 1.11), for unlike these the woman does not want to eat with the guests. The perfumed oil (μύρον), which she brings in her alabaster flask, has its place both in the Hellenistic symposia (cf. Xenophon, *Symposium* 2.3–4) and at the eschatic banquet of the nations on Mount Zion (cf. Isaiah 25.6^{LXX}: πίονται εὐφροσύνην, πίονται οἶνον, χρίσονται μύρον ["they will drink joy, they will drink wine, they will anoint themselves with oil"]). An ἀλάβαστρον μύρου, which is spoken of in v. 37c and in Mark 14.3, was evidently a common utensil, for this designation is widely attested in ancient literature (e.g., Herodotus 3.20; Alciphron, *Epistulae* 4.14.4; Lucian of Samosata, *Dialogi meretricii* 14.2; see also Ps.-Lucian, *Asinus* 51). Even Indian pearl divers can utilize it. They use it as a lure when fishing for oysters (Philostratus, *Vita Apollonii* 3.57.1). The woman places herself at the foot end of the couch of Jesus and thus occupies the place that is appointed for slaves (cf. Seneca *De beneficiis* 3.27.1: *servus, qui cenanti ad pedes steterat* ["a slave who placed himself at the feet of the one eating"]; Petronius, *Satyricon* 68.4).

The main storyline in v. 38b-e is also comprised of four subactions, which all take place at Jesus's feet (ἤρξατο βρέχειν . . . ἐξέμασσεν . . . κατεφίλει . . . ἤλειφεν). Jesus recapitulates these four actions in vv. 44e, f, 45b, 46b. Surprisingly there is much speculation about their meaning in the literature, although Luke has Jesus expressly state how they are to be understood in v. 47b. In these four actions nothing other than the great love that the woman has toward Jesus comes to expression (ἠγάπησεν πολύ).

As a group these actions only occur here. As individual actions, some of them are found outside the New Testament:

An epigram attributed to Asclepiades speaks of *wetting* (βρέχειν) *through tears* in a revealing manner: "I wet (the crown) with tears; those in love weep easily. But the door opens, the beloved comes out, let the tears drop on his head so that his blond head becomes soaked in my so salty dew" (Anthologia Graeca 5.145; see also *IG* 14: 1422.5: δακρύοισιν ἔβρεχαν ὅλον τάφον ["they wet the whole burial site with tears"]).

The *kissing of the feet* can be a gesture of submission and homage (cf. G. Stählin, ThWNT 9: 119–20n73). In Xenophon, *Cyropaedia* 7.5.32 two military leaders kiss the hands and feet of their ruler Cyrus and "weep strongly for joy and relief" (πολλὰ δακρύοντες ἅμα χαρᾷ καὶ εὐφραινόμενοι); see also Dionysius of Halicarnassus, *Antiquitates romanae* 8.54.1 (Veturia threw herself to the ground, took Marcius's feet with both hands, and kissed them); Polybius 15.1.7; Heliodorus, *Aethiopica* 10.34.6 (expression of thanksgiving); *SGUÄ* I: 4323.5.

However, it was also used as a means of (erotic) flattery; cf. Epictetus, *Dissertationes* 4.1.17 (οὐδέποτέ σου τὸ δουλάριον ἐκολάκευσας; οὐδέποτ' αὐτοῦ τοὺς πόδας κατεφίλησας; ["Have you never flirted with your young slave? Have you never kissed his feet?"]); Longus, *Daphnis and Chloe* 4.16.1; 17.1. Aristophanes, *Vespae* 608 connects it with the anointing of the feet and other affectionate actions (a daughter to the father—but only because she wants his money). The latter is also often practiced in the context of symposia (cf. Athenaeus, *Deipnosophistae* 12.78 [553a]: "Among the Athenians it was customary τοὺς πόδας τῶν τρυφώντων ἐναλείφειν μύροις [to rub with oil the feet of the ones eating]," and the following dialogue on this topic; see also Antiphanes, Fragment 154 [Kock 1880–1888]). Thus, it certainly did not belong "in the sphere of perverse customs" (so Bovon I: 392).

39 The inner monologue of the Pharisee stands in the same place as the Pharisaic criticism of the (meal-)fellowship with "tax collectors and sinners" in 5.30; 15.2 and also fulfills the same form-critical function within the controversy dialogue. With the help of the readers' recollection, Luke has the inner monologue connect to the acclamation of v. 16 and call into question the designation of Jesus as a "great prophet" pronounced there. His view is based on a combination of two unspoken presuppositions—first, on an image of a prophet that ascribes to a prophet the ability to see through people and recognize what is hidden (cf. 1 Samuel 9.19-20; John 4.17-19; later Jewish and Christian texts can be found in G. Friedrich, ThWNT 6: 845n400), and second, on the social stigmatization of a woman who is regarded as a "sinner." From the fact that Jesus does not avoid the touch of the woman, the Pharisee thinks he can already infer almost syllogistically that he is not a prophet, because he does not recognize the τίς καὶ ποταπή (see also Philo, *Legum allegoriae* 1.91 concerning the Spirit) of the woman. Luke seasons this reaction with a powerful shot of irony, for the readers know, of course, that the Pharisee is correct—Jesus is, indeed, no prophet—but in a completely different way than he thinks: Jesus is the authentic representative of God's salvific presence in Israel. Therefore, he also knows, of course, that the woman is a "sinner" (in v. 40 it will be shown that he also knows the thoughts of the Pharisee). For this reason he can also allow her to touch him.

40 As in 5.31 and 15.3ff, here too Jesus answers the Pharisaic criticism of his nearness to (tax collectors and) sinners with a parable. However, Luke has never formulated the introduction as memorably as he does here. As an announcement of a communication, ἔχω . . . εἰπεῖν is attested almost as a formula in the Hellenistic environment of the New Testament (e.g., Plato, *Apologia* 34a; *Alcibiades I*, 119a; Philo, *De virtutibus* 211; Plutarch, *Moralia* 434d; Epictetus, *Dissertationes* 2.24.19; 3.22.2; never in the

LXX). The Pharisee Simon is the first person who addresses Jesus with διδάσκαλε (literally: "teacher"; for the translation, cf. John 1.38) in the Gospel of Luke (cf. subsequently Luke 9.38; 10.25; 11.45; 12.13; 18.18; 19.39; 20.21, 28, 39; 21.7). In Luke it is always outsiders who address Jesus in this way, and never the disciples (see 5.5; 9.49, on the one hand, and Mark 4.39; 9.38; 10.35; 13.1, on the other side). Surprisingly, such an address is nowhere attested in the Greek writings of early Judaism, while it is frequently found in pagan Greek works (e.g., Athenaeus, *Deipnosophistae* 9.36 [386e]; Galen, *De nervorum dissectione*, ed. Kühn 1964, II: 624; Lucian of Samosata, *Gallus* 10; Diogenes Laertius 6.69). This address is nowhere attested in the density with which it is encountered in the Gospels, however. Here, it is probably due to the translation of Aramaic רַבִּי or רַבּוּנִי as an address to Jesus (cf. John 1.38; 20.16; see further F. Hahn 1964 or Karrer 1998, 229).

41-43 The parable that Jesus narrates in these verses belongs to the so-called paradigmatic decisions (see also 2 Samuel 12.1-15; 4 Ezra 4.10-21), which are also found in Matthew 21.28-31 and Luke 10.25-37 (cf. Bultmann 1995, 198–99; K. Berger 1973b, 20–25). It is common to them that the narrative leads to a question addressed to the hearers that exhorts them to take a position. They then do so in the sense of the logic of the plot (v. 43; see also 2 Samuel 12.5-6; 4 Ezra 4.19; Matthew 21.31; Luke 10.37a), and after this, the narrator comments on the position that is taken (vv. 44-47; see also 2 Samuel 12.7-12; 4 Ezra 4.20-21; Matthew 21.31-32; Luke 10.37b).

41-42 The story that is narrated in this parable is an ideal-typical construction. Moreover, it displays close correspondences with other parables of the Jesus tradition in the figure constellations and plot (cf. e.g., Matthew 20.1-16; 21.28-32; Luke 10.25-37; 15.11-32; 18.9-14). All the stories share the fact that the interaction between the narrative figures takes place in the form of a "dramatic triangle" (see also Sellin 1974/1975, 180). A master of action (here: the creditor) is juxtaposed with a pair of narrative twins whose *formal status* is the same at the beginning of the action (here: both are debtors), while their *functional roles* differ from each other (here: one owes ten times more than the other). The identically formed presentation of the twins in v. 41 and 18.10 should be noted: δύο . . . ὁ εἷς . . . ὁ δὲ ἕτερος (cf. also the same narrative structure in 23.32, 39-43: κακοῦργοι δύο . . . εἷς . . . ὁ ἕτερος). At the end of the narrative this allocation of roles is then reversed. The 'twin' who stood at a greater distance from the master of action at the beginning stands nearer to him at the end. All the narratives also share the fact that the 'twins' always communicate only with the master of action and never with each other.

Parables that thematize the remission of debts are also found elsewhere in the New Testament (Matthew 18.23-35) and in rabbinic literature (cf. Bill. I: 798ff). In all cases the financial remission of debts in the narrated world refers to the forgiveness of sins in the world under discussion. The semantic precondition was first that the terms for "monetary debt" and "sins" were interchangeable (cf. e.g., Luke 13.2/4; 11.4 diff. Matthew 6.12; Greek Apocalypse of Enoch 6.3: ὀφειλέτης ἁμαρτίας μεγάλης ["debtors of a great sin"]; see also M. Wolter, *EWNT* 2: 1344ff) and second that the verbs χαρίζεσθαι and ἀφιέναι could designate both the remission of a monetary debt and the forgiveness (therefore perhaps better: "remission") of sins (cf. Philo, *De specialibus legibus* 2.39; Josephus, *Antiquitates judaicae* 6.144; Colossians 2.13; 3.13; and Matthew 18.27).

That a money creditor would simply release his insolvent debtors (on ἀποδοῦναι as a *terminus technicus* for the payment of debts, cf. 12.59) from paying the owed sum probably did not happen often in reality, but it was also not completely unthinkable (cf., in addition to Matthew 18.27, the example in Bill. I: 798–99). Thus, we have an extremely extravagant narrative move before us here. That God is recognizable in the creditor, as interpreters of the parable usually assume, does not yet emerge, of course, from the constructed case as such.

In itself the example is not yet comprehensible. Its meaning is only disclosed in **42b-43** with Jesus's question and the answer of the Pharisee (who represents the readers here). The fact that the one who πλεῖον ἀγαπήσει (v. 42b) is identical with the πλεῖον ἐχαρίσατο (v. 43b) makes clear which aspect is decisive. The remission of *great* debts can change *great* distance into *great* nearness. This quantitative accentuation is what matters, and in this respect the parable solely wants to explain the behavior of the woman described in v. 38. This intention is also expressed in the taking up of πλεῖον (vv. 42b, 43b) through πολλαί and πολύ (v. 47b) in contrast to ὀλίγον (v. 47c). The Pharisee Simon gets entirely left out and therefore one may not identify him with the 'small' debtor of the parable. This is also opposed by the continuation, since it distinguishes Simon from the woman not by the fact that he has done *less* than her; rather, he has done *nothing at all* (see also Hofius 1990, 176).

44-47 transfer the example to the level of the subject matter—namely, the behavior of the "sinner" narrated in v. 38. In vv. 44d-46 Jesus first compares the woman with the Pharisee in the form of a threefold syncrisis. The linguistic structure of the three pairs is carefully carried out. The three lines are identically constructed on each side. Every Pharisee-line begins with the mention of what the Pharisee did not give (water, kiss, oil) and ends with the negated predicate (2×: οὐκ ἔδωκας and οὐκ ἤλειψας). On the other side, the woman-lines always begin with an adversative αὕτη δέ. In them Jesus describes the woman with recourse to her four actions narrated in v. 38. The wetting of Jesus's feet with tears and the wiping with her hair (v. 38b, c) are summarized in v. 44e. The very extensive terminological correspondence that Luke establishes between his original narrative and its subsequent reproduction by Jesus is conspicuous. Of the twenty-three words in v. 38b-d, no less than seventeen reappear in vv. 44e, 45b, 46b, and among these all the action verbs and nouns appear.

Jesus himself stands, of course, at the center of the comparison, which is especially recognizable in the fact that in all six cola we find an enclitic personal pronoun that refers to him (μου or μοι). The extraordinary nature of the actions that the woman does to Jesus is further intensified rhetorically by the fact that the non-actions of the Pharisee are described not only as the omission of them, but also as surpassed by the actions of the woman in material respects:

- not even *water* / with *tears*: v. 44d-e (for the rendering of διδόναι ἐπί [v. 44d] with "pour on" cf. Ezekiel 24.8; Hofius 1990, 172–73);
- not even a (normal, i.e., short greeting) *kiss* / she kisses *the feet unceasingly*: v. 45; for the intensive meaning of καταφιλεῖν, cf. Xenophon, *Memorabilia* 2.6.33: "φιλεῖν the beautiful, but καταφιλείν the good." The first person εἰσῆλθον contradicts the course of action described in vv. 36-37 and is therefore wrongly corrected to εἰσῆλθεν in some manuscripts; it is explained, however, by the situation described in v. 45a (see also Jülicher 1976, II: 296; the assumption of translation error [Jeremias 1960] is unnecessary);
- not even the *head* with *(cheap olive) oil* (ἔλαιον) / the *feet* with *(expensive) aromatic oil* (μύρον): v. 46.

The listing of the actions that Simon left undone (vv. , 45a, 46a) does not want to accuse the Pharisee of failing to fulfill his obligations as a host, for such attentions in relation to eating guests were by no means generally common and such actions were certainly not expected from the *host* (for *the washing of feet,* cf. Hofius 1990, 173ff with the modifications by C. Burchard, *JSHRZ* II/4, 646n7/1b on Joseph and Aseneth 7.1; Thomas 1991, 35ff; for *the kiss,* cf. G. Stählin, ThWNT 9: 118ff, 124ff; for *the anointing of the head*, see Hofius 1990, 173; see also Schürmann; Marshall). Thus the comparison does not wish to scold the Pharisee (Jülicher 1976, II: 297 already pointed to the fact "that a σύ is never juxtaposed with the αὕτη"), but "exclusively . . . illustrates . . . the completely extraordinary greatness of the woman's deeds of love; the omissions of another person help in this" (Jülicher 1976, II: 297).

In **47** Jesus connects the message of the parable with the actions of the woman and draws the conclusion that follows from this (cf. also the analogous use of οὗ χάριν in Philo, *Legum allegoriae* 3.6, 10, 50, 81 and elsewhere). To be sure, the result formulated in v. 47a contradicts both the message of the parable and the slope of v. 47b. While here (in the parable and in v. 47b) the love *follows* the remission of debts or sins, there (in v. 47a) it *precedes* it. It is not the forgiveness of sins that motivates to love, but *because* the woman has loved, her sins are forgiven. Some interpreters want to weaken this contradiction by having the ὅτι-sentence designate not the causal basis for the forgiveness of sins but rather the basis for knowledge of it. In this interpretation the devotion that the woman brings to Jesus is said to reveal that her many sins are forgiven (e.g., Fitzmyer; Drexler 1968; Wilckens 1973, 404ff; Johnson). Although this interpretation is certainly possible linguistically (cf. Zerwick 1966, 422, 427), it is made impossible through v. 48, for only now does the woman learn of the forgiveness of her sins (see also Delobel 1966, 471; Taeger 1986, 194; for the understanding of ἀφέωνται see at 5.20), so that the actions narrated in v. 38 and interpreted as "loving" in v. 47a provide the causal basis for the forgiveness of her sins. In v. 47b the slope is then reversed again and love is made subsequent to forgiveness. Because the perspective of the parable is taken up again, the statement formulated here is often understood as a pre-Lukan continuation of v. 43b (e.g., Heininger 1991, 88; Melzer-Keller 1997, 218). This is contradicted, however, by the fact that Luke not only uses a different verb (ἀφιέναι instead of χαρίζεσθαι), but also by the fact that the adjective ὀλίγον fits not with the comparative πλεῖον (vv. 42b, 43b) but with πολύ (v. 47a).

The contradiction between the intention of the parable and v. 47b, on the one hand, and v. 47a, on the other hand, is obvious. In the literature this is usually solved with reference to the tradition history. It is said to have arisen because Luke integrated two different traditions or supplemented an existing tradition (cf. e.g., Braumann 1963/1964, 488ff; Heininger 1991, 87–88; Delobel 1992). Indeed, it looks like there is probably no other way to explain this tension.

48-49 call to mind the sequence of 5.20-21. The pronouncement of the forgiveness of sins by Jesus (v. 48; for the understanding of ἀφέωνται, see at 5.20) evokes the disconcertment of the other participants in the meal who are now mentioned for the first time. They react similarly to the scribes and Pharisees in 5.21. They ask about the legitimacy of Jesus's claim to be able to forgive sins and in this way to claim for himself an exclusive right of God. Unlike before, however, Luke has them invoke neither the accusation of blasphemy nor the rationale that it is God alone who can forgive sins. However, it is questionable whether one can infer from this that Luke wanted to express a greater openness to Jesus's claim here (cf. e.g., Schürmann; Nolland; Löning 1997/2006, I: 225), for one can also understand the allusion as an inclusive recurrence. The partial word-for-word repetition of the disconcertment with reference to the identity of Jesus (ἤρχαντο . . . λέγειν . . . τίς οὗτός ἐστιν ὅς + forgiveness of sins) suffices. In this way Luke refers to the identical question in 5.21. He need not explicitly convey again the accusation reported there and its rationale because it is present in the background. By placing the question about Jesus's identity in the mouth of the other participants in the meal, Luke puts them in the same box as the scribes and the Pharisees of 5.21 and makes clear that nothing has changed since this episode.

50 The actions of the woman described in v. 38 experience yet another interpretation in v. 50b. They are now portrayed additionally as a visualization of her faith. Identical phrasings are found in the same position elsewhere only at the end of healing stories (cf. Mark 5.34parr.; 10.52 par. Luke 18.42; Luke 17.19). There is, of course, again a special closeness to Luke 5.20, where faith and forgiveness of sins are connected with each other in a quite analogous way. The same understanding of faith is common to all the texts mentioned (see also Luke 7.9; 8.50; Mark 5.36). It always precedes the intervention of Jesus and is understood as trust in his saving power that is directed toward his person. In this way Luke also allows new light to fall on the understanding of the actions of the woman. They express that she regards Jesus as her "savior." They have nothing to do with "remorse" or the like (*pace* Neale 1991, 145 and many others). Rather, Luke views them as something like christological actions of confession that are concerned with Jesus's identity. In the background stands a general early Christian use of language that brings "faith" (πίστις/ πιστεύειν) and "salvation" (σωτηρία/σῴζειν) into a direct nexus of conduct and consequences (cf. Luke 8.12 diff. Mark 4.15; Luke 8.48, 50; 17.19; Acts 14.9; 15.11; 16.31; Romans 1.16; 10.10; 1 Corinthians 1.21; Ephesians 2.8; 2 Timothy 3.15; 1 Peter 1.5, 9; see also James 2.14). This reflects the fact that early Christianity was a conversion religion. The concluding wish of peace in v. 50c is already attested in the Old Testament as a farewell greeting (cf. Judges 18.6; 1 Samuel 1.17; 20.42; 29.7^LXX; 2 Samuel 15.9; 2 Kings 5.19; Judith 8.35; and elsewhere; in the New Testament it also occurs in Acts 16.36; James 2.16). Verse 50b brings to light what actually distinguishes the Pharisee and the sinner woman from each other, namely faith—she has it and he does not.

The narrative stages the difference between the Pharisee and the woman sinner through the opposition of the actions of confession with which the woman expresses her awareness of the identity of Jesus (v. 38), on the one side, and the Pharisee's lack of awareness ("not even a prophet";

v. 39), which is documented in his 'non-actions' (vv. 44, 45a, 46a), on the other side. Thus, both—the woman sinner and the Pharisee—stand almost ideal-typically for the alternative possibilities for how one can behave toward Jesus (see also at 10.38-42 and 23.39-43).

8.1–9.50: The Preparation for the Journey to Jerusalem

With the summary διώδευεν κατὰ πόλιν καὶ κώμην κηρύσσων καὶ εὐαγγελιζόμενος τὴν βασιλείαν τοῦ θεοῦ Luke opens a narrative space that reaches to 9.50, for in 9.51 the peregrination of Jesus receives a specific goal—Jerusalem. The narrative perspective is expanded once more vis-à-vis 4.44, for now the restriction via the qualification "Judea" found there is lacking. This expansion finds its narrative abutment in the fact that Jesus extends his activity to the region of the Gentile Gerasenes on the other side of the Lake of Gennesaret (8.26-39).

Nevertheless, Jerusalem as the goal of the peregrination of Jesus is also already present in this section—not yet on the authorial level of presentation but in the fact that Jesus already announces the Jerusalem events here (9.22, 44; indirectly in v. 41), that Moses and Elijah speak with him about it on the mountain of the transfiguration (9.31), and that he instructs the disciples regarding discipleship (9.23-27).

One can add to this the fact that Luke already has the end of the story of Jesus in view in 8.1-3. This is revealed in the list of women in vv. 2-3, which Luke has constructed on the basis of Mark 15.40-41 (see also Hentschel 2007, 221ff). Here and there Mary Magdalene stands at the head of a series of three women mentioned by name and "many other women" (ἄλλαι πολλαί or ἕτεραι πολλαί), about whom it is said that they "supported" (διηκόνουν) "him" (Mark 15.41) or "them" (Luke 8.3). Accordingly, when Luke speaks generally of women who had come with Jesus from Galilee in 23.49, 55, he means those women named in 8.2-3. Because he had mentioned their names in chapter 8, he does not need to repeat them in chapter 23. The backward reference is also unmistakable in 24.10, for here Luke, deviating from Mark 16.1, replaces Salome with Joanna and mentions "additional (women) with him." Plus, unlike the circle of the twelve (8.1), the women (8.2-3) immediately disappear again into a narrative oblivion from which Luke only brings them back again after the death of Jesus.

Finally, the characters in the narrative also change. The Pharisees (and scribes) take a break for a time; only in 11.37-54 do they temporarily return to the narrative, and they are then more regularly present again after 13.31 or 14.1. By contrast, episodes that present Jesus in the circle of his disciples now become more frequent.

In this section (and in what follows up to 9.50), Luke orients himself very closely again to the presentation of the Gospel of Mark (Mark 4.1–9.1). With the exception of 8.1-3 there are no episodes in this portion of the Gospel of Luke that do not have a parallel in Mark 4.1–9.1. And from the converse perspective there are also only minor deviations.

The parable of the mustard seed (Mark 4.30-32) and the Nazareth pericope (Mark 6.1-6a) are located elsewhere in Luke (13.18-19 and 4.16-30).

In addition to Mark 4.24b (see Luke 6.38b) Luke lacks above all Mark 4.26-29 (the parable of the self-growing seed), Mark 4.33-34 (the summary of Jesus's parable speech), Mark 6.17-29 (the narrative of the death of the Baptist), and all the material from Mark 6.45–8.26 (the so-called great omission). The latter results in the fact that in Luke the so-called confession of Peter (Luke 9.18-21 par. Mark 8.27-30) directly follows the feeding of the 5,000 (Luke 9.10-17 par. Mark 6.30-44).

8.1-3: Jesus and His Followers on a Peregrination of Proclamation

¹And it happened in the following (time) **that he wandered around city by city and village by village, preaching and gospeling the kingdom of God, and the twelve** (were) **with him ²and some women who had been healed from evil spirits and sicknesses—Mary, called Magdalene, from whom seven demons had gone out, ³and Joanna, the wife of Chuza, an administrative official of Herod, and Susanna—and many other** (women), **who supported them from their financial means.**

The summary is comprised of a single sentence and is usually regarded as a redactional composition, for which one can invoke the numerous peculiarities of Lukan language as evidence (cf. the compilation in Melzer-Keller 1997, 194–96; Radl). On the basis of the points of contact with Matthew 9.35, v. 1 is sometimes traced back to Q or to another common *Vorlage* (e.g., Schürmann; Marshall; Schmithals; see also Prieur 1996, 182–83). This, however, is rather unlikely, since κηρύσσων τὸ εὐαγγέλιον τῆς βασιλείας in Matthew 9.35 is just as much an unmistakable linguistic peculiarity of the first evangelist (cf. further Matthew 4.23; 24.14) as the expressions κηρύσσειν and εὐαγγελίζεσθαι τὴν βασιλείαν τοῦ θεοῦ (1c) are characteristic of Luke (cf. further Luke 4.23; 9.2; 16.16; Acts 8.12; 20.25; 28.32; nowhere else in the New Testament). This is not, of course, to say that Luke invented each and every one of the details about the women in vv. 2-3; besides being based on Mark 15.40-41 (see above), at least in part they are probably based on pieces of information about individuals that managed to be recorded in the Gospel of Luke before they were forgotten.

1 The phrasing of the introduction in 1a corresponds to the phrasing of 5.17 (see further there); 17.11; 24.15. The temporal specification ἐν τῷ καθεξῆς is elliptical; one must supply χρόνῳ (see the parallel to ἐν τῷ ἑξῆς in 7.11 and Martyrdom of Polycarp 22.3). In this way Luke places the readers at the beginning of a stretch of time whose end initially remains unspecified. In 1b he transfers this unspecificity to the map. The iterative imperfect διώδευεν (in the New Testament the verb only occurs elsewhere in Acts 17.1) and the distributive κατά (πόλιν καὶ κώμην; see also Josephus, *Antiquitates judaicae* 11.172; 14.160; BDR §224.3), on the one hand, widen the angle of narration vis-à-vis 4.44 and, on the other hand, characterize the proclamation peregrination of Jesus as directionless (the text does not indicate that Luke wants to restrict the peregrination of Jesus to Galilee). Finally, it also fits this that in describing Jesus's activity as κηρύσσειν and εὐαγγελίζεσθαι τὴν βασιλείαν τοῦ θεοῦ (v. 1c) Luke makes recourse to the comprehensive categories with which he had already summarized Jesus's commission in 4.18, 43-44. The structure of v. 1b-c is reproduced exactly in 9.6 and 13.22 (see also Jeremias 1980, 175). Luke then explicitly emphasizes that Jesus is accompanied by the twelve, who as such have not played a role since their "election" in 6.13 (in the Sermon on the Plain and in Nain Luke always had only unspecific disciples be present; 6.20; 7.11). He ensures their presence with Jesus already here because he wants them to witness the instruction on the topic of 'hearing (and doing)' in 8.4-21 and Jesus's power described in 8.22-56 before they are sent out in 9.1. The Markan phrasing of the specification of the circle of the twelve (ἵνα ὦσιν μετ' αὐτοῦ; Mark 3.14) probably continues to have an effect in the phrase σὺν αὐτῷ; for the Lukan preference for σύν (75 of 127 New Testament attestations) instead of μετά, cf. Jeremias 1980, 63. Luke realizes the other specifications of the purposes of the circle of the twelve mentioned in Mark 3.14 (ἵνα ἀποστέλλῃ αὐτοὺς κηρύσσειν) in 9.1-6.

2-3 The syntactical connections in these two verses are somewhat unclear. Most considerations probably favor the view that καὶ ἕτεραι πολλαί (v. 3c) does not continue the series of women mentioned in vv. 2c-3d but rather lies on the same level of the text as the relative clause ἃ ἦσαν τεθεραπευμέναι . . . (v. 2b). Thus, in the Lukan understanding, the women mentioned in v. 3c refer to a different group than the women spoken of in vv. 2c-3b. Otherwise, one would have to assume that Luke imagines that Jesus was exclusively accompanied by previously sick women. Therefore, he probably related this information solely to the three named women. It cannot be clarified with ultimate certainty whether the concluding relative sentence αἵτινες διηκόνουν αὐτοῖς . . . (v. 3d) should refer to all the women, i.e., including those named in vv. 2b-3d, or solely to the ἕτεραι πολλαί of v. 3c. One should show restraint toward overly precise affirmations and generalizations, however, for just as it is unlikely that Jesus was accompanied exclusively by previously sick and possessed women, so it is improbable that there were only financially solvent women around him. This applies both to the historical and the literary levels.

The talk of "evil spirits" (πνευμάτων πονηρῶν) is unusual (א Θ *pc* therefore change it to the more common πνευμάτων ἀκαθάρτων). Apart from the not entirely pertinent Q parallel Luke 11.26 par. Matthew 12.45 (comparative), this designation appears only in Luke in the New Testament (see also 7.21; Acts 19.12, 13, 15, 16).

The fact that people apparently liked to have demons turn up as an "evil seven" is already attested in ancient Near Eastern texts (cf. W 22652 in Weiher 1983, 15–21, vs. II.2–9: "Being seven, they were . . . born in the mountain of the sunset; being seven, they grew up . . . in the mountain of the sunrise; in the crevices of the earth they sit [around]; from the undeveloped land of the earth they raise [?] themselves"); Thompson 1903, 64–65, 77; see also Nicomachus of Gerasa, *Theologoumena arithmeticae* 57.8 [de Falco 1922]; Testament of Reuben 2.1–9 mentions "seven spirits of straying" (πνεύματα τῆς πλάνης), which "were given against humans"; see also the seven plagues in Deuteronomy 28.22, 27-28; Luke 11.26 par. Matthew 12.45; Testament of Solomon 8.1.

Whence Luke has the lists with the names of the three women cannot be determined. There are also lists of three women—at whose head Mary Magdalene stands as here—in the vicinity of the tomb of Jesus (Mark 15.40 par. Matthew 27.56; Mark 16.1 par./diff. Luke 24.10 [Salome is replaced by Joanna]); cf. further John 20.1-2, 11-18. Mary (Hebrew Miriam) probably received the byname "Magdalene" from her hometown Magdala. The only known place of this name is today's el-Meğdel, which was located on the western shore of the Lake of Gennesaret ca. 5 kilometers north of Tiberias and was connected with Magdala for the first time in the sixth century (Theodosius, *De situ terrae sanctae* 2 [CChr.SL 175.115]); in Josephus the place is mentioned many times as Tarichaea (cf. especially *Bellum judaicum* 3.462ff; Genesis Rabbah 79.6 and Kopp 1964, 246ff and Tsafrir 1994, 173). Apart from the aforementioned texts that connect Mary Magdalene with the burial of Jesus and the discovery of the empty tomb, we know nothing about her. Her identification with the "woman sinner" of Luke 7.36-50, the women mentioned in Mark 14.3-9; Luke 10.38-42; and John 12.1-8, let alone the adulteress of John 7.53–8.11, are plucked out of the air. With regard to the two other women we know nothing about Susanna, whereas the name Joanna appears once more in Luke 24.10 (see above). That Luke introduces her as wife of an official who worked for Herod Antipas and thus defines her via the occupation and social status of her husband (for ἐπίτροπος with the genitive of the employer, cf. 2 Maccabees 11.1; 14.2; Josephus, *Bellum judaicum* 1.592; *Antiquitates judaicae* 11.61; 17.252; Matthew 20.8; Acts of John 73.74; the name Chuza is also attested on Nabatean and Syrian inscriptions, cf. W. Bauer 1988, 1763) is intended to express that the influence of Jesus extends into the higher levels of society.

Much has been written about the character of the διακονία that the women gave to Jesus and his companions (the reading αὐτοῖς [B D K W Γ Δ Θ *f¹³* and others] is, to be sure, only negligibly better attested than αὐτῷ [ℵ A L Ψ *f¹* 33 Marcion and others], but it is probably the more difficult variant theologically, since the changing of the plural into the singular is easier to explain than the reverse; see also Hentschel 2007, 225). Luke certainly thought less of "general care for their physical well-being" (Hengel 1963, 248–49) or the like (see also Witherington 1979, 246 and the criticism by Sim 1989, 56ff), but simply of material support that they provided for Jesus and his disciples (see also Hentschel 2007, 232). But one also should not exaggerate this generosity and speak of a "renunciation of their assets" (Melzer-Keller 1997, 201), for Luke certainly does not wish to give the impression that the women separated themselves from "all their possessions" in order to "live in poverty and needlessness" (Melzer-Keller 1997, 201, 202). Rather, the partitive ἐκ (τῶν ὑπαρχόντων) with the *dativus commodi* αὐτοῖς and the linguistic parallels clearly show that Luke thinks simply of something like donations; cf. e.g., Tobit 4.7AB (ἐκ τῶν ὑπαρχόντων σοι ποίει ἐλεημοσύνην ["Do mercy/give alms from your financial means"]); Isocrates, *Areopagiticus* 24 (ἐκ τῶν ἑκάστοις ὑπαρχόντων . . . τοῖς κοινοῖς ἐπαρκεῖν ["To help the fellowship . . . from the financial means that each one has"]); for the subject, see also Polybius 38.8.4 (to take ten talents ἐκ τῶν ἰδίων ὑπαρχόντων); 2 Chronicles 31.3 (the portion of the king [μερὶς τοῦ βασιλέως] for the financing of offerings came ἐκ τῶν ὑπαρχόντων αὐτοῦ); Constitutiones apostolicae 5.1 (ἐκ τῶν ὑπαρχόντων ὑμῶν . . . διακονήσατε τοῖς ἁγίοις ["Serve the saints . . . from your financial means!"]); 8.42. These parallels also refute the assumption that τὰ ὑπάρχοντα refers not only to the material means but also the "personal abilities" of the women (S. Bieberstein 1998, 67; see also Luke 12.15; Acts 3.6; 4.32, 37 and the references in W. Bauer 1988, 1670). Finally, there is also no indication that Luke gives a paraenetic overtone to this note and presents the women supporters of the Jesus movement as models for rich women in his own community (so e.g., Schneider; Horn 1986, 117; Melzer-Keller 1997, 211). Rather, conversely, he more likely projects existing conditions back into the time of Jesus (see also Melzer-Keller 1997, 210)—which does not, of course, rule out the possibility that Luke reproduces a historically reliable piece of information here.

8.4-21: On the Proper Hearing of the Word

The coherence of this section is established through the multiple repetitions (vv. 8, 10, 12-15, 18, 21) of the word "to hear" (ἀκούειν). Its theme is the proper "how" (πῶς) of hearing (cf. v. 18a diff. Mark 4.24a). It consists in the fact that one "does" what one "hears" (v. 21c) or—stated with recourse to the imagery of the parable—that one "bears fruit" (v. 15c). The narrative sequence is subdivided into three sections, which are marked by the change of Jesus's dialogue partner (see also Radl). First, it is a *great crowd* to whom Jesus narrates the parable of the fourfold fate of the seed (vv. 4-8). After this he explains the meaning of the parable (vv. 9-18) to the *disciples*, and, finally, Jesus finds himself again in the midst of the *crowd* (vv. 19-21). Luke obtains this division by removing the concluding scene with Jesus's saying about his mother and his brothers (vv. 19-21 par. Mark 3.31-35) from the Markan order and placing it here.

8.4-8: The Parable of the Fate of the Seed

⁴But when a great crowd was gathered, and they came to him from all the towns, he spoke through a parable: ⁵"A sower went out to sow his seed. And when he sowed, part fell on the way; and it was trampled, and the birds of heaven ate it up. ⁶And some fell on rocky ground; and it came up and withered, because it had no moisture. ⁷And some fell in the midst of thorns; and when the thorns came up with (it), they choked it. ⁸But some fell on the good soil; and it came up and yielded a hundredfold of fruit." As he said this, he called out, "Whoever has ears to hear should hear!"

With the parable taken over from Mark 4.3-9 Luke provides a concrete example of Jesus's proclamation of the kingdom of God (cf. also the taking up again of the term in v. 10b). The parable (vv. 5-8b) has a parallel in Gospel of Thomas 9, and Horman 1979, 341ff thinks that it is based on the same source as Mark 4.3-8.

The narrative is composed of four parts, which Luke, with the help of shortenings, has given a greater uniformity of form than he found in his *Vorlage*.

In the case of some of them we are dealing, admittedly, with negative minor agreements: καὶ καρπὸν οὐκ ἔδωκεν (Mark 4.7c) is lacking in v. 7 par. Matthew 13.7; ἀναβαίνοντα καὶ αὐξανόμενα (Mark 4.8) is lacking in v. 8 par. Matthew 13.8; see also ἀκούετε in Mark 4.3 (lacking in v. 5 par. Matthew 13.3b). Further examples include ἐν τῷ σπείρειν αὐτόν (v. 5b par. Matthew 13.4) instead of ἐν τῷ σπείρειν without subject (Mark 4.4); ὁ ἔχων (v. 8d par. Matthew 13.9) instead of ὃς ἔχει

(Mark 4.9); see further Schramm 1971, 114ff; Neirynck 1974b, 87–88; 1991, 31; Ennulat 1994, 117ff.

4 forms, together with vv. 8c-d, the frame. The structure of the scene recalls 5.1 and 6.17 (for the distributive κατά, cf. BDR §224.3). Unlike what we find in Mark 4.1, the scene does not take place at the sea (see at 5.1). The καί between the two genitive absolutes has an explanatory function (καί *epexegeticum*; cf. BDR §442.6), for the sequence of the narrated events only makes sense in this way.

5 narrates what happens during the sowing or immediately thereafter. For the imagery, cf. already Hesiod, *Opera et dies* 467–71: "If you begin to sow . . . , a younger assistant should . . . drive away the birds behind and hide the seed." There has especially been discussion about whether the plowing took place before or after the sowing (cf., on the one hand, Dalman 1926 and Jeremias 1966–1967, and, on the other hand, White 1964, 300–307). Plowing probably took place both before *and* after the sowing (cf. Payne 1979; von Gemünden 1993, 214); see also Jubilees 11.11: "And Prince Mastema sent crows and birds so that they might eat the seed which was being sown in the earth. . . . Before they plowed in the seed, the crows picked it off the surface of the earth" (but cf. also the technical innovation described in v. 23: "And they made implements above the ground . . . so that they might place seed upon it. And the seed would go down from within it onto the point of the plow, and it would be hidden in the earth. And therefore they were not afraid of the crows"; translated by O. S. Wintermute, *OTP* II: 78-79).

The narrator wants to make clear that this part of the seed does not even germinate. Unlike Mark, Luke says that this part of the seed was "trampled" (κατεπατήθη) and shows in this way that he probably understood the phrasing παρὰ τὴν ὁδόν in the sense of "*on* the way" (and not beside it; cf. the parallels for such usage in W. Bauer 1988, 1236; for the image, see also 5.13; 7.6).

6 looks at a considerably later point in time. The period of growth has advanced so far in the meantime that the seed has come up (v. 6b). The seed grains that have fallen on shallow ground, i.e., on a thin topsoil under which there is soon rock, are in view. Luke has deleted the biological detail of Mark 4.5-6 and in this way deprived the narrative of a temporal accentuation, namely that seedlings that cannot form roots (e.g., for the reasons mentioned in Mark 4.5b-c) grow more quickly toward the light and bring forth visible shoots earlier than all others. Further, Luke describes the reason for their withering in a more trivial manner. The specific causality of Mark 4.6b ("because it had no root") is transformed into the general and quite tautological explanation: 'It withers because it is not moist enough.'

In **7** this temporal distance is extended again, for the occurrence described in v. 7b only takes place when the sowed wheat has already reached a certain height. In some places of the field, weeds, whose seeds were plowed under with the seeds that were sown, have also come up. They now take away the light from the grain stalks found between them and take away the nutrients of the ground that they need for the formation of the fruit and for the ripening process. For ἄκανθαι one must imagine some sort of thorny undergrowth (W. Bauer 1988, 56: "*ononis spinosa*, restharrow"). According to Genesis 3.18, they belong, together with thistles (τρίβολοι), to the curse of the ground (see also Isaiah 5.6; 7.23-24; 32.13; Job 31.40). Accordingly, Jeremiah 4.3 warns: μὴ σπείρητε ἐπ' ἀκάνθαις ("Do not sow on thorns!").

In **8b** the end of the growth period is reached: the seed that has fallen on "good," i.e., fruitful, land (**8a**) produces fruit in the end. This is just as certain as the fact that only failure was visible previously. By speaking simply of a hundredfold yield of the seed, Luke has simplified the Markan differentiation of the multiplication of the yield into thirty, sixty, and one hundred. It is controversial in the literature whether this is a realistic number or an exaggeration that bursts the image field of the parable and functions as a gateway to its subject matter (cf. e.g., G. Lohfink 1985; Klauck 1978, 191; McIver 1994). Comparable numbers are mentioned in some texts (Genesis 26.12: Isaac harvests a 100-fold "for the Lord had blessed him"; Herodotus 1.193.3 regarding Babylon: 200-fold, in good years 300-fold; 4.198.3 regarding the land of the Euesperides: 100-fold, of Cinyps: 300-fold; Theophrastus, *Historia Plantarum* 8.7.4 regarding Babylon: 50-to 100-fold; Varro, *De re rustica* 1.44.2 regarding Syria: 100-fold; Strabo 15.3.11 regarding Susa: 100-fold; Pliny, *Naturalis historia* 18.21.94–95 regarding Susa: 150-fold). Others speak simply of a four- to fivefold yield (e.g., Columella, *De re rustica* 3.3.4; b. Ketubbot 112a). McIver 1994 rightly points to the fact that the first numbers mentioned always refer to "exotic locations." Therefore, there is probably more in favor of the view that the narrator of the parable has it end with a yield that bursts the image in order to build a bridge for the readers to the reference of the imagery. This same narrative technique can already be observed in 3.17, where the talk of "unquenchable fire" had this same function (both here and there the hyperbolic information also comes at the end; cf. also 12.37, 46; 19.27).

The concluding frame in **8c-d** is formed by a call to attention that is also found in this or similar form—in addition to its occurrence in the synoptic parallels—in Matthew 11.5; 13.9, 43; Mark 4.23; Luke 14.35; Revelation 2.7, 11, 17, 29; 3.6, 13, 22; 13.9 (see also Gospel of Thomas 8, 21, 24, 63, 65, 96).

For the understanding of the narrative it is essential that one pay attention to the temporal structure that underlies the scenic sequence. Although Luke has reduced the contours of this temporal structure vis-à-vis the Markan version in v. 6, it is still clearly recognizable in the Lukan version. There are not "four perspectives" (Lührmann 1987) juxtaposed with one another, but rather a description—in quick time as it were—of what took place in every growth period in every field in the Mediterranean world (and everywhere else, of course, where there was or is no mechanized and industrial agriculture). For months one can observe only losses and yet the farmer can be certain at every point in time that the sown seed will bring rich fruit at the end. Thus, with reference to that yearly experience, the parable wants to convey that the ultimate success of the sowing is not in question, even though nothing but failure can be observed thus far.

8.9-18: The Interpretation of the Parable for the Disciples

⁹But his disciples asked him what this parable meant. ¹⁰But he said, "It is given to you to know the mysteries of the kingdom of God; but to the rest (it is given) **in parables, so that they see without seeing and hear without understanding.**

¹¹Now, this is the parable: The seed is the word of God. ¹²The ones on the path are those who have heard; then the devil comes and takes away the word from their hearts, so that they do not come to faith and be saved. ¹³The ones on the rocky ground are the ones who receive the word with joy when they hear it, but they have no root. They believe for a time, and in the moment of testing they fall away. ¹⁴And that which has fallen among the thorns—these are the ones who have heard and are increasingly choked by the cares, riches, and pleasures of life, and do not come to completion. ¹⁵But that which is in the good soil—these are the ones who have heard the word with a good and noble heart; they hold it fast and bear fruit in steadfastness.

¹⁶No one who has lit a lamp hides it with a vessel or places it under a bed, but he places it on a lampstand [in order that those entering may see the light]. ¹⁷For there is nothing hidden that will not become manifest, and nothing hidden that will not become known and come to light. ¹⁸Therefore, pay attention to how you hear. For whoever has, to him will be given; and whoever does not have, from him even that which he thinks he has will be taken away."

Form-critically this is a kind of school dialogue. As often in Luke (cf. at 1.34), it is introduced with a question of the disciples (v. 9), which Jesus then answers. From ὑμῖν and their demarcation from "the rest" (v. 10) it follows that Jesus addresses the disciples through v. 18. It is unclear whether Luke—as in 6.20ff; 12.1ff—presupposes that the crowd listens also (so e.g., Nolland). However, the scenic ambiguity probably plays no role (in 15.3ff only the Pharisees are addressed without Luke having previously removed the tax collectors and sinners). Here Luke features Jesus's instruction of disciples and non-public proclamation. The speech is structured via two participles in v. 10d-e. Together with the concluding saying in v. 18, the allegorical interpretation of the parable of the fate of the seed (vv. 11-15) thematizes the hearing (v. 10e; see at 8.4-21), while the image of the lamp with its interpretation (vv. 16-17), which follows without a transition, takes up the topic of seeing (v. 10d/v. 16c).

The parabolic saying of the lamp (v. 16) is repeated once again in 11.33, which points to a Mark–Q overlap. However, the Q-version can no longer be reconstructed (and certainly not with the help of Matthew 5.15). The parallel found in Gospel of Thomas 33.2–3 is very clearly dependent on the Lukan version, for here too the final clause about seeing the light occurs, which is attested only in Luke 8.16; 11.33.

The saying about the hidden thing that must come to light (v. 17; cf. Luke 12.2 par. Matthew 10.26) also apparently has a parallel in Q. Moreover, it is attested in Gospel of Thomas 5.2 and 6.5–6 (with an older Greek version in P. Oxy. IV, 654.29–31). Like Luke 8.17, Gospel of Thomas 5.2 has the future and therefore is probably dependent on the Lukan redaction (cf. Schröter 1997a, 369ff).

The saying about the correspondence between having and receiving (v. 18b), which gives the rationale for the exhortation to proper hearing, is found in a completely different context in Q (Luke 19.26 par. Matthew 25.29) and is also found in Gospel of Thomas 41 (cf. Schrage 1964; Schröter 1997a, 329ff).

There are spectacular minor agreements in vv. 9-10. In Matthew and Luke it is *(a)* not οἱ περὶ αὐτὸν σὺν τοῖς δώδεκα (Mark 4.10) who ask Jesus but οἱ μαθηταί (v. 9a par. Matthew 13.10a). The answer of Jesus is *(b)* introduced with ὁ δὲ . . . εἶπεν (v. 10a par. Matthew 13.11a) instead of with καὶ ἔλεγεν αὐτοῖς (Mark 4.11a). It reads *(c)* not ὑμῖν τὸ μυστήριον δέδοται τῆς βασιλείας τοῦ θεοῦ (Mark 4.11b), but ὑμῖν δέδοται γνῶναι τὰ μυστήρια τῆς βασιλείας τοῦ θεοῦ/τῶν οὐρανῶν (v. 10b par. Matthew 13b). The last Matthew–Luke agreement against Mark is especially difficult to explain without the assumption either that both had before them a post-Markan recension of the Gospel of Mark known to us or that they reproduce the phrasing of another source (possibly Q; contrast Fusco 1982: *une forme plus archaïque que dans Mc*); cf. further the mention of the heart (καρδία αὐτῶν/αὐτοῦ in v. 12c par. Matthew 13.19 diff. Mark 4.15) and Neirynck 1974b, 90ff; 1991, 32ff; Rauscher 1990, 37ff; Ennulat 1994, 123ff, 128ff).

9 Unlike in Mark 4.10a, Jesus and the disciples do not go into a house in order to be alone. Therefore, unlike in Mark 4.11, the crowd is also not designated as "those outside" (ἐκεῖνοι οἱ ἔξω) but as "the rest" (this same constellation is also found in Ephesians 2.3; 1 Thessalonians 4.13; 5.6; see also Luke 18.9; Acts 5.13). Rather, from out of the crowd Luke has the disciples ask about the meaning of the parable that was just narrated. The readers should apparently imagine that the disciples and crowd stand around Jesus in concentric circles.

10 From the Markan parable theory Luke takes up the quotation of Isaiah 6.9-10, though only in greatly abbreviated form. He has Paul pronounce the hardening judgment omitted here only at the end of his narrative (Acts 28.26-27). This alters the thematic orientation of the statement. While in Mark it continued to have the function of explaining the rejection of the proclamation of Jesus and the post-Easter Christian message of salvation, in Luke it becomes the introduction to the interpretation of the parable for the disciples that begins in v. 11. Thus, it is intended to ground the special position of the circle of disciples. This intention finds its linguistic expression in the fact that the phrasing δέδοται + dative of the person + designation of a doing (mostly in the infinitive) always designates an award or allowance bestowed from a higher position (cf. e.g., Tobit 5.20; Bel and the Dragon 25–26; Xenophon, *Hellenica* 6.6.36; *Anabasis* 6.6.36; Plato, *Symposium* 183b; Diogenes Laertius 2.67; often with ἐξουσία: Athenaeus, *Deipnosophistae* 4.22 [143d]; Herodianus Historicus 1.10.5; *Epistulae Pythagorae*, ed. Städele 1980, 7.1). Thus, δέδοται is a *passivum divinum*. For Luke the identity of the circle of disciples is determined in this way by a privilege granted by God (Bock I: 727–28 is entirely wrong in this respect). The phrasing μυστήρια τῆς βασιλείας τοῦ θεοῦ finds its closest counterpart in the speech about the μυστήρια τοῦ θεοῦ, the non-recognition of which is a characteristic of the godless according to Wisdom of Solomon 2.22 (cf. further Testament of Levi 2.10; Joseph and Aseneth 16.14; Philo, *Legum allegoriae* 3.3; 3 Baruch 1.8; Greek Apocalypse of Ezra 1.5; 1 Corinthians 2.1 among others; see also Ephesians 1.9: τὸ μυστήριον τοῦ θελήματος αὐτου; 6.19; Colossians 2.2; Revelation 1.20; 17.7); syntagms with μυστήριον/μυστήρια + genitive are not found anywhere else with the frequency with which they occur in the New Testament.

Verse 10c (τοῖς δὲ λοιποῖς ἐν παραβολαῖς) is elliptical; a verb of speaking must be supplied (such as λαλῶ; Matthew 13.13). It follows that the opposition is between "the ones who know the mysteries of the reign of God" (on the side of the disciples) and "in parables" (on the side of the rest). The latter refers to the proclamation of the reign of God, which Luke had spoken of in v. 1 and given an example of in vv. 4-8. The fact that παραβολαί conceal mysteries is generally known and also thematized, e.g., in Sirach 39.3 (see also the reference to Clement of Alexandria, *Stromateis* 5.10.63; Ps.-Clementine Homilies 19.20 in Davies/Allison, 2001–2004, II: 388–89). One can also ask whether ἵνα in 10d should be understood as final ("in order that") or consecutive ("so that" [I have translated it in this way]; cf. BDR §391.5 and Luke 9.45; John 9.2; Romans 5.20; 2 Corinthians 1.17; 1 Thessalonians 5.4; Revelation 9.20; 13.13). The difference is not especially great, for if Jesus knows that the non-disciples do not understand his parables and he nevertheless continues to speak in parables, the consecutive meaning receives a telic sense. What is at issue is clear. Jesus begins to give contours to the circle of disciples and to specify the characteristics of proper discipleship.

11 The equating of the seed with the word of God, behind which there implicitly stands the identification of the sowing with the proclamation, makes a metaphoric connection—which was firmly established in the ancient world—between sowing and speaking or, rather, between words and seeds (cf. Klauck 1978, 192ff).

Socrates says in Plato "that rhetoric reaps fruit from what it has sown" (τὴν ῥητορικὴν καρπὸν ὧν ἔσπειρε θερίζειν; *Phaedrus* 206d; cf. then also 276e: φυτεύειν τε καὶ σπείρειν . . . λόγους ["to plant and sow words"] as well as the whole context from 276b), and Plutarch can speak of sowing and reaping words (σπείροντες λόγους καὶ θερίζοντες; *Moralia* 394e). Analogously Ps.-Plutarch, *Moralia* 2b compares the raising of children with agriculture: "The nature (sc. of the child) is comparable to the arable land, the upbringer to the farmer, but exhortations and instructions of the words to the seed (σπέρματι δ᾽ αἱ τῶν λόγων ὑποθῆκαι καὶ τὰ παραγγέλματα)"; cf. also Xenophon, *Hellenica* 5.1.25; Aristotle, *Politeia Athenaion* 14.14; Chrysippus, *SVF* II: 746, 747; Dionysius of Halicarnassus, *Antiquitates romanae* 3.35.4; 11.27.1; Plutarch, *Pompeius* 18.1; *Cicero* 3.6; *Caesar* 29.5; 60.2; *Moralia* 398–99; 399a; Seneca, *Epistulae morales* 38.2; James 1.21. In terms of subject matter 4 Ezra 9.31 is similar: ". . . I sow in you my law; it will bring fruit in you." Isaiah 55.10-11, which is repeatedly mentioned as an Old Testament parallel, is not a parallel, for there it is rain and snow that are compared with the word of God (see also G. Lohfink 1985, 216). The same applies to texts that describe the sapiential nexus between conduct and consequences with the help of the image of sowing and reaping (Job 4.8; Proverbs 22.8; Sirach 7.3; Hosea 8.7; 10.12; Testament of Levi 13.6; 3 Baruch 15.2; 4 Ezra 4.28-29; 1 Corinthians 9.11; 2 Corinthians 9.6; Galatians 6.7-8).

To be sure, in **12-15** Luke does not consistently sustain this image (this was also already the case in Mark 4.15-20). For unlike in the aforementioned texts, it is, contrary to expectation, not the field on which it is sown that is equated with the people who hear the word. Rather, it looks as if it is suddenly the people themselves who are "sown" and fall "on the way" (v. 12), "on the rocky ground" (v. 13), "among the thorns" (v. 12), and "in the good earth" (v. 15). It corresponds to this that the arable land is identified with the external life circumstances of the humans. The interpretation appears to orient itself more toward metaphorical ideas as expressed in 4 Ezra 8.41: "For as the farmer sows seeds on the earth and plants many plants, but not everything that was sown . . . remained preserved, and not everything that was planted put down roots, so those who are sown in the world will not all remain preserved."

Interpreting the picture of the birds that take away the grains of seed, **12** speaks of those who (acoustically) hear the proclamation of the word but do not receive it. Here a direct missionary experience is described, namely that among many people the proclamation of the message of Christ remains without any resonance from the start. This experience is mythically traced back to the activity of the "devil" who wants to hinder—so Luke supplements his *Vorlage*—the hearers of the word from "coming to faith and being saved" (πιστεύσαντες σωθῶσιν). The nexus of conduct and consequences is transferred to the nexus of faith and salvation, which reflects early Christian usage (cf. the texts mentioned at 7.50).

13 then takes a later point in time into view, for here there is talk of people who, unlike those mentioned previously, initially reacted affirmatively to the word of the proclamation (πιστεύουσιν; v. 13d) and received it (v. 13b); the acceptance of the Christian message of salvation is also designated as τὸν λόγον δέχεσθαι in Acts 8.14; 11.1; 17.11; 1 Thessalonians 1.6 (with μετὰ χαρᾶς as here); 2.13; James 1.21; see also 2 Thessalonians 2.10. Further, a common early Christian experience is described in relation to them as well, namely that a—presumably not small—number of members of Christian communities turned away from them again (ἀφίστημι [v. 13e] without attribute is found in this sense in 1 Maccabees 11.43; Daniel 9.9[Theodotion]; Greek Apocalypse of Enoch 5.4; in the Septuagint frequently with reference to the turning away of Israel from its God: e.g., Joshua 22.18, 23 and elsewhere; Hebrews 3.12; see also 1 Timothy 4.1) after a period of time (πρὸς καιρόν [v. 13d] in the sense of "temporarily" or more generally as a designation of a short time is also found in Philo, *De posteritate Caini* 121; *De specialibus legibus* 2.205; Josephus, *Bellum judaicum* 6.32, 117; 1 Corinthians 7.5; 1 Thessalonians 2.17; Hebrews 11.25). Luke traces back this situation to two coactive causes. For the description of the 'exterior' cause the Markan phrasing "tribulation and persecution because of the word" (Mark 4.17) is weakened to "in the moment of testing" (ἐν καιρῷ πειρασμοῦ; cf. also ἐν καιρῷ θλίψεως, which is frequent in the Septuagint: Judges 10.14; 2 Ezra 19.27 [= Nehemiah 9.27]; Esther

4.17r; 8.12s; Psalm^LXX 36.39; Sirach 2.11; 22.23; 35.24; 37.4; Isaiah 33.2; Jeremiah 15.11). The term πειρασμός interprets an experience of reality as a crisis into which God leads the persons who belong to him in order to test the quality of their faith (cf. the texts mentioned at 4.13 and at 11.4c; with qualifications, see also S. S. Brown 1969, 12ff). The question of which particular experiences are in view remains open. The lack of a "root" is mentioned as the 'inner' cause that, on account of the associations bound up with it in everyday life, can be presented as the metaphorical cause for the turning away from faith (cf. also the use of this same metaphor in Colossians 2.7; Ephesians 3.17; see also Philo, *De posteritate Caini* 163). In v. 6 there was, by contrast, talk of withering on account of the absence of moisture, and this does not fit the interpretation insofar as in it there is talk of a punctiliar crisis as an 'external cause' (ἐν καιρῷ πειρασμοῦ)— from the picture of the absence of a root one would have to think of trees that a storm knocks down—that brings about the failure. In this incoherence it becomes recognizable that it is less the case that Luke interprets his own parable narrative and more the case that he reworks the interpretation in Mark 4.14-20 (see also W. C. Robinson 1980, 133).

We can first characterize the hearers of the word, who are spoken of in **14,** with the help of v. 13, for the contours of the scenarios described there are present under the surface. Like the hearers addressed in the preceding verse, those of v. 14 have received the word with joy, but unlike them they have believed not only for a time and have not fallen away "in the moment of testing." The changed perspective finds expression in the participle πορευόμενοι, which points to a continuing process; linguistically it is probably a Septuagintism (e.g., 2 Samuel 15.12; Proverbs 4.18; Jonah 1.11; see also Acts 9.31 and F. Hauck/S. Schulz, ThWNT 6: 570.10ff; 573.19–20; W. Radl, *EWNT* 3: 327; Zedda 1974, 105ff).

The picture of the impact of the thorns is transferred to a sort of tribulation list. Similar listings in the Hellenistic environment of early Christianity place together life circumstances and other external factors that divert one from a morally perfect life (Luke has replaced the Markan ἐπιθυμίαι with ἡδοναί because precisely the ἡδονή has a fixed place in such lists, namely time and again in connection with wealth); cf. the presentation of the material in G. Stählin, ThWNT 6: 320–21; see also Dio Chrysostom 1.21; 6.29; 17.18; Plutarch, *Alexander* 5.5; Epictetus, *Dissertationes* 3.24.71; for Hellenistic Judaism, see, e.g., Philo, *De congressu eruditionis gratia* 27; *De fuga et inventione* 25; *De praemiis et poenis* 24. Acts of John 68 provides a Christianized version where "cares (μέριμνα), children, parents, fame, poverty, flattery, youthful vigor, beauty, boasting, desires (ἐπιθυμία), riches (πλοῦτος), anger, pride . . ." are mentioned as "hindrances (ἐμπόδια) to human reason," which impair the "true" faith.

For cares see also the cross-connection with Luke 12.22ff; 21.34; 1 Corinthians 7.32-34 with the parallels in Strecker/Schnelle 2001/1996, II/1: 301ff. Thus, in contrast to the two other groups, here Luke has in mind hearers who still believe but allow themselves to be ruled by the aforementioned life circumstances so that they "do not come to ripeness" (οὐ τελεσφοροῦσιν). This verb, which is a New Testament *hapax legomenon*, can—like the synonym καρποφορεῖν (see at v. 15)—both designate the fruit-bearing of plants (e.g., Theophrastus, *Historia plantarum* 8.7.6; Strabo 2.1.16; Philo, *De vita Mosis* 1.226; see also 4 Maccabees 13.20) and be transferred to human life conduct (e.g., Philo, *Legum allegoriae* 1.76; *De praemiis et poenis* 126; Epictetus, *Dissertationes* 4.8.36; see also Ps.-Longinus, *De sublimitate* 14.3). Thus, Luke carries out an ethical *interpretatio hellenistica* of the Markan interpretation of the parable. From the tribulation list he will subsequently thematize again paraenetically the dangers of cares and riches (cf. 10.41; 12.22-30 and 12.13-21, 33-34; 16.1-31; 18.22-25).

15 The description of the fourth group is formulated in such a way that the antithesis to the three groups mentioned previously explicitly comes to expression. The hearing "with a noble and good heart" points back to v. 12 and distinguishes this group from those out of whose "heart" Satan had robbed the word. With the lexical pair καλὸς καὶ ἀγαθός Luke takes up the ethical excellence ideal of καλοκἀγαθία, an ideal that was accepted in his Greek environment (cf. W. Grundmann, ThWNT 3: 540–43; it is not found elsewhere in the New Testament; in the Septuagint it occurs in 2 Maccabees 15.12; 4 Maccabees 1.10; 3.18; 4.1; 11.22; 13.2; 15.9; Tobit 5.4; 7.7; 9.6א). The demarcation from the rootless is expressed by Luke in v. 13 with the help of the opposition of (ἐν καιρῷ πειρασμοῦ) ἀφίστανται, on the one hand, and κατέχουσιν . . . ἐν ὑπομονῇ, on the other hand; for κατέχω as semantic opposition in the sense of "hold fast, preserve" (cf. the tradition, the gospel, or the Christian confession) cf. 1 Corinthians 11.2; 15.2; Hebrews 3.6, 14; 10.23, and for ὑπομονή as a virtue that has to be preserved precisely ἐν πειρασμοῖς, cf. Testament of Joseph 2.7; James 1.2-3, 12; Revelation 3.10; Acts of Paul 25; see also Wolter 1978, 140ff; Spicq 1994, III: 414ff. It is not by chance, therefore, that this key word is also found again at the end of the persecution paraenesis in 21.19. The demarcation from the people described in v. 14 is recognizable in the antithesis between οὐ τελεσφοροῦσιν and καρποφοροῦσιν. Like τελεσφορεῖν, the image of bearing fruit is used time and again as a metaphorical designation for the results of human action (e.g., Proverbs 1.31; Isaiah 5.2, 4, 7; Jeremiah 2.21^LXX; Jeremiah 17.10; in the New Testament: Romans 7.4-5; Colossians 1.6, 10).

Luke furnishes the interpretation of the parable with a much more profiled pragmatics than was the case in Mark 4.14-20. It is graspable in vv. 14-15. Luke has readers in view for whom the fate of the word narrated in v. 12 and v. 13 is no longer an issue, but for whom the two possibilities described in v. 14 and v. 15 remain relevant. This may also be the reason for introducing the interpretation in these two verses with the help of a *nominativus pendens* (cf. Zerwick 1966, 25[14]ff). Beyond this, the interpretation is configured as a paraenetic admonition speech that sets "what is ruinous" (βλαβερόν) and "what is useful" (συμφέρον) over against each other, warning against the one and recommending the other (cf. Aristotle, *Rhetorica* 1.3.5).

16 The parabolic saying of the lamp, which immediately follows the interpretation of the parable in Luke, refers to the paraenetic instruction contained in vv. (14-)15 and reinforces it with a simple common sense argument. Not to let a καρποφορεῖν follow the ἀκούειν of the word would be just as absurd as if one first lit a lamp and then prevented it from shining (see also 5.39 [further here]; 9.62; 11.33 and Dupont 1985, II: 1042–43). Thus, the concern is that the word should not remain hidden in the hearts but rather be made visible through actions on all sides (cf. the talk of the "light of good works" in Testament of Benjamin 5.3). The further proclamation of the word (so Schürmann 1970, 39; Radl) is not specifically in view here. It is controversial text-critically whether the final clause in 16c belonged to the original text, for it is lacking in two manuscript of the top category ($\mathfrak{P}^{75}$ B). The phrasing corresponds to Luke 11.33c, with the exception of a word transposition. Thus, it could have been added here in order to adjust the two Lukan versions of the parabolic saying to each other. However, a subsequent omission to adjust it to Mark 4.21 and Matthew 5.15 is also conceivable. Should the sentence be original at this place, it would direct the picture in a certain direction (see also Dupont 1985, II: 1037–38). One primarily lights a lamp in order that people in the house do not sit in darkness (in this vein explicitly Matthew 5.15c) and not with consideration for possible visitors. When Luke, by contrast, places the "entering ones" in the foreground, he strains the logic of the imagery for the sake of his paraenetic interest. When outsiders come into the community (for εἰσπορευόμενοι in this sense, cf. Acts 28.30), the word of God meets them in the light of the believers' way of life. The use of "to see the light" as a conversion term in Philo, *De virtutibus* 179 points in the same direction.

17 The proverb-like saying, which is less awkwardly formulated than Mark 4.22, does not refer to the subsequent making public or proclamation of the mysteries, the knowledge of which is said to be still reserved for the disciples alone according to v. 10 (*pace* Marshall; Green; Radl;

and others). Rather, it furnishes the paraenetic instruction formulated in vv. 14-16 with an additional argument, namely that it will in any case come out whether or not one has heard the word "with a noble and good heart" (v. 15b) (see also Schweizer; Bock). Luke may even have the final judgment in view here (like Paul with the same phrasing in 1 Corinthians 3.13: the work of every one φανερὸν γενήσεται, ἡ γὰρ ἡμέρα δηλώσει). The continuation at least speaks for this reference.

18 In 18a the paraenetic intention that guides the interpretation of the parable is brought to a point in a summarizing manner. For this reason Luke deletes the intervening comment of the narrator from Mark 4.24a and with the help of the so-called οὖν *paraeneticum* immediately attaches the exhortation to what precedes (cf. W. Nauck 1958, 134–35). The imperative βλέπετε often introduces warning exhortations; cf. especially 21.8 (βλέπετε μὴ πλανηθῆτε); Ephesians 5.15 (βλέπετε οὖν . . . πῶς περιπατεῖτε), as well as Mark 13.5, 9; Acts 13.40; 1 Corinthians 8.9; 16.10; Colossians 2.8; Hebrews 3.12; 12.25; and elsewhere. Luke changes the Markan τί to πῶς and in this way stresses that it depends not on the object but on the proper manner of hearing (here πῶς is therefore precisely *not* "= τί" [*pace* BDR §436.3]). What this manner of hearing consists in already emerged from vv. 14-15—in not letting oneself be choked by the tribulations of everyday life but in τελεσφορεῖν and καρποφορεῖν. The readers know from 6.27-38 what actions are concretely in view.

There is a distant analogy in 4 Ezra 7.25: *vacua vacuis et plena plenis* ("the empty to the empty and the full to the full") to the maxim-like justification in v. 18b-c (see also 19.26), which Luke—by omitting Mark 4.24b—has directly follow the exhortation to proper hearing. In v. 18c Luke has inserted δοκεῖ in order to attenuate the logical paradox, for one cannot actually take away anything from the person who has nothing. The exhortation of v. 18a is given judgment-paraenetic emphasis by describing the different results of the two ways of hearing with recourse to the nexus of conduct and consequences—just like at the conclusion of the Sermon on the Plain and in the parable of the unfruitful fig tree (cf. 6.46-49; 13.9: in all cases the positive outcome precedes the negative one). In both initial subordinate clauses "fruits" could be added to ἔχῃ. In v. 18b the fruit-bearing hearers are in view (v. 15), whereas v. 18c describes the fate of those whose hearing remains without fruit (v. 14). Accordingly, "giving" and "taking" are metaphors for the allocation of salvation and unsalvation in the final judgment.

8.19-21: Jesus's Mother and His Brothers

¹⁹But his mother and his brothers came to him; because of the crowd, however, they could not get to him. ²⁰And he was told, "Your mother and your brothers are standing outside and want to see you." ²¹But he answered and said to them, "My mother and my brothers—these are the ones who hear and do the word of God."

Luke concludes the scene with the help of a chreia (pronouncement story), for which Mark 3.31-35 was shortened and moved to this place. Verses 20-21 have a parallel in Gospel of Thomas 99.1–2 that corresponds to the Matthean version ("to do the will of my father").

The following minor agreements are noteworthy: ἐστήκασιν (v. 20b par. Matthew 12.47) is without Markan equivalent; ὁ δέ . . . εἶπεν πρὸς αὐτούς / τῷ λέγοντι αὐτῷ (v. 21 par. Matthew 12.48) instead of καὶ . . . αὐτοῖς λέγει (Mark 3.33); cf. further Neirynck 1974b, 85ff; 1991, 30; Ennulat 1994, 111ff.

19-20 Luke uses one of his typical words (παραγίνομαι; v. 19a: 28 of the 35 attestations in the New Testament are in Luke) to introduce the mother and brothers of Jesus onto the scene. But it is also unmistakable that the introduction of episodic sequences through 'so-and-so' παρεγένετο/ παρεγένοντο πρός is also characteristic of the Septuagint's style of narration (cf. Genesis 50.16; Exodus 2.18; Joshua 22.15; Judges 8.15; Samuel 15.13; 22.11; 2 Samuel 15.13; and elsewhere; see also Luke 11.6). Unlike Mark 3.21, Luke does not mention a reason for the coming of Jesus's mother and brothers. The fact that they are what they are evidently suffices as a plausible motivation for a visit. Accordingly, there is no discord between Jesus and his physical family. On the other hand, however, he does not present them as "model disciples" (*pace* Fitzmyer I: 723). For Luke too, it is crucial that Jesus and his family members do not meet. Unlike Mark 3.31, Luke does not simply leave Jesus's mother and brothers standing outside (narratively and symbolically) and send for Jesus in order to call him out, but he assigns to them the intention of wanting to come to their son and brother themselves (this is evident from οὐκ ἠδύναντο [19b])—which he then, of course, has fail due to the crowd surrounding Jesus (v. 19b; cf. also the comparable scenario in 5.19 [likewise with διὰ τὸν ὄχλον]).

21 Jesus's answer redefines his interfamilial relations and in this way transcends the individual situation. In the sentence, "my mother and my brothers" (v. 21b) is the topic and "those who hear and do the word of God" (v. 21c) is the comment. Therefore, Jesus does not merely make "those of physical descent models for those who hear the word of God and keep it" (Fitzmyer I: 725), nor is the concern simply with "his true relatives" (Marshall 332; see also Schneider). Rather, he redefines the intensional meaning of "my mother and my brothers." The social nearness that this designates is based no longer on biological criteria but on ethical criteria. The discussion of the syntax of the answer of Jesus (cf. especially Fitzmyer; Nolland; Bock) is based on false presuppositions, because it starts from the reference of v. 21b. Jesus's answer annuls the meaning of the physical relations (this is often wrongly weakened in the commentaries; cf. e.g., Fitzmyer; Nolland; Radl; contrast, rightly, Wiefel), for the persons who are called mother and brothers by the narrator in v. 20 and by unnamed narrative figures in v. 20 are this for Jesus only insofar as they fulfill the condition formulated in v. 21c. Comparable redefinitions occur especially in the context of conversions (e.g., Joseph and Aseneth 12.12–15; Philo, *De specialibus legibus* 1.52; *Quis rerum divinarum heres sit* 26–27; Josephus, *Bellum judaicum* 2.120 concerning the Essenes: "But the children of others whom they . . . receive they view as relatives [συγγενεῖς]"; see also 2.122), and the formation of the family metaphor in early Christianity is probably due to this context (cf. Sandness 1994). In 18.28-30 the same topic—now with reference to the disciples of Jesus—is taken up again at the end of the journey that Jesus makes with them to Jerusalem, which results in a clear *inclusio* (see also at 21.32). The phrasing "hear and do the word of God," which is placed emphatically at the end, calls to mind not only James 1.22-25 but especially the end of the Sermon on the Plain (6.46-49); for further discussion of the lexical pair "hear and do," see at 6.46-49.

8.22-56: Further Demonstrations of Jesus's δύναμις and ἐξουσία

Luke aligns himself further with the order of the Gospel of Mark and has the cycle—stemming from Mark 4.35–5.43—of three or four episodes follow in which Jesus demonstrates anew the ἐξουσία and δύναμις present in him (cf. 4.36), namely over wind and water (vv. 22-25), over a legion of demons (vv. 26-39), and over sickness and death (vv. 43-48 and 40-42, 49-56). While Luke sets off this episode sequence from 8.4-21 through the introductory temporal specification in v. 22, he explicitly takes up the connection between faith and salvation stressed there (8.12 diff. Mark 4.15) in two more places (8.48, 50; see also v. 25).

8.22-25: Jesus's Power over Wind and Water

²²**But it happened one day that he got into a boat and his disciples also. And he said to them, "Let us go to the other side." And they**

went out. ²³As they sailed there, he fell asleep, and a storm came down upon the sea, and they were swamped and fell into danger. ²⁴But they came to him, woke him, and said, "Master, Master, we are perishing!" But he stood up, rebuked the wind and the troubled water, and they settled down, and it became calm. ²⁵But he said to them, "Where is your faith?" But they fell into fear and marveled and said to one another, "Who is this that he commands the winds and water and they obey him?"

Form-critically the episode can be classified as a sea rescue miracle. Luke does not completely take over the structure of the Markan *Vorlage*, since in Luke Jesus's falling asleep belongs to the *introduction* (vv. 22-23a). There follows the expositional *portrayal* of the distress (vv. 23b-24b), the *removal of the distress* (v. 24c-d), and a relatively extensive *finale* (v. 25). Luke also makes the usual shortenings (most strongly in the exposition; he always deletes the word μέγας [Mark 4.37a, 39e, 41a]). Further, unlike in Mark, the story does not take place at night but during the day.

The following minor agreements are noteworthy: In Matthew 8.23 Jesus and the disciples also begin their crossing in the evening; ἐμβαίνειν (ἐνέβη/ἐμβάντι) . . . εἰς (τὸ) πλοῖον (v. 22a par. Matthew 8.23) instead of ὡς ἦν ἐν τῷ πλοίῳ (Mark 4.36); οἱ μαθηταὶ αὐτοῦ (v. 22a par. Matthew 8.23) has no Markan equivalent; προσελθόντες . . . (δι)ήγειραν . . . λέγοντες (v. 24a par. Matthew 8.25) instead of ἐγείρουσιν . . . καὶ λέγουσιν (Mar 4.38); ἐθαύμασαν λέγοντες (v. 25c par. Matthew 8.27) instead of καὶ ἔλεγον (Mark 4.41); cf. further Neirynck 1974b, 95ff; 1991, 35–36; Ennulat 1994, 137ff.

22 With the help of the temporal specification ἐν μιᾷ τῶν ἡμερῶν (see further at 5.17), which is characteristic of episodic narration, Luke creates distance from the preceding scene, which he had not located—as Mark 4.1 had—at the sea, and coordinates the following sequence of events only to the time of the preaching itinerancy of Jesus outlined in 8.1.

23 In the exposition Luke rearranges the sequence narrated in Mark 4.37-38a (see also John 1.4-5) by reporting Jesus's falling asleep before the storm breaks out and the ship falls into danger at sea. This is more plausible with regard to the narrated sequence of events, but by doing this Luke removes a special accent of his *Vorlage*. Jesus is not presented as the one who sleeps unfazed by the raging of the chaos elements, but as someone who initially is just as suddenly struck by the emerging storm as the disciples.

The center of the narrative in **24** portrays the different reactions of the disciples and Jesus to the crisis. The disciples wake Jesus neither with

the accusation that he does not concern himself with the distress (Mark
4.38) nor with a petition for salvation (Matthew 8.25 and in many other
comparable narratives; cf. Theissen 1987, 108–9), but solely with their
own interpretation of the situation (ἀπολλύμεθα; v. 24b); for the address
of Jesus as ἐπιστάτα, see at 5.5. Jesus's reaction (v. 24c) refutes, however, the evaluation of the disciples. He deals with the chaos elements
in the same way as God once did at creation according to Psalm 104.6-7
(". . . the waters stand over the mountains, before your rebuke [LXX: ἀπὸ
ἐπιτιμήσεώς σου] they flee"; see also Psalm 18.16; 65.8; 89.9-10; 104.6-7;
106.9; 107.29; Job 26.12ᴸˣˣ; for ἐπιτιμᾶν, see also at 4.35). Analogously,
among the Greeks it is the deities who have power over wind and waves
(cf. Hesiod, *Theogonia* 253: Kymodoke; Homeric Hymns 33.8–15 and
Plutarch, *Moralia* 426c: the Dioscuri). But they can also delegate this
power to certain humans; cf. Iamblichus, *De vita Pythagorica* 135, where
the following is adduced as support for the piety of Pythagoras (*De vita
Pythagorica* 134, 137): "He at once brought storm and hail to rest, flood
and sea waters he stilled, so that his friends passed through without effort"
(see also Porphyry, *Vita Pythagorae* 29 and Talbert/Hayes 1995, 329–30;
Kollmann 1996, 273; Aus 2000; Strelan 2000). The motif of the passenger
who saves is related tradition-historically; cf. Jonah 1.3-16; Plutarch, *Caesar* 38.2–4; b. Berakhot 13b (Bill. I: 452).

25 After the confirmation of the miracle (v. 24d), Jesus and the disciples
comment on the reaction of the respective other(s). First, Jesus asks—in
a phrasing that is weakened vis-à-vis the strict scolding of Mark 4.40—
about the whereabouts of the faith of the disciples (v. 25a). After 8.12 they
should have known that faith saves (see then also vv. 48, 50), and therefore
their interpretation of the situation in v. 24b was false in light of the presence of Jesus in the boat. Conversely, in v. 25b-d the disciples react in a
way that makes clear their deficit in this respect. Luke not only has them
articulate the usual fear in the face of the epiphany of the numinous, as
Mark 4.41 does, but in Luke they also "marvel" at the miracle (θαυμάζειν:
motif of wonder; cf. Theissen 1987, 78ff and at 1.63). Through this he
places them in a series with the relatives of Elisabeth (1.63), the shepherds (2.18), Jesus's parents (2.33), and the inhabitants of Nazareth (4.22;
see also the other attestations mentioned at 1.63) and in this way makes
a characterization at the same time. The disciples notice that something
extraordinary has taken place without understanding it in its full significance. In the concluding question about Jesus's identity, Luke intensifies
this difference even further by having the disciples describe the event with
words that designate God's power over the elements of nature (in addition
to the texts mentioned at v. 24c, see Job 38.34ᴸˣˣ; 2 Maccabees 9.8).

8.26-39: Jesus's Power over a Legion of Demons

[26]And they sailed into the region of the Gerasenes, which was located opposite Galilee. [27]But when he reached land a man from the city met him who had demons. For quite a while he had worn no garment and stayed not in a house but in the tombs. [28]When he saw Jesus he cried out, fell before him, and called out with a loud voice, "What do I have to do with you, Jesus, Son of God, the Most High? I ask you, do not torment me!" [29]For he had commanded the unclean spirit to come out of the man. For it had held him seized for a long time; and he was bound with chains and shackles and guarded, but he always burst the chains and was driven by the demon into isolated regions. [30]And Jesus asked him, "What is your name?" And he said, "Legion," for many demons had entered into him. [31]And they asked him not to command them to go off into the underworld. [32]But there was there a great herd of pigs, which was grazing on the mountain. And they asked him to allow them to go into them. And he allowed them. [33]The demons came out of the man and went into the pigs. And the herd rushed down the cliff into the sea and drowned. [34]But when the swineherds saw what had happened they fled and related (it) in city and countryside. [35]And they came out to see what had happened. And they came to Jesus and found the man from whom the demons had come out, sitting fully clothed and sober minded at Jesus's feet, and they were seized with fear. [36]The ones who had seen how the possessed man had been healed related it to them. [37]And the whole crowd from the region of the Gerasenes asked him to go away from them, for they had been seized by great fear. And he got into a boat and returned.

[38]But the man from whom the demons had come out asked him to be allowed to remain with him. But he sent him forth and said, [39]"Go back to your house and tell what God has done for you." And he went forth and proclaimed in the whole city what Jesus had done for him.

Luke carried over the narrative of the exorcism in the region of the Gerasenes from Mark 5.1-50 with minor changes. The most conspicuous feature is that Luke describes the behavior of the possessed man before his encounter with Jesus not only in v. 27b-c (where it would have its sensible location; cf. Mark 5.3-5), but also again in vv. 29b-d, i.e., after the episode's course of action had long begun.

Form-critically it is an exorcism narrative that is lavishly configured in all its subparts. After the *introduction* (v. 26), the possessed man is introduced in detail (*exposition*; vv. 27, 29b-d). The dialogue between the exorcist and the demons as well as the description of their end (vv. 28-29a, 30-33) form the *center*, which is interlaced with expositional elements.

There then follows a detailed narration of the regional population's reaction to the exorcism (vv. 34-37) as the *finale*. The narrative is concluded with an epilogue, which consists of a dialogue between Jesus and the healed man and another note of dissemination (vv. 38-39).

The following minor agreements are noteworthy: τῆς θαλάσσης and ἐκ τοῦ πλοίου (Mark 5.1, 2) are lacking in vv. 26, 27 par. Matthew 8.28; δαιμόνια (v. 27a) or δαιμονιζόμενοι (Matthew 8.28) instead of ἐν πνεύματι ἀκαθάρτῳ (Mark 5.2); cf. further Neirynck 1974b, 97ff; 1991, 37–38; Ennulat 1994, 145ff.

26 Gerasa (today's Ǧeraš) belongs to the cities of the Decapolis founded in the middle of the first century CE (cf. Mark 5.20). It is located ca. fifty-five kilometers southeast of the Lake of Gennesaret in the "mountains of Gilead" (Genesis 31.21, 23, 25). Eusebius designates the place as πόλις ἐπίσημος τῆς Ἀραβίας ("a famous city in Arabia," *Onomasticon*, GCS XI/1, *Eusebius Werke* III/1: 64.4; see also Möller/Schmitt 1976, 71–72; S. Applebaum/A. Segal, *NEAEHL* II: 470–79; Hoffmann/Kerner 2002; Lichtenberger 2003, 191ff). The territory that belongs to it also does not reach to the Lake of Gennesaret, and the statement that it is located "opposite" Galilee (ἀντιπέρα, which takes up εἰς τὸ πέραν τῆς λίμνης from v. 22) is also not accurate. Luke certainly knew that the Gerasenes were not Jews (especially since the Decapolis is mentioned in Mark 5.20). Thus, we have here the only episode in the Lukan story of Jesus that brings Jesus into contact with non-Jews prior to the passion narrative and that takes place outside of the land inhabited by Jews. Further, it is not the case that Jesus was driven there by the storm; rather, he sought out this region with full intention (cf. v. 22).

The topographical evidence was already known in the time of the ancient church (cf. Origen, *Commentarii in evangelium Joannis* 6.41 on John 1.28 [GCS X, *Origenes Werke* IV: 150.8]: "a city that had neither a sea nor a lake in the vicinity") and led in the textual tradition to readings that alleviated this problem: Γαδαρηνῶν (in v. 26: A W Ψ *f¹³* 𝔐 sy; in v. 37: ℵ² A W Ψ 𝔐 sy) has presumably wandered in from Matthew 8.28 and refers to Gadara, which is located just ten kilometers southeast of the Lake of Gennesaret. It is, however, separated from the lake by the Yarmuk valley (cf. T. Weber 2002; Lichtenberger 2003, 83ff). For his part, Origen brought *Gergesa* into the conversation "in whose vicinity there was also a hillside on the Lake" (GCS X, *Origenes Werke* IV: 150.15–16). Moreover, the name is said to mean παροικία ἐκβεβληκότων "exile of the one driven out." This placement then found entrance into the textual tradition (in v. 26: ℵ L Θ Ξ *f¹* 33 and Epiph among others; in v. 37: ℵ*,c [C²] L P Θ *f¹,¹³* 33 among others), but it is clear from the manner of Origen's presentation that he did not find this variant in any manuscript (*pace* Fitzmyer). Therefore, not only better manuscript evidence (in v. 26: 𝔓⁷⁵ B D latt sy^hmg [sa]; in v. 37: 𝔓⁷⁵ B C* D 0279 579 *pc* latt [sa]) but also the geographic location, which makes this reading the *lectio difficillima* (see also Lagrange 1895; Zahn 1902; Annen 1976, 201–2; Baarda 1969) support the originality of Gerasa in Mark 5.1 and in our text. The identification with *Kursi* (*Khersa*), which is located on the eastern shore of the lake, probably reaches back at least into the early Byzantine period, since the existence of a monastery and a lodging for pilgrims is already attested for it here (cf. Tzaferis 1989; V. Tzaferis, *NEAEHL* III: 893–96; Tsafrir et al. 1994, 104).

27 Luke has made the Markan *genitivus absolutus* into a *participium coniunctum* in the object case required by ὑπαντάω in order to avoid the linguistically inelegant repetition of the personal pronoun (cf. BDR §423.2; see also Appian, *Bella civilia* 4.17.134: ἐξιόντι δὲ τῷ στρατῷ πρὸ πυλῶν αἰθίοψ ὑπήντησε ["an Ethiopian met the departing troop before the gates"]). Luke mentions the possession of the man with the help of a phrasing that is widespread especially in the New Testament (see at 7.33) and after this portrays the conspicuous behaviors that result from this or, rather, that form the epistemological basis for the corresponding diagnoses. Here he tears apart the description that he found in Mark 5.3-5 (the difference that Busse 1979, 207 postulates "between the general sickness image in v. 27 and the detailed sickness image in v. 29" does not, of course, exist).

When it initially says in v. 27b that the man had no longer worn an over-garment (ἱμάτιον) for quite a while already (on χρόνος ἱκανός, see at 20.9), this merely indicates that he runs around in the undershirt (χιτών; for the distinction from ἱμάτιον, see at 3.11; 6.29). Thus, there can be no talk of "nakedness" (Radl I: 554; see also Bock). Luke presumably derived this information from Mark 5.15 where the healed person is designated not only as "sober minded" but also as "outer-garmented" (ἱματισμένος; see v. 35d). This habit and the constant dwelling in tombs mentioned in v. 27c (i.e., among the dead) rather than in houses (i.e., among the living) would be regarded today as a symptom of a severe psychosis. Within an understanding of reality that included the notion of personal beings that bring individual people under their power and can rule them against their will, it stood to reason, of course, to trace back such behavior to demonic possession. That ἐν τοῖς μνήμασιν should be understood as a conscious allusion to Isaiah 65.4 ("people who . . . sit in tombs and spend the night in hidden places, who eat pork and have abominable broth in their vessels") in order to "portray the possessed man as a model of paganism" (cf. Merklein 1992, 1027) is entirely improbable, since v. 29c-d shows that this behavior is also regarded as pathological by the compatriots of the possessed person. For a cultural-anthropological interpretation of the description of the possessed person that goes beyond this, cf. Karris 1991.

28 recounts the encounter of the exorcist with the possessed man or, rather, with the demon that has taken possession of him and reacts, as in 4.34, with a mix of defense (see at 4:34: τί ἐμοὶ καὶ σοί;) and submission. While this reaction precedes the command to come out in 4.34-35, the sequence is reversed here (v. 29a). The falling down before Jesus in v. 28a and his titling as υἱὸς τοῦ θεοῦ τοῦ ὑψίστου should be regarded as actions of submission, which call to mind 1.32 (see there), on the one hand, and Acts 16.17, on the other hand. In Acts 16.7, a πύθων-spirit—which is pagan, as here—continually designates Paul and his companions as δοῦλοι τοῦ θεοῦ τοῦ ὑψίστου. In both cases Luke (and before him also Mark 5.7) has a pagan demon speak of God in the style of the Septuagint, for the expression ὁ θεὸς ὁ ὕψιστος (thus with double article) as a translation of Hebrew אֵל עֶלְיוֹן comes from it (Genesis 14.18, 19, 20, 22; 1/3 Ezra 6.30; 8.19, 21; Judith 13.18; Psalm^LXX 56.3; 77.35, 56; Daniel^LXX 5, tit; Daniel^Theodotion 4.2; 5.18, 21; see also 1/3 Ezra 9.46; Daniel 3.93; Joseph and Aseneth 8.2; 9.1 and in Luke 1.32), since the double article is always lacking in the numerous (also pagan) θεὸς-ὕψιστος inscriptions that have been found in the eastern Mediterranean (cf. S. Mitchell 1999, esp. 128ff). The petition to the victor not to prepare torments for the conquered one is also part of the submission. For βασανίζειν in a comparable context, cf. Philostratus, *Vita Apollonii* 4.25.5: after Apollonius unmasked a woman as a φάσμα "apparition," it says, "δακρύοντι ἐῴκει . . . καὶ ἐδεῖτο μὴ βασανίζειν αὐτό (It looked as if it wept . . . and asked [him] not to torment it) and not to compel it to admit what it is"—namely, a vampire. Within the New Testament narrative this request has no other function than to express the complete inferiority of the demon; that is also the reason why the narrative does not have to include whether Jesus grants it.

29 The sequence of the events and the order of the narrative no longer run parallel (cf. the overview in Green 337), for unlike in 4.35, Jesus reacts not with a combination of command to silence and command to come out. Instead, the reader learns that Jesus's command to come out already preceded the submission of the demon (v. 29a; this is the same in Mark 5.8). This undramatic manner of narration probably has its basis in the fact that the story does *not* continue, as in 4.35, with the coming out of the demon but rather is followed first by another dialogue, which—if it directly followed an explicit command to come out—would call the effectiveness of this command into question.

But Luke also adds retrospectively another piece of the sick person's medical history (v. 29b-d), which would actually have had its place in the introduction of the man in v. 27. Verse 29b functions as a heading (without a counterpart in Mark). With regard to what follows in v. 29c-d συναρπάζω (only in Luke in the New Testament) could have the meaning of the violent snatching away along with the demon; in any case the verb is often used with reference to people who are dragged somewhere against their will (as, e.g., in all the other Lukan attestations: Acts 6.12; 19.29; 27.15; see also Philo, *In Flaccum* 95; Josephus, *Antiquitates judaicae* 19.157; and elsewhere). In the present case this can be seen in the fact that the sick person is repeatedly torn away from his home and wanders around in regions that lack people (29d), which his family also cannot prevent through the use of massive physical coercive measures (v. 29c; ἀλύσεις and πέδαι are also combined with each other in Polybius 3.82.8; Dionysius of Halicarnassus, *Antiquitates romanae* 6.26.2; 27.3; 79.2).

Luke has presumably added this extensive retrospective into the sick person's story in order to heighten the tension, for with it the question of how Jesus will react to the demon's request from v. 28c is left open over a long narrative distance.

30 Correspondingly, Luke must renominalize the subject of the sentence with which he takes up the narrative thread again. Because Jesus rules the demon, he can compel him to mention his name (for this motif, cf. *PGM* IV: 3037ff; Testament of Solomon 2.1; 25.1–2). The fact that the demon is named "Legion" has sometimes been understood as an anti-Roman feature (cf. Theissen 1992, 116–17 with older literature; Karris 1991, 47–48)—especially since the *legio X fretensis*, which was stationed in Jerusalem, had a boar as its heraldic animal (this would fit vv. 32-33) and the cities of the Decapolis, which included Gerasa, were allied with Rome (cf. Bietenhard 1977; Lichtenberger 2003, 1ff). Even if this aspect was once connected with the assignment of this name within the tradition history of the narrative—which is by no means certain—it plays no role in Luke, for it is evident from the explanation for the name that "Legion" is merely intended to stand for a great number (so to speak an 'army' of demons; v. 30c; see also Mark 5.9; Matthew 26.53).

31 Then again, with the request not to be sent into the ἄβυσσος Luke ascribes a linguistic competency colored in a Jewish manner to the demons. Outside the New Testament, this term, which designates—within the framework of the three-story worldview—the sphere under the earth (e.g., Testament of Levi 3.9; Jubilees 2.2, 16 [Greek fragment in each case]), is used as a substantive, with one exception, only in Jewish texts. Only Diogenes Laertius 4.27 speaks of the "black abyss of the (underworld god) Pluto"; apart from this text, pagan Greek literature knows of ἄβυσσος only as an adjective in the sense of "without ground, groundless" (in Euripides, *Phoenissae* 1605 it is a characteristic of Tartarus; for late ancient attestations, cf. J. Jeremias, ThWNT 1: 9; see also J. Schneider, *RAC* 1:

60ff). Philo of Alexandria uses ἄβυσσος to designate empty space due to its unendingness (*De opificio mundi* 29, 32). In the Septuagint ἄβυσσος is usually a translation of תְּהוֹם (e.g., Genesis 1.2; 7.11; 8.2; Psalm^LXX 32.7; 35.7; 70.20; 106.26) and designates the chaotic primeval flood, so that the ἄβυσσος is often envisaged as filled with water. Through this and in view of the fate that is given to the demons in v. 33, their request to be permitted not to go into the ἄβυσσος but into the pigs receives a significant portion of irony. The conception of the abyss as a place of punishment probably stands in the background. The wicked are kept in it until the judgment (Greek Apocalypse of Enoch 9.4; Jubilees 5.10; see also Greek Apocalypse of Enoch 21.7–10: the eternal prison of the angels; Jubilees 10.7, 9 [Greek fragment in each case]; 7.29; Greek Apocalypse of Ezra 4.21: the twelve plagues of the abyss); cf. also *PGM* IV: 1245–48: ἔξελθε, δαῖμων . . . καὶ παραδίδωμί σε εἰς τὸ μέλαν χάος ἐν ταῖς ἀπωλείαις ("Come out demon . . . and I hand you over into the dark chaos in perdition"). In the New Testament there is talk of the abyss in Romans 10.7 (quotation of Psalm 107.26) and a number of times in Revelation. There it is the place from which the locust demons, who fall over the earth, rise (9.1-2; according to 9.11, their "king" is an "angel of the abyss" named Abaddon [Hebrew] or Apollyon [Greek]). The beast that rules the entire earth has risen from it (11.7; 17.8), and Satan will be shut up in it in it again for 1,000 years (20.1, 3). Testament of Solomon 1.12 places a comparable request in the mouth of a demon who has just been conquered: "I will give you the silver and gold of the whole earth—only do not bring me to Solomon."

32 Other exorcism stories also have a demon formulate a so-called concession request (cf. Bultmann 1995, 239). In Testament of Solomon 5.11 the demon Asmodaeus asks his exorcists: ἀξιῶ δέ σε, βασιλεῦ Σολομῶν, μή με κατακρίνῃς εἰς ὕδωρ ("I entreat you, King Solomon, condemn me not into the water"); see also b. Pesahim 112b–113a where a female demon says to the exorcist, "I ask you, give me a certain time," after which she receives permission to wander around in the nights preceding the Sabbath and Wednesday. In view of the outcome of the story the request to be permitted to go into a herd of pigs proves, of course, to be a downright comical error. The presence of a herd of pigs, i.e., animals that the Torah has declared to be unclean (cf. Leviticus 11.7; Deuteronomy 14.8), is another indication that the narrative takes place outside of the land inhabited by Jews. That healing takes place in the way of a transference of sicknesses or demonic possession to other people, objects, or animals is not unknown in the environment of the New Testament (cf. e.g., Wohlstein 1894, 31: "Go away and fall on the gazelles on the mountains . . . and on the horses"; see also Berger/Colpe 1987, 47).

33 Form-critically this verse, like 4.35c, narrates the outwardly visible sign of the success of the exorcism (see further there). With respect to the intention of the narrative, considerations that are sometimes advanced in the commentaries ('the poor pigs!'; 'the immense economic ioss!') are just as erroneous as the moralistic apologetic that wants to disburden Jesus from such accusations (e.g., the cynical remark in Bock I, 777: "the removal of evil is always costly"), or the objection against the credibility of the narrative with the argument that pigs can, after all, swim. Rather, the narrative is only rightly understood when one recognizes that it seeks to portray a paradigmatic event, namely that with Jesus the rule of the demons has fundamentally come to an end—and not only in Israel, but also in pagan territory.

34-37 narrate the finale, which differs in multiple respects from corresponding texts in other exorcism and healing stories.

Already in **34** the information in v. 34a that the swineherds fled (ἔφυγον; so also already Mark 5.14) on account of what has happened (for the substantivized participle τὸ γεγονός, see at 2.15) is sent ahead of the note of dissemination (v. 34b), which belongs to the topics of such narratives (see at 1.65 and Theissen 1987, 81). This is undoubtedly a behavior that is plausible as a reaction to the encounter with the *mysterium tremendum*. One can discuss whether this remark should emphasize once more the extraordinary character of the event or whether it wants to illustrate the *pagan* population's lack of understanding regarding the activity of Jesus. Presumably both are not false. πόλις and ἀγροί as a lexical pair in the sense of "everywhere" is also found, e.g., in Philo, *De specialibus legibus* 2.19, 116, 119; Sibylline Oracles 3.237; Plutarch, *Pompeius* 47.3; Herodianus Historicus 8.1.4; see also Mark 6.56.

35 Luke recounts first the reaction of those among whom the news of the events was disseminated. He had already reported such reactions following a note of dissemination in 1.66 and (summarily) in 5.15. Luke's hand is clearly recognizable in the correspondence with 2.15 (διέλθωμεν . . . καὶ . . . ἴδωμεν). The description of the one who was previously possessed as "completely clothed and sober minded" (v. 35c), which is antithetically related to the portrayal of his behavior in vv. 27b, 29c-d, functions as a genre-typical demonstration of the success of the healing, as this is often found at the end of healing stories (in Luke see 1.64; 4.39; 5.25; 13.13; Acts 3.8; 14.10), but never in exorcisms with the exception of this text. Luke embeds this presentation in the participial construction καθήμενον . . . παρὰ τούς πόδας τοῦ Ἰησοῦ (diff. Mark 5.15) and in this way places the healed man in the position of a student (cf. Luke 10.39; Acts 22.3; see also Plato, *Protagoras* 310c; 2 Corinthians 4.38; 6.1; m. Avot 1.4). It does not yet, however, make him a "disciple" (Annen 1976,

207; Kirchschläger 1981, 129), and it is just as little said that the healed man listens to Jesus's word (*pace* Pesch 1972, 62). The associative references in this direction are probably intended, but they remain very vague. For Luke the time for the inclusion of the Gentiles into the people of God is still a long way off, and, therefore, he must keep Jesus and the Gerasene demoniac at a distance (see also vv. 38-39). That the Gerasenes fall into fear when they see the scene with the man who was previously possessed (the narrator presupposes that they recognize him as such) does not distinguish them from the Jews, for Luke had already reported the exact same thing as a reaction to Jesus's deeds of power in 4.36; 5.26; 7.16.

36 An ἀπαγγέλλειν occurs again. It differs from the ἀπαγγέλλειν in 34b in the fact that it is aimed at the "how" of the healing. In this way Luke lets the entire story that he had narrated from v. 27 pass once more before the ears of the newcomers and, in so doing, gives it a clear sense of direction: πῶς ἐσώθη ὁ δαιμονισθείς. With this specification of the theme, Luke identifies the narrative as a story of the liberation of a person from demonic possession and in this way makes the fate of the pigs into a part of this story. In Mark 5.16 the two still stood unconnected alongside each other.

37 After the story has been brought to mind again in this way, there is again a reaction to the event—now from the side of the earwitnesses. For this Luke has the entire population of the environment turn up, namely—in clear distinction from Mark 5.17—not only the Gerasenes but also the people from the neighboring territories (for this understanding of περίχωρος + genitive plural, cf. Judith 3.7; Herodianus Grammaticus, *De prosodia catholica*, ed. Lentz/Ludwich 1965, I: 297.40; for the phrasing πᾶν τὸ πλῆθος + genitive, see at 1.10). In this way he stages in a very conscious manner an encounter of Jesus with a non-Jewish population of representative scope. They interpret Jesus's deed of power as an epiphany of the divine and therefore become afraid just like the Jews in 4.36; 5.26; 7.16 (37b), but they react differently than these with a sort of 'anti-acclamation.' They ask Jesus to go away from them (v. 37a). If we compare this request with what Luke writes in the aforementioned texts about the reactions of the Jewish population his concern becomes clear. He wants to show that the Gentiles' understanding of Jesus remains miles behind that of the Jews. It is still a long way to the statement of Acts 28.26-28.

With v. 37c Luke brings the readers and Jesus back again to the place left in v. 22 (ὑπέστρεψεν is Lukan idiolect: 32 of 35 attestations for this verb occur in Luke–Acts) and ends in this way the only episode of his story of Jesus that takes place in a non-Jewish region.

38-39 The story still has an epilogue, however, which is not entirely coordinated narratively with the end of the main narrative because its

beginning takes place within the narrated time before v. 37c. This incoherence has its reason in the fact that Luke was evidently concerned to
have the healed man disseminate his story only *after* Jesus had left the
region of the Gerasenes; in the Markan *Vorlage* this demarcation is not so
clearly drawn.

38 The readers can interpret without effort the request to be permitted
to remain with Jesus (εἶναι σὺν αὐτῷ) as a wish to be received into the circle of the twelve called "apostles" (6.13), for according to 8.1 they are said
to be with Jesus (σὺν αὐτῷ). Jesus, of course, must reject this request also
in Luke since, first, there is no free space in the circle of the twelve and,
second, the time of the Gentiles is still a long way off. For ἀπέλυσεν . . .
αὐτόν, see also 14.4.

In **39** Luke reconfigures Mark 5.19-20 in a way that lets the accent
with which he furnishes the note of dissemination stand out clearly. The
commission that Jesus gives the healed man (v. 39a) and its *implementation* (v. 39b) differ in multiple ways. *(a)* He should go into his house, but
he goes through "the whole city" (καθ' ὅλην τὴν πόλιν). *(b)* He should
"tell" (διηγοῦ), but he "proclaims" (κηρύσσων). *(c)* The content of this
proclamation is almost identical in wording—with the exception of the
respective last word that Luke places, of course with full intention, emphatically at the end. While Jesus exhorted the healed man to tell what *God*
did for him, he proclaims what *Jesus* did for him. This is not an "interesting mix-up" (Busse 1979, 213), for the decisive christological point, with
which Luke is concerned here and which also surfaces clearly in texts
such as 1.17, 76; 5.17-26; 7.16, becomes graspable precisely in this substitution, namely that in the activity of Jesus none other than God himself
is present (see also 9.43a; 18.43). And for this reason Luke can also say
that the healed man "proclaims." He carries out the commission to speak
of God by speaking of Jesus. In this way the Gerasene liberated from the
demons becomes the first person who "proclaims" Jesus, both long before
the apostles and other witnesses of Jesus, who do not begin to do so until
after Easter (cf. Acts 8.5; 9.20; 10.42; 19.13; 28.31; see also Luke 24.47),
and outside the Jewish land.

8.40-56: Jesus's Power over Sickness and Death

**⁴⁰When Jesus returned the crowd welcomed him, for all were waiting
for him. ⁴¹And behold, there came a man named Jairus; he was a synagogue leader. He fell at Jesus's feet and asked him to come into his
house, ⁴²for he had an only daughter; she was about twelve years old
and was dying.**

While he went, the people pressed upon him. [43]**And a woman who had a flow of blood for twelve years and could not be healed by anyone** [44]**came up to him from behind and touched the fringe of his garment, and immediately her bleeding stopped.** [45]**And Jesus said, "Who touched me?" When all denied it, Peter said, "Master, the people are pressing around you."** [46]**But Jesus said, "Someone touched me, for I noticed that a power has gone out from me."** [47]**When the woman saw that she had not remained unnoticed, she came trembling and fell down before him and told before the whole people the reason for which she had touched him and how she had been immediately healed.** [48]**And he said to her, "Daughter, your faith has healed you. Go forth in peace."**

[49]**While he was still speaking, one of the people of the synagogue leader came and said, "Your daughter is dead, trouble the teacher no longer."** [50]**But when Jesus heard this, he answered him, "Do not fear, only believe, and she will be saved."** [51]**And when he had reached the house he did not let anyone enter with him except Peter and John and James and the father of the child and the mother.** [52]**And all were weeping and lamenting her. But he said, "Stop weeping, for she is not dead, but she is sleeping."** [53]**And they laughed at him, for they knew that she had died.** [54]**But he took her hand and called out, "Girl, rise!"** [55]**And her spirit returned, and she rose immediately, and he directed that someone bring her something to eat.** [56]**And her parents were astonished. But he commanded them to tell no one what had happened.**

Luke aligns himself further with the order of the Gospel of Mark and recounts, in line with Mark 5.21-43, how Jesus heals a woman from her constant bleeding and how he raises the daughter of the Jewish synagogue leader Jairus from the dead. In doing so, Luke also takes over the typical Markan sandwich construction with the intercalation of the two episodes. We can no longer say why the episodes were originally joined with each other in this manner. Perhaps the twelve years that occurs in both stories (Mark 5.25, 42: the woman was already sick for as many years as the girl had lived) provided the occasion. Luke gives the inserted episode the function of increasing the narrative tension of the frame story by inserting καὶ αὐτὴ ἀπέθνῃσκεν in v. 42b. In this way he makes the healing urgent and lets the readers perceive the dialogue with the healed woman as a temporal delay.

Beyond this, however, Luke has also given the two episodes a common denominator, for both Jairus and the woman with a blood flow are examples of the salvific effect of faith in Luke. With reference to the woman, Luke already found the connection between faith and salvation in Mark (v. 48b), whereas he establishes it for the first time in relation to Jairus (v. 50b diff. Mark 5.36). Luke presumably viewed the narrative of the raising of the daughter of Jairus (vv. 40-42c, 49-56) as a counterpart to the narrative of the raising of the youth in Nain. There it was the *only son* of a *mother*, here the *only* (v. 42 diff. 5.23) *daughter* of a *father* (see however, also at 9.38). In the structure of the narrative, the *exposition* (vv. 41-53), which follows a short *introduction* (v. 40), makes a raising-from-the-dead story out of a healing story on account of the delay through the conversation with the healed woman. There then follows the description of the saving action (*center*; v. 54-55) and the *finale* (vv. 55c-56), which consists of an instruction for the demonstration of the success of the healing, a note of wonder, and a command to be silent. From a form-critical perspective the narrative corresponds to the type of raising stories (cf. the inventory of the genre-specific elements in Fischbach 1992, 22ff) known from 2 Kings 4.8-37; John 11.1-44 (see also Acts 9.36; Leviticus Rabbah 10 [cf. Bill. I: 560]), in which the miracle worker is called to the person who has died (cf. v. 42). By contrast, Luke 7.11-17 represents the type of encounter between miracle worker and funeral procession that is especially common in non-Jewish texts.

The story of the healing of the woman with a blood flow (v. 42-48) can be understood within the Lukan story of Jesus as a narrative elaboration of Luke 6.19b-c: "For power went out from him and healed all" (cf. also 8.46). The distinctiveness of its structure consists especially in the fact that in relation to the *introduction* (v. 42c), *exposition* (v. 43), and *center* (v. 44), the *finale* (vv. 45-48) is very extensively elaborated. An allusion to this narrative is found in Acts of Pilate 7 where the woman has the name Bernice (Latin: Veronica).

The only minor agreements worth noting are: προσελθοῦσα (v. 44a par. Matthew 9.20) instead of ἐλθοῦσα ἐν τῷ ὄχλῳ (Mark 5.27); τοῦ κρασπέδου (v. 44a par. Matthew 9.20) is without a Markan equivalent; cf. further Neirynck 1974b, 101ff; 1991, 39ff; A. Fuchs 1992a, 5ff; Ennulat 1994, 150ff.

With ἐν δὲ τῷ ὑποστρέφειν **40** connects to ὑπέστρεψεν in v. 37 (see further there) and leads Jesus back again into the same context in which he found himself before the start of the boat trip, namely in the midst of a great crowd (cf. 8.4, 19). With the help of the *coniugatio periphrastica*, which Luke also uses in 1.21 with reference to the waiting people (see BDR §353; for the use in the Gospel of Luke, see Verboomen 1992), he apparently wants to evoke the impression that the people have waited for Jesus the whole time. ἀποδέχεσθαι also fits with this. In the New Testament this word occurs only in Luke (see also W. Grundmann, ThWNT 2: 54). In 9.11 the process is reversed. Luke is evidently concerned to present the relation between Jesus and the Jewish ὄχλος not only as amicable but as heartfelt.

41 New narrative figures are also introduced with the same words (ἀνὴρ ᾧ ὄνομα + name) in Appian, *Iberica* (= *Hispania*) 236; Philostratus, *Vitae sophistarum* 1.512 (cf. further at 1.26).

The name Ἰάϊρος (or Ἰάειρος) is the Graecised version of Hebrew יָאִיר ("may God enlighten"; cf. Numbers 32.41; Deuteronomy 3.14; Joshua 13.30; and elsewhere) or יָעִיר ("may God awaken"; cf. 2 Samuel 2.19[?]; 1 Chronicles 20.5). In Greek it is also attested in 1/3 Ezra 5.31; Josephus, *Bellum judaicum* 2.447, and on a number of ossuaries (cf. Ilan 2002, 111). The possibility that the tradition of the name in connection with the raising narrative may have its basis in the last of these meanings cannot be ruled out (see also Pesch 1970a).

The fact that Luke introduces Jairus with his function within the Jewish synagogue (v. 41b) is not necessary for the narrative and probably functions as a foil for his humble falling at Jesus's feet, which is a gesture of submission (v. 41c; cf. e.g., Vita Aesopi 3 where it uses almost the same words about a slave [!]: πεσὼν παρὰ τοὺς πόδας τοῦ δεσπότου παρεκάλει ["Falling at the feet of the master he entreated"]). The Lukan designation ἄρχων τῆς συναγωγῆς does not express that Jairus "in Luke . . . as distinct from Mark . . . shares his function as leader of a synagogue with no one" (so Busse 1979, 226). Verse 49 alone already contradicts this. While ἀρχισυνάγωγος is literarily attested only in early Christianity (see also Mark 5.35, 36, 38; Luke 13.14; Acts 13.15; 18.8, 17; Justin, *Dialogus cum Tryphone* 137.2), ἄρχοντες τῆς συναγωγῆς is used in the Septuagint for Hebrew נְשִׂיאֵי הָעֵדָה (Exodus 16.22; 34.31; Numbers 31.13; 32.2; Joshua 9.15; 22.30; see also Numbers 16.2). There are numerous epigraphical attestations for both designations, however; cf. for ἀρχισυνάγωγος, e.g., *CIJ* 336, 383, 504, 587; and for ἄρχοντες τῆς συναγωγῆς, e.g., *CIJ* 343, 384, 390 (see also *CIJ* I, XCVIIff; Schürer 1973–1987, 436: it is said that a ἀρχισυνάγωγος led the worship service, while an ἄρχων was occupied with the synagogue leadership "in general"). One and the same person could apparently also be both (cf. *CIJ* 265, 553, 833); on the other hand, in a synagogue there were also evidently always multiple ἄρχοντες and ἀρχισυνάγωγοι (cf. Acts 13.15; 14.2D). There were also ἀρχισυνάγωγοι in associations (cf. W. Schrage, ThWNT 7: 842ff; Schürer 1973–1987, 436). The petition to come into the house of the synagogue leader is presumably meant to be understood as a sideways glance to the story of the faith of the centurion in 7.1-10, for it forms the exact counterpart to 7.6c.

42 In v. 42a Luke explains the behavior of Jairus to the readers. What Jesus is meant to do in his house can remain unstated, for the readers can supply this without effort from, e.g., 7.3. Specifications of age and time with ὡς ἐτῶν are uncommon in literature (with considerable difficulty I found Testament of Levi 2.2; Joseph and Aseneth 1.4 v. l; 27.1 v. l; Galen, _De locis affectis_, ed. Kühn 1964, VIII: 64, 194; Cyranides, ed. Kaimakis 1976, 1.1 [line 33]; see also Luke 3.23); however, they occur abundantly in papyri and inscriptions (cf. Preisigke 1925–1931, I: 607). Luke also adds μονογενής in 9.38 (see also 7.12). The imperfect ἀπέθνῃσκεν should be understood as conative (cf. BDR §326).

That Jesus complies with the request is regarded by Luke as such a given that he merely conveys this information in v. 42b as an adverbial phrase. It is related to the introduction of an insertion for whose narrative staging Luke needs a crowd (cf. v. 45d).

With the introduction of a woman who suffers from a "blood flow" for twelve years **43** presents the course setting for a healing story. Although a ῥύσις αἵματος can also be caused by wounds (e.g., Diodorus Siculus 4.11.6; Plutarch, _Brutus_ 13.5; see also Aristotle, _De generatione animalium_ 727a13: concerning nosebleeds; for its use in professional medical literature, see Weissenrieder 2003), the remark on the duration of the sickness indicates that the narrative envisages a woman who suffers from bleedings even outside of her monthly period (see also Leviticus 15.25; 20.18; Philo, _De fuga et inventione_ 188, 190). According to the halakah on discharges, this causes her to be in a state of lasting impurity (cf. Leviticus 15.19-24, 25-28; see also 11QTemple 48.15–17; Josephus, _Bellum judaicum_ 5.227; _Contra Apionem_ 2.103; m. Niddah passim). Although this aspect plays no role in the narrative, everyone who knows Leviticus 15 would probably have read the narrative in the light of this text. The explicit statement that previous attempts at healing have failed is a favorite _topos_ in narratives such as this one (cf. e.g., Aelian, _De natura animalium_ 9.33; Weinreich 1969, 195–96; Kollmann 1996, 230).

The comment ἰατροῖς προσαναλώσασα ὅλον τὸν βίον, which further intensifies the desperate situation of the woman, reads like an epitome of Mark 5.26. It is attested in only part of the textual tradition, however (ℵ[*,C] A L W Θ Ξ [Ψ] ƒ[1,13] 33 [1424] 𝔐 [lat sy^{c.p.h} bo]). The absence of these words in 𝔓75 B (D) 0279 sy^s sa armen georg; Orig is nevertheless much better attested. It is therefore probable that it was added later.

44 portrays a "contact healing" (cf. ἅπτεσθαι as in 6.19; Mark 6.56 par. Matthew 14.36; see also Wells 1998, 195ff) that takes place without out Jesus's knowledge and assistance; for this reason the narrative has the woman approach him "from behind" (see also 7.38). The dynamistic worldview is in the background again (see further at 6.19). Acts 19.12 (see also Acts 5.15) also presupposes that not only the touch of the miracle worker himself but also the touch of his clothing alone or objects with which he had contact mediate healing power. Here the following principle applies: "the lesser the healing contact, the greater the overflowing power seems" (Theissen 1987, 71). The κράσπεδον of Jesus's garment that the woman touches certainly does not refer to one of the tassels (Hebrew צִיצָת) that were to be attached to the four corners of the outergarment according to Numbers 15.38-39; Deuteronomy 22.12 (*pace* Marshall; Bovon). The narrative says nothing of a submission involving falling at the feet or the like. What is in mind is probably merely one of the lower-hanging ends of Jesus's garment (see also Plutarch, *Tiberius et Caius Gracchus* 19.5; Appian, *Bella civilia* 1.2.16; Zechariah 8.23). That the healing takes place "immediately" belongs to the topics of healing stories (παραχρῆμα is a typical Lukan term; see further at 1.64).

The exchange of words narrated in **45-46** depends on the fact that the readers know more than the narrative figures (including Jesus), for they can immediately answer the question that Jesus poses. What is initially hidden from them, however, in contrast to Mark 5.30, is the reason of knowledge that has led Jesus to his question, for the information that describes how Jesus recognized that someone touched him is saved by Luke until the conclusion (v. 46c). The explanation that he places in Jesus's mouth implies not only a material conception of δύναμις but also makes clear that the touch must have taken place under special circumstances, for otherwise no "power" would have gone out from Jesus (Luke uses here the same ἐξέρχεσθαι ἀπό phrasing that he uses elsewhere for the coming out of demons; cf. 4.35, 41; 8.2, 29, 35, 38; 11.24; Acts 16.18). Against this background, the superficial attempt at explanation that Peter gives in v. 45c-d (for the address of Jesus as ἐπιστάτα, cf. at 5.5) has the narrative function of ensuring the exceptional character of the touch by the woman. Peter's reference to the crowd that presses upon Jesus is based on the misunderstanding that what had happened was a touch that did not involve the transfer of healing power. This also indicates that δύναμις does not flow every time Jesus is touched, but only under a certain presupposition. Jesus will say what this is in v. 48.

In v. 45c Luke explicitly emphasizes that no one admitted that they were the one who touched Jesus (ἀρνουμένων δὲ πάντων), and except for the woman who had been healed by now, all are also correct in this. The continuation in v. 47a makes clear that the woman was seeking to touch Jesus secretly. The narrative says nothing about the reasons, evidently because they were so plausible in light of the woman's sickness that every reader could effortlessly supply them on their own with the help of their cultural basic knowledge (see at v. 43). The woman could not be certain whether Jesus would not interpret the touch by her as infection with her uncleanness and react accordingly.

47 The Lukan dramaturgy of the narrative brings it about that Jesus's explanation of v. 46c leads the woman to the recognition that her action has not remained unnoticed (v. 47a). Her immediate reaction (trembling and falling before Jesus's feet; v. 47b) is an analogy to 5.8 (see further there; cf. also the respective introductions with ἰδών/ἰδοῦσα) and shows that the woman recognizes Jesus as God's representative. As in 8.36, it also comes here to a narrative-internal ἀπαγγέλλειν of the healing, namely "before the whole people" (v. 47c). For this reason, one should preferably not designate it as a "confession" (so Fitzmyer; Nolland; Bock; and others). For the conclusion of the narrative, it is of decisive significance that with the paraphrasing formulation δι' ἣν αἰτίαν (v. 47c) the narrator refers back to the description of the sickness in v. 43 (the "reasons" also include, of course, the fact that the woman promised herself healing from the touch, but this is such a given that Luke can omit the inner monologue from Mark 5.28).

In **48** Luke narrates the reaction to the ἀπαγγέλλειν of the healing. However, unlike in the Markan *Vorlage,* the reaction does not come from the side of the public hearers of the narrative but from the side of Jesus. With the same words as in 7.50 he interprets the expectation that guided the action of the woman and the image of Jesus underlying this expectation as saving faith. His reaction stands at the same place at which notes of wonder or acclamation stand elsewhere. Nevertheless, one should probably not assign to it the intention of warding off exaggerated praise (*pace* Robbins 1987, 512–13; the attestation of Plutarch, *Moralia* 542c adduced by Robbins occurs in a completely different context and has a completely different orientation). Rather, here too "faith" has a christological substructure and is nothing other than the certainty that salvation and healing are accessible in Jesus. That was also already the topic of 5.20; 7.9; 8.25; see also in 8.50 below. For the concluding wish of peace, see at 7.50.

In **49** Luke takes up the interrupted narrative of the synagogue leader and his deathly ill daughter. He increases the dramatic tension by allowing the two episodes to merge into each other (the events described in v. 48 and v. 49 proceed synchronically) and introducing, like Mark 5.34, the bringer of the news of her death with the help of a historical present (v. 49a; apart from this Luke has not taken over a single one of the Markan historical presents; see also at 24.36). The phrasing τις παρὰ τοῦ . . . designates a family member (see also Mark 3.21; 1 Maccabees 9.44, 58; 13.52; BDR §237$_2$). When the exhortation not to bother Jesus further is grounded with reference to the death of the girl, this represents an element that belongs to the topics of miracle stories—namely, the motif of the underestimation of the miracle worker. The words of the messenger assume that Jesus can perhaps heal sick people but cannot make dead people alive again (see also Philostratus, *Vita Apollonii* 4.45.1: the people think that Apollonius merely wants to deliver a funeral oration; Epidaurus W 9.10 [Herzog 1931, 12]; Phlegon, *De mirabilibus* 2.7; Acts 3.5; and v. 53).

50 Jesus's response sets φοβεῖσθαι and πιστεύειν over against each other and in this way makes a semantic profiling of "believe" that had also already characterized the theologically profiled use of אמן hiphil in the Old Testament; cf. Genesis 15.1/6; Isaiah 7.4/9 (in each case with "fear not!"; for the New Testament, see also Mark 4.40). "Faith" is understood here as trusting that God will save from a desperate situation that appears hopeless (see also Exodus 14.30-31; 2 Chronicles 20.20; Psalm 78.32; 116.10; Jonah 4.4). The exhortation "fear not!" also precedes God's saving intervention in Genesis 21.17; Exodus 14.13; Numbers 21.34; Deuteronomy 20.3-4; Joshua 8.1; 11.6; 2 Kings 19.6; Isaiah 35.4. And as in 8.48; Daniel 6.24 it is also presupposed in our text that faith leads to salvation (for the connection between πιστεύειν and σῴζειν in Luke and in the New Testament, see at 7.50).

51 Luke makes a scenic simplification of Mark 5.37, 38a, 40b-c. Unlike in Mark 5.37, John is named before James (so also 9.28 and Acts 1.13; diff. 5.10; 6.14; 9.54), but that should not be overinterpreted (as e.g., in Marshall; Fitzmyer; Radl). The fact that the crowd is hindered from entering the house comes into contact with a motif that often occurs in healing stories (cf. Mark 7.33; 8.23; Acts 9.40; see Bultmann 1995, 239; Theissen 1987, 70–71). The realization of the miracle action is meant to remain hidden from the public so that the aura of mystery surrounding it is not destroyed (see also at v. 56b).

52 Luke describes first the common mourning rituals (the lexical pair κλαίεν and κόπτεσθαι is also found in Aesop, *Fabulae*, ed. Hausrath/ Hunger 1970, 221; Josephus, *Antiquitates judaicae* 13.399). As in 7.13 (see further there), Jesus exhorts the mourners with the imperative present μὴ κλαίετε to stop weeping (see also 23.28). Unlike there, however, he provides a justification (οὐ γὰρ ἀπέθανεν ἀλλὰ καθεύδει), concerning which it has sometimes been claimed that it is "meant not just euphemistically but eschatologically" because Jesus "in the face of the dead girl (denies) the power of death" (Kertelge 1970, 116; see also Wiefel; Nolland). Although this is undoubtedly an incorrect interpretation, "sleep" also does not simply stand as a metaphor for "dead" here (cf. in this sense 1 Corinthians 7.39; 11.30; 15.6, 18, 20, 51; 1 Thessalonians 4.13, 14, 15; 5.10; 2 Peter 3.4 and Hoffmann 1978, 186ff), for after all, the two verbs are set over against each other (see also Marshall). Rather, Jesus makes another interpretation of the situation in which the girl is found, and his statement is nothing other than the indirect announcement that the girl will get up again in the near future—for this is precisely what distinguishes sleep from death; cf. also Ovid, *Fasti* 6.746–48, where in a similar situation Aesculapius says, *Nulla causa doloris, namque pio iuveni vitam sine vulnere reddam et cedent arti tristia fata meae* ("There is no reason for sorrow, for I will give back life without harm to the pious youth, and the sad fate will yield to my art").

53 provides again the motif of the underestimation of the miracle worker ("laugh [at]" in comparable contexts is also found in Genesis 18.12; Acts of John 60; see already at v. 49). Luke explains the reaction of the mourners with the phrasing εἰδότες ὅτι ἀπέθανεν and thus agrees with their understanding of reality. Therefore, for him the girl was not merely almost dead but completely dead (*pace* Weissenrieder 2003, 267).

54 The taking of the hand (κρατεῖν τῆς χειρός; see also Mark 5.41 par. Matthew 9.25) by the miracle worker is also attested, besides Acts 9.41 (raising of Tabitha) in New Testament healing stories (Mark 1.31; 9.27; Acts 3.7), namely always when it says that the sick "rise" and/or the healer "raises" them (ἀνίστημι and/or ἐγείρω). Hence, what is in mind is obviously not a touch for the transfer of healing power as in the case of the woman with a blood flow (see at v. 44), but a helping and saving gesture (see also 1 Enoch 48.10; 71.3; Apocalypse of Abraham 11.1; see also Psalm 73.23; Isaiah 41.13; 42.6). A reference to Jesus's own resurrection is not even recognizable in the distance. But the girl is pulled back from death into life only through Jesus's word, which Luke, unlike Mark 5.41, very consciously does not defamiliarize to a ῥῆσις βαρβαρική ("incomprehensible speech"; see Theissen 1987, 73). What he previously wrote about the authority (ἐξουσία) of Jesus's word (see at 4.32, 36; 7.7, 14) would become untrustworthy if he would bind it to the sound of the words.

In **55** Luke narrates the consequences. First, as a supplement to Mark 5.42 he has the πνεῦμα of the girl immediately return into her (v. 55a; on παραχρῆμα, see at vv. 44, 47 and above all at 1.64), which certainly means not simply the replacement of the breath but the return of that which is called πνεῦμα ζωῆς/רוּחַ חַיִּים, e.g., in Genesis 6.17; 7.15; Ezekiel 1.21; 10.17; 37.5 (see also Judith 10.13; in the New Testament: Revelation 11.11) and which leaves a person at his or her death (cf. Psalm 143.7; 146.4; Matthew 27.50; John 19.30; see E. Schweizer, ThWNT 6: 358.33ff; 362.14ff; 367.4ff). There is also talk of the ἐπιστρέφειν of the πνεῦμα of a person in Judges 15.19 (Samson, who is, to be sure, barely still alive and would be only almost dead from thirst; cf. also 1 Kings 17.21: Elijah asks for the return of the נֶפֶשׁ/ψυχή into the dead child). 55b establishes the success of the words of Jesus according to its visible side. Whether Jesus's instruction to let the girl eat is intended to be understood as a genre-typical demonstration of the success of the healing (as 4.39; 5.25; see at 1.64) is not entirely certain, since for that the girl would have had to actually eat (cf. the parallel in the healing from a distance by R. Hanina ben Dosa [y. Berakhot 5.5; Bill. II: 10]). Schiffer 2001, 151ff connects this with the age of the girl and infers that the narrative intended for her to have suffered from a sickness that is called *anorexia nervosa* today. This interpretation, however, is just as much plucked out of the air as every other diagnosis.

56 Vis-à-vis Mark 5.42 Luke places emphasis on the fact that only the parents (and not also the three disciples who are likewise present) react with genre-typical wonder (v. 56a; for the term, see also at 2.47; for the subject matter, see Theissen 1987, 78ff). Luke relates the command to maintain secrecy, which Jesus places on the parents in v. 56b, more precisely to the healing *process* (τὸ γεγονός as in 2.15; see further there); in Mark 5.42 the *result* stood in the foreground. The view that Luke intended this command to be understood as a distancing of Jesus from a perception of his person and task oriented to such deeds of power (e.g., Nolland; Bock; Radl) can be fairly safely excluded in light of the previous course of his story of Jesus, which has not dealt with such stories in a sparing manner. Therefore, one can say nothing more than that Luke brings in the command to be silent against his other tendency at this point because he found it as a saying of Jesus in Mark 5.42.

9.1-36: The Preparation of the Disciples for Discipleship

The structure and function of chapter 9 present many problems for interpreters of Luke. This is recognizable in the great number of very different structuring proposals (cf. e.g., Green 352ff; Radl I: 578) and in the great number of articles with the term "composition" (or the like) in the title. It is more or less common to all the investigations that they view the episodes narrated here as "*Vorspiel*," "preview," or "prelude" to the section that begins in 9.51, which is regarded as the 'travel narrative' or 'central section.'

Luke continues to follow the Markan order; between the last events narrated (par. Mark 5.21-43) and the sending out of the disciples that follows in vv. 1-6 (par. Mark 6.6b-13), only the narrative of the visit of Jesus in Nazareth (Mark 6.1-6a), which Luke had moved earlier to 4.16-30, is missing. For the overall understanding of this episode it is, of course, decisive that between v. 17 and v. 18 the section Mark 6.45–8.26 is lacking (the so-called great omission). Only Bethsaida in v. 10 remains from Mark 6.45; 8.22, i.e., from the two wing pericopes of this textual complex. From this one can infer that Luke was not working with a version of the Gospel of Mark that did not (yet) contain 6.45–8.26, but that he consciously left out this part of his *Vorlage* (beyond this Luke 11.16 shows that Luke knew Mark 8.11). In two other places Luke has also streamlined the Markan presentation. Between the disciples' departure and return (v. 6/v. 10) he omitted the narrative of the death of John the Baptist (Mark 6.17-29 par. Matthew 14.3-12), and the boat trip of Mark 6.32 is lacking between the return of the disciples and the narrative of the feeding of the 5,000 (v. 10/v. 12b).

Through these shortenings there emerges a narrative collecting basin that obtains its coherence through the fact that it places the disciples' instruction in discipleship at the center. The christological question is also oriented toward the disciple theme (in this respect the readers learn nothing that they have not long known). Luke not only makes the feeding of the 5,000 (vv. 12b-17) into a disciple story, but he also corrects his Markan *Vorlage* in a very central point. Since via the omission of Mark 6.45–8.26 the so-called confession of Peter directly follows the feeding of the 5,000, Luke reverses the statement of Mark 6.52 and has the disciples come to insight precisely "about the bread!" Verses 7-9 is also only indirectly a story of Jesus, for there the concern is with who Herod and his environment take Jesus to be.

Moreover, one should not miss a whole series of cross-connections to the Emmaus episode (Luke 24.13-35), where the disciples also come to insight "over the bread" (see also Tannehill 1986, I: 289–90; Just 1993, 16ff; cf. also Gillman 2002; B. P. Robinson 1984): *(a)* "The day began to recline" (ἤρξατο κλίνειν; 9.12 diff. Mark 6.35); "the day had already reclined" (κέκλικεν; 24.29). *(b)* Jesus "takes" "bread," "blesses," "breaks" it and "gives it to the disciples/them" (9.16; 24.30). *(c)* The disciples subsequently recognize him (9.18-20; 24.31). *(d)* Jesus speaks about his fate, "The Son of Man δεῖ πολλὰ παθεῖν . . . and on the third day ἐγερθῆναι" (9.22); "the Messiah ἔδει ταῦτα παθεῖν . . . and εἰσελθεῖν εἰς τὴν δόξαν αὐτοῦ" (24.26). In chapter 9 the reference to death and resurrection thus stands *after* the bread and recognition scene, while it *precedes* it in chapter 24. If one also includes the broader context, *(e)* the two sendings of the twelve in 9.1-6 (for the κηρύσσειν of the reign of God; v. 2) and the remaining eleven in 24.47 (for the κηρύσσειν of "repentance for the forgiveness of sins among all nations") can easily be integrated into this structure. However, the suggestion that Luke also makes a bridge from the *five loaves and two fish* of 9.13 to the *bread* that Jesus breaks in 24.31 and the *fish* that Jesus eats a piece of in 24.42-43 (Gillmann 2002, 168–69) goes beyond what can be assumed with some probability. This results in the following mirror-image juxtaposition:

Sending of the twelve for the κηρύσσειν
of the reign of God (9.1-6)

ἡ δὲ ἡμέρα ἤρξατο κλίνειν (9.12)
Bread action of Jesus (9.16)
Recognition by the disciples (9.18-20)

"The Son of Man δεῖ παθεῖν   "The Messiah ἔδει παθεῖν
and rise" (9.21-22)   and enter into his δόξα" (24.26)

                                     κέκλικεν ἤδη ἡ ἡμέρα (24.29)
                                     Bread action of Jesus (24.30-31)
                                     Recognition by the disciples (24.31)

                                     κέκλικεν ἤδη ἡ ἡμέρα (24.29)
                                     Bread action of Jesus (24.30-31)
                                     Recognition by the disciples (24.31)

Jesus's passion and resurrection fate forms the axis between the two narrative sequences not only on the level of the text but also on the level of the
events. This connection is also recognizable in the fact that in 24.44-46 the
Lukan Jesus explicitly points the eleven to his earlier announcements of
the passion and the resurrection ("my words that I said to you when I was
still with you"; v. 44), the first of which is found precisely in 9.22. One can
therefore say that 9.1-22 is called to mind in chapter 24, thus actualizing
above all the sequence of sayings in 9.23-27 with their pronounced temporal slope (see at 9.23-27) for the time of Jesus's absence.

9.1-6: The Commission of the Twelve

[1]And he called the twelve together and gave them power and authority over all demons and to heal sicknesses. [2]And he sent them out to
proclaim the reign of God and to make well. [3]And he said to them,
"Take nothing on the way, neither staff nor a provision bag, neither
bread nor money, nor (should you) have two undergarments. [4]And if
you come into a house—remain there and move on from there. [5]And
all who do not receive you—go out from that town and shake off the
dust from your feet as a witness against them." [6]But they went off and
went through village by village. In doing so they gospeled and healed
everywhere.

The episode consists of a narrative frame in which the narrator reports that Jesus commissions the twelve with proclaiming the kingdom of God and healing the sick (vv. 1-2) and that the disciples then also do this (v. 6). Embedded in this frame is a three-part speech of Jesus, which gives the disciples instructions for their behavior on the way.

The dependence on Mark 6.7-13 is clearly recognizable. The problem, however, consists in the fact that there is yet another commission in Luke 10.1-12 that only partially touches upon Mark 6.7-13 and in the fact that the parallels in Matthew 9.37–10.15 overlap both with Mark 6.7-13 and with non-Markan elements in Luke 9.1-6. In the framework of the two-source theory this situation is explained with the assumption of a Mark–Q overlap (cf. Fleddermann 1995, 101–26; Laufen 1980, 201ff). Further, it is assumed with relatively great unanimity (exception: A. Fuchs 1992b) that in Luke 10.1-12 the version handed down in Q dominates, that there was originally only a single speech, and that the minor agreements in Luke 9.1-6 par. Matthew 9.37–10.15 vis-à-vis Mark 6.7-13 go back for the most part to the influence of the Q-version.

Of these minor agreements the following are significant: νόσους/νόσον (v. 1b par. Matthew 10.1) is without a Markan equivalent (cf. Tuckett 1984, 135–36); κηρύσσειν + βασιλεία (v. 2a par. Matthew 10.7) is without Markan equivalent; direct speech in the instructions on equipment v. 3 par. Matthew 10.9-10 (instead of indirect speech as in Mark 6.8); no taking of a staff (ῥάβδος; v. 3b par. Matthew 10.10 diff. Mark 6.8); ἐξερχόμενοι . . . τῆς πόλεως ἐκείνης (v. 5b par. Matthew 10.14) instead of ἐκπορευόμενοι ἐκεῖθεν (Mark 6.11); τὸν κονιορτόν (v. 5c par. Matthew 10.14) instead of τὸν χοῦν τὸν ὑποκάτω (Mark 6.11); cf. further Schramm 1971, 26ff; Neirynck 1974b, 106ff; 1991, 42ff; Ennulat 1994, 162–63.

There is controversial discussion over what the Q-version looked like (cf. the proposals of Hoffmann 1972, 263ff; *CEQ* 158ff) or whether it can be reconstructed at all (it certainly cannot!) and whether the Markan version is literarily dependent upon Q (so Fleddermann 1995) or not.

1 The new scene follows the preceding episode abruptly, for narratively Jesus is actually still in the house of Jairus. At any rate, the calling together of the twelve (the addition of ἀποστόλους by ℵ C* L Θ Ξ Ψ and others is certainly secondary) makes a clear caesura, for as such the disciples of Jesus last appeared in 8.1. It is, hence, this level of narration to which Luke returns (συγκαλεῖν is a Lukanism: 7 of the 8 New Testament attestations appear in Luke). Jesus now lets the disciples participate in those attributes with which God had previously equipped only him (cf. 4.14, 32, 36; 5.17, 24; 6.19; 8.46; ἐξουσία and δύναμις are also found as a lexical pair outside the New Testament; see at 4.36). The consequence is that the disciples can and may do something that was previously reserved for Jesus alone. For the phrasing ἐξουσίαν διδόναι, see, at 4.6 (in the New Testament, cf. also Mark 11.28parr.; John 5.27; 17.2; Acts 8.19; 2 Corinthians 10.8; 13.10); for δύναμιν διδόναι, see e.g., 2 Chronicles 17.2; Daniel 2.23[Theodotion]; Josephus, *Antiquitates judaicae* 12.393 (for the embedding of this linguistic use in the context of the authorization of envoys and mediators, cf. with further attestations Wolter 1988b, 31ff).

ἐπί indicates to what the authority of the disciples extends (cf. also Testament of Reuben 5.1 in connection with this same lexical pair; see also at 10.19). This is also connected with a qualification, for their ἐξουσία does not yet extend to the forgiveness of sins as with Jesus (cf. 5.24); this is not added until after Easter (cf. 24.47). The joining of θεραπεύειν with the accusative direct object νόσον or νόσους (so also Matthew 4.23; 9.35; 10.1) occurs frequently in pagan Greek texts (e.g., Isocrates, *Aegineticus* 26, 29; Diodorus Siculus 1.82.1; Strabo 5.3.1; 8.3.32; 8.6.15; Galen, *De methodo medendi*, ed. Kühn 1964, X: 509; in Jewish sources only in Josephus, *Antiquitates judaicae* 17.150). Otherwise θεραπεύειν always refers only to people (Matthew 4.24; 8.7; 10.8; 12.22; Mark 1.34par.; 3.10par.; Luke 4.40; 7.21; 10.9; and elsewhere). We are dealing with an infinitive of purpose that is joined zeugmatically—passing over the prepositional phrase—with ἔδωκεν αὐτοῖς . . . (cf. BDR §390.1b; §479.2; and, e.g., 1 Maccabees 1.13 [ἔδωκεν αὐτοῖς ἐξουσίαν ποιῆσαι τὰ δικαιώματα τῶν ἐθνῶν ("He gave them authority to enact the legal regulations of the Gentiles")]; 10.6 [ἔδωκεν αὐτῷ ἐξουσίαν συναγαγεῖν δυνάμεις ("He gave them authority to gather armed forces")]).

2 With the sending out (ἀποστέλλειν) the twelve are given a function that corresponds to their designation as ἀπόστολοι in 6.13. Their commission consists in doing exactly what Jesus has previously done, namely in proclaiming the reign of God and healing the sick (cf. then also 10.9 and the summaries in 4.40; 6.18-19; 7.21-22; 8.2). Both aspects are also connected with each other in Matthew 10.7-8, so quite a bit speaks for the view that Luke already found this joining in Q.

In many manuscripts ἰᾶσθαι occurs with the object τοὺς ἀσθενεῖς (‭א‬ A D L Ξ Ψ and others) or τοὺς ἀσθενοῦντας (C W Θ *f¹³* 𝔐). Although these readings, taken together, are better attested, more speaks for the original lack of an object (so only in B sy[s,c]), because one can actually explain only a subsequent addition (adjustment to the other Lukan uses of ἰᾶσθαι and/or establishment of symmetry to the proclamation commission) and not a subsequent deletion.

Unlike in Mark 6.7 (and unlike the seventy-two in Luke 10.1) the twelve are not sent out in groups of two, and as distinct from 10.1 they also are not meant to announce the coming of Jesus.

3 The general instruction to take "nothing" on the journey is specified in a five-member catalogue. In comparison to the version in Mark it is conspicuous that in Luke the taking of a staff (ῥάβδος) is forbidden, while it is explicitly allowed in Mark 6.8. Since Matthew 10.10 also prohibits the staff, quite a bit speaks for the view that here the Q-version—which is older than Mark 6.8—is preserved, which is much more radical than the Markan version. All five objects belonged to the typical equipment of travelers: a "staff" (that is longer than a man) as a support and weapon against robbers and wild animals (cf. e. g., Philo, *Quaestiones et solutions in Exodum* 1.19: "one needs a staff in order to support oneself on it and to drive away poisonous reptiles and other wild animals"; C. Schneider, ThWNT 6: 969) and a "provision bag" (πήρα) for storing foodstuffs or the like (see, e.g., Judith 10.5; 13.10; it was "carried on the left hip on a strap placed over the right shoulder": W. Michaelis, ThWNT 6: 119 following F. Wotke, PRE 19.563) are often mentioned alongside each other in these contexts (cf. m. Yebamot 16.7d; b. Shabbat 31a; b. Baba Batra 133b [all texts in Bill. I: 565; see also Hoffmann 1972, 314–15]; especially also about Cynics: Diogenes Laertius 6.13 about Antisthenes and Diodorus of Aspendus; Apuleius, *Apologia* 22: *pera et baculum* "provision sack and staff" are for Diogenes and Antisthenes what the diadem is for kings; see also Apuleius, *Florida* 14; Dio Chrysostom 64.18; Alciphron, *Epistulae* 3.19.5; Epictetus, *Dissertationes* 3.22.10, 50; Lucian of Samosata, *Demonax* 48; *De morte Peregrini* 24; *Fugativi* 32; *Cataplus* 3 and 19 [πήρα . . . καὶ ξύλον ("provision sack and staff")]; Julianus Imperator, *Orationes* 9.18).

The instruction to take no "bread" (ἄρτος) as a provision for the way also fits this context, for this was usually transported in the aforementioned "provision sack" (cf. Athenaeus, *Deipnosophistae* 10.19 [422b–c]: ἐν πήρᾳ φέροις ἄρτους ἄν ["in a provision sack you can carry bread"]; Longus 3.11.2; Philostratus, *Vita Apollonii* 4.10.1 about Apollonius: πήραν ἔφερε καὶ ἄρτου ἐν αὐτῇ τρύφος ["he carried a provision sack and a piece of bread in it"]; Suidas, s. v. πήρα: ἡ θήκη τῶν ἄρτων ["the container for the bread"]). Taking along bread is also prohibited only in Mark 6.8 and not also in Luke 10.4 and Matthew 10.9-10 (this instruction was therefore probably not in Q); contrast also Didache 11.6: when an itinerant apostle moves on "he should receive nothing except bread until he stays overnight."

It is rather unlikely that Luke thinks of silver coins in the prohibition against taking along ἀργύριον and in this way softens the instruction of his *Vorlage* concerning this (Mark 6.8 even prohibits the bringing along of copper coins of little value [χαλκός], i.e., "small change" [Luz 1985–2002, II: 87]; Matthew 10.9 prohibits the *acquisition* of "gold, silver, and copper"). It is more conceivable that Luke generalizes the Markan version and has Jesus speak very generally of "money" (for ἀργύριον in this sense, see also Matthew 25.18; Mark 14.11; Luke 19.15, 23; Acts 8.20; see also W. Bauer 1988, 210–11).

The last member of the equipment rule is not dependent upon αἴρετε syntactically but is parallel to it (ἔχειν is an imperative infinitive like Romans 12.15; Philippians 3.16; cf. BDR §389₃). A distributive ἀνά is found only in a part of the textual tradition. This, to be sure, is probably a secondary addition. Not only is it more poorly attested (A C³ D W Θ Ψ *f*¹,¹³ 𝔐 against ℵ B C* L Ξ and others), but further, it is probably a result of semantic pedantry. It clarifies that the concern here is not with the number of the χιτῶνες of the entire circle of the twelve but of every single one of them. A χιτών is actually the undergarment over which a ἱμάτιον was worn when applicable (see further at 3.10-11). According to Diogenes Laertius 6.102, the Cynic Menedemus wore a dark grey, footlength χιτών, but this piece of clothing has nothing to do with the "cloak" (τρίβων; cf. Diogenes Laertius 4.52; 6.13; Plutarch, *Moralia* 332a) that was otherwise typical for Cynics. According to Dionysius of Halicarnassus, *Antiquitates romanae* 9.59.4, Fabius Vibulanus extorted, *inter alia*, two tunics per soldier from the Aequans for his army. Although Josephus, *Antiquitates judaicae* 17.136, which is often mentioned in this context, is comparable only to a limited extent (cf. Radl), it is nevertheless evident from it and from Mark 6.9 that wearing two tunics over each other (presumably as protection against the cold) was not especially uncommon (see also Bill. I: 566). However, Luke and Matthew 10.10 are concerned with the *possession* of two undergarments, i.e., taking a change of shirt is prohibited. The twelve are to bring with them only what they carry on their bodies.

Taken altogether, the radicality of this instruction differs from everything that is known from the environment of Jesus and early Christianity. The twelve are not even permitted to bring with them what was indispensable for someone traveling by foot at that time in order to make provision for his or her existential survival on the way (see also Hoffmann 1972, 314). There is no group whose ethos even comes close to the rigorousness of this demand (cf. the further radicalizations in 10.4). Böttrich 2003 is therefore right to ascribe to it the character of a symbolic action. It finds its theological complementary counterpart in Luke 12.22-31 par. Matthew 6.25-34. Whether it has a historical basis must, of course, remain open.

4 The renunciation of every existential self-securing has the consequence that Jesus's messengers were dependent upon the care and hospitality of other people who invited them into their houses (and thus made visible the reception of the message; cf. Matthew 10.40-42; 25.34-40). The instruction in v. 4b must be joined with 1.7c and prohibits moving to a different house (possibly because it is more comfortable there or has better food). This presupposes a longer stay of the missionaries in a town (Didache 11.4–5 is decidedly different: "Every apostle who comes to you should not remain more than one day—if necessary also one more. But if he remains three days, he is a false prophet"). From this it can be inferred that this instruction is already related to post-Easter processes of founding communities and can be interpreted as an early witness of the history of Christian institutionalization (cf. also the analogous use of μένειν in Acts 9.43; 16.15; 18.3; 21.8).

5 reflects the opposite case. The missionaries find no resonance with their message in a town (cf. Mark 6.11b par. Matthew 10.14), and correspondingly, there is also no house in which they are received with hospitality. The use of δέχεσθαι in the context of ancient hospitality ethics is in the background here (see above all at 16.4; cf. further Xenophon, *Oeconomicus* 5.8; Plutarch, *Agis et Cleomenes* 34.4 and Luke 9.48, 53; 10.8, 10 and parallels; see also Matthew 10.41; 11.14; John 4.45; 2 Corinthians 7.15; Galatians 6.14; Colossians 4.10; Hebrews 11.31; W. Grundmann, ThWNT 2: 50–51). The reaction to which Jesus exhorts the messengers in this case is a symbolic action (see also Nehemiah 5.13; Acts 13.51; 18.6). It is meant to express the radical breaking of all fellowship (cf. esp. Delebecque 1982) and is based on an *a minore ad maius* logic. Those who act in this way demonstrate that they want nothing more to do with something as insignificant and guiltless as the dust of a town—how much less with their inhabitants! The widespread opinion that Jews practiced such a gesture when they returned from foreign territory into the land of Israel is not attested in the texts mentioned in Bill. I: 571.

The phrasing εἰς μαρτύριον ἐπ' αὐτούς is not easy to understand because μαρτυρ- ἐπί + accusative of person is not attested elsewhere. The final judgment is probably in view, and in this context the function of the witness for the prosecution is assigned to the shaking off of the dust (like the queen of the south and the Ninevites in Luke 11.31-32 par.; see also Delebecque 1982, 183).

In **6** Luke reports the carrying out of the commission issued in v. 2 in a very summary manner. For διέρχεσθαι as a typical Lukan word, see at 2.15. When there is talk here of the εὐαγγελίζεσθαι of the twelve, this means the same thing as κηρύσσειν τὴν βασιλείαν τοῦ θεοῦ in v. 2. Luke sends the disciples via the "villages" (for the distributive interpretation of κατὰ τὰς κώμας, cf. BDR §224.3). However, it is certainly not intended (*pace* Wiefel and Schürmann I: 504) to keep them away from the "towns" (πόλεις) as places for proclamation reserved for Jesus.

9.7-9: The Perplexity of Herod

⁷But the tetrarch Herod heard of all these events, and he was per-
plexed, for some said, "John has been raised from the dead," ⁸but
others, "Elijah has appeared," and yet others, "one of the old prophets has risen." ⁹But Herod said, "John I had beheaded, but who is this
about whom I hear such things?" And he wanted to see him.

The sideways glance to Herod Antipas seeks to create room for the time
of the disciples' proclamation and healing activity without having the narration accompany them. Thus, it primarily has the function of producing
narrative time in order to bridge the time that has elapsed between the
sending out and the return of the twelve. Luke has possibly deleted the
episode of the death of John the Baptist (Mark 6.17-29 par. Matthew 14.3-
12) because it ran counter to the ideal of historiographic "brevity" (τάχος;
Lucian of Samosata, *Quomodo historia conscribenda sit* 56); cf. in this
sense *Quomodo historia conscribenda sit* 56: "One needs only to suggest
secondary and unimportant things but one should report the great events;
much can also be completely omitted."

Luke has undoubtedly used Mark 6.14-16. However, he changes his
Vorlage by placing Herod Antipas at the center. Unlike Mark 6.14c-15,
Luke does not report about the speculations regarding Jesus's identity in
three independent main sentences. Instead, he embeds it in an infinitive
construction (διὰ τὸ λέγεσθαι) and disempowers it to an explanation for
Herod's perplexity (διηπόρει). Moreover, he also changes the thrust of his
Vorlage at a very substantial point: Herod understands Jesus explicitly *not*
as John *redivivus* (v. 9b diff. Mark 6.16), but he instead leaves the question
of Jesus's identity open.

The most conspicuous minor agreement is undoubtedly that Herod Antipas is
called ὁ τετραάρχης (v. 7a par. Matthew 14.1) instead of ὁ βασιλεύς (Mark 6.14).
This agreement cannot be interpreted without further ado as independent corrections of the historically incorrect Markan designation, for on the one hand, Matthew himself calls Herod βασιλεύς a bit later (14.9), and on the other hand, the
title τετραάρχης is additionally attested for Herod only in later Christian texts (cf.
Ennulat 1994, 164); see further Neirynck 1974b, 111; 1991, 44–45.

7a Luke introduces Herod, the territorial sovereign of Jesus, as τετραάρχης
and in this way makes a connection to 3.1 (Herod as τετρααρχῶν τῆς
Γαλιλαίας). From 3.19-20 the readers also know concerning him that
he was a villain and had thrown John the Baptist into prison. With τὰ
γινόμενα πάντα Luke summarizes everything that he had recounted about

Jesus since 4.14 (see also 13.17), and both here and there the present participle—as distinct from the retrospective aorist in 4.23 (with ἀκούειν) and 24.18—accentuates the incompleteness of the activity of Jesus.

In **7b-8** Herod Antipas is described as one who permanently cannot make heads or tails of what he hears about Jesus (διηπόρει as a durative imperfect; this verb occurs in the New Testament also in Acts 2.12; 5.24; 10.17). As grounds for his perplexity Luke mentions a series of different opinions that were being circulated with regard to Jesus's identity. Of course, what all three speculations have in common is the fact that they regard Jesus as a prophetic figure.

Through the reproduction of the speculation that God raised John the Baptist from the dead (v. 7c; ἠγέρθη is meant to be a *passivum divinum*) the readers learn for the first time about the death of Jesus's forerunner, and they will soon learn also that Herod had him beheaded. The question of whereupon such an opinion is based may not be answered with reference to the notion of the individual resurrection of martyrs (*pace* Pesch 1973, 222–23; K. Berger 1976, 15–22; for criticism cf. Nützel 1976), for there the resurrection is always accompanied by the exaltation into God's heavenly world (e.g., Wisdom of Solomon 2–5; 4 Maccabees 5.36-37; 9.7-8; 13.16-17; 17.17-18; Philippians 1.23; 2.8-9; Revelation 11.11-13). Rather, it is completely adequate as an explanation that Luke invents the voice of the people here and it can be thought capable of "something preposterous" (Schürmann I: 507). This is not, of course, to say that this opinion actually existed (*pace* Marshall; Radl).

Behind the second speculation, according to which the prophet Elijah has taken form in Jesus (v. 8a; see also Matthew 9.33), stands the Jewish conception of *Elias redivivus* (see at 1.17) developed in connection with Malachi 3.1, 23.

There is only a rather small tradition-historical basis (5 Ezra 2.18: Jeremiah, Isaiah, Daniel; see further K. Berger 1976, 256 nn. 72–73; 2 Maccabees 15.12-16 does not count, for we are dealing here with a dream) for the third speculation (v. 8b), which sees in Jesus not a certain prophet (such as Elijah) but one of the other (cf. BDR §306[11]) "old" prophets having returned (according to Philo, *De somniis* 2.172; Josephus, *Bellum judaicum* 6.109; *Antiquitates judaicae* 12.413 this refers to the preexilic prophets; in Didache 11.11 the concern is probably with Christian prophets).

All three opinions are, of course, false, and the readers know this; likewise, Luke knows that the readers know this. Thus, the topic of these lines is not Jesus himself but the reaction to Jesus.

9 Unlike Mark 6.16, Luke has Herod contradict the opinion circulated among the people that Jesus is the Baptist come back to life with the argument that he himself had the Baptist beheaded. Luke has Herod speak here in the so-called causative active, for it is unlikely that he put his own hand to the task (cf. Kühner/Gerth 1890–1898, II/1, 99–100; Moulton/Turner 1963, III: 52–53; see, e.g., also 7.5; 20.9, 16; 22.11; 24.9). It is also noteworthy that Luke neatly differentiates with respect to what his narrative figures regard as possible (see at v. 7c). A tetrarch does not believe such preposterous things as the common people do. However, everything else remains open of course, and Luke can therefore place the same question in the mouth of Herod as he places in the disciples' mouths in 8.25. Just as the disciples could not understand how to interpret Jesus's power over the forces of chaos, so Herod cannot explain what he hears about Jesus (the present ἀκούω corresponds to the present τὰ γινόμενα in v. 7a). The question picks up διηπόρει from v. 7b and makes clear that Herod's perplexity also continues beyond the end of this episode. The readers can infer from the concluding note (v. 9c) that Herod hopes to receive information about Jesus's identity from a personal encounter with him (see also 19.3 of Zacchaeus: ἐζήτει ἰδεῖν τὸν Ἰησοῦν τίς ἐστιν; see also Philo, *De mutatione nominum* 7). This wish is fulfilled in 23.8 where it also says why Herod wanted to "see" him. But the readers do not know this yet.

9.10-17: The Disciples Make the People Satiated

[10]**After the apostles had returned, they told him everything that they had done. And he took them to himself and withdrew alone with them to a town named Bethsaida.** [11]**But the people learned about this and followed him. And he welcomed them and spoke to them about the reign of God, and he made well the ones who needed healing.**

[12]**The day began to recline, and the twelve came to him and said, "Send away the people in order they may go into the surrounding villages and farms and stop off and find provisions, for we are in an uninhabited place here."** [13]**But he said to them, "You give them** (something) **to eat!" They replied, "We have no more than five loaves and two fish; unless we go and buy food for this whole people."** [14]**For there were about 5,000 men. He, however, said to his disciples, "Have them recline in eating groups of about fifty."** [15]**And they did so and had all recline.** [16]**And he took the five loaves and the two fish, looked up to heaven, blessed them and broke** (them) **and gave** (them) **to the disciples in order that they set** (them) **before the crowd.** [17]**And all ate and became satiated. And what was left over to them was gathered— twelve baskets full of broken pieces.**

The structure of the narrative is clearly recognizable: v. 10a establishes the connection with 9.1-6. The *introduction* (vv. 10b-11) constructs the scene, the *exposition* (vv. 12-14a) develops the problem that is then overcome in the *center* (vv. 14b-17). The note in v. 17c serves the visible *demonstration* of the miracle story.

Form-critically this narrative was regarded earlier as a "nature miracle" (e.g., Bultmann 1995, 230ff). Today, under the influence of Theissen 1987, 111ff., it is sometimes called a "gift miracle" (e.g., Lührmann 1987, 119; Radl I: 595), namely alongside John 2.1-11; Luke 5.1-11; 1 Kings 17.7-16; 2 Kings 4.42-44. But this designation makes determinative for the form a certain social interaction that actually plays no role in the individual examples of the genre. Therefore, perhaps one should instead speak of a miraculous overcoming of situations of material deprivation (see also Lührmann 1987).

Like the parallel in Mathew 14.13-21, the narrative of the feeding of the 5,000 in Luke is based literarily on Mark 6.30-44. The feeding of the 4,000 with seven loaves and a pair of fish narrated in Mark 8.1-9 par. Matthew 15.32-38 has left no traces in the Lukan version. The situation is somewhat different in relation to the version handed down in John 6.1-5. In that regard we find Mark–John agreements against Matthew and Luke, on the one hand, and yet also Johannine agreements with Matthew–Luke minor agreements (see below). Two Mark–Matthew–John agreements against Luke should also be registered (πολὺς ὄχλος Mark 6.34/Matthew 14.14/John 6.5; χόρτος Mark 6.39/Matthew 14.19/John 6.10). From this and from the agreements in the plot one can conclude that all six literary versions arose from the same narrative.

The shape of this original narrative cannot be reconstructed, of course, but the points of contact with 2 Kings 4.42-44, where it is narrated that Elisha makes one hundred people satiated with twenty loaves, are unmistakable. Jesus gives the disciples/Elisha gives the servant the commission to distribute the bread; their/his objection that the bread is not sufficient; renewal of the commission; all eat, and there still remains something left over.

The complexity of the source question is increased further through the high number of minor agreements, especially in vv. 10-11 (see Neirynck 1982/1991/2001, II: 75–94; A. Fuchs 1997): cf. in the first instance: ὑπεχώρησεν or ἀνεχώρησεν (v. 10 par. Matthew 14.13) instead of ἀπῆλθον (Mark 6.32); καὶ εἶδον αὐτοὺς ὑπάγοντας καὶ ἐπέγνωσαν (Mark 6.33a) is lacking in v. 10b par. Matthew 14.3; οἱ ὄχλοι ἠκολούθησαν αὐτῷ (v. 11a par. Matthew 14.13; see also John 6.2a: ἠκολούθει δὲ αὐτῷ ὄχλος πολύς) instead of πολλοὶ . . . συνέδραμον ἐκεῖ καὶ προῆλθον αὐτούς (Mark 6.33); the lack of Mark 6.34c with the allusion to Numbers 27.17 or 1 Kings 22.17; the note that Jesus heals sick people (v. 11d par. Matthew 14.14c). Beyond this, mention should be made of the following minor agreements: the designation of the 5,000 as ὄχλος (v. 12c, 16d par. Matthew 14.15c, 19d) instead of αὐτοί (Mark 6.36a, 41d); the lack of φάγωσιν Mark 6.36c (see also John 6.5d) in v. 12e par. Matthew 14.15e; the lack of Mark 6.37c-38c (the 200 denarii from v. 37c are found, however, in John 6.7b); βρώματα (v. 13e par. Matthew 14.15e) instead of ἄρτους (Mark 6.37d); ὡσεί with 5,000 (v. 14a par. Matthew 14.21; see also John 6.10d: ὡς) is without a Markan equivalent; συμπόσια συμπόσια (Mark 6.39) is lacking in v. 14 par. Matthew 14.19; τοὺς ἄρτους (Mark 6.41c) is lacking in v. 16c par. Matthew 14.19c; the far-reaching omission of Mark 6.40 (ἀνέπεσαν has, however, remained in John 6.10d); Mark 6.41e ("and the two fish he divided for all") is lacking in v. 16 par. Matthew 14.19; τὸ περισσεῦσαν . . . κλασμάτων (v. 17b par. Matthew 14.20b [τὸ περισσεῦον]; see also John 6.12c: τὰ περισσεύσαντα κλάσματα) instead of κλάσματα (Mark 6.43a); see further Schramm 1971, 129–30; Neirynck 1974b, 112ff; 1991, 45ff; Ennulat 1994, 167ff.

The search for an explanation of this evidence has produced a plethora of hypotheses (cf. the overview in Ennulat 1994, 168). For the Lukan narrative it can—in addition to the aforementioned dependence on Mark 6.30-44—be regarded as rather certain that it arose independently of Matthew 14.13-1. On the other hand, most of the minor agreements (above all the extensive agreements of the Matthew–Luke version against Mark 6.32-34, 37c-38c) cannot be explained as independent redactions of the Mark-*Vorlage*. Moreover, they make it unlikely that Matthew and Luke combined the Markan narrative with an *oral* tradition alongside Mark independently of each other. In this case, there remains only two explanatory possibilities. Either the narrative was also contained in Q (on this with Fitzmyer I: 763: "This is not impossible, but can scarcely be proved"), or there was a secondary "revision of the Markan text . . . that lay before Matthew and Luke respectively" (Ennulat 1994, 179).

10a is the counterpart to v. 6. Luke had already combined ὑποστρέφειν (see at 1.56) and διηγεῖσθαι with each other in 8.39 (the latter both here and there in the place of a Markan ἀπαγγέλλειν).

In **10b-11** Luke constructs the scene for the following episodes. First, he has Jesus withdraw together with the twelve. Unlike in the parallels, however, Jesus does not use a boat to do so. With this change Luke probably wants to reconfigure somewhat more plausibly the very unrealistic presentation of Mark 6.32-31 (the inhabitants of the cities see Jesus and the disciples set off in the boat, run by foot around the sea, and come before them to the landing place). In Luke Jesus and the twelve do not arrive "in an isolated place" (so Mark 6.32) but in a "town named Bethsaida" (v. 10b). Luke has taken this name from Mark 6.45; 8.22 (see the introductory comments on 9.1-36). The phrasing καλουμένης Βηθσαϊδά makes clear that Luke does not know the place, and he also assumes that it is unknown to his readers.

According to John 1.44; 12.21, Bethsaida (Hebrew בֵּית צַיְדָא), which Herod Philip renamed Iulias (Josephus, *Antiquitates judaicae* 18.28), was the hometown of Peter, Andrew, and Philip. However, Josephus localizes it not in Galilee but in the Gaulanitis. It is probably identical with today's et-Tell, which is located about 2.5 kilometers north of the Lake of Gennesaret (cf. Kuhn/Arav 1991; Arav/Freund 1995/1999; Rottloff/Schipper 2002; Tsafrir 1994, 85).

With this localization, however, Luke incurs a certain narrative incoherence, for according to vv. 12-13 all the participants find themselves not in a town but "in an isolated place." This incoherence is also reflected in the numerous variants of the textual tradition (cf. the apparatus).

In 11b Jesus receives the crowd that has followed him in the same way as they had greeted him in 8.40 (see further there). The last sentence of Luke–Acts, where it says of Paul that he "welcomed" every visitor "and proclaimed the reign of God" (ἀπεδέχετο . . . κηρύσσων τὴν βασιλείαν τοῦ θεοῦ; Acts 28.30-31), will be reminiscent of the terminology of this verse. In any case, Luke presents Jesus in an activity that is typical for him (cf. 4.43; 5.17; 6.18-19; 7.21-22; 8.1-2).

In **12** the action is set into motion, with the authorial description of an existing situation of hardship not functioning as the point that stimulates the action but rather as an initiative of the disciples. The narrator himself notes only the time of day. However, with this the problem that will soon be named by the disciples is already announced to the attentive reader who still has vv. 10-11a in his or her ear. Luke has presumably consciously reconfigured the *Vorlage* of Mark 6.35 (ὥρας πολλῆς γενομένης is the only Markan genitive absolute that Luke does not adopt; cf. Cadbury 1969, 133), for in 24.29 he will speak again of the κλίνειν of the day (see the introductory comments on 9.1-36; for the phrasing, cf. Judges 19.8, 9A [with καταλύειν as in v. 12d], 11A; Jeremiah 6.4). While Mark speaks very generally of Jesus's μαθηταί, Luke probably intentionally has "the twelve" appear, for in v. 17c he also ends the narrative with this number (see at v. 17c). Unlike in Mark 6.36, the twelve are not concerned that the people *buy* for themselves something to eat; rather, they suggest that the crowd go in order *to stop off* in the surrounding villages and farms and get provisions for themselves *there* (see also Schenke 1983, 167). The justification that Luke reformulates and moves backward—ὧδε ἐν ἐρήμῳ τόπῳ ἐσμέν—receives through this a secondary meaning: 'From us they find neither lodging nor provisions.' καταλύειν and ἐπισιτισμός are semantically isotopic, for both require people who are on journeys (cf., on the one hand, Genesis 19.2; 24.23, 25; Testament of Levi 9.5; Joseph and Aseneth 3.2; Plato, *Gorgias* 447b; Plutarch, *Moralia* 850d; Luke 19.7; see also at 2.7 on κατάλυμα; and, on the other hand, Genesis 42.25; 45.21; Exodus 12.39; Joshua 1.11; Xenophon, *Anabasis* 1.5.9; Plutarch, *Moralia* 327e).

13-14a Whether Luke has changed the Markan word order and moved the personal pronoun ὑμεῖς backward is text-critically doubtful (B b 1* against ℵ A C D L W Ξ Ψ *f*[1,13] 33 𝔐 it). Either way the narrative makes a surprising turn, for Jesus's countersuggestion in v. 13a lies completely outside of the spectrum of possible reactions that could be expected on the basis of the initiative of the twelve. An allusion to the similar instruction in 2 Kings 4.42c is not intended, for the opposition to the suggestion of the disciples and, if applicable, the emphasis of the personal pronoun ὑμεῖς give the exhortation of Jesus a completely different orientation. The *twelve* should adopt the role of the host vis-à-vis the crowd, for the people whom Jesus welcomed and whom he told about the reign of God (v. 11) should become satiated (χορτασθῆναι; v. 17) where *they* are—and not elsewhere. The disciples' reference to the limited amount of the food at their disposal (v. 13b; the two fish belonged already to the pre-Markan elements of the narrative, namely as the common accompaniment of bread; Marshall 360: "a relish like a modern sandwich filling"; see also Körtner 1984; Bill. I: 683–84) and the information that "about 5,000 men" had to be fed (v. 14a) accomplishes exactly what an exposition in a miracle story needs to accomplish narratively. It characterizes the hardship that needs to be removed by the action of the miracle worker (cf. Theissen 1987, 61–62). The disciples' deliberation—formulated in response and with an undertone of slight indignation (εἰ μήτι + subjunctive is also found in 1 Corinthians 7.5; 2 Corinthians 13.5; cf. BDR §376₃)—that Jesus's suggestion could only be realized if they went shopping (v. 13c) can be placed under the rubric of 'unsatisfactory attempts to find a solution,' which also belong to the expositional motifs of miracle stories. However, it is not the case that this deliberation of the disciples is not carried out because it would be "completely unrealistic" or "a completely failed undertaking" (Radl I: 601 in dependence on van Iersel 1964/1965, 190; Busse 1979, 238), but because Jesus wills that the disciples make the people satiated with the means that are at their disposal. The situation of need that is set up in the exposition therefore applies not to the people but to the disciples, who at Jesus's instruction should feed 5,000 men with five loaves and two fish. Therefore, from the continuation of the narrative the readers await the answer to the burning question—how will the twelve manage to implement Jesus's exhortation?

14b-15 Luke leaves the focusing on the twelve (the change from the δώδεκα to the μαθηταί is overinterpreted in Schenke 1983, 168) and gives

Jesus the role of the host who assigns places to the guests. Here Luke breaks himself away from the orientation to the arrangement of Israel's camp in the wilderness that still shimmers through in the *Vorlage* Mark 6.39-40. The choice of κατακλίνειν, which elsewhere always describes reclining to eat in a house (cf. 7.36; 14.8 24.30; nowhere else in the New Testament), and of κλισία as a metonymic designation for table fellowship (see also Josephus, *Antiquitates judaicae* 12.96; 3 Maccabees 6.31; Plutarch, *Moralia* 149b; see also P. Mich. 243.7; 246.13), together with the size of the groups into which the crowd is divided, more likely indicates that here the meal celebrations of the Lukan period stand in the background as a model (see also Radl).

16 Jesus does what every Jewish *paterfamilias* does at the beginning of a meal. He takes the bread in the hand, speaks the grace, "breaks" the bread, and extends the pieces to the other meal participants. This practice is probably also responsible for the overlaps with the reports of the Last Supper of Jesus (Mark 14.22-24parr.) and of Jesus's bread action in Emmaus (Luke 24.30). In each case we find "taking" (λαμβάνειν) bread, "blessing"/"thanking" (εὐλογεῖν/εὐχαριστεῖν; for the relationship of the two terms, cf. J. M. Robinson 1964: the εὐχαριστεῖν has grown out of the εὐλογεῖν), "breaking" ([κατα]κλᾶν), and "giving" (διδόναι) to the disciples (see also Mark 8.6 par. Matthew 15.36). According to m. Berakhot 6.1, the grace spoken over the bread ran as follows: "Praised be Yhwh, our God, the king of the world, who causes bread to rise from the earth." Many interpreters want to see in this correspondence an allusion to the Eucharistic meal, which was anchored in Jesus's Last Supper with his disciples on the eve of his death and included the interpretation of the bread and wine as "body" or "flesh" and as "blood" of Jesus (cf. 1 Corinthians 11.23-25; Mark 14.22-24parr.; see also John 6.51, 53-56; Ignatius of Antioch, *To the Philadelphians* 4; *To the Smyrnaeans* 7.1; Didache 9.1–10.6; Justin, *Apologia i* 66–67; e.g., Wanke 1973a, 45ff; van Iersel 1964/1965; Schenke 1983, 172–73). There is no evidence at all in the text for this, however, since the specified overlaps "are restricted to what is common to every meal" (Lührmann 1987, 120), whereas the all-conclusive interpretation is lacking.

There are admittedly two peculiarities: unlike in the other meal scenes, Jesus looks up to heaven in all three versions of this narrative after taking the bread. This is a common gesture of making contact with God, which is attested in the environment of early Christianity in every possible form of communication with God (prayers of petition and thanks, hymns, eulogies, etc.).

Psalm 123.1-2; Daniel 4.31 (= 4.34^Theodotion^: "I raise my eyes to heaven . . . and praise the Most High [καὶ τῷ ὑψίστῳ εὐλόγησα]"); Josephus, *Antiquitates judaicae* 11.64 (with a following εὐχαριστεῖν), 162 (with a following petition for salvation; see also Job 22.26; Susanna 35^Theodotion^); Apocalypse of Moses 42.8 (see also Susanna 9; Acts 7.55); Joseph and Aseneth 11.19; 4 Baruch 6.5; 1/3 Ezra 4.58; John 11.41; 17.1. Josephus, *Antiquitates judaicae* 11.143 also belongs in this context (Ezra does not want to look up to heaven because he is ashamed of the sins of the people; see also Greek Apocalypse of Enoch 13.5, Luke 18.13). In non-Christian texts: Xenophon, *Cyropaedia* 6.4.9; Chariton of Aphrodisias 3.3.4; 8.7.2 (εἰς τὸν οὐρανὸν ἀναβλέψας εὐφήμει τοὺς θεούς ["looking up to heaven he praises the gods"]); Plutarch, *Marcellus* 7.3; Epictetus, *Dissertationes* 2.17.29 (εἰς τὸν οὐρανὸν ἀναβλέπειν ὡς φίλον τοῦ θεοῦ μηδὲν φοβούμενον τῶν συμβῆναι δυναμένων ["to look up to heaven as a friend of God, not being afraid of the things that could happen"]); Antonius Liberalis, *Metamorphōseōn synagōgē* 5.4; cf. also the contrary texts mentioned at 18.13.

Although this gesture is nowhere attested as a "thaumaturgical motif" (*pace* Pesch 1980, I: 352), its use at this point should probably be brought into connection with the following miracle (see also Mark 7.34). Beyond that, Luke supplies the object αὐτούς to εὐλόγησεν, which relates the praise (spoken "over the bread"), which is always directed to God in Jewish meals, to the food (see, however, also Mark 8.7 with regard to the fish; D it sy^[s],c^ have wanted to correct this by adding ἐπ' before αὐτούς; see Brock 1963). The parallel in 1 Corinthians 10.16 ("the cup of blessing ὃ εὐλογοῦμεν") does not rule out the possibility that we are dealing with an accusative of respect (Marshall; BDR §160). However, it is probably more likely that Luke wanted the blessing of the food to be understood as causative for the event narrated in v. 17 (see also Fitzmyer). Because Jesus blessed the five loaves and two fish, they were sufficient for 5,000 people.

17 There is a narrative gap between vv. 16 and 17a-b, for it is not recounted what the disciples do with the bread. Instead, the narrative jumps right to the eating of the crowd. Luke evidently wants to evoke the impression that the food multiplies among the hands of the disciples to the extent that—as the demonstration of the success in v. 17c makes clear—more is left over afterward than before. How this takes place in detail is left—as so often—to the imagination of the readers (see also at 2.5-6; 4.30; 7.10, 37-38). Plus, within the narrative only the disciples have realized that the food has multiplied in a miraculous way, for only they—and not the 5,000 people—know that there was only five loaves and two fish to distribute. For this reason the absence of an acclamation from the side of the crowd is not very surprising. From the side of the disciples, Peter speaks representatively for the others in v. 20b. Unlike Mark 6.44, Luke ends the story not with the number of eaters but with the amount left over and places the concluding point with the number twelve, which is fraught with meaning. In this way he first has the narrative point back to v. 12 (a basket is assigned, so to speak, to each of the twelve named there) and then forward to the post-Easter sending of the apostles (cf. Luke 24.47-48; Acts 1.8). There too the twelve act in Jesus's commission and hand on nothing other than what they have. Through this it becomes possible for the readers to perceive the event described in v. 17c as a proleptic symbol of the post-Easter mission success (see also Fitzmyer I: 769: "They each bring back a basketful *and now have enough to feed still others*").

9.18-22: The Christological Insight of the Disciples and Jesus's First Announcement of the Passion and the Resurrection

[18]**And it happened when he was praying by himself alone that the disciples were with him, and he asked them, "Who do the people say that I am?"** [19]**And they answered and said, "John the Baptist, but others Elijah, and yet others** (say), **'one of the old prophets has risen.'"** [20]**And he said to them, "But you, whom do you regard me to be?" And Peter answered and said, "the Anointed One of God."** [21]**But he rebuked them and commanded** (them) **to say this to no one,** [22]**and said, "The Son of Man must suffer much and be rejected by the elders and chief priests and scribes and be killed and be raised on the third day."**

Due to the omission of Mark 6.45–8.26, the disciples' confession of Jesus as the Messiah follows directly after the feeding of the 5,000. Thus, here, in direct contradiction to Mark 6.52, they recognize the identity of Jesus (v. 20b) "ἐπὶ τοῖς ἄρτοις." The episode is not narrated in order for the readers to learn through Peter that Jesus is the "Anointed One of God," for they have already known this for a long time. Rather, what they learn is that the disciples too have now finally grasped this.

Luke's *Vorlage* was Mark 8.27-33, though Luke localizes the scene neither in the villages of Caesarea Philippi nor "on the way" (Mark 8.27) and vv. 32-33 is lacking in Luke.

The evaluation of v. 22 is controversial, for here there are a few striking agreements with Matthew 16.21 against Mark 8.31: ἀπό (instead of ὑπό); in each case τῶν is lacking before ἀρχιερέων and γραμματέων; τῇ τρίτῃ ἡμέρᾳ ἐγερθῆναι (instead of μετὰ τρεῖς ἡμέρας ἀναστῆναι). The following explanations have been proposed as solutions: Lukan dependence on Matthew 16.21 (e.g., Goulder 1989, I: 48ff, 438–39; Farmer 1990; Gundry 1999, 105ff); Lukan redaction (e.g., Neirynck 1982/1991/2001, II: 43–48, III: 295–306); tradition alongside of Mark (Schramm 1971, 130ff); "post-Markan textual changes" (Ennulat 1994, 195). With the exception of the first proposal mentioned, everything else is conceivable.

18 For the phrasing of the introduction, see at 5.12. The Lukan manner of narration evokes the impression that the crowd has moved away by now and Jesus is found again with his disciples in the same situation as between v. 10 and v. 11. The portrayal of Jesus praying "by himself" recalls 5.16 and 6.12 (κατὰ μόνας has the same function here as the wilderness or the mountain there); the *coniugatio periphrastica* εἶναι . . . προσευχόμενον indicates a longer duration of the prayer and lets the narrative come to rest. Jesus's question to the disciples about whom the "people" regard him to be suddenly calls to mind once again the feeding of the 5,000, for Luke replaces—certainly not unintentionally—the Markan οἱ ἄνθρωποι with οἱ ὄχλοι and refers in this way to vv. 11a, 12c, 16e (see also Feldkämper 1978, 110).

On the other hand, the answer of the disciples in **19** also makes clear that Luke does not think only of the 5,000 from vv. 11-17, for it repeats with slight modification the public opinion about Jesus that was already related in vv. 7-8.

20 Peter answers the question about whom the *disciples* regard Jesus to be representatively for all. The designation "Anointed One of God" (ὁ χριστὸς τοῦ θεοῦ; diff. Mark 8.29) is nothing new for the readers, for Luke had already spoken of Jesus as χριστὸς κυρίου in 2.26 (for the tradition-historical background and context of the title, see there). By now the readers are also in position to connect this statement with 3.22 and with the quotation of Isaiah 61.1 in 4.18 and fill it with content on the basis of these two texts. Jesus is the Spirit-anointed messianic king of Israel (see also Acts 4.27; 10.38). The genitive can be interpreted both as a *genitivus subiectivus* (cf. 1 Samuel 10.1; 15.17; 2 Samuel 12.7; 2 Kings 9.6; Acts 10.38) and as a genitive of belonging (as with ὁ ἅγιος τοῦ θεοῦ; 4.34par.; cf. BDR §162).

21 The command to silence immediately follows. Plutarch, *Aemillius Paullus* 13.6, ἐπετίμησεν αὐτοῖς καὶ παρήγγειλε μηδὲν πολυπραγμονεῖν ("he rebuked them and commanded [them] not to interfere"; see also 2 Timothy 4.2) is comparable linguistically. Unlike Mark, who also covers the divine sonship of Jesus with a command to silence (cf. Mark 3.11-12; 9.9), Luke relates the command to silence only to the title χριστός (see also at 4.41 where the reasons for this are discussed). Keeping this secret is limited to the period up to the resurrection of Jesus. Correspondingly, the first time that this is made known publicly (explicitly for "the whole house of Israel"!) does not take place until Acts 2.36.

22 The first announcement of the passion and the resurrection of Jesus follows almost without a transition. In 24.6-7 Luke will put the reminder of it in the mouth of the angels in the empty tomb. Two aspects are decisive for the understanding of the thematic connection with the disciples' confession of Jesus as the Messiah and Jesus's command to silence.

First, Luke 24.19-27, 44-47; Acts 2.29-36; 3.18 make clear that Jesus's messiahship can be understood as according to Scripture only after his passion and resurrection, and this means: as determined by the prior establishment (δεῖ or ἔδει; see at 4.43) by God's plan of salvation (βουλή; see at 7.30). Therefore, for Luke the δεῖ of the passion and resurrection (cf. also Luke 17.25; 24.7, 26; Acts 3.21; 17.3) and the δεῖ of the fulfillment of Scripture (Luke 22.37; 24.44; Acts 1.16) are christologically isotopic, and in this sense the note on the fulfillment of Scripture in 18.31b also corresponds to the δεῖ in v. 22a. *Second*, Jesus's resurrection from the dead creates for the very first time the presupposition for the unique character of his messiahship, as it was described in 1.33 (see further there). That Jesus's regency over Israel will be eternal in duration and surpasses in this way the traditional Jewish conception of the Messiah is possible not before but only after Easter.

When Luke, following Mark 8.31, speaks of ἀποδοκιμάζεσθαι (v. 22b; see also 17.25), he uses a verb that is also used to describe the fate of Jesus in Mark 12.10parr. and 1 Peter 2.4, 7 (see also Acts 4.11; Gospel of Thomas 66), namely with recourse to the metaphor of the rejection of the eventual cornerstone by the builders according to Psalm 118.22 (see also at 20.17). The groups of the elders, chief priests, and scribes, whom Mark introduces separately, are combined to a single group in Luke (and Matthew) on account of the absence of the definite article between them. In 20.1, however, he separates them again from one another (but cf. then again 22.66: the "council of elders of the people, chief priests, and scribes"). Comparable three-member listings also appear in 19.47; 22.52; Acts 4.5. With this series Luke merely wants to bring together the whole Jewish ruling class (see also Neirynck 1982/1991/2001, II: 45–46). The Lukan–Matthean "on the third day" (so also Matthew 17.23; 20.19; Luke 18.33; 24.7, 46; Acts 10.40; 1 Corinthians 15.4; see also Luke 13.32) means the same period of time as the Markan "after three days" (so also Matthew 27.63; Mark 9.31; 10.34), for begun days (the so-called border days) were always counted as full days in New Testament times.

9.23-27: Instruction in Discipleship

[23]**But he said to all, "If anyone wants to come after me, he must deny himself and take up his cross daily and follow me. **[24]**For whoever wants**

to save his life will lose it; but whoever loses his life for my sake, he will save it. [25]For what does a person profit if he obtains the whole world but gives away or harms himself? [26]For whoever is ashamed of me and my words, of him the Son of Man will be ashamed when he comes in his glory and (in the glory) of the Father and of the holy angels. [27]Truly, I say to you: Among those who stand here there are some who will not taste death before they see the reign of God."

The circle of hearers is now expanded again. The textual complex is composed of a compilation of predominantly symbouleutic sayings of very different provenances (vv. 23-26; only v. 27 is epideictic). Luke has taken them over from Mark 8.34–9.1 (with the exception of Mark 8.37) and lightly reworked them. There are parallels in Q to v. 23b par. Mark 8.34b (Luke 14.27 par. Matthew 10.38), to v. 24 par. Mark 8.35 (Luke 17.33 par. Matthew 10.39 with another parallel in John 12.25), and to v. 26 par. Mark 8.38 (Luke 12.9 par. Matthew 10.33). The parallel to v. 23b in Gospel of Thomas 55.2 is based on Luke 14.27 par. Matthew 10.38 (cf. Schröter 1997a, 379ff). Since the Q parallels are found in different contexts, Mark was probably the first to put the sayings together. In doing so he created a paraenetic slope that is also still clearly identifiable in the Lukan version. Verse 23 communicates to the public the conditions for entering into the discipleship of Jesus. Thus, the concern here is with the *adoption* of a certain orientation of existence. Verses 24-26 then turn to the narrower circle of those who have decided for discipleship, and exhort them to *maintain* this orientation of existence. The coherence is established through the reference to Jesus with the help of recurrent pronouns: ἀκολουθεῖν μοι (v. 23), ἕνεκεν ἐμοῦ (v. 24b), and ἐπαισχύνεσθαι με καὶ τοὺς ἐμοὺς λόγους (v. 26a).

The only noteworthy minor agreements are the absence of καὶ τοῦ εὐαγγελίου Mark 8.35 (v. 24 par. Matthew 16.25), the absence of ἐν τῇ γενεᾷ ταύτῃ τῇ μοιχαλίδι καὶ ἁμαρτωλῷ καί (Mark 8.38) in v. 26 par. Matthew 16.26; the authorial transition καὶ ἔλεγεν αὐτοῖς at the beginning of Mark 9.1 is absent in v. 27 par. Matthew 16.28; ἐληλυθυῖαν at the end of Mark 9.1 is lacking in v. 27 par. Matthew 16.28; cf. further Neirynck 1974b, 121ff; 1991, 50–51; Ennulat 1994, 196ff; there is also a parallel in Q to v. 23b-c, which Luke reproduces in 14.27 (see further there).

23 If Luke had Mark 8.34 as *Vorlage*, it is clear whom he meant with "all," namely the disciples and the crowd. The ὄχλος is thus suddenly there again; whence it has come remains unstated. Jesus now declares in relation to the crowd what everyone must be prepared to do who wants to join him.

In 5.11, 27-28 it had already become clear that entering into discipleship entailed "leaving everything" (see then also 18.28-29 and 14.26). It is now said what is required on the journey of discipleship. In this sense the three imperatives in v. 23c-e do not lie on the same level. Rather, the first two concretize the third; they are therefore aorist, whereas ἀκολουθείτο, the third imperative, is present.

The joining of (ἀπ)αρνεῖσθαι with the reflexive pronoun ἑαυτόν or the like is only attested elsewhere in 2 Timothy 2.13: "If we are unfaithful (ἀπιστοῦμεν), he (sc. Christ) remains faithful (πιστός), ἀρνήσασθαι γὰρ ἑαυτὸν οὐ δύναται." The verb occurs with a personal object in the sense of "deny the connection with someone" or "reject someone" in Joseph and Aseneth 12.12 ("My father and my mother denied me [ἠρνήσαντό με] and said, Aseneth is not our daughter [οὐκ ἔστιν ἡμῶν θυγάτηρ]"); Acts 3.14; 7.35; 1 John 2.21, 23; 2 Peter 2.1; Jude 1.4; see also the personification in 4 Maccabees 5.35; often with reference to gods in the sense of a contestation of their deity and refusal to worship them as God: Philo, *De special-ibus legibus* 2.255; Josephus, *Contra Apionem* 1.191; see also Sibylline Oracles 4.27. In this sense it can also describe the apotreptic aspect of a conversion pro-cess ("to break away from") as, e.g., in 4 Maccabees 8.7 (τὸν πάτριον . . . θεσμόν ["the ancestral . . . ordinance"]); 10.5 (τὴν εὐγενῆ ἀδελφότητα ["the noble broth-erliness"]); Isaiah 31.7 (τὰ χειροποίητα αὐτῶν ["their hand-made (i.e., self-made) things"]); Babrius, *Fabulae Aesopae*, ed. Crusius/Müller 1897, 152; Lucian of Samosata, *De morte Peregrini* 13 (the Christians deny the Greek gods [θεοὺς . . . τοὺς Ἑλληνικοὺς ἀπαρνήσωνται] and worship "that suspended sophist"); Acts 2.13; 3.7 (cf. also Fridrichsen 1994, 264ff; Spicq 1994, I: 1999). The use in the context of the "denial" of Jesus by Peter (Mark 14.30-31parr. 72parr.; John 13.38) corresponds most closely to Joseph and Aseneth 12.12 (see above). When Peter says, "I do not know the person" (Matthew 26.72, 74), this is the 'denial of Jesus'; Luke 12.9 par. Matthew 10.33 belongs in this same context.

When we place this exhortation to self-denial in this framework, it immediately becomes clear that what is required is actually impossible. Entrance into discipleship means that one leaves not only everything else (5.11, 27-28; 14.26) but also breaks away from *oneself* and no longer cares for oneself. The radical character of this demand goes far beyond what is grasped with the term "conversion," for there the self of the converted always continues to exist as an element of continuity. But even this is sup-posed to remain behind.

In the exhortation in 23d we are dealing with a metaphor whose imag-ery is taken from the practice that offenders condemned to crucifixion had to carry the crossbeam (the *patibulum*) to the execution site themselves (attestations at 23.26). It is often overlooked that there is talk here not of Jesus's cross but of every follower having to take up *his own* cross. For this reason the reference to Simon of Cyrene's carrying of the cross of Jesus (see at 23.26; e.g., Fitzmyer; Schneider; Kremer) is misleading, because he does not carry *his own* cross (see also 14.27) but Jesus's cross.

It is, of course, only from the perspective of Jesus's death on the cross that this exhortation becomes a metaphor that describes the distinguishing feature of following Jesus, and therefore it is also probable that it arose only after Easter, even though the existence also of a Q-version (cf. 14.27 par. Matthew 10.38) shows that it is very old. It also corresponds to this that there is not a single non-Christian text from antiquity that uses the phrasing "to take up/carry one's cross" in a figurative sense. According to this, following Jesus presupposes the readiness to go the way of one condemned to death "who has finished with his life" (J. Schneider, ThWNT 7: 579). Nevertheless, Fridrichsen also rightly points out that not only death as the end of this way determines the semantic profile of the metaphor but also the contemporary social image of the punishment of crucifixion as a dishonoring and shameful one: "The 'cross' is . . . the visible sign of the position of the one judged, the sign of shame that made him the object of everyone's contempt and rejection" (Fridrichsen 1994, 43; see also Hengel 1977; H.-W. Kuhn 1982, 758ff; C. Strecker 1999, 264ff). That this aspect guides precisely the Lukan reception of this exhortation is recognizable in the fact that Luke adds καθ' ἡμέραν vis-à-vis the Markan *Vorlage* (see also 11.3; for the subject, see 1 Corinthians 15.31). This is not, of course, an attempt to mitigate the demand of Jesus within the framework of the delay of the parousia and convert it into the small change of the hindrances of everyday Christian life (so, e.g., Schürmann; Fitzmyer; Wiefel; Bovon). Rather, the opposite is the case, for Luke further escalates what is being said—discipleship means not merely going the metaphorical way to execution or shame *once* but rather doing so "daily."

24 As justification there follows a twofold antithetical statement that constructs a new understanding of reality that reverses the meaning of the terms in relation to the conventional understanding of reality (for the juxtaposition of σῴζειν and ἀπολλύναι and the understanding of ψυχή as "life," see at 6.9). Verse 24a gives the impression that a *topos* is taken up here that is known from the speeches of generals.

In such speeches the soldiers are exhorted before battle to stake their life courageously, for—so the justification goes—precisely the one who wants to save his life by flight will die; cf. already Homer, *Ilias* 2.357–59 ("But if anyone inexpressibly longs to return homeward / let him only touch his well-benched black ship / that death and fate overtake him first before all"); 5.529–32; 15.564; Xenophon, *Cyropaedia* 3.3.45 ("whoever wants to survive and attempts to flee is foolish, for he knows that the victors survive, whereas those fleeing are more likely to die than the steadfast"); *Anabasis* 3.1.43 ("all those who strive in times of war to preserve their life in every imaginable way mostly die an ignominious and pitiful death"); Polybius 3.63.6–7; cf. J. B. Bauer 1972 with additional attestations. In Tyrtaeus, Fragment 8.12ff (Diehl 1948–1952) something completely different is found than what W. Bauer 1988, s.v. ἀπόλλυμι 1b cites.

If one read v. 24a from the perspective of this *topos* one could still think that here there is talk of "saving" and "losing" only the *physical* life. However, the continuation in v. 24b shows that there is talk of losing and gaining life in a double sense. The verbs whose semantics are at issue here are chiastically arranged, which increases the antithesis. Suddenly an understanding of life that is completely different than the physical understanding comes into view: a life that is paradoxically born from the death of the physical life; thus, a life beyond the physical life, which is promised to the one (οὗτος) who loses his physical life ἕνεκεν ἐμοῦ (for this aspect of the interpretation of suffering in early Christianity and its tradition-historical presuppositions, cf. Satake 1976; M. Wolter, *TRE* 20: 679–80). The semantic expansion that the understanding of "save/lose life" in v. 24a experiences in light of v. 24b is unmistakable, and it also transcends the framework of the *topos* sketched above. Just as there is a life that one can win in the loss of physical life, so there is also a life that one can lose when one saves the physical life. Both are, of course, the same life—namely, the life that is mediated through the belonging to Jesus Christ, that reaches beyond death and that endures forever (so John 12.25 *expressis verbis*), which cannot be said of any physical life. This ambiguity of the understanding of 'life' and its semantic surroundings also occurs elsewhere in early Christianity (cf. e.g., 17.33b; 21.19; John 5.24-25; 8.51; Romans 6.13; 2 Corinthians 2.15-16; Colossians 2.13; 2 Timothy 2.11). It has its basis in the fact that Christian faith is an understanding of reality that defines the whole world anew from the standpoint of Jesus Christ and provides all concepts with new meanings.

25 There follows a justification that is formulated as a rhetorical question. Vis-à-vis Mark 8.36 Luke has changed not only the syntax but also the wording insofar as, *inter alia*, he replaces the phrasing ζημιωθῆναι τὴν ψυχὴν αὐτοῦ (sc. of the person) with ἑαυτὸν . . . ἀπολέσας ἢ ζημιωθείς. The connection with the preceding verse—which runs via the term ψυχή in Mark—is established in Luke through ἀπολλύναι. Thematically the justification refers only to v. 24a, with "wanting to save one's life" being taken up by "gaining the whole world" (v. 25b) and ἀπολέσει αὐτήν by ἑαυτὸν . . . ἀπολέσας ἢ ζημιωθείς (v. 25c). Rhetorically we are dealing with a comparison of values that is formulated in a proverb-like saying that relativizes the importance of riches (ὀφείλειν, κερδαίνειν, and ἀπολλύναι have a common semantic reference in business and finance; cf. M. Wolter, *EWNT* 2: 1344ff; Spicq 1994, II: 157ff). The concern is to support the statement of v. 24a through a parabolic saying by elaborating on the difference of the two kinds of "life" spoken of there with the help of the difference described in v. 25b-c. Just as even the possession of the whole world (i.e., the greatest accumulation of riches and power that one can imagine) is worth nothing if obtaining it entails the destruction or damaging of one's own life (for the Lukan ἑαυτόν . . . ἀπολέσας ἢ ζημιωθείς in v. 25c, cf. 4 Maccabees 6.14; Philo, *Quod deterius potiori insidiari soleat* 52; Plutarch, *Fabius Maximus* 12.3; Epictetus, *Dissertationes* 4.2.1; Aelian, *Varia historia* 3.23; Sextus, *Pythagoreorum Sententiae* 477), so the saving of (physical) life is worth nothing if it entails the loss of ("real") life. The pragmatic of this comparison thus goes even beyond the intention of the example stories of the foolish farmer (12.15-21) and the rich man (16.19-31). Further, Luke does not merely have Jesus warn against riches, for the assumed case is purely hypothetical due to its hyperbolic character.

26 reads v. 24a into the situation of the followers of Jesus (see also 12.9; v. 24b is developed in 12.8). The opposition of "wanting to save one's life" and "losing it" is explained with the help of the two scenarios that are taken into view here. Verse 26a describes the situation of those who are "persecuted" (this ranges from social discrimination to death) as disciples of Jesus (v. 24b: ἕνεκεν ἐμοῦ) and want to escape this threat by withdrawing from him—i.e., "want to save their life." Several decades later and from another perspective Pliny the Younger, *Epistulae* 10.96.3–6 describes this same nexus (cf. Thraede 2004; for the use of [ἐπ]αισχύνεσθαι with this meaning, see also 2 Timothy 1.8, 12; 1 Peter 4.16 [in each case in connection with "suffering"]). Verse 26b then states how and why it is the case that precisely these "will lose" their life. The final judgment is in view, i.e., the decision about the allocation of salvation and unsalvation or, in other words, the salvation of life and the loss of life depends on how one has behaved in relation to Jesus. Whoever has dissociated himself from Jesus in order to save his life—i.e., has *not* denied himself and has put down his cross again; v. 23c-e—will lose it at this moment because Jesus, who in the role of the Son of Man functions as accuser, witness, and judge in one, now dissociates himself from *him*. This takes place in the presence of God and the angels because the "glory" (δόξα; see at 2.9) that represents them comes down to earth at the parousia of the Son of Man and is present in his judgment (v. 26c diff. Mark 8.38; see also 21.27 diff. Mark 13.26-27). Luke will formulate this correspondence once again in 12.8-9.

By contrast, in **27** the salvation side is then taken into view. While Mark 9.1 still emphasizes the temporal nearness of the dawning of the reign of God, Luke has removed the temporal aspect through the deletion of the last three words and reconfigured the announcement of Jesus into a salvation saying over some of those present. "To see" (v. 27c) means not merely 'to observe' or 'to recognize,' but 'to experience' (see Psalm 27.13; 89.49; 98.3; Jeremiah 5.12; Ezekiel 39.21; 1 Enoch 102.9; 103.10; Luke 2.26; 17.22; Acts 2.27, 31; 13.36–37; cf. W. Bauer 1988, 445, 1172). As in the parallel in John 3.3 ("whoever has not been born ἄνωθεν cannot see the reign of God"; see also Targum Isaiah 53.10: "they will see the reign of their Annointed"), the concern here is with the marked experience of the salvation of the reign of God. But with this a decision is also made about the identity of the τινές. They are the ones who have followed Jesus under the conditions mentioned in v. 23 and have not been "ashamed" of Jesus and his words (v. 26). But what does Luke have in mind when he has Jesus announce that these τινές will experience the reality of the reign of God during their lifetime (οὐ μὴ γεύσωνται θανάτου; the same metaphor occurs in Anthologia Graeca 7.662; Sibylline Oracles 1.82; 4 Ezra 6.26; John 8.52; Hebrews 2.9; Bill. I: 751–52; for the translation, see BDR §169.3)? The connection that Luke establishes between the βασιλεία and the circle of the disciples provides the answer. It is "handed over" to them (cf. 12.32; 22.29), and in Acts the proclamation of the reign of God and the proclamation of Christ by the "witnesses" are identified with each other (cf. Acts 8.5/12; 19.8/10; 20.25; 28.23/31; see also Wolter 1995a, 543, 549ff). One can infer from this that with "seeing (= experiencing) the reign of God" in 27c Luke very likely alludes to the witnessing of the disciples with regard to the resurrection of Jesus (Luke 24.36-49) and to their being equipped with the Holy Spirit for the proclamation of Christ and of the reign of God (Acts 2.1-13).

9.28-36: The Revelation of the δόξα of Jesus before the Disciples

[28]And it happened about eight days after these words that he took Peter and John and James to himself and went up the mountain to pray. [29]And it happened while he was praying that the appearance of his face became different and his clothing shone in white radiance. [30]And behold, two men conversed with him; they were Moses and Elijah. [31]They appeared in glory and discussed his departure that he was to fulfill in Jerusalem. [32]But Peter and his companions were overwhelmed by sleep. When they awoke, they saw his glory and the two men standing with him. [33]And when they departed from him, Peter said to Jesus, "Master, it is good that we are here; so let us build three tents: one for you, one for Moses, and one for Elijah"— without knowing what he said. [34]While he said this, a cloud formed

and overshadowed them. But they were afraid as they entered into the cloud. ³⁵And a voice sounded from the cloud that said, "This is my son, the chosen one. Listen to him!" ³⁶And when the voice had sounded, it was found that Jesus was alone.

And they became silent and told no one in those days anything of what they had seen.

In the narrative of the so-called transfiguration of Jesus, God's "glory" (δόξα) becomes manifest (vv. 31-32) on the earth again for the first time since 2.9, again at night (cf. v. 37). Beyond this, the heavenly voice speaks for the first time since 3.22. It now unveils Jesus's identity as God's son to the three disciples who are present (v. 36; see also Fitzmyer I: 793). Finally, there is talk of Jesus's "departure" (ἔξοδος) in Jerusalem for the first time *expressis verbis* (v. 31).

Luke interweaves the story of Jesus with the story of the disciples, who are represented here by the three who had been called first (5.1-11) and who stand in the center from v. 32 onward. He characterizes them through two events that point far into the narrative future. First, they see Jesus's δόξα (v. 32) and learn through the heavenly voice that he is God's son (v. 35). However, through v. 36 this knowledge is immediately blocked narratively. The disciples will pass it on only after Easter and Jesus's ascension (more precisely, at Pentecost; cf. Acts 2.14ff). Second, Luke has the three disciples fall asleep so that they do not learn precisely that information that is new within the story of Jesus—namely, that Moses and Elijah speak with Jesus about his impending "departure" in Jerusalem (vv. 31-32). This deficit will only be removed on the day of Easter (cf. 24.26-27, 44-48). Even in this episode, Christology does not play an independent role, for the question of Herod (9.9) has long been answered from the perspective of the readers. Rather, the question of the identity of Jesus is narrated again as part of the story of the disciples (v. 35).

In both parts there are elements that are specific to the form of appearance stories (attestations ad loc.): ὀφθέντες ἐν δόξῃ in the first part (v. 31) and the appearance of a cloud (v. 34b) and the fear of the disciples (v. 34c) in the second part.

The number of minor agreements is relatively great. The following are especially conspicuous: τοῦ προσώπου (or τὸ πρόσωπον) αὐτοῦ (v. 29b par. Matthew 17.2) is lacking in Mark; the lack of Mark 9.3b at the end of v. 29 (par. Matthew 17.2 fin.); ἰδού (v. 30a par. Matthew 17.3) is without Markan equivalent; the order Μωϋσῆς καὶ Ἠλίας (v. 30b par. Matthew 17.3) instead of Ἠλίας σὺν Μωϋσεῖ (Mark 9.4); the *genitivus absolutus* (ταῦτα δὲ/ἔτι) αὐτοῦ λέγοντος/λαλοῦντος at the appearance of the cloud (v. 34a par. Matthew 17.5) has no Markan counterpart; λέγουσα

(v. 35a par. Matthew 17.5) is without a Markan equivalent; cf. further Neirynck 1982/1991/2001, I: 797–810; 1974b, 123ff; 1991, 51–52; Niemand 1989; Ennulat 1994, 200ff. Neither the minor agreements, nor the additions (above all vv. 31-33a, 34b, 36b-c), nor other differences require the assumption that Luke reworked additional traditions alongside Mark 9.2-8 (differently especially Reid 1993; for criticism, cf. Miller 1998).

Second Peter 1.16-18 presents a paraphrase of the event. The literary reworking of synoptic texts is, of course, less likely than knowledge of oral tradition alongside or subsequent to the literary tradition. Apocalypse of Peter 15–17 is based literarily on all three synoptic versions.

28 Thus far no one has been able to explain why Luke makes "after about eight days" out of the Markan temporal specification ("after six days"). A connection with Leviticus 23.36 (festival of tabernacles), Genesis 17.12 (circumcision; see also Luke 1.59; 2.21; Acts 7.8), or John 20.26 (last appearance of Jesus in Jerusalem) is not recognizable. After 6.12, this is the second "mountain prayer of Jesus" (Conzelmann 1977, 51); the last one then follows in 22.39-46 on the Mount of Olives. In v. 37 the readers will learn that this prayer also took place at night. Unlike Mark, here too Luke uses the definite article and in this way evokes the impression that the readers know which mountain is in view (its identification with Mount Tabor [Ğebel et-tōr] is attested literarily for the first time in the fourth century in Cyril of Jerusalem, *Catecheses* 12.16). However, with quite a bit of certainty one can ascribe to Luke the intention of wanting to remind the readers of 6.12 and to awaken in them the expectation that something important is about to take place. Unlike at that time, however, Jesus does not withdraw alone to the mountain now, but rather takes with him the three disciples who had been called first (par. Mark 9.2; see also 5.1-11) and whom he had already singled out in 8.51 (par. Mark 5.37). Here they represent the entire circle of disciples. Interpretations that want to find a Moses typology in this narrative (see, however, at v. 29) refer to the fact that Moses also took three named companions with him when he ascended Mount Sinai according to Exodus 24.9.

29-31 During the prayer of Jesus, an event is set in motion that calls to mind 3.21-22, on the one hand, but also sets its own accents, on the other hand. It is common to both narratives, first, that heavenly instances come down upon or to Jesus—in 3.22a the Spirit in the form of a dove and in 9.30-31 Moses and Elijah. Later the heavenly voice joins in each case (3.22b-c; 9.34).

29 What Mark 9.2 had presented as a "transformation" (μεταμορφοῦσθαι) of Jesus (for the tradition-historical background, cf. Zeller 1999) Luke reduces to a changing of Jesus's face, while mostly taking over the shining of the clothing. In v. 32 Luke interprets the appearance of Jesus as a visible appearance of "his glory" (δόξα; see also 9.26; 21.27; 24.26 with reference to parousia and resurrection). Insofar as white is the color of God in Jewish basic knowledge (cf. Daniel 7.9; 1 Enoch 14.20), this event is suitable for revealing to the disciples Jesus's belonging to the heavenly world (see also 2 Maccabees 11.8; Liber antiquitatum biblicarum 64.6; Apocalypse of Elijah 39.11–12; Mark 16.5parr.; Acts 1.10; Revelation 3.4-5, 18; 4.4; 6.11; 7.9; 5 Ezra 2.40; J.-A. Bühner, *EWNT* 2: 865–66). That it is precisely the *face and clothing* upon which this identity is recognizable is shown by 1 Enoch 71.1 ("My spirit was translated, and rose to heaven, and I saw the children of the holy angels . . . and their white garments and their clothing and the brightness of their face like snow"). Above all it is this combination and the absence of the motif of white clothing in Exodus 34.29-30, 33-35 that make it unlikely that Moses is meant to be typologically surpassed by Jesus here.

30-31 The expansion of the scene to Moses and Elijah who converse with Jesus initially follows the same goal as v. 29. It shows that Jesus interacts with the inhabitants of heaven as an equal. Therefore, he does not become afraid like people otherwise do when there are appearances (see at 1.12, 28; 2.9).

There has been much discussion over the question of why the narrative has Moses and Elijah of all people turn up (cf. Reid 1993, 121ff; Zeller 1999, 318ff), for they never form a pair elsewhere—with something of an exception in Revelation 11.6, where the deeds of Elijah and Moses are ascribed to the two endtime prophets. In Luke—which reverses their order vis-à-vis Mark—they most likely stand for the entirety of Scripture in the sense of Law and Prophets (see at 16.16a-b), which begins with "Moses" (i.e., with the Torah) and ends in Malachi 3.23-24 with "Elijah." For Luke "Moses and Elijah" are, so to speak, the "A and Ω" of Scripture. This assumption is supported above all by the fact that in Luke Moses and Elijah speak of Jesus's "departure" in Jerusalem as a fulfillment event (ἤμελλεν πληροῦν; cf. BDR §356.1), for precisely this is the specific quality that Jesus's death and resurrection receive from the perspective of Scripture (i.e., from the standpoint of "Moses and Elijah"; cf. especially 24.44-46 and yet also 18.31-33; 24.27). Therefore, ἔξοδος probably means not merely the death (as, e.g., in Wisdom of Solomon 3.2; 7.6; Testament of Naphtali 1.1; 2 Peter 1.15), but rather the whole event of death and resurrection (the term finds its complementary counterpart in the talk of Jesus's εἴσοδος in Acts 13.24).

32 The disciples stand at the center in the second part of the episode. Luke has let them fall asleep (v. 32a; the phrasing βεβαρημένοι ὕπνῳ is also found in Anthologia Graeca 7.290; 16.98) so that they catch nothing of Jesus's speech with Moses and Elijah, and he can send them unsuspectingly upon the way to Jerusalem. On two other occasions Jesus announces to them what awaits him without them gaining even the slightest understanding of this (9.44-45; 18.31-34). They will understand the meaning of this event only on the basis of the Easter exposition of 'Moses and Elijah' ("Law and Prophets") by Jesus himself (cf. 24.26-27, 32, 44-46). This narrative intention of the sleeping of the disciples also comes to expression in the perception with which Luke has them wake up (v. 32b). The previously described scene is recapitulated in a revealing way. While the key word δόξα refers summarily to v. 29, v. 30a is repeated almost word for word—though with a significant exception. From the συλλαλεῖν of the "two men . . . with him (sc. Jesus)" only a συνιστάναι remains. This makes clear once more that Luke wants the disciples to have heard nothing of the conversation.

33 Their false estimation of the situation also comes to expression in the fact that Peter suggests that they make three tents. In both v. 33c (ἡμᾶς) and v. 33d (ποιήσωμεν) the first person plural refers only to the three disciples. The καλόν of their presence finds its explanation in the fact that they can build tents for Jesus, Moses, and Elijah (καί has telic meaning: see BDR §442.3₉). Although Luke had the disciples see Jesus's δόξα when they woke up in v. 32b, it is not very likely that he wanted to allude via the suggestion of Peter to the tent of meeting that was filled with the δόξα κυρίου according to Exodus 40.34 (see also Numbers 16.19; 20.6). This is contradicted already by the fact that Luke explicitly has this suggestion coincide with Moses's and Elijah's departure from Jesus and by the fact that Peter wants to build *three* tents (for the address of Jesus as ἐπιστάτα, see at 5.5). It is probably no longer possible to reconstruct what this suggestion was meant to express (cf. the overview of the proposed interpretations in Marshall; J. P. Heil 2000, 116ff). The majority of the arguments still speak for the assumption that Peter (at least in Luke) is concerned to keep Moses and Elijah on the mountain and make Jesus's fellowship with them and the earthly presence of his δόξα permanent, for σκηναί are there to make possible a longer stay. However, with this Peter has fundamentally misunderstood the situation, for Moses and Elijah have appeared only temporarily and Jesus still has to come to a violent death in Jerusalem before he can definitively enter into his δόξα (cf. 24.26). Therefore, the short commentary of the narrator in v. 33e (cf. Sheeley 1992, 89, 111) also makes clear that Peter (and with him the disciples as a whole) is meant to be 'unmasked' by means of this suggestion. Luke demonstrates that the disciples of Jesus follow on the way to Jerusalem without having the slightest idea of what fate awaits him there.

34 The cloud is a theophany motif, which Luke—like every other reader of the Bible—knows especially from the Exodus tradition (cf. Exodus 16.10; 19.9, 16; 24.15-16, 18; 34.5; 40.34-38; Leviticus 16.2; Numbers 11.25; 17.7; Deuteronomy 31.15; and elsewhere as well as Jubilees 1.2; Liber antiquitatum biblicarum 13.1; Josephus, *Antiquitates judaicae* 3.310: ἡ νεφέλη . . . ἐσήμαινε τὴν ἐπιφάνειαν τοῦ θεοῦ ["the cloud designates the appearance of God"]; see also J. P. Heil 2000, 132ff). Correspondingly, through an addition vis-à-vis Mark 9.7, Luke has the disciples be filled with the usual fear (v. 34c; cf. the documentation at 1.12). It emerges from v. 34c that the cloud not only slid over "them" but, as in Exodus 40.35; Numbers 9.18, 22; 10.36, set down upon them in such a way that they were enveloped in it. Who is meant by "they" is even more unclear in Luke than in the Markan version (cf. the overview in J. P. Heil 2000, 129–30). Does it refer to Moses and Elijah (and Jesus?) (so, e.g., Marshall; Wiefel; J. P. Heil 2000, 266–67), or does it refer also or only to the disciples (and Jesus?) (so, e.g., Bock; Radl; Reid 1993, 137)? This ambiguity arises especially through the Lukan insertion of v. 34c, for there it is clearly presupposed that the disciples are at least also found in the cloud (the contestation of this fact in J. P. Heil 2000, 267 is unconvincing). By contrast, the Markan version more likely evokes the impression that only Moses and Elijah (and Jesus) were enveloped by it (see also J. P. Heil 2000, 131: the cloud functions here both as "oracular cloud" and—with reference to Testament of Abraham B 8.1–3; Josephus, *Antiquitates judaicae* 4.326; 1 Thessalonians 4.17; Acts 1.9-10 [see J. P. Heil 2000, 145ff]—as "vehicular cloud").

35 God speaks "from" a cloud not only to Moses on Sinai (cf. Exodus 24.16: ἐκ μέσου τῆς νεφέλης ["from the middle of the cloud"]), but following Job 38.1 also to Job; cf. Testament of Job 42.3 (διὰ τῆς νεφέλης ["through the cloud"]); 11Q10 XL, 6 ("from the wind and the cloud").

The content of the speech of God is composed of two parts. In the first part (35b) God identifies Jesus in front of the disciples as his Son, with the Markan ὁ ἀγαπητός (so also Luke 3.22) being replaced by the attributive participle ὁ ἐκλελεγμένος. The perfect expresses that this designates an already existing status of Jesus. The phrasing highlights the singularity of Jesus and elevates him above all previous mediators between God and his people about whom it was said that God "chose" them (Moses: Psalm 106.23; Aaron: Psalm 105.26; David: Psalm 89.20-21; the servant of God: Isaiah 43.10; see also at 23.35): for none of them were made the "Son" of God. That Luke takes up Isaiah 42.21 (see also 44.1-2; 49.7) with the phrasing, as is often assumed (cf. e.g., Nolland; Bock; Radl), is rather doubtful, for in the Septuagint version of this text there is always only talk of the election of Israel.

This message to the disciples now becomes the basis for the second part of the speech of God (v. 35c). The exhortation to listen to Jesus (αὐτοῦ ἀκούετε) is probably meant to allude to Deuteronomy 18.15—i.e., to the announcement that in the future God will raise up for Israel "a prophet like me (sc. Moses)," and to the exhortation addressed to Israel "you shall listen to him" (αὐτοῦ ἀκούσεσθε). This assumption is supported, first, by the fact that vis-à-vis Mark 9.7 (ἀκούετε αὐτοῦ) Luke conforms the word order to Deuteronomy 18.15 and, second, that in Acts 3.22 he quotes Deuteronomy 18.15^LXX *expressis verbis* with reference to Jesus. Within the Lukan story of Jesus this exhortation refers, initially, to the journey to Jerusalem that the disciples will go on with Jesus. It is nothing less than God's confirmation of the instruction that they will receive from Jesus on the way (see also Tannehill 1986, 224).

In **36a** Luke summarizes Mark 9.8. He describes the situation from the perspective of the outside observer with a view to vv. 30-33. Accordingly, μόνος means without Moses and Elijah; cf. BDR §404.1 for the punctiliar meaning of the temporal specification ἐν τῷ γενέσθαι τὴν φωνήν (ἐν τῷ + aorist infinitive occurs only in Luke in the New Testament: Luke 2.27; 3.21; 9.34; 14.1; 19.15; 24.30; Acts 11.15). **36b** is a new phrasing of Mark 9.9-10a (Luke completely omits the rest of Mark 9.9-13). Here the narrator leaves the concrete situation behind him and adopts a bird's eye view that looks far into the narrated future. The temporal specification ἐν ἐκείναις ταῖς ἡμέραις corresponds to the Markan "not before the Son of Man is raised from the dead" (Mark 9.9c) and is based on the knowledge of how the story of Jesus will conclude—namely, that the disciples will end their silence after the expiration "of those days." As in Mark this takes into view the time after Easter, but unlike in Mark, this time does not lie outside the narrative in Luke, for he will report it in Acts. This forward look simultaneously shows that Luke situates the entire episode on a narrative level that leads beyond Jesus's ἔξοδος (v. 31) and comes into contact with the overall understanding of Luke–Acts.

9.37-50: The Inability of the Disciples

All the episodes of this narrative collecting basin make the inability of the disciples visible (see also Tannehill 1986, 225ff; Green). They are not able to drive out an epilepsy demon (v. 40). They do not grasp Jesus's announcement of his passion (v. 45). They want to prevent someone who does not belong to them from successfully (sic!; cf. v. 40) exorcising demons (v. 49). This section's centeredness on the disciples is also expressed in the fact that with the last saying Luke narrows the phrasing of Mark 9.40 to the disciples.

9.37-45 . . . at the Driving Out of an Epilepsy Demon

[37]**And it happened on the next day, when they came down from the mountain, a great crowd came to him.** [38]**And look, a man from the crowd called out, "Rabbi, I beg you, look at my son, for he is the only one I have!** [39]**For look, a spirit takes hold of him and suddenly he shrieks, and it pulls him to-and-fro with foaming** (at the mouth), **and it almost never withdraws from him and constantly tortures him.** [40]**And I asked your disciples to drive it out but they were not able."** [41]**And Jesus answered and said, "O unbelieving and twisted generation! How long will I still be with you come to your aid? Bring your son here!"** [42]**And just as he approached, the demon threw him to the ground and convulsed him. But Jesus rebuked the unclean spirit and healed the boy and gave him back to his father.** [43]**But all were astonished at the majesty of God.**

But while all marveled at all he was doing, he said to his disciples, [44]**"You—put these words in your ears, for the Son of Man will be handed over into human hands!"** [45]**But they did not understand this saying, and it remained veiled to them, so that they did not comprehend it. And they were afraid to ask him about this saying.**

The form of the narrative in vv. 37-43a resembles 7.1-10, for in both texts a healing story (cf. v. 42d: ἰάσατο τὸν παῖδα) and a chreia (pronouncement story) are combined with each other. Both levels overlap in v. 40. As part of the chreia this verse is the trigger for the concluding dictum of Jesus (v. 41a-c), while within the healing story it functions as a pointer to previously unsuccessful healing attempts. This already exhausts the commonalities between the two narratives, however, for unlike in 7.1-10, we have here an exorcism story that is fully developed in terms of its form with an *introduction* (v. 37), *exposition* (vv. 38-42b), *center* (v. 42c-e), and *finale* with a motif of wonder (v. 43). It is conspicuous that the center with the actual exorcism action is narrated much more concisely vis-à-vis the portrayal of the need (vv. 39-40, 42a-b).

The episode is based on Mark 9.14-29, but there it is narrated much more expansively. It is interesting what Luke has omitted and what he has not. Luke has especially deleted those elments that do not belong to the constitutive form-elements of exorcism narratives such as the exchange of words about faith (9.23-24) and the conversation with the disciples (9.28-29). He has even radically shortened the center, i.e., the description of the actual miracle. This makes it all the more conspicuous that Luke not only takes over the apophthegmatic elements in vv. 40-41c in their complete scope from Mark 9.18b-19c, but even expands them. One can infer from this that he had special interest precisely in this part of the narrative. This narrative thread is taken up again via the specification of the situation in v. 43b and continued with another announcement of the passion.

As minor agreements one must especially mention the extensive passages from Mark 9.14-29 that are lacking in Matthew and Luke (see Vaganay 1954)—namely, vv. 14b-16, 20d-21, 22c-25a, 25c-3, 26b-27. In addition, the following minor agreements deserve mention: λέγων (v. 38a par. Matthew 17.15) is lacking in Mark; οὐκ ἠδυνήθησαν (v. 40c par. Matthew 17.16) instead of οὐκ ἴσχυσαν (Mark 9.18); Ἰησοῦς εἶπεν (v. 41a par. Matthew 17.17) instead of αὐτοῖς λέγει (Mark 9.19); καὶ διεστραμμένη (v. 41b par. Matthew 17.17) is without Markan equivalent; ὧδε (v. 41d par. Matthew 17.17) instead of πρός με (Mark 9.19); ὁ Ἰησοῦς (v. 42c par. Matthew 17.18) has no Markan counterpart; καὶ ἰάσατο τὸν παῖδα or καὶ ἐθεραπεύθη ὁ παῖς (v. 42d par. Matthew 17.18) is lacking in Mark; see further Neirynck 1974b, 126ff; 1991, 53ff; Ennulat 1994, 208ff. Viewed as a whole, a monocausal explanation certainly misses the mark. Rather, one must assume that some minor agreements are due to chance, i.e., independent Luke–Matthew redaction, some to the influence of independent oral tradition, and some were probably found by Luke and Matthew in their Gospel of Mark.

37 First, the readers learn in passing that the event narrated in vv. 28-36 had taken place in the night (the adverb ἑξῆς occurs only in Luke in the New Testament; see at 7.11). Luke need not have carried over the specification of the situation from Mark 9.9a (so Fitzmyer; Bovon), for it results necessarily from v. 28. If Jesus climbs a mountain, he must—at least at this point of time—also come down again. The same thing happens as previously when Jesus had withdrawn for a certain time alone or with his disciples: a great crowd seeks him or is already waiting for him (cf. also 4.42; 6.17; 8.40; 9.11).

38 Luke singles out a man from the crowd. The form of his narrative presentation corresponds to 19.39. Luke apparently imagines that the man calls out from the crowd (for ἀπὸ τοῦ ὄχλου, see also Mark 7.17, 33). Moreover, the man calls to mind Jairus (8.41-42). Both here and there a father asks Jesus for help in relation to his sick child (for the address of Jesus as διδάσκαλος, see at 7.40), and both here and there it is the only child—or, more specifically, the only daughter/the only son (Luke thus pays attention to the balance of genders also on this level; see at 2.22-39 and section 4.4.3 in the introduction). This feature is lacking in Mark 9.17. Comparable constellations were already found in 7.2 (the slave of the centurion was ἔντιμος to him) and 7.12 (the μονογενὴς υἱός of the widow). They all have the narrative function of further underlining the urgency of the request or the greatness of the need. Against the *Vorlage* Luke has also added ἐπιβλέψαι ἐπί as the content of the request. In this way he takes up a language usage that describes God's salvific turning and saving intervention for the sake of his people or individual pious persons in the Septuagint and extracanonical Jewish literature (as imperative: 1 Kings 8.28; Tobit 3.3; Judith 13.4; Psalm^LXX 12.4; 69.17; 83.10); word combinations with ἐλεεῖν and cognates are common (Tobit 3.15; Judith 6.19; Psalm^LXX 25.16; 85.16; 118.132; Joseph and Aseneth 11.18; see also Isaiah 66.2; Ezekiel 36.9; Luke 1.48 with a connection to 1 Samuel 1.11). The man asks Jesus for what is traditionally expected from God. We are thus dealing here with the same christological subtext that was already observable in 7.22.

In **39** the father describes the sickness of his son. From the portrayal of the symptoms in v. 39b-c (see also v. 42a-b) epilepsy was already inferred in the time of the early church (cf. Origen, *Commentarium in evangelium Matthaei* 13.6 on Matthew 17.14 [GCS XL, *Origenes Werke* X: 193.12ff]; see Dölger 1934; Wohlers 1999b). Epilepsy is also traced back to demonic possession elsewhere; cf. Aretaeus of Cappadocia, *De causis et signis acutorum morborum* 1.4.2 (Hude 1958, 38.29–30); Lucian of Samosata, *Philopseudes* 16; Testament of Solomon 18.21. The thesis that the demonic interpretation of epilepsy is "a genuine Christian notion" (Wohlers 1999b, 128) is unlikely, for the ancient sources attest the existence of this explanation in subliterary popular medicine. It is, of course, by no means certain whether Luke himself in his presentation thought of ἐπιληψία (this term had already long established itself as a medical *terminus technicus* at the time of the New Testament) or the so-called sacred disease (this designation occurs for the first time in Heraclitus, Fragment 46; cf. the excursus on the history of the term in Wohlers 1999b, 122ff).

40 Already in 2 Kings 4.31, the disciple is not able to perform a miracle healing; only the prophet himself is in a position to do so. This narrative motif belongs to the expositional motifs of miracle stories. Here it has the function of illustrating the special difficulty of the task (cf. also Aelian, *De natura animalium* 9.33 and for the more general background, see at 8.43; the narrative in Lucian of Samosata, *Philopseudes* 36, which is often mentioned as a parallel, pursues a different intention).

Beyond this function, this information also opens yet another possibility for understanding if it is read on the narrative level of the story of the disciples. For in that case it falls into the light of 9.1, where Luke reported that Jesus had given the disciples δύναμις and ἐξουσία ("over all [sic!] demons)". Since this passage does not lie so far back that the readers could not recall it, a certain tension arises (cf. also Plummer; Green 388: "Why not this one?").

41 Jesus's annoyed exclamation resembles the sweeping verdicts about his contemporaries (see at 7.31) who close themselves to his message;

cf. Luke 11.29 par. Matthew 12.39; 16.4 (γενεὰ πονηρὰ καὶ μοιχαλίς); 12.45 (γεν. αὕτη πονηρά); Mark 8.38 (γεν. αὕτη ἡ μοιχαλίς); there are analogies outside the Jesus tradition in Deuteronomy 32.5 (γεν. σκολιὰ καὶ διεστραμμένη ["a crooked and perverse generation"]); 1 Enoch 93.9 ("rebellious generation"); Jubilees 23.14, 15 ("evil generation"); 1Q28b III: 7 ("generation of wickedness"); Acts 2.40 (γεν. σκολιά); Philippians 2.15 (quotation of Deuteronomy 32.5). The supplementation of the Markan γεν. ἄπιστος (Mark 9.19) with καὶ διεστραμμένη, which is also found in Matthew 17.17, may go back to Deuteronomy 32.5 (see above); the possibility that Luke and Matthew made this change independently of one another cannot be ruled out.

The addressee of this lament is certainly not the father, for he had documented his faith in an unmistakable way with the petition that Jesus look at his son (ἐπιβλέψαι; see at v. 38). The crowd also does not come into consideration, for it does not appear in the narrative, or if it does, it is represented by the father (see at v. 38). Therefore, as in the synoptic counterparts, Jesus's words can only be properly understood as a reaction (cf. ἀποκριθείς) to the communication about the failure of the disciples. The occasion and reason for the lament would then be that the disciples did not make use of the δύναμις and ἐξουσία for the driving out of demons that was bestowed upon them in 9.1 (see also Davies/Allison 2001–2004, I: 723). Against this background, the rhetorical question in 41c, which calls to mind again the mention of the "departure" (ἔξοδος) of Jesus that occurred shortly before (v. 31), makes good sense (see also Tannehill 1986, 226). Jesus himself will continue to be with his disciples for only a limited time, and they are still not in a position to continue his mission without him. This orientation also makes it likely that the phrasing ἀνέξομαι ὑμῶν should be translated not with "put up with, endure" (as, e.g., in Colossians 3.13; Ephesians 4.2), but in the sense of "help out, liberate from a desperate situation" (as in Isaiah 46.4; 63.15). Cf. also Moessner 1986, 237; there is, however, certainly not an echo of Moses's lament in Deuteronomy 1.12, for first, we find here not ἕως πότε but πῶς, and second, the content of the lament is entirely different.

With the last words of v. 41 the narrative is brought back from the narrative level of the pronouncement story to the level of the exorcism story. **42a-b** ensures that it really arrives there (here the exorcism story is still at the narrative stage of the exposition). Unlike in Mark 9.20, the renewed attack of the demon upon the youth is not interpreted as a consequence of the encounter with Jesus. Rather, in Luke the portrayal primarily has the function of reminding the readers—after the apophthegmatic digression—that they are in an exorcism story. After this Luke hurries to the end of the narrative, for he rigorously cuts down the Markan narrative of the healing of the youth (Mark 9.25-27) from fifty-seven to eighteen words and reports only what is absolutely necessary in v. 42c-e—namely, the *exorcism action* (v. 42c; on ἐπιτιμᾶν as an exorcistic *terminus technicus*, see at 4.35 and 4.39, 41; 8.24), the establishment of the result (v. 42d; in the New Testament only Luke has ἰάσατο: see also 14.4; 22.51; Acts 28.8), and the restitution—which calls to mind 7.5—of the youth to his original social role, which establishes a narrative *inclusio* with the request of the father in v. 38. Now the son no longer belongs to the (unclean) spirit, but—as must be the case—to his father.

43a Luke concludes the narrative with a concise report of wonder (see at 1.65; for ἐκπλήσσομαι, see at 2.48; 4.32). It comes into contact above all with the form-critically analogous texts in 7.16; 8.39; 18.43, for here too Jesus's deeds are traced back to God. μεγαλειότης is also attested as a predicate of God in Jeremiah 40(33).9; Josephus, *Antiquitates judaicae* 8.111; *Contra Apionem* 2.168 (but see also 1/3 Ezra 1.4: concerning Solomon; Acts 19.27: Artemis; 2 Peter 1.16: Jesus's transfiguration). It has its basis in the fact that God does "great deeds" (μεγάλεια; cf. Deuteronomy 11.2; Psalm^{LXX} 70.19; 2 Maccabees 3.34; 7.17, 22; Tobit 11.15; Sirach^{LXX} 17.8, 10; 18.4; 36.7; see also Luke 1.49); cf. further Spicq 1994, II: 457ff.

43b-45 Entirely unlike Mark, who first sends Jesus and the disciples on a journey through Galilee (9.30), Luke narrates the announcement of the handing over of the Son of Man "into the hands of humans" as an epilogue to the healing story. The narrative goal is again to present the disciples as lacking understanding. This is recognizable in the fact that vis-à-vis his *Vorlage*, Luke shortens the statement about Jesus's own fate by removing the announcement of the death and resurrection of Jesus after three days, whereas he expands the description of the disciples' lack of understanding. This results in the fact that in Luke there are actually only two announcements of the passion *and* the resurrection of Jesus, namely in 9.22 and 18.31-33.

One minor agreement deserves to be mentioned: μέλλει . . . παραδίδοσθαι (v. 44b par. Matthew 17.22) instead of παραδίδοται (Mark 9.31); cf. further Neirynck 1974b, 130; 1991, 55; Ennulat 1994, 188ff; Farmer 1990, 561ff.

43b Luke makes the wonder of the πάντες (on θαυμάζειν, see at 1.63; see further 2.18; 4.22; Mark 5.20), narrated in v. 43a, into the starting situation for a saying of Jesus directed to his disciples. When he makes the entire doing of Jesus (ἐπὶ πᾶσιν οἷς ἐποίει) into the object of the marveling (W and 𝔐 replace the durative imperfect with the punctiliar aorist and in this way take only the preceding healing into view), he builds on the generalization that is already present in μεγαλειότης τοῦ θεοῦ.

44 The introductory words in v. 44a have a distant analogy in Exodus 17.14 ("Write this for remembrance [εἰς μνημοσύνην] in a book and give [it] into the ears of Joshua [δὸς εἰς τὰ ὦτα of Joshua] . . ."). It is thus an exhortation to pay attention to τοὺς λόγους τούτους. The question is only: Which words are meant? All recent commentaries refer them to the passion prediction in v. 44b (older proposals supporting v. 43b are rightly rejected). However, the particle γάρ in v. 44b speaks against this interpretation. It turns the handing over of the Son of Man into a rationale for the exhortation and not into the content "of these words" (in this case one would expect a recitative ὅτι). The demonstrative pronoun can therefore only be understood anaphorically and only the words that Jesus has just said come into consideration as the reference, namely the words about his temporally limited presence with the disciples that were related in v. 41b-c. Luke now has him provide the explanation for this here. This orientation also makes it intelligible that Luke has taken only this part from Mark 9.31. The handing over of the Son of Man explains why Jesus can soon no longer help the disciples.

45 Luke says no less than three times that the disciples do not comprehend the meaning of this announcement (the same is true in 18.34 after the second announcement of the passion and the resurrection). This repetition is possibly caused by 8.9-10, for there Jesus had assured the disciples that the secrets of the reign of God would be revealed to them. Moreover, a consecutive ἵνα (cf. BDR §391.5 and the parallels mentioned at 8.10c) occur both here and there, and vis-à-vis 8.9 it is now explicitly emphasized that the disciples do *not* ask. The participle παρακεκαλυμμένον is not a *passivum divinum* (*pace* Marshall; Fitzmyer), for here Jesus presents the announcement in such a way that it wants to be understood (see also Tannehill 1986, 227; Green)—even though the disciples founder on it. We are dealing with the same lack of understanding that the Emmaus disciples have not yet overcome and that will only be removed by having Jesus himself explain to them the meaning of his fate from Scripture (cf. 24.26-27, 44-46).

9.46-50: . . . and Also Otherwise

⁴⁶**And there arose among them the thought of who of them was the greatest.** ⁴⁷**Jesus, however, knew the thought of their heart; he took a child and placed it beside himself** ⁴⁸**and said to them, "Whoever receives this child for my name's sake receives me. And whoever**

receives me receives the one who sent me. For the one who is the smallest among you all, this one is great."

⁴⁹John answered, however, and said, "Master, we saw someone driving out demons in your name and we hindered him (from doing this) **because he did not follow with us." ⁵⁰But Jesus said to him, "Do not hinder** (him)**, for whoever is not against you is for you."**

While a change of scene is made in Mark 9.33 (Jesus and the disciples come to Capernaum), Luke continues the narrative at the same place. Form-critically we are dealing with two thematically independent chreiae, but Luke has joined them together with the help of the introductory ἀποκριθείς in v. 49. In both cases the disciples are corrected and instructed. The Lukan text has undoubtedly arisen using Mark 9.33-37, 38-41.

Noteworthy minor agreements are above all the lack of Mark 9.35 and ἐναγκαλισάμενος αὐτό from Mark 9.36b (v. 48a par. Matthew 18.3); see further: ὃς ἐὰν δέξηται (v. 48b par. Matthew 18.5) instead of ὃς ἄν . . . δέχηται (Mark 9.37); οὗτός ἐστιν μέγας/ὁ μείζων (v. 48d par. Matthew 18.4) is without Markan equivalent; cf. further Neirynck 1974b, 131–32; 1991, 55–56; Ennulat 1994, 214ff. Nothing certain can be said about their emergence. The only thing that is reasonably certain is probably that v. 48d goes back to Luke himself (the Matthean equivalent stands in Matthew 18.4). For vv. 47-48c, knowledge of a tradition alongside Mark 9.33-37 is not excluded. This could certainly have been Q, especially since Mark 9.37b has a parallel in Luke 10.16 par. Matthew 10.40 (cf. Fleddermann 1995, 153ff). Verses 49-50 are probably based exclusively on Mark 9.38-41.

46-48 The framing through the pair of antithetical concepts "great-small" and its reference to the circle of disciples at the beginning and the end establishes the coherence of the text: μείζων αὐτῶν (v. 46b); μικρότερος ἐν πᾶσιν ὑμῖν and μέγας (v. 48d). In vv. 47b-48c the chreia about the "receiving" of the child is embedded within this frame. The child functions here as a material symbol for 'being small' and via this characteristic joins the small scene with the frame. Form-critically it is an 'action chreia' (πρακτικὴ χρεία; cf. with analogies outside the New Testament Robbins 1983, 62ff).

46 That Luke has a "thought" (διαλογισμός) arise in the disciples as such already signals nothing good (see at 2.35). Its content comes into tension with what was just said by Jesus insofar as the disciples are not interested in *Jesus's* fate but are occupied with *themselves*. In terms of subject matter the concern is with the same question that the disciples will occupy themselves with before Jesus goes to the Mount of Olives (22.24), which Luke characterizes there as φιλονεικία (for the substantivization of interrogative questions with τό as a Lukan peculiarity, see at 1.72): Who is the highest ranking disciple? From a purely linguistic perspective one could also translate v. 46b with "who was greater than they," but on the basis of ἐν πᾶσιν ὑμῖν in v. 48d αὐτῶν should be connected not with μείζων but with τίς (in Koine the comparative stands for the superlative, which is largely lacking; cf. BDR §60, §244).

47 The introduction to the answer of Jesus is not surprising, for the fact that Jesus knows and makes known the thoughts hidden in human hearts is already known to the readers from 2.35; 5.22; and 6.8 (see further ad loc.). The fact that in Luke Jesus places the child not in the midst of the disciples, as in the synoptic parallels, but at his side (a position of trust according to Sirach 12.12; see also 1/3 Ezra 9.43; differently in Daniel 2.2) should not give him the place of honor (*pace* Marshall; Fitzmyer) but prepares for the following opposition (see also Nolland).

48a-c In the Lukan version of the word Jesus speaks not of an arbitrary child as in Mark 9.37 (ἓν τῶν τοιούτων παιδίων) and Matthew 18.5 (ἓν παιδίον τοιοῦτο) but of *this specific* child (τοῦτο τὸ παιδίον). For this reason δέχεσθαι cannot refer to hospitality as in Matthew 10.40-41 ("δέχεσθαι you/a prophet/a righteous person"). Nor does this text speak about homeless orphan children (cf. Bill. I: 774; similarly also W. Bauer 1988, 355: "of the reception of the defenseless"; rightly opposed by P. Müller 1992, 219). A charitable action is not envisaged at all here, for there is no indication at all that the child is in need or without means. The phrasing παιδίον δέχεσθαι is semantically completely ambiguous; cf. Josephus, *Antiquitates judaicae* 3.63: on the greeting of children by the guest; Aelius Aristides, *Panathenaicus* 18: on the reception of the newborn by the midwife. What is decisive for the understanding is, first of all, the fact that here the child is not meant to illustrate the situation of being 'small' or 'insignificant' within the general societal context (i.e., in relation to adults or in relation to the disciples). Rather, the Lukan Jesus compares it with himself (therefore he has also placed the child beside him in v. 47b). Next to him, whom the readers know to be "great" ever since 1.32, the child is "small." Against this background it does not really matter what specific action one has παιδίον δέχεσθαι refer to. What is important is only that v. 48b-c refers to one and the same action: Whoever 'receives' (whatever this should mean) this child, receives Jesus himself (v. 48b) and with him God (v. 48c), because Jesus represents God.

The action of παιδίον δέχεσθαι is, of course, furnished with a specifying qualification: the linking of a child via Jesus to God only occurs if the reception of the child takes place ἐπὶ τῷ ὀνόματι of Jesus.

The phrasing ἐπὶ τῷ ὀνόματι (or ἐν τῷ ὀνόματι and εἰς τὸ ὄνομα) is the Greek translation of Hebrew לְשֵׁם. The Hebrew syntagm functions as a preposition that indicates the "fundamental reference" of an action (Hartmann 1992a, 44) and can best be translated with "for the sake of" or "with reference to"; cf. e.g., in the Old Testament: Joshua 9.9 ("out of a very distant land we have come as your slaves לְשֵׁם יְהוָה [LXX: ἐν ὀνόματι κυρίου], your God"); 1 Kings 8.20 ("I . . . have built a house לְשֵׁם יְהוָה [LXX: τῷ ὀνόματι κυρίου], the God of Israel"; see also 3.2; 5.17, 19; 8.17; Sirach 47.13); in *rabbinic literature*: b. Yevamot 39b (a man should not receive the wife of his brother לְשֵׁם her beauty and not לְשֵׁם sleeping with her, but לְשֵׁם the commandment of God); b. Yevamot 45b (when someone purchases a slave from a Gentile and this one comes to him before and receives the immersion bath לְשֵׁם a free man, he purchases himself as a free man); m. Zevachim 4.6 (an offering is offered לְשֵׁם six things: לְשֵׁם the offering; לְשֵׁם the one offering; לְשֵׁם הַשֵּׁם [thus 'for God's sake']; לְשֵׁם the altar fire; לְשֵׁם the smoke; לְשֵׁם the good pleasure); m. Avot 4.11 (each assembly that takes place לְשֵׁם of heaven will endure; Matthew 18.20; 1 Corinthians 5.4 are based on this); t. Avodah Zarah 3.13 (a Samaritan circumcises לְשֵׁם of Mount Gerizim). In early Christianity this phrasing is closely connected with baptism (cf. Matthew 28.19; Acts 2.38; 8.16; 10.48; 19.5; Romans 6.3; 1 Corinthians 1.13, 15; 6.11; 10.2; Galatians 3.27), viz. probably from the beginning with the intention of demarcating baptism 'for the sake of Jesus' from the baptism of John the Baptist. The original prepositional meaning is still recognizable especially in Mark 9.41 (ἐν ὀνόματι ὅτι Χριστοῦ ἐστε); cf. further Matthew 10.41-42; Hebrews 16.10; see also at Luke 9.49. For the use of this expression in healings and exorcisms, see at v. 49 below. Cf. also Brandt 1891; Hartman 1992a, 39–52; Ruck-Schröder 1999.

To receive a child 'for the sake of Jesus' can thus mean 'because Jesus commanded it' or 'because the child belongs to Jesus' or 'because one does this on the basis of one's understanding of the message of Jesus.' Thus, not the reception of the child as such reaches to heaven but only the motivation of this action through the reference to Jesus. For this reason, quite a bit speaks for the view that here the child is meant to express the contrast and in this way illustrate in a hyperbolic manner the decisive meaning of 'for the sake of Jesus.' Even if someone receives something as small and insignificant as a child, they receive—insofar as they do it ἐπὶ τῷ ὀνόματι of Jesus—God.

In **48d** the example is tied back to the opening question of v. 46b (cf. the correspondence μείζων—μέγας), which Jesus now answers. On the social ladder of the circle of disciples the one who possesses the smallest prestige stands at the top (for the use of μέγας as an absolute predicate noun with reference to people, see at 1.32). Thus, as in v. 24, a semantic counterworld is constructed, which leads in this case to the ascriptions of social status being turned into their opposite.

49-50 The entire narrative section is concluded with a chreia that Luke has taken over from Mark 9.38-41 and shortened.

49 Luke also reports later that the sick are healed and demons are driven out "in the name of Jesus" (always ἐν τῷ ὀνόματι), namely by the seventy-two (10.17), by Peter (Acts 3.6; 4.7, 10), and by Paul (Acts 16.18). That he does not merely think of a summoning whose technique includes mentioning the name of Jesus (so Kollmann 1996, 335) is shown by the failure of the sons of Sceva in Acts 19.13-16. Here, ἐν τῷ ὀνόματι thus means the same as ἐπὶ τῷ ὀνόματι in v. 48 (cf. the excursus at v. 48 and the exchange of the two expressions in Mark 9.38-39), and the foreign exorcist is in this way shown to be belonging to Jesus. In v. 49b Luke thus has John describe an accurate situation (for the address of Jesus as ἐπιστάτα, see at 5.5). The argument with which John justifies the intervention of the disciples against the other exorcist (the interpretation of ἐκωλύομεν as *imperfectum de conatu* is unnecessary) receives its profile through the fact that two prepositional expressions are set over against each other: ἐν τῷ ὀνόματί σου (v. 49b) and μεθ' ἡμῶν (v. 49d). The difference consists above all in the fact the Markan οὐκ ἠκολούθει ἡμῖν is meant inclusively (Jesus and the disciples), whereas in the Lukan οὐκ ἀκολουθεῖ μεθ' ἡμῶν it is clear that the concern here is exclusively with the circle of disciples. In this way, however, John not only plays off Jesus and the circle of disciples against each other, but he also makes belonging to the circle of disciples the criterion for an action "in the name of Jesus."

50 In the reproduction of the answer of Jesus Luke has skipped over Mark 9.39c so that the exhortation μὴ κωλύετε is immediately justified by the proverbial saying taken over from Mark 9.40. Luke probably took it over from general usage, for it has also left traces elsewhere; cf. Cicero, *Pro Ligario* 33 ("We heard you [sc. Caesar] say that we regard all as opponents who are not with us [*nobiscum*], while you regard all who are not against you [*contra te*] as yours [*tuos*]"); Suetonius, *Divus Julius* 75.1 (*medios et neutrius partis suorum sibi numero futuros pronuntiavit* ["he made known that he would count the neutrals, i.e., those of no party, in the future to his"]). P. Oxy. X, 1224 (176), Fragment 2ʳ 1.2–5 ("And pray for your enemies. For whoever is not [against y]ou is for you [ὁ γὰρ μὴ ὢν (κατὰ ὑμ)ῶν ὑπὲρ ὑμῶν ἐστιν]. [The one who today] is distant—tomorrow he will be [near to you]") comes from the fourth century.

Through this shortening Luke transcends the individual situation; moreover he replaces the Markan first person ("against us—for us") with the second person ("against you—for you"). In this way he not only sets Jesus over against the circle of disciples, but he also removes him completely from the discussion of the issue at stake, which corresponds to the tendency of his reworking of v. 49d (see above). Thus, the concern is not with Jesus but solely with the circle of disciples. In the process the foreign exorcist becomes a type of the one who 'is not against you,' whom one can certainly let be for this reason.

From the profile of the Lukan redaction it is often inferred that Luke wants to read the scene into his own present in an allegorizing manner and with the help of Jesus's answer takes a stance in favor of a relaxed attitude toward intra-Christian pluralism (e.g., Schürmann; Marshall; Radl; cf. Lührmann 1987, 166, who already does so for the Markan *Vorlage*: "Here the problem of heresy and orthodoxy is suggested"). Perhaps. There is no contradiction to Luke 11.23 par. Matthew 12.30 ("Whoever is not with me is against me. . . ."), for there the concern is not with the circle of disciples but with Jesus's exclusive claim vis-à-vis the public, a claim that does not allow for indifference. In that regard the two statements even complement each other.

Bibliography

Finding a Work in the Bibliography

In the English translation, works have been referenced in three different ways. First, a small number of works have been referenced using abbreviations, which are explained below. Second, select commentaries on Luke, which are listed below, have been referenced by last name alone. Third, most literature has been referenced by author date in the main text, e.g., Schröter 2014. If necessary, works from the same year have been distinguished through the addition of a letter, e.g., Wolter 2005a and 2005b. While the bibliography sometimes includes earlier publication dates in square brackets, e.g., Bultmann, R. 1995 [1921], this information is not included in the body of the translation, e.g., Bultmann 1995. For the most part, standard works such as ThWNT have been referenced by abbreviations in the main text and not included in the bibliography.

(1) Abbreviations

The abbreviations used in this work are primarily based on the list of abbreviations in the second edition of the *Theologische Realenzyklopädie*, compiled by S. M. Schwertner (Berlin: Walter de Gruyter, 1994). For abbreviations not found there, Michael Wolter also refers the readers of the German version to *Abkürzungen Theologie und Religionswissenschaften nach RGG⁴* (edited by the editorial team of *RGG⁴*; Tübingen: Mohr, 2007). For the English version we have also consulted the *IATG3— Internationales Abkürzungsverzeichnis für Theologie und Grenzgebiete*, compiled by S. M. Schwertner (Berlin: Walter de Gruyter, 2014) and the second edition of the SBL Handbook of Style (Atlanta: SBL Press, 2014).

For the main text and bibliography, special note should be made of the following abbreviations, some of which differ from the conventions adopted in the aforementioned works.

ABD	*Anchor Bible Dictionary.* Edited by D. N. Freedman. 6 vols. New York: Doubleday, 1992.
AJEC	Ancient Judaism and Early Christianity
ARB.CL	Académie Royale de Belgique. Classe des Lettres.
BBR	*Bulletin for Biblical Research*
BBTS	*Bulletin of the General Theological Seminary of Bangor Theological Seminary*
BDR	F. Blass, A. Debrunner. Grammatik des neutestamentlichen Griechisch. Bearbeitet von F. Rehkopf. 14th edition. Göttingen: Vandenhoeck & Ruprecht, 1976.
BGU	*Berliner Ägyptische Urkunden. Griechische Urkunden.*
BiAth	Biblioteca di Athenaeum
BibPat	*Biblia Patristica. Index des citations et allusions bibliques dans la littérature patristique.* Edited by Centre d'analyse et de documentation patristiques. Vol. I: *Des origines à Clément d'Alexandrie et Tertullien.* Paris: Centre National de la Recherche Scientifique, 1975
Bill.	*Kommentar zum Neuen Testament aus Talmud und Midrasch.* Paul Billerbeck
BiTS	Biblical Tools and Studies
BoC	*The Beginnings of Christianity.* Edited by F. J. Foakes Jackson and K. Lake. London: Macmillan, 1920–1933.
BVBi	Beiträge zum Verstehen der Bibel
CChr.SL	Corpus Christianorum Series Latina
CEQ	*The Critical Edition of Q.* Edited by J. M. Robinson, P. Hoffmann, and J. S. Kloppenborg. Leuven: Leuven University Press, 2000. (see also IQP).
CIC.Dig	Corpus Iuris Civilis. Digestae
CIG	*Corpus inscriptionem graecarum.* Edited by A. Boeckh. 4 vols. Berlin, 1828–1877.
CIJ	*Corpus Inscriptionum Judaicarum*
CSEL	Corpus scriptorium ecclesiasticorum Latinorum
CuBR	*Currents in Biblical Research*
DNP	*Der neue Pauly.* Edited by H. Cancik, H. Schneider, and M. Landfester. Stuttgart: Metzler, 1996ff.
EBR	*Encyclopedia of the Bible and Its Reception.* Edited by H.-J. Klauck, D. Allison et al. Walter de Gruyter, 2009ff.
EKL	*Evangelisches Kirchenlexikon.* 2nd edition (1962). Edited by H. Brunotte and O. Weber. 3rd edition (1986–1997). Edited by E. Fahlbusch. Göttingen: Vandenhoeck & Ruprecht.

EWNT	*Exegetisches Wörterbuch zum Neuen Testament.* Edited by H. R. Balz and G. Schneider. Stuttgart: Kohlhammer, 1980–1983.
FGH	*Die Fragmente der griechischen Historiker.* Edited by F. Jacoby.
FilNeo	*Filología Theologica*
GAStL	*The Gospel According to St. Luke.* Edited by The American and British Committees of the International Greek New Testament Project. 2 vols. Oxford: Oxford University Press, 1983–1987.
GCS	Die griechischen christlichen Schriftsteller der ersten drei Jahrhunderte
HBiSt	Herders Biblische Studien
IG	*Inscriptiones Graecae*
IQP	International Q Project (see also *CEQ*)
JPeTh.S	Journal of Pentecostal Theology. Supplement Series
JSHRZ	*Jüdische Schriften aus hellenistisch-römischer Zeit*
KP	Der Kleine Pauly
KTU	Die keilalphabetischen Texte aus Ugarit. Vol. 1. Edited by M. Dietrich and J. Sanmartin. Neukirchen-Vluyn: Neukirchen, 1976.
LAW	*Lexicon der Alten Welt*
LNTS	Library of New Testament Studies
LPTB	Linzer Philosophisch-Theologische Beiträge
LSJ	Liddell, H. G., R. Scott, and H. S. Jones. *A Greek English Lexicon.* 9th edition. Oxford: Clarendon Press, 1992.
NHC	Nag Hammadi Codices
NBL	Neues Bibel-Lexikon
NEAEHL	*The New Encyclopedia of Archaeological Excavations in the Holy Land.* Edited by E. Stern. New York: Simon & Schuster, 1993–2008.
NTMon	New Testament Monographs
NTR	*New Theological Review*
OGIS	Orientalis Graeci inscriptiones selectae
OPIAC	Occasional Papers of the Institute for Antiquity and Christianity
OTP	*The Old Testament Pseudepigrapha.* Edited by J. H. Charlesworth. 2 vols. Garden City: Doubleday, 1983–1985.
PEMBS	*Proceedings. Eastern Great Lakes and Midwest Biblical Societies*
PG	*Patrologia Graeca.* Edited by J.-P. Migne. 162 vols. Paris: Minge, 1857–1886.
PGM	*Papyri Graecae Magicae*
PL	Patrologiae cursus completus. Accurante Jacques-Paul Migne. Series Latina
PRE	Paulys Real-Encyclopädie der classichen Alterthumswissenschaft
P.S.I.	Papiri greci e latini. Pubblicazioni della Società italiana per la ricerca dei papiri greci e latini in Egitto. Firenze: Ariani, 1912.
ProBi	Protokolle zur Bibel
RAC	*Reallexikon für Antike und Christentum*

RGG⁴	*Religion in Geschichte und Gegenwart*. 4th edition. Edited by H. D. Betz et al. Tübingen: Mohr Siebeck, 1998–2007.
rell.	Reliqui, i.e., the remaining manuscripts
SacPag	Sacra Pagina
SBG	Studies in Biblical Greek
SGUÄ	*Sammelbuch griechischer Urkunden aus Ägypten*
SIG	Sylloge Inscriptionum Graecarum
StBL	Studies in Biblical Literature
SVF	Stoicorum Veterum Fragmenta
TAPA	*Transactions of the American Philological Association*
ThBNT	*Theologisches Begriffslexikon zum Neuen Testament*
TWNT	*Theologisches Wörtenbuch zum Neuen Testament*. Edited by G. Kittel and G. Friedrich. Stuttgart: Kohlhammer, 1932–1979.
ThGespr	*Theologisches Gespräch*
TLG #E	*Thesaurus Linguae Graecae*, edition E
TPINTC	Trinity Press International New Testament Commentaries
TRE	*Theologische Realenzyklopädie*
TrinJ	*Trinity Journal*
VEccl	*Verbum et Ecclesia*
W&W	*Word & World*
ZBK.WK	Zürcher Werkkommentare zur Bibel

(2) Commentaries on Luke

Bock, D. L. 1994–1996. *Luke*. 2 vols. BECNT 3. Grand Rapids: Baker.

Bossuyt, P., and J. Radermakers. 1999. *Jésus, parole de la grâce selon Saint Luc*. 2 vols. 3rd edition. Brussels: Institut d'Etudes Theologiques.

Bovon, F. 1989–2009. *Das Evangelium nach Lukas*. Neukirchen-Vluyn: Neukirchener.

Caird, G. B. 1977. *The Gospel of St. Luke*. PNTC. Harmondsworth: Penguin.

Creed, J. M. 1960 [1930]. *The Gospel according to St. Luke*. London: Macmillan.

Danker, F. W. 1988. *Jesus and the New Age: A Commentary on St. Luke's Gospel*. 2nd edition. Philadelphia: Fortress Press.

Eckey, W. 2004. *Das Lukas-Evangelium*. 2 vols. Neukirchen-Vluyn: Neukirchener.

Ellis, E. E. 1987. *The Gospel of Luke*. 2nd edition. Grand Rapids: Eerdmans.

Ernst, J. 1993. *Das Evangelium nach Lukas*. 6th edition. RNT. Regensburg: Pustet.

Evans, C. A. 1995. *Luke*. NIBC 3. Peabody, Mass.: Hendrickson.

Evans, C. F. 1990. *Saint Luke*. TPINTC. London: SCM Press.

Fitzmyer, J. A. 1981/1985. *The Gospel according to Luke*. 2 vols. AncB 28–28a. New York: Doubleday.

Geldenhuys, N. 1950. *Commentary on the Gospel of Luke*. London: Marshall, Morgan & Scott.

Green, J. B. 1997. *The Gospel of Luke*. NIC. Grand Rapids: Eerdmans.

Grundmann, W. 1984. *Das Evangelium nach Lukas*. 10th edition. ThHK 3. Berlin: Evangelische Verlagsanstalt.

Johnson, L. T. 1991. *The Gospel of Luke*. SacPag 3. Collegeville, Minn.: Liturgical Press.

Just, A. A. 1996/1997. *Luke*. 2 vols. St. Louis, Mo.: Concordia.

Klein, H. 2006. *Das Lukasevangelium*. KEK I/3. Göttingen: Vandenhoeck & Ruprecht.

Klostermann, E. 1975 [²1929]. *Das Lukasevangelium*. 3rd edition. HNT 5. Tübingen: Mohr.

Kremer, J. 2000. *Lukasevangelium*. 3rd edition. NEB.NT 3. Würzburg: Echter.

Lagrange, M.-J. 1948. *Évangile selon Saint Luc*. 7th edition. EtB. Paris: Gabalda.

LaVerdiere, E. 1985. "No Room for Them in the Inn." *Emmanuel* 91: 552–57.

Marshall, I. H. 1978. *The Gospel of Luke*. NIGTC. Grand Rapids: Eerdmans.

Meynet, R. 2005. *L'évangile de Luc*. Paris: Gabalda.

Nolland, J. 1989–1993. *Luke*. 3 vols. WBC 35A–C. Dallas: Word Books.

Petzke, G. 1990. *Das Sondergut des Evangeliums nach Lukas*. ZBK.WK. Zürich: Theologischer Verlag.

Plummer, A. 1953 [⁵1922]. *The Gospel according to S. Luke*. ICC. Edinburgh: T&T Clark.

Radl, W. 2003. *Das Evangelium nach Lukas I*. Freiburg i.Br.: Herder.

Sabourin, L. 1992. *L'évangile de Luc*. 2nd edition. Rome: Pontificia Università Gregoriana.

Schlatter, A. 1960. *Das Evangelium des Lukas*. 2nd edition. Stuttgart: Calver.

Schmid, J. 1960. *Das Evangelium nach Lukas*. 4th edition. RNT 3. Regensburg: Pustet.

Schmithals, W. 1980. *Das Evangelium nach Lukas*. ZBK.NT 3/1. Zürich: Theologischer.

Schneider, G. 1984. *Das Evangelium nach Lukas*. 2 vols. 2nd edition. ÖTK 3/1–2. Gütersloh: Mohn.

Schürmann, H. 1990⁴/1994. *Das Lukasevangelium*. Vol. I and II/I. HThK 3/1–2. Freiburg i.Br.: Herder.

Schweizer, E. 1982. *Das Evangelium nach Lukas*. NTD 3. Göttingen: Vandenhoeck & Ruprecht.

Stein, R. H. 1992. *Luke*. NAC 24. Nashville: Broadman.

Talbert, C. H. 2002. *Reading Luke: A Literary and Theological Commentary*. 2nd edition. Macon, Ga.: Smyth & Helwys.

Tannehill, R. C. 1996. *Luke*. ANTC. Nashville: Abingdon.

Tiede, D. L. 1988. *Luke*. Minneapolis: Augsburg.

Tresmontant, C. 1987. *L'évangile de Luc*. Paris: O.E.I.L.

Weiss, B. 1901 [⁷1885]. *Die Evangelien des Markus und Lukas*. 9th edition. KEK I/2. Göttingen: Vandenhoeck & Ruprecht.

Weiss, J. 1892. "Evangelium des Lukas." Pages 271–666 in *Die Evangelien des Markus und Lukas*. 8th edition. Edited by B. Weiss and J. Weiss. KEK I/2. Göttingen: Vandenhoeck & Ruprecht.

Wellhausen, J. 1904. *Das Evangelium Lucae übersetzt und erklärt*. Berlin: Reimer.

Wiefel, W. 1988. *Das Evangelium nach Lukas*. ThHK 3. Berlin: Evangelische Verlagsanstalt.

Zahn, T. 1988 [³/⁴1920]. *Das Evangelium des Lucas*. KNT 3. Wuppertal Brockhaus.

(3) Literature

Aalen, S. 1966–1967. "St. Luke's Cospel and the Last Chapters of I Enoch." *NTS* 13: 1–13.

Abadie, P. 1999. "Les généalogies de Jésus en Matthieu et Luc." *LV(L)* 48: 47–60.

Abel, E. L. 1974. "The Genealogies of Jesus Ο ΧΡΙΣΤΟΣ." *NTS* 20: 203–10.

Adams, B. 1964. *Paramoné und verwandte Texte: Studien zum Dienstvertrag im Rechte der Papyri*. Berlin: Walter de Gruyter.

Aejmelaeus, L. 1985. *Wachen vor dem Ende: Die traditionsgeschichtlichen Wurzeln von 1 Thess. 5:1-11 und Luk 21:34-36*. SESJ 44. Helsinki: Kirjapaino Raamattutalo.

Ahn, Y.-S. 2006. *The Reign of God and Rome in Luke's Passion Narrative*. Bib. Int.S 80. Leiden: Brill.

Aicher, G. 1908. *Kamel und Nadelöhr*. Münster: Aschendorff.

Aichinger, H. 1978. "Zur Traditionsgeschichte der Epileptiker-Perikope." Pages 114–43 in *Probleme der Forschung*. SNTU.A 3. Vienna: Herold.

Akaabiam, T. H. 1999. *The Proclamation of the Good News: A Study of Luke 24 in Tiv Context*. EHS.T 673. Frankfurt am Main: Peter Lang.

Aland, K. 1967. "Die Bedeutung des 𝔓⁷⁵ for the Text of the New Testament." Pages 155–72 in *Studien zur Überlieferung des Neuen Testaments und seines Textes*. ANTF 2. Berlin: Walter de Gruyter.

———. 1979. "Der Schluß des Markusevangeliums." Pages 246–83 in *Neutestamentliche Entwürfe*. TB 63. Munich: Kaiser.

———. 1987. "Alter und Entstehung des D-Textes im Neuen Testament." Pages 37–61 in *Miscellània papirològica Ramón Roca-Puig en el seu vuitantè aniversari*. Edited by S. Janeras. Barcelona: Fundació Salvador Vives Casajuana.

———. 2001. *Synopsis Quattuor Evangeliorum*. 15th edition. Stuttgart: Deutsche Bibelgesellschaft.

Albertz, R. 1983. "Die 'Antrittspredigt' Jesu im Lukasevangelium auf ihrem alttestamentlichen Hintergrund." *ZNW* 74: 182–206.

Aletti, J.-N. 1983. "Jésus à Nazareth (Lc 4,16-30)." Pages 431–51 in *À cause de l'évangile: Festschrift Jacques Dupont*. Paris: Cerf.

———. 1989a. *L'art de raconter Jésus Christ. L'écriture narrative de l'évangile de Luc*. Paris: Éditions du Seuil.

————. 1989b. "Parabole des mines et/ou parabole du roi." Pages 309–32 in *Les Paraboles évangéliques: Perspectives nouvelles. XIIe congrès de l'ACFEB, Lyon (1987)*. Edited by J. Delorme. LeDiv 135. Paris: Cerf.

Alexander, L. 1993. *The Preface to Luke's Gospel*. MSSNTS 78. Cambridge: Cambridge University Press.

Alliata, E. 1984. "La krypte di Lc 11,33 e le grotte ripostiglio della antiche case palestinesi." *SBF/LA* 34: 53–66.

Allison, D. C. 1983. "Matthew 23:39 = Luke 13:35b as a Conditional Prophecy." *JSNT* 18: 75–84.

————. 1987. "The Eye is the Lamp of the Body." *NTS* 33: 61–83.

————. 1988. "Was There a 'Lukan Community'?" *IBSt* 10: 62–70.

————. 1989/1990. "'The hairs on your head are all numbered.'" *ExpT* 101: 334–36.

————. 2002. "Rejecting Violent Judgment: Luke 9:52 and Its Relatives." *JBL* 121: 459–78.

Amon, J. E. 1997. "Settling out of Court." Pages 269–413 in *Q 12:49-59*. Edited by S. Carruth. Leuven: Peeters.

Amphoux, C.-B. 1991–1992. "Les premières éditions de Luc." *EthL* 67/68: 312–27, 38–48.

Anderson, R. H. 1997. "Theophilus: A Proposal." *EvQ* 69: 195–215.

Annas, J., ed., and R. Woolf, trans. 2001. *Cicero, On Moral Ends*. Cambridge: Cambridge University Press.

Annen, F. 1976. *Heil für die Heiden*. FTS 20. Frankfurt am Main: Knecht.

Applebaum, S. 1979. *Jews and Greeks in Ancient Cyrene*. Leiden: Brill.

Arav, R., and R. A. Freund, eds. 1995/1999. *Bethsaida: A City by the North Shore of the Sea of Galilee*. Kirksville, Mo.: Thomas Jefferson State University Press.

Arbesmann, R. 1929. *Das Fasten bei den Griechen und Römern*. Giessen: Töpelmann.

Arens, E. 1976. *The HΛΘON-Sayings in the Synoptic Tradition*. OBO 10. Göttingen: Vandenhoeck & Ruprecht.

Ascough, R. S. 1993. "Rejection and Repentance: Peter and the People in Luke's Passion Narrative." *Bib.* 74: 349–65.

Ash, H. B. 1977. *Res Rustica*. Vol. 1. LCL 361. Cambridge, Mass.: Harvard University Press.

Attridge, H. W. 2000. "'Seeking' and 'Asking' in Q, Thomas, and John." Pages 295–302 in *From Quest to Q: Festschrift James M. Robinson*. Edited by J. M. Asgeirsson, K. de Troyer, and M. M. Meyer. BEThL 146. Leuven: Peeters.

Auffret, P. 1978. "Note sur la structure littéraire de Lc I. 67-79." *NTS* 24: 248–58.

Aune, D. E. 1996. "Luke 20:34-36: A 'Gnosticized' Logion of Jesus?" Pages 187–202 in *Geschichte–Tradition–Reflexion: Festschrift Martin Hengel*. Vol. 3. Edited by H. Cancik, H. Lichtenberger, and P. Schäfer. Tübingen: Mohr.

————. 1997–1998. *Revelation 1–5 / 6–16 / 17–22*. WBC 52A–C. Nashville: T. Nelson.

————. 2002. "Luke 1.1-4: Historical or Scientific Prooimion?" Pages 138–48 in *Paul, Luke and the Graeco-Roman World: Festschrift Alexander J.M.*

Wedderburn. Edited by A. J. M. Wedderburn and A. Christophersen. JSNT.S 217. London: Sheffield Academic.

Aus, R. D. 1985. "Luke 15:1-32 and R. Eliezer ben Hyrcanus's Rise to Fame." *JBL* 104: 443–69.

———. 1994. *Samuel, Saul and Jesus: Three Early Palestinian Jewish Christian Gospel Haggadoth*. SFSHJ 105. Atlanta: Scholars Press.

———. 2000. *The Stilling of the Storm*. Binghampton, N. Y.: Global Publications.

———. 2003. *My Name is "Legion."* Lanham, Md.: University Press of America.

Ausbüttel, A. 1998. *Die Verwaltung des römischen Kaiserreiches*. Darmstadt: Wissenschaftliche Buchgesellschaft.

Avigad, N. 1962. "A Depository of Inscribed Ossuaries in the Kidron Valley." *IEJ* 12: 1–12.

Avni, G. 1994. "Three New Burial Caves of the Second Temple Period in Aceldama." Pages 206–18 in *Ancient Jerusalem Revealed*. Edited by H. Geva. Jerusalem: Israel Exploration Society.

Baarda, T. 1969. "Gadarenes, Gerasenes, Gergesenes and the 'Diatessaron' Traditions." Pages 181–97 in *Neotestamentica et Semitica: Festschrift Matthew Black*. Edited by E. E. Ellis. Edinburgh: T&T Clark.

———. 1975. "Luke 12,13-14: Text and Transmission from Marcion to Augustine." Pages 107–62 in *Christianity, Judaism and Other Greco-Roman Cults: Festschrift Morton Smith*. Vol. 1. Edited by J. Neusner. Leiden: Brill.

———. 1988. "Luke 22:42-47a: The Emperor Julian as a Witness to the Text of Luke." *NT* 30: 289–96.

Baarlink, H. 1982. "Ein gnädiges Jahr des Herrn–und Tage der Vergeltung." *ZNW* 73: 204–20.

Backhaus, K. 1991. *Die "Jüngerkreise" des Täufers Johannes*. PaThSt 19. Paderborn: Schöningh.

———. 2007. "Lukas der Maler: Die Apostelgeschichte als intentionale Geschichte der christlichen Erstepoche." Pages 30–66 in *Historiographie und fiktionales Erzählen*. Edited by K. Backhaus and G. Häfner. BThSt 86. Neukirchen-Vluyn: Neukirchener.

Baergen, R. A. 2006. "Servant, Manager or Slave? Reading the Parable of the Rich Man and His Steward (Luke 16:1-8a) through the Lens of Ancient Slavery." *StudRel/SciRel* 35: 25–38.

Bagatti, B. 1969/2002. *Excavations in Nazareth*. 2 vols. Jerusalem: Franciscan Printing Press.

Bagnall, R. G. 2000. "Jesus Reads a Book." *JThS* 51: 577–88.

Bagnall, R. S., and K. A. Worp. 2001. "Household Accounts: SB I 5224 Revised." *BASPap* 38: 7–20.

Bailey, K. E. 1976. *Poet and Peasant: A Literary-cultural Approach to the Parables in Luke*. Grand Rapids: Eerdmans.

———. 1992. *Finding the Lost*. St. Louis, Mo.: Concordia.

———. 2003. *Jacob and the Prodigal*. Downers Grove, Ill.: InterVarsity.

Ballard, P. H. 1972. "Reasons for Refusing the Great Supper." *JThS NS* 23: 341–50.

Baltensweiler, H. 1984. "'Wer nicht gegen uns (euch) ist, ist für uns (euch)!'" *ThZ* 40: 130–36.

Bammel, E. 1986. "The Cambridge Pericope: The Addition to Luke 6.4 in Codex Bezae." *NTS* 32: 404–26.

Barigazzi, A., ed. 1966. *Favorinus, Opere*. Florence: Le Monnier.

Barr, J. 1988. "Abba Isn't Daddy." *JThS* 39: 28–47.

Barrett, C. K. 1958. "Luke XXII.15: To Eat the Passover." *JThS* 9: 305–7.

———. 1992. "The Third Gospel as a Preface to Acts? Some Reflections." Pages 1451–66 in *The Four Gospels 1992: Festschrift Frans Neirynck*. Vol. 2. Edited by F. van Segbroeck, C. M. Tuckett, G. van Belle, and J. Verheyden. BEThL 100. Leuven: Peeters.

———. 1994/1998. *The Acts of the Apostles*. 2 vols. ICC. London: T&T Clark.

Barrett, C. K., and C.-J. Thornton. 1991. *Texte zur Umwelt des Neuen Testaments*. 2nd edition. Tübingen: Mohr.

Bartsch, H.-W. 1974. "Jesu Schwertwort, Lukas xxii.35-38." *NTS* 20: 190–203.

———. 1984. *Codex Bezae versus Codex Sinaiticus im Lukasevangelium*. Hildesheim: Olms.

Batten, A. 1998. "Patience Breeds Wisdom: Q 6:40 in Context." *CBQ* 60: 641–56.

Bauckham, R. 1977. "Synoptic Parousia Parables and the Apocalypse." *NTS* 23: 162–76.

———. 1990. *Jude and the Relatives of Jesus in the Early Church*. Edinburgh: T&T Clark.

———. 1991a. "More on Kainam: The Son of Arpachshad in Luke's Genealogy." *EThL* 67: 95–103.

———. 1991b. "The Rich Man and Lazarus." *NTS* 37: 225–46.

———. 1997. "Anna of the Tribe of Asher (Luke 2:36-38)." *RB* 104: 161–91.

———. 1998. "For Whom Were Gospels Written?" Pages 9–48 in *The Gospel for All Christians: Rethinking the Gospel Audiences*. Edited by R. Bauckham. Grand Rapids: Eerdmans.

Bauer, J. B. 1960. "ΠΟΛΛΟΙ Luk 1,1." *NT* 4: 263–66.

———. 1972. "'Wer sein Leben retten will' Mark 8,35 Parr." Pages 43–46 in *Scholia biblica et patristica*. Graz: Akademische Druck- und Verlagsanstalt.

Bauer, U. 1998. "Der Anfang der Endzeitrede in der Logienquelle (Q 17)." Pages 79–101 in *Wenn drei das Gleiche sagen*. Edited by S. H. Brandenburger and T. Hieke. Münster: Lit.

Bauer, W. 1988. *Griechisch-deutsches Wörterbuch zu den Schriften des Neuen Testaments und der übrigen urchristlichen Literatur*. 6th edition. Berlin: Walter de Gruyter.

Baum, A. D. 1993. *Lukas als Historiker der letzten Jesusreise*. Wuppertal: Brockhaus.

Beardslee, W. A. 1979. "Saving One's Life by Losing It." *JAAR* 47: 57–72.

Beavis, M. A. 1992. "Ancient Slavery as an Interpretive Context for the New Testament Servant Parables." *JBL* 111: 37–54.

Beck, B. E. 1981. "'Imitatio Christi' and the Lukan Passion Narrative." Pages 28–47 in *Suffering and Martyrdom in the New Testament: Studies Presented to G. M. Styler by the Cambridge New Testament Seminar*. Edited by W. Horbury and B. McNeil. Cambridge: Cambridge University Press.

Becker, J. 1981. *Das Evangelium nach Johannes*. Vol. 2. Gütersloh: Mohn.

———. 1996. *Jesus von Nazaret*. Berlin: Walter de Gruyter.

Bellinzoni, A. J. 1998. "The Gospel of Luke in the Second Century CE." Pages 59–76 in *Literary Studies in Luke–Acts: Festschrift Joseph B. Tyson*. Edited by R. P. Thompson and T. E. Phillips. Macon, Ga.: Mercer University Press.

———. 2005. "The Gospel of Luke in the Apostolic Fathers: An Overview." Pages 45–68 in *The New Testament and the Apostolic Fathers*. Vol. 2, *Trajectories through the New Testament and the Apostolic Fathers*. Edited by A. Gregory and C. Tuckett. Oxford: Oxford University Press.

Ben-David, A. 1974. *Talmudische Ökonomie I*. Hildesheim: Olms.

Bendemann, R. von. 2000. "Liebe und Sündenvergebung." *BZ NF* 44: 161-82.

———. 2001. *Zwischen ΔΟΞΑ und ΣΤΑΥΡΟΣ. Eine exegetische Untersuchung der Texte des sogenannten Reiseberichts im Lukasevangelium*. BZNW. Berlin: Walter de Gruyter.

Bengel, J. A. 1855. *Gnomon Novi Testamenti*. 3rd edition. Tübingen: Fues.

Benko, S. 1967. "The Magnificat: A History of the Controversy." *JBL* 86: 263–75.

Benoit, P. 1956–1957. "L'Enfance de Jean-Baptiste selon Luc 1." *NTS* 3: 169–94.

Bergemann, T. 1993. *Q auf dem Prüfstand*. FRLANT 158. Göttingen: Vandenhoeck & Ruprecht.

Berger, K. 1972. *Die Gesetzesauslegung Jesu*. WMANT 40. Neukirchen-Vluyn: Neukirchener.

———. 1973a. "'Gnade' im frühen Christentum." *NedThT* 27: 1–25.

———. 1973b. "Materialien zu Form und Überlieferungsgeschichte neutestamentlicher Gleichnisse." *NT* 15: 1–37.

———. 1976. *Die Auferstehung des Propheten und die Erhöhung des Menschensohnes*. StUNT 13. Göttingen: Vandenhoeck & Ruprecht.

———. 1977a. "Almosen für Israel: Zum historischen Kontext der Paulinischen Kollekte." *NTS* 23: 180–204.

———. 1977b. "Gleichnisse als Texte. Zum lukanischen Gleichnis vom 'verlorenen Sohn' (Lk 15,11-32)." Pages 61–74 in *Imago Linguae: Festschrift for Fritz Paepcke*. Edited by K.-H. Bender, K. Berger, and M. Wandruszka. Munich: Fink.

———. 1980. "Hellenistisch-heidnische Prodigien und die Vorzeichen in der jüdischen und christlichen Apokalyptik." Pages 1428–69 in *ANRW* II: 23/2.

———. 1984a. *Formgeschichte des Neuen Testaments*. Heidelberg: Quelle & Meyer.

———. 1984b. "Hellenistische Gattungen im Neuen Testament." Pages 1031–432 and 1831–85 in *ANRW* II: 25/2.

———. 1985. "Das Canticum Simeonis (Lk 2:29-32)." *NT* 27: 27–39.

———. 1988. "Jesus als Pharisäer und frühe Christen als Pharisäer." *NT* 30: 231–62.

———. 1996. "Jesus als Nasoräer / Nasiräer." *NT* 41: 322–35.

———. 2005. *Formen und Gattungen im Neuen Testament*. Tübingen: Francke.

Berger, K., and C. Colpe. 1987. *Religionsgeschichtliches Textbuch zum Neuen Testament*. NTD.T 1. Göttingen: Vandenhoeck & Ruprecht.

Berger, P. L. 1991. *Auf den Spuren der Engel*. 3rd edition. Frankfurt am Main: Fischer.

Berger, P. L., and T. Luckmann. 1966. *The Social Construction of Reality: A Treatise in the Sociology of Knowledge*. New York: Doubleday.

Berger, P.-R. 1983. "Luke 2,14: ἄνθρωποι εὐδοκίας. Die auf Gottes Weisung mit Wohlgefallen beschenkten Menschen." *ZNW* 74: 129–44.

Bergier, J.-F. 1989. *Die Geschichte vom Salz*. Frankfurt: Campus.

Bergson, L. 1965. *Der griechische Alexanderroman*. Stockholm: Almqvist & Wiksell.

Bernabé Ubieta, C. 2000. "Mary Magdalene and the Seven Demons in Social-Scientific Perspective." Pages 203–23 in *Transformative Encounters: Jesus and Women Re-Viewed*. Edited by I. R. Kitzberger. Bib.Int.S 43. Leiden: Brill.

Berthelot, M., and C.-E. Ruelle. 1887–1888. *Collection des anciens alchimistes grecs*. Paris: Steinheil.

Betz, H. D. 1972. *Der Apostel Paulus und die Sokratische Tradition*. Tübingen: Mohr Siebeck.

———. 1978. "De Tranquillitate animi [*Moralia* 464e–477f]." Pages 198–230 in *Plutarch's Ethical Writings and Early Christian Literature*. Leiden: Brill.

———. 1992. "The Sermon on the Mount and Q." Pages 249–69 in *Synoptische Studien*. Tübingen: Mohr.

———. 1995. *The Sermon on the Mount*. Hermeneia. Philadelphia: Fortress.

Betz, O. 1964. "The Dichotomized Servant and the End of Judas Iscariot." *RdQ* 5: 43–58.

Beutler, J. 1991. "Punkt oder Komma?" *BZ* NF 35: 231–33.

Beyer, K. 1962. *Semitische Syntax im Neuen Testament*. StUNT 1. Göttingen: Vandenhoeck & Ruprecht.

Bickermann, E. 1985. "Die römische Kaiserapotheose [1929]." Pages 1–34 in *Religions and Politics in the Hellenistic and Roman Periods*. BiAth 5. Como: Edizioni New Press.

———. 1988. "Das leere Grab." Pages 271–84 in *Zur neutestamentlichen Überlieferung von der Auferstehung Jesu*. Edited by P. Hoffmann. WdF 522. Darmstadt: Wissenschaftliche Buchgesellschaft.

Bieberstein, K., and H. Bloedhorn. 1994. *Jerusalem: Grundzüge der Baugeschichte vom Chalkolithikum bis zur Frühzeit der osmanischen Herrschaft*. 3 vols. BTAVO.B 100. Wiesbaden: Reichert.

Bieberstein, S. 1998. *Verschwiegene Jüngerinnen—vergessene Zeuginnen*. 38 vols. NTOA. Freiburg: Göttingen.

Bielinski, K. 2003. *Jesus vor Herodes in Lk 23,6-12*. SBB 50. Stuttgart: Katholisches Bibelwerk.

Bietenhard, H. 1951. *Die himmlische Welt im Urchristentum und Spätjudentum*. WUNT 2. Tübingen: Mohr.

———. 1977. "Die syrische Dekapolis von Pompejus bis Trajan." Pages 220–61 in *ANRW* II: 8.

Bikerman, E. 1937. "ΑΝΑΔΕΙΞΙΣ." Pages 117–24 in *Mélanges Émile Boisacq*. Brussels: Secrétariat des éd. de l'Institut.

Billings, B. S. 2006. *Do This in Remembrance of Me: The Disputed Words in the Lukan Institution Narrative (Luke 22.19b-20)*. LNTS 314. London: T&T Clark.

Bindemann, W. 1995. "Ungerechte als Vorbilder?" *ThLZ* 120: 955–70.

Binder, D. D. 1999. *Into the Temple Courts: The Place of the Synagogues in the Second Temple Period*. Atlanta: Scholars Press.

Binder, H. 1988. *Das Gleichnis von dem Richter und der Witwe Lk 18,1-8*. Neukirchen-Vluyn: Neukirchener.

Bivin, B. 1992. "The Miraculous Catch." *Jerusalem Perspectives* 5: 7–10.

Blaschke, A. 1998. *Beschneidung. Zeugnisse der Bibel und verwandter Texte*. TANZ 28. Tübingen: Francke.

Blau, L. 1898. *Das altjüdische Zauberwesen*. Straussburg: Teubner.

Blinzler, J. 1953. "Die literarische Eigenart des sogenannten Reiseberichts im Lukasevangelium." Pages 20–52 in *Synoptische Studien: Festschrift Alfred Wikenhauser*. Munich: Zink.

———. 1954–1955. "Ὀθόνια und andere Stoffbezeichnungen im 'Wäschekatalog' des Ägypters Theophanes und im Neuen Testament." *Ph*. 99: 158–66.

———. 1957/1958. "Die Niedermetzelung von Galiläer durch Pilatus." *NT* 2: 24–49.

Blomberg, C. L. 1983. "Midrash, Chiasmus, and the Outline of Luke's Central Section." Pages 217–61 in *Gospel Perspectives*. Vol. 3. Edited by R. T. France and D. Wenham. Sheffield: JSOT.

Blomqvist, J. 1979. *Das sogenannte καί adversativum: Zur Semantik einer griechischen Partikel*. AUU. SGU 13. Uppsala: Almqvist & Wiksell.

Blum, M. 2004. *". . . denn sie wissen nicht, was sie tun."* NTA NF 46. Münster: Aschendorff.

Blumenthal, C. 2005. "Zur 'Zinne des Tempels.'" *ZNW* 96: 274–83.

Böcher, O. 1970. *Dämonenfurcht und Dämonenabwehr*. BWANT 90. Stuttgart: Kohlhammer.

———. 1971/1972. "Aß Johannes der Täufer kein Brot (Luk. VII.33)?" *NTS* 18: 90–92.

Bock, D. L. 1987. *Proclamation from Prophecy and Pattern*. JSNT.S 12. Sheffield: Sheffield Academic Press.

Bockmuehl, M. 1998. "'Let the Dead Bury Their Dead.'" *JThS* 49: 553–81.

———. 2003. "'Leave the Dead to Bury Their Own Dead.'" *JSNT* 26: 241–42.

Böhl, F. 1987. "Das Fasten an Montagen und Donerstagen." *BZ NF* 31: 247–50.

Böhlemann, P. 1997. *Jesus und der Täufer. Schlüssel zur Theologie und Ethik des Lukas*. MSSNTS 99. Cambridge: Cambridge University Press.

Böhler, D. 1998. "Jesus als Davidssohn bei Lukas und Micha." *Bib*. 79: 532–38.

Böhm, M. 1999. *Samarien und die Samaritai bei Lukas*. WUNT 2/111. Tübingen: Mohr.

Boismard, M. É. 1997. *En quête du proto-Luc*. Paris: Gabalda.

———. 2002. "La parabole de l'intendant infidèle en Lc 16,1-9." Pages 451–54 in *San Luca Evangelista. Testimone della fede che unisce. I. L'unità letteraria e teologica dell'opera di Luca*. Edited by G. Leonarde. Padova: Istituto per la storia ecclesiastica padovana.

Bolkestein, H. 1967 [1939]. *Wohltätigkeit und Armenpflege im vorchristlichen Altertum*. Groningen: Bouma.

Bonnard, P. 1980. "Approche historico-critique de Luc 15." Pages 93–103 in *Anamnesis: Recherches sur le Nouveau Testament*. Edited by P. Bonnard. Geneva: Revue de Theologie et de Philosophie.

Bons, E. 1994. "Das Sterbewort Jesu nach Lk 23,46 und sein alttestamentlicher Hintergrund." *BZ NF* 38: 93–101.

Booth, R. P. 1986. *Jesus and the Laws of Purity*. Sheffield: JSOT.

Borg, M. J. 1992. "Luke 19,42-44 and Jesus as Prophet?" *Forum* 8: 99–112.

Bork, H. D. 1977. "Lateinisch-romanisch auris/auricula/auditus und die partitiven Diminutiva." *Glotta* 55: 120–56.

Bormann, L. 2001. *Recht, Gerechtigkeit und Religion im Lukasevangelium*. StUNT 24. Göttingen: Vandenhoeck & Ruprecht.

Bornhäuser, K. 1934. *Studien zum Sondergut des Lukas*. Gütersloh: Bertelsmann.

Borse, U. 1997. "Der lukanische Verzicht auf Betanien." *SNTU.A* 22: 5-24.

Bösen, W. 1980. *Jesusmahl, Eucharistisches Mahl, Endzeitmahl. Ein Beitrag zur Theologie des Lukas*. SBS 97. Stuttgart: Katholisches Bibelwerk.

Bosold, I. 1978. *Pazifismus und prophetische Provokation: Das Grußverbot Lk 10,4b und sein historischer Kontext*. SBS 90. Stuttgart: Katholisches Bibelwerk.

Bottini, G. C. 2001. "Luca 18,31-33. Il mistero del Figlio dell'uomo." Pages 705–14 in *Mysterium Regni. Ministerium Verbi. Scritti in onore di Mons. Vittorio Fusco*. Edited by E. Franco. SRivBib 38. Bologna: EDB.

Böttrich, C. 2001. *Petrus: Fischer, Fels und Funktionär*. BG 2. Leipzig: Evangelische Verlagsanstalt.

———. 2003. "Ideal oder Zeichen? Besitzverzicht bei Lukas am Beispiel der 'Ausrüstungsregel.'" *NTS* 49: 372–92.

———. 2005. "Proexistenz im Leben und Sterben: Jesu Tod bei Lukas." Pages 413–36 in *Deutungen des Todes Jesu*. Edited by J. Frey and J. Schröter. WUNT 181. Tübingen: Mohr Siebeck.

Bovon, F. 1993. "Wetterkundliches bei den Synoptikern (Lk 12,54-56 par.)." *BThZ* 10: 175–86.

———. 2000. "Tracing the Trajectory of Luke 13,22-30 back to Q." Pages 285–94 in *From Quest to Q: Festschrift James M. Robinson*. Edited by J. M. Asgeirsson, K. de Troyer, and M. M. Meyer. BEThL 146. Leuven: Peeters.

———. 2002–2013. *Luke*. 3 vols. Hermeneia. Minneapolis: Fortress.

———. 2003. "The Lukan Story of the Passion of Jesus (Luke 22-23)." Pages 74–105 in *Studies in Early Christianity*. WUNT 161. Tübingen: Mohr.

———. 2005. "The Reception and Use of the Gospel of Luke in the Second Century CE." Pages 379–400 in *Reading Luke: Interpretation, Reflection, Formation*. Edited by C. G. Bartholomew, J. B. Green, and A. C. Thiselton. Milton Keynes: Paternoster.

———. 2006. *Luke the Theologian: Fifty-five Years of Research (1950–2005)*. 2nd edition. Waco, Tex.: Baylor University Press.

Brandenburger, E. 1973. *Frieden im Neuen Testament.* Gütersloh: Mohn.

Brandt, W. 1891. "ONOMA en de Doopsformule in het Nieuwe Testament." *ThT* 25: 565–610.

Braude, W. G., trans. 1959. *The Midrash on Psalms.* Vol. 1. New Haven: Yale University Press.

Braumann, G. 1963/1864. "Die Schuldner und die Sünderin." *NTS* 10: 487-93.

———. 1980. "Tot–lebendig–verloren–gefunden (Lk 15,24 and 32)." Pages 156–64 in *Wort in der Zeit. Neutestamentliche Studien: Festschrift Karl Heinrich Rengstorf.* Edited by W. Haubeck and M. Bachmann. Leiden: Brill.

Braun, W. 1992. "Symposium or Anti-Symposium? Reflections on Luke 14:1-24." *TJT* 8: 70–84.

———. 1995. *Feasting and Social Rhetoric in Luke 14.* MSSNTS 85. Cambridge: Cambridge University Press.

Braunert, H. 1980. "Der römischen Provinzialzensus und der Schätzungsbericht des Lukas-Evangeliums." Pages 213–37 in *Politik, Recht und Gesellschaft in der griechisch-römischen Antike.* Edited by K. Telschow and M. Zahrnt. Stuttgart: Klett-Cotta.

Brawley, R. L. 1987. *Luke–Acts and the Jews.* SBLMS 33. Atlanta: Scholars Press.

———. 1992. "Canon and Community." *SBL.SP* 31: 419–34.

———. 1995. *Text to Text Pours Forth Speech: Voices of Scripture in Luke–Acts.* Bloomington, Ind.: Indiana University Press.

Breytenbach, C. 1985. "Das Markusevangelium als episodische Erzählung. Mit Überlegungen zum Aufbau des zweiten Evangeliums." Pages 137–69 in *Der Erzähler des Evangeliums. Methodische Neuansätze in der Markusforschung.* Edited by F. Hahn. SBS 118/119. Stuttgart: Katholisches Bibelwerk.

———. 1999. "Gnädigstimmen und opferkultische Sühne im Urchristentum und seiner Umwelt." Pages 419–42 in *Das Urchristentum in seiner literarischen Geschichte: Festschrift Jürgen Becker.* Edited by U. Mell and U. B. Müller. BZNW 100. Berlin: Walter de Gruyter.

Bridge, S. L. 2003. *"Where the Eagles Are Gathered": The Deliverance of the Elect in Lukan Eschatology.* JSNT.S 240. Sheffield: Sheffield Academic.

Brock, S. P. 1963. "A Note on Luke IX.16 (D)." *JThS* 14: 391–92.

Brodie, T. L. 1986. "Towards Unravelling Luke's Use of the Old Testament: Luke 7.11-17 as an *Imitatio* of 1 Kings 17.17-24." *NTS* 32: 247–67.

———. 1989a. "The Departure for Jerusalem (Luke 9,51-56) as a Rhetorical Imitation of Elijah's Departure for the Jordan." *Bib.* 70: 96–109.

———. 1989b. "Luke 9:57-62: A Systematic Adaption of the Divine Challenge to Elijah (1 Kings 19)." *SBLSP* 28: 237–45.

———. 1992. "Not Q but Elijah: The Saving of the Centurion's Servant (Luke 7:1-10) as an Internalization of the Saving of the Widow and her Child (1 Kings 17:1-16)." *IBSt* 14: 54–71.

Broer, I. 1986. *Die Seligpreisungen der Bergpredigt.* BBB 61. Königstein: Hanstein.

———. 1998/2001. *Einleitung in das Neue Testament.* 2 vols. NEB.E 2/1–2. Würzburg: Echter.

Brooke, G. J. 1995. "4Q500 1 and the Use of Scripture in the Parable of the Vineyard." *DSD* 2: 268–94.

Brown, R. E. 1978. "Luke's Method in the Annunciation Narrative of Chapter One." Pages 126–38 in *Perspectives in Luke–Acts*. Edited by C. H. Talbert. Edinburgh: Clark.

———. 1993. *The Birth of the Messiah*. New York: Doubleday.

———. 1994. *The Death of the Messiah: From Gethsemane to the Grave. A Commentary on the Passion Narratives in the Four Gospels*. 2 vols. New York: Doubleday.

———. 1997. *An Introduction to the New Testament*. New York: Doubleday.

Brown, S. 1969. *Apostasy and Perseverance in the Theology of Luke*. AnBib 36. Rome: Pontifical Biblical Institute.

Brox, N. 1969. "Zu den persönlichen Notizen der Pastoralbriefe." *BZ NF* 13: 76–94.

Bruhn, W., and M. Tilke. 1955. *Kostümgeschichte in Bildern*. Tübingen: Wasmuth.

Brun, L. 1932. "Die Berufung der ersten Jünger in der evangelischen Tradition." *SO* 11: 35–54.

———. 1933. "Engel und Blutschweiß Lc 22.43-44." *ZNW* 32: 265–76.

Bruners, W. 1977. *Die Reinigung der zehn Aussätzigen und die Heilung des Samariters Lk 17,11-19*. FzB 23. Stuttgart: Katholisches Bibelwerk.

Brunner, H. 1988. *Altägyptische Weisheit. Lehren für das Leben*. Darmstadt: Wissenschaftiche Buchgesellschaft.

Brunt, P. A. 1981. "The Revenues of Rome." *JRS* 71: 163–72.

Büchele, A. 1978. *Der Tod Jesu im Lukasevangelium*. FTS 26. Frankfurt am Main: Knecht.

Buckhanon Crowder, S. 2002. *Simon of Cyrene: A Case of Roman Conscription*. StBL 46. New York: Lang.

Buckwalter, H. D. 1996. *The Character and Purpose of Luke's Christology*. MSSNTS 89. Cambridge: Cambridge University Press.

Buffière, F. 1962. *Allégories d'Homère*. Paris: Les Belles Lettres.

Bühner, J.-A. 1977. *Der Gesandte und sein Weg im 4: Evangelium*. WUNT 2/2. Tübingen: Mohr.

Buitenwerf, R. 2003. *Book III of the Sibylline Oracles and Its Social Setting: With an Introduction, Translation, and Commentary*. Leiden: Brill.

Bultmann, R. 1995 [1921]. *Die Geschichte der synoptischen Tradition*. 10th edition. FRLANT 29. Göttingen: Vandenhoeck & Ruprecht.

Burchard, C. 1970. *Der dreizehnte Zeuge: Traditions- und kompositionsgeschichtliche Untersuchungen zu Lukas' Darstellung der Frühzeit des Paulus*. FRLANT 103. Göttingen: Vandenhoeck & Ruprecht.

———. 1985. "A Note on Ῥῆμα in JosAs 17:1-2; Luke 2:15, 17; Acts 10:37." *NT* 27: 281–95.

———. 1998. *Studien zur Theologie, Sprache und Umwelt des Neuen Testaments*. WUNT 107. Tübingen: Mohr.

Burger, C. 1970. *Jesus als Davidssohn*. FRLANT 98. Göttingen: Vanderhoeck & Ruprecht.

Burnett, A. 1998. *Roman Provincial Coinage*. Vol. I/1–2. 2nd edition. London: British Museum Press.

———. 1999. *Roman Provincial Coinage*. Vol. II/1–2. London: British Museum Press.

Burridge, R. A. 1998. "About People, by People, for People: Gospel Genre and Audiences." Pages 113–45 in *The Gospel for All Christians*. Edited by R. Bauckham. Grand Rapids: Eerdmans.

Busch, P. 1966. *Der gefallene Drache: Mythenexegese am Beispiel von Apokalypse 12*. Tübingen: Francke.

Busse, U. 1978. *Das Nazareth-Manifest Jesu*. SBS 91. Stuttgart: Katholisches Bibelwerk.

———. 1979. *Die Wunder des Propheten Jesus*. 2nd edition. FzB 24. Stuttgart: Katholisches Bibelwerk.

———. 1991. "Das 'Evangelium' des Lukas: Die Funktion der Vorgeschichte im lukanischen Doppelwerk." Pages 161–77 in *Der Treue Gottes trauen. Beiträge zum Werk des Lukas: Festschrift Gerhard Schneider*. Edited by C. Bussmann and W. Radl. Freiburg: Herder.

———. 1994. "Die Engelrede Lk 1,13-17 und ihre Vorgeschichte." Pages 163–77 in *Nach den Anfängen fragen: Festschrift Gerhard Dautzenberg*. Edited by C. P. Mayer. Giessen: Selbstverlag des Fachbereichs Evangelische Theologie und Katholische Theologie und deren Didaktik.

———. 1998. "Dechiffrierung eines lukanischen Schlüsseltextes (Lk 19,11-27)." Pages 423–41 in *Von Jesus zum Christus. Christologische Studien: Festschrift Paul Hoffmann*. Edited by R. Hoppe and U. Busse. BZNW 93. Berlin: Walter de Gruyter.

———. 2005. "Begegnung mit dem Wort nach Lk 5,1-11." Pages 113–29 in *Luke and His Readers: Festschrift Adelbert Denaux*. Edited by R. Bieringer, G. Van Belle, and J. Verheyden. BEThL 182. Leuvenx: Peeters.

Buth, R. 1984. "Hebrew Tenses and the Magnificat." *JSNT* 21: 67–83.

Cadbury, H. J. 1925. "Lexical Notes on Luke–Acts I." *JBL* 44: 214–27.

———. 1926. "Lexical Notes on Luke–Acts II. Recent Arguments for Medical Language." *JBL* 45: 190–206.

———. 1933. "Lexical Notes on Luke–Acts V: Luke and the Horse-Doctors." *JBL* 52: 55–65.

———. 1969 [1920]. *The Style and Literary Method of Luke*. HThS 6. New York: Kraus.

Cairns, D. L. 1993. *Aidōs: The Psychology and Ethics of Honour and Shame in Ancient Greek Literature*. Oxford: Clarendon.

Callan, T. 1985. "The Preface of Luke–Acts and Historiography." *NTS* 31: 576–81.

Cameron, R. 1990. "What Have You Come Out to See?" *Semeia* 49: 35–69.

———. 1996. "The Sayings Gospel Q and the Quest of the Historical Jesus." *HThR* 89: 351–54.

Cancik, H. 1982. "Die Berufung des Johannes." *Der altsprachl. Unterricht* 25: 45–62.

————. 1997. "The History of Culture, Religion, and Institutions in Ancient Historiography: Philological Observations Concerning Luke's History." *JBL* 116: 673–95.

Caragounis, C. C. 1974. " Ὀψώνιον: A Reconsideration of Its Meaning." *NT* 16: 35–57.

Carlston, C. E. 1975. "Reminiscence and Redaction in Luke 15:11-32." *JBL* 95: 368–90.

Carmignac, J. 1969. *Recherches sur le "Notre Père."* Paris: Letouzey & Ané.

Carpinelli, F. G. 1999. "Do This as *My* Memorial (Luke 22:19): Lucan Soteriology of Atonement." *CBQ* 61: 74–91.

Carras, G. P. 1997. "A Pentateuchal Echo in Jesus' Prayer on the Cross: Intertextuality between Numbers 15,22-31 and Luke 23,34a." Pages 605–16 in *The Scriptures in the Gospels*. Edited by C. M. Tuckett. BEThL 131. Leuven: Peeters.

Carroll, J. T. 1988. "Luke's Portrayal of the Pharisees." *CBQ* 50: 604–21.

————. 1990. "Luke's Crucifixion Scene." Pages 108–24, 194–203 in *Reimagining the Death of the Lukan Jesus*. Edited by D. D. Sylva. BBB 73. Frankfurt am Main: Hain.

Carruth, S., and A. Garsky. 1996. *Q 11:2b-4*. Edited by S. D. Anderson. Leuven: Peeters.

Carruth, S., and J. M. Robinson. 1996. *Q 4:1-13,16: The Temptations of Jesus, Nazara*. Edited by C. Heil. Leuven: Peeters.

Casey, M. 1985. "The Jackals and the Son of Man." *JSNT* 23: 3–22.

Catchpole, D. R. 1977. "The Son of Man's Search for Faith (Luke XVIII 8b)." *NT* 19: 81–104.

————. 1981. "On Doing Violence to the Kingdom." *IrBSt* 3: 77–92.

————. 1983. "Q and 'The Friend at Midnight.'" *JBL* 34: 407–24.

————. 1984. "The 'Triumphal Entry.'" Pages 319–34 in *Jesus and the Politics of His Day*. Edited by E. Bammel and C. F. D. Moule. Cambridge: Cambridge University Press.

————. 1989. "Q, Prayer, and the Kingdom." *JThS* 40: 377–88.

————. 1991. "The Mission Charge in Q." *Semeia* 55: 147–74.

————. 1992. "The Centurion's Faith and Its Function in Q." Pages 517–40 in *The Four Gospels 1992: Festschrift Frans Neirynck*. Vol. 2. Edited by F. van Segbroeck, C. M. Tuckett, G. van Belle, and J. Verheyden. BEThL 100. Leuven: Peeters.

————. 1993a. "The Annointed One in Nazareth." Pages 231–51 in *From Jesus to John: Festschrift Marinus de Jonge*. Edited by M. C. De Boer. Sheffield: JSOT.

————. 1993b. "The Beginning of Q: A Proposal." Pages 60–78 in *The Quest for Q*. Edinburgh: T&T Clark.

Cavallin, C. 1985. "'Bienheureux seras-tu . . . à la résurrection des justes.' Le macarisme de lc 14,14." Pages 531–46 in *À cause de l'évangile: Festschrift Jacques Dupont*. LeDiv 123. Paris: Cerf.

Cerfaux, L. 1985. "À propos de Lc., VIII,15." Pages 111–22 in *Recueil Lucien Cerfaux III*. 2nd edition. BEThL 71. Leuven: Peeters.

Chance, J. B. 1988. *Jerusalem, the Temple, and the New Age in Luke–Acts*. Macon, Ga.: Mercer University Press.

Charlesworth, J. H., ed. 1983–1985. *The Old Testament Pseudepigrapha*. 2 vols. New York: Doubleday.

Charlesworth, J. H., H. Lichtenberger, and G. Oegema, eds. 1998. *Qumran-Messianism*. Tübingen: Mohr.

Chen, D. G. 2006. *God as Father in Luke–Acts*. StBL 92. New York: Lang.

Chenu, B. 2003. *Disciples d'Emmaüs*. Paris: Bayard.

Cheong, C.-S. A. 2001. *A Dialogic Reading of the Steward Parable (Luke 16:1-9)*. StBL 28. New York: Lang.

Chilton, B. 1979. *God in Strength*. SNTU.B 1. Freistadt: Plöchl.

Cho, Y. 2003. "Spirit and Kingdom in Luke–Acts." *AJPS* 6: 173–97.

Chow, S. 1995. *The Sign of Jonah Reconsidered*. CB.NT 27. Stockholm: Almqvist & Wiksell.

Christ, F. 1970. *Jesus Sophia*. AThANT 57. Zürich: Fischer.

Clemen, C. 1973 [1924]. *Religionsgeschichtliche Erklärung des Neuen Testaments*. Berlin: Walter de Gruyter.

Clivaz, C. 2002. "Douze noms pour une main: nouveaux regards sur Judas à partir de Lc 22.21-2." *NTS* 48: 400–416.

———. 2003. "Quand le récit fait parler le discours (Luc 22,28-30)." Pages 368–85 in *La Bible en récits. L'exégèse biblique à l'heure du lecteur*. Edited by D. Marguerat. MoBi 48. Geneva: Labor et Fides.

———. 2005. "The Angel and the Sweat Like 'Drops of Blood' (Lk 22:43-44): $\mathfrak{P}^{69}$ and f^{13}." *HThR* 98: 419–40.

Cohn-Sherbok, D. M. 1979. "An Analysis of Jesus' Arguments concerning the Plucking of Grain on the Sabbath." *JSNT* 2: 31–41.

Coleridge, M. 1993. *The Birth of the Lucan Narrative: Narrative as Christology in Luke 1–2*. JSNT.S 88. Sheffield: Sheffield Academic.

———. 1997. "'You Are Witnesses' (Luke 24:48): Who Sees What in Luke." *ABR* 45: 1–19.

Collins, J. N. 1990. *Diakonia: Re-Interpreting the Ancient Sources*. Oxford: Oxford University Press.

Collins, R. F. 1976. "Luke 3:21-22, Baptism or Anointing?" *BiTod* 84: 821–32.

Conzelmann, H. 1977. *Die Mitte der Zeit*. 6th edition. BHTh 17. Tübingen: Mohr.

Correns, D. 1963. "Die Verzehntung der Raute, Lk 11,42 und MSchebi 9,1." *NT* 6: 110–12.

———. 2005. *Die Mischnah*. Wiesbaden: Marix.

Cortés, J. B. 1984. "The Greek Text of Luke 18:14a." *CBQ* 46: 255–73.

Cortés, J. B., and F. M. Gatti. 1987. "On the Meaning of Luke 16:16." *JBL* 106: 247–49.

Cosgrove, C. H. 1984. "The Divine δεῖ in Luke–Acts." *NT* 26: 168–90.

———. 2005. "A Woman's Unbound Hair in the Greco-Roman World, with Special Reference to the Story of the 'Sinful Woman' in Luke 7:36-50." *JBL*: 675–92.

Cotter, W. J. 1987. "The Parable of the Children in the Marketplace, Q (Lk) 7:31-35." *NT* 29: 289–304.

———. 1989. "Children Sitting in the Agora." *Forum* 5: 63–82.

———. 2005. "The Parable of the Feisty Widow and the Threatened Judge (Luk 18.1-8)." *NTS* 51: 328–43.

Coulot, C. 1982. "La structuration de la péricope de l'homme riche et ses différentes lectures." *RSR* 56: 240–52.

Craghan, J. F. 1967. "A Redactional Study of Lk 7,21 in the Light of Dt 19,15." *CBQ* 29: 47–61 (353–67).

Creech, R. R. 1990. "The Most Excellent Narratee: The Significance of Theophilus in Luke–Acts." Pages 107–26 in *With Steadfast Purpose: Festschrift Henry Jackson Flanders*. Edited by N. H. Keathley. Waco, Tex: Baylor University Press.

Croatto, J. S. 2005. "Jesus, Prophet Like Elijah, and Prophet-Teacher Like Moses in Luke–Acts." *JBL* 124: 451–65.

Crook, Z. A. 2000. "The Synoptic Parables of the Mustard Seed and the Leaven: A Test-Case for the Two-Document, Two-Gospel, and Farrer-Goulder Hypotheses." *JSNT* 78: 23–48.

Crossan, J. D. 1992. "Jesus and the Leper." *Forum* 8: 177–90.

Crowe, J. 1977. "The Laos at the Cross: Luke's Crucifixion Scene." Pages 75–101 in *The Language of the Cross*. Edited by A. Lacomara. Chicago: Franciscan Herald Press.

Crump, D. M. 1992a. *Jesus the Intercessor: Prayer and Christology in Luke–Acts*. WUNT 2/49. Tübingen: Mohr.

———. 1992b. "Jesus, the Victorious Scribal-Intercessor in Luke's Gospel." *NTS* 38: 51–65.

Crusius, O., and C. F. T. Müller, eds. 1897. *Babrii Fabulae Aesopeae*. Leipzig: Teubner.

Cukrowski, K. L. 1997. "'Blessed is the King': Roman Triumph and Jesus' Triumphal Entry in Luke 19:37-40." *BBTS* 87: 3–14.

Culpepper, R. A. 1999. "Parable as Commentary: The Twice-Given Vineyard." *PRSt* 26: 147–68.

Cunningham, S. 1997. *"Through Many Tribulations": The Theology of Persecution in Luke–Acts*. JSNT.S 142. Sheffield: Sheffield Academic.

Curkpatrick, S. 2002. "Dissonance in Luke 18:1-8." *JBL* 121: 107–21.

———. 2003. "A Parable Frame-up and Its Audacious Reframing." *NTS* 49: 22–38.

d'Angelo, M. R. 1990. "Women in Luke–Acts: A Redactional View." *JBL* 109: 441–61.

d'Arms, J. H. 1990. "The Roman Ckonvivium and the Idea of Equality." Pages 308–20 in *Sympotica: A Symposium on the Symposion*. Edited by O. Murray. Oxford: Clarendon.

Dalman, G. 1921. *Orte und Wege Jesu*. 2nd edition. BFChTh.M 1. Gütersloh: Bertelsmann.

———. 1926. "Viererlei Acker." *PJ* 22: 120–32.

———. 1930. *Die Worte Jesu*. Vol. 1. 2nd edition. Leipzig: Hinrichs.

———. 1964 [1928–1942]. *Arbeit und Sitte in Palästina*. 7 vols. BFChTh.M 14. Hildesheim: Olms.

————. 1989 [²1905]. *Grammatik des jüdisch-palästinischen Aramäisch nach den Idiomen des palästinischen Talmud, des Onkelostargum und Prophetentargum und der jerusalemischen Targume*. Darmstadt: Wissenschaftliche Buchgesellschaft.

Danker, F. W. 1960–1961. "The *huios* Phrases in the New Testament." *NTS* 7: 94.

Darr, J. A. 1993. "Narrator as Character: Mapping a Reader-Oriented Approach to Narration in Luke–Acts." *Semeia* 63: 43–60.

————. 1998. *Herod the Fox: Audience Criticism and Lukan Characterization*. JSNT.S 163. Sheffield: Sheffield Academic.

Dauer, A. 1984. *Johannes und Lukas*. FzB 50. Stuttgart: Katholisches Bibelwerk.

————. 1990. *Beobachtungen zur literarischen Arbeitstechnik des Lukas*. BBB 79. Frankfurt am Main: Hain.

————. 1992. "Luke 24,12—Ein Produkt lukanischer Redaktion?" Pages 1697–716 in *The Four Gospels 1992: Festschrift Frans Neirynck*. Vol. 2. Edited by F. van Segbroeck, C. M. Tuckett, G. van Belle, and J. Verheyden. BEThL 100. Leuven: Peeters.

————. 1994. "Zur Authenzizität von Lk 24,12." *EThL* 70: 294–318.

Dautzenberg, G. 1966. *Sein Leben bewahren*. StANT 14. Munich: Kösel.

Davies, W. D., and D. C. Allison. 2001–2004. *A Critical and Exegetical Commentary on the Gospel according to St Matthew*. 3 vols. ICC. London: A&C Black.

Dawsey, J. M. 1984. "Confrontation in the Temple: Luke 19:45–20:47." *PRSt* 11: 153–56.

————. 1986. *The Lukan Voice: Confusion and Irony in Luke's Gospel*. Macon, Ga.: Mercer University Press.

————. 1991. "The Origin of Luke's Positive Perception of the Temple." *PRSt* 18: 5–22.

Deatrick, E. P. 1962. "Salt, Soil, Savior." *BA* 25: 41–48.

Decock, P. B. 2002. "The Breaking of Bread in Luke 24." *Neotest.* 36: 39–56.

Degenhardt, H.-J. 1965. *Lukas—Evangelist der Armen*. Stuttgart: Katholisches Bibelwerk.

Deichgräber, R. 1967. *Gotteshymnus und Christushymnus in der frühen Christenheit*. StUNT 5. Göttingen: Vandenhoeck & Ruprecht.

Deines, R. 1993. *Jüdische Steingefäße und pharisäische Frömmigkeit*. WUNT 2/52. Tübingen: Mohr.

————. 1997. *Die Pharisäer*. WUNT 101. Tübingen: Mohr.

Deissmann, A. 1923. *Licht vom Osten*. 4th edition. Tübingen: Mohr.

Delatte, A. 1939. *Anecdota Atheniensia et alia*. Vol. 2. Liége: Faculté de Philosophie.

Delebecque, É. 1976. *Études grecques sur l'évangile de Luc*. CEA. Paris: Belles Lettres.

————. 1982. "'Secouez la poussière de vos pieds . . .'" *RB* 89: 177–84.

Delling, G. 1962. "Das Gleichnis vom gottlosen Richter." *ZNW* 53: 1–25.

————. 1963. "Partizipiale Gottesprädikationen in den Briefen des Neuen Testaments." *StTh* 17: 1–59.

————. 1972/1973. "Die Jesusgeschichte in der Verkündigung nach Acta." *NTS* 19: 373–89.

Delobel, J. 1966. "L'onction par la pécheresse." *EThL* 42: 415–75.

————. 1985. "Luke 6,5 in Codex Bezae." Pages 453–77 in *À cause de l'évangile: Festschrift Jacques Dupont*. LeDiv 123. Paris: Cerf.

————. 1989. "La rédaction de Lc., IV,14-16a et le 'Bericht vom Anfang.'" Pages 113–33, 306–12 in *The Gospel of Luke*. 2nd edition. Edited by F. Neirynck. BEThL 32. Leuven: Peeters.

————. 1992. "Lk 7,47 in Its Context." Pages 1581–90 in *The Four Gospels 1992: Festschrift Frans Neirynck*. Vol. 2. Edited by F. van Segbroeck, C. M. Tuckett, G. van Belle, and J. Verheyden. BEThL 100. Leuven: Peeters.

————. 1997. "Luke 23:34a: A Perpetual Text-critical Crux?" Pages 25–36 in *Sayings of Jesus: Canonical and Non-Canonical: Festschrift Tjitze Baarda*. Edited by W. L. Petersen, J. S. Vos, and H. J. de Jonge. NT.S 89. Leiden: Brill.

Deltombe, F. 1982. "Désormais tu rendras la vie à des hommes (Luc V,10)." *RB* 89: 492–97.

Demel, S. 1991. "Jesu Umgang mit Frauen nach dem Lukasevangelium." *BN* 57: 41–45.

Denaux, A. 1989. "L'hypocrise des Pharisiens et le dessein de Dieu: Analyse de Lc., XIII,31-33." Pages 155–95, 316–23 in *L'évangile de Luc–The Gospel of Luke*. 2nd edition. Edited by F. Neirynck. BEThL 32. Leuven: Leuven University Press.

————. 1993. "The Delineation of the Lukan Travel Narrative within the Overall Structure of the Gospel of Luke." Pages 357–92 in *The Synoptic Gospels*. Edited by C. Focant. BEThL 110. Leuven: Peeters.

————. 1997. "Old Testament Models for the Lukan Travel Narrative." Pages 271–305 in *The Scriptures in the Gospels*. Edited by C. M. Tuckett. BEThL 131. Leuven: Peeters.

————. 2001. "The Parable of the Talents/Pounds (Q 19,2-27): A Reconstruction of the Q Text." Pages 429–60 in *The Sayings Source Q and the Historical Jesus*. Edited by A. Lindemann. BEThL 158. Leuven: Peeters.

————. 2002. "The Parable of the King-Judge (Lk 19,12-28) and Its Relation to the Entry Story (Lk 19,29-44)." *ZNW* 93: 35–57.

Denis, A.-M., ed. 1970. *Fragmenta Pseudepigraphorum quae supersunt Graeca*. Leiden: Brill.

Denk, J. 1904. "Camelus: 1. Kamel, 2. Schiffstau." *ZNW* 5: 256–57.

Derrett, J. D. M. 1970. *Law in the New Testament*. London: Darton, Longman & Todd.

————. 1971. "Law in the New Testament: The Palm Sunday Colt." *NT* 13: 241–58.

————. 1972a. "'Eating up the Houses of Widows.'" *NT* 14: 1–9.

————. 1972b. "'Take Thy Bond . . . and Write Fifty' (Luke XVI.6): The Nature of the Bond." *JThS* 23: 438–40.

————. 1982. "The Friend at Midnight." Pages 31–41 in *Studies in the New Testament*. Vol. 3. Leiden: Brill.

————. 1993. "Getting on Top of a Demon (Luke 4:39)." *EvQ* 65: 99–109.

————. 1995. "Luke 6:5D Reexamined." *NT* 37: 232–48.

————. 2002. "Choosing the Lowest Seat: Lk 14,7-11." *EstB* 60: 147–68.

Despotis, A. 2009. *The Parable of the Rich Man and Lazarus: A Comparative Study on Patristic and Modern Interpretation (in Greek).* Bibliotheca Biblica 43. Thessaloniki: Pournaras Press.

Dexinger, F. 1992. "Der Ursprung der Samaritaner im Spiegel der frühen Quellen." Pages 67–140 in *Die Samaritaner.* Edited by F. Dexinger and R. Pummer. WdF 604. Darmstadt: Wissenschaftliche Buchgesellschaft.

Dibelius, M. 1911. *Die urchristliche Überlieferung von Johannes dem Täufer.* FRLANT 15. Göttingen: Vandenhoeck & Ruprecht.

————. 1953 [1932]. "Jungfrauensohn und Krippenkind." Pages 1–78 in *Botschaft und Geschichte.* Tübingen: Mohr.

————. 1968. *Aufsätze zur Apostelgeschichte.* 5th edition. Edited by H. Greeven. FRLANT 60. Göttingen: Vandenhoeck & Ruprecht.

————. 1971. *Die Formgeschichte des Evangeliums.* 6th edition. Tübingen: Mohr.

Dieckmann, H. 1925. "Das fünfzehnte Jahr des Caesar Tiberius." *Bib.* 6: 63–67.

Diefenbach, M. 1993. *Die Komposition des Lukasevangelium unter Berücksichtigung antiker Rhetorikelemente.* FThSt 43. Frankfurt am Main: Knecht.

Diehl, E. 1948–1952. *Anthologia Lyrica Graeca.* 2 Vols. 3rd edition. Leipzig: Teubner.

Diels, H. 1879. *Doxographi Graeci.* Berlin: Reimer.

Dietrich, W. 1972. *Das Petrusbild der lukanischen Schriften.* BWANT 94. Stuttgart: Kohlhammer.

Dihle, A. 1962. *Die Goldene Regel.* SAW 7. Göttingen: Vandenhoeck & Ruprecht.

————. 1968. *Der Kanon der zwei Tugenden.* Cologne: Westdeutscher.

Dillmann, R. 1994. "Das Lukasevangelium als Tendenzschrift. Leserlenkung und Leseintention in Lk 1,1-4." *BZ NF* 38: 86–93.

————. 2000. "Die lukanische Kindheitsgeschichte als Aktualisierung frühjüdischer Armenfrömmigkeit." *SNTU.A* 25: 76–97.

Dillon, R. J. 1978. *From Eye-Witnesses to Ministers of the Word: Tradition and Composition in Luke 24.* AnBib 82. Rome: Biblical Institute Press.

————. 1991. "Ravens, Lillies, and the Kingdom of God (Matthew 6:25-33/Luke 12:22-31)." *CBQ* 55: 605–27.

————. 2007. "Simeon as a Lucan Spokesman (Lk 2,29-35)." Pages 189–217 in *"Il verbo di Dio è vivo": Festschrift Albert Vanhoye.* AnBib 165. Rome: Pontifical Biblical Institute.

Dindorf, W., ed. 1964. *Aristides.* Vol. 1. Hildesheim: Olms.

————. 1969. *Harpocrationis Lexicon in decem oratores Atticos.* Groningen: Bouma.

Doble, P. 1996. *The Paradox of Salvation.* MSSNTS 87. Cambridge: Cambridge University Press.

Dobson, B. 1974. "The Significance of the Centurion and 'Primipilaris' in the Roman Army and Administration." Pages 392-434 in *ANRW* II: 2/1.

Doering, L. 1999. *Schabbat.* TSAJ 78. Tübingen: Mohr.

Dölger, F. J. 1925. *Sol Salutis: Gebet und Gesang im christlichen Altertum, mit besonder Rücksicht auf die Ostung in Gebet und Liturgie.* 2nd edition. LF 4/5. Münster: Aschendorff.

———. 1934. "Der Einfluss des Origenes auf die Beurteilung der Epilepsie und Mondsucht im christlichen Ahertiim." *Antike und Christentum* 4: 95–109.

Dömer, M. 1978. *Das Heil Gottes: Studien zur Theologie des lukanischen Doppelwerks.* BBB 51. Cologne: Hanstein.

Donahue, J. 1971. "Tax Collectors and Sinners: An Attempt at Identification." *CBQ* 33: 39–61.

Dormeyer, D. 1974. "Literarische und theologische Analyse der Parabel Lukas 14,15-24." *BiLe* 15: 206–19.

———. 1989. *Evangelium als literarische und theologische Gattung.* EdF 263. Darmstadt: Wissenschaftliche Buchgesellschaft.

———. 2004. "Die Apotheose in Seneca 'Apocolocyntosis' und die Himmelfahrt Lk 24,50-53; Acts 1,9-11." Pages 125–42 in *Testimony and Interpretation: Festschrift Petr Pokorný.* Edited by J. Mrázek and J. Roskovec. JSNT.S 272. London: T&T Clark.

Dörrfuss, E. M. 1991. "'Wie eine Taube.'" *BN* 57: 7–13.

Downing, F. G. 1992. "The Ambiguity of the 'Pharisee and the Toll-Collector': Luke (18:9-14) in the Greco-Roman World of Late Antiquity." *CBQ* 54: 80–99.

Dreizehnter, A. 1978. *Die rhetorische Zahl: Quellenkristische Untersuchungen anhand der Zahlen 70 und 700.* Munich: Beck.

Drexler, H. 1967. "Zu Lukas 16,1-7." *ZNW* 58: 286–88.

———. 1968. "Die große Sünderin Lucas 7,36-50." *ZNW* 59: 159–73.

Drury, J. 1976. *Tradition and Design in Luke's Gospel.* London: Darton, Longman & Todd.

Duff, P. B. 1992. "The March of the Divine Warrior and the Advent of the Greco-Roman King." *JBL* 111: 55–71.

Dumoulin, P. 1999. "La parabole de la veuve, de Ben Sira 35,11-24 à Luc 18,1-8." Pages 169–79 in *Treasures of Wisdom: Festschrift Maurice Gilbert.* Edited by N. Calduch-Benages and J. Vermeylen. BEThL 143. Leuven: Peeters.

Dunn, J. D. G. 1988. *Romans 9–16.* WBC 38. Dallas, Tex.: Word Books.

———. 2003. "Altering the Default Setting: Re-envisaging the Early Transmission of the Jesus Tradition." *NTS* 49: 139–75.

Duplacy, J. 1981. "Le véritable disciple: Un essai d'analyse sémantique de Luc 6,43-49." *RSR* 69: 71–86.

———. 1987. "L'histoire la plus ancienne et la forme originale du texte en Luc 22,43-44." Pages 349–85 in *Études de critique textuelle du Nouveau Testament.* Edited by J. Duplacy. Leuven: Peeters.

———. 1989. "P75 (*Pap. Bodmer XIV–XV*) et les formes les plus anciennes du texte de Luc." Pages 21–38 in *L'évangile de Luc–The Gospel of Luke.* Edited by F. Neirynck. BEThL 2. Leuven: Leuven University Press.

Dupont, J. 1957–1973. *Les Béatitudes.* 3 vols. 2nd edition. Paris: Gabalda.

———. 1967. "'Beaucoup viendront du levant et du couchant . . .' (Matthieu 8,11-12; Luc 13,28-29)." *ScEc* 19: 153–67.

————. 1969. *Die Versuchung Jesu in der Wüste*. SBS 37. Stuttgart: Katholisches Bibelwerk.

————. 1975. "Le couple parabolique du sénevé et du levain." Pages 331–45 in *Jesus Christus in Historie und Theologie: Festschrift Hans Conzelmann*. Edited by G. Strecker. Tübingen: Mohr.

————. 1984. "Le maître et son serviteur (Luc 17,7-10)." *EThL* 60: 233–51.

————. 1985. *Études sur les évangiles synoptiques*. 2 vols. BEThL 70A–B. Leuve: Peeters.

————. 1991. "Le riche publicain Zachée est aussi un fils d'Abraham (Luc 19,1-10)." Pages 265–76 in *Der Treue Gottes Trauen: Beiträge zum Werk des Lukas: Festschrift Gerhard Schneider*. Edited by C. Bussmann and W. Radl. Freiburg: Herder.

Dussaut, L. 1987. "Le triptyque des apparitions en Luc 24." *RB* 94: 161–213.

Ebener, D. 1981. *Die Griechische Anthologie*. Berlin: Aufbau.

Ebner, M. 1998. *Jesus—ein Weisheitslehrer?* HBS 15. Freiburg im Breisgau: Herder.

Eckstein, H.-J. 2002. "Die Wirklichkeit der Auferstehung Jesu. Lukas 24.34 als Beispiel früher formelhafter Zeugnisse." Pages 1–30 in *Die Wirklichkeit der Auferstehung*. Edited by H.-J. Eckstein and M. Welker. Neukirchen-Vluyn: Neukirchener.

Eco, U. 1987. *Lector in fabula: Die Mitarbeit der Interpretation in erzählenden Texten*. Munich: Hanser.

Edelstein, E. J., and L. Edelstein. 1945. *Asclepius*. Vol. 1. Baltimore: John's Hopkins Press.

Edwards, J. R. 2002. "The Gospel of the Ebionites and the Gospel of Luke." *NTS* 48: 568–86.

Edwards, R. A. 1969. "The Eschatological Correlative as a Gattung in the New Testament." *ZNW* 60: 9–20.

————. 1971. *The Sign of Jonah in the Theology of the Evangelists and Q*. SBT. 2nd Ser. 18. London: SCM Press.

Egelkraut, H. L. 1976. *Jesus' Mission to Jerusalem: A Redaction Critical Study of the Travel Narrative in the Gospel of Luke*. EHS.T 80. Frankfurt am Main: Peter Lang.

Ehrhardt, A. 1958. "Parakatatheke." *ZSRG.R* 75: 32–90.

Ehrman, B. D., and M. A. Plunkett. 1983. "The Angel and the Agony: The Textual Problem of Luke 22:43-44." *CBQ* 45: 401–16.

Ehrman, B. D., and Z. Pleše. 2011. *The Apocryphal Gospels: Texts and Translations*. Oxford: Oxford University Press.

Elbert, P. 2004. "An Observation on Luke's Composition and Narrative Style of Questions." *CBQ* 66: 98–109.

Elliott, J. H. 1994. "The Evil Eye and the Sermon on the Mount." *Bib.Int.* 2: 51–84.

Elliott, J. K. 1971/1972. "Does Luke 2.41-52 Anticipate the Resurrection?" *ET* 83: 87–89.

————. 1973. "Did the Lord's Prayer Originate with John the Baptist?" *ThZ* 29: 215.

————. 1988. "Anna's Age (Luke 2:36-37)." *NT* 30: 100–102.

Ellis, E. E. 1975. "The Composition of Luke 9 and the Source of Its Christology." Pages 120–27 in *Current Issues in Biblical and Patristic Interpretation: Festschrift Merrill C. Tenney*. Edited by G. F. Hawthorne. Grand Rapids: Eerdmans.

Emmrich, M. 2000. "The Lucan Account of the Beelzebul Controversy." *WThJ* 62: 267–79.

Engelbrecht, J. 1989. "The Empty Tomb (Lk 24:1-12) in Historical Perspective." *Neotest.* 23: 235–49.

Ennulat, A. 1994. *Die "Minor Agreements."* WUNT 2/62. Tübingen: Mohr.

Erdmann, G. 1932. *Die Vorgeschichten des Lukas- und Matthäusevangeliums und Vergils vierte Ekloge*. FRLANT NF 30. Göttingen: Vandenhoeck & Ruprecht.

Erickson, R. J. 1993. "The Jailing of John and the Baptism of Jesus: Luke 3.19-21." *JETS* 36: 455–66.

Erlemann, K. 1988. *Das Bild Gottes in den synoptischen Gleichnissen*. BWANT 126. Stuttgart: Kohlhammer.

————. 1995. *Naherwartung und Parusieverzögerung im Neuen Testament*. TANZ 17. Tübingen: Francke.

Ernst, J. 1978. "Gastmahlgespräche: Luk. 14,1-24." Pages 57–78 in *Die Kirche des Anfangs: Festschrift Heinz Schürmann*. Edited by R. Schnackenburg, J. Ernst, and J. Wanke. Freiburg: Herder.

————. 1989. *Johannes der Täufer*. BZNW 53. Berlin: Walter de Gruyter.

————. 1991a. *Lukas. Ein theologisches Portrait*. 2nd edition. Düsseldorf: Patmos.

————. 1991b. "Der Spruch von den 'frommen' Sündern und den 'unfrommen' Gerechten (Lk 7,29f)." Pages 197–213 in *Der Treue Gottes trauen. Beiträge zum Werk des Lukas: Festschrift Gerhard Schneider*. Edited by C. Bussmann and W. Radl. Freiburg: Herder.

Esler, P. F. 1987. *Community and Gospel in Luke–Acts*. MSSNTS 57. Cambridge: Cambridge University Press.

Evans, C. A. 1989. *To See and Not Perceive: Isaiah 6.9-10 in Early Jewish and Christian Interpretation*. Sheffield: JSOT Press.

————. 1992. "Predictions of the Destruction of the Herodian Temple in the Pseudepigrapha, Qumran Scrolls, and Related Texts." *JSPE* 10: 89–147.

————. 1993a. "'He set his face': On the Meaning of Luk 9:51." Pages 92–105 in *Luke and Scripture: The Function of Sacred Tradition in Luke–Acts*. Edited by C. A. Evans and J. A. Sanders. Minneapolis: Fortress.

————. 1993b. "The Twelve Thrones of Israel: Scripture and Politics in Luke 22:24-30." Pages 154–70 in *Luke and Scripture: The Function of Sacred Tradition in Luke–Acts*. Edited by C. A. Evans and J. A. Sanders. Minneapolis: Fortress.

————. 1994. "The Pharisee and the Publican: Luke 18,9-14 and Deuteronomy 26." Pages 342–55 in *The Gospels and the Scriptures of Israel*. Edited by C. A. Evans and W. R. Stegner. JSNT.S 104. Sheffield: Sheffield Academic.

————. 1996. "Jesus' Parable of the Tenant Farmers in Light of Lease Agreements in Antiquity." *JSPE* 14: 65–83.

Evans, C. F. 1955. "The Central Section of St. Luke's Gospel." Pages 37–53 in *Studies in the Gospels: Essays in Memory of R. H. Lightfoot.* Edited by D. Nineham. Oxford: Blackwell.

Eynde, S. van den 2005. "Come and Hate? On the Interpretation of Luk 14,26." Pages 283–97 in *Luke and His Readers: Festschrift Adelbert Denaux.* Edited by R. Bieringer, G. van Belle, and J. Verheyden. BEThL 182. Leuven: Peeters.

Fabricius, C. 1985. "Zu παραχρῆμα bei Lukas." *Eranos* 83: 62–66.

Falcetta, A. 2003. *The Call of Nazareth.* CRB 53. Paris: Gabalda.

Falco, V. de. 1922. *Theologoumena arithmeticae.* Leipzig: Teubner.

Fanning, B. M. 1990. *Verbal Aspect in New Testament Greek.* OTM. Oxford: Clarendon.

Farmer, W. R. 1961/1962. "Notes on a Literary and Form-critical Analysis of Some of the Synoptic Material Peculiar to Luke." *NTS* 8: 301–16.

———. 1976 [1964]. *The Synoptic Problem: A Critical Analysis.* Dillsboro: Western North Carolina Press.

———. 1990. "The Passion Prediction Passages and the Synoptic Problem." *NTS* 36: 558–70.

———. 1998. "The Present State of the Synoptic Problem." Pages 11–36 in *Literary Studies in Luke–Acts: Festschrift J. B. Tyson.* Edited by R. P. Thompson and T. E. Phillips. Macon, Ga.: Mercer University Press.

Farris, M. 1999. "A Tale of Two Taxations (Luke 18:10-14)." Pages 23–33 in *Jesus and His Parables.* Edited by V. G. Shillington. Edinburgh: T&T Clark.

Farris, S. C. 1981. "On Discerning Semitic Sources in Luke 1-2." Pages 201–37 in *Gospel Perspectives.* Vol. 2. Edited by R. T. France and D. Wenham. Sheffield: JSOT.

———. 1985. *The Hymns of Luke's Infancy Narratives.* JSNT.S 9. Sheffield: Sheffield Academic.

Fassl, P. 1981. "'Und er lobte den ungerechten Verwalter' (Lk 16,8a)." Pages 109–43 in *Eschatologie: Festschrift Engelbert Neuhäusler.* Edited by R. Kilian, K. Funk, and P. Fassl. St. Ottilien: EOS.

Feine, P. 1891. *Eine vorkanonisch Überlieferung des Lukas in Evangelium und Apostelgeschichte.* Gotha: Perthes.

Feldkämper, L. 1978. *Der betende Jesus als Heilsmittler nach Lukas.* Vol. 29. VMStA. St. Augustin: Steyler.

Feldmeier, R. 1987. *Die Krisis des Gottessohnes.* WUNT 2/21. Tübingen: Mohr.

———. 1992. *Die Christen als Fremde.* WUNT 64. Tübingen: Mohr.

Fernández Marcos, N. 1987. "La unción de Salomón y la entrada de Jesús en Jerusalén: 1 Re 1,33-40 / Lc 19,35-40." *Bib.* 68: 89–97.

Festa, N., ed. 1902. *Mythographi Graeci.* Vol. 3/2. Leipzig: Teubner.

Feuillet, A. 1959. "Le récit lucanien de la tentation (Lc 4,1-13)." *Bib.* 40: 613–31.

———. 1981. "La double venue du règne de Dieu et du fils de l'homme en Luc XVII,20—XVIII,8." *RThom* 81: 5–33.

Fischbach, S. M. 1992. *Totenerweckungen.* FzB 69. Stuttgart: Katholisches Bibelwerk.

Fischer, M. 2001. "Kapharnaum: Eine Retrospektive." *JAC* 44: 142–67.

Fischer, U. 1978. *Eschatologie und Jenseitserwartung im hellenistischen Diasporajudentum*. BZNW 44. Berlin: Walter de Gruyter.

Fitzmyer, J. A. 1962. "Papyrus Bodmer XIV: Some Features of Our Oldest Text of Luke." *CBQ* 24: 170–79.

———. 1964. "The Story of the Dishonest Manager (Lk 16:1-13)." *TS* 25: 23–42.

———. 1978. "The Composition of Luke, Chapter 9." Pages 139–52 in *Perspectives in Luke–Acts*. Edited by C. H. Talbert. Edinburgh: T&T Clark.

———. 1981. "The Virginal Conception of Jesus in the New Testament." Pages 41-78 in *To Advance the Gospel*. New York: Crossroad.

———. 1989. *Luke the Theologian*. New York: Paulist Press.

———. 2003. "And Lead Us Not into Temptation." *Bib.* 84: 259–73.

Flebbe, J. 2005. "Alter und neuer Wein bei Lukas." *ZNW* 96: 171–87.

Fleckenstein, K.-H., ed. 2003. *Emmaus in Judäa: Geschichte–Exegese–Archäologie*. BAZ 11. Gießen: Brunnen.

Fleddermann, H. T. 1982. "A Warning about the Scribes." *CBQ* 44: 52–67.

———. 1989. "The Mustard Seed and the Leaven in Q, the Synoptics, and Thomas." *SBLSP* 28: 216–36.

———. 1995. *Mark and Q: A Study of the Overlap Texts*. BEThL 122. Leuven: Peeters.

———. 2003. "Mid-level Techniques in Luke's Redaction of Q." *EThL* 79: 53–71.

———. 2005a. *Q. A Reconstruction and Commentary*. BiTS 1. Leuven: Peeters.

———. 2005b. "Three Friends at Midnight (Luke 11.5-8)." Pages 265–82 in *Luke and His Readers: Festschrift Adelbert Denaux*. Edited by R. Bieringer, G. van Belle, and J. Verheyden. BEThL 182. Leuven: Peeters.

Fletcher-Louis, C. H. T. 1997. *Luke–Acts: Angels, Christology and Soteriology*. WUNT 2/94. Tübingen: Mohr.

———. 2000. "Jesus Inspects His Priestly War Party (Luke 14.25-35)." Pages 126–43 in *The Old Testament in the New Testament: Festschrift J. Lionel North*. Edited by S. Moyise. JSNT.S 189. Sheffield: Sheffield Academic.

———. 2003. "'Leave the Dead to Bury Their Own Dead.'" *JSNT* 26: 39–68.

Flückiger, F. 1972. "Luk. 21,20-24 und die Zerstörung Jerusalems." *ThZ* 28: 385–90.

Flückiger-Guggenheim, D. 1984. *Göttliche Gäste: Die Einkehr von Göttern und Heroen in der griechischen Mythologie*. Bern: Lang.

Flusser, D. 1981. "'Sie wissen nicht, was sie tun.'" Pages 393–410 in *Kontinuität und Einheit: Festschrift Franz Mussner*. Edited by P.-G. Müller and W. Stencer. Freiburg: Herder.

Focke, F. 1923. "Synkrisis." *Hermes* 58: 327–68.

Forbes, G. W. 2000. *The God of Old: The Role of the Lukan Parables in the Purpose of Luke's Gospel*. JSNT.S 198. Sheffield: Sheffield Academic.

Ford, R. C. 1920–1921. "St. Luke and Lucius of Cyrene." *ET* 32: 219–20.

Forestell, J. T. 1961. "The Old Testament Background of the Magnificat." *MarSt* 12: 205–44.

Foster, R. A., and W. D. Shiell. 1997. "The Parable of the Sower and the Seed in Luke 8:1-10: Jesus' Parable of Parables." *RExp* 94: 259–67.

Fowl, S. E. 1993. "Receiving the Kingdom of God as a Child: Children and Riches in Luke 18.15ff." *NTS* 39: 153–58.

Fraenkel, E. 1960. "Eine Anfangsformel attischer Reden." *Glotta* 39: 1–5.

Frankenmölle, H. 1983. "Die Offenbarung an die Unmündigen." Pages 80–108 in *Biblische Handlungsanweisungen*. Mainz: Grünewald.

Franz, G. 1995. "The Parable of the Two Builders." *ABW* 3: 6–11.

Freed, E. D. 1987. "The Parable of the Judge and the Widow (Luke 18.1-8)." *NTS* 33: 38–60.

Frenschkowski, M. 1997. *Offenbarung und Epiphanie*. Vol. 2. WUNT 2/80. Tübingen: Mohr.

Freudenberger, R. 1968–1969. "Zum Text der zweiten Vaterunserbitte." *NTS* 15: 419–32.

Fridrichsen, A. 1928. "Randbemerkungen zur Kindheitsgeschichte bei Lukas." *SO* 6: 33–38.

———. 1994. *Exegetical Writings: A Selection*. Translated by C. C. Caragounis and T. Fornberg. WUNT 76. Tübingen: Mohr.

Friedl, A. 1996. *Das eschatologische Gericht in Bildern aus dem Alltag*. ÖBS 14. Frankfurt am Main: Lang.

Friedrich, G. 1973. "Lk 9,51 und die Entrückungschristologie des Lukas." Pages 48–77 in *Orientierung an Jesus: Festschrift Josef Schmid*. Edited by P. Hoffmann, N. Brox, and W. Pesch. Freiburg: Herder.

Friedrichsen, T. A. 1989. "The Matthew-Luke Agreements against Mark: A Survey of Recent Studies." Pages 335–92 in *L'évangile de Luc–The Gospel of Luke*. Edited by F. Neirynck. BEThL 2. Leuven: Leuven University Press.

———. 1992. "'Minor' and 'Major' Matthew-Luke Agreements against Mark 4,30-32." Pages 649–76 in *The Four Gospels 1992: Festschrift Frans Neirynck*. Vol. 2. Edited by F. van Segbroeck, C. M. Tuckett, G. van Belle, and J. Verheyden. BEThL 100. Leuven: Peeters.

———. 1996. "Luke 9,22—A Matthean Foreign Body?" *EThL* 72: 398–407.

———. 2001a. "A Note on καὶ διχοτομήσει αὐτόν (Luke 12:46 and the Parallel in Matthew 24:51)." *CBQ* 63: 258–64.

———. 2001b. "The Parable of the Mustard Seed Mark 4,30-32 and Q 13,18-19." *EThL* 57: 297–317.

———. 2003. "A Note on the Lamp Saying, Mark 4,21 and Q 11,33." *EThL* 79: 423–30.

———. 2005. "The Temple, a Pharisee, a Tax Collector, and the Kingdom of God." *JBL* 124: 89–119.

Fuchs, A. 1980a. *Die Entwicklung der Beelzebulkontroverse bei den Synoptikern*. SNTU.B 5. Linz: SNTU.

———. 1980b. "Die Überscheidungen von Mk und 'Q' nach B. H. Streeter und E. P. Sanders und ihre wahre Bedeutung (Mk 1,1-8 Par.)." Pages 28–81 in *Wort in der Zeit. Neutestamentliche Studien: Festschrift Karl Heinrich Rengstorf*. Edited by W. Haubeck and M. Bachmann. Leiden: Brill.

———. 1992a. "Schrittweises Wachstum: Zur Entwicklung der Perikope Mk 5,21-43 par Mt 9,18-26 par Lk 8,40-56." *SNTU* 17: 5–53.

————. 1992b. "Die synoptische Aussendungsrede in quellenkritischer und traditionsgeschichtlicher Sicht." *SNTU.A* 17: 77–168.

————. 1994. "Das Zeichen des Jona: Vom Rückfall." *SNTU.A* 19: 131–60.

————. 1997. "Die Agreement-Redaktion von Mk 6,32-44 par Mt 14,13-21 par Lk 9,10b-17." *SNTU.A* 22: 181–203.

————. 1998. "Die agreements der Einzugsperikope." *SNTU.A* 13: 215–27.

————. 2001a. "Die Frage nach der Vollmacht Jesu." *SNTU.A* 26: 27–58.

————. 2001b. "Mehr als Davids Sohn." *SNTU.A* 26: 111–28.

————. 2001c. "Die Pharisäerfrage nach der Kaisersteuer Mk 12,13-17 par Mt 22,15-22 par Lk 20,20-26." *SNTU.A* 26: 59–110.

————. 2001d. "Die Sadduzäerfrage Mk 12,18-27 par Mt 22,23-33 par Lk 20,27-40." *SNTU.A* 26: 83–110.

————. 2002. "Das Verhältnis der synoptischen agreements zur johanneischen Tradition, untersucht anhand der messianischen Perikope Mk 6,32-44 par Mt 14,13-21 par Lk 9,10b-17; John 6,1-5." *SNTU.A* 27: 85–115.

————. 2004–2007. *Spuren von Deuteromarkus*. 5 vols. SNTU [N.F.] 1–5. Münster: Lit.

————. 2006. "Zum Stand der Synoptischen Frage—H. Klein. Fortschritt in kleinen Schritten." *SNTU* 31: 203–41.

————. 2009. "Plädoyer für das Gestrige?—Anfragen an Michael Wolter." *SNTU* 34: 207–46.

Fuchs, G. 2003. *Der Becher des Sonnengottes: zur Entwicklung des Motivs "Becher des Zorns."* BVBi 4. Münster: Lit.

Fuller, M. E. 2006. *The Restoration of Israel: Israel's Re-gathering and the Fate of the Nations in Early Jewish Literature and Luke–Acts*. BZNW 138. Berlin: Walter de Gruyter.

Funk, R. W. 1973. "The Looking-Glass Tree Is for the Birds." *Int.* 27: 3–9.

Furlani, J., ed. 1968. *Fontes Iuris Romani Antejustiniani*. Florence: G. Barberà.

Fusco, V. 1982. "L'accord mineur Mt 13,11a / Lc 8,10a contre Mc 4,11a." Pages 355–61 in *Logia. Mémorial Joseph Coppens*. Edited by J. Delobel and T. Baarda. BEThL 59. Leuven: Peeters.

————. 1992. "'Point of View' and 'Implicit Reader' in Two Eschatological Texts: Luke 19,11-28; Acts 1,6-8." Pages 1677–96 in *The Four Gospels 1992: Festschrift Frans Neirynck*. Vol. 2. Edited by F. van Segbroeck, C. M. Tuckett, G. van Belle, and J. Verheyden. BEThL 100. Leuven: Peeters.

————. 1993a. "Le discours eschatologique lucanien: 'Rédaction' et 'composition.'" Pages 311–55 in *The Synoptic Gospels*. Edited by C. Focant. BEThL 110. Leuven: Peeters.

————. 1993b. "Problems of Structure in Luke's Eschatological Discourse (Lk 21:7-36)." Pages 72–92, 225–32 in *Luke and Acts: Festschrift Emilio Raco*. Edited by G. Marconi and G. O'Collins. New York: Paulist Press.

Gagnon, R. A. J. 1993. "Statistical Analysis and the Case of the Double Delegation in Luke 7:3-7." *CBQ* 55: 709–31.

————. 1994. "Luke's Motives for Redaction in the Account of the Double Delegation in Luke 7:1-10." *NT* 36: 122–45.

Gaiser, F. J. 1996. "'Your Faith Has Made You Well': Healing and Salvation in Luke 17:12-19." *W&W* 16: 291–301.

Ganser-Kerperin, H. 2000. *Das Zeugnis des Tempels. Studien zur Bedeutung des Tempelmotivs im lukanischen Doppelwerk.* NTA NF 36. Münster: Aschendorff.

Garland, D. E. 1979. *The Intention of Matthew 23.* Leiden: Brill.

Garrett, S. R. 1989. *The Demise of the Devil: Magic and the Demonic in Luke's Writings.* Minneapolis: Fortress.

———. 1991. "'Lest the Light in You Be Darkness.'" *JBL* 110: 93–105.

Gathercole, S. 2003a. "Jesus' Eschatological Vision of the Fall of Satan." *ZNW* 94: 143–63.

———. 2003b. "The Justification of Wisdom." *NTS* 49: 476–88.

———. 2005. "The Heavenly ἀνατολή (Luke 1:78-9)." *JThS* 56: 471–88.

Gauger, J.-D., ed. 2002. *Sibyllinische Weissagungen: Griechisch–Deutsch.* 2nd edition. Düsseldorf: Artemis & Winkler.

Gault, J. A. 1990. "The Discourse Function of KAI ΕΓΕΝΕΤΟ in Luke and Acts." *OPTAT* 4: 388–99.

Geffcken, J. 1967. *Die oracula subyllina.* Leipzig: Hinrichs.

Geiger, R. 1973. *Die Lukanischen Endzeitreden.* EHS.T 16. Bern: Peter Lang.

Gemünden, P. von. 1993. *Vegetationsmetaphorik im Neuen Testament und seiner Umwelt.* NTOA 18. Göttingen: Vandenhoeck & Ruprecht.

George, A. 1970. "Le parallèle entre Jean-Baptiste et Jésus en Lc 1-2." Pages 147–71 in *Mélanges bibliques en hommage au R.P. Béda Rigaux.* Gembloux: Duculot.

———. 1978. *Études sur l'oeuvre de Luc.* Paris: Gabalda.

Gérard, J.-P. 1995. "Les riches dans la communauté lucanienne." *EThL* 71: 71–106.

Gerber, D. 2003a. "(. . .) comme il leur avait été dit. À propos des derniers mots de Luc 2,8-20." Pages 151–59 in *Raconter, interpréter, annoncer: Festschrift Daniel Marguerat.* Edited by E. Steffek and Y. Bourquin. MoBi 47. Geneva: Labor et Fides.

———. 2003b. "Le *Magnificat,* le *Benedictus,* le *Gloria* et le *Nunc Dimittis*: Quatre Hymnes en réseau pour une introduction en surplomb à Luc-Actes." Pages 353–67 in *La Bible en récits. L'exégèse biblique à l'heure du lecteur.* Edited by D. Marguerat. MoBi 48. Paris

———. 2004. "Luc 19,41-44: La mise en perspective d'un oracle de jugement." Pages 219–36 in *Le jugement dans l'un et l'autre Testament. II. Mélanges offerts à Jacques Schlosser.* Edited by C. Coulot, D. Fricker, and J. Doré. LeDiv 198. Paris: Cerf.

Gerhardsson, B. 1966. *The Testing of God's Son.* CB.NT 2/1. Lund: Gleerup.

Gerits, H. 1981. "Le message pascal au tombeau (Lc 24,1-12)." *EstTeol* 8: 3–63.

Gero, S. 1976. "The Spirit as a Dove at the Baptism of Jesus." *NT* 18: 17–35.

Gerstenberger, E. 1962. "The Woe Oracles of the Prophets." *JBL* 81: 249–63.

Giblin, C. H. 1971. "'The Things of God' in the Question Concerning Tribute to Caesar." *CBQ* 33: 510–27.

————. 1985. *The Destruction of Jerusalem according to Luke's Gospel*. AnBib 107. Rome: Biblical Institute Press.

Gibson, J. B. 1995. *The Temptations of Jesus in Early Christianity*. JSNT.S 112. Sheffield: Sheffield Academic.

Gibson, M. 1911. *The Commentaries of Isho'dad of Merv, Bishop of Ḥadatha (c. 850 A.D.)*. Vol. 1. Cambridge: Cambridge University Press.

Gielen, M. 1998. "'Und führe uns nicht in Versuchung.'" *ZNW* 89: 201–16.

Giesen, H. 1988. "Verantwortung des Christen in der Gegenwart und Heilsvollendung. Ethik und Eschatologie nach Lk 13,24 und 16,16." *ThG(M)* 31: 218–28.

————. 2005. "'Noch heute wirst du mit mir im Paradies sein' (Lk 23,43)." Pages 151–57 in *"Licht zur Erleuchtung der Heiden und Herrlichkeit für dein Volk Israel": Festschrift Josef Zmijewski*. Edited by C. G. Müller. BBB 151. Hamburg: Philo.

Gigon, O. 1953. *Kommentar zum ersten Buch von Xenophons Memorabilien*. Basel: Reinhardt.

Gill, D. 1991. "Socrates and Jesus on Non-Retaliation and Love of Enemies." *HBT* 18: 246–62.

Gillman, J. 1991. *Possessions and the Life of Faith: A Reading of Luke–Acts*. Collegeville, Minn.: Liturgical Press.

————. 2002. "The Emmaus Story in Luke–Acts Revisited." Pages 165–88 in *Resurrection in the New Testament: Festschrift Jan Lambrecht*. Edited by R. Bieringer, V. Koperski, and B. Lataire. BEThL 165. Leuven: Peeters.

Glombitza, O. 1962. "Der zwölfjährige Jesus. Luk. ii 40-52: Ein Beitrag zur Exegese der lukanischen Vorgeschichte." *NT* 5: 1–4.

————. 1971. "Die christologische Aussage des Lukas in seiner Gestaltung der drei Nachfolgeworte Lukas IX 57-62." *NovT*: 14-23.

Gnilka, J. 1962. "Der Hymnus des Zacharias." *BZ NF* 6: 215–38.

————. 1978/1979. *Das Evangelium nach Markus*. 2 vols. EKK 2. Zürich: Benziger.

Göbl, R. 1978. *Antike Numismatik*. 2 vols. Munich: Battenberg.

Goldenberg, R. 1979. "The Jewish Sabbath in the Roman World up to the Time of Constantine the Great." Pages 414–47 in *ANRW* II: 19/1.

Good, R. S. 1983. "Jesus, Protagonist of the Old, in Lk 5:33-39." *NT* 25: 19–36.

Goodspeed, E. J. 1954. "Was Theophilus Luke's Publisher?" *JBL* 73: 84.

Goor, A. 1965. "The History of the Fig in the Holy Land from Ancient Times to the Present Day." *EcBot* 19: 124–35.

Gordon, C. H. 1977. "Paternity at Two Levels." *JBL* 96: 101.

Goulder, M. D. 1989. *Luke: A New Paradigm*. 2 vols. JSNT.S 20. Sheffield Sheffield Academic.

————. 2003. "Two Significant Minor Agreements." *NT* 45: 365–73.

Gourgues, M. 1985. "Deux miracles de foi." Pages 229–49 in *À cause de l'évangile: Festschrift Jacques Dupont*. LeDiv 123. Paris: Cerf.

————. 1992. "Regroupement littéraire et équilibrage théologique. Le cas de Lc 13,1-9." Pages 1591–602 iin *The Four Gospels 1992: Festschrift Frans*

Neirynck. Vol. 2. Edited by F. van Segbroeck, C. M. Tuckett, G. van Belle, and J. Verheyden. BEThL 100. Leuven: Peeters..

———. 2002. "Du centurion de Capharnaüm au centurion de Césarée." Pages 259–70 in *Forschungen zum Neuen Testament und seiner Umwelt: Festschrift Albert Fuchs*. Edited by C. Niemand. LPTB 7. Frankfurt am Main: Lang.

Gowler, D. B. 1991. *Host, Guest, Enemy and Friend: Portraits of the Pharisees in Luke and Acts*. New York: Lang.

———. 1993. "Hospitality and Characterization in Luke 11:37-54." *Semeia* 64: 213–51.

———. 2003. "Text, Culture, and Ideology in Luke 7:1-10." Pages 89–125 in *Fabrics of Discourse: Festschrift Vernon K. Robbins*. Edited by D. B. Gowler, L. G. Bloomquist, and D. F. Watson. Harrisburg: Trinity International.

———. 2005. "'At His Gate Lay a Poor Man': A Dialogic Reading of Luke 16:16." *JBL* 106: 247–49.

Gradl, H.-G. 2005a. "Von den Kosten des Reichtums: Die Beispielerzählung vom reichen Mann und armen Lazarus (Lk 16,19-31) textpragmatisch gelesen." *MThZ* 56: 305–17.

———. 2005b. *Zwischen Arm und Reich: Das lukanische Doppelwerk in leserorientierter und textpragmatischer Perspektive*. Würzburg: Echter.

Grangaard, B. R. 1999. *Conflict and Authority in Luke 19:47 to 21:4*. StBL 8. New York: Peter Lang.

Grässer, E. 1977. *Das Problem der Parusieverzögerung in den synoptischen Evangelien und in der Apostelgeschichte*. 3rd edition. BZNW 22. Berlin: Walter de Gruyter.

———. 1985. *Der Alte Bund im Neuen*. WUNT 35. Tübingen: Mohr.

———. 1997. *An die Hebräer*. Vol. 3. EKK XVII/3. Neukirchen-Vluyn: Neukirchener.

Gray, R. 1993. *Prophetic Figures in Late Second Temple Jewish Palestine: The Evidence from Josephus* New York: Oxford University Press.

Green, D., and R. Lattimore, eds. 1960. *Greek Tragdies*. Vol. 1. 2nd edition. Chicago: University of Chicago Press.

Green, J. B. 1986. "Jesus on the Mount of Olives (Luke 22.39-46)." *JSNT* 26: 29–48.

———. 1987. "Preparation for Passover (Luke 22:7-13)." *NT* 29: 305–19.

———. 1988. *The Death of Jesus*. WUNT 2/33. Tübingen: Mohr.

———. 1989. "Jesus and a Daughter of Abraham (Luke 13:10-17)." *CBQ* 51: 643–54.

———. 1992. "The Social Status of Mary in Luke 1,5-2,52." *Bib.* 73: 457–72.

———. 1994. "The Demise of the Temple as 'Culture Center' in Luke–Acts." *RB* 101: 495–515.

———. 1995. *The Theology of the Gospel of Luke*. Cambridge: Cambridge University Press.

Green, M. P. 1983. "The Meaning of Cross-Bearing." *BS* 140: 117–33.

Greeven, H. 1982. "'Wer unter euch . . . ?'" Pages 238–55 in *Gleichnisse Jesu*. Edited by W. Harnisch. WdF 366. Darmstadt: Wissenschaftliche Buchgesellschaft.

Gregory, A. 2003. *The Reception of Luke and Acts in the Period before Irenaeus.* WUNT 2/169. Tübingen: Mohr.

———. 2005a. "Looking for Luke in the Second Century." Pages 401–15 in *Reading Luke: Interpretation, Reflection, Formation.* Edited by C. G. Bartholomew, J. B. Green, and A. C. Thiselton. Milton Keynes: Paternoster.

———. 2005b. "Prior or Posterior? The *Gospel of the Ebionites* and the Gospel of Luke." *NTS* 51: 344–60.

Grelot, P. 1981. "Étude critique de Luc 10,19." *RSR* 69: 87–100.

———. 1984. "L'arrière-plan araméen du 'Pater.'" *RB* 91: 531–56.

———. 1986. "Le cantique de Siméon (Luc II,29-32)." *RB* 93: 481–509.

Gressmann, H. 1911. "Salzdüngung in den Evangelien." *ThLZ* 32: 156–57.

———. 1918. *Vom reichen Mann und armen Lazarus.* APAW.PH 118/7. Berlin: Reimer.

Grimm, J., and W. Grimm. 1854. *Deutsches Wörterbuch.* Vol. 1. Leipzig: Hirzel.

Grimm, W. 1972. "Zum Hintergrund von Mt 8,11f / Lk 13,28f." *BZ NF* 16: 255–56.

———. 1973. "Der Dank für die empfangene Offenbarung bei Jesus und Josephus. Parallelen zu Mt 11,25-27." *BZ NF* 17: 249–56.

———. 1984. *Jesus und das Danielbuch. I. Jesu Einspruch gegen das Offenbarungssystem Daniels.* ANTJ 6. Franfurt am Main: Lang.

Grindlay, B. W. 1987. "Zacchaeus and David." *ExpT* 99: 46–47.

Gruenewald, M. 1961. "A Rabbinic Parallel to Luke 14,12." Pages 47–48 in *Der Friede: Idee und Verwirklichung—The Search for Peace: Festschrift Adolf Leschnitzer.* Edited by E. Fromm and H. Herzfeld. Heidelberg: Schneider.

Guenther, H. O. 1989. "When 'Eagles' Draw Together." *Forum* 5: 140–50.

Gueuret, A. 1989. "Le pharisien et le publicain (Lc 18,9-14)." Pages 289–308 in *Les paraboles évangéliques: Perspectives nouvelles. XIIe congrès de l'ACFEB, Lyon (1987).* Edited by J. Delorme. Paris: Cerf.

Guillaume, J. M. 1979. *Luc interprète des anciennes traditions sur la résurrection de Jésus.* EtB. Paris: Librairie Lecoffre.

Guillet, J. 1981. "Luc 22,29. Une formule johannique dans l'évangile de Luc?" *RSR* 69: 113–22.

Gulick, C. B. 1928. *Athenaeus: The Deipnosophists.* Vol. 2. LCL. London: Heinemann.

Gundry, R. H. 1995. "A Rejoinder on Matthean Foreign Bodies in Luke 10,25-28." *EThL* 71: 139–50.

———. 1999. "The Refusal of Matthean Foreign Bodies to be Exorcised from Luke 9,22; 10,25-28." *EThL* 75: 104–22.

Gunkel, H. 1921. "Die Lieder in der Kindheitsgeschichte Jesu bei Lukas." Pages 43–60 in *Festgabe von Fachgenossen und Freunden A. von Harnack zum siebzigsten Geburtstag dargebracht.* Tübingen: Mohr.

Gunter, J. J. 1980. "The Meaning and Origin of the Name 'Judas Thomas.'" *Muséon* 93: 113–48.

Güttgemanns, E. 1977. "Narrative Analyse des Streitgesprächs über den 'Zinsgroschen.'" *Ling-Bibl* 41/42: 88–105.

Guy, L. 1997. "The Interplay of the Present and Future in the Kingdom of God (Luke 19:11-14)." *TynB* 48: 119–37.

Haacker, K. 1986. "Mut zum Bitten: Eine Auslegung von Lukas 11,5-8." *ThBeitr* 17: 1–6.

———. 1987. "Erst unter Quirinius?" *BN* 38/39: 39–43.

———. 1988. "Verwendung und Vermeidung des Apostelbegriffs im lukanischen Werk." *NT* 30: 9–38.

———. 1994. "Das Gleichnis von der bittenden Witwe (Lk 18,1-8)." *ThBeitr* 25: 277–84.

Haapa, E. 1983. "Zur Selbsteinschätzung des Hauptmanns von Kapharnaum im Lukasevangelium." Pages 69–76 in *Glaube und Gerechtigkeit. In memoriam Rafael Gyllenberg*. Edited by J. Kiilunen. Helsinki: Suomen eksegeettinen seura.

Haas, H. 1922. *"Das Scherflein der Witwe" und seine Entsprechung in Tripitaka*. Leipzig: Hinrichs.

Habbe, J. 1996. *Palästina zur Zeit Jesu*. Neukirchen-Vluyn: Neukirchener.

Habicht, C. 1970. *Gottmenschentum und griechische Städte*. 2nd edition. Zet. 14. Munich: Beck.

Hagene, S. 2003. *Zeiten der Wiederherstellung*. NTA NF 42. Münster: Aschendorff.

Hahn, F. 1964. *Christologische Hoheitstitel*. 2nd edition. FRLANT 83. Göttingen: Vandenhoeck & Ruprecht.

———. 1970. "Das Gleichnis von der Einladung zum Festmahl." Pages 51–82 in *Verborum Veritas: Festschrift Gustav Stählin*. Edited by O. Böcher and K. Haacker. Wuppertal: Brockhaus.

———. 1971. "Die Bildworte vom neuen Flicken und vom jungen Wein (Mk. 2,21f parr)." *EvTh* 31: 357–75.

———. 1973. "Die Wort vom Licht Lk 11,33-36." Pages 107–38 in *Orientierung an Jesus: Festschrift Josef Schmid*. Edited by P. Hoffmann, N. Brox, and W. Pesch. Freiburg: Herder.

———. 1985. "Jesu Wort vom bergeversetzenden Glauben." *ZNW* 76: 149–69.

Hahneman, G. M. 1992. *The Muratorian Fragment and the Development of the Canon*. Oxford: Clarendon.

Halleux, R., and J. Schramp. 1985. *Les lapidaires grecs*. Paris: Les Belles Lettres.

Hamel, E. 1979. "Le Magnificat et le renversement des situations." *Gr.* 60: 55–84.

Hamm, D. 1988. "Luke 19:8 Once Again." *JBL* 107: 431–37.

———. 1991. "Zachaeus Revisited Once More." *Bib.* 72: 249–52.

———. 1994. "What the Samaritan Leper Sees: The Narrative Christology of Luke 17:11-19." *CBQ* 56: 273–87.

———. 2003. "The Tamid Service in Luke–Acts." *CBQ* 65: 215–31.

Hamm, M. D. 1987. "The Freeing of the Bent Woman and the Restoration of Israel." *JSNT* 31: 23–44.

Hampel, V. 1990. *Menschensohn und historischer Jesus*. Neukirchen-Vluyn: Neukirchener.

Hands, A. R. 1968. *Charities and Social Aid in Greece and Rome*. London: Thames & Hudson.

Hann, R. R. 1985. "Christos Kyrios in PsSol. 17.32." *NTS* 31: 620–27.

Harmansa, H.-K. 1995. *Die Zeit der Entscheidung: Lk 13,1-9 also Beispiel für das lukanische Verständnis der Gerichtspredigt Jesu an Israel.* ETS 69. Leipzig: Benno.

Harmon, S. R. 2001. "Zechariah's Unbelief and Early Jewish-Christian Relations." *BTB* 31: 10–16.

Harnack, A. von. 1904. "Über einige Worte Jesu, die nicht in den kanonischen Evangelien stehen, nebst einem Anhang über die ursprüngliche Gestalt des Vaterunsers." Pages 170–208 in *SPAW.PH 1904/1.* Heidelberg: Winter.

―――. 1906. *Lukas der Arzt: Der Verfasser des dritten Evangeliums und der Apostelgeschichte.* Leipzig: Hinrichs.

―――. 1931. "Das Magnificat der Elisabet (Luk. 1,46-55) nebst einigen Bemerkungen zu Luk. 1 und 2." Pages 62–85 in *Studie zur Geschichte des Neuen Testaments und der Alten Kirche I.* AKG 19. Berlin: Walter de Gruyter.

―――. 1980. *Kleine Schriften zur Alten Kirche.* Vol. 1, *Berliner Akademieschriften 1890–1907.* Edited by J. Dummer. Opuscula IX/1. Leipzig: Zentralantiquariat der Deutschen Demokratischen Republik.

―――. 1990. *Marcion: The Gospel of the Alien God.* Durham, N.C.: Labrynth Press.

―――. 1996 [1921/1924]. *Marcion. Das Evangelium vom fremden Gott. Eine Monographie zur Geschichte der Grundlegung der katholischen Kirche.* 2nd edition. Darmstadt: Wissenschaftliche Buchgesellschaft.

Harnisch, W. 1973. *Eschatologische Existenz.* FRLANT 110. Göttingen: Vandenhoek & Ruprecht.

―――. 1985. *Die Gleichniserzählungen Jesu.* UTB 1343. Göttingen: Vandenhoeck & Ruprecht.

Harrill, J. A. 1996. "The Indentured Labor of the Prodigal Son (Luke 15,15)." *JBL*: 714–17.

Harrington, J. M. 2000. *The Lukan Passion Narrative: The Markan Material in Luke 22.54–23.25. A Historical Survey: 1891–1997.* NTTS 30. Leiden: Brill.

Harris, R. 1927. *The Twelve Apostles.* Cambridge: Heffer.

Harrison, J. R. 2003. "Paul's Language of Grace in Its Graeco-Roman Context." WUNT 2/172. Tübingen: Mohr.

Hart, H. S. 1984. "The Coin of 'Render unto Caesar . . .'" Pages 241–48 in *Jesus and the Politics of His Day.* Edited by E. Bammel and C. F. D. Moule. Cambridge: Cambridge University Press.

Hartman, L. 1963. "A Linguistic Examination of Luke 21,13." Pages 57–75 in *Testimonium linguae.* Lund: Gleerup.

―――. 1966. *Prophecy Interpreted: The Formation of Some Jewish Apocalyptic Texts and of the Eschatological Discourse Mark 13 par.* CB.NT 1. Lund: Gleerup.

―――. 1992a. *"Auf den Namen des Herrn Jesus": Die Taufe in den neutestamentlichen Schriften.* SBS 148. Stuttgart: Katholisches Bibelwerk.

―――. 1992b. "Reading Luke 17,20-37." Pages 1663–75 in *The Four Gospels 1992: Festschrift Frans Neirynck.* Vol. 2. Edited by F. van Segbroeck, C. M. Tuckett, G. van Belle, and J. Verheyden. BEThL 100. Leuven: Peeters.

Harvey, A. E. 1982. "'The Workman Is Worthy of His Hire': Fortunes of a Proverb in the Early Church." *NT* 24: 209–21.

Hatch, E., and H. A. Redpath. 1975 [1897]. *A Concordance to the Septuagint and Other Greek Versions of the Old Testament*. 2 vols. Graz: Akademische Druck- und Verlagsanstalt.

Haubeck, W. 1985. *Loskauf durch Christus*. Giessen: Brunnen.

———. 2004. "Das Gleichnis vom ungerechten Richter und der Witwe (Lukas 18,1-8)." *ThGespr* 28: 157–68.

Hausrath, A., and H. Hunger. 1970. *Corpus gabularum Aesopicarum*. Leipzig: Teubner.

Hay, D. M. 1973. *Glory at the Right Hand: Psalm 110 in Early Christianity*. SBL. MS 18. Nashville: Abingdon.

Head, P. M. 2004. "Papyrological Perspectives on Luke's Predecessors (Luke 1:1)." Pages 30–45 in *The New Testament in Its First Century Setting: Festschrift B[ruce] W. Winter*. Edited by P. J. Williams. Grand Rapids: Eerdmans.

Heater, H. 1986. "A Textual Note on Luke 3.33." *JSNT* 28: 25–29.

Hedrick, C. W. 1994. *Parables as Poetic Fictions*. Peabody, Mass.: Hendrickson.

———. 1999. "An Unfinished Story about a Fig Tree in a Vineyard (Luke 13:6-9)." *PRSt* 26: 169–92.

Heil, C., ed. 1997. *Q 12:8-12*. Leuven: Peeters.

———. 1998. "'Πάντες ἐργάται ἀδικίας' Revisited." Pages 261–76 in *Von Jesus zum Christus: Christologische Studien: Festschrift Paul Hoffmann*. Edited by R. Hoppe and U. Busse. BZNW 93. Berlin: Walter de Gruyter.

———. 2001. "Die Q-Rekonstruktion des Internationalen Q-Projekts." *NT* 43: 128–43.

———. 2002. "Einleitung." Pages 11–28 in *Die Spruchquelle Q: Studienausgabe Griechisch und Deutsch*. Edited by P. Hoffman and C. Heil. Darmstadt: Wissenschaftliche Buchgesellschaft.

———. 2003. *Lukas und Q*. BZNW 111. Berlin: Walter de Gruyter.

Heil, C., and T. Klampfl. 2005. "Theophilus (Luke 1.3; Acts 1.1)." Pages 7–28 in *"Licht zur Erleuchtung der Heiden und Herrlichkeit für dein Volk Israel": Festschrift Josef Zmijewski*. Edited by C. G. Müller. BBB 151. Hamburg: Philo.

Heil, J. P. 1989. "Reader-Response and the Irony of Jesus before the Sanhedrin in Luke 22:66-71." *CBQ* 51: 271–84.

———. 1991. "Reader-Response and the Irony of the Trial of Jesus in Luke 23:1-25." *ScEs* 43: 175–86.

———. 1999. *The Meal Scenes in Luke–Acts*. SBL.MS 52. Atlanta, Ga.: SBL.

———. 2000. *The Transfiguration of Jesus*. AnBib 144. Rome: Pontifical Biblical Institute.

Heiligenthal, R. 1983a. *Werke als Zeichen*. WUNT 2/9. Tübingen: Mohr.

———. 1983b. "Werke der Barmherzigkeit oder Almosen?" *NT* 25: 289–301.

———. 1995. "Wehrlosigkeit oder Selbstschutz? Aspekte zum Verständnis des lukanischen Schwertwortes." *NTS* 41: 39–58.

Heininger, B. 1991. *Metaphorik, Erzählstruktur und szenisch-dramatische Gestaltung in den Sondergutgleichnissen bei Lukas.* NTA NF 24. Münster: Aschendorff.

———. 2005. "Familienkonflikte: Der zwölfjährige Jesus im Tempel (Lk 2,41-52)." Pages 49–72 in *"Licht zur Erleuchtung der Heiden und Herrlichkeit für dein Volk Israel": Festschrift Josef Zmijewski.* Edited by C. G. Müller. BBB 151. Hamburg: Philo.

Heitsch, E. 1964. *Die griechischen Dichterfragmente der römischen Kaiserzeit.* Vol. 2. Göttingen: Vandenhoeck & Ruprecht.

Helmreich, G. 1968. *Galeni De usu partium libri XVII.* Amsterdam: Hakkert.

Hemer, C. J. 1984. "ἐπιούσιος." *JSNT* 22: 81–94.

———. 1990. *The Book of Acts in the Setting of Hellenistic History.* Winona Lake, Ind.: Eisenbrauns.

Hengel, M. 1963. "Maria Magdalena und die Frauen als Zeugen." Pages 243–56 in *Abraham unser Vater: Festschrift Otto Michel.* Edited by O. Betz, M. Hengel, and P. Schmidt. Leiden: Brill.

———. 1968a. "Das Gleichnis von den Weingärtnern Mc 12,1-12 im Lichte der Zenonpapyri und der rabbinischen Gleichnisse." *ZNW* 59: 1–39.

———. 1968b. *Nachfolge und Charisma.* BZNW 34. Berlin: Walter de Gruyter.

———. 1973. *Judentum und Hellenismus.* 2nd edition. WUNT 10. Tübingen: Mohr.

———. 1977. *Crucifixion in the Ancient World and the Folly of the Message of the Cross.* Philadelphia: Fortress.

———. 1984. *Evangelienüberschriften.* SHAW.PH 3. Heidelberg: C. Winter.

———. 1993. "'Setze dich zu meiner Rechten!' Die Inthronisation Christi zur Rechten Gottes und Psalm 110,1." Pages 108–94 in *Le Trône de Dieu.* Edited by M. Philonenko. WUNT 69. Tübingen: Mohr.

———. 1997. "Der Finger und die Herrschaft Gottes in Lk 11,20." Pages 87–106 in *La main de Dieu. Die Hand Gottes.* Edited by R. Kieffer and J. Bergman. WUNT 94. Tübingen: Mohr.

Hengstl, J. 1972. *Private Arbeitsverhältnisse freier Personen in den hellenistischen Papyri bis Diokletian.* Bonn: Habelt.

———. 1978. *Griechische Papyri aus Ägypten als Zeugnisse des öffentlichen und privaten Lebens: Griechisch-deutsch.* Munich: Heimeran.

———. 2004. "Griechische Papyri und Ostraka." Pages 119–24 in *Neues Testament und Antike Kultur.* Vol. 1. Edited by K. Erlemann, K.-O. Noethlichs, K. Scherberich, and J. Zangenberg. Neukirchen-Vluyn: Neukircher.

Henten, J. W. van. 2005. "Jewish Martyrs and the Lukan Passion Narrative Revisited." Pages 325–44 in *Luke and His Readers: Festschrift Adelbert Denaux.* Edited by R. Bieringer, G. van Belle, and J. Verheyden. BEThL 182. Leuven: Peeters.

Hentschel, A. 2007. *Diakonia im Neuen Testament.* WUNT 2/226. Tübingen: Mohf-Siebeck.

Herkommer, E. 1968. "Die Topoi in den Proömien der römischen Geschichtswerke." Ph.D. diss, University of Tübingen.

Hermanson, E. A. 1999. "Kings Are Lions, but Herod Is a Fox." *BiTr* 50: 235–40.

Herrenbrück, F. 1981. "Wer waren die 'Zöllner'?" *ZNW* 72: 178–94.

———. 1987. "Zum Vorwurf der Kollaboration des Zöllners mit Rom." *ZNW* 78: 186–99.

———. 1990. *Jesus und die Zöllner*. WUNT 2/41. Tübingen: Mohr.

———. 1996. "Steuerpacht und Moral." Pages 2221–97 in *ANRW* II: 26/3.

Herrmann, W. 1999. "Baal Zebub." Pages 154–56 in *Dictionary of Deities and Demons in the Bible*. 2nd edition. Edited by K. van der Toorn. New York: Brill.

Hertford, R. T. 1971. *Pirke Aboth. The Ethics of the Talmud: Sayings of the Fathers*. New York: Schocken.

Herzog, R. 1922. "Das delphische Orakel als ethischer Preisrichter." Pages 149–58 in *Der junge Platon*. Edited by E. Hornseffer. Gießen: Töpelmann.

———. 1931. *Die Wunderheilungen von Epidauros*. Ph.S 22/3. Leipzig: Dieterich.

Heusler, E. 2000. *Kapitalprozesse im lukanischen Doppelwerk*. NTA NF 38. Münster: Aschendorff.

Heutger, N. 1983. "Münzen im Lukasevangelium." *BZ NF* 27: 97–101.

Hezser, C. 1996. "Die Verwendung der hellenistischen Gattung Chrie im frühen Christentum und Judentum." *JSJ* 27: 371–439.

Hicks, J. M. 1991. "The Parable of the Persistent Widow (Luke 18:1-8)." *RestQ* 33: 209–23.

Hieke, T. 1997. "Judging the Time." Pages 159–268 in *Q 12:49-59*. Edited by S. Carruth. Leuven: Peeters.

———, ed. 2001. *Q 6:20-12: The Beatitudes for the Poor, Hungry, and Mourning*. Leuven: Peeters.

Hilhorst, A. 1983. "The Wounds of the Risen Jesus." *EstB* 41: 165–67.

Hill, D. 1971. "The Rejection of Jesus in Nazareth (Lk iv 16-30)." *NT* 13: 161–80.

Hills, J. V. 1992. "Luke 10.18—Who Saw Satan Fall?" *JSNT* 46: 25–40.

Hiltbrunner, O. 2005. *Gastfreundschaft in der Antike und im frühen Christentum*. Darmstadt: Wissenschaftiche Buchgesellschaft.

Hintzen, J. 1991. *Verkündigung und Wahrnehmung: Über das Verhältnis von Evangelium und Leser am Beispiel Lk 16,19-31 im Rahmen des lukanischen Doppelwerkes*. BBB 81. Frankfurt am Main: Hain.

Hirschmüller, M. 1994. "Der Zensus des Quirinius nach der Darstellung des Josephus." *JETh* 8: 33–68.

Hobart, W. K. 2004 [1882]. *The Medical Language of St. Luke*. Piscataway, N.J.: Gorgias.

Hock, R. F. 1987. "Lazarus and Micyllus: Greco-Roman Backgrounds to Luke 16:19-31." *JBL* 106: 447–63.

———. 2002. "Romancing the Parables of Jesus." *PRS* 29: 11–37.

———. 2003. "The Parable of the Foolish Rich Man (Luke 12:16-20) and Graeco-Roman Conventions of Thought and Behavior." Pages 181–96 in *Early Christianity and Classical Culture: Festschrift Abraham J. Malherbe*. Edited by J. T. Fitzgerald. NT.S 110. Atlanta: Society of Biblical Literature.

Hock, R. F., and E. N. O'Neil. 1986. *The Chreia in Ancient Rhetoric*. Vol.1, *The Progymnasmata*. SBL.TT 27. Atlanta: Scholars Press.

Hoehner, H. W. 1972. *Herod Antipas*. Cambridge: Cambridge University Press.

Hoeren, T. 1995. "Das Gleichnis vom ungerechten Verwalter (Lukas 16.1-8a)." *NTS* 41: 620–29.

Hoffmann, A., and S. Kerner, eds. 2002. *Gadara, Gerasa und die Dekapolis.* Mainz: Zabern.

Hoffmann, P. 1972. *Studien zur Theologie der Logienquelle.* NTA NF 8. Münster: Aschendorff.

———. 1978. *Die Toten in Christus.* 3rd edition. Münster: Aschendorff.

———. 1995. *Tradition und Situation: Studien zur Jesusüberlieferung in der Logienquelle und den synoptischen Evangelien.* NTA NF 28. Münster: Aschendorff.

———. 1998a. "Herrscher in oder Richter über Israel? Mt 19,28 / Lk 22,28-30 in der synoptischen Überlieferung." Pages 253–64 in *Ja und Nein: Festschrift Wolfgang Schrage.* Edited by K. Wengst, G. Sass, K. Kriener, and R. Stuhlmann. Neukirchen-Vluyn: Neukirchener.

———. 1998b. "Der Menschensohn in Lukas 12.8." *NTS* 44: 357–79.

———. 1998c. *Q 22:28, 30: You Will Judge the Twelve Tribes of Israel.* Edited by C. Heil. Leuven: Peeters.

———. 2001. "Mutmaßungen über Q." Pages 255–88 in *The Sayings Source Q and the Historical Jesus.* Edited by A. Lindemann. BEThL 158. Leuven: Peeters.

Hoffmann, P., and V. Eid. 1979. *Jesus von Nazareth und eine christliche Moral.* 3rd edition. QD 66. Freiburg: Herder.

Hofius, O. 1977/1978. "Alttestamentliche Motive im Gleichnis vom verlorenen Sohn." *NTS* 24: 240–48.

———. 1990. "Fußwaschung als Erweis der Liebe." *ZNW* 81: 170–77.

Hofrichter, P. 1993. "Parallelen zum 24: Gesang der Ilias in den Engelerscheinungen des lukanischen Doppelwerkes." *ProBi* 2: 60–76.

Holgate, D. A. 1999. *Prodigality, Liberality and Meanness: The Prodigal Son in Greco-Roman Perspective.* JSNT.S 187. Sheffield: Sheffield Academic.

Holloway, P. A. 2005. "Left Behind: Jesus' Consolation of His Disciples in John 13.31-17.26." *ZNW* 96: 1–34.

Holmén, T. 1996. "The Alternatives of the Kingdom: Encountering the Semantic Restrictions of Luke 17,20-21 (ἐντὸς ὑμῶν)." *ZNW* 87: 204–29.

Holst, R. 1976. "The One Anointing of Jesus." *JBL* 95: 435–46.

Holtz, T. 1964. "Die Standespredigt Johannes des Täufers." Pages 461–74 in *Ruf und Antwort: Festschrift Emil Fuchs.* Leipzig: Koehler & Amelang.

———. 1968. *Untersuchung über die alttestamentlichen Zitate bei Lukas.* Vol. 104. TU. Berlin: Akademie.

Hombert, M., and C. Préaux. 1952. *Recherches sur le recensement dans l'Égypte romaine.* Leiden: Brill.

Hommel, H. 1983/1984. *Sebasmata.* 2 vols. WUNT 31–32. Tübingen: Mohr.

Hood, R. T. 1961. "The Genealogies of Jesus." Pages 1–15 in *Early Christian Origins: Festschrift Harold R. Willoughby.* Edited by A. P. Wikgren. Chicago: Quadrangle Books.

Hoover, R. W. 1998. "Selected Special Lukan Material in the Passion Narrative: Luke 23:33-43, 47b-49." *Forum NS* 1: 119–27.

Hoppe, R. 1998. "Das Gastmahlgleichnis Jesu (Mt 22,1-10 / Lk 14,16-24) und seine vorevangelische Traditionsgeschichte." Pages 277–93 in *Von Jesus zum Christus: Christologische Studien: Festschrift Paul Hoffmann*. Edited by R. Hoppe and U. Busse. BZNW 93. Berlin: Walter de Gruyter.

———. 2005. "Tischgespräche und Nachfolgebedingungen." Pages 115–30 in *Licht zur Erleuchtung der Heiden und Herrlichkeit für dein Volk Israel: Festschrift Josef Zmijewski*. Edited by C. G. Müller. BBB 151. Hamburg: Philo.

Horbury, W. 1998. *Jews and Christians in Contact and Controversy*. Edinburgh: T&T Clark.

Horman, J. 1979. "The Source of the Version of the Parable of the Sower in the Gospel of Thomas." *NT* 21: 326–43.

Horn, F. W. 1986. *Glaube und Handeln in der Theologie des Lukas*. 2nd edition. GTA 26. Göttingen: Vandenhoeck & Ruprecht.

———. 1992. *Das Angeld des Geistes*. FRLANT 154. Göttingen: Vandenhoeck & Ruprecht.

———. 2002. "Die politische Umkehr in der Verkündigung Jesu." Pages 53–70 in *Forschungen zum Neuen Testament und seiner Umwelt: Festschrift Albert Fuchs*. Edited by C. Niemand. LPTB 7. Frankfurt am Main: Lang.

Horsley, G. H. R. 1981. *New Documents Illustrating Early Christianity: A Review of the Greek Inscriptions and Papyri Published in 1976*. Vol. 1. North Ryde: Macquaire University.

Horst, P. W. van der. 1977. "Peter's Shadow: The Religio-Historical Background to Acts 5:15." *NTS* 23: 204–12.

———. 1991. *Ancient Jewish Epitaphs*. Kampen: Kok

———. 1997. "'The Finger of God.'" Pages 89–103 in *Sayings of Jesus: Canonical and Non-Canonical: Festschrift Tjitze Baarda*. Edited by W. L. Petersen, J. S. Vos, and H. J. de Jonge. NT.S 89. Leiden: Brill.

———. 2006. "Abraham's Bosom, the Place Where He Belonged: A Short Note on ἀπενεχθῆναι in Luke 16.22." *NTS* 52: 142–44.

Hospodar, B. 1956. "Meta Spoudes in Lk 1,39." *CBQ* 18: 14–18.

Hossfeld, F.-L., and E. Zenger. 2000. *Psalmen 51–100*. Freiburg: Herder.

———. 2005. *Psalms 2: A Commentary on Psalms 51–100*. Translated by L. M. Maloney. Minneapolis: Fortress.

Houzet, P. 1992. "Les serviteurs de l'évangile (Luc 17,5-10) sont-ils inutiles?" *RB* 99: 335–72.

Huber, K. 1995a. *Jesus in Auseinandersetzung*. FzB 75. Stuttgart: Katholisches Bibelwerk.

———. 1995b. "ΩΣ ΠΕΡΙΣΤΕΡΑ." *ProBi* 4: 87–101.

———. 1998. "'Zeichen des Jona' und 'mehr als Jona.'" *ProBi* 7: 77–94.

Hude, K. 1958. *Aretaeus*. Berlin: Akademie.

Hughes, F. W. 1993. "The Parable of the Rich Man and Lazarus (Luke 16.19-31) and Graeco-Roman Rhetoric." Pages 29–41 in *Rhetoric and the New Testament: Essays from the 1992 Heidelberg Conference*. Edited by S. E. Porter and T. H. Olbricht. JSNT.S 90. Sheffield: Sheffield Academic.

Hultgren, A. J. 1991. "Jesus and Gnosis: The Saying on Hindering Others in Luke 11:52 and Its Parallels." *Forum* 7: 165–82.

————. 2000. *The Parables of Jesus: A Commentary.* Grand Rapids: Eerdmans.

Hultgren, S. 2002. *Narrative Elements in the Double Tradition: A Study of Their Place within the Framework of the Gospel Narrative.* BZNW 113. Berlin: Walter de Gruyter.

Hundeshagen, F. 2002. *Wenn doch auch du erkannt hättest, was dir zum Frieden dient.* ETS 85. Leipzig: Benno.

Hunzinger, C.-H. 1960. "Unbekannte Gleichnisse Jesu aus dem Thomas-Evangelium." Pages 209–20 in *Judentum, Urchristentum, Kirche: Festschrift Joachim Jeremias.* Edited by E. Eltester. BZNW 26. Berlin: Walter de Gruyter.

Huuhtanen, P. 1977. "Die Perikope vom 'reichen Jüngling' unter Berücksichtigung der Akzentuierung des Lukas." *SNTU.A* 2: 79–98.

Hyldahl, N. 1961. "Die Versuchung auf der Zinne des Tempels." *StTh* 15: 113–27.

Ideler, J. L. 1841–1842. *Physici et medici Graeci minores.* Berlin: Reimar.

Iersel, B. van. 1960. "The Finding of Jesus in the Temple." *NT* 4: 161–73.

————. 1964. *"Der Sohn" in den synoptischen Jesusworten.* 2nd edition. NT.S 3. Leiden: Brill.

————. 1964/1965. "Die wunderbare Speisung und das Abendmahl in der synoptischen Tradition." *NT* 7: 167–94.

Ilan, T. 2002. *Lexicon of Jewish Names in Late Antiquity.* Vol. 1. TSAJ 91. Tübingen: Mohr.

Ireland, D. J. 1989. "A History of Recent Interpretation of the Parable of the Unjust Steward (Luke 16:1-13)." *WThJ* 51: 293–318.

————. 1992. *Stewardship and the Kingdom of God.* NT.S. 70. Leiden: Brill.

Itgenshorst, T. 2005. *Tota illa pompa: der Triumph in der römischen Republik.* Göttingen: Vandenhoeck & Ruprecht.

Jacobson, A. D. 1995. "Divided Families and Christian Origins." Pages 361–80 in *The Gospel Behind the Gospels.* Edited by R. A. Piper. NT.S. 75. Leiden: Brill.

Jacoby, A. 1921. "ΑΝΑΤΟΛΗ ΕΞ ΥΨΟΥΣ." *ZNW* 20: 205–14.

Janse, M. 1996. "L'importance de la position d'un mot 'accessoire' (à propos de Luc 1.3)." *Bib.* 77: 93–97.

Jarvis, P. G. 1965/1966. "Expounding the Parables V: The Tower-builder and the King Going to War (Luke 14,25-33)." *ExpT* 77: 196–98.

Jellicoe, S. 1959/1960. "St. Luke and the 'Seventy(two).'" *NTS* 6: 319–21.

Jenni, E. 1992. "Kausativ und Funktionsverbgefüge: Sprachliche Bemerkungen zur Bitte: 'Führe uns nicht in Versuchung.'" *ThZ* 48: 77–88.

Jeremias, J. 1925. "Der Eckstein." *Angelos* 1: 65–70.

————. 1930. "Κεφαλὴ γωνίας— Ἀκρογωνιαῖος." *ZNW* 29: 264–80.

————. 1936. "Die Zinne des Tempels (Mt 4,5: Lk 4,9)." *ZDPV* 59: 195–208.

————. 1937. "Eckstein–Schlußstein." *ZNW* 36: 154–57.

————. 1939. "Beobachtungen zu neutestamentlichen Stellen an Hand des neugefundenen griechischen Henoch-Textes." *ZNW* 38: 115–24.

————. 1958. *Heiligengräber in Jesu Umwelt (Mt. 23, 29; Lk. 11, 47): Eine Untersuchung zur Volksreligion der Zeit Jesu.* Göttingen: Vandenhoeck & Ruprecht.

————. 1960. "Lukas 7 45: ΕΙΣΗΔΘΟΝ." *ZNT* 51: 131.

————. 1961. "Drei weitere jüdische Heiligengraber." *ZNW* 52: 95–101.

————. 1965. *Unbekannte Jesusworte*. 4th edition. Gütersloh: Mohn.

————. 1966. *Abba: Studien zur neutestamentlichen Theologie und Zeitgeschichte*. Göttingen: Vandenhoeck & Ruprecht.

————. 1966-1967. "Paliistinakundliches zum Gleichnis vom Siiemann (Mark iv. 3-8 Par.)." *NTS* 13: 48-53.

————. 1967. *Die Abendmahlsworte Jesu*. 4th edition. Göttingen: Vandenhoeck & Ruprecht.

————. 1969. *Jerusalem zur Zeit Jesu*. 3rd edition. Göttingen: Vandenhoeck & Ruprecht.

————. 1977. *Die Gleichnisse Jesu*. 9th edition. Göttingen: Vandenhoeck & Ruprecht.

————. 1980. *Die Sprache des Lukasevangeliums*. KEK.S. Göttingen: Vandenhoeck & Ruprecht.

Jervell, J. 1998. *Die Apostelgeschichte*. KEK 3. Göttingen: Vandenhoeck & Ruprecht.

Johnson, A. F. 1979. "Assurance for Man: The Fallacy of Translating ANAIDEIA by 'Persistence' in Luke 11:5-8." *JETS* 22: 123–31.

Johnson, L. T. 1977. *The Literary Function of Possessions in Luke–Acts*. SBL.DS 39. Missoula, Mont.: Scholars Press.

————. 1982. "The Lukan Kingship Parable (Lk. 19:11-27)." *NT* 24: 139–59.

Johnson, M. D. 1969. *The Purpose of the Biblical Genealogies*. MSSNTS 8. Cambridge: Cambridge University Press.

Johnson, S. E. 1935. "A Note on Luke 13:1-5." *AThR* 17: 91–95.

Johnson, S. R., ed. 2002. *Q 7:1-10: The Centurion's Faith in Jesus' Word*. Leuven: Peeters.

Jonge, H. J. de. 1978. "Sonship, Wisdom, Infancy: Luke II.41-51a." *NTS* 24: 317–54.

————. 1997. "The Sayings on Confessing and Denying Jesus in Q 12:8-9 and Mark 8:38." Pages 105–21 in *Sayings of Jesus: Canonical and Non-Canonical: Festschrift Tjitze Baarda*. Edited by W. L. Petersen, J. S. Vos, and H. J. de Jonge. Leiden: Brill.

Joosten, J. 2003. "'Père, j'ai péché envers le ciel et devant toi': Remarques exégétiques et textuelles sur Luc 15.18, 21." *RHPhR* 83: 145–56.

Joüon, P. 1936. "Luc 23,11: ἐσθῆτα λαμπράν." *RSR* 26: 80–85.

Judge, P. J. 1989. "Luke 7.1-10: Sources and Redaction." Pages 473–90 in *L'evangile de Luc–The Gospel of Luke*. Edited by F. Neirynck. Leuven: Leuven University Press.

Jülicher, A. 1976 [²1910]. *Die Gleichnisreden Jesu, zwei Teile in einem Band*. Darmstadt: Wissenschaftiche Buchgesellschaft.

Jung, C.-W. 2004. *The Original Language of the Lukan Infancy Narrative*. JSNT.S 267. London: T&T Clark.

Jung, F. 2002. ΣΩΤΗΡ: *Studien zur Rezeption eines hellenistischen Ehrentitels im Neuen Testament*. NTA.NF 39. Münster: Aschendorff.

Just, A. A. 1993. *The Ongoing Feast: Table Fellowship and Eschatology at Emmaus*. Collegeville, Minn.: Liturgical Press.

Kaestli, J.-D. 1969. *L'eschatologie dans l'oeuvre de Luc*. NSTh 22. Geneva: Labor et Fides.

Kähler, C. 1995. *Jesu Gleichnisse als Poesie und Therapie*. WUNT 78. Tübingen: Mohr.

Kaibel, G. 1965 [1878]. *Epigrammata graeca: ex lapidibus conlecta*. Hildesheim: Olms.

Kaimakis, D. 1976. *Die Kyraniden*. Meisenheim an Glan: Hein.

Kany, R. 1986. "Der lukanische Bericht von Tod und Auferstehugn Jesu aus der Sicht eines hellenistischen Romanlesers." *NT* 28: 75–90.

Kariamadam, P. 1985. *The Zacchaeus Story*. Kerala: Pontifical Institute of Theology and Philosophy.

———. 1987. "The Composition and Meaning of the Lucan Travel Narrative (Lk. 9,51–19,46)." *BiBh* 13: 179–98.

———. 1997. "Transfiguration and Jesus' Ascended Glory: An Explanation of Lk. 9:28-36." *BiBh* 23: 1–13.

Karrer, M. 1991. *Der Gesalbte: Die Grundlagen des Christustitel*. Göttingen: Vandenhoeck & Ruprecht.

———. 1998. *Jesus Christus im Neuen Testament*. NTD.E 11. Göttingen: Vandenhoeck & Ruprecht.

———. 2002. "Jesus der Retter (Sôtêr). Zur Aufnahme eines hellenistischen Prädikats im Neuen Testament." *ZNW* 93: 153–76.

Karris, R. J. 1985. *Luke, Artist and Theologian: Luke's Passion Account as Literature*. New York: Paulist Press.

———. 1986. "Luke 23:47 and the Lucan View of Jesus' Death." *JBL* 105: 65–74.

———. 1991. "Luke 8:26-39: Jesus, the Pigs, and Human Transformation." *NTR* 4: 39–51.

———. 1995. "Luke 13:10-17 and God's Promises to Israel." Pages 98–115 in *Divine Promises to the Fathers in the Three Monotheistic Religions*. Edited by A. Niccacci. SBF 40. Jerusalem: Franciscan.

Käsemann, E. 1970. *Exegetische Versuche und Besinnungen*. 6th edition. Göttingen: Vandenhoek & Ruprecht.

Käser, W. 1963. "Exegetische und theologische Erwägungen zur Seligpreisung der Kinderlosen Lc 23,29b." *ZNW* 54: 240–54.

Kato, T. 1997. *La pensée sociale de Luc-Actes*. EHPhR 76. Paris: Presses universitaires de France.

Kaut, T. 1990. *Befreier und befreites Volk. Traditions- und redaktionsgeschichtliche Untersuchungen zu Magnifikat und Benediktus im Kontext der lukanischen Kindheitsgeschichte*. BBB 77. Frankfurt am Main: Hain.

Keck, F. 1976. *Die öffentliche Abschiedsrede Jesu in Lk 20,45—21,36*. FzB 25. Stuttgart: Katholisches Bibelwerk.

Keck, L. E. 1970/1971. "The Spirit and the Dove." *NTS* 17: 41–67.

Kee, H. C. 1967/1968. "The Terminology of Mark's Exorcism Stories." *NTS* 14: 232–46.

Kelhoffer, J. 2000. *Miracle and Mission: The Authentication of Missionaries and their Message in the Longer Ending of Mark*. WUNT 2/112. Tübingen: Mohr.

———. 2004. "'How Soon a Book' Revisited: ΕΥΑΓΓΕΛΙΟΝ as a Reference to 'Gospel' Materials in the First Half of the Second Century." *ZNW* 95: 1–34.

Kellermann, U. 2007. *Das Achtzehn-Bitten-Gebet*. Neukirchen-Vluyn: Neukirchener.

Kelly, J. F. 1974. "The Patristic Biography of Luke." *BiTod* 74: 113–19.

Kennel, G. 1995. *Frühchristliche Hymnen? Gattungskritische Studien zur Frage nach den Liedern der frühen Christenheit*. WMANT 71. Neukirchen-Vluyn: Neukirchener.

Kenyon, F. G. 1935. *The Chester Beatty Biblical Papyri*. Vol. 5. London: Walker.

Kenyon, K. M., and T. A. Holland. 1960–1982. *Excavations at Jericho*. Vols. 1–4. London: British School of Archaeology in Jerusalem.

Kertelge, K. 1970. *Die Wunder Jesu im Markusevangelium*. StANT 23. München: Kösel.

Kezbere, I. 2007. *Umstrittener Monotheismus: Wahre und falsche Apotheose im lukanischen Doppelwerk*. NTOA/StUNT 60. Göttingen: Vandenhoeck & Ruprecht.

Kienast, D. 1982. *Augustus: Prinzeps und Monarch*. Darmstadt: Wissenschaftliche Buchgesellschaft.

Kierdorf, W. 1986. "'Funus' und 'consecratio.' Zu Terminologie und Ablauf der römischen Kaiserapotheose." *Chiron* 16: 43–69.

Kiilunen, J. 1989. *Das Doppelgebot der Liebe in synoptischer Sicht*. STAT 250. Helsinki: Suomalainen Tiedeakatemia.

———. 2002. "'Minor Agreements' und die Hypothese von Lukas' Kenntnis des Matthäusevangeliums." Pages 165–202 in *Fair Play: Festschrift Heikki Räisänen*. Leiden: Brill.

Kilgallen, J. J. 1982. "What Kind of Servants Are We? (Luke 17,10)." *Bib.* 63: 549–51.

———. 1986. "The Sadducees and Resurrection from the Dead: Luke 20,27-40." *Bib.* 67: 478–95.

———. 1991. "A Proposal for Interpreting Luke 7.36-50." *Bib.* 72: 305–30.

———. 1993. "The Return of the Unclean Spirit." *Bib.* 74: 45–59.

———. 1998a. "Forgiveness of Sins (Luke 7:36-50)." *NT* 40: 105–16.

———. 1998b. "The Importance of the Redactor in Luke 18,9-14." *Bib.* 79: 69–75.

———. 1999. "Jesus' First Trial: Messiah and Son of God (Luke 22,66-71)." *Bib.* 80: 401–14.

———. 2001a. "A Comment on Luke 1:31-35." *ExpT* 112: 413–14.

———. 2001b. "Faith and Forgiveness: Luke 7,36-50." *RB* 108: 214–27.

———. 2001c. "The Obligation to Heal (Luke 13,10-17)." *Bib.* 82: 402–9.

———. 2002. "The Parable of the Fig Tree (Luke 13,6-9)." Pages 439–49 in *San Luca Evangelista. Testimone della fede che unisce*. Vol. 1, *L'unità letteraria e teologica dell'opera di Luca*. Edited by G. Leonarde. Padova: Istituto per la storia ecclesiastica padovana.

———. 2003a. "The Unity of Luke 17,1-10." *EThL* 79: 157–65.

————. 2003b. "What Does It Mean to Say: 'Wisdom Is Justified by Her Children'?" *ChiSt* 42: 205–11.

————. 2005a. "Faith and Forgiveness: Luke 7,36-50." *RB* 112: 372–84.

————. 2005b. "What Does It Mean to Say That There Are Additions in Luke 7,36-50." *Bib.* 86: 529–35.

————. 2006. "Luke 18,11—Pharisees and Lucan Irony." *RB* 113: 53–64.

Kilpatrick, G. D. 1965. "ΛΑΟΙ at Luke 11.31 and Acts IV.25, 27." *JThS NS* 16: 127.

————. 1979. "Three Problems of New Testament Text." *NT* 21: 289-92.

Kim, H.-S. 1993. *Die Geisttaufe des Messias: Eine kompositionsgeschichtliche Untersuchung zu einem Leitmotiv des lukanischen Doppelwerks.* SKP 81. Frankfurt am Main: Lang.

Kim, K.-J. 1998. *Stewardship and Almsgiving in Luke's Theology.* JSNT.S 155. Sheffield: Sheffield Academic.

Kimball, C. A. 1993. "Jesus' Exposition of Scripture in Luke 20:9-19." *BBR* 3: 77–92.

————. 1994. *Jesus' Exposition of the Old Testament in Luke's Gospel.* JSNT.S 94. Sheffield: Sheffield Academic.

Kingsbury, J. D. 1991. *Conflict in Luke.* Minneapolis: Augsburg Fortress.

Kinman, B. 1993. "Luke's Exoneration of John the Baptist." *JThS* 44: 595–98.

————. 1994. "'The Stones Will Cry Out' (Luke 19,40)—Joy or Judgment?" *Bib.* 75: 232–35.

————. 1995. *Jesus' Entry into Jerusalem.* AGJU 28. Leiden: Brill.

————. 1999a. "Debtor's Prison and the Future of Israel (Luke 12:57-59)." *JETS* 42: 411–25.

————. 1999b. "Parousia, Jesus' 'a-triumphal' Entry, and the Fate of Jerusalem (Luke 19:28-44)." *JBL* 118: 279–94.

Kirchschläger, W. 1981. *Jesu exorzistisches Wirken aus der Sicht des Lukas.* ÖBS 3. Klosterneuburg: Österreichisches Katholisches Bibelwerk.

Kirk, A. 1998a. *The Composition of the Sayings Source: Genre, Synchrony, and Wisdom Redaction in Q.* NT.S 91. Leiden: Brill

————. 1998b. "Upbraiding Wisdom: John's Speech and the Beginning of Q (Q 3:7-9, 16-17)." *NT* 40: 1–16.

————. 2003. "'Love Your Enemies,' the Golden Rule, and Ancient Reciprocity (Luke 6:27-35)." *JBL* 122: 667–86.

Klassen, W. 1980/1981. "'A Child of Peace' (Luke 10.6) in First Century Context." *NTS* 27: 488–506.

————. 1996. *Judas: Betrayer or Friend of Jesus?* Minneapolis: Augsburg Fortress.

Klauck, H.-J. 1978. *Allegorie und Allegorese in synoptischen Gleichnistexten.* NTA NF 13. Münster: Aschendorff.

————. 1981. "Die Frage der Sündenvergebung in der Perikope von der Heilung des Gelähmten (Mk 2,1-12 parr)." *BZ NF* 25: 223–48.

————. 1982. *Herrenmahl und hellenistischer Kult.* Münster: Aschendorff.

————. 1986. "Die Armut der Jünger in der Sicht des Lukas." *Clar.* 26: 5–47.

————. 1987. *Judas—ein Jünger des Herrn.* QD 111. Freiburg: Herder.

————. 1997. "Gottesfürchtige im Magnifikat?" *NTS* 43: 134–39.

Klauser, T. 1958. "Studien zur Entstehungsgeschichte der christlichen Kunst I." *JAC* 1: 20–51.

Klausner, J. 1952. *Jesus von Nazareth*. 3rd edition. Jerusalem: Jewish Publishing House.

Klawans, J. 2000. *Impurity and Sin in Ancient Judaism*. Oxford: Oxford University Press.

Klein, G. 1961. *Die zwölf Apostel. Ursprung und Gehalt einer Idee*. Göttingen: Vanderhoeck & Ruprecht.

————. 1964. "Die Prüfung der Zeit (Lukas 12.54-56)." *ZThK* 61: 373–90.

————. 1969. *Rekonstruktion und Interpretation*. BEvTh 50. Munich: Kaiser.

————. 1972. "Die Verfolgung der Apostel, Luk 11,49." Pages 113–24 in *Neues Testament und Geschichte: Festschrift Oscar Cullmann*. Edited by H. Baltensweiler and B. Reicke. Tübingen: Mohr.

————. 1997. "Eschatologie und Schöpfung bei Lukas: Eine kosmische Liturgie im dritten Evangelium." Pages 145–54 in *Eschatologie und Schöpfung: Festschrift Erich Gräßer*. Edited by M. Evang, H. Merklein, and M. Wolter. BZNW 89. Berlin: Walter de Gruyter.

Klein, H. 1972. "Zur Frage nach dem Abfassungsort der Lukasschriften." *EvTh* 32: 467–77.

————. 1976. "Die lukanisch-johanneische Passionstradition." *ZNW* 67: 155–86.

————. 1987. *Barmherzigkeit gegenüber den Elenden und Geächteten. Studien zur Botschaft des lukanischen Sondergutes*. BThSt 10. Neukirchen-Vluyn: Neukirchener.

————. 1996a. "Am ersten Sabbat: Eine Konjektur zu Lk 6,1." *ZNW* 87: 290–93.

————. 1996b. "Gerichtsankündigung und Liebesforderung: Lk 6.24-6 and 27 innerhalb der Botschaft des frühen Christentums." *NTS* 42: 421–33.

————. 2005. *Lukasstudien*. FRLANT 209. Göttingen: Vandenhoeck & Ruprecht.

Klein, P. 1980. "Die lukanische Weherufe Lk 6.24-26." *ZNW* 71: 150–59.

Klemm, H. G. 1969–1970. "Das Wort von der Selbstbestattung der toten: Beobachtungen zur Auslegungsgeschichte von Mt. VIII. 22 par." *NTS* 16: 60–75.

————. 1982. "De Censu Caesaris." *NT* 24: 234–54.

Klijn, A. F. J. 1966. "The Question of the Rich Young Man in a Jewish-Christian Gospel." *NT* 8: 149–55.

————. 1970. "John XIV 22 and the Name Judas Thomas." Pages 88–96 in *Studies in John: Festschrift J. N. Sevenster*. NT.S 24. Leiden: Brill.

————. 2002. "Matthew 11:25 // Luke 10:21." Pages 3–14 in *New Testament Textual Criticism: Festschrift Bruce M. Metzger*. Edited by E. J. Epp and G. D. Fee. Oxford: Clarendon.

Klingbeil, G. A. 2000. "The Finger of God in the Old Testament." *ZAW* 112: 409–15.

Klinghardt, M. 1988. *Gesetz und Volk Gottes: Das lukanische Verständnis des Gesetzes nach Herkunft, Funktion und seinem Ort in der Geschichte des Urchristentums*. WUNT 2/32. Tübingen: Mohr.

————. 2006. "Markion vs. Lukas: Plädoyer für die Wiederaufnahme eines alten Falles." *NTS* 52: 484–513.

Klink, E. W. 2004. "The Gospel Community Debate: State of the Question." *CuBR* 3: 60–85.

Kloft, H. 1988. "Gedanken zum Ptochòs." Pages 81–106 in *Soziale Randgruppen und Außenseiter im Altertum*. Edited by I. Weiler and H. Grassl. Graz: Leykam.

Kloppenborg, J. S. 1989. "The Dishonoured Master (Luke 16,1-8a)." *Bib.* 70: 474–95.

———. 1992. "*Exitus clari viri*. The Death of Jesus in Luke." *TJT* 8: 106–20.

———. 2006. *The Tenants in the Vineyard*. WUNT 195. Tübingen: Mohr.

Klostermann, E. 1971. *Das Markusevangelium*. 4th–5th edition. HNT 3. Tübingen: Mohr.

Klumbies, P.-G. 1989. "Die Sabbatheilungen Jesu nach Markus und Lukas." Pages 165–78 in *Jesu Rede von Gott und ihre Nachgeschichte im frühen Christentum: Festschrift Willi Marxen*. Edited by D.-A. Koch, G. Sellin, and A. Lindemann. Gütersloh: Mohn.

———. 2003. "Das Sterben Jesu als Schauspiel nach Lk 23,44-49." *BZ NF* 47: 186–205.

———. 2007. "Himmelfahrt und Apotheose Jesu in Luke 24,50-53." *Klio* 89: 147–60.

Klutz, T. 2004. *The Exorcism Stories in Luke–Acts*. MSSNTS 129. Cambridge: Cambridge University Press.

Knowles, M. P. 2003. "Reciprocity and 'Favour' in the Parable of the Undeserving Servant (Luke 17.7-10)." *NTS* 49: 256–60.

Knox, J. 1942. *Marcion and the New Testament: An Essay in the Early History of the Canon*. Chicago: University of Chicago Press.

Kobert, R. 1972. "Kamel und Schiffstau: zu Markus 10,25 (Par.) und Koran 7,40/38." *Bib.* 53: 229–33.

Koch, D.-A. 1989. "Jesu Tischgemeinschaft mit Zöllnern und Sündern." Pages 57–73 in *Jesu Rede von Gott und ihre Nachgeschichte im frühen Christentum: Festschrift Willi Marxsen*. Edited by D.-A. Koch, G. Sellin, and A. Lindemann. Gütersloh: Mohn.

Koch, K. 1979. "Offenbaren wird sich das Reich Gottes: Die Malkuta Jahwäs im Profeten-Targum." *NTS* 25: 158–65.

Kock, T. 1880–1888. *Comicorum atticorum fragmenta*. Leipzig: Teubner.

Kodell, J. 1969. "Luke's Use of Laos, 'People,' Especially in the Jerusalem Narrative (Lk 19,28–24,53)." *CBQ* 31: 327–43.

Koenen, K. 1995. *Jahwe wird kommen, zu herrschen über die Erde: Ps 90–110 als Komposition*. BBB 101. Weinheim: Beltz Athenaum.

Koep, L. 1952. *Das himmlische Buch in Antike und Christentum*. Bonn: Hanstein.

Koester, H. 1990. *Ancient Christian Gospels*. London: SCM Press.

Koet, B. J. 1989. "'Today This Scripture Has Been Fulfilled in Your Ears.'" Pages 24–55 in *Five Studies on Interpretation of Scripture in Luke–Acts*. SNTA 14. Leuven: Leuven University Press.

———. 1992. "Simeons Worte (Lk 2,29-32, 34c-35) und Israels Geschick." Pages 1549–69 in *The Four Gospels 1992: Festschrift Frans Neirynck*. Vol.

2. Edited by F. van Segbroeck, C. M. Tuckett, G. van Belle, and J. Verheyden. BEThL 100. Leuven: Peeters.

———. 1998. "Holy Place and Hannah's Prayer: A Comparison of LAB 50-51 and Luke 22:22-39 à propos 1 Samuel 1–2." Pages 45–72 in *Sanctity of Time and Space in Tradition and Modernity*. Edited by A. Houtman, M. J. H. M. Poorthuis, and J. Schwartz. Leiden: Brill.

Kogler, F. 1988. *Das Doppelgleichnis vom Senfkorn und vom Sauerteig in seiner traditionsgeschichtlichen Entwicklung*. FzB 59. Stuttgart: Katholisches Bibelwerk.

Köhler, L., and W. Baumgartner. 2004 [^{3}1967–1995]. *Hebräisches und aramäisches Lexikon zum Alten Testament*. 2 vols. 3rd edition. Leiden: Brill.

Kollmann, B. 1990. "Lk 12,35-38—ein Gleichnis der Logienquelle." *ZNW* 81: 254–61.

———. 1996. *Jesus und die Christen als Wundertäter*. FRLANT 170. Göttingen: Vandenhoeck & Ruprecht.

———. 1997. "Jesu Verbot des Richtens und die Gemeindedisziplin." *ZNW* 88: 170–86.

König, R. 1967. "Institution." Pages 142–48 in *Soziologie*. Frankfurt am Main: Fischer.

Konradt, M. 2003. *Gericht und Gemeinde: Eine Studie zur Bedeutung und Funktion von Gerichtsaussagen im Rahmen der paulinischen Ekklesiologie und Ethik im 1 Thess und 1 Kor*. BZNW 117. Berlin: Walter de Gruyter.

———. 2006. "Gott oder Mammon: Besitzethos und Diakonie im frühen Christentum." Pages 107–54 in *Diakonie und Ökonomie. Orientierungen im Europa des Wandels*. Edited by C. Sigrist. Zürich: Theologischer Verlag.

Kopp, C. 1964. *Die Heiligen Stätten der Evangelien*. 2nd edition. Regensburg: Pustet.

Korn, J. H. 1937. ΠΕΙΡΑΣΜΟΣ. Stuttgart: Kohlhammer.

Korn, M. 1993. *Die Geschichte Jesu in veränderter Zeit*. WUNT 2/51. Tübingen: Mohr.

Korting, G. 2004. *Das Vaterunser und die Unheilabwehr: Ein Beitrag zur* ἐπιούσιον-*Debatte (Mt 6,11/Lk 11,3)*. NTA.NF 48. Münster: Aschendorff.

Körtner, U. H. J. 1984. "Das Fischmotiv im Speisungswunder." *ZNW* 75: 24–35.

———. 1998. "Papiasfragmente." Pages 3–103 in *Papiasfragmente: Hirt des Hermas*. Edited by U. H. J. Körtner and M. Leutzsch. Darmstadt: Wissenschaftiche Buchgesellschaft.

Kosch, D. 1989. *Die eschatologische Tora des Menschensohnes*. NTOA 12. Göttingen: Vandenhoeck & Ruprecht.

Kowalski, B. 2002/2003. "Forschungsgeschichtlicher Überblick: Sprache und Stil des Lukasevangeliums." *SNTU* 27/28: 41–83, 27–64.

Kozar, J. V. 1990. "The Function of the Character of Elizabeth as the Omniscent Narrator's Reliable Vehicle in the First Chapter of the Gospel of Luke." *PEMBS* 10: 214–22.

Kraeling, C. H. 1935. *A Greek Fragment of Tatian's Diatessaron, from Dura*. London: Christophers.

Krämer, M. 1972. *Das Rätsel der Parabel vom ungerechten Verwalter Lk 16,1-13.* BSRel 5. Zürich: PAS.

Kratz, R. 1979. *Rettungswunder.* EHS.T 123. Frankfurt am Main: Peter Lang.

Kraus, W. 2003. "Das jüdische Evangelium und seine griechischen Leser. Zum lukanischen Verständnis der Passion Jesu." Pages 29–43 in *Die bleibende Gegenwart des Evangeliums: Festschrift Otto Merk.* Edited by R. Gebauer and M. Meiser. MThSt 76. Marburg: Elwert.

Krauss, S. 1899. "Die Zahl der biblischen Volkerschaften." *ZAW* 19: 1–14.

———. 1900. "Zur Zahl der biblischen Volkerschaften." *ZAW* 20: 38–43.

———. 1925. "Die Instruktion Jesu an die Apostel." *Angelos* 1: 96–102.

———. 1966 [1910–1912]. *Talmudische Archäologie.* Hildesheim: Olms.

Kreuzer, S. 1985. "Der Zwang des Boten—Beobachtungen zu Lk 14,23 und 1 Kor 9,16." *ZNW* 76: 123–28.

Krieger, K. S. 1997. "Die Historizität des Census des Quirinius." *BN* 87: 17–23.

Kroll, W., ed. 1958 [1926]. *Historia Alexandri Magni.* Berlin: Weidemann.

———. ed. 1973. *Vettii Valentis Anthologiarum libri.* Dublin: Weidmann.

Krückemeier, N. 2004. "Der zwölfjährige Jesus im Tempel (Lk 2.40-52) und die biografische Literatur der hellenistischen Antike." *NTS* 50: 307–19.

Kruger, H. A. J. 1997. "A Sword over His Head or in His Hand? Luke 22,35-38." Pages 597–604 in *The Scriptures in the Gospels.* Edited by C. M. Tuckett. BEThL 131. Leuven: Peeters.

Küchler, M. 1979. *Frühjüdische Weisheitstraditionen: zum Fortgang weisheitlichen Denkens im Bereich des frühjüdischen Jahweglaubens.* Freiburg: Universitätsverlag.

———. 2007. *Jerusalem. Ein Handbuch und Studienreiseführer zur Heiligen Stadt.* Göttingen: Vandenhoeck & Ruprecht.

Kügler, J. 1995. "Die Windeln Jesu als Zeichen." *BN* 77: 20–28.

———. 1997. *Pharao und Christus? Religionsgeschichtliche Untersuchung zur Frage einer Verbindung zwischen altägyptischer Königstheologie und neutestamentlicher Christologie im Lukasevangelium.* BBB 113. Bodenheim: Philo.

Kühlewein, J. 1976. "Nächster." Pages 786–91 in *Theologisches Handwörterbuch zum Alten Testament* 2. Edited by Ernst Jenni and Claus Westermann. Munich: Kaiser.

Kuhn, G. 1923. "The Geschlechtsregister Jesu bei Lukas und Matthäus, nach ihrer Herkunft untersucht." *ZNW* 22: 206–28.

Kuhn, H.-W. 1959. "Das Reittier Jesu in der Einzugsgeschichte des Markusevangeliums." *ZNW* 50: 82–91.

———. 1976. "Der Gekreuzigte von Giv^cat ha-Mivtar." Pages 303–34 in *Theologia Crucis—Signum Crucis: Festschrift Erich Dinkler.* Edited by C. Andresen and G. Klein. Tübingen: Mohr.

———. 1980. "Nachfolge nach Ostern." Pages 105–32 in *Kirche: Festschrift Günter Bornkamm.* Edited by D. Lührmann and G. Strecker. Tübingen: Mohr.

———. 1982. "Die Kreuzesstrafe während der frühen Kaiserzeit." Pages 648–793 in *ANRW* II: 25/1.

————. 1995. "Bethsaida in the Gospels: The Feeding Story in Luke 9 and the Q Saying in Luke 10." Pages 243–56 in *Bethsaida: A City by the North Shore of the Sea of Galilee*. Edited by R. Arav and R. A. Freund. Kirksville, Mo.: Thomas Jefferson University Press.

Kuhn, H.-W., and R. R. Arav. 1991. "The Bethsaida Excavations: Historical and Archaeological Approaches." Pages 77–106 in *The Future of Early Christianity: Festschrift Helmut Koester*. Edited by B. A. Pearson, A. T. Kraabel, G. W. E. Nickelsburg. and N. R. Petersen. Minneapolis: Fortress.

Kuhn, K. A. 2003. "Beginning the Witness: The αὐτόπται καὶ ὑπηρέται of Luke's Infancy Narrative." *NTS* 49: 237–55.

Kühn, K. G., ed. 1964 [1921]. *Claudii Galeni Opera omnia*. Hildesheim: Olms.

Kühner, R., and B. Gerth. 1890–1898. *Ausführliche Grammatik der griechischen Sprache*. Vol. I/1–II/2. 3rd edition. Hannover: Hahnsche Buchhandlung.

Kühschelm, R. 1983. *Jüngerverfolgung und Geschick Jesu*. ÖBS 5. Klosterneuburg: Österreichisches Katholisches Bibelwerk.

Kümmel, W. G. 1956 [1945]. *Verheißung und Erfüllung*. 3rd edition. AThANT 6. Zürich: Zwingli-Verlag.

————. 1973. *Einleitung in das Neue Testament*. 17th edition. Heidelberg: Quelle und Meyer.

————. 1974. "'Das Gesetz und die Propheten gehen bis Johannes'—Luke 16,16 im Zusammenhang der heilsgeschichtlichen Theologie der Lukasschriften." Pages 398–415 in *Das Lukas-Evangelium*. Edited by G. Braumann. WdF 280. Darmstadt: Wissenschaftliche Buchgesellschaft.

————. 1978. "Jesu Antwort an Johannes den Täufer." Pages 177–200 in *Heilsgeschehen und Geschichte*. Vol. 2. Marburg: Elwert.

Künzl, E. 1988. *Der römische Triumph: Siegesfeiern im antiken Rom*. Munich: Beck.

Kurth, C. 2000. *"Die Stimmen der Propheten erfüllt." Jesu Geschick und "die" Juden nach der Darstellung des Lukas*. BWANT 148. Stuttgart: Kohlhammer.

Kurz, W. S. 1980. "Luke–Acts and Historiography in the Greek Bible." *SBLSP* 19: 283–300.

————. 1984. "Luke 3:23-38 and Greco-Roman and Biblical Genealogies." Pages 169–87 in *Luke–Acts*. Edited by C. H. Talbert. New York: Crossroad.

————. 1985. "Luke 22:14-38 and Greco-Roman and Biblical Farewell Addresses." *JBL* 104: 251–68.

————. 1987. "Narrative Approaches to Luke–Acts." *Bib.* 62: 195–220.

————. 1993. *Reading Luke–Acts: Dynamics of Biblical Narrative*. Louisville, Ky.: Westminster John Knox.

Kusch, E. 1978. *Neues Testament–Neuer Bund? Eine Fehlübersetzung wird korrigiert*. Neukirchen-Vluyn: Neukirchener.

Kvalbein, H. 1997. "Die Wunder der Endzeit." *ZNW* 88: 111–25.

Kwong, I. S. C. 2005. *The Word Order of the Gospel of Luke*. London: T&T Clark.

Lacy, P. H. de, ed. 1978–1984. *Galeni de placitis Hippocratis et Platonis*. Berlin: Akademie.

Lagrange, M.-J. 1895. "Origène, la critique textuelle et la tradition topographique." *RB* 4: 501–24.

————. 1912. "Le sens du Luc, I,1, d'après les papyrus." *BALAC* 2: 96–100.

Lambrecht, J. 1967. *Die Redaktion der Markus-Apokalypse.* Rome: Papstliches Bibelinstitut.

————. 1981. *Once More Astonished: The Parables of Jesus.* New York: Crossroad.

————. 1985. "Reading and Rereading Lk 18,31–22,6." Pages 585–612 in *À cause de l'évangile: Festschrift Jacques Dupont.* LeDiv 123. Paris: Cerf.

————. 1992. "John the Baptist and Jesus in Mark 1.1-15: Markan Redaction of Q?" *NTS* 38: 357–84.

————. 2003. *Understanding What One Reads: New Testament Essays.* Edited by V. Koperski. Leuven: Peeters.

————. 2005a. " 'But you too.' A Note on Luke 1,76." *EThL* 81: 487–90.

————. 2005b. "A Note on Luke 15,1-32." Pages 299–306 in *Luke and His Readers: Festschrift Adelbert Denaux.* Edited by R. Bieringer, G. van Belle, and J. Verheyden. BEThL 182. Leuven: Peeters.

Lämmert, E. 1975. *Bauformen des Erzählens.* 6th edition. Stuttgart: Metzler.

Lampe, G. W. H. 1984. "The Two Swords (Luke 22:35-38)." Pages 335–51 in *Jesus and the Politics of His Day.* Edited by E. Bammel and C. F. D. Moule. Cambridge: Cambridge University Press.

Landes, G. M. 1996. "Jonah in Luke." Pages 133–63 in *A Gift of God in Due Season: Festschrift James A. Sanders.* Edited by D. M. Carr and R. D. Weis. Sheffield: Sheffield Academic.

Landis, S. 1994. *Das Verhältnis des Johannesevangeliums zu den Synoptikern: Am Beispiel von Mt 8,5-13; Lk 7,1-10; Joh 4,46-54.* BZNW 74. Berlin: Walter de Gruyter.

Landmesser, C. 2002. "Die Rückkehr ins Leben nach dem Gleichnis vom verlorenen Sohn." *ZThK* 99: 239–61.

Landry, D. T. 1995. "Narrative Logic in the Annunciation to Mary (Luke 1:26-28)." *JBL* 114: 65–79.

Landry, D. T., and B. May. 2000. "Honor Restored: New Light on the Parable of the Prudent Steward (Luke 16:1-8a)." *JBL* 119: 287–309.

Lang, B. 1982. "Grußverbot oder Besuchsverbot?" *BZ NF* 26: 75–79.

Laufen, R. 1980. *Die Doppelüberlieferungen der Logienquelle und des Markusevangeliums.* BBB 54. Königstein: Hanstein.

Laum, B. 1914. *Stiftungen in der griechischen und römischen Antike.* Vol. 2. Leipzig: Teubner.

Laurentin, R. 1966. *Jésus au temple: Mystère de Pâques et foi de Marie en Luc 2,48-50.* EtB. Paris: Gabalda.

————. 1967. *Struktur und Theologie der lukanischen Kindheitsgeschichte.* Stuttgart: Katholisches Bibelwerk.

Lausberg, H. 1949. *Elemente der literarischen Rhetorik.* Munich: Hueber.

————. 1973. *Handbuch der literarischen Rhetorik.* 2 vols. 2nd edition. Munich: Hueber.

————. 1998. *Handbook of Literary Rhetoric: A Foundation for Literary Study.* Edited by D. E. Orton and R. D. Anderson. Translated by M. T. Bliss, A. Jansen, and D. E. Orton. Leiden: Brill.

Leaney, A. R. C. 1956. "The Lucan Text of the Lord's Prayer (Lk XI 2-4)." *NT* 1: 103–11.

Lebourlier, J. 1992. "*Entos hymnōn*: Le sens 'au milieu de vous' est-il possible?" *Bib.* 73: 259–62.

Lee, B. T. 2005. *Apuleius' Florida: A Commentary*. Berlin: Walter de Gruyter.

Lee, J. A. L. 1991. "A Non-Aramaism in Luke 6:7." *NT* 33: 28–34.

Lefebvre, P. 1998. "Anne de la tribu d'Asher: Le bonheur d'une femme (Lc 2,36-38)." *SémBib* 91: 3–32.

Lefort, L. T. 1938. "Le nom du mauvais riche (Luc 16.19) et la tradition copte." *ZNW* 37: 65–72.

Legare, C. 1983. "Jésus et la pécheresse." *SémBib* 29: 19–45.

Légasse, S. 1976. "Le logion sur le fils révélateur." Pages 245–74 in *La notion biblique de Dieu*. Edited by J. Coppens. BEThL 41. Leuven: Peeters.

Legrand, L. 1982. "On l'appela du nom de Jésus (Luc, II,21)." *RB* 89: 481–91.

Lehnardt, A. 2002. *Qaddish. Untersuchungen zur Entstehung und Rezeption eines rabbinischen Gebetes*. TSAJ 87. Tübingen: Mohr.

Lehtipuu, O. 1999. "Characterization and Persuasion: The Rich Man and the Poor Man in Luke 16.19-31." Pages 73–105 in *Characterization in the Gospels: Reconceiving Narrative Criticism*. Edited by D. M. Rhoads and K. Syreeni. Sheffield: Sheffield Academic.

———. 2007. *The Afterlife Imagery in Luke's Story of the Rich Man and Lazarus*. NT.S 123. Leiden: Brill.

Leinhäupl-Wilke, A. 2007. "Zu Gast bei Lukas. Einblicke in die lukanische Mahlkonzeption am Beispiel von Lk 7,36-50." Pages 91–120 in *Herrenmahl und Gruppenidentität*. Edited by M. Ebner. QD 221. Freiburg im Breisgau: Herder.

Lémonon, J.-P. 1981. *Pilate et le gouvernement de la Judée*. Paris: Gabalda.

Lentz, A., and A. Ludwich, eds. 1965. *Herodiani technici Reliquae*. Hildesheim: Olms.

Lentzen-Deis, F. 1969. "Das Motive der 'Himmelsoffnung' in verschiedenen Gattungen der Umweltliteratur des Neuen Testaments." *Bib.* 50: 301–27.

———. 1970. *Die Taufe Jesu nach den Synoptikern*. FTS 4. Frankfurt am Main: Knecht.

Lenz, F. W., and C. A. Behr, eds. 1976. *Aelius Aristides, Opera quae exstant omnia*. Lugduni Batavorum: Brill.

Léon-Dufour, X. 1983. *Abendmahl und Abschiedsrede im Neuen Testament*. Stuttgart: Katholisches Bibelwerk.

Leonhard, C. 2002. "Vaterunser II." *TRE* 34: 512–15.

Leslie, S. 1929. *The Greek Anthology*. London: Ernest Benn.

Leppä, H. 2005. "Luke's Account of the Lord's Supper." Pages 364–73 in *Lux Humana, Lux Aeterna: Festschrift Lars Aejmelaeus*. Edited by A. Mustakallio, H. Leppä, and H. Räisänen. SESJ 89. Helsinki: Finnish Exegetical Society.

Leutsch, E. van, and F. W. Schneidewin. 1958 [1839–1851]. *Corpus paroemiographorum Graecorum*. Hildesheim: Olms.

Lewis, N., Y. Yadin, and J. C. Greenfield. 1989. "The Documents from the Bar Kokhba Period in the Cave of Letters." Jerusalem: Israel Exploration Society.

Lichtenberger, A. 2003. *Kulte und Kultur der Dekapolis*. ADPV 29. Wiesbaden: Harrassowitz.

Liebenberg, J. 1993. "The Function of the *Standespredigt* in Luke 3:1-20." *Neotest.* 27: 55–67.

Lifshitz, B. 1967. *Donateurs et fondateurs dans les synagogues juives*. Paris: Gabalda.

Lignée, H. 1974. "La mission des Soixante-douze." *ASeign* 45: 64–74.

Lindemann, A. 1983. "Die Kinder und die Gottesherrschaft." *WuD* 17: 77–104.

———. 1992. *Die Clemensbriefe*. HNT 17. Tübingen: Mohr.

———. 1993. "Samaria und Samaritaner im Neuen Testament." *WuD* 22: 51–76.

———. 1994. "Literatur zu den Synoptischen Evangelien 1984–1991." *ThR* 59: 41–100, 113–85, 252–84 (on Luke in particular, see 252–81).

———. 1999. "Einheit und Vielfalt im lukanischen Doppelwerk: Beobachtungen zu Reden, Wundererzählungen und Mahlberichten." Pages 225–53 in *The Unity of Luke–Acts*. Edited by J. Verheyden. BEThL 142. Leuven: Leuven University Press.

———. 2002. "Jesus als der Christus bei Paulus und Lukas." Pages 429–61 in *Der historische Jesus. Tendenzen und Perspektiven der gegenwärtigen Forschung*. Edited by J. Schröter and R. Brucker. Berlin: Walter de Gruyter.

———. 2004/2005. "Literatur zu den Synoptischen Evangelien 1992–2000." *ThR* 69/70: 182–227, 241–72, 44–80 ("Das Lukasevangelium").

Lindhagen, C. 1950. "Die Wurzel ΣΑΠ- im NT und AT." *UUA* 40: 26–69.

Linke, K. 1977. *Die Fragmente des Grammatikers Dionysios Thrax*. Berlin: Walter de Gruyter.

Linnemann, E. 1960. "Überlegungen zur Parabel vom großen Abendmahl." *ZNW* 51: 246–55.

Linton, O. 1975/1976. "The Parable of the Children's Game." *NTS* 22: 159–79.

Lipsius, R. A. 1884. "Die Acten des Lukas." Pages 354–71 in *Die apokryphen Apostelgeschichten und Apostellegenden*. Vol. II/2. Braunschweig: Schwetschke.

Lipsius, R. A., and M. Bonnet, eds. 1959 [1891–1903]. *Acta Apostolorum Apocrypha*. 3 vols. Darmstadt: Wissenschaftliche Buchgesellschaft.

Littré, E. ed. 1853. "Hippocrates, De mulierum affectibus I–III." Pages 10-462 in *Oeuvres completes d'Hippocrate*. Vol. 8. Paris: Baillière.

Litwak, K. D. 2005. *Echoes of Scripture in Luke–Acts*. JSNT.S 282. Sheffield: Sheffield Academic.

———. 2006. Περὶ τῶν πεπληροφορημένων ἐν ἡμῖν πραγμάτων. Concerning the Things Fulfilled or Accomplished." *RB* 113: 37–52.

Lohfink, G. 1971. *Die Himmelfahrt Jesu*. StANT 26. Munich: Kösel.

———. 1975a. "'Ich habe gesündigt gegen den Himmel und gegen dich': Eine Exegese von Lk 15.18, 21." *ThQ* 155: 51–52.

———. 1975b. *Die Sammlung Israels*. StANT 39. Munich: Kösel.

————. 1985. "Die Metaphorik der Aussat im Gleichnis vom Sämann (Mk 4,3-9)." Pages 211–28 in *À cause de l'évangile: Festschrift Jacques Dupont*. LeDiv 123. Paris: Cerf.

Lohfink, N. 1994. "Psalmen im Neuen Testament: Die Lieder in der Kindheitsgeschichte bei Lukas." Pages 105–25 in *Neue Wege der Psalmenforschung: Festschrift Walter Beyerlin*. HBiSt 1. Freiburg: Herder.

Lohmeyer, M. 1995. *Der Apostelbegriff im Neuen Testament*. SBB 29. Stuttgart: Katholisches Bibelwerk.

Lohse, E. 1961. *Die Auferstehung Jesu Christi im Zeugnis des Lukasevangelium*. BSt 31. Neukirchen-Vluyn: Neukirchener.

Löning, K. 1997/2006. *Das Geschichtswerk des Lukas*. 2 vols. Stuttgart: Kohlhammer.

————. 2000. "Gottes Barmherzigkeit und die pharisäische Sabbat-Observanz. Zu den Sabbat-Therapien im lukanischen Reisebericht." Pages 218–40 in *Das Drama der Barmherzigkeit Gottes*. Edited by R. Scoralick. SBS 183. Stuttgart: Katholisches Bibelwerk.

————. 2004. "Die Auseinandersetzung mit dem Pharisäismus in den Weherufen bei Matthäus (Mt 23) und Lukas (Lk 11,37-53)." Pages 217–34 in *"Dies ist das Buch . . .": Festschrift Hubert Frankenmölle*. Edited by R. Kampling. Paderborn: Schöningh.

Loos, H. van der. 1965. *The Miracles of Jesus*. NT.S 9. Leiden: Brill.

Lövestam, E. 1963. *Spiritual Wakefulness in the New Testament*. AUL.T 53/3. Lund: Gleerup.

————. 1968. *Spiritus Blasphemia*. Lund: Gleerup.

————. 1995. *Jesus and 'This Generation.'* Stockholm: Almqvist & Wiksell.

Löw, I. 1928. *Die Flora der Juden*. Vol. 1. Vienna: Löwit.

Lührmann, D. 1969. *Die Redaktion der Logienquelle*. WMANT 33. Neukirchen-Vluyn: Neukirchener.

————. 1971. "Epiphaneia: Zur Bedeutungsgeschichte eines griechischen Wortes." Pages 185–99 in *Tradition und Glaube: Festschrift Karl Georg Kuhn*. Edited by G. Jeremias, H.-W. Kuhn, and H. Stegemann. Göttingen: Vandenhoeck & Ruprecht.

————. 1972a. "Liebet eure Feinde." *ZThK* 69: 412–38.

————. 1972b. "Noah and Lot (Lk 17,26-29)—ein Nachtrag." *ZNW* 63: 130–32.

————. 1987. *Das Markusevangelium*. HNT 3. Tübingen: Mohr.

Lull, D. J. 1986. "The Servant-Benefactor as a Model of Greatness." *NT* 28: 289–305.

Luz, U. 1985–2002. *Das Evangelium nach Matthäus*. 4 vols. EKK 1. Neukirchen-Vluyn: Neukirchener.

Lyonnet, S. 1939. "Χαῖρε κεχαριτωμένη." *Bib.* 20: 131–41.

————. 1964. "Der Verkündigungsbericht und die Gottesmutterschaft Marias." *ORPB* 65: 129–38, 164–70, 193–99.

Mach, M. 1992. *Entwicklungsstadien des jüdischen Engelglaubens in vorrabbinischer Zeit*. Tübingen: Mohr.

MacLaurin, E. C. B. 1978. "Beelzeboul." *NT* 20: 156–60.

Macoby, H. 1982. "The Washing of Cups." *JSNT* 14: 3–15.

Maddox, R. 1982. *The Purpose of Luke–Acts*. FRLANT 126. Göttingen: Vanden-hoeck & Ruprecht.

Mahnke, H. 1978. *Die Versuchungsgeschichte im Rahmen der synoptischen Evangelien*. BET 9. Frankfurt am Main: Lang.

Mahoney, M. 1980. "Luke 21,14-15: Editorial Rewriting or Authenticity." *IThQ* 47: 220–38.

Maier, J. 1995–1996. *Die Qumran-Essener: Die Texte von Toten Meer*. 3 vols. München: Reinhardt.

Main, E. 1996. "Les Sadducéens et la résurrection des morts: Comparaison entre Mc 12,18-27 et Lc 20,27-38." *RB* 103: 411–40.

Mainville, O. 1991. *L'esprit dans l'oeuvre de Luc*. CTHP 45. Quebec: Fides.

———. 1999. "Le péché contre l'esprit annoncé en Lc 12.10, commis en Ac 4.16-18." *NTS* 45: 38–50.

———. 2003. "De Jésus prophète au Christ glorieux: Le récit d'Emmaüs comme lieu de passage identitaire et fonctionnel." Pages 160–68 in *Raconter, inter-préter, annoncer: Festschrift Daniel Marguerat*. Edited by E. Steffek and Y. Bourquin. MoBi 47. Geneva: Labor et Fides.

———. 2005. "De Jésus à l'Église: Étude rédactionelle de Luc 24." *NTS* 51: 192–211.

Maisch, I. 1971. *Die Heilung des Gelähmten*. SBS 52. Stuttgart: Katholisches Bibelwerk.

Malherbe, A. J. 1977. *The Cynic Epistles: A Study Edition*. Missoula, Mont.: Scholars Press.

———. 1996. "The Christianization of a Topos (Luke 12:13-34)." *NT* 38: 123–35.

Malina, B. J., and J. H. Neyrey. 1991. "Honor and Shame in Luke–Acts." Pages 25–65 in *The Social World of Luke–Acts: Models for Interpretation*. Edited by J. H. Neyrey. Peabody, Mass.: Hendrickson.

Manitius, K. 1894. *In Arati et Eudoxi Phaenomena commentariorum libri tres*. Leipzig: Teubner.

Manns, F. 1996. "Un document judéo-chrétien: La source propre à Luc." *BeO* 38: 43–62.

Mansion, J. 1930. "Sur le sens d'un mot grec: ἀνατάσσω." *BFPUL* 44: 261–67.

Manson, T. W. 1949. *The Sayings of Jesus as Recorded in the Gospels according to St. Matthew and St. Luke*. London: SCM Press.

Marchant, E. C. 2002. *Memorabilia and Oeconomicus*. LCL 168. Cambridge, Mass.: Harvard University Press.

Marcus, J. 1988. "Entering into the Kingly Power of God." *JBL* 107: 663–75.

———. 1995. "Jesus' Baptismal Vision." *NTS* 41: 512–21.

Marcus, R. 1961. *Philo. Supplement I: Questions and Answers on Genesis*. LCL. Cambridge, Mass.: Harvard University Press.

Marguerat, D. 1999. *La première histoire du Christianisme*. LeDiv 180. Paris: Cerf.

———. ed. 2009. *Reception of Paulinism in Acts: Reception du Paulinisme dans le Actes de Apôtres*. BEThL 229. Leuven: Peeters.

Markschies, C. 1993. "Sessio ad Dexteram." Pages 252–317 in *Le Trône de Dieu*. Edited by M. Philonenko. WUNT 69. Tübingen: Mohr.

————. 2015. *Christian Theology and Its Institutions in the Early Roman Empire: Prolegommena to a History of Early Christian Theology*. Translated by W. Coppins. BMSEC 3. Waco, Tex.: Baylor University Press.

Marquardt, J. 1957 [²1884]. *Römische Staatsverwaltung*. Vol. 2. 3rd edition. Darmstadt: Wissenschaftiche Buchgesellschaft.

Marshall, I. H. 1968. "Luke XVI—Who Commended the Unjust Steward?" *JThS NS* 19: 617–19.

————. 1969. "Tradition and Theology in Luke (Luke 8:5-15)." *TynB* 20: 56–75.

————. 1983. "Luke and His 'Gospel.'" Pages 289–308 in *Das Evangelium und die Evangelien*. Edited by P. Stuhlmacher. Tübingen: Mohr.

————. 1991. "The Interpretation of the Magnifikat: Luke 1:46-55." Pages 181–96 in *Der Treue Gottes trauen: Beiträge zum Werk des Lukas: Festschrift Gerhard Schneider*. Edited by C. Bussmann and W. Radl. Freiburg: Herder.

————. 1993. "Acts and the 'Former Treatise.'" Pages 163–82 in *The Book of Acts in Its First Century Setting*. Vol. 1, *Ancient Literary Setting*. Edited by B. Winter and A. D. Clark. Grand Rapids: Carlisle.

Martin, J. 1931. *Symposion: Die Geschichte einer literarischen Form*. Stud. zu Gesch. u. Kultur des Altertums 17/1–2. Paderborn: Schöningh.

Martin, R. P. 1978. "The Pericope of the Healing of the 'Centurion's' Servant/Son (Matt 8:5-13 par. Luke 7:1-10)." Pages 14–22 in *Unity and Diversity in New Testament Theology: Festschrift George E. Ladd*. Edited by R. A. Guelich. Grand Rapids: Eerdmans.

Martin, V., and G. de Budé, eds. 1962. *Eschine Discours*. 2 vols. Paris: Les Belles Lettres.

Martin, V., and R. Kasser. 1961. *Papyrus Bodmer XIV: Évangile de Luc chap. 3–24*. Geneva: Bibliotheca Bodmeriana.

Martínez, F. G., and E. J. C. Tigchelaar. 1998. *The Dead Sea Scrolls: Study Edition*. Vol. 2. Grand Rapids: Eerdmans.

März, C.-P. 1974. *Das Wort Gottes bei Lukas*. Leipzig: Benno.

————. 1990. "Zur Vorgeschichte von Lk 12,35-48." Pages 166–78 in *Christus bezeugen: Festschrift Wolfgang Trilling*. Edited by K. Kertelge, T. Holtz, and C.-P. März. Freiburg: Herder.

————. 1992. "Das Gleichnis vom Dieb." Pages 633–48 in *The Four Gospels 1992: Festschrift Frans Neirynck*. Vol. 2. Edited by F. van Segbroeck, C. M. Tuckett, G. van Belle, and J. Verheyden. BEThL 100. Leuven: Peeters.

————. 2005. "Zur lukanischen Rezeption der Gerichtspredigt Jesu in Q." Pages 1–24 in *Luke and his Readers: Festschrift Adelbert Denaux*. Edited by R. Bieringer, G. van Belle, and J. Verheyden. BEThL 182. Leuven: Peeters.

Matera, F. J. 1985. "The Death of Jesus according to Luke." *CBQ* 47: 469–85.

————. 1989a. "Jesus before the ΠΡΕΣΒΥΤΕΡΙΟΝ." Pages 517–33 in *L'évangile de Luc–The Gospel of Luke*. 2nd edition. Edited by F. Neirynck. BEThL 32. Leuven: Leuven University Press.

————. 1989b. "Luke 23,1-25: Jesus before Pilate, Herod, and Israel." Pages 535–51 in *L'évangile de Luc–The Gospel of Luke*. 2nd edition. Edited by F. Neirynck. BEThL 32. Leuven: Leuven University Press.

————. 1993. "Jesus' Journey to Jerusalem." *JSNT* 51: 57–77.

Mathieu, Y. 2004. *La figure de Pierre dans l'oeuvre de Luc.* EtB.NS 52. Paris: Gabalda.

Matson, D. L. 1996. *Household Conversion Narratives in Acts.* JSNT.S 123. Sheffield: Sheffield Academic.

Matson, M. A. 2001. *In Dialogue with Another Gospel? The Influence of the Fourth Gospel on the Passion Narrative of the Gospel of Luke.* SBL.DS 178. Atlanta: Society of Biblical Literature.

Mattill, A. J. 1979. *Luke and the Last Things.* Dillsboro: Western North Carolina Press.

Mayer, E. 1996. *Die Reiseerzählung des Lukas (Lk 9,51–9,10).* EHS.T 554. Frankfurt am Main: Peter Lang.

Mayer-Haas, A. J. 2003. *"Geschenk aus Gottes Schatzkammer" (bSchab 10b). Jesus und der Sabbat im Spiegel der neutestamentlichen Schriften.* NTA NF 43. Münster: Aschendorff.

Mayordomo-Marín, M. 1998. *Den Anfang hören. Leserorientierte Evangelienexegese am Beispiel von Matthäus 1–2.* FRLANT 180. Göttingen: Vandenhoeck & Ruprecht.

Mayser, E. 1926/1934. *Grammatik der griechischen Papyri aus der Ptolemäerzeit.* Vol. II/1–3. Berlin: Teubner.

———. ²1970/²1938/²1936. *Grammatik der griechischen Papyri aus der Ptolemäerzeit.* Vol. I/1–3. Berlin: Teubner.

McCane, B. R. 1990. "'Let the dead bury their own dead.'" *HThR* 83: 31–43.

McCown, C. C. 1939. "Luke's Translation of Semitic into Hellenistic Custom." *JBL* 58: 213–20.

McDermott, J. M. 1977. "Luke, XII, 8-9: Stone of Scandal." *RB* 84: 523–37.

McGaughy, L. C. 1999. "Infancy Narratives and Hellenistic Lives: Luke 1–2." *Forum NF* 2: 25–39.

McIver, R. K. 1994. "One Hundred-fold Yield—Miraculous or Mundane?" *NTS* 40: 606–8.

McKnight, S. 1999. "Public Declaration or Final Judgment? Matthew 10:26-27 = Luke 12:2-3 as a Case of Creative Redaction." Pages 363–83 in *Authenticating the Words of Jesus.* Edited by B. Chilton and C. A. Evans. NTTS 28/1. Leiden: Brill.

McNamara, M. 1966. *The New Testament and the Palestinian Targum to the Pentateuch.* AnBib 27. Rome: Pontifical Biblical Institute.

McNicol, A. J., D. L. Dungen, and D. Barrett, eds. 1996. *Beyond the Q Impasse—Luke's Use of Matthew: A Demonstration by the Research Team of the International Institute for Gospel Studies.* Valley Forge, Penn.: Trinity International.

Meeûs, X. de. 1961. "Composition de Lc., XIV et genre symposiaque." *EThL* 37: 847–70.

Meinertz, M. 1957. "Dieses Geschlecht im Neuen Testament." *BZ NF* 1: 283–89.

Meiser, M. 1998. *Die Reaktion des Volkes auf Jesus.* BZNW 96. Berlin: Walter de Gruyter.

———. 2001. "Das Alte Testament im lukanischen Doppelwerk." Pages 167–95 in *Im Brennpunkt: Die Septuaginta. Studien zur Entstehung und Bedeutung der Griechischen Bibel.* Edited by H.-J. Fabry and U. Offerhaus. BWANT 153. Stuttgart: Kohlhammer.

Mekkattukunnel, A. G. 2001. *The Priestly Blessing of the Risen Christ: An Exegetico-Theological Analysis of Luke 24,50-53.* EHS.T 714. Bern: Peter Lang.

Mell, U. 1994. *Die "anderen" Winzer.* WUNT 77. Tübingen: Mohr.

Melzer-Keller, H. 1997. *Jesus und die Frauen.* HBSt 14. Freiburg im Breisgau: Herder.

Méndez-Moratalla, F. 2004. *The Paradigm of Conversion in Luke.* JSNT.S 252. London: T&T Clark.

Menoud, P. H. 1975. "Le sens du verbe BIAZETAI dans Luc 16.16." Pages 125–30 in *Jésus-Christ et la foi.* Neuchâtel: Delachaux et Niestlé.

Merkel, H. 1994. "Israel im lukanischen Werk." *NTS* 40: 371–98.

Merkel, J. 1905. "Die Begnadigung am Passahfeste." *ZNW* 6: 293–316.

Merklein, H. 1977. "'Dieser ging als Gerechter nach Hause . . .' Das Gottesbild Jesu und die Haltung der Menschen nach Lk 18,9-14." *BiKi* 32: 34–42.

———. 1984. *Die Gottesherrschaft als Handlungsprinzip: Untersuchung zur Ethik Jesu.* 3rd edition. FzB 34. Würzburg: Echter.

———. 1992. "Die Heilung des Besessenen von Gerasa." Pages 1017–37 in *The Four Gospels 1992: Festschrift Frans Neirynck.* Vol. 2. Edited by F. van Segbroeck, C. M. Tuckett, G. van Belle, and J. Verheyden. BEThL 100. Leuven: Peeters.

———. 1998. "Ägyptische Einflüsse auf die messianische Sohn-Gottes-Aussage des Neuen Testaments." in *Zwischen Jesus und Paulus II.* WUNT 105. Tübingen: Mohr.

Metzger, B. M. 1958/1959. "Seventy or Seventy-two Disciples?" *NTS* 5: 299–306.

———. 1971. *A Textual Commentary on the Greek New Testament.* London: United Bible Societies.

Meynet, R. 1981. "Au coeur du texte: Analyse rhétorique de l'aveugle de Jéricho selon saint Luc." *NRTh* 103: 696–710.

———. 1985. "Dieu donne son nom à Jésus. Analyse rhétorique de Lc 1,26-56 et de 1 Sam 2,1-10." *Bib.* 66: 39–72.

———. 2005. "Le vin de la nouvelle alliance. La parabole du vieux et du neuf (Lc 5,36-37) dans son contexte." *Gr.* 86: 5–27.

Mézange, C. 2000. "Simon le Zélote était-il un révolutionnaire?" *Bib* 81: 489–506.

Michaelis, W. 1964. "Lukas und die Anfang der Kindertaufe." Pages 187–93 in *Apophoreta: Festschrift Ernst Haenchen.* Edited by W. Eltester. BZNW 30. Berlin: Töpelmann.

Michel, O. 1959–1960. "Eine philologische Frage zur Einzugsgeschichte." *NTS* 6: 81–82.

———. 1975. *Der Brief an die Hebräer.* 7th edition. KEK 13. Göttingen: Vandenhoeck & Ruprecht.

Michel, V. 2003. "Emmaus in Lukas 24,13: Textkritik und Lokalisierungsversuche." Pages 124–41 in *Emmaus in Judäa: Geschichte, Exegese, Archäologie.* Edited by K.-H. Fleckenstein, M. Louhivuori, and R. Riesner. Giessen: Brunnen.

Miller, R. J. 1988. "Elijah, John, and Jesus in the Gospel of Luke." *NTS* 34: 611–22.

———. 1998. "Source Criticism and the Limits of Certainty: The Lukan Transfiguration Story as a Test Case." *EThL* 74: 127–44.

Mills, W. E. 1994. *Bibliographies for Biblical Research: New Testament Series.* Vol. 3, *The Gospel of Luke.* Lewiston, N.Y.: Mellen.

Milot, L. 1985. "Guérison d'une femme infirme un jour de sabbat (Luc 13,10-17)." *SémBib* 39: 23–33.

Minear, P. S. 1964/1965. "A Note on Luke xxii 36." *NT* 7: 128–34.

———. 1974. "A Note on Luke 17:7-10." *JBL* 93: 82–87.

Mineshige, K. 2003. *Besitzverzicht und Almosen bei Lukas.* WUNT 2/163. Tübingen: Mohr Siebeck.

Minnen, P. van. 2001. "Luke 4,17-20 and the Handling of Ancient Books." *JThS* 52: 689–90.

Mitchell, A. C. 1990. "Zachaeus Revisited." *Bib.* 71: 153–76.

———. 1991. "The Use of συκοφαντεῖν in Luke 19,8." *Bib.* 72: 546–47.

Mitchell, M. 2005. "Patristic Counter-Evidence to the Claim that 'The Gospels Were Written for All Christians.'" *NTS* 51: 36–79.

Mitchell, S. 1998. "Wer waren die Gottesfürchtigen?" *Chiron* 28: 55–64.

———. 1999. The Cult of Theos Hypsistos between Pagans, Jews, and Christians. Pages 81–148 in *Pagan Monotheism in Late Antiquity.* Edited by P. Athanassiadi and M. Frede. Oxford: Clarendon.

Mittelstaedt, A. 2006. *Lukas als Historiker. Zur Datierung des lukanischen Doppelwerkes.* TANZ 43. Tübingen: Francke.

Mittmann-Richert, U. 1996. *Magifikat und Benedictus.* WUNT 2/90. Tübingen: Mohr.

Mitton, C. L. 1972/1973. "New Wine in Old Wine Skins. IV. Leaven." *ExpT* 84: 339–43.

Miyoshi, M. 1974. *Der Anfang des Reiseberichts.* AnBib 60. Rome: Pontifical Biblical Institute.

———. 1978. "Jesu Darstellung oder Reinigung im Tempel unter Berücksichtigung von 'Nunc Dimittis' Lk II 22-38." *AJBI* 4: 85–115.

Moessner, D. P. 1986. "'The Christ Must Suffer': New Light on the Jesus—Peter, Stephen, Paul Parallels in Luke–Acts." *NT* 28: 220–56.

———. 1989. *Lord of the Banquet: The Literary and Theological Significance of the Lukan Travel Narrative.* Minneapolis: Fortress.

———. 1992. "The Meaning of ΚΑΘΕΞΗΣ in the Lukan Prologue as a Key to the Distinctive Contribution of Luke's Narrative among the 'Many.'" Pages 1513–28 in *The Four Gospels 1992: Festschrift Frans Neirynck.* Vol. 2. Edited by F. van Segbroeck, C. M. Tuckett, G. van Belle, and J. Verheyden. BEThL 100. Leuven: Peeters.

———. 1996. "'Eyewitnesses,' 'Informed Contemporaries,' and 'Unknowing Inquirers': Josephus' Criteria for Authentic Historiography and the Meaning of ΠΑΡΑΚΟΛΟΥΘΕΩ." *NT* 38: 105–22.

————. 1999. "The Appeal and Power of Poetics (Luke 1:1-4)." Pages 84–123 in *Jesus and the Heritage of Israel: Luke's Narrative Claim upon Israel's Legacy*. Edited by D. P. Moessner. Harrisburg: Trinity International.

Möller, C., and G. Schmitt. 1976. *Siedlungen Palästinas nach Flavius Josephus*. BTAVO.B 19. Wiesbaden: Reichert.

Mommsen, T. 1899. *Römisches Strafrecht*. Leipzig: Duncker & Humblot.

Moo, D. J. 1983. *The Old Testament in the Gospel Passion Narratives*. Sheffield: Almond Press.

Moore, T. S. 1997. "The Lucan Great Commission and the Isaianic Servant." *BS* 154: 47–60.

Mora, V. 1983. *Le signe de Jonas*. Paris: Cerf.

Moretti, L. ed. 1967/1976. *Iscrizioni storiche ellenistiche*. 2 vols. Florence: La Nuova Italia. Morgan, R. 1994. "Flesh is Precious: The Significance of Luke 24.36-43." Pages 8–20 in *Resurrection: Festschrift Leslie Houlden*. Edited by Stephen C. Barton and Graham Stanton. London: SPCK.

Morgen, M. 1997. "Lc 17,20-37 et Lc 21,8-11.20-24. Arrière-fond scripturaire." Pages 307–26 in *The Scriptures in the Gospels*. Edited by C. M. Tuckett. BEThL 131. Leuven: Peeters.

Morgenthaler, R. 1948. *Die lukanische Geschichtsschreibung als Zeugnis*. 2 vols. AThANT 14–15. Zürich: Zwingli-Verlag.

————. 1993. *Lukas und Quintilian*. Zürich: Gotthelf.

Mott, S. C. 1975. "The Power of Giving and Receiving." Pages 60–72 in *Current Issues in Biblical and Patristic Interpretation: Festschrift Merrill C. Tenney*. Edited by G. F. Hawthorne. Grand Rapids: Eerdmans.

Moule, C. F. D. 1959 [1953]. *An Idiom Book of New Testament Greek*. 2nd edition. Cambridge: Cambridge University Press.

Moulton, J. H., and G. Milligan. 1963. *The Vocabulary of the Greek Testament: Illustrated from the Papyri and Other Non-literay Sources*. London: Hodder & Stoughton.

Moulton, J. H., and N. Turner. 1963. *A Grammar of New Testament Greek*. Vol. 3, *Syntax*. Edinburgh: T&T Clark.

Moxnes, H. 1988. *The Economy of the Kingdom*. Philadelphia: Fortress.

Muddiman, J. 1972. "A Note on Reading Luke XXIV.12." *EThL* 48: 542–58.

Mullach, F. W. A. 1860–1881. *Fragmenta Philosophorum Graecum*. Paris: Didot.

Müller, C. F. T. 1965. *Geographi Graeci Minores*. Hildesheim: Olms.

Müller, C. G. 2001. *Mehr als ein Prophet: Die Charakterzeichnung Johannes des Täufers im lukanischen Erzählwerk*. HBiSt 31. Freiburg: Herder.

————. 2003. "'Ungefähr 30': Anmerkungen zur Altersangabe Jesu im Lukasevangelium (Lk 3.23)." *NTS* 49: 489–504.

————. 2005. "Josef von Arimathäa und die Grablegung Jesu (Lk 23,50-56)." Pages 179–98 in *"Licht zur Erleuchtung der Heiden und Herrlichkeit für dein Volk Israel": Festschrift Josef Zmijewski*. Edited by C. G. Müller. BBB 151. Hamburg: Philo.

Müller, I. 1993. *Humoralmedizin*. Heidelberg: Haug.

Müller, K. 1969. *Anstoss und Gericht; eine Studie zum jüdischen Hintergrund des paulinischen Skandalon-Begriffs*. Munich: Kösel.

———. 1979. "Jesus vor Herodes." Pages 111–41 in *Zur Geschichte des Urchristentums*. Edited by G. Dautzenberg. QD 87. Freiburg: Herder.

———. 1994. "Gott als Richter und die Erscheinungsweisen seiner Gerichte in den Schriften des Frühjudentums." Pages 23–53 in *Weltgericht und Weltvollendung: Zukunftsbilder im Neuen Testament*. Edited by H.-J. Klauck. Freiburg: Herder.

———. 2003. "Das Vaterunser als jüdisches Gebet." Pages 159–204 in *Identität durch Gebet*. Edited by A. Gerhards. Paderborn: Schöningh.

Müller, P. 1992. *In der Mitte der Gemeinde: Kinder im Neuen Testament*. Neukirchen-Vluyn: Neukirchener.

Müller, U. B. 1974. "Vision und Botschaft. Erwägung zur prophetischen Struktur der Verkündigung Jesu." *ZThK* 71: 416–48.

———. 1996. "';Sohn Gottes'—ein messianischer Hoheitstitel Jesu." *ZNW* 87: 1–32.

———. 1998. *Die Entstehung des Glaubens an die Auferstehung Jesu*. SBS 172. Stuttgart: Katholisches Bibelwerk.

Müller, V. 1994. "The Prehistory of the 'Good Shepherd.'" *JNES* 3: 87–90.

Muñoz Iglesias, S. 1984. "El procedimiento literario del anuncio previo en la Biblia." *EstB* 42: 21–70.

Mussies, G. 1978. "The Sense of συλλογίζεσθαι at Luke XX 5." Pages 59–76 in *Miscellanea Neotestamentica*. Vol. 2. Edited by T. Baarda, A. F. J. Klijn, and W. C. van Unnik. Leiden: Brill.

———. 1988. "Vernoemen in de antieke wereld. De historische achergrond van Luk. 1,59-63." *NedThT* 42: 114–25.

Mussner, F. 1967. "Das 'Gleichnis' vom gestrengen Mahlherrn (Lk 13,22-30)." Pages 113–24 in *Praesentia salutis: Gesammelte Studien zu Fragen und Themen des Neuen Testamentes*. Düsseldorf: Patmos.

———. 2002. "Die Skepsis des Menschensohn. Zu Lk 18,8b." Pages 271–75 in *Forschungen zum Neuen Testament und seiner Umwelt: Festschrift Albert Fuchs*. Edited by C. Niemand. LPTB 7. Frankfurt am Main: Lang.

Myllykoski, M. 1991. "The Material Common to Luke and John." Pages 115–56 in *Luke–Acts: Scandanavian Perspectives*. Edited by P. Luomanen. Helsinki: Finnish Exegetical Society.

———. 2005. "On the Way to Emmaus (Luke 24:13-35): Narrative and Ideological Aspects of Fiction." Pages 92–115 in *Lux Humana, Lux Aeterna. Festschrift Lars Aejmelaeus*. Edited by A. Mustakallio, H. Leppä, and H. Räisänen. SESJ 89. Helsinki: Finnish Exegetical Society.

Nauck, A. 1963. *Aristophanis Byzantii Grammatici Alexandrine Fragmenta*. Hildesheim: Olms.

Nauck, W. 1955. "Freude im Leiden." *ZNW* 46: 68–80.

———. 1958. "Das οὖν paräneticum." *ZNW* 49: 134–35.

Nave, G. D. 2002. *The Role and Function of Repentance in Luke–Acts*. SBL.AB 4. Atlanta: Society of Biblical Literature.

Neale, D. A. 1991. *None but the Sinners*. JSNT.S 58. Sheffield: Sheffield Academic.

Nebe, G. 1989. *Prophetische Züge im Bilde Jesu bei Lukas*. BWANT 127. Stuttgart: Kohlhammer.

———. 1992. "Das ἔσται in Luke 11,36 —ein neuer Deutungsvorschlag." *ZNW* 83: 108–14.

Negoiță, A., and C. Daniel. 1967. "L'énigme du levain." *NT* 9: 306–14.

Neirynck, F. 1974a. "Les accords mineurs et la rédaction des évangiles: L'épisode du paralytique (Mt., IX, 1-8/Lc., V,17-26, par. Mc., II,1-12)." *EThL* 50: 215–30.

———. 1974b. *The Minor Agreements of Matthew and Luke against Mark with a Cumulative List*. BEThL 37. Leuven: Peeters.

———. 1982/1991/2001. *Evangelica*. 3 vols. BEThL 60/99/150. Leuven: Peeters.

———. 1991. *The Minor Agreements in a Horizontal-Line Synopsis*. SNTA 15. Leuven: Leuven University Press.

———. 2001. *Q-Parallels. Q-Synopsis and IQP/CritEd Parallels*. Leuven: Leuven University Press.

———. 2002. "Luke 24.12: An Anti-docetic Interpretation?" Pages 145–58 in *New Testament Textual Criticism and Exegesis: Festschrift Joël Delobel*. Edited by A. Denaux. BEThL 161. Leuven: Peeters.

Nellessen, E. 1976. *Zeugnis für Jesus und das Wort: Exegetische Untersuchungen zum lukanischen Zeugnisbegriff*. BBB 43. Cologne: Hanstein.

Nelson, P. K. 1991. "The Flow of Thought in Luke 22.24-27." *JSNT* 43: 113–23.

———. 1993. "Luke 22:29-30 and the Time Frame for Dining and Ruling." *TynB* 44: 351–61.

———. 1994a. *Leadership and Discipleship: A Study of Luke 22:24-30*. SBL.DS 138. Atlanta: Scholars Press.

———. 1994b. "The Unitary Character of Luke 22.24-30." *NTS* 40: 609–19.

Nestle, E. 1903. "Ein Andreasbrief im Neuen Testament?" *ZNW* 4: 270–72.

———. 1913. "Otterngezüchte." *ZNW* 14: 267–68.

Netzer, E. 1991. *Masada III: The Yigael Yadin Excavations, 1963–1965: Final Reports III*. Jerusalem: Israel Exploration Society.

Neumann, P. K. D. 1973. "Das Wort, das geschehen ist . . . Zum Problem der Wortempfangsterminologie in Jer. I-XXV." *VT* 23: 171–217.

Neusner, J. 1988. *The Mishnah: A New Translation*. New Haven: Yale University Press.

Neyrey, J. H. 1980. "The Absence of Jesus' Emotions—the Lucan Redaction of Lk 22,39-46." *Bib.* 61: 153–71.

———. 1983. "Jesus' Address to the Women of Jerusalem (Lk. 23.27-31)." *NTS* 29: 74–86.

———. 1985. *The Passion According to Luke*. New York: Paulist Press.

Nickau, K. 1966a. *Ammonii qui dicitur liber de adfinium vocabulorum differentia*. Leipzig: Teubner.

———. 1966b. *Ammonius—De adfinium vocabulorum–differentia*. Leipzig: Teubner.

Nicklas, T. 2002. "Das Agraphon vom 'Sabbatarbeiter' und sein Kontext. Lk. 6:1-11 in der Textform des Codex Bezae Cantabrigiensis (D)." *NovT* 44: 160–75.

Niebuhr, K.-W. 1997. "Die Werke des eschatologischen Freudenboten." Pages 637–46 in *The Scriptures in the Gospels*. Edited by C. M. Tuckett. BEThL 131. Leuven: Peeters.

Nielsen, A. E. 2000. *Until It Is Fulfilled: Lukan Eschatology According to Luke 22 and Acts 20*. WUNT 2/126. Tübingen: Mohr.

Niemand, C. 1989. *Studien zu den Minor Agreements der synoptischen Verklärungsperikopen*. EHS.T 352. Frankfurt am Main: Lang.

Niese, B. 1892. *Flavii Iosephi opera*. Vol. 3. Berlin: Weidmann.

Nijman, M., and K. W. Worp. 1999. "Ἐπιούσιος in a Documentary Papyrus?" *NT* 41: 231–34.

Nilsson, M. P. 1950. *Geschichte der Griechischen Religion*. Vol. 2. Munich: Beck.

Nissen, A. 1974. *Gott und der Nächste im antiken Judentum*. WUNT 15. Tübingen: Mohr.

Noack, B. 1948. *Das Gottesreich bei Lukas. Eine Studie zu Luk. 17,20-24*. SyBU 10. Uppsala: Gleerup.

Noël, F. 1997. "The Double Commandment of Love in Lk 10,27." Pages 559–70 in *The Scriptures in the Gospels*. Edited by C. M. Tuckett. BEThL 131. Leuven: Peeters

———. 2004. *The Travel Narrative in the Gospel of Luke*. CBRA 5. Brussels: Koninklijke Vlaamse Academie voor Wetenschappen en Kunsten van België.

Noël, T. 1989. "The Parable of the Wedding Guests." *PRSt* 16: 17–27.

Nolland, J. 1979a. "Classical and Rabbinic Parallels to 'Physician, Heal Yourself' (Lk IV 23)." *NT* 21: 193–209.

———. 1979b. "Impressed Unbelievers as Witnesses to Christ (Luke 4:22a)." *JBL* 98: 219–29.

———. 1984. "Words of Grace (Luke 4,22)." *Blb.* 65: 44–60.

Noorda, S. J. 1982. "'Cure Yourself, Doctor!' (Luke 4,23). Classical Parallels to an Alleged Saying of Jesus." Pages 459–67 in *Logia: Mémorial Joseph Coppens*. Edited by J. Delobel and T. Baarda. BEThL 59. Leuven: Peeters.

Norden, E. 1913. *Agnostos Theos*. Leipzig: Teubner.

———. 1958 [1924]. *Die Geburt des Kindes. Geschichte einer religiösen Idee*. Darmstadt: Wissenschaftliche Buchgesellschaft.

Nordheim, E. von. 1980/1985. *Die Lehre der Alten*. 2 vols. ALGHJ 13/18. Leiden: Brill.

North, J. L. 2005. "Praying for a Good Spirit: Text, Context and Meaning of Luke 11.13." *JSNT* 28: 167–88.

Novenson, M. 2012. *Christ among the Messiahs: Christ Language in Paul and Messiah Language in Ancient Judaism*. Oxford: Oxford University Press.

Nützel, J. M. 1976. "Zum Schicksal der eschatologischen Propheten." *BZ NF* 20: 59–94.

———. 1980. *Jesus als Offenbarer Gottes nach den lukanischen Schriften*. FzB 39. Stuttgart: Katholisches Bibelwerk.

Ó Fearghail, F. 1984. "Rejection in Nazareth: Lk 4,22." *ZNW* 75: 60–72.

————. 1989. "The Imitation of the Septuagint in Luke's Infancy Narrative." *PIBA* 12: 58–78.

————. 1991. *The Introduction to Luke–Acts*. AnBib 126. Rome: Pontifical Biblical Institute.

————. 1993. "Announcement or Call? Literary Form and Purpose in Luke 1:26-38." *PIBA* 16: 20–35.

Oakman, D. E. 1987. "The Buying Power of Two Denarii: A Comment on Luke 10:35." *Forum* 3: 33–38.

Oberlinner, L. 1975. *Historische Überlieferung und christologische Aussage. Zur Frage der "Bruder" Jesu in der Synopse*. FzB 19. Stuttgart: Katholisches Bibelwerk.

————. 2003. "Begegnungen mit Jesus: Der Pharisäer und die Sünderin nach Lk 7,36-50." Pages 253–78 in *Liebe, Macht und Religion. Gedenkschrift für Helmut Merklein*. Edited by M. Gielen and J. Kügler. Stuttgart: Katholisches Bibelwerk.

O'Day, G. R. 2004. "'There the ? Will Gather Together,' (Luke 17:37)." Pages 288–303 in *Literary Encounters with the Reign of God*. Edited by S. H. Ringe and H. C. P. Kim. New York: T&T Clark.

Oegema, G. 1998. *The Anointed and His People: Messianic Expectations from the Maccabees to Bar Kochba*. Sheffield: Sheffield Academic.

O'Hanlon, J. 1981. "The Story of Zachaeus and the Lukan Ethic." *JSNT* 12: 2–26.

Öhler, M. 1997. *Elia im Neuen Testament*. BZNW 88. Berlin: Walter de Gruyter.

Ollrog, W.-H. 1979. *Paulus und seine Mitarbeiter*. Neukirchen-Vluyn: Neukirchener.

Olrik, A. 1982. "Epische Gesetze der Volksdichtung." Pages 58–69 in *Gleichnisse Jesu*. Edited by W. Harnisch. Darmstadt: Wissenschaftiche Buchgesellschaft.

Olsson, B. 2004. "The Canticle of the Heavenly Host (Luke 2.14) in History and Culture." *NTS* 50: 146–66.

Olsthoorn, M. F. 1975. *The Jewish Background and the Synoptic Setting of Mt 6,25-33 and Lk 12,22-31*. SBFA 10. Jerusalem: Studium Biblicum Franciscanum.

Omerzu, H. 2003. "Das traditionsgeschichtliche Verhältnis der Begegnungen von Jesus mit Herodes Antipas und Paulus mit Agrippa II." *SNTU.A* 28: 121–45.

Onuki, T. 2000. "Tollwut in Q? Ein Versuch über Mt 12.43-5 / Lk 11.24-6." *NTS* 46: 358–74.

Orelli, J. K. 1816. *Memnonis Historiarum Heracleae Ponti*. Leipzig: Weidemann.

Osten-Sacken, P. von der. 1973. "Zur Christologie des lukanischen Reiseberichts." *EvTh* 33: 476–96.

Ostmeyer, K.-H. 2006. *Kommunikation mit Gott und Christus*. WUNT 197. Tübingen: Mohr.

O'Toole, R. F. 1983. "Luke's Position on Politics and Society in Luke–Acts." Pages 1–17 in *Political Issues in Luke–Acts*. Edited by R. J. Cassidy and P. J. Scharper. Maryknoll, N. Y.: Orbis.

————. 1987. "Luke's Message in Luke 9:1-50." *CBQ* 49: 74–89.

————. 1991. "The Literary Form of Luke 19:1-10." *JBL* 110: 107–16.

————. 1992. "Some Exegetical Reflections on Luke 13,10-17." *Bib.* 73: 84–107.

———. 1995. "Does Luke Also Portray Jesus as the Christ in Luke 4.16-30?" *Bib.* 76: 498–522.

———. 2004. *Luke's Presentation of Jesus: A Christology*. SubBi 25. Rome: Pontifical Biblical Institute.

Nickau, K. 1966. *Ammonii qui dicitur liber de adfinium vocabulorum differentia*. Leipzig: Teubner.

Novenson, M. 2012. *Christ Among the Messiahs: Christ Language in Paul and Messiah Language in Ancient Judaism*. Oxford: Oxford University Press.

Pack, R. A. 1963. *Onirocriticon libri V*. Leipzig: Teubner.

Paffenroth, K. 1997. *The Story of Jesus according to L*. JSNT.S 147. Sheffield: Sheffield Academic.

Palme, B. 1993. "Die ägyptische κατ' οἰκίαν ἀπογραφή und Lk 2,1-5." *ProBi* 2: 1–24.

———. 1994. "Neues zum ägyptischen Provinzialzensus." *ProBi* 3: 1–7.

Palmer, H. 1976. "Just Married, Cannot Come." *NT* 18: 241–57.

Panier, L. 1984. *Récit et commentaires de la tentation de Jésus au désert*. Paris: Cerf.

———. 1989. "La parabole des mines. Lecture sémiotique." Pages 333–47 in *Les Paraboles évangéliques: Perspectives nouvelles. XIIe congrès de l'ACFEB, Lyon (1987)*. Edited by J. Delorme. LeDiv 135. Paris: Cerf.

———. 2005. "Récit et figure dans la parabole des mines." *SémBib* 117: 30–45.

Parente, M. I., ed. 1980. *Speusippus Frammenti*. Naples: Bibliopolis.

Parker, S. B. 1988. "The Birth Announcement." Pages 133–49 in *Ascribe to the Lord: Biblical and Other Studies in Memory of Peter C. Craigie*. Edited by L. M. Eslinger and G. Taylor. Sheffield: JSOT.

Parrot, A. 1939. "Le 'Bon Pasteur.'" Pages 171–82 in *Mélanges syriens offerts á M. Réne Dussaud*. Vol. 1. Paris: Paul Geuthner.

Parsons, M. C. 1986. "Narrative Closure and Openness in the Plot of the Third Gospel: The Sense of an Ending in Luke 24:50-53." *SBLSP* 25: 201–23.

———. 1987. *The Departure of Jesus in Luke–Acts: The Ascension Narratives in Context*. JSNT.S 21. Sheffield: Sheffield Academic.

———. 2001. "'Short in Stature': Luke's Physical Description of Zachaeus." *NTS* 47: 50–57.

Parsons, M. C., and R. I. Pervo. 1993. *Rethinking the Unity of Luke and Acts*. Minneapolis: Fortress.

Patella, M. 1999. *The Death of Jesus: The Diabolic Force and the Ministering Angel*. CRB 43. Paris: Gabalda.

Paton, W. R. 1913. "Ἀγωνία (Agony)." *CIR* 27: 194.

Patte, D. 1997. "Whither Critical New Testament Studies for a New Day: Some Reflections on Luke 17:11-19." Pages 277–93 in *Putting Body and Soul Together: Festschrift Robin Scroggs*. Edited by V. Wiles, A. R. Brown, and G. F. Snyder. Valley Forge, Penn.: Trinity International.

Paulsen, H. 1997. "Die Witwe und der Richter (Lk 18,1-8)." Pages 113–38 in *Zur Literatur und Geschichte des frühen Christentums*. WUNT 99. Tübingen: Mohr.

Payne, P. B. 1979. "The Order of Sowing and Ploughing in the Parable of the Sower." *NTS* 25: 123–29.

Pearson, B. A. 1999. "The Lucan Censuses, Revisited." *CBQ* 61: 262–82.

Peels, H. G. L. 2001. "The Blood 'from Abel to Zechariah' [Matthew 23.35; Luke 11.50f.] and the Canon of the Old Testament." *ZAW* 113: 583–601.

Pellegrini, S. 2004. "Ein 'ungetreuer' οἰκονόμος (Luke 16.1-13)." *BZ NF* 48: 161–78.

Peppink, S. P. 1937–1939. *Athenæi Dipnosophistarum epitome.* Leiden: Brill.

Peres, I. 2003. *Griechische Grabinschriften und neutestamentliche Eschatologie.* WUNT 157. Tübingen: Mohr.

Perrot, C. 1988. "The Reading of the Bible in the Ancient Synagogue." Pages 137–59 in *Mikra: Text, Translation, Reading and Interpretation of the Hebrew Bible in Ancient Judaism and Early Christianity.* Edited by M. J. Mulder and H. Sysling. Assen: Van Gorcum.

Pesch, R. 1968. "'Kind warum hast du so an uns getan?' [Luke 2.48]." *BZ NF* 12: 245–48.

———. 1969. *Der reiche Fischfang.* Düsseldorf: Patmos.

———. 1970a. "Jairus (Mark 5,22/Lk 8,41)." *BZ NF* 14: 252–56.

———. 1970b. *Jesu ureigene Taten?* QD 52. Freiburg: Herder.

———. 1972. *Der Besessene von Gerasa.* SBS 56. Stuttgart: Katholisches Bibelwerk.

———. 1973. "Zur Entstehung des Glaubens an die Auferstehung Iesu." *ThQ* 153: 201–28.

———. 1980. *Das Markusevangelium.* 2 vols. HThK 2. Freiburg i.Br.: Herder.

———, ed. 1981. *Zur Theologie der Kindheitsgeschichten.* Munich: Schnell & Steiner.

———. 1989. "La rédaction lucanienne du logion des pêcheurs d'hommes (Lc., V,10c)." Pages 135–54, 313–15 in *L'évangile de Luc–The Gospel of Luke.* 2nd edition. Edited by F. Neirynck. Leuven: Leuven University Press.

Pesonen, A. 2000. "The Weeping Sinner: A Short Story by Luke?" *Neotest.* 34: 87–102.

Petersen, S. 2006. "Die Evangelienüberschriften und die Entstehung des neutestamentlichen Kanons." *ZNW* 97: 250–74.

Peterson, E. 1929/1930. "Die Einholung des Kyrios." *ZSTh* 7: 682–702.

Petracca, V. 2003. *Gott oder das Geld. Die Besitzethik des Lukas.* TANZ 39. Tübingen: Francke.

Petzer, J. H. 1984. "Luke 22:19b-20 and the Structure of the Passage." *NT* 26: 249–52.

———. 1992. "Anti-Judaism and the Textual Problem of Luke 23:34." *FilNeo* 5: 199–203.

Petzer, K. 1991. "Style and Text in the Lucan Narrative of the Institution of the Lord's Supper (Luke 22.19b-20)." *NTS* 37: 113–29.

Philippidis, L. J. 1929. *Die "Goldene Regel."* Leipzig: Klein.

Philonenko, M. 1988. "La parabole sur la lampe (Luc 11,33-36) et les horoscopes qoumrâniens." *ZNW* 79: 145–51.

———. 2002. *Das Vaterunser.* UTB 2312. Tübingen: Mohr.

Pietersma, A. 1994. *The Apocryphon of Jannes and Jambres, the Magicians: P. Chester Beatty XVI (with new editions of Papyrus Vindobonensis Greek inv. 29456 + 29828 verso and British Library Cotton Tiberius B. v f. 87).* Leiden: Brill.

Pilhofer, P. 1995. *Die erste christliche Gemeinde Europas.* Vol. 1. WUNT 87. Tübingen: Mohr.

Piper, J. 1979. *"Love Your Enemies."* MSSNTS 38. Cambridge: Cambridge University Press.

Piper, R. 1982. "Matthew 7,7-11 par. Luke 11,9-13." Pages 411–18 in *Logia. Mémorial Joseph Coppens.* Edited by J. Delobel and T. Baarda. BEThL 59. Leuven: Peeters.

Pitre, B. J. 2001. "Blessing the Barren and Warning the Fecund." *JSNT* 81: 59–80.

Pittner, B. 1991. *Studien zum lukanischen Sondergut.* Vol. 18. ETS. Leipzig: Benno.

Plessis, I. J. de. 1974. "Once More: The Purpose of Luke's Prologue." *NT* 16: 259–71.

———. 1994. "The Saving Significance of Jesus and His Death on the Cross in Luke's Gospel—Focussing on Luke 22:19-20." *Neotest.* 28: 523–40.

———. 2000. "The Lukan Audience–Rediscovered?" *Neotest.* 34: 243–61.

Plevnik, J. 1987. "The Eyewitnesses of the Risen Jesus in Luke 24." *CBQ* 49: 90–103.

———. 1991. "Son of Man Seated at the Right Hand of God: Luke 22.69 in Lucan Soteriology." *Bib.* 72: 331–47.

Plisch, U.-K. 2002. "Was ist 'das Zeichen des Jona'?" Pages 399–409 in *For the Children, Perfect Instruction: Festschrift Hans-Martin Schenke.* Edited by H.-G. Bethge. NHS 54. Leiden: Brill.

Plümacher, E. 1983. "Acta-Forschung 1974–1982." *ThR NF* 48: 1–56.

———. 1984. "Acta-Forschung 1974–1982." *ThR NF* 49: 105-69.

———. 2004. *Geschichte und Geschichten. Studien zur Apostelgeschichte und zu den Johannesakten.* Edited by J. Schröter and R. Brucker. WUNT 170. Tübingen: Mohr.

Pöhlmann, W. 1979. "Die Absichtung des Verlorenen Sohnes (Lk 15,12f.) und die erzählte Welt der Parabel." *ZNW* 70: 194–213.

———. 1993. *Der Verlorene Sohn und das Haus.* WUNT 68. Tübingen: Mohr.

Pokorný, P. 1973/1974. "The Temptation Stories and Their Intention." *NTS* 20: 115–27.

———. 1990. "Luke 15,11-32 und die lukanische Soteriologie." Pages 179–92 in *Christus bezeugen: Festschrift Wolfgang Trilling.* Edited by K. Kertelge, T. Holtz, and C.-P. März. Freiburg: Herder.

———. 1998. *Theologie der lukanischen Schriften.* FRLANT 174. Göttingen: Vandenhoeck & Ruprecht.

Pomeroy, A. J., ed. 1999. *Arius, Didymus: Epitome of Stoic Ethics.* Atlanta: Society of Biblical Literature.

Poon, W. C. K. 2003. "Superabundant Table Fellowship in the Kingdom: The Feeding of the Five Thousand and the Meal Motif in Luke." *ExpT* 114: 224–30.

Porter, S. E. 1987. "The Parable of the Unjust Steward (Luke 16.1-13)." Pages 127–53 in *The Bible in Three Dimensions*. Edited by D. J. A. Clines. JSOT.S 87. Sheffield: Sheffield Academic.

———. 1989. *Verbal Aspect in the Greek of the New Testament, with Reference to Tense and Mood*. SBG 1. New York: Lang.

———. 1992. "'In the Vicinity of Jericho': Luke 18:35 in the Light of Its Synoptic Parallels." *BBR* 2: 91–104.

———. 1999. *The Paul of Acts: Essays in Literary Criticism, Rhetoric, and Theology*. WUNT 115. Tübingen: Mohr.

———. 2002. "The Reasons for the Lukan Census." Pages 165–88 in *Paul, Luke and the Graeco-Roman World: Festschrift Alexander J. M. Wedderburn*. Edited by A. J. M. Wedderburn and A. Christophersen. JSNT.S 217. London: T&T Clark.

Potterie, I. de la. 1970. "Le titre KYRIOS appliqué à Jésus dans l'évangile de Luc." Pages 117–46 in *Mélanges bibliques en hommage au R.P. Béda Rigaux*. Edited by A.-L. Descamps and A. de Halleaux. Gembloux: Duculot.

———. 1985. "La parabole du prétendant à la royauté (Lc 19,11-28)." Pages 613–41 in *À cause de l'évangile: Festschrift Jacques Dupont*. LeDiv 123. Paris: Cerf.

———. 1987. "Κεχαριτωμένη en Lc 1.28." *Bib.* 68: 357–82.

Powell, J. U. 1925. *Collectanea Alexandrina: Reliquiae minores Poetarum Graecorum Aetatis Ptolemaicae 323–146 A.C.* Oxford: Clarendon.

Powell, M. A. 2004. "The Forgotten Famine: Personal Responsibility in Luke's Parable of 'the Prodigal Son.'" Pages 265–87 in *Literary Encounters with the Reign of God*. Edited by S. H. Ringe and H. C. P. Kim. New York: T&T Clark.

Preisigke, F. 1915. *Fachwörter des öffentlichen Verwaltungsdienstes Ägyptens in den griechischen Papyrusurkunden der ptolemäisch-römischen Zeit*. Göttingen: Vandenhoeck & Ruprecht.

———. 1925–1931. *Wörterbuch der griechischen Papyrusurkunden* 3. Berlin: Selbstverlag der Erben.

Preisigke, F., E. Kiessling, and W. J. R. Rübsam, eds. 1969–1971. *Wörterbuch der griechischen Papyrusurkunden: Supplementum I*. Amsterdam: Hakkert.

Prell, M. 1997. *Sozialökonomische Untersuchungen zur Armut im antiken Rom: von den Gracchen bis Kaiser Diokletian*. Stuttgart. Steiner.

Prieur, A. 1996. *Die Verkündigung der Gottesherrschaft*. WUNT 2/89. Tübingen: Mohr.

Puig I Tàrrech, A. 2001. "Une parabole à l'image antithétique." Pages 681–93 in *The Sayings Source Q and the Historical Jesus*. Edited by A. Lindemann. Leuven: Leuven University Press.

Quarles, C. L. 1999. "The Authenticity of the Parable of the Warring King: A Response to the Jesus Seminar." Pages 409–29 in *Authenticating the Words of Jesus*. Edited by B. Chilton and C. A. Evans. NTTS 28/2. Leiden: Brill.

Rackham, R. 2006. *Natural History. Books 8–11*. LCL. Cambridge, Mass.: Harvard University Press.

Radermacher, L. 1967. *Demetrii Phalerei Qui Dicitur de Elocutione Libellus*. Leipzig: Teubner.

Radl, W. 1986. "Ein 'doppeltes Leiden' in Lk 13,11? Zu einer Notiz von Günther Schwarz." *BN* 31: 35–36.

———. 1988a. *Das Lukas-Evangelium*. EdF 261. Darmstadt: Wissenschaftliche Buchgesellschaft.

———. 1988b. "Sonderüberlieferungen bei Lukas? Traditionsgeschichtliche Fragen zu Lk 22,67f; 23,2 und 23,6-12." Pages 131–47 in *Der Prozeß gegen Jesus*. Edited by K. Kertelge. QD 112. Freiburg: Herder.

———. 1996. *Der Ursprung Jesu. Traditionsgeschichtliche Untersuchungen zu Lukas 1–2*. HBSt 7. Freiburg im Breisgau: Herder.

———. 1999. "Die Beziehungen der Vorgeschichte zur Apostelgeschichte. Dargestellt an Lk 2,22-39." Pages 297–312 in *The Unity of Luke–Acts*. Edited by J. Verheyden. BEThL 142. Leuven: Peeters.

———. 2005. "Von der Habsucht und dem törichten Reichen (Lk 12,13-21)." Pages 103–14 in *"Licht der Erleuchtung der Heiden und Herrlichkeit für dein Volk Israel": Festschrift Josef Zmijewski*. Edited by C. G. Müller. BBB 151. Hamburg: Philo.

Räisänen, H. 1989. *Die Mutter Jesu im Neuen Testament*. 2nd edition. STAT.B 247. Helsinki: Suomalainen Tiedeakatemia.

———. 1991. "The Redemption of Israel." Pages 94–114 in *Luke–Acts: Scandinavian Perspectives*. Edited by P. Luomanen. SESJ 54. Helsinki: Finnish Exegetical Society.

———. 1992. "The Prodigal Gentile and His Jewish Christian Brother Lk 15,11-32." Pages 1617–36 in *The Four Gospels 1992: Festschrift Frans Neirynck*. Vol. 2. Edited by F. van Segbroeck, C. M. Tuckett, G. van Belle, and J. Verheyden. BEThL 100. Leuven: Peeters.

Rakocy, W. 2005. "The Sense of the Logion about the Sign of Jonah in the Gospel According to St Luke (11:29b-30)." *RTK* 52: 81–94.

Ramlot, M.-L. 1964. "Les généalogies bibliques: Un genre littéraire oriental." *BVC* 60: 53–70.

Ramsey, G. W. 1990. "Plots, Gaps, Repetitions, and Ambiguity in Luke 15." *PRS* 17: 33–42.

Randellini, L. 1974. "I'inno di giubilo: Mt 11,25-30; Lc. 10,20-24." *RivBib* 22: 183–235.

Rau, E. 1990. *Reden in Vollmacht: Hintergrund, Form, und Anliegen der Gleichnisse Jesu*. FRLANT 149. Göttingen: Vandenhoeck & Ruprecht.

Rauscher, J. 1990. *Vom Messiasgeheimnis zur Lehre der Kirche*. Desselbrunn: Rauscher.

Ravens, D. A. S. 1988. "The Setting of Luke's Account of the Anointing: Luke 7.2–8.3." *NTS* 34: 282–92.

———. 1990. "Luke 9.7-62 and the Prophetic Role of Jesus." *NTS* 36: 119–29.

———. 1991. "Zachaeus: The Final Part of a Lucan Triptych?" *JSNT* 41: 19–32.

Razzano, M. 2003. "Le discours de Jésus à Nazareth et la question du Jubilé (Lc 4,16-30)." *Hokhma* 82: 25–55.

Read-Heimerdinger, J., and J. Rius-Camps. 2002. "Emmaous or Oulammaous? Luke's Use of the Jewish Scriptures in the Text of Luke in Codex Bezae." *RCatT* 27: 23–42.

Reece, S. 2002. "Seven Stades to Emmaus." *NTS* 48: 262–66.

Reeg, G. 1989. *Die Ortsnamen Israels nach der rabbinischen Literatur*. BTAVO.B 51. Wiesbaden: Reichert.

Regul, J. 1969. *Die antimarcionitischen Evangelienprologe*. VL 6. Freiburg: Herder.

Rehkopf, F. 1959. *Die lukanische Sonderquelle*. WUNT 5. Tübingen: Mohr.

Reicke, B. 1974. "Die Fastenfrage nach Luk. 5,33-39." *ThZ* 30: 321–28.

Reid, B. E. 1993. *The Transfiguration: A Source- and Redaction-Critical Study of Luke 9:28–36*. CRB 32. Paris: Gabalda.

———. 1996. *Choosing the Better Part? Women in the Gospel of Luke*. Collegeville, Minn.: Liturgical Press.

Reinbold, W. 1994. *Der älteste Bericht über den Tod Jesu*. BZNW 69. Berlin: Walter de Gruyter.

Reinmuth, E. 1994. *Pseudo-Philo und Lukas*. WUNT 74. Tübingen: Mohr.

———. 2005. "Alles muss raus: Die Parabel Lk 16,1-8 ist moralischer als ihre Auslegungen." Pages 223–31 in *Kontexte der Schrift: Festschrift Ekkehard W. und Wolfgang Stegemann*. Vol. 2. Edited by G. Gelardini and C. Strecker. Stuttgart: Kohlhammer.

Reiser, M. 1990. *Die Gerichtspredigt Jesu*. NTA NF 23. Münster: Aschendorff.

———. 2000. "Numismatik und Neues Testament." *Bib.* 81: 457–88.

Rengstorf, K. H. 1963. "Die στολαί der Schriftgelehrten." Pages 383–404 in *Abraham unser Vater: Festschrift Otto Michel*. Edited by O. Betz, M. Hengel, and P. Schmidt. Leiden: Brill.

———. 1967. *Die Re-Investitur des Verlorenen Sohnes in der Gleichniserzählung Jesu Luk. 15,11-32*. VAFLNW.G 137. Cologne: Westdeutscher.

Rese, M. 1969. *Alttestamentliche Motive in der Christologie des Lukas*. StNT 1. Gütersloh: Mohn.

———. 1975/1976. "Zur Problematik von Kurz- und Langtext in Luk. XII.17ff." *NTS* 22: 15–31.

———. 1985. "Das Lukasevangelium: Ein Forschungsbericht." Pages 2258–328 in *ANRW* II: 25/3.

———. 1989. "Einige Überlegungen zu Lukas XIII, 31-33." Pages 201–25, 421–22 in *Jésus aux origines de la christologie*. 2nd edition. Edited by J. Dupont. BEThL 40. Leuven: Peeters.

Reymond, S. 2003. "Une histoire sans fin: les pèlerins d'Emmaüs." Pages 123–41 in *Quand la Bible se raconte*. Edited by D. Marguerat. Paris: Cerf.

Reynolds, J., and R. Tannenbaum. 1987. *Jews and God-fearers at Aphrodisias*. Cambridge: Cambridge Philological Society.

Riches, J. 1987. "Die Synoptiker und ihre Gemeinden." Pages 160–84 in *Die Anfänge des Christentums: Alte Welt und neue Hoffnung*. Edited by J. Becker. Stuttgart: Kohlhammer.

Riedo-Emenegger, C. 2005. *Prophetisch-messianische Provokateure der Pax Romana: Jesus von Nazaret und andere Störenfriede im Konflikt mit dem Römischen Reich.* Göttingen: Vandenhoeck & Ruprecht.

Riesenfeld, H. 1963. "Zu μακροθυμεῖν (Lk 18,7)." Pages 214–17 in *Neutestamentliche Aufsätze: Festschrift Josef Schmid.* Edited by J. Blinzler, O. Kuss, and F. Mussner. Regensburg: Pustet.

———. 1991. "Le règne de Dieu, parmi vous ou en vous? (Luc 17,20-21)." *RB* 98: 190–98.

Riesner, R. 1993. "Prägung und Herkunft der lukanischen Sondergutüberlieferung." *ThBeitr* 24: 228–48.

———. 1999. "Das Lokalkolorit des Lukas-Sonderguts: Italisch oder palästinisch-juden-christlich?" *SBFLA* 49: 51–64.

———. 2003. "Die Emmaus-Erzählung (Lk 24,13-35): Lukanische Theologie, judenchristliche Tradition und palästinische Topographie." Pages 150–208 in *Emmaus in Judäa: Geschichte, Exegese, Archäologie.* Edited by K.-H. Fleckenstein, M. Louhivuori, and R. Riesner. Giessen: Brunnen.

Rigaux, B. 1970. "La petite apocalypse de Luc (XVII,22-37)." Pages 407–38 in *Ecclesia a Spiritu Sancto edocta: Festschrift Gérard Philips.* BEThL 27. Gembloux: Duculot.

Riley, G. J. 1995. "Influence of Thomas Christianity on Luke 12,14 and 5,39." *HThR* 88: 229–35.

Rist, J. M. 2005. "Luke 2:2: Making Sense of the Date of Jesus' Birth." *JThS NS* 56: 489–91.

Ritschl, A. 1846. *Das Evangelium Marcions und das kanonische Evangelium des Lucas.* Tübingen: Ostander.

Robbins, V. K. 1978. "By Land and by Sea: The We-Passages of Acts and Ancient Sea Voyages." Pages 215–42 in *Perspectives on Luke–Acts.* Edited by C. H. Talbert. Edinburgh: T&T Clark.

———. 1983. "Pronouncement Stories and Jesus' Blessing of the Children." *Semeia* 29: 43–74.

———. 1987. "The Woman Who Touched Jesus' Garment." *NTS* 33: 502–15.

———. 1991a. "Beelzebul Controversy in Mark and Luke." *Forum* 7: 261–77.

———. 1991b. "The Social Location of the Implied Author of Luke–Acts." Pages 305–32 in *The Social World of Luke–Acts: Models for Interpretation.* Edited by J. H. Neyrey. Peabody, Mass.: Hendrickson.

———. 1994. "Introduction: Using Rhetorical Discussions of the Chreia to Interpret Pronouncement Stories." *Semeia* 64: vii–xvii.

———. 1998. "From Enthymeme to Theology in Luke 11:1-13." Pages 191–214 in *Literary Studies in Luke–Acts: Festschrift Joseph B. Tyson.* Edited by R. P. Thompson and T. E. Phillips. Macon, Ga.: Mercer University Press.

Roberts, C. H. 1948. "The Kingdom of Heaven (Lk. XVII.21)." *HThR* 41: 1–8.

Robinson, B. P. 1984. "The Place of the Emmaus Story in Luke–Acts." *NTS* 30: 481–97.

Robinson, J. M. 1964. "Die Hodajot-Formel in Gebet und Hymnus des Frühchristentums." Pages 194–235 in *Apophoreta: Festschrift Ernst Haenchen.* Edited by W. Eltester. BZNW 30. Berlin: Walter de Gruyter.

————. 1998. "The Sequence of Q: The Lament over Jerusalem." Pages 225–69 in *Von Jesus zum Christus: Christologische Studien: Festschrift Paul Hoffmann*. Edited by R. Hoppe and U. Busse. BZNW 93. Berlin: Walter de Gruyter.

Robinson, J. M., P. Hoffmann, and J. S. Kloppenborg, eds. 2000. *The Critical Edition of Q*. Minneapolis: Fortress.

Robinson, W. C. 1980. "On Preaching the Word of God (Luke 8:4-21)." Pages 131–38 in *Studies in Luke–Acts*. Edited by L. E. Keck and J. L. Martyn. Minneapolis: Fortress.

Rochais, G. 1981. *Les récits de résurrection des morts dans le Nouveau Testament*. SNTSMS 40. Cambridge: Cambridge University Press.

Rodríguez, A. A. 1993. "La vocación de Maria a la maternidad (Lc 1,26-38)." *Eph.Mar.* 43: 153–73.

Rohrbaugh, R. L. 1991. "The Pre-industrial City in Luke–Acts." Pages 125–49 in *The Social World of Luke–Acts*. Edited by J. H. Neyrey. Peabody, Mass.: Hendrickson.

Rolland, P. 1993. "Lecture par couches rédactionnelles de l'épisode de l'épileptique." Pages 451–58 in *The Synoptic Gospels*. Edited by C. Focant. BEThL 110. Leuven: Peeters.

Roloff, J. 1965. *Apostolat—Verkündigung—Kirche*. Gütersloh: Mohn.

————. 1989. "Beobachtungen zur Überlieferungsgeschichte von Offb 3,20." Pages 452–66 in *Vom Urchristentum zu Jesus: Festschrift Joachim Gnilka*. Edited by H. Frankenmölle and K. Kertelge. Freiburg: Herder.

Rose, V. 1967. *Aristotelis qui ferebantur librorum fragmenta: Aristoteles pseudepigraphus*. Stuttgart: Teubner.

Rosen, K. 1995. "Jesu Geburtsdatum, der Census des Quirinius und eine jüdische Steuererklärung aus dem Jahre 127nC." *JAC* 38: 5–15.

Ross, J. M. 1987. "The Genuineness of Luke 24:12." *ExpT* 98: 107–08.

Rostovtzeff, M. 1910. *Studien zur Geschichte des römischen Kolonats*. Leipzig: Teubner.

————. 1934. "Οὑς δεξιὸν ἀποτέμνειν." *ZNW* 33: 196–99.

Roth, D. T. 2015. *The Text of Marcion's Gospel*. Leiden: Brill.

Rothschild, C. K. 2004. *Luke–Acts and the Rhetoric of History*. WUNT 2/175. Tübingen: Mohr.

Rottloff, A., and F. Schipper. 2002. "Das hellenistisch-frührömische Bethsaida." *ProBi* 11: 127–47.

Rousseau, F. 1986. "Les structures du Benedictus (Luc 1,68-79)." *NTS* 32: 268–82.

Rowe, C. K. 2006. *Early Narrative Christology: The Lord in the Gospel of Luke*. BZNW 139. Berlin: Walter de Gruyter.

Royse, R. 1981. "A Philonic Use of ΠΑΝΔΟΧΕΙΟΝ (Luke X 34)." *NT* 23: 193–94.

Ruck-Schröder, A. 1999. *Der Name Gottes und der Name Jesu*. Neukirchen-Vluyn: Neukirchener.

Rudman, D. 2004. "Authority and Right of Disposal in Luke 4.6." *NTS* 50: 778–86.

Ruelle, C.-É. 1898. *Les Lapidaires de l'antiquité et du moyen âge*. Paris: Leroux.

Rüger, H. P. 1969. "'Mit welchem Maß ihr meßt wird euch gemessen werden.'" *ZNW* 60: 174–82.

―――. 1973. "Μαμωνᾶς." *ZNW* 64: 127–31.

―――. 1981. "ΝΑΖΑΡΕΘ / ΝΑΖΑΡΑ ΝΑΖΑΡΗΝΟΣ / ΝΑΖΩΡΑΙΟΣ." *ZNW* 72: 257–63.

Ruis-Camps, J. 1999. "Simón (Pedro) se autoexcluye de la llamada de Jesús al seguimiento." *EstB* 57: 565–87.

Ruiz, G. 1984. "El clamor de las piedras (Lc 19,40–Hab 2,11)." *EE* 59: 297–312.

Ruppert, L. 1973. *Der leidende Gerechte und seine Feinde: Eine Wortfelduntersuchung*. Würzberg: Echter.

Rusam, D. 2003. *Das Alte Testament bei Lukas*. BZNW 112. Berlin: Walter de Gruyter.

―――. 2004. "Sah Jesus wirklich den Satan vom Himmel fallen (Lk 10,18)? Auf der Suche nach einem neuen Differenzkriterium." *NTS* 50: 87–105.

Rüstow, A. 1960. "ΕΝΤΟΣ ΥΜΩΝ ΕΣΤΙΝ." *ZNW* 51: 197–224.

Rydbeck, L. 1967. *Fachprosa, vermeintliche Volkssprache und Neues Testament* AUU 5. Uppsala: Almquist & Wiksell.

Safrai, S. 1981. *Die Wallfahrt im Zeitalter des Zweiten Tempels*. Neukirchen-Vluyn: Neukirchener.

―――. 1990. "Sabbath Breakers?" *Jerusalem Perspectives* 3: 3–5.

Salo, K. 1991. *Luke's Treatment of the Law*. AASF.DHL 57. Helsinki Suomalainen Tiedeakatemia.

Sanday, W. 1911. "The Conditions under Which the Gospels Were Written in Their Bearing upon Some Difficulties of the Synoptic Problem." Pages 1–26 in *Studies in the Synoptic Gospels*. Oxford: Clarendon Press.

Sandback, F. H. ed. 1969. *Moralia, Vol XV: Fragments*. Cambridge, Mass.: Harvard University Press.

Sanders, J. A. 1974. "The Ethic of Election in Luke's Great Banquet Parable." Pages 241–57 in *Essays in Old Testament Ethics. J. Philip Hyatt, In Memoriam*. Edited by J. L. Crenshaw and J. T. Willis. New York: KTAV.

―――. 1993. "From Isaiah 61 to Luke 4." Pages 46–69 in *Luke and Scripture: The Function of Sacred Tradition in Luke–Acts*. Edited by C. A. Evans and J. A. Sanders. Minneapolis: Fortress.

Sanders, J. T. 1987. *The Jews in Luke–Acts*. London: SCM Press.

Sandiyagu, V. R. 2006. "ἕτερος and ἄλλος in Luke." *NT* 48: 105–30.

Sandnes, K. O. 1994. *A New Family: Conversion and Ecclesiology in the Early Church with Cross-Cultural Comparisons*. New York: Lang.

Satake, A. 1976. "Das Leiden der Jünger 'um Meinetwillen.'" *ZNW* 67: 4–19.

Sato, M. 1988. *Q und Prophetie*. WUNT 2/29. Tübingen: Mohr.

Sauer, J. 1985. "Traditionsgeschichtliche Erwägungen zu den synoptischen und paulinischen Aussagen über Feindesliebe und Wiedervergeltungsverzicht." *ZNW* 76: 1–28.

Scaer, P. J. 2005. *The Lukan Passion and the Praiseworthy Death*. NTMon 10. Sheffield: Sheffield Phoenix Press.

Scheffler, E. H. 1990. "The Social Ethics of the Lucan Baptist (Lk 3:10-14)." *Neotest.* 24: 21–36.

Schelbert, G. 1981. "Sprachgeschichtliches zu 'Abba.'" Pages 395–447 in *Mélanges Dominique Barthélemy*. Edited by P. Casetti, O. Keel, and A. Schenker. Göttingen: Vandenhoeck & Ruprecht.

———. 1993. "Abba, Vater! Stand der Frage." *FZPhTh* 40: 259–81.

Schiffer, B. 2001. *Fliessende Identität: Körper und Geschlechter im Wandel. Symbole von Krankheit und Heilung feministisch-theologisch gedeutet im Kontext postmoderner Körper- und Geschlechterkonstruktionen*. Frankfurt am Main: Lang.

Schinkel, D. 1999. "Das Magnifikat Lk 1,46-55—ein Hymnus in Harlekinsjacke?" *ZNW* 90: 273–79.

Schleiermacher, F. D. E. 1999. *Die christliche Sitte nach den Grundsätzen der evangelischen Kirche im Zusammenhang dargestellt*. Edited by W. E. Müller. Part 1. Waltrop: Spenner.

———. 2001. "Ueber die Schriften des Lukas ein kritischer Versuch." Pages 1–180 in *Kritische Gesamtausgabe. I/8: Exegetische Schriften*. Edited by H. Patsch and D. Schmid. Berlin: Walter de Gruyter.

Schlosser, J. 1973. "Les jours de Noé et de Lot." *RB* 80: 13–36.

———. 1980. *Le règne de Dieu dans les dits de Jésus*. 2 vols. Paris: Gabalda.

———. 1982. "La genèse de Luc, XXII,25-27." *RB* 89: 52–70.

———. 1983. "Lk 17,2 und die Logienquelle." *SNTU.A* 8: 70–78.

———. 1989. "Le pharisien et le publicain (Lc 18,9-14)." Pages 271–88 in *Les paraboles évangéliques: Perspectives nouvelles. XIIe congrès de l'ACFEB, Lyon (1987)*. Edited by J. Delorme. Paris: Cerf.

———. 1998. "Q 11,23 et la christologie." Pages 217–24 in *Von Jesus zum Christus. Christologische Studien: Festschrift Paul Hoffmann*. Edited by R. Hoppe and U. Busse. BZNW 93. Berlin: Walter de Gruyter.

———. 2002. "Les tentations de Jésus et la cause de Dieu." *RSR* 76: 403–25.

Schmahl, G. 1974. "Lk 2,41-52 und die Kindheitserzählung des Thomas 19,1-5." *BiLe* 15: 249–58.

Schmeller, T. 1999. "Die Radikalität der Logienquelle: Raben, Lilien und die Freiheit vom Sorgen (Q 12,22-32)." *BiKi* 54: 85–88.

Schmid, U. 1999. "Eklektische Textkonstitution als theologische Rekonstruktion: Zur Heilsbedeutung des Todes Jesu bei Lukas." Pages 577–84 in *The Unity of Luke–Acts*. Edited by J. Verheyden. BEThL 142. Leuven: Peeters.

———. 2002. "Marcions Evangelium und die neutestamentlichen Evangelien." Pages 66–77 in *Marcion und seine kirchengeschichtliche Wirkung*. Edited by G. May, K. Greschat, and M. Meiser. TU 150. Berlin: Walter de Gruyter.

Schmidt, D. 1977. "The LXX Gattung 'Prophetie Correlative.'" *JBL* 96: 517–22.

———. 1983. "Luke's 'Innocent' Jesus." Pages 111–21 in *Political Issues in Luke–Acts*. Edited by R. J. Cassidy and P. J. Scharper. Maryknoll, N.Y.: Orbis.

Schmidt, K. L. 1964 [1919]. *Der Rahmen der Geschichte Jesu*. Darmstadt: Wissenschaftiche Buchgesellschaft.

Schmidt, W., L. Nix, H. Schöne, and J. L. Heiberg, eds. 1976. *Heronis Alexandrini opera quae supersunt omnia*. Stuttgart: Teubner.

Schmithals, W. 1973. "Die Weihnachtsgeschichte Lukas 2,1-20." Pages 281–97 in *Festschrift Ernst Fuchs*. Edited by G. Ebeling, E. Jüngel, and G. Schunack. Tübingen: Mohr.

———. 1985. *Einleitung in die drei ersten Evangelien*. Berlin: Walter de Gruyter.

Schmitt, G. 1978. "Das Zeichen des Jona." *ZNW* 69: 123–29.

———. 1995. *Siedlungen Palästinas in griechisch-römischer Zeit*. BTAVO.B 93. Wiesbaden: Reichert.

Schnackenburg, R. 1970. "Der eschatologische Abschnitt Lk 17,20-37." Pages 213–34 in *Mélanges bibliques en hommage au R. P. Béda Rigaux*. Edited by A.-L. Descamps and A. de Halleux. Gembloux: Duculot.

———. 1991. "Lk 13,31-33. Eine Studie zur lukanischen Redaktion und Theologie." Pages 229–41 in *Der Treue Gottes Trauen. Beiträge zum Werk des Lukas: Festschrift Gerhard Schneider*. Edited by C. Bussmann and W. Radl. Freiburg: Herder.

Schneemelcher, W., ed. 1963. *New Testament Apocrypha*. Vol. 1. English Translation edited by R. McL. Wilson. Philadelphia: Westminster.

———. 1990. *Neutestamentliche Apokryphen*. Vol. 1, *Evangelien*. 6th edition. Tübingen: Mohr.

Schneider, G. 1969. *Verleugnung, Verspottung und Verhör Jesu nach Lukas 22.54-71*. StANT 22. Munich: Kösel.

———. 1970. "Das Bildwort von der Lampe." *ZNW* 61: 183–209.

———. 1972. "Die Davidssohnfrage." *Bib.* 53: 65–90.

———. 1973. *Die Passion Jesu nach den drei älteren Evangelien*. BiH 11. München: Kösel.

———. 1975. *Parusiegleichnisse im Lukasevangelium*. SBS 74. Stuttgart: Katholisches Bibelwerk.

———. 1985. *Lukas, Theologe der Heilsgeschichte*. BBB 59. Königstein: Hanstein.

———. 1988. "Das Verfahren gegen Jesus in der Sicht des dritten Evangeliums (Lk 22,54–23,25)." Pages 111–30 in *Der Prozeß gegen Jesus*. Edited by K. Kertelge. QD 112. Freiburg: Herder.

———. 1992. "Imitatio Dei als Motiv der 'Ethik Jesu.'" Pages 155–67 in *Jesusüberlieferung und Christologie*. NT.S 67. Leiden: Brill.

Schnelle, U. 2007. *Einleitung in das Neue Testament*. 6th edition. Göttingen: Vandenhoeck & Ruprecht.

Schnider, F. 1980. "Ausschließen und ausgeschlossen werden. Beobachtungen zur Struktur des Gleichnisses vom Pharisäer und Zöllner Lk 18,10-14a." *BZ NF* 24: 42–56.

———. 1981. "Die Himmelfahrt Jesu—Ende oder Anfang?" Pages 158–72 in *Kontinuität und Einheit: Festschrift Franz Mussner*. Edited by P. G. Müller and W. Stencer. Freiburg: Herder.

Schnider, F., and W. Stenger. 1971. *Johannes und die Synoptiker*. Munich: Katholisches Bibelwerk.

———. 1972. "Beobachtungen zur Struktur der Emmausperikope." *BZ NF* 16: 94–114.

————. 1979. "Die offene Tür und die unüberstreitbare Kluft: Strukturanalytische Überlegungen zum Gleichnis vom reichen Mann und armen Lazarus (Lk 16,19-31)." *NTS* 25: 273–83.

Scholtissek, K. 1992. *Die Vollmacht Jesu. Traditions- und redaktionsgeschichtliche Analysen zu einem Leitmotiv markinischer Christologie.* NTA 25. Münster: Aschendorff.

Schöner, E. 1964. *Das Viererschema in der antiken Humoralpathologie.* Wiesbaden: Steiner.

Schottroff, L. 1971. "Das Gleichnis vom verlorenen Sohn." *ZThK* 68: 27–52.

————. 1973. "Die Erzählung vom Pharisäer und Zöllner als Beispiel für die theologische Kunst des Überredens." Pages 439–61 in *Neues Testament und christliche Existenz: Festschrift Herbert Braun.* Edited by H. D. Betz and L. Schottroff. Tübingen: Mohr.

————. 1975. "Gewaltverzicht und Feindesliebe in der urchristlichen Jesustradition." Pages 197–221 in *Jesus Christus in Historie und Theologie: Festschrift Hans Conzelmann.* Edited by G. Strecker. Tübingen: Mohr.

————. 1978. "Das Magnifikat und die älteste Tradition über Jesus von Nazaret." *EvTh* 38: 293–312.

————. 1987. "Das Gleichnis vom großen Gastmahl in der Logienquelle." *EvTh* 47: 192–211.

Schottroff, L., and W. Stegemann. 1978. *Jesus von Nazareth—Hoffnung der Armen.* UB 639. Stuttgart: Kohlhammer.

Schottroff, W. 1982. "Die Ituraer." *ZDPV* 98: 125–52.

————. 1996. "Das Gleichnis von den bösen Weingärtnern (Mk 12,1-9 parr.). Ein Beitrag zur Geschichte der Bodenpacht in Palästina." *ZDPV* 112: 18–48.

Schrage, W. 1964. *Das Verhältnis des Thomas-Evangeliums zur synoptischen Tradition und zu den koptischen Evangelienübersetzungen.* BZNW 29. Berlin: Walter de Gruyter.

Schramm, T. 1971. *Der Markus-Stoff bei Lukas.* SNTSMS 14. Cambridge: Cambridge University Press.

Schreck, C. J. 1989. "The Nazareth Pericope. Luke 4,16-30 in Recent Study." Pages 399–471 in *L'évangile de Luc–The Gospel of Luke.* 2nd edition. Edited by F. Neirynck. Leuven: Leuven University Press.

Schreiber, S. 2002. "'Ars moriendi' in Lk 23,39-43." Pages 277–97 in *Forschungen zum Neuen Testament und seiner Umwelt: Festschrift Albert Fuchs.* Edited by C. Niemand. LPTB 7. Frankfurt am Main: Lang.

Schroer, S. 1986. "Der Geist, die Weisheit und die Taube." *FZPhTh* 33: 197–225.

Schröter, J. 1997a. *Erinnerung an Jesu Worte: Studien zur Rezeption der Logienüberlieferung in Markus, Q und Thomas.* WMANT 76. Neukirchen-Vluyn: Neukirchener.

————. 1997b. "Erwägungen zum Gesetzesverständnis in Q anhand von Q 16,16-18." Pages 441–58 in *The Scriptures in the Gospels.* Edited by C. M. Tuckett. BEThL 131. Leuven: Peeters.

————. 2000. "Sterben für die Freunde." Pages 263–87 in *Religionsgeschichte des Neuen Testaments: Festschrift Klaus Berger.* Edited by A. van Dobbeler, K. Erlemann, and R. Heiligenthal. Tübingen: Francke.

———. 2003. "Die Bedeutung der Q-Überlieferung für die Interpretation der frühen Jesustradition." *ZNW* 94: 38–67.

———. 2006. *Das Abendmahl: Frühchristliche Deutungen und Impulse für die Gegenwart*. SBS 210. Stuttgart: Katholisches Bibelwerk.

———. 2007. *Von Jesus zum Neuen Testament. Studien zur urchristlichen Theologiegeschichte und zur Entstehung des neutestamentlichen Kanons*. WUNT 204. Tübingen: Mohr.

———. 2013. *From Jesus to the New Testament*. Translated by W. Coppins. BMSEC 1. Waco, Tex.: Baylor University Press.

———. 2014. *Jesus of Nazareth: Jew from Galilee, Savior of the World*. Translated by W. Coppins and S. B. Pounds. Waco, Tex.: Baylor University Press.

Schubert, P. 1988. "Structur und Bedeutung von Lukas 24." Pages 331–59 in *Zur neutestamentlichen Überlieferung von der Auferstehung Jesu*. Edited by P. Hoffmann. WdF 522. Darmstadt: Wissenschaftliche Buchgesellschaft.

Schult, H. 1971. "Amos 7,15a und die Legitimation des Außenseiters." Pages 462–78 in *Probleme Biblischer Theologie: Festschrift Gerhard von Rad*. Edited by H. W. Wolff. Munich: Kaiser.

Schürer, E. 1973–1987. *The History of the Jewish People in the Age of Jesus Christ (175 BC–AD 135): A New English Version Revised and Edited by G. Vermes, F. Millar, and M. Black*. 3 vols. Edinburgh: T&T Clark.

Schürmann, H. 1953. *Der Paschamahlbericht Lk 22,(7-14.)15-18*. NTA 19/5. Münster: Aschendorff.

———. 1957. *Jesu Abschiedsrede Lk 22,21-38*. NTA 20/5. Münster: Aschendorff.

———. 1968. *Traditionsgeschichtliche Untersuchungen zu den synoptischen Evangelien*. Düsseldorf: Patmos.

———. 1970. *Ursprung und Gestalt*. Düsseldorf: Patmos.

Schwankl, O. 1987. *Die Sadduzäerfrage (Mk 12,18-27 parr)*. BBB 66. Frankfurt am Main: Athenäum.

Schwarz, G. 1981. "τὸ δὲ ἄχυρον κατακαύσει." *ZNW* 72: 264–71.

———. 1990. "ΟΙ ΔΕ ΟΦΘΑΛΜΟΙ ΑΥΤΩΝ ΕΚΡΑΤΟΥΝΤΟ?" *BN* 55: 16–17.

———. 1991. "FILLIPPON KAI BARUOLOMAION?" *BN* 56: 26–30.

———. 1992. "ΤΟ ΠΤΕΡΥΓΙΟ ΤΟΥ ΙΕΡΟ." *BN* 61: 33–35.

———. 1996. "'Ein Rohr, vom Wind bewegt'?" *BN* 83: 19–21.

———. 1997. "'Wie eine Taube'?" *BN* 89: 27–29.

Schweizer, E. 1963. "'Er wird Nazoräer heissen.'" Pages 51–55 in *Neotestamentica: deutsche und englische Aufsatze 1951–1963*. Zürich: Zwingli.

———. 1981. "Zum Aufbau von Lukas 1 und 2." Pages 309–35 in *Intergerini Parietis Septum: Festschrift Markus Barth*. Edited by D. Y. Hadidian. Pittsburgh: Pickwick.

Schwemer, A. M. 1994. "Elija als Araber." Pages 108–57 in *Die Heiden. Juden, Christen und das Problem des Fremden*. Edited by R. Feldmeier and U. Heckel. Tübingen: Mohr.

———. 1996. *Studien zu den frühjudischen Prophetenlegenden*. Vol. 2. TSAJ 50. Tübingen: Mohr Siebeck.

————. 2001. "Der Auferstandene und die Emmausjünger." Pages 95–117 in *Auferstehun–Resurrection*. Edited by F. Avemarie and H. Lichtenberger. WUNT 135. Tübingen: Mohr.

Seccombe, D. P. 1982. *Possessions and the Poor in Luke–Acts*. SNTU.B 6. Linz: SNTU.

Seeley, D. 1990. *The Noble Death: Graeco-Roman Martyrology and Paul's Concept of Salvation*. Sheffield: JSOT.

Segbroeck, F. van. 1989. *The Gospel of Luke: A Cumulative Bibliography 1973–1988*. BEThL 88. Leuven: Leuven University Press.

Seim, T. K. 1994. *The Double Message: Patterns of Gender in Luke–Acts*. Edinburgh: T&T Clark.

————. 2002. "Conflicting Voices, Irony and Reiteration: An Exploration of the Narrational Structure of Luke 24:1-35 and Its Theological Implications." Pages 151–64 in *Fair Play: Festschrift Heikki Räisänen*. Edited by I. Dunderberg, C. M. Tuckett, and K. Syreeni. NT.S 103. Leiden: Brill.

Sellew, P. 1987. "The Last Supper Discourse in Luke 22:21-38." *Forum* 3: 70–95.

————. 1992. "Interior Monologue as a Narrative Device in the Parables of Luke." *JBL* 111: 239–53.

Sellin, G. 1974/1975. "Lukas als Gleichniserzähler." *ZNW* 65/66: 166–89, 19–60.

————. 1978. "Komposition, Quellen und Funktion des lukanischen Reiseberichtes." *NT* 20: 100–35.

Semanet, G. 1993. "Le fils de la veuve: Deux récits de résurrection." Pages 247–66 in *Le temps de la lecture: Festschrift Jean Delorme*. Edited by L. Panier. LeDiv 155. Paris: Cerf.

Seng, E. W. 1978. "Der reiche Tor." *NT* 20: 136–55.

Senior, D. 1989. *The Passion of Jesus in the Gospel of Luke*. Wilmington, Del.: M. Glazier.

Sevenich-Bax, E. 1993. *Israels Konfrontation mit den letzten Boten der Weisheit*. MThA 21. Altenberge: Orlos.

Seybold, K. 1996. *Die Psalmen*. Tübingen: Mohr.

Seybold, K., and U. Müller. 1978. *Krankheit und Heilung*. Stuttgart: Kohlhammer.

Shantz, C. 2001. "Wisdom Is as Wisdom Does: The Use of Folk Proverbs in Q 7:31-35." *TJT* 17: 249–62.

Shauf, S. 2005. *Theology as History, History as Theology: Paul in Ephesus in Acts 19*. BZNW 133. Berlin: Walter de Gruyter.

Sheeley, S. M. 1992. *Narrative Asides in Luke–Acts*. JSNT.S 72. Sheffield: Sheffield Academic.

Shellard, B. 1995. "The Relationship of Luke and John." *JThS* 46: 71–98.

————. 2002. "New Light on Luke: Its Purpose, Sources and Literary Context." *JSNT.S* 215. London: Sheffield Academic Press.

Shepherd, W. H. 1994. *The Narrative Function of the Holy Spirit as a Character in Luke–Acts*. SBL.DS 147. Atlanta: Scholars Press.

Sherwin-White, A. N. 1963. *Roman Society and Roman Law in the New Testament*. Oxford: Clarendon.

Shirock, R. 1992. "Whose Exorcists Are They? The Referents of οἱ υἱοὶ ὑμῶν at Matthew 12.27/Luke 11.19." *JSNT* 46: 41–51.

Sibinga, J. S. 1997. "The Making of Luke 23:26-56." *RB* 104: 378–404.

Siegert, F. 1973. "Gottesfürchtige und Sympathisanten." *JSJ* 4: 109–64.

Siffer-Wiederhold, N. 2005. "Le projet littéraire de Luc d'après le prologue de l'évangile (Lc 1.1-4)." *RSR* 79: 39–54.

Siker, J. S. 1992. "'First to the Gentiles'. A Literary Analysis of Luke 4:16-30." *JBL* 111: 73–90.

Sim, D. C. 1989. "The Women Followers of Jesus: The Implications of Luke 8:1-3." *HeyJ* 30: 51–62.

———. 2001. "The Gospels for All Christians? A Response to Richard Bauckham." *JSNT* 84: 3–27.

Singer, C. 1998. "La difficulté d'être disciple. Luc 14/25-35." *ETR* 73: 21–36.

Sloan, I. 1993. "The Greatest and the Youngest: Greco-Roman Reciprocity in the Farewell Address, Luke 22:24-30." *SR* 22: 63–73.

Smith, D. E. 1987. "Table Fellowship as a Literary Motiv in the Gospel of Luke." *JBL* 106: 613–38.

———. 1991. "The Messianic Banquet Reconsidered." Pages 64–73 in *The Future of Early Christianity: Festschrift Helmut Koester*. Edited by B. A. Pearson, A. T. Kraabel, G. W. E. Nickelsburg, and N. R. Petersen. Minneapolis: Fortress.

Smith, M. D. 2000. "Of Jesus and Quirinius." *CBQ* 62: 278–93.

Smyth, K. 1987. "'Peace on Earth to Men . . .' (Lk 2.14)." *IrBSt* 9: 27–34.

Snodgrass, K. 1983. *The Parable of the Wicked Tenants*. WUNT 27. Tübingen: Mohr.

———. 1997. "*Anaideia* and the Friend at Midnight." *JBL* 116: 505–13.

———. 1998. "Common Life with Jesus: The Parable of the Banquet in Luke 14:16-24." Pages 186–201 in *Common Life in the Early Church: Festschrift Graydon F. Snyder*. Edited by J. V. Hills and R. B. Gardner. Harrisville: Trinity International.

Soards, M. L. 1985a. "The Silence of Jesus before Herod: An Interpretative Suggestion." *ABR* 33: 41–45.

———. 1985b. "Tradition, Composition, and Theology in Luke's Account of Jesus before Herod Antipas." *Bib.* 66: 344–64.

———. 1986. "'And the Lord Turned and Looked Straight at Peter': Understanding Luke 22,61." *Bib.* 67: 518–19.

———. 1987a. "A Literary Analysis of the Origin and Purpose of Luke's Account of the Mockery of Jesus." *BZ NF* 31: 110–16.

———. 1987b. *The Passion according to Luke: The Special Material of Luke 22*. JSNT.S 14. Sheffield: Sheffield Academic Press.

———. 1987c. "Tradition, Composition, and Theology in Jesus' Speech to the 'Daughters of Jerusalem' (Luke 23,26-32)." *Bib.* 68: 221–44.

Söding, T. 1992. "Die Tempelaktion Jesu." *TThZ* 101: 36–64.

Spengel, L. von, ed. 1953–1956. *Rhetores Graeci*. 3 vols. Leipzig: Teubner.

Spicq, C. 1961. "La parabole de la veuve obstiné et du juge inerte, aux décisions impromptues (Lc. xviii,1-8)." *RB* 68: 68–90.

———. 1994. *Theological Lexicon of the New Testament*. 3 vols. Peabody, Mass.: Hendrickson.

Spitta, F. 1906. "Die chronologischen Notizen und die Hymnen in Lc 1 u. 2."
    ZNW 7: 281–317.
Spitznagel, A. 1977. "Rolle und Status." Pages 401–9 in Handbuch psycholo-
    gischer Grundbegriffe. Edited by T. Hermann, P. R. Hofstätter, and H. P.
    Huber. Munich: Kösel.
Squires, J. T. 1993. The Plan of God in Luke–Acts. MSSNTS 76. Cambridge:
    Cambridge University Press.
Städele, A. 1980. Die Briefe des Pythagoras und der Pythagoreer. Meisenheim
    am Glan: Hain.
Stählin, G. 1930. Skandalon: Untersuchung zur Geschichte eines biblischen
    Begriffs. Gütersloh: Bertelsmann.
———. 1973. "Um mitzusterben und mitzuleben." Pages 503–21 in Neues Tes-
    tament und christliche Existenz: Festschrift Herbert Braun. Edited by H. D.
    Betz and L. Schottroff. Tübingen: Mohr.
Steck, O. H. 1967. Israel und das gewaltsame Geschick der Propheten. WMANT
    23. Neukirchen-Vluyn: Neukirchener.
Steele, E. S. 1984. "Luke 11:37-54—A Modified Hellenistic Symposium?" JBL
    103: 379–94.
Stegemann, W. 1991a. " 'Licht der Völker' bei Lukas." Pages 81–97 in Der Treue
    Gottes trauen: Beiträge zum Werk des Lukas: Festschrift Gerhard Schneider.
    Edited by C. Bussmann and W. Radl. Freiburg: Herder.
———. 1991b. Zwischen Synagoge und Obrigkeit. FRLANT 152. Göttingen:
    Vandenhoeck & Ruprecht.
———. 1993. "Jesus als Messias in der Theologie des Lukas." Pages 21–40 in
    Messias-Vorstellungen bei Juden und Christen. Edited by E. Stegemann.
    Stuttgart: Kohlhammer.
Stegner, W. R. 1976. "Lucan Priority in the Feeding of the Five Thousand." BR
    21: 19–28.
Stein, R. H. 1989. "Luke 14:26 and the Question of Authenticity." Forum 5:
    187–92.
Steinhauser, M. G. 1981. Doppelbildworte in den synoptischen Evangelien. FzB
    44. Stuttgart: Katholisches Bibelwerk.
Stemberger, G. 1987. "Pesachhaggada und Abendmahlsberichte des Neuen Testa-
    ments." Kairos 29: 147–58.
———. 1991. Pharisäer, Sadduzäer, Essener. SBS 144. Stuttgart: Katholisches
    Bibelwerk.
Stemm, S. von. 1997. "Der betende Sünder vor Gott: Lk 18,9-14." Pages 579–
    89 in The Scriptures in the Gospels. Edited by C. M. Tuckett. BEThL 131.
    Leuven: Peeters.
Stenger, W. 1986. "Die Seligpreisung der Geschmähten." Kairos 28: 33–60.
———. 1988. "Gebt dem Kaiser, was des Kaisers ist . . . !" BBB 68. Frankfurt
    am Main: Athenäum.
Sterling, G. 1992. Historiography and Self-Definition: Josephos, Luke–Acts and
    Apologetic Historiography. NT.S 64. Leiden: Brill.
———. 1993. "Jesus as Exorcist: An Analysis of Matthew 17:14-20; Mark 9:14-
    29; Luke 9:37-43a." CBQ 55: 467–93.

———. 2001. "*Mors philosophi*: The Death of Jesus in Luke." *HThR* 94: 383–402.

Stettberger, H. 2005a. *Mahlmetaphorik im Evangelium des Lukas*. Münster: Lit.

———. 2005b. *Nichts haben—alles geben? Eine kognitiv-linguistisch orientierte Studie zur Besitzethik im lukanischen Doppelwerk*. HBiSt 45. Freiburg: Herder.

Steyn, G. J. 1989. "The Occurrence of 'Kainam' in Luke's Genealogy: Evidence of Septuagint Influence?" *EThL* 65: 409–11.

———. 1990. "Intertexual Similarities between Septuagint Pretexts and Luke's Gospel." *Neotest*. 24: 229–46.

———. 1991. "A Short Reply." *EthL* 65: 103–4.

Stock, A. 1978. *Textentfaltungen. Semiotische Experimente mit einer biblischen Geschichte*. Düsseldorf: Patmos.

Stock, K. 1980. "Die Berufung Marias (Lk 1,26-38)." *Bib*. 61: 457–91.

Storme, A. 1992. *Béthanie*. 3rd edition. Jerusalem: Franciscan.

Strauss, M. L. 1995. *The Davidic Messiah in Luke–Acts*. JSNTSup 110. Sheffield: Sheffield Academic.

Strecker, C. 1999. *Die liminale Theologie des Paulus. Zugänge zur paulinischen Theologie aus kulturanthropologischer Perspektive*. FRLANT 185. Göttingen: Vandenhoeck & Ruprecht.

Strecker, G. 1984. *Die Bergpredigt*. Göttingen: Vandenhoek & Ruprecht.

———, ed. 1993. *Minor Agreements: Symposium Göttingen 1991*. GTA 50. Göttingen: Vandenhoeck & Ruprecht.

Strecker, G., and U. Schnelle. 2001/1996. *Neuer Wettstein*. Vol. I and II/1–2. Berlin: Walter de Gruyter.

Streeter, B. H. 1924. *The Four Gospels: A Study of Origins*. London: Macmillan.

Strelan, R. 2000. "A Greater Than Caesar: Storm Stories in Lucan and Mark." *ZNW* 91: 166–79.

———. 2003. "Elizabeth, Are You Hiding? (Luke 1:24)." *Neotest*. 37: 87–95.

Strobel, A. 1958. "Lukas der Antiochener (Bemerkungen zu Act 11,28D)." *ZNW* 49: 131–34.

———. 1961a. "In dieser Nacht (Luk 17,34)." *ZThK* 58: 16–29.

———. 1961b. *Untersuchungen zum eschatologischen Verzögerungsproblem*. NT.S 2. Leiden: Brill.

———. 1962. "Der Gruß an Maria (Lc 1,28): Eine philologische Betrachtung zu seinem Sinngehalt." *ZNW* 53: 86–110.

———. 1964. "Maße und Gewichte." Page 1163 in *Biblisch-historisches Handwörterbuch*. Edited by B. Reicke and L. Rost. Vol. 2. Göttingen: Vandenhoeck & Ruprecht.

———. 1995. "Plädoyer für Lukas: Zur Stimmigkeit des chronistischen Rahmens von Lk 3,1." *NTS* 41: 466–69.

Strotmann, A. 1991. *Mein Vater bist du! (Sir 51,10): Zur Bedeutung der Vaterschaft Gottes in kanonischen und nichtkanonischen Schriften*. FTS 39. Frankfurt am Main: Knecht.

Stubbs, J. 2002. "A Certain Woman Raised Her Voice: The Use of Grammatical Structure and the Origins of Texts." *Neotest*. 36: 21–37.

Stuhlmacher, P. 1992/1999. *Biblische Theologie des Neuen Testaments*. 2 vols. Göttingen: Vandenhoeck & Ruprecht.

Stuhlmann, R. 1983 *Das eschatologische Maß im Neuen Testament*. FRLANT 132. Göttingen: Vandenhoek & Ruprecht.

Sussman, L. A. 1987. *The Major Declamations Ascribed to Quintilian: A Translation*. Frankfurt am Main: Lang.

———. 1994. *The Declamations of Calpurnius Flaccus: Text, Translation, and Commentary*. Leiden: Brill.

Sweetland, D. M. 1984. "Discipleship and Persecution: A Study of Luke 12,1-12." *Bib.* 65: 61–80.

Sylva, D. D. 1986. "The Temple Curtain and Jesus' Death in the Gospel of Luke." *JBL* 105: 239–50.

———. 1987. "The Cryptic Clause *en tois tou patros mou dei einai me* in Luke 2,49b." *ZNW* 78: 132–40.

Taeger, J.-W. 1986. *Der Mensch und sein Heil: Studien zum Bild des Menschen und zur Sicht der Bekehrung bei Lukas*. Gütersloh: Mohn.

Talbert, C. H., and J. H. Hayes. 1995. "A Theology of Sea Storms in Luke–Acts." *SBL.SP* 131: 321–36.

Tanghe, V. 1984. "Abraham, son fils et son envoyé (Luc 16,19-31)." *RB* 91: 557–77.

Tannehill, R. C. 1972. "The Mission of Jesus according to Luke IV 16-30." Pages 51–75 in *Jesus in Nazareth*. Edited by E. Gräßer. BZNW 40. Berlin: Walter de Gruyter.

———. 1974. "The Magnifikat as Poem." *JBL* 93: 263–75.

———. 1986. *The Narrative Unity of Luke–Acts*. Vol. 1, *The Gospel of Luke*. Philadelphia: Fortress.

———. 1992. "The Lukan Discourse on Invitations (Luke 14,7-24)." Pages 1603–16 in *The Four Gospels 1992: Festschrift Frans Neirynck*. Vol. 2. Edited by F. van Segbroeck, C. M. Tuckett, G. van Belle, and J. Verheyden. BEThL 100. Leuven: Peeters.

———. 1993. "The Story of Zacchaeus as Rhetoric." *Semeia* 64: 201–11.

Taylor, J. E. 1998. "Golgotha." *NTS* 44: 180–203.

Taylor, N. H. 2001. "The Temptation of Jesus on the Mountain: A Palestinian Christian Polemic against Agrippa I." *JSNT* 83: 27–49.

Taylor, V. 1972. *The Passion Narrative of St Luke*. SNTSMS 19. Cambridge: Cambridge University Press.

Terry, M. 1899. *The Sibylline Oracles: Translated from the Greek into English Blank Verse*. New York: Eaton & Mains.

Theissen, G. 1979. *Studien zur Soziologie des Urchristentums*. Tübingen: Mohr.

———. 1983. *The Miracle Stories of the Early Christian Tradition*. Translated by F. McDonagh. Minneapolis: Fortress.

———. 1987. *Urchristliche Wundergeschichten*. 5th edition. StNT 8. Gütersloh: Mohn.

———. 1992. *Lokalkolorit und Zeitgeschichte in den Evangelien*. 2nd edition. Freiburg: Universitätsverlag Freiburg.

————. 2003. "Das Zeichen des Jona." Pages 181–93 in *Der Freund des Menschen: Festschrift Georg Christian Macholz*. Edited by A. Meinhold and A. Berlejung. Neukirchen-Vluyn: Neukirchener.

Theobald, M. 1984. "Die Anfänge der Kirche. Zur Struktur von Lk. 5.1–6.19." *NTS* 30: 91–108.

————. 2005. "'Ich sah den Satan aus dem Himmel stürzen . . .': Überlieferungskritische Beobachtungen zu Lk 10.18-20." *BZ NF* 49: 174–90.

————. 2006. "Paschamahl und Eucharistiefeier: Zur heilsgeschichtlichen Relevanz der Abendmahlsszenerie bei Lukas (Lk 22,14-38)." Pages 133–80 in *"Für alle Zeiten zur Erinnerung" (Jos 4,7): Beiträge zu einer biblischen Gedächniskultur: Festschrift Franz Mußner*. Edited by M. Theobald, R. Hoppe, and Pope Benedict. SBS 209. Stuttgart: Katholisches Bibelwerk.

Thiede, C.-P. 2004. "Die Wiederentdeckung von Emmaus bei Jerusalem." *ZAC* 8: 593–99.

Thoma, C., and S. Lauer. 1986. *Die Gleichnisse der Rabbinen*. Vol. 1. Bern: Lang.

Thomas, J. C. 1991. *Footwashing in John 13 and the Johannine Community*. JSNT.S 61. Sheffield: Sheffield Academic.

Thompson, G. P. 1960. "Called–Proved–Obedient." *JThS* 11: 1–12.

Thompson, R. C. 1903. *The Devils and Evil Spirits of Babylonia*. Vol. 1. London: Luzac.

Thornton, C.-J. 1991. *Der Zeuge des Zeugen: Lukas als Historiker der Paulusreisen*. WUNT 56. Tübingen: Mohr.

Thraede, K. 2004. "Noch einmal: Plinius d. J. und die Christen." *ZNW* 95: 102–28.

Thrall, M. E. 2004. *2 Corinthians 8–13*. ICC. London: T&T Clark.

————. 1962. *Greek Particles in the New Testament*. NTTS 3. Leiden: Brill.

Thurston, B. 2001. "Who Was Anna? Luke 2:36-38." *PRS* 28: 47–55.

Tiede, D. L. 1980. *Prophecy and History in Luke–Acts*. Philadelphia: Fortress.

Tilborg, S. van. 2002. "The Meaning of the Word γαμῶ in Lk 14:20; 17:27; Mk 12:25 and in a Number of Early Jewish and Christian Authors." *HTS* 58: 802–10.

Tilborg, S. van, and P. C. Counet. 2000. *Jesus' Appearances and Disappearances in Luke 24*. Bib.Int.S 45. Leiden: Brill.

Tilly, M. 1991. "Kanaanäer, Händler und der Tempel in Jerusalem." *BN* 57: 30–36.

Topel, L. J. 1998. "The Tarnished Golden Rule (Luke 6:31)." *TS* 59: 475–85.

————. 2001. *Children of a Compassionate God: A Theological Exegesis of Luke 6:20-49*. Collegeville, Minn.: Liturgical Press.

————. 2003. "What Kind of a Sign are Vultures? Luke 17,37b." *Bib.* 84: 403–11.

Trites, A. A. 1987. "The Transfiguration in the Theology of Luke." Pages 71–81 in *The Glory of Christ in the New Testament: Studies in Christology in Memory of George Bradford Caird*. Edited by L. D. Hurst and N. T. Wright. Oxford: Clarendon.

Trummer, P. 1991. *Die blutende Frau*. Freiburg: Herder.

Tsafrir, Y., L. di Segni, J. Green, I. Roll, and T. Tsuk. 1994. *Tabula Imperii Romani: Iudaea. Palaestina*. Jerusalem: Israel Academy of Sciences and Humanities.

Tuckett, C. M. 1982. "Luke 14,16-30, Isaiah and Q." Pages 343–54 in *Logia. Mémorial Joseph Coppens*. Edited by J. Delobel and T. Baarda. BEThL 59. Leuven: Peeters.

———. 1983. *The Revival of the Griesbach Hypothesis*. MSSNTS 44. Cambridge: Cambridge University Press.

———. 1984. "On the Relationship Between Matthew and Luke." *NTS* 30: 130–42.

———. 1989. "Q, Prayer, and the Kingdom." *JThS* 40: 367–76.

———. 1992. "The Temptation Narrative in Q." Pages 479–507 in *The Four Gospels 1992: Festschrift Frans Neirynck*. Vol. 2. Edited by F. van Segbroeck, C. M. Tuckett, G. van Belle, and J. Verheyden. BEThL 100. Leuven: Peeters.

———. 1995. "The Lukan Son of Man." Pages 198–217 in *Luke's Literary Achievement*. Edited by C. M. Tuckett. JSNT.S 116. Sheffield: Sheffield Academic.

———. 1996. *Q and the History of Early Christianity*. Edinburgh: T&T Clark.

———. 2000. "Q 12,8 Once Again." Pages 171–88 in *From Quest to Q: Festschrift James M. Robinson*. Edited by J. M. Asgeirsson, K. de Troyer, and M. M. Meyer. BEThL 146. Leuven: Peeters.

———. 2002. "Luke 22,43-44: The 'Agony' in the Garden and Luke's Gospel." Pages 131–44 in *New Testament Textual Criticism and Exegesis: Festschrift Joël Delobel*. Edited by A. Denaux. BEThL 161. Leuven: Peeters.

———. 2004. *Luke*. London: T&T Clark.

Turner, E. G., and J. W. B. Barns, eds. 1957. *The Oxyrhynchus Papyri XXIV*. London: Egypt Exploration Society.

Tyson, J. B. 1978. "Source Criticism of the Gospel of Luke." Pages 24–39 in *Perspectives on Luke–Acts*. Edited by C. H. Talbert. Edinburgh: T&T Clark.

———. 1986. *The Death of Jesus in Luke–Acts*. Columbia: University of South Carolina Press.

———. 1990. "The Birth Narratives and the Beginning of Luke's Gospel." *Semeia* 52: 103–20.

———. 2006. *Marcion and Luke–Acts: A Defining Struggle*. Columbia: University of South Carolina Press.

Tzaferis, V., ed. 1989. *Excavations at Capernaum*. Vol. 1. Winona Lake, Ind.: Eisenbrauns.

Ulrichs, K. F. 1999. "Some Notes on Ears in Luke–Acts, especially in Lk 4:21." *BN* 98: 28–31.

Unnik, W. C. van. 1966. "Die Motivierung der Feindesliebe in Lukas VI 32-35." *NT* 8: 284–300.

———. 1973. "Once More: St. Luke's Prologue." *Neotest.* 7: 7–26.

———. 1973–1983. *Sparsa Collecta*. 3 vols. NT.S 29–31. Leiden: Brill.

Untergassmair, F. G. 1980. *Kreuzweg und Kreuzigung Jesu*. PT 10. Paderborn: Schöningh.

———. 1991. "Der Spruch vom 'grünen und dürren Holz' (Lk 23,31)." *SNTU.A* 16: 55–87.

————. 1996. "Zur Problematik der lukanischen Passionsgeschichte. Jesus vor Herodes (Lk 23,6-12)." Pages 273–92 in *Schrift und Tradition: Festschrift Josef Ernst*. Edited by K. Backhaus and F. G. Untergassmair. Paderborn: Schöningh.

Uro, R. 1987. *Sheep among the Wolves*. AASF 47. Helsinki: Suomalainen Tiedeakatemia.

————. 1990. *Neither Here nor There: Luke 17:20-21 and Related Sayings in Thomas, Mark and Q*. OPIAC 20. Claremont, Calif.: Institute for Antiquity and Christianity.

————. 2000. "'Washing the outside of the Cup.'" Pages 303–22 in *From Quest to Q: Festschrift James M. Robinson*. Edited by J. M. Asgeirsson, K. de Troyer, and M. M. Meyer. BEThL 146. Leuven: Peeters.

Usener, H. 1900. "Beiläufige Bemerkungen." *RhMus* 55: 286–87.

Usener, H., and L. Radermacher. 1965. *Dionysii Halicarnasei quae exstant opuscula*. Stuttgart: Teubner.

Vaganay, L. 1954. "Les accords négatifs de Matthieu-Luc contre Marc: L'épisode de l'enfant épileptique." Pages 405–25 in *Le problème synoptique: une hypothèse de travail*. Tournai: Desclée.

Vahrenhorst, M. 1998. "'Se non è vero, è ben trovato': Die Frauen und das leere Grab." *ZNW* 89: 282–88.

Vanhoye, A. 1965–1966. "Structure du 'Benedictus.'" *NTS* 12: 382–89.

Velsen, A. de. 1965 [1853]. *Tryphonis Grammatici Alexandrini fragmenta*. Amsterdam: Hakkert.

Verboomen, A. 1992. *L'imparfait périphrastique dans l'évangile de Luc et dans la Septante*. ARB.CL 10. Leuven: Peeters.

Verheyden, J. 1989. "The Source(s) of Luke 21." Pages 491–516 in *L'évangile de Luc–The Gospel of Luke*. 2nd edition. Edited by F. Neirynck. BEThL 32. Leuven: Leuven University Press.

————. 1999. "The Unity of Luke–Acts: What Are We Up To?" Pages 3–56 in *The Unity of Luke–Acts*. Edited by J. Verheyden. BEThL 142. Leuven: Leuven University Press.

————. 2003. "The Canon Muratori: A Matter of Dispute." Pages 487–556 in *The Biblical Canons (Fiftieth Colloquium Biblicum Lovaniense)*. Edited by J.-M. Auwers. BEThL 163. Leuven: Leuven University Press.

Versnel, H. S. 1970. *Triumphus: An Inquiry into the Origin, Development and Meaning of the Roman Triumph*. Leiden: Brill.

————. 2005. "Making Sense of Jesus' Death. The Pagan Contribution." Pages 215–94 in *Deutungen des Todes Jesu*. Edited by J. Frey and J. Schröter. WUNT 181. Tübingen: Mohr.

Veyries, A. 1884. *Les figures criophores dans l'art grec, l'art gréco-romain et l'art chrétien*. Paris: Thorin.

Via, D. O. 1967. *The Parables: Their Literary and Existential Dimension*. Philadelphia: Fortress.

————. 1970. *Die Gleichnisse Jesu*. Translated by E. Güttgemanns. BEvTh 57. München: Kaiser.

Victor, U. 2009. "Textkritischer Kommentar zu ausgewählten Stellen des Lukas- und des Johannesevangeliums." *NT* 51: 30–77.

Vielhauer, P. 1965. *Aufsätze zum Neuen Testament*. TB 31. Munich: Kaiser.

Vinzent, M. 2002. "Der Schluß des Lukasevangelium bei Marcion." Pages 79–94 in *Marcion und seine kirchengeschichtliche Wirkung*. Edited by G. May, K. Greschat, and M. Meiser. TU 150. Berlin: Walter de Gruyter.

Viviano, B. T. 2000. "The Least in the Kingdom." *CBQ* 62: 41–54.

Vogel, M. 1996. *Das Heil des Bundes*. TANZ 18. Tübingen: Francke.

Vogels, W. 1983. "A Semiotic Study of Luke 7.11-17." *EeT(O)* 14: 273–92.

Vogt, J. 1990. *Aspekte erzählender Prosa*. 7th edition. Opladen: Westdeutscher.

Vögtle, A. 1971. *Das Evangelium und die Evangelien*. KBANT. Düsseldorf: Patmos.

———. 1977. *Was Weihnachten bedeutet*. Freiburg: Herder.

———. 1989. "Ein 'unablässiger Stachel' (Mt 5,3[9]b-42 par. Lk 6.29-30)." Pages 53–70 in *Neues Testament und Ethik: Festschrift Rudolf Schnackenburg*. Edited by H. Merklein. Freiburg: Herder.

———. 1994. *Die "Gretchenfrage" des Menschensohnproblems. Bilanz und Perspektive*. QD 152. Freiburg: Herder.

———. 1996. *Gott und seine Gäste*. BThSt 29. Neukirchen-Vluyn: Neukirchener.

Volgers, A., and C. Zamagni, eds. 2004. *Erotapokriseis: Early Christian Question-and-Answer Literature in Context*. Leuven: Peeters.

Völkel, M. 1973a. "Der Anfang in Galiläa." *ZNW* 64: 222–32.

———. 1973b. "Anmerkungen zur lukanischen Fassung der Täuferanfrage Luk 7.18-23." Pages 166–73 in *Festgabe für Karl Heinrich Rengstorf zum 70. Geburtstag*. Edited by W. Dietrich. Theokr. 2. Leiden: Brill.

———. 1974. "Exegetische Erwägungen zum Verständnis des Begriffs καθεξῆς im lukanischen Prolog." *NTS* 20: 289–99.

———. 1978. "'Freund der Zöllner und Sünder.'" *ZNW* 69: 1–10.

Vollenweider, S. 1988. "'Ich sah den Satan wie einen Blitz vom Himmel fallen' (Lk 10,18)." *ZNW* 79: 187–203.

———. 1994. "Die waagschalen von Leben und Tod: Zum antiken Hintergrund von Phil 1,21–26." *ZNW* 85: 93–115.

Volz, P. 1934. *Die Eschatologie der jüdischen Gemeinde im neutestamentlichen Zeitalter*. 2nd edition. Tübingen: Mohr.

Wachsmann, S., ed. 1990. *The Excavations of an Ancient Boat in the Sea of Galilee [Lake Kinneret]*. Jerusalem: Israel Antiquities Authority.

Wachsmuth, C., and O. Hense, eds. 1958 [1884–1912]. *Joannis Stobaei Anthologium*. Berlin: Weidmann.

Waetjen, H. C. 2001. "The Subversion of 'World' by the Parable of the Friend at Midnight." *JBL* 120: 703–21.

Wagner, J. R. 1997. "Psalm 118 in Luke–Acts: Tracing a Narrative Thread." Pages 154–78 in *Early Christian Interpretation of the Scriptures of Israel*. Edited by C. A. Evans and J. A. Sanders. JSNT.S 148. Sheffield: Sheffield Academic.

Wagner, V. 2001. "Mit der Herkunft Jesu aus Nazaret gegen die Geltung des Gesetzes?" *ZNW* 92: 273–82.

Wainwright, A. W. 1977/1978. "Luke and the Restoration of the Kingdom to Israel." *ET* 89: 76–79.

Walaskay, P. W. 1975. "The Trial and Death of Jesus in the Gospel of Luke." *JBL* 94: 81–93.

Waldmann, W. 1902. *Die Feindesliebe in der antiken Welt und im Christenthum.* Vienna: Mayer.

Wall, R. W. 1987. "'The Finger of God': Deuteronomy 9.10 and Luke 11.20." *NTS* 33: 144–50.

Wallace, R. W. 1989. "ΟΡΘΡΟΣ." *TAPA* 119: 201–7.

Walz, C. 1968 [1832–1836]. *Rhetores Graeci.* Osnabruck: Zeller.

Wander, B. 1998. *Gottesfürchtige und Sympathisanten.* Tübingen: Mohr.

Wanke, J. 1973a. *Beobachtungen zum Eucharistieverständnis des Lukas auf Grund der lukanischen Mahlberichte.* ETS 8. Leipzig: Benno.

———. 1973b. *Die Emmauserzählung.* ETS 31. Leipzig: Benno.

———. 1974. "'. . . wie sie ihn beim Brotbrechen erkannten': Zur Auslegung der Emmaeuserzählung Lk 24,13-35." *BZ NF* 18: 180–92.

———. 1981. *"Bezugs- und Kommentarworte" in den synoptischen Evangelien.* ETS 44. Leipzig: Benno.

Wargnies, P. 2003. "Théophile ouvre l'évangile (Luc 1–4)." *NRTh* 125: 77–88.

Wasserberg, G. 1998. *Aus Israels Mitte—Heil für die Welt: Eine narrative-exegetische Studie zur Theologie des Lukas.* BZNW 92. Berlin: Walter de Gruyter.

Watt, J. M. 1999. "Pronouns of Shame and Disgrace in Luke 22.63-64." Pages 223–34 in *Discourse Analysis and the New Testament.* Edited by S. E. Porter and J. T. Reed. Sheffield: Sheffield Academic.

Wattles, J. 1996. *The Golden Rule.* Oxford: Oxford University Press.

Weatherly, J. A. 1994. *Jewish Responsibility for the Death of Jesus in Luke–Acts.* JSNT.S 106. Sheffield: Sheffield Academic.

Webb, R. L. 1991a. "The Activity of John the Baptist's Expected Figure at the Threshing Floor (Matthew 3.12 = Luke 3.17)." *JSNT* 43: 103–11.

———. 1991b. *John the Baptizer and Prophet.* JSNT.S 62. Sheffield: Sheffield Academic.

Weber, K. 1993. "Is There a Qumran Parallel to *Matthew* 24,51 // *Luke* 12,46?" *RdQ* 16: 657–63.

Weber, T. 2002. *Gadara Decapolitana.* Wiesbaden: Harrassowitz.

Wedderburn, A. J. M. 2002. "The 'We'-Passages in Acts: On the Horns of a Dilemma." *ZNW* 93: 78–98.

Weder, H. 1984. *Die Gleichnisse Jesu als Metaphern.* 3rd edition. FRLANT 120. Göttingen: Vandenhoeck & Ruprecht.

Wegener, E. P. 1942. *Some Oxford Papyri [P. Oxford].* Leiden: Brill.

Wegner, U. 1985. *Der Hauptmann von Kafarnaum.* WUNT 2/14. Tübingen: Mohr.

Wehnert, J. 1989. *Die Wir-Passagen der Apostelgeschichte. Ein lukanisches Stil-mittel aus jüdischer Tradition.* GTA 40. Göttingen: Vandenhoeck & Ruprecht.

Wehr, L. 1998. "Die Rettung der 'Kleinen.' Der Auftrag der Jüngergemeinde nach Lc 17,1-10." Pages 65–83 in *Für euch Bischof-mit euch Christ: Festschrift*

Friedrich Kardinal Wetter. Edited by M. Weitlauff and P. Neuner. St. Ottilien: EOS.

Weiher, E. von. 1983. *Spätbabylonische Texte aus Uruk*. Vol. 2. Berlin: Mann.

Weihs, A. 2003. *Jesus und das Schicksal der Propheten*. BThSt 61. Neukirchen-Vluyn: Neukirchener.

Weinert, F. D. 1977. "The Parable of the Throne Claimant (Luke 19:12, 14-15a, 27) Reconsidered." *CBQ* 39: 505–14.

———. 1982. "Luke, the Temple and Jesus' Saying about Jerusalem's Abandoned House (Luke 13:34-35)." *CBQ* 44: 68–76.

———. 1983. "The Multiple Meanings of Luke 2:49 and their Significance." *BTB* 13: 19–22.

Weinreich, O. 1969 [1909]. *Antike Heilungswunder*. RVV 8/1. Berlin: Walter de Gruyter.

Weiser, A. 1971. *Die Knechtsgleichnisse der synoptischen Evangelien*. StANT 29. Munich: Kösel.

———. 1996. "Zuvorkommendes Erbarmen (Lk 15,20)." Pages 259–71 in *Schrift und Tradition: Festschrift Josef Ernst*. Edited by K. Backhaus and F. G. Untergassmair. Paderborn: Schöningh.

Weiss, B. 1889 [¹1886]. *Lehrbuch der Einleitung in das Neue Testament*. 2nd edition. Berlin: Hertz.

———. 1907. *Die Quellen des Lukasevangeliums*. Stuttgart: Cotta.

Weiss, W. 1989. *"Eine neue Lehre in Vollmacht": Die Streit- und Schulgespräche des Markusevangeliums*. BZNW 52. Berlin: Walter de Gruyter.

Weissenrieder, A. 2002. "Die Plage der Unreinheit? Das antike Krankheitskonstrukt 'Blutfluss' in Lk 8,43-48." Pages 75–85 in *Jesus in neuen Kontexten*. Edited by W. Stegemann. Stuttgart: Kohlhammer.

———. 2003. *Images of Illness in the Gospel of Luke*. WUNT 2/164. Tübingen: Mohr.

Weizsäcker, C. 1901 [1864]. *Untersuchungen über die evangelische Geschichte, ihre Quellen und den Gang ihrer Entwicklung*. 2nd edition. Tübingen: Mohr.

Welker, M., and M. Wolter. 1999. "Die Unscheinbarkeit des Reiches Gottes." Pages 103–16 in *Marburger Jahrbuch Theologie*. Vol. 11, *Reich Gottes*. Edited by W. Härle and R. Preul. Marburg: Elwert Verlag.

Wells, L. 1998. *The Greek Language of Healing from Homer to New Testament Times*. BZNW 83. Berlin: Walter de Gruyter.

Welzen, H. 1989. "Loosening and Binding: Luke 13.10-21 as Programme and Anti-programme of the Gospel of Luke." Pages 175–87 in *Intertexuality in Biblical Writings: Festschrift Bas van Iersel*. Edited by S. Draisma. Kampen: Kok.

Wendland, E. R. 1996. "Finding Some Lost Aspects of Meaning in Christ's Parables of the Lost and Found (Luke 15)." *TrinJ* 17: 19–65.

———. 1997. "'Blessed Is the Man Who Will Eat at the Feast in the Kingdom of God' (Lk 14:15)." *Neotest.* 31: 159–94.

Wenk, M. 2000. *Community-Forming Power: The Socio-Ethical Role of the Spirit in Luke–Acts*. JPeTh.S 19. Sheffield: Sheffield Academic.

Weren, W. 1981. "The Lord's Supper: An Inquiry into the Coherence in Lk 22,14-38." Pages 9–26 in *Fides sacramenti, sacramentum fidei. Studies in honor of Pieter Smulders*. Edited by Hans Jörg auf der Mauer. Assen: Van Gorcum.

West, M. L. 1994. *Greek Lyric Poetry: The Poems and Fragments of the Greek Iambic, Elegiac, and Melic Poets (Excluding Pindar and Bacchylides) down to 450 BC*. Oxford: Oxford University Press.

Westermann, C. 1971. *Grundformen prophetischer Rede*. 4th edition. BEvTh 31. Munich: Kaiser.

Wettstein, J. J. 1962 [1751/1752]. *Novum Testamentum Graecum Editionis Receptae*. 2 vols. Graz: A Concordance to the Septuagint and Other Greek Versions of the Old Testament.

White, K. D. 1964. "The Parable of the Sower." *JThS NS* 13: 300–307.

Whitlark, J. A., and M. C. Parsons. 2006. "The 'Seven' Last Words: A Numerical Motivation for the Insertion of Luke 23.34a." *NTS* 52: 188–204.

Wifstrand, A. 1964/1965. "Lukas XVIII.7." *NTS* 11: 72–74.

Wilcken, U. 1957. *Urkunden der Ptolemäerzeit*. Vol. 2, *Papyri aus Oberägypten*. Berlin: Walter de Gruyter.

Wilckens, U. 1973. "Vergebung für die Sünderin (Lk 7,36-50)." Pages 394–424 in *Orientierung an Jesus: Festschrift Josef Schmid*. Edited by P. Hoffmann, N. Brox, and W. Pesch. Freiburg: Herder.

———. 1998. *Das Evangelium nach Johannes*. NTD 4. Göttingen: Vandenhoeck & Ruprecht.

Wilkens, W. 1974. "Die Versuchungsgeschichte Luk. 4.1-13 und die Komposition des Evangeliums." *ThZ* 30: 262–72.

———. 1976. "Die Auslassung von Mark. 6.45–8.26 bei Lukas im Licht der Komposition Luk. 9,1-50." *ThZ* 32: 193–200.

Wilkinson, J. 1980. "The Case of the Bent Woman." Pages 70–80 in *Health and Healing: Studies in New Testament Principles and Practice*. Edinburgh: Handsel.

Williams, D. S. 1989. "Reconsidering Marcion's Gospel." *JBL* 108: 477–96.

Wilson, S. G. 1973. *The Gentiles and the Gentile Mission in Luke–Acts*. MSSNTS 23. Cambridge: Cambridge University Press.

———. 1983. *Luke and the Law*. MSSNTS 50. Cambridge: Cambridge University Press.

Winandy, J. 1998. "Du *kataluma* à la crèche." *NTS* 44: 618–22.

Wink, W. 1989. "Jesus' Reply to John." *Forum* 5: 121–28.

Winter, P. 1954/1955a. "The Cultural Background of the Narrative in Luke I and II." *JQR* 45/46: 159–67.

———. 1954/1955b. "Magnificat and Benedictus—Maccabaean Psalms?" *BJRL* 37: 328–47.

Witherington III, B. 1979. "On the Road with Mary Magdalene, Joanna, Susanna, and Other Disciples—Luke 8.1-3." *ZNW* 70: 243–48.

———. 1984. *Women in the Ministry of Jesus*. MSSNTS 51. Cambridge: Cambridge University Press.

Wohlers, M. 1999a. "'Aussätzige reinigt' (Mt 10,8). Aussatz in antiker Medizin, Judentum und frühem Christentum." Pages 294–304 in *Text und Geschichte:*

Festschrift Dieter Lührmann. Edited by S. Maser and E. Schlarb. MThSt 50. Marburg: Elwert.

———. 1999b. *Heilige Krankheit. Epilepsie in antiker Medizin, Astrologie und Religion*. Marburg: Elwert

Wohlstein, J. 1894. "Über einige aramaische Inschriften auf Throngefässen des Koniglichen Museums zu Berlin." *ZA* 9: 11–41.

Wolter, M. 1978. *Rechtfertigung und zukünftiges Heil: Untersuchungen zu Röm 5,1–11*. BZNW 43. Berlin: Walter de Gruyter.

———. 1988a. "Die anonymen Schriften des Neuen Testaments. Annäherungsversuch an ein literarisches Phänomen." *ZNW* 79: 1–16.

———. 1988b. *Die Pastoralbriefe als Paulustradition*. FRLANT 146. Göttingen: Vandenhoeck & Ruprecht.

———. 1989. "Paulus, der bekehrte Gottesfeind. Zum Verständnis von 1.Tim 1:13." *NT* 31: 48–66.

———. 1990. "Der Apostel und seine Gemeinden als Teilhaber am Leidensgeschick Jesu Christi: Beobachtungen zur paulinischen Theologie." *NTS* 36: 535–57.

———. 1992. "Inschriftliche Heilungsberichte und neutestamentliche Wundererzählungen." Pages 135–75 in *Studien und Texte zur Formgeschichte*. Edited by K. Berger. TANZ 7. Tübingen: Francke.

———. 1995a. "'Reich Gottes' bei Lukas." *New Testament Studies* 41: 451–563.

———. 1995b. "'Was heisset nu Gottes reich?'" *ZNW* 86: 5–19.

———. 1997a. "Ethos und Identität in paulinischen Gemeinden." *NTS* 43: 430–44.

———. 1997b. "Israels Zukunft und die Parusieverzögerung bei Lukas." Pages 405–26 in *Eschatologie und Schöpfung: Festschrift Erich Gräßer*. Edited by M. Evang, H. Merklein, and M. Wolter. BZNW. Berlin: Walter de Gruyter.

———. 1998a. "Die Juden und die Obrigkeit bei Lukas." Pages 277–90 in *Ja und Nein: Festschrift Wolfgang Schrage*. Neukirchen-Vluyn: Neukirchener.

———. 1998b. "Wann wurde Maria schwanger?" Pages 405–22 in *Von Jesus zum Christus: Christologische Studien: Festschrift Paul Hoffmann*. Edited by R. Hoppe and U. Busse. BZNW 93. Berlin: Walter de Gruyter.

———. 2000a. "Erstmals unter Quirinius! Zum Verständnis." *BN* 102: 35–41.

———. 2000b. "Die Hirten in der Weichnachtsgeschichte (Lk 2,8-20)." Pages 501–17 in *Religionsgeschichte des Neuen Testaments: Festschrift Klaus Berger*. Edited by A. von Dobbeler, K. Erlemann, and R. Heiligenthal. Tübingen: Francke.

———. 2002a. "'Gericht' und 'Heil' bei Jesus von Nazareth und Johannes dem Täufer." Pages 355–92 in *Der historische Jesus: Tendenzen und Perspektiven der gegenwärtigen Forschung*. Edited by J. Schröter and R. Brucker. BZNW 114. Berlin: Walter de Gruyter.

———. 2002b. "Lk 15 als Streitgespräch." *EThL* 78: 25–56.

———. 2003/2004. "Reconstructing Q?" *ET* 115: 115–19.

———. 2004a. "'Ihr sollt aber wissen . . .' Das Anakoluth nach ἵνα δὲ εἰδῆτε in Mark 2.10-11 parr." *ZNW* 95: 269–75.

————. 2004b. "Das lukanische Doppelwerk als Epochengeschichte." Pages 185–207 in *Die Apostelgeschichte und die hellenistische Geschichtsschreibung: Festschrift Eckhard Plümacher*. Edited by C. Breytenbach and J. Schröter. AJEC 57. Leiden: Brill.

————. 2005a. "Apokalyptik als Redeform im Neuen Testament." *NTS* 51: 171–91.

————. 2005b. "Der Heilstod Jesu als theologisches Argument." Pages 297–313 in *Deutungen des Todes Jesu*. Edited by J. Frey and J. Schröter. 181 WUNT. Tübingen: Mohr.

————. 2011. "Bed. II. New Testament." Pages 730–31 in *EBR* 3. Berlin: Walter de Gruyter.

Woods, E. J. 2001. *The "Finger of God" and Pneumatology in Luke–Acts*. JSNT.S 205. Sheffield: Sheffield Academic.

Wrege, H. T. 1968. *Die Überlieferungsgeschichte der Bergpredigt*. WUNT 9. Tübingen: Mohr.

Wright, A. G. 1982. "The Widow's Mites: Praise or Lament?" *CBQ* 44: 256–65.

Wuellner, W. H. 1967. *The Meaning of "Fishers of Men."* Philadelphia: Westminster.

————. 1991. "The Rhetorical Genre of Jesus' Sermon." Pages 93–118 in *Persuasive Artistry: Festschrift George A. Kennedy*. Edited by D. Watson. Sheffield: Sheffield Academic.

Yamasaki, G. 2006. "Point of View in a Gospel Story: What Difference Does It Make? Luke 19:1-10 as a Test Case." *JBL* 125: 89–105.

York, J. O. 1991. *The Last Shall be First: The Rhetoric of Reversal in Luke*. JSNT.S 46. Sheffield: Sheffield Academic.

Youtie, H. C. 1977. "P. Mich. Inv. 855: Letter from Herakleides to Nemesion." *ZPE* 27: 147–50.

Ytterbrink, M. 2004. *The Third Gospel for the First Time: Luke within the Context of Ancient Biography*. Lund: Lund University.

Zahn, T. 1902. "Das Land der Gadarener, Gerasener oder Gergesener." *NKZ* 13: 923–45.

————. 1904. *Grundriss der Geschichte des Neutestamentlichen Kanons*. 2nd edition. Leipzig: Deichert.

Zedda, S. 1974. "Πορευόμενοι συμπνίγονται (Lc 8,14)." *ED* 27: 92–108.

Zeller, D. 1969. *Die Redaktion der Logienquelle*. WMANT 33. Neukirchen-Vluyn: Neukirchener.

————. 1971/1972. "Das Logion Mt 8,11f / Lk 13,28 und das Motiv der 'Völkerwallfahrt.'" *BZ NF* 15/16: 222–37, 84–93.

————. 1977a. "Die Bildlogik des Gleichnisses Mt 11,16f/Lk 7,31f." *ZNW* 68: 252–57.

————. 1977b. *Die weisheitlichen Mahnsprüche bei den Synoptikern*. FzB 17. Würzburg: Echter.

————. 1985. "Entrückung zur Ankunft als Menschensohn (Lk 13,34f.; 11,29f)." Pages 513–30 in *À cause de l'évangile: Festschrift Jacques Dupont*. LeDiv 123. Paris: Cerf.

————. 1992. "Geburtsankündigung und Geburtsverkündigung." Pages 59–134 in *Studien und Texte zur Formgeschichte*. Edited by K. Berger. TANZ 7. Tübingen: Francke.

————. 1999. "Bedeutung und religionsgeschichtlicher Hintergrund der Verwandlung Jesu." Pages 303–21 in *Authenticating the Activities of Jesus*. Edited by B. D. Chilton and C. A. Evans. NTTS 28/2. Leiden: Brill.

Zerwick, M. 1959. "Die Parabel vom Thronanwärter." *Bib.* 40: 654–74.

————. 1966. *Graecitas Biblica*. 5th edition. Rome: Pontifical Biblical Institute.

Ziegler, I. 1903. *Die Königsgleichnisse des Midrasch, beleuchtet durch die römische Kaiserzeit*. Breslau: Schottlaender.

Ziesler, J. A. 1978/1979. "Luke and the Pharisees." *NTS* 25: 146–57.

Zimmermann, C. 2007. *Die Namen des Vaters: Studien zu ausgewählten neutestamentlichen Gottesbezeichnungen vor ihrem frühjüdischen und paganen Sprachhorizont*. AJEC 69. Leiden: Brill.

Zimmermann, H., and K. Kliesch. 1982. *Neutestamentliche Methodenlehre*. 7th edition. Stuttgart: Katholisches Bibelwerk.

Zimmermann, J. 1998. "Observations on 4Q246—The 'Son of God.'" Pages 175–90 in *Qumran-Messianism*. Edited by J. H. Charlesworth, H. Lichtenberger, and G. Oegema. Tübingen: Mohr.

Zimmermann, R. 2001. *Geschlechtermetaphorik und Gottverhältnis: Traditionsgeschichte und Theologie eines Bildfeldes in Urchristentum und antiker Umwelt*. WUNT 2/122. Tübingen: Mohr.

Zmijewski, J. 1972. *Die Eschatologiereden des Lukas-Evangeliums*. BBB 40. Bonn: Hanstein.

Zohary, M. 1995. *Pflanzen der Bibel*. 3rd edition. Stuttgart: Calwer.

Zuckschwerdt, E. 1975. "Nazōraios in Matth. 2,23." *ThZ* 31: 65–77.

Zwickel, W. 1994. "Emmaus: Ein neuer Versuch." *BN* 74: 33–36.

Zwiep, A. W. 1996. "The Text of the Ascension Narratives." *NTS* 42: 219–44.

————. 1997. *The Ascension of the Messiah in Lukan Christology*. NT.S 87. Leiden: Brill.

Zyl, H. C. van. 2002. "The Soteriological Meaning of Jesus' Death in Luke–Acts. A Survey of Possibilities." *VEccl* 23: 533–57.